D0558269

Risk Management and Insurance in Canada

Coleen Clark

Captus Press

Risk Management and Insurance in Canada

© 2010 by Coleen Clark and Captus Press Inc.

All rights reserved. No part of this book may be reproduced, stored in a retrieval system, or transmitted, in any form or by any means, electronic, mechanical, photocopying, recording, or otherwise, without prior written permission of the copyright holders.

Captus Press Inc.
Units 14 & 15, 1600 Steeles Avenue West,
Concord, Ontario   L4K 4M2
Telephone: (416) 736–5537
Fax: (416) 736–5793
Email: Info@captus.com
Internet: www.captus.com

Library and Archives Canada Cataloguing in Publication
Clark, Coleen, 1947–
        Risk management and insurance in Canada / Coleen Clark.

Includes bibliographical references and index.
ISBN 978-1-55322-216-3

1. Risk (Insurance) — Canada — Textbooks. 2. Risk management — Canada — Textbooks. I. Title.

HG8054.5.C53 2010   368'.971   C2010-904740-0

Canada   We acknowledge the financial support of the Government of Canada through the Book Publishing Industry Development Program (BPIDP) for our publishing activities.

0 9 8 7 6 5 4
Printed in Canada

Contents

Acknowledgments

Acknowledgments

In addition to thanking Jason Wormald at Captus Press for his support and guidance, I thank all the anonymous reviewers who provided valuable feedback. I also thank the hundreds of students at Ryerson University enrolled in FIN 512, "Risk Management and Insurance", for their candid requests for clarification. For this project, I reserve very special thanks to two people in particular.

Perminder Bhogal was my teaching assistant during the Fall, 2005 semester when this book was originally being drafted and, again, in the Fall of 2008, as the working draft was revised for publication. Perminder, I can honestly say I couldn't have done it without you. Your creativity, honest feedback, timely turnaround and willingness to research that which did not want to be found, will forever leave me in your debt. Thank you.

Giulio Iacobelli was a student in FIN 512 "Risk Management and Insurance" in the Fall of 2002. He was working for a life insurance company at the time and I will always be grateful for his comment, "You have to start by understanding the policies. If you don't understand the policies, you can't understand insurance." Later, although no longer a student, Giulio never failed to help me understand fundamental issues when I looked to him for help and guidance. As a result, in 2007, Giulio developed this course for Ryerson's Distance Education program and then went on to teach it in Continuing Education. In 2008 and 2009, when the draft was being revised, Giulio was again available for in-depth discussions and explorations of possibilities. I am also forever in your debt. Thank you.

Introduction

When we think of something being a risk or risky, we often think of the possibility of losing something. Does risk management always mean "buy insurance"? Is that the only way a risk can be managed? Well, no. If asked what other ways could there be to manage risk, most people could easily suggest, for example, seat belts, speed limits, smoke detectors, not smoking, eating well and regular exercise...

In talking about risk management, something is not considered a risk if it is certain to happen. Using this definition, dying, therefore, is not a risk since it is a certainty for everyone. Where is the risk in dying then? The risk is that of a premature death — or, more specifically, dying while there are people who are still financially dependent on a significant breadwinner in a family.

Some losses are a result of risks that are not recognized as risks, including:

- the recent loss of 96 lives in the crash of a Polish aircraft — among the dead was the Polish president and his wife, the chief of general staff, senior military leaders, the president of the National Bank of Poland, the deputy foreign minister, Polish government officials, 12 members of the Polish parliament and senior members of the Polish clergy.
- the recent oil spill in the Gulf of Mexico that resulted from the failure of the blowout preventer after the oil rig exploded and sunk. At the time of this writing, the spill threatens the livelihoods of the fishermen in the Gulf Coast seafood industry, one of the largest in the world, as well as the lives of hundreds of species of wildlife (including birds, dolphins, shrimp, oysters and crabs in the four states that border the Gulf). There is some fear that if the spill continues, it could enter the Gulf Stream and move up the eastern coast of the United States.
- a volcano in a small northern European city erupts and brings air travel in norther Europe for four or five days.

Why then should someone study risk management? The primary reason is to be able to recognize a risk exposure and to then assess the alternatives for dealing with it. The three events outlined above happened in less than two weeks in April 2010. While many might have predicted a plane crash or an oil spill, a volcano disrupting air travel for such an extended period was far less foreseeable.

What can be learned from these events?

- Some companies, having learned from their past or from the past of others, never allow all senior executives to fly in the same plane (or even enter the same elevator) at the same time.
- The oil spill happened as the American president was considering ending an embargo on domestic offshore drilling of oil and gas in order to decrease American reliance on imported oil and gas. Just before the Gulf spill, the U.S. Department of the Interior Department was quoted as calculating a Gulf of Mexico "spill rate" of 0.001% of oil production — much less than the normal seepage of oil into the world's oceans by natural processes. In 2005, Hurricane Katrina destroyed oil and gas platforms, but produced no significant oil spills and broke no submerged pipelines.
- And the volcano? What can we learn from this since just about no one would have predicted something like this? Always travel with a contingency plan and enough financial resources to implement the plan.

This book is designed to provide an introduction to all aspects of risk management and offer an in-depth survey of commonly-available insurance contracts to absorb some of the risk exposures.

Since insurance policies are "just" contracts, an understanding of the rights and obligations of both parties to an insurance contract helps ensure that an individual or organization has the appropriate type and amount of coverage. In addition, the insurance industry is a large part of the Canadian economy and provides employment for some 235,000 Canadians, so an understanding of the basic operations of this industry is useful for students who may pursue a career in insurance.

In addition to providing a survey course covering risk management and insurance, this text also meets the specific requirements for insurance set by the Financial Planning Standards Council (FPSC) for the Certified Financial Planner© (CFP©) national examination.

Insurance is a complex industry and it works rather differently from many other industries since it holds investments to fulfil future obligations. For houses and cars, the future obligation is measured in a year or two, but for life and disability insurance, the future is measured in decades. Further, your own annual automobile policy premiums are not enough to pay for your car if you completely demolish it in an accident. And what if you failed to notice a stop sign and caused an accident that results in a million dollar law suit? Even if you are older and have been paying premiums for many years, the accumulated and invested total of your own premiums will not cover this payout. To deal with this, insurance companies group people in various risk categories and charge premiums that they believe reflects the risk of each category so they can cover loss payouts as they arise.

Chapter 1: Risk, Risk Management and Insurance introduces risk — the definition, what types of risk are there, what risks are faced by individuals and businesses and what causes losses. This takes us into the six steps of the risk management process and the tools that are available to manage various risks. The fundamental mathematics of insurance and the pooling of losses concept explain how insurance companies are able to develop premiums for individual people and individual organizations that enable insurers to have the funds available to pay out large losses, as required. The chapter concludes with an overview of the insurance industry and its place in the Canadian economy.

Chapter 2: Backdrop to Insurance and Insurance Law provides a brief history of insurance, the basic characteristics of insurance, a description of an insurable risk and the five principles of insurance that are reflected in all insurance contracts. Since insurance policies are contracts, the chapter provides an overview of the elements of a valid contract, an outline of the parts of an insurance policy and an illustration using a sample term life policy. The chapter concludes with a look at negligence, since insurance can provide protection in such cases.

Chapter 3: Automobile Insurance is the first of several chapters to look at policies in detail and is the first of three chapters covering Property and Casualty (P & C) / General Insurance. Auto insurance in Canada varies a great deal by province and territory since some jurisdictions provide government-run coverage for the mandatory coverage; some provide no-fault insurance (each party is compensated by his or her own insurance company regardless of fault); and some limit the right to sue for pain and suffering. The chapter also looks at the factors that determine the premium before looking at the basic elements found in the various policies across Canada.

Chapter 4: Homeowners Insurance is much more straight-forward in that policies vary from company to company, but not very much. A sample policy provides the details of coverage for the homeowner's property in Section I, while Section II outlines the coverage on the insured's coverage for liability to other people and their property. The chapter concludes with a description of other types of insurance coverages available, such as the two types of mortgage insurance, tenants insurance, title insurance and identity theft and fraud.

Chapter 5: Commercial Insurance expands on the descriptions in Auto and Homeowners Insurance to outline the various insurance coverages available to organizations of all types and sizes.

Chapter 6: Health Care is the first chapter in the Life and Health Insurance sector. Health insurance in Canada is provided by each province and territory and all are governed by the *Canada Health Act*, which sets the minimum standards for all jurisdictions. The chapter goes on to look at optional coverage provided by each jurisdiction. In Canada, wait times and a shortage of doctors are issues and the chapter provides an overview of some of the ways these issues are being addressed. The chapter concludes with Supplementary Health Care Plans that can be purchased by individuals or organizations for their employees as well as Travel Insurance and Long-term Care Insurance.

Chapter 7: Income Protection Plans covers the plans provided by governments (Workers' Compensation, Employment Insurance and the Canada Pension Plan) before looking at private disability plans in detail. When buying individual disability insurance, it is important to understand the various ways policies can differ as well as optional riders available to make sure a person has the coverage they expect to have should they need to collect the benefit. Group disability plans are offered by employers. The way that disability benefits are taxed depends on who pays the premium and the taxability of the premium which greatly affects the amount of coverage a person should and can get. The chapter concludes with an overview of Critical Illness Insurance.

Chapter 8: Life Insurance begins with a discussion of whether a person needs life insurance and, if yes, how much he or she should buy. All life insurance policies have common elements, though there are differences between temporary and permanent policies. Term insurance provides temporary coverage for a defined period of time while permanent insurance policies, such as whole life, provide coverage for one's entire life and also provide a savings component. This savings component is held in a Reserve, where it accumulates before tax and can be used in several ways — to increase the savings and/or the death benefit coverage, to be paid out in cash as a non-taxable Dividend and/or to pay the premiums for a while. The savings component greatly increases the cost of insurance coverage in the early years of the policy compared to a term policy, but becomes cheaper later in life as the cost of term insurance increases — reflecting the increased likelihood of dying as a person ages. The chapter concludes with an overview of Segregated Funds, offered only by insurance companies, and a comparison with Mutual Funds.

Chapter 9: Insurance Operations describes the unique processes associated with insurance companies — underwriting (selecting and classifying applicants), claim settlement, production (sales and marketing) and rate making (setting the premium). Included in production is an outline of the requirements for becoming licensed to sell general insurance (property and casualty), and life and health insurance. Rate making looks at the pricing of general insurance, and life and health insurance. Using a five-year policy as an example, an illustration of the pricing of a life insurance policy shows how an insurance company can figure out how much the same annual premium needs to be over the entire life of a person in order to have enough money in their reserve to pay out the face value when someone dies.

Chapter 9 goes on to look at other aspects of insurance operations. The Office of the Superintendent of Insurance (OSFI) oversees the financial results of insurance companies to anticipate when a company is getting into financial difficulty. Investments of insurance companies reflect the long-term nature of their future obligations while Accounting in insurance companies reflects the unique nature of their operations. Finally Reinsurance is illustrated to show how insurance companies share large risks with other insurance companies to reduce their own loss exposures.

Risk, Risk Management and Insurance

Learning Objectives

After completing this chapter, students will be able to

A. Understand the **meaning of risk** and distinguish between the different types of risk.

B. Recognize the steps involved in the **risk management process** and know the various ways of dealing with risk.

C. Understand the **rationale behind insurance rates**.

D. Know the **importance of the industry** in the Canadian economy.

Introduction

When dealing with the topics of risk management and insurance, it is easy to assume that these two terms are synonymous — that the only way to manage risk is to insure it. We will spend a lot of time on insurance and insurance contracts. However, when faced with the possibility of a loss, it is important to begin by understanding exactly what **risk exposures** are involved, how the losses might occur, and how these losses might be prevented or reduced before deciding to insure against them. Certain risk exposures cannot be avoided, others can be avoided, and some, though unavoidable, may result in losses that can be reduced. We begin by understanding the concept of risk.

We then look at the first of two fundamental principles that explain how insurance can work.

1. The **law of large numbers** explains how insurance companies can charge a relatively small premium for large loss exposures.
2. An insurance policy is a contract.

The **first principle** uses the Law of Large Numbers to explain how insurers can figure out how much to charge different classes of insureds. For example, an insurance company cannot know whether or not *you* will have a car accident. So it does the next best thing, from its own point of view, and classifies drivers according to age, marital status, driving history, etc. It then charges all the people in each class of drivers the same amount based on its own history of people in each class.

There are several steps to be taken to understand how insurers arrive at the premiums they charge insureds. This chapter will show how insurance companies are able to make large payouts to a small number of people. We will look at this issue of setting rates (ratemaking) in Chapter 9 when we look at life insurance premiums and reserves.

The **second principle**, that an insurance policy is a contract, is covered in Chapter 2.

An overview of the insurance industry provides a picture of its importance in the Canadian economy. The insurance industry holds 7.5% of the assets of the 22 industries in Canada while having some 14% of the operating profit margin. It employs more than 230,000 people.

Risk

We know that it is risky to drive in a major snowstorm. We know that it is risky to smoke in bed. We know our families would suffer financial hardship if a significant breadwinner were to die prematurely. We know we would suffer financial hardship if an injury kept us off work for several weeks. What exactly are all the risks we face as individuals?

What about a business? What if a customer slips and falls on a slippery floor? What if a product causes someone to get sick? What if the entire research and development team were killed in a plane crash? What other risks do businesses face?

Let's begin by defining *risk* in order to better understand the risk exposures we face.

What is Risk?

Risk has different meanings depending on the point of view. Some people see risk as an undesirable event or as an expected or possible loss. The *Oxford English Dictionary* defines risk as a "hazard, danger; exposure to mischance or peril". Others see risk as a statistical probability of something happening, or as a variance from expectations based on the possibility of a number of outcomes (as in the investment industry where the concept of the **risk/return tradeoff** — the more risk one is willing to accept, the higher the *possible* return — is intended to be used to make investment decisions that are in line with one's own risk tolerance).

Peter Bernstein, author of *Against the Gods: The Remarkable Story of Risk*,[1] commenting[2] on the mortgage meltdown (before the market meltdown), quotes Elroy Dimson of the London Business School, who defines *risk* as meaning that more things *can* happen than *will* happen That is, we don't know what will happen. The result is that we can formulate probabilities of possible outcomes but we cannot know in advance the true range of outcomes — our forecasts are wrong from time to time. He goes on to ask, "How will we deal with surprises — outcomes different from what we expect? What are the consequences of being wrong in our expectations?" Bernstein then defines *risk* as "the chance of being wrong — not always in an adverse direction, but always in a direction different from what we expected". He goes on to define *risk management* as "a process of dealing with the consequences of being wrong" and states "**risk management** should concentrate either on limiting the size of the bet or on finding ways to hedge the bet so you are not wiped out if you take the wrong side".

For our purposes, *risk* is defined as an **uncertainty** about the occurrence of a loss — if there is uncertainty about a loss, there is a risk and, conversely, if a loss in a given situation is a certainty, then there is no risk since the loss is a sure thing. This is why insurance companies usually require a medical before a person can buy individual life insurance (individual as opposed to life insurance through a group plan at work where a physical examination is generally not required since the plan is usually available to everyone and the combined health risks should average out). Insurers are looking for pre-existing conditions. If they find one (diabetes, for example), they might be prepared to give you a life insurance policy but with an **exclusion** for complications arising from this disease if the disease is likely to shorten your life. Alternatively, with a smoker for instance, there is no pre-existing condition, but since smoking increases the chance of a **premature death,** the insurer might either decline to give the life insurance policy or will charge a higher premium to reflect the increased risk of early demise.

Categories or Types of Risk

There are many ways of categorizing risks in order to predict the **probability of a loss** occurring. In order to ensure that all possible risk exposures have been recognized and acknowledged, it is important to understand the following:

---

1   *Against the Gods: The Remarkable Story of Risk*, Peter L. Bernstein, John Wiley & Sons, Inc., 1996, New York.
2   "What Happens if We're Wrong?" Peter L. Bernstein, *New York Times*, June 22, 2008. Peter L. Bernstein, a financial consultant and economic historian, is the editor of the *Economics & Portfolio Strategy* newsletter.

- The types of risks you, your family and/or your company can face and the frequency or likelihood of their occurring.
- Your perception of risk since a worst-case scenario can occur when a risk is not even acknowledged as such. The devastation caused by Hurricane Katrina in New Orleans in September 2005 is a prime example of a risk that wasn't acknowledged even though there were people who predicted losses of this magnitude for many years. Some people are **risk takers** while others are **risk averse**, and some people are even **risk seekers**. As a result, two people of opposite nature can look at the same investment opportunity and come to very different conclusions about the probability of making money or incurring a loss — their nature and attitude toward risk affects their interpretation of the risk/return tradeoff concept.

There are several types of risk exposures and a risk exposure can belong to more than one category — the categories are not mutually exclusive. The various views are useful when deciding on the appropriate tools to manage risk exposures.

Exogenous and Endogenous Risks

One way of categorizing risks is to look at how much control we have over them. **Exogenous risks** are risks over which we have no control and which are not affected by our actions. Earthquakes or hurricanes are examples of exogenous risks.

Endogenous risks, on the other hand, are risks that are dependent on our actions. Smoking in bed, jay-walking, not studying for an exam, and cutting in and out of heavy traffic are examples of endogenous risks. Some risks are a combination of the two — a car accident, for example. While a driver has no control over other drivers (the exogenous portion), the probability of an accident happening is strongly influenced by the driver's behaviour and ability (endogenous).

Objective and Subjective Risks

Risk assessment can also be based on external factors or on more personal, subjective factors. An **objective risk** is a risk that is determined by analysing past experiences and calculating the **mean** (average) of the losses and the **standard deviation** (the average difference of each loss from this average) of the actual losses from the expected losses for a particular risk exposure. For example, insurance companies keep track of drivers in various categories. They may, from tracking this for many years, come to the conclusion that drivers over the age of 50 are, on average, less likely to have an accident than drivers under the age of 50. Insurers then calculate their expected losses for a year for this age group and compare them to the actual losses for all drivers in this category. The more observations the insurer can use to evaluate the risk (the more drivers in the group of over-50s), the lower the objective risk (the more accurate their prediction). Insurers can calculate the **objective probability** of a loss by tracking various classes of drivers over several years. The insurer will never know exactly how many claims and the average or total value of the claims it will pay out, but it can estimate both the number and the amount with a large degree of accuracy.

The investment industry also uses the mean and standard deviation to estimate risk (hence the risk/return tradeoff). However, there are a couple of limitations to this:

- If the standard deviation doesn't cover enough years, it will not reflect the effect of a long bull market such as the one we have just experienced. In a *Toronto Star* article[3], Ellen Roseman pointed out that the 10-year annualized change in the TSX composite index was 3.3% while the average three-month T-bill yield over the same 10-year period was 3.5%. If dividends are included, the total return of Canadian stocks is just over 5%. She goes on to suggest that looking at a 10-year holding period isn't enough. Since stocks outperform T-bills in the long run, 15 or

---

3   "Here's the lowdown on your losses", Ellen Roseman, *The Toronto Star*, January 14, 2009.

20 years might be closer to the mark. The same can be said for calculating the standard deviation to achieve an assessment of the risk.

- Using a standard deviation based on historical data can never measure 100% of the risk. The insurance industry knows this better than the investment industry. As Bernstein said above, risk means the chance of being wrong, of the forecasts being wrong from time to time, of failing to take into account the tails of the bell curve, which happen only 1% of the time, or less.

A **subjective risk** means the uncertainty is based on a person's mental condition or state of mind and the resulting **subjective probability** is based on an individual's personal estimate of a **chance of loss**. For instance, driving accidents often occur because people fall asleep at the wheel — their subjective (personal) assessment was inaccurate. They were too tired to drive but they didn't realize it. And some drivers cannot accurately assess safe driving speeds in bad weather conditions.

Insurance companies use **inductive reasoning** to come to conclusions about objective risks — they analyse past data to predict future losses as described in the prior example about drivers. Alternatively, **deductive reasoning** can be used with probabilities where the probability is obvious from the nature of the event. For example, the probability of drawing a red card from a deck of cards is 50%. This concept is being used when laws deem that a driver is impaired with a blood alcohol concentration level of .08 although some people might not be fit to drive at .06.

Pure and Speculative Risks

Some risks provide opportunities for gain while some do not. **Pure risk** refers to risks where there is a chance of a loss or no loss, but no chance of a gain — these risks are generally insurable. For example, either your home burns or it doesn't; you die in an airplane crash or not; your car is damaged by another driver or it isn't. In all these examples, there is a loss or not, but there is no gain or profit. Insurance companies are concerned with pure risks and the chances of loss involved with this type of risk. A person who buys a new home automatically takes on the chance of a loss from perils such as fire, damage from a storm, vandalism, and broken water pipes. When discussing pure risk, we distinguish between the risks that affect individuals and those that affect businesses.

Speculative risk describes situations where there is the possibility of a loss but also the possibility of a gain. For example, an investment in common stock can either return a profit or sustain a loss; you could leave a secure job to start your own business, which could fail or succeed. In most instances, speculative risks are not insurable since they involve a voluntary acceptance of that risk.

Pure Risk for Individuals

Individuals are exposed to three broad categories of pure risk:

- **Property risk** is the risk of damage to or loss of one's auto, home, and personal belongings as a result of a fire, an accident, an earthquake, theft, etc. The insured can face both direct losses and indirect losses:
  - A **direct loss** is the damage to or loss of the property. For example, if an individual's house burns down, the owner loses the value of the building and its contents.
  - People can also face **indirect losses,** such as the need to rent another space while their house is being rebuilt or repaired. In addition, the person will have to spend a lot of time making decisions and shopping while the house is reconstructed and the contents are replaced. People cannot insure the value of their personal time, but they can insure the value of the building, its physical contents, and the cost of renting temporary living space.

- **Personal risk** come from the possibility of such things as
  - poor health (being unable to work and having unexpected additional expenses),
  - outliving one's personal savings in retirement,
  - unemployment (which governments generally insure — at least for salaried people), and

- premature death (the premature death of a family wage earner will have a range of financial consequences as a result of the loss of future income stream: mortgage, college expenses, day-to-day expenses, funeral/final expenses).

- **Liability risk** arises from a person's responsibility for harming someone or damaging their property. If someone causes damage or loss to someone else because of their own negligence, they are responsible for compensating that person for the loss.

Pure Risk for Businesses

A business is exposed to property risks, loss of key people and liability risks. But it can also face a number of other risks that could cause it to suffer a loss. These risks include such things as the following:

- **Financial risks**:
  - **Exchange rate risk** arises from changes in foreign exchange rates and affects businesses that import and export.
  - **Interest rate risk** is the risk faced by the holder of a fixed income instrument such as a bond whose price falls when interest rates increase. For a deposit-taking institution, it arises from the difference between the assets it invests in (loans to individuals and businesses) and the cost of its funds (deposits).
  - **Commodity price risk** arises from changes in commodity prices such as oil, gas, electricity, copper, etc. It affects both users and producers. Should you sign a five-year contract with a gas supplier or just take your chances with current prices? If the gas supplier sets the rate low and rates go up, the supplier will suffer losses but consumers gain (assuming the supplier does not go bankrupt). If the reverse happens, consumers pay more than they would have but they have the security of knowing what they will be paying.

- **Credit risk** is the risk that a receivable will become uncollectible and affects both borrowers and lending institutions.

- **Operational risks** can cause a loss of revenue or added costs and are the result of:
  - internal or external fraud (covered in Chapter 5: Commercial Insurance),
  - poor management and lack of supervision with inadequate accountability and internal control,
  - technology failures,
  - errors in forecasting and reporting,
  - inadequate document retention or record keeping,
  - workplace safety and employment practices failure (covered in Chapter 5: Commercial Insurance and Chapter 7, under Workers' Compensation),
  - damage to physical assets and loss of production due to equipment failure (covered in Chapter 5: Commercial Insurance),
  - product liability when a product does not work properly or harms someone (covered in Chapter 5: Commercial Insurance),

- **Strategic risks** are risks over which the business has no control, such as changes in government policy and regulations, macro-economic events, social and natural emergencies, unexpected input cost fluctuations, and relationships with other businesses. Strategic risks can also arise because a company fails to see that a change in direction is in order or that a major product is about to become obsolete.

- **Risk to reputation** can cause customers, both businesses and individuals, to change suppliers: "I never shop at XYZ because they ..." In order to prevent or reduce these losses, businesses set up operational guidelines, quality control techniques, and management programs that are designed to reduce the chances of negative events happening.

Business owners also face the possibility of direct losses — the value of the building and its contents, employer injury and illness, liability claims and the legal costs involved in defending against these claims. Indirect losses include the loss of profits and the need to rent other space in order to continue operations while the building is reconstructed.

Dynamic and Static Risks

Another way of looking at risk exposures is to look at the economy. **Dynamic risks** come from changes in the economy and are often insured by governments (in the form of employment insurance for employees). For example, imagine that you own a small business, have an unsecured loan at a major bank, and are required to make monthly interest payments only. The Bank of Canada decides to increase its rate and your bank not only does the same to its interest rates, but also decides that it has too many of your type of loan — your loan is now deemed to be high risk. So the bank calls your loan and you are out looking for another loan and possibly out of business. **Static risks**, on the other hand, are risks that are not connected to changes in the economy, and are a form of pure risk. For example, imagine you are a small business owner who has a very large customer go bankrupt. The receivable becomes uncollectible, thereby increasing your "days" receivables and in a few months, your "days old" receivables as well. If other customers cannot provide enough business to justify your loan, your bank might decide to lower your allowable loan balance or might even call in the loan.

Fundamental and Particular Risks

Some risks are borne by individuals alone, while some risks are shared risks. **Fundamental risks** affect large numbers of people and are caused by economic, social, political, and sometimes physical occurrences. These group risks may even affect the population as a whole, for example, an earthquake that causes major damage to an entire city — this natural disaster causes losses that affect the entire population of that city. **Particular risks**, on the other hand, affect only individuals and not a large group of people or the entire population. For example, lightning from a major thunderstorm may cause property damage to only one person's home. If it strikes a generating station and knocks out power to many homes, then it is a particular risk to the power company, who now has to repair the building and equipment, and a fundamental risk for individuals who experience inconvenience, discomfort, spoiled food and lost income but do not have to repair their homes (thinking of the power outage in August 2003 caused, not by lightening, but by an under-maintained power grid and a hot summer day).

It is important to make the distinction between fundamental and particular risks since governments and charities usually step in to offer financial assistance for losses resulting from a fundamental risk — that is, fundamental risks are often "insured" by governments while individuals are usually on his/her own to deal with the losses from a particular risk.

Social and Private Insurance

Lastly, we can look at who makes the decision to be insured for individuals and society as a whole. **Social insurance** is insurance required by governments, and employees, employers, or both contribute to the fund. It includes Workers' Compensation, Employment Insurance, and Canada Pension Plan retirement, disability, and death benefits. Old Age Security pension and Guaranteed Income Supplement are forms of **public assistance** since they are paid out of general tax revenues and are not tied to employment and contributions. **Private insurance** is primarily voluntary and is mostly provided by private insurers, not governments. An exception to this is auto insurance since basic levels are mandatory and, in some provinces, some of it is covered by government plans, as we will see in Chapter 3. However, this is not considered to be social insurance because there is not a "fund" out of which benefits are paid.

Perils and Hazards

Now let's look at the cause of losses and how these causes can be increased or moderated.

• A **peril** is the cause of a loss, such as a fire, windstorm, theft, explosion, or riot.

- A **hazard** is something that increases the likelihood or probable severity of a loss. For example, storing gasoline in a home basement is a hazard that increases the severity of the loss should there be a fire — the fire would be the peril. There are four types of hazards:
  1. physical hazards,
  2. moral hazards,
  3. morale hazards, and
  4. legal hazards.

1. Physical Hazards

Physical hazards are physical conditions that increase the chance of a loss, for example, an icy, un-salted walkway increases the chance of someone slipping on the ice and being injured, while faulty wiring in an old building increases the chance of a fire.

2. Moral Hazards

Moral hazards are character defects that allow insured people to be dishonest and either intentionally cause a loss or exaggerate the amount of the loss. In other words, this character defect leads these people to believe that it is acceptable to defraud an insurance company. For example, I might leave my wallet on the dashboard of my parked car, thereby encouraging someone to break into my car. I might then overstate the amount of cash that was in it.

3. Morale Hazards

Morale hazards arise from the insured's indifference to a loss because of the existence of insurance. These are careless or negligent acts that will increase the chance of loss. If the contents of my car are fully insured against theft, I might be less diligent in locking it up and taking other precautions against theft — a morale hazard. If I make a false theft claim, however, it is moral hazard.

4. Legal Hazards

Legal hazards are defined as the characteristics of the legal system that increase the frequency and/or severity of a loss. Legislatures and the courts may enact laws that

- favour plaintiffs (successfully suing McDonald's for getting fat on their food), or
- increase the chance of loss for someone who could be affected by this law (Certain zoning restrictions or by-laws may affect a business owner who suffers a financial loss by having to abide by new laws. For example, the owner of a building may have to rebuild to a higher standard to meet new building codes if the building is destroyed in a fire; a bar owner may have to add a heated, ventilated room for smokers.)

Is Insurance a Form of Gambling?

Some people are reluctant to carry insurance because they believe it is merely a form of gambling — you pay premiums and may or may not "win" by collecting insurance proceeds. What is the difference between gambling and insurance? Insurance transfers an existing risk to an insurance company while gambling creates a new speculative risk.

People often over-insure because they don't understand that the fundamental purpose of insurance is to prevent **catastrophic losses**, and that small losses should just be absorbed although the definition of *small* varies between people based on their level of income, job security and risk preference. In this context, insurance is certainly not gambling — you are paying the insurance company in the hope that you will never have to ask it to fulfil its part of the bargain. But if you do have a loss, the insurance company it there to make sure it isn't a catastrophic loss.

Risk Management

My 92-year-old Uncle Ralph asked me recently, "What is risk management?" He is still very mentally alert and extremely curious about many things. This is a man who taught art in the Ontario public school system for 30 years and then retired to Vancouver Island. He's more or less computer literate but not nearly as good as his wife, Aunt Marge. He couldn't begin to imagine what I am writing about and brought it up in a second conversation for clarification.

Indeed, the world has changed a lot since he was working and raising a family. He was a teen-ager during the Depression and fought during the Second World War so he knows something about risk. But risk management? That is a mystery to him. Let's examine the process of managing risk.

The Risk Management Process

Risk management is the process of identifying and assessing risks or **loss exposures,** including their probability and severity, and then taking steps to eliminate or reduce them using one or more of the risk management tools available. For example, when buying a home, one of the first steps is to have a home inspector examine the home to look for problems that are present or could arise in the future. This inspection gives home buyers information they need to determine if they want to purchase the home, whether the asking price is reasonable or should be lowered, or to know what costs they will have to incur at what point in the future if they do go ahead with the purchase.

The Six Steps in the Risk Management Process

The risk management process involves six steps:

1. Determine the objectives.
2. Identify the risks.
3. Evaluate the potential losses.
4. Consider the alternatives and choose the appropriate risk management technique.
5. Implement the risk management technique.
6. Perform ongoing evaluation and review.

1. Determine the Objectives

The first step in the risk management process is to determine what it is that you are trying to achieve with this process. In some cases the main objective might be to avoid the risk altogether. But many risk exposures are unavoidable and can only be controlled or reduced.

Individuals can have different objectives than businesses. Individuals' objectives will focus on reducing or avoiding losses to themselves, their property, and their families. Businesses generally have these same objectives but also the actual survival, continuation, and growth of business operations, revenue, and profits.

2. Identify the Risks

Once objectives in the risk management process have been determined, it is time to try to identify every risk exposure (even though it is virtually impossible to determine every possible risk) and to prioritize potential liabilities, which could range from a common cold and cancer to natural disasters and negligence on the part of ourselves or an employee.

Businesses face different risks than individuals do and therefore use a number of different and more sophisticated techniques to identify risks. These techniques range from computer programs to mathematical matrices that predict the probability of a loss and the amount of that loss. Insurance brokers and agents are also very useful for helping businesses determine the range of risk exposures. In Chapter 5, we look at commercial insurance and will see the great variety of insurance coverages available to offset various risks to businesses.

3. Evaluate the Potential Losses

After identifying the risks involved, it is necessary to review them in light of their possible severity (the **maximum** *possible* loss), their frequency, and the probability of their occurring (the **maximum** *probable* loss) — some risks may be highly unlikely to occur but would cause a major loss for the individual or the company if they did. Possible losses can be categorized as

(a) **critical losses**, having serious financial exposure for the enterprise, possibly leading to bank-ruptcy;

(b) **material losses**, having serious financial exposure leading to a reduced standard of living;

(c) **minor losses**, having financial consequences that are minor and manageable; and

(d) **insurable risks**, which can be covered by insurance.

The assessment also has to determine the **maximum** *acceptable* loss — the maximum loss the family or organization could experience without unacceptable financial consequences. As mentioned earlier, the purpose of insurance is to provide coverage against catastrophic losses. While the definition of *catastrophic* varies from person to person and from organization to organization, insurance is not intended to provide coverage against all possible losses — just the ones that have unacceptable consequences. Critical and material losses have, in virtually all situations, unacceptable consequences.

Risk evaluation will vary for people and businesses since the likelihood of an earthquake in San Francisco is much more likely than in Toronto. The risk of a strike from the union of a car manufacturer is higher than the risk of a strike from a small non-unionized company. While earthquakes and labour strikes are not usually covered by private insurers, they nonetheless need to be recognized as possible risks. Once the risks have been identified and evaluated, we move on to formulate a plan to deal with those risks that have unacceptable consequences.

4. Consider the Alternatives and Choose the Risk Management Technique

Once the risks have been identified and assessed for probability and severity, it is time to identify the technique that could be best used to avoid or control these risks. Each technique will then have to be evaluated to determine how effective and costly it would be to implement. On the following page we look at the risk management tools that are available to individuals and businesses.

The choice of risk management technique is both a personal decision as well as an economic one. For instance, one way to avoid being involved in an airplane disaster is to avoid flying. But for a business traveler, this would not be possible. Or if a person wants to avoid snow and icy weather, she may choose to live in Florida as opposed to Toronto. But this decision may not make sense from an economic standpoint — she may not be able to get a green card to work in the United States, and she may have a personal preference for staying in Toronto.

5. Implement the Technique

Once the appropriate technique has been selected, the next step is to implement it for each risk exposure.

6. Perform Ongoing Evaluation and Review

The final step in the risk management process is to regularly review and evaluate the risk management techniques that have been chosen and implemented. The frequency of this review will depend on the type of risk and the techniques involved. For example, a large city with many city trucks and cars may decide to **self-insure** on the collision benefits of its vehicle insurance, meaning the city will pay the costs of damage to its fleet out of operating costs. It will set up a special fund to handle major expenses as they occur while saving the cost of the premium.

However, a decision like this requires a careful analysis of the insurance claims as compared to the insurance premiums over a lengthy period of time. Furthermore, this may leave employees without coverage should a company encounter financial difficulties. For example, when Eaton's went bankrupt, it turned out that the company was self-insured on its disability policies and employees who were collecting disability benefit found themselves with no income until they were able to start collecting their pension (which, for some, was a long wait).

Risk Management Tools

There are five ways of handling risk:

1. Avoid the risk.
2. Control the risk.
3. Retain the risk.
4. Share the risk.
5. Insure the risk.

1. Risk Avoidance

The first method of risk management is the avoidance of the risk altogether — that way, there is no risk. This means that we can prevent the risk by not doing the action that could cause the loss. One way of avoiding an airplane accident, for example, is not to fly. A company can eliminate the risk of product liability by ceasing production of the product.

2. Loss Control

The next tool for risk management is to control the risk exposure, that is, **risk reduction** to both reduce the possible *severity* of a loss (loss reduction) and reduce the *probability* of a loss (loss prevention).

Loss Reduction

This involves reducing the **severity** of the loss by taking precautions. For example, drivers can wear seat belts and drive at slower speeds, people can install smoke detectors in their homes, couples may fly on separate flights thinking that if one of the planes crashes, their children will not lose both parents.

Loss Prevention

This involves reducing the **frequency** of the loss. For example, people leave on lights in their homes when they are out to discourage potential thieves who would break in only if they thought there was no one home. Workplace accidents are reduced when the space is kept clean and organized.

3. Risk Retention

Risk retention involves retaining all or part of a certain risk. This may be *voluntary or involuntary* on behalf of the individual or business. Risk retention may also be *intentional or unintentional*. For example, if you insure your home with replacement insurance of $200,000 when the value of the home is really $300,000, you are under-insured by $100,000. If you know that you are under-insured by $100,000 then you have voluntarily and intentionally done so. But if you don't realize this fact, then you may be doing it out of ignorance and have unintentionally retained part of the risk.

4. Risk Sharing — Non-Insurance Transfers

Risk transfer allows an individual or business to shift the financial responsibility to another party for a fee. This may be done through the use of insurance or via other non-insurance methods such as incorporating a business, hedging, and hold-harmless clauses.

- **Incorporating a business** means an individual can limit the amount of potential losses — losses are limited to the amount the individual has invested but, unless personal assets have been used as a guarantee, personal assets are not at risk if the business encounters serious financial difficulties.
- **Hedging** is another example of a non-insurance transfer that can be done to reduce the risk of foreign currency exposure for companies. A company may purchase goods and services from companies in other countries using other currencies. In order to avoid any risks relating to fluctuations in currency prices, the company may enter into futures contracts that allow the company to know the exact currency price it will be receiving or will have to pay in the future.
- **Hold-harmless clauses** in contracts also transfer risk. In a publishing agreement, a publisher might insert a clause stating that the author is liable if there is a lawsuit for plagiarism. A company might have a hold-harmless clause in a building contract so that any losses during construction are the responsibility of the construction company.

5. Risk Transfers — Insurance

Insurance allows people or businesses to transfer all or a part of the risk to an insurance company by paying a premium or fee for that protection. This is known as "pooling" the risk, allowing a few individuals or companies to spread the risk over a larger group. For example, an individual who has disability insurance pays a premium to protect him- or herself from a reduction or loss of wages due to an injury or illness. The premiums are paid by a large group of people who are buying the disability coverage. In return for receiving the premiums, the insurance company will make disability payments to a smaller group of insured people who have become disabled. The risk of disability is transferred from the individual to the insurance company that is providing the coverage.

Examples of How Some Personal Risks Might Be Managed

		Probability of a Loss			
		Low		**High**	
Size of Loss	**Small**	Retain	*You lose a cheap watch.*	Retain	*You don't have collision insurance on your 12-year-old Honda, which you use to deliver pizzas.*
	Large	Insure	*Your house burns down completely.*	Avoid	*You decide to not buy an expensive car because you can't afford to insure it.*
				Reduce	*You take public transportation to work and leave the expensive car at home when the weather is really bad.*

Rationale for Insuring and Insurance Rates

The decision to insure or not can be looked at using the following:

- **decision theory** which chooses the minimum expected value or cost; and
- **minimax regret theory** which states that one should always minimize the maximum possible loss or regret.

To understand why rates are different for different people or companies, we look at the role of individual risk.

We will look at two drivers who are in different risk categories and show why the premium will be higher for the person in the higher risk category. We expand this to view the consequences of putting drivers of the same risk category into one class. Based on these illustrations, we will draw some conclusions about risk management.

Decision Theory and Minimax Regret Theory

Decision theory and the minimax regret theory explain why we insure even when the chance of loss is very low or negligible but not impossible.

Decision Theory

Individuals and corporations can use decision theory to help them choose whether they should purchase insurance or retain the risk. Most of decision theory is concerned with identifying the best decision to take, assuming a fully informed, fully rationale decision maker who is able to predict, estimate, and calculate with perfect accuracy. Decision theory arrives at a decision by calculating the **expected value** of the alternatives and selecting the one that incurs the lowest costs. The idea of expected value is that, when faced with a number of actions, each of which could give rise to more than one possible outcome with different probabilities, the rational procedure is to

- identify all possible outcomes,
- determine the value (positive or negative) of all possible outcomes,
- determine the probabilities that each outcome has of occurring, and
- multiply each value by its probability to arrive at an expected value for each outcome.

The action to be chosen should be the one that gives rise to the highest total expected value or the least amount of loss.

Let's look at a simple example. Assume we have just bought a car costing $30,000, that is, our loss exposure on the car is a maximum of $30,000. The question is, should we have **collision coverage** on the car that will reimburse us if the car is completely destroyed? For now, we will look at only two options — no loss and total loss. Let's assume the probability of the car being completely destroyed is 0.1% and therefore the probability that it will not be completely destroyed is 99.9% (100% – 0.1%). We can either insure the car or not insure it, thus retaining the risk of a total loss. Let's furthermore assume it costs $400 to have collision insurance. Using decision theory, we will calculate the expected value of both insuring the risk and retaining the risk.

	No Loss Occurs			Loss Occurs			Expected Value	
Insure	−$400	99.9%	−399.60	−$ 400	0.1%	−0.40	−400.00	*(−399.60 − 0.40)*
Retain	$ 0	99.9%	0.00	−$30,000	0.1%	−30.00	−30.00	*(+ 0.00 − 30.00)*

This analysis suggests we should *not* insure the car because the expected value of retaining the risk is so much lower than insuring the risk. However, there are two difficulties with this analysis:

1. The **pure premium** in this example is $30 — the probability of a total loss times the amount of the loss. The **gross premium** (what the insured pays) of $400 is obtained by adding **loading costs** — operating expenses, sales commissions, profits, and contingencies. Because loading costs are added to the pure premium to arrive at the gross premium, using the expected value to decide whether or not to insure will *always* tell us to retain the loss.

2. If we decide to retain the risk and a loss occurs, the loss can be very large.

Minimax Regret Theory

This theory is based on **Pascal's Wager**. Blaise Pascal, 1623 to 1662, was a philosopher and gambler who was also religious. He asked the question, "God is, or he is not?" He reasoned that people believe or they don't, so logic cannot supply an answer. Instead, he asked what would happen if you had to gamble on the correct answer. Let's put the possible consequences in a table.

Type of Life Lived	God Is	God Is Not
Pure and pious life	Tolerable life, safe for eternity	No afterlife consequences
Immoral and decadent life	Tolerable life, damned for eternity	No afterlife consequences

If there is no God, the consequences of the kind of life you live affect only your life now. However, if there is a God, the consequences of living an immoral and decadent life are atrocious. Pascal concluded that, whether there is a God or not, one has to live one's life as if God does exist in order to minimize the risk of eternal regret.

In the same way, the minimax regret strategy leads us to want to *minimize our maximum loss* or *minimize our maximum regret*. What is the maximum loss for each option of insuring or retaining the risk?

	No Loss	Loss Occurs	Maximum Loss
Insure	−$400	$ 400	−$ 400
Retain	$ 0	−$30,000	−$30,000

Using this approach, we *will insure* because it provides the lowest potential for regret. This also explains why we choose to retain some risk exposures when the *frequency of loss* (**probability of a loss**) is high and the *amount of the loss* (**severity of the loss**) is low. The cost to insure these risks is very high — the pure premium will be high because the probability of loss is high and then loading expenses are added to it to arrive at the gross premium.

Risk Classification and Expected Value

Why is home insurance cheaper than auto insurance for each dollar of insurance? Why does insurance cost more for poorer drivers? The explanation is a combination of the probability of a loss and the amount of the possible loss.

Let's expand the auto example above and assume two drivers, Alice and Joe. Alice has had several moving violations. None of them seemed too serious at the time. Once, she drifted through a stop sign on a quiet street. Another time she make an illegal left turn when there was no one coming in the opposite direction. And once she was ticketed for running a red light when she deliberately ran a yellow light but the light turned red just before she entered the intersection. Joe, on the other hand, is a model driver with a few parking tickets to his name but no moving violations. Let's also add the possibility of two different levels of partial losses and that each person has a probability of experiencing each loss as shown in the following table. This data is used to calculate

- the expected loss (the expected value) for each, and
- the standard deviation, which is often used as a measure of risk because it measures how much variation there is for each value from the average (mean) value. The higher the standard deviation, the higher the probability that the extreme outcomes will occur.

Amount of loss	Alice (A)		Joe (J)		
	Probability of loss		Probability of loss		
X	P_A	XP_A	P_J	XP_J	
$ 0	40%	$ 0	69%	$ 0	
5,000	30%	1,500	20%	1,000	
10,000	20%	2,000	10%	1,000	
30,000	10%	3,000	1%	300	
Expected Value	100%	**$6,500**	100%	**$2,300**	= Expected Payout (Loss)
Standard Deviation*		$8,675		$4,326	= Amount of Uncertainty about the amount of the payout

* The calculation of **Alice's Standard Deviation** is as follows:

1. Subtract each outcome, X, from the Expected Value, E(x), to get the difference of each outcome from the Expected Value.
2. Square the each difference because we don't care if the outcome is above or below the Expected Value.
3. Multiply the squared difference from step 2 by the weight for each outcome.
4. Add the weighted, squared differences. This is the Variance.
5. Take the square root of the Variance to get the Standard Deviation.

		Step 1	Step 2	Step 3	
X	E(x)	Difference	Difference squared	P_A	Diff ^{2} x P_A
$ 0	$6,500	$6,500	$42,250,000	0.4	$16,900,000
5,000	6,500	1,500	2,250,000	0.3	675,000
10,000	6,500	−3,500	12,250,000	0.2	2,450,000
30,000	6,500	−23,500	552,250,000	0.1	55,225,000
				Step 4 →	$75,250,000
				Step 5 →	$8,675

We can summarize the expected payout for Alice and Joe as well as the range of expected payouts.

		Alice	Joe
Expected payout		$ 6,500	$2,300
Standard deviation (σ)		$ 8,675	$4,326
Range: E(payout) + / − 1 σ	66% of the time or 2 years out of 3, the insurer can expect to pay out:	from $−2,175 to $15,175	from −$2,025 to $6,175

In this simplified example, we can see that Alice, with her poor driving record, has a *higher expected value,* that is, a **higher outcome**, which means the insurer can expect to have to pay out more for Alice than for Joe. In addition, Alice's higher standard deviation makes the outcome more unpredictable. We can expect that the outcomes for Joe will be closer to $2,300, while Alice's outcomes will be closer to $6,500 because there is more variations in the outcomes for Alice.

So we can expect that Alice's insurance rates will be higher than Joe's for two reasons:

1. Her poor driving record makes her expected value higher, that is, her insurer can *expect* to pay out more for her.
2. Her insurer can be less certain about how much it will have to pay out for Alice as reflected in the higher standard deviation for her.

Pooling of Losses and the Law of Large Numbers

The **Law of Large Numbers** states that the more observations there are, the higher is the probability that the *actual* number of observations will be close to the *expected* number of observations. For example, if you throw a die once, there is a 1/6 chance of getting a 4. And the more times you throw it, the more you can expect that a 4 will come up 1/6 of the time. This explains how insurance for a group of people can decrease the cost for each person and still provide a profit for the insurer. For example, a large company with many employees can offer the same group life insurance coverage and health care coverage to all its employees, ranging in age from 18 to 65, because both the company and the insurer absorb the risk of early death in some people.

Let's take our previous example and look at it in more detail. Let's put Alice in a class with another driver, Pete, who has a driving record similar to Alice's. And let's reduce the possible outcomes into only two: no accidents or an accident costing $6,500.

First let's look at Alice by herself.

Amount of loss	Probability of loss	
X	P_A	XP_A
$ 0	40%	$ 0
6,500	60%	3,900
Expected Value	100%	$3,900
Standard Deviation		$3,184

Now we will add Pete.

Pete and Alice agree to share the total costs if either or both have an accident, meaning each will pay half if there is any cost. The cost that each pays can also be called the **average loss** for each. The possibilities are summarized in the first four columns of the following table, which goes on to calculate the expected value and standard deviation for both.

Possible Outcomes	Cost		Probability for each	Calculation of probability	Expected cost	Calculation of Expected cost
	Total	Each				
Neither Alice nor Pete has an accident	$ 0	$ 0	16%	.40 × .40	$ 0	0 × .16
Alice has an accident but Pete does not	6,500	3,250	24%	.40 × .60	780	3,250 × .24
Pete has an accident but Alice does not	6,500	3,250	24%	.60 × .40	780	3,250 × .24
Both have an accident	13,000	6,500	36%	.60 × .60	2,340	6,500 × .36
Expected Value			100%		$3,900	
Standard Deviation					$2,252	

By combining their possible outcomes,

- the probability distribution for each has changed,
- the probability of no loss has dropped for both (from 40% to 16%),
- the *expected loss has remained the same*, and
- the *standard deviation has decreased significantly* from $3,184 to $2,252, a drop of 29% (932 ÷ 3,184).

While the cost (expected value) for each remains the same, the risk (standard deviation) has decreased for both, meaning that *accident costs* have become more predictable for both — pooling has reduced the uncertainty, which is the definition of risk — uncertainty as to the outcome as described earlier.

And if we add a third person into the same risk pool? Without showing the details of the calculation, the expected value remains at $3,900 while the standard deviation drops to $1,838 — a further reduction in uncertainty.

As the number of participants in this risk class increases, the expected outcome remains the same but the standard deviation continues to drop until the probability that the average outcome will be different from the expected outcome becomes negligible. This illustrates the Law of Large Numbers. In statistical terms, this reflects the **Central Limit Theorem,** meaning the distribution of the average outcome becomes more symmetric, that is, more bell-shaped. This is how insurers are able to predict losses for various classes of drivers and charge premiums for each risk class that reflects the predicted losses.

Conclusions about Risk Management

We can now draw some conclusions about risk management.

1. **Don't risk more than you can afford to lose.**
   Select an appropriate amount of insurance — evaluate the risk to determine if the severity of the loss is enough to mean we should insure or use another risk management technique. The severity is far more important than the probability that a loss will occur. A wealthy person might decide to not insure his car since a wealthy person could, presumably, easily afford to replace it. But most of us should insure.

2. **Don't risk a lot for a little.**
   Some homeowners' policies have a requirement that the homeowner must have at least 80% of the replacement value of the home insured in order to collect 100% of a partial loss. This 80% rule (called a **co-insurance clause**) is designed to discourage people from deliberately underinsuring since a total loss is very unlikely, that is, it has a very low probability of happening. Therefore, it may seem tempting to insure a home for only 80% of its value but homeowners' insurance is relatively cheap. On a $200,000 home the premium might be only $600. It doesn't make sense to expose yourself to a $40,000 loss (20% of $200,000) in order to save $120 (20% of $600) a year.

3. **The best buys in insurance cover those losses that are least likely to happen.**
   This explains why
   - the cost per dollar of insurance on a house is so much cheaper than on a car;
   - auto insurance is cheaper for people with good driving records than for people with bad driving records;
   - moving violations increase the cost of auto insurance — they imply you are not a good driver, especially if there are several moving violations;
   - auto insurance is more expensive in large cities than for drivers in rural communities, and
   - life insurance and disability insurance are cheaper for non-smokers than for smokers.

We will look more closely at **ratemaking** (insurance pricing) as we look at each type of insurance in later chapters.

The Insurance Industry

We turn now to the insurance industry to see its environment, size, types of companies and to find out how consumers are protected. An overview of compliance requirements in the insurance industry provides insight into the environment in which the insurance industry operates. Data on the assets, operating revenue and operating profit margin of the twenty-two industries in Canada shows the size of both this and the financial services sector as a whole relative to the other industries.

Primer on Insurance Compliance in Canada

The following material was prepared by Dale W. Scott, B. Com., LL.B., M.B.A., Senior Advisor, General Electric Company.[4]

A. Background

The insurance industry and its participants, products and sales practices are heavily regulated in all industrialized countries.

---

4   Reproduced with permission of author.

Compliance is a critical, front-line business function within an insurance company. In the past few years, insurance compliance has become more complex. The size, capability and prestige of insurance company compliance departments has grown substantially in response to the increased number and complexity of laws and regulations, the increased complexity (and commensurate risks) of the insurance industry and its products, and corporate failures such as Enron and Worldcom.

In Canada, the insurance industry, including life insurance companies, their products and agents, are regulated by both the federal and provincial governments. There are specific, comprehensive and complex insurance statutes and regulations, as well as general business and consumer-protection laws applicable to all businesses.

In the financial services industry, including insurance, the term **compliance** or **legislative compliance management** is used to refer to the legal requirement that companies, products and sales agents must comply with all applicable laws and regulations, both federal and provincial.

Federal

Federal regulatory requirements focus on the financial health, minimum capitalization requirements, risk management, and management and governance of insurance companies. This is commonly referred to as **prudential regulation** and the objective is to ensure the insurance company manages its risks effectively and always has adequate capital and liquidity to pay the claims of policyholders, even in extreme circumstances, such as natural disasters (for example, hurricanes) or disease pandemics.

Provincial

Provincial regulation focuses on the **insurance products** (that is, the terms and pricing of insurance policies) and on the **marketing and sales practices** of insurance companies and agents. Insurance agents and brokers must meet provincial qualifications and licensing requirements. This is commonly referred to as **market conduct regulation** and focuses on protecting customers from misleading or deceptive sales practices, such as understating the costs of policy premiums or overstating the amount of benefits payable to policyholders, commonly referred to as "mis-selling".

B. Federal Regulation and Compliance

The federal regulator is the **Office of the Superintendent of Financial Institutions (Canada) (OSFI)** [www.osfi-bsif.gc.ca], which is an agency of the Department of Finance.

OSFI's activities can be divided into two broad areas: **regulation and supervision**. Regulation is a legislative function, involving the issuance and enforcement of laws and regulations with which insurance companies must comply. Supervision involves assessing of the financial and operational health and soundness of insurance companies.

OSFI refers to its comprehensive array of laws, regulations and guidelines as the **Supervisory Framework**, which is intended to systematically evaluate an insurance company's risk profile, financial condition, risk management processes, and compliance with applicable laws and regulations.

Two key features of the OSFI compliance system put a very strong onus on the insurance company and its internal compliance function and staff:

1. It is a self-regulatory system, that is, the insurance company, not the regulator, is responsible for compliance with the Supervisory Framework and all laws and regulations; OSFI relies on reports and annual audits to assess the quality of the compliance; and

2. the insurance company's internal compliance department, systems, policies and procedures must operate on a continuous, daily basis. Compliance operates non-stop.

The following lists some of the key business, financial, risk management and legal areas that are subject to OSFI regulation and compliance requirements for insurance companies:

- Risk Management — identifying all risks, on an enterprise-wide basis, including financial, operational and legal risks, such as investment risk, credit risk, foreign exchange risk, risk of natural disasters, disease pandemics or terrorism,
- Outsourcing,
- Capital and Liquidity Adequacy (sufficient to pay all claims as the become payable),
- Record keeping,
- Accounting and Financial Reporting,
- Actuarial Requirements, and
- Anti-money laundering and Terrorism Financing.

OSFI reviews reports from the insurance companies on a monthly and quarterly basis and conducts an annual on-site audit. If there are regulatory or compliance deficiencies, OSFI has the authority to levy fines and financial penalties, and to require the insurance company to prepare, file and complete a remediation plan within a specified time period. If the insurance company is at risk of insolvency or inability to pay claims, OSFI can seize the institution and take over its day-to-day management (thankfully, a very rare occurrence in Canada because of our strong regulatory system).

C. Provincial Regulation and Compliance

Insurance agents and brokers must qualify and be licensed in the province in which they reside and sell policies. Insurance companies and their policies and sales practices must comply with the laws of the province in which the policy is sold and the policyholder resides.

The Canadian Council of Insurance Regulators (CCIR) [www.ccir-ccrra.org] is an inter-jurisdictional association of regulators of insurance. Its mandate is to facilitate and promote an effective regulatory system in Canada to serve the public interest. CCIR works co-operatively with other financial services regulators to enhance consumer protection and to develop and harmonize insurance policy and regulation across jurisdictions. Complete contact information for the following membership is provided on CCIR's website.

Table 1.1   CCIR's Membership

Regular Members	
Alberta	• Insurance and Financial Institutions, Alberta Finance, Edmonton, Alta.
British Columbia	• Financial Institutions Commission, Surrey B.C.
Manitoba	• Financial Institutions Regulation Branch, Winnipeg, Man.
Nova Scotia	• Office of Insurance, Credit Unions and Trust and Loan Companies, Department of Finance, Halifax, N.S.
New Brunswick	• Department of Justice — Insurance Branch, Fredericton, N.B.
Newfoundland and Labrador	• Department of Government Services, St. John's, Nfld.
Northwest Territories and Nunavut	• Department of Finance, G.N.W.T., Yellowknife, N.W.T.
Ontario	• Superintendent of Financial Services, Financial Services Commission of Ontario, North York, Ont.
Prince Edward Island	• Office of the Attorney General, Charlottetown, P.E.I.
Québec	• Autorité des marchés financiers, Québec, P.Q.
Saskatchewan	• Saskatchewan Financial Services Commission, Financial Institutions Division, Regina, Sask.
Yukon	• Department of Community Services, Whitehorse, Y.T.
Associate Member: Federal Government	• Office of the Superintendent of Financial Institutions Canada, Ottawa, Ont.

With respect to compliance, insurance companies are required to ensure their policies, agents and sales practices comply with applicable provincial laws and regulations. Usually, this compliance is handled as an integral part of the insurance company's product-development and marketing and sales functions.

Federal/OSFI compliance is usually a head office function involving risk managers, accountants, actuaries, lawyers and paralegals. Conversely, provincial compliance usually involves compliance officers operating in cooperation with product development and marketing at the business-unit level.

Industry Data

As shown in Table 1.2, the financial sector has over 50% of total assets of all industries and less than 10% of operating revenue due mainly to very large investments in loans (Table 1.3).

Table 1.2   Size of All Industries in Canada at December 31, 2008 ($ millions)

	Assets		Operating Revenue		Operating Profit Margin
Non-financial industries					
Agriculture, forestry, fishing and hunting	74,889	1.2%	41,321	1.3%	4.3%
Oil and gas extraction and support activities	464,509	7.3%	207,817	6.6%	18.1%
Mining (except oil and gas)	113,832	1.8%	35,381	1.1%	25.4%
Utilities	71,520	1.1%	67,295	2.1%	5.9%
Construction	173,161	2.7%	242,541	7.7%	5.1%
Manufacturing	700,414	11.0%	709,374	22.5%	6.5%
Wholesale trade	229,533	3.6%	502,792	15.9%	3.8%
Retail trade	186,376	2.9%	444,594	14.1%	4.1%
Transportation and warehousing	173,098	2.7%	136,996	4.3%	9.1%
Information and cultural industries	165,487	2.6%	92,158	2.9%	15.6%
Real estate and rental and leasing	286,100	4.5%	71,016	2.2%	19.1%
Professional, scientific and technical services	145,530	2.3%	106,301	3.4%	5.7%
Administrative and support, waste management and remediation services	58,282	0.9%	70,568	2.2%	5.6%
Educational, healthcare and social assistance services	38,807	0.6%	34,821	1.1%	15.1%
Arts, entertainment and recreation	20,190	0.3%	11,793	0.4%	7.4%
Accommodation and food services	50,591	0.8%	58,577	1.9%	5.6%
Repair, maintenance and personal services	23,234	0.4%	28,416	0.9%	6.1%
	2,975,553	**46.9%**	**2,861,761**	**90.6%**	**7.4%**
Finance and Insurance Industries					
Non-depository credit intermediation	180,099	2.8%	24,695	0.8%	35.8%
Insurance carriers and related activities	432,569	6.8%	94,155	3.0%	18.3%
Activities related to credit intermediation	44,749	0.7%	5,264	0.2%	16.8%
Depository credit intermediation	2,441,866	38.5%	119,717	3.8%	20.8%
Securities, commodity contracts, and other financial investments and related activities	264,711	4.2%	52,583	1.7%	40.6%
	3,363,994	**53.1%**	**296,414**	**9.4%**	**24.7%**
Total, all industries	**6,339,547**	**100.0%**	**3,158,175**	**100.0%**	**9.1%**

Source: Statistics Canada (www.statcan.ca), *Quarterly Financial Statistics for Enterprises*, Fourth Quarter 2008, Tables 1-1, 1-3, and 2-1, Catalogue no. 61-008-X

Table 1.3   Balance Sheet and Income Statements for the Finance and Insurance Industries, December 31, 2008 ($ millions)

	Total	Insurance	Banking	Investment Services	Other Consumer & Business Credit	Other Financial Services
Assets						
Investments & accounts with affiliates	295,756	62,891	141,742	55,926	31,847	3,350
Portfolio investments	822,805	235,397	458,038	104,573	9,297	15,500
Loans	1,499,888	49,772	1,332,727	13,651	87,426	16,312
Capital assets	65,217	10,094	10,883	19,684	23,890	666
Other, net	680,328	74,415	498,476	70,877	27,639	8,921
	3,363,994	432,569	2,441,866	264,711	180,099	44,749
	100.0%	12.9%	72.6%	7.9%	5.4%	1.3%
Liabilities						
Deposits	1,569,703	6,590	1,528,128	24	5,892	29,069
Actuarial liabilities	173,273	173,273	0	0	0	0
Loans & borrowings	325,460	31,582	70,852	82,311	136,797	3,918
A/P & Other	844,358	105,326	670,614	53,912	8,994	5,512
	2,912,794	316,771	2,269,594	136,247	151,683	38,499
Equity	451,200	115,798	172,272	128,464	28,416	6,250
	3,363,994	432,569	2,441,866	264,711	180,099	44,749
Revenue						
Sales of goods & services	54,365	4,911	25,262	20,725	2,100	1,367
Premiums & annuities	70,656	70,656	0	0	0	0
Interest & dividends	128,346	13,668	85,977	13,927	13,086	1,688
Other	43,050	4,920	8,478	17,932	9,511	2,209
	296,417	94,155	119,717	52,584	24,697	5,264
	100.0%	31.8%	40.4%	17.7%	8.3%	1.8%
Operating expenses						
Depreciation & amortization	11,018	876	2,267	2,044	5,561	270
Insurance & annuities	50,565	50,565	0	0	0	0
Interest	44,460	212	41,781	516	900	1,051
Other	117,264	25,521	50,617	28,674	9,393	3,059
	223,307	77,174	94,665	31,234	15,854	4,380
Operating profit	73,110	16,981	25,052	21,350	8,843	884
Interest, gains or losses	24,904	5,515	9,413	2,954	6,743	279
Income tax	11,808	3,800	4,015	2,745	1,015	233
Equity in affiliates' earnings	−4,655	−2,772	−32	−1,790	−36	−25
Net profit before extraordinary gains	41,053	10,438	11,656	17,441	1,121	397
	100.0%	25.4%	28.4%	42.5%	2.7%	1.0%
Using net profit before extraordinary gains						
Return on assets (ROA)	1.2%	2.4%	0.5%	6.6%	0.6%	0.9%
Return on equity (ROE)	9.1%	9.0%	6.8%	13.6%	3.9%	6.4%

Source: Statistics Canada (www.statcan.ca), *Quarterly Financial Statistics for Enterprises*, Fourth Quarter 2008, Tables 22-1, 23-1, 24-1, 25-1, and 26-1, Catalogue no. 61-008-X

Table 1.3 shows that the largest by:
- Assets is Banking with 72.6% of the Total Assets (total of the five listed),
- Revenue is Banking with 40.4%, and
- Net Profit is Investment Services with 42.5% of Total Net Profit, Banking at 28.4% and Insurance at 25.4%. Investment Services has by far the largest return on assets (ROA) at 6.6% and return on equity (ROE) at 13.6%.

Terms Used in Tables 1.2 and 1.3

Table 1.2	Table 1.3	Industry includes:
• Depository credit intermediation	• Banking	• Chartered banks, trust companies, deposit-accepting mortgage companies, credit unions
• Insurance carriers and related activities	• Insurance	
• Securities, commodity contracts, and other financial investments and related activities	• Investment services	• Stock brokers and investment managers
• Non-depository credit intermediation	• Other consumer and business credit	• Companies providing credit cards, sales financing and consumer lending without providing other banking services
• Activities related to credit intermediation	• Other financial services	• Central credit unions, loan brokers and other financial transaction processing such as cheque processing

Types of Insurance Companies

There are two kinds of insurance operations and they operate quite differently due to the character of their respective liabilities.

- **Property and Casualty (P & C) Insurers** cover risk exposures to physical property as well as liability resulting from damage to other people — bodily harm or death and damage to their property.
- **Life and Health Insurers** cover risks to one's own person that have financial implications. These risks include death, sickness or injury that makes a person unable to work, and health costs not covered by provincial plans. In addition, life insurance companies handle Registered Retirement Savings Plans (RRSPs) and annuities such as those one buys at retirement.

The following tables provide some financial information for both sides of the industry.

Canadian Life and Health Insurers

Table 1.4   Premium Income in Canada — 2007 ($ millions)

	Total		Group		Individual	
Life insurance	14,397	20%	3,477	8%	10,920	37%
Annuities	34,303	47%	17,984	41%	16,319	55%
Health Insurance*	24,803	34%	22,444	51%	2,359	8%
	73,503	100%	43,905	100%	29,598	100%

Group health insurance includes premium equivalents (benefit payments and administration fees) of $8,171 million for uninsured contracts administered by life insurance companies.

	Registration		Ownership	
Canadian companies	70,504	96%	62,736	85%
Foreign branches	2,999	4%	10,767	15%
	73,503	100%	73,503	100%

Source: Canadian Life and Health Insurance Association (CLHIA) [www.clhia.ca] Facts 2008 page 17, 24

Table 1.5   Premium Income and Assets — Worldwide Business — 2007 ($ millions)

	Premium Income		Assets	
Canadian income	70,504	*48%*	417,000	*47%*
Other	77,656	*52%*	466,420	*53%*
World-wide income	148,160	*100%*	883,420	*100%*
	16.8%		*100.0%*	

Source: CLHIA, *Facts 2008*, page 25

Table 1.6   Policy Payments and Premium Income — 2007 ($ millions)

	Policy Payments		Premium Income	
Life insurance benefits	7,081	*12.3%*	14,397	*19.6%*
Annuities	28,591	*49.5%*	34,303	*46.7%*
Health Insurance	19,553	*33.9%*	24,803	*33.7%*
Policyholder dividends	2,510	*4.3%*		
	57,735	*100.0%*	73,503	*100.0%*
	78.5%		*100.0%*	

Source: CLHIA, *Facts 2008*, pages 14, 17

Property and Casualty Insurers

Table 1.7   Claims and Net Premiums Written — 2006 ($ millions)

	Claims		Net Premiums Written		Assets	
Auto — all	10,968	*54.0%*	16,590	*47.4%*		
Commercial property	2,173	*10.7%*	4,985	*14.3%*		
Personal Property	3,556	*17.5%*	5,621	*16.1%*		
Liability	2,577	*12.7%*	4,826	*13.8%*		
Accident, Sickness	274	*1.3%*	765	*2.2%*	72,988	Canadian
Other	778	*3.8%*	2,177	*6.2%*	29,900	Foreign
	20,326	*100.0%*	34,964	*100.0%*	102,888	Total
	20%		*34%*		*100%*	
	58%		*100%*			

Source: Insurance Bureau of Canada (IBC) [www.ibc.ca], *Facts 2008*, pp. 6, 7, 11, 16, 17.

And, finally...

Table 1.8   Top 5 Natural Disasters since 1992 ($2006 adjusted for inflation)

Southern Quebec	January, 1998	Ice storm	$1,763,818,000
Ontario	August, 2005	Wind/rainstorm	$509,813,000
Alberta	June, 2005	Flooding	$305,888,000
Quebec	July, 1996	Flooding	$254,230,000
Manitoba	August, 1993	Flooding	$235,581,000

Source: IBC, *Facts 2008*, pp. 20, 21.

There are two types of **ownership** of insurance companies:

- **Stock insurance companies** are corporations which have shares — they have shareholders who elect a board of directors to manage the company and a second board of directors is elected by the policyholders. Stock insurers can raise new investment capital for expansion by selling shares as well as through issuing bonds and using retained earnings. They pay traditional dividends to their shareholders as well as insurance dividends, a refund of premiums, to policyholders.

- **Mutual insurance companies** are owned by the policyholders. They have no capital stock so their net income is paid out as a dividend (refund of premiums) if it is not retained to finance future growth. The board of directors is elected by the policyholders. Their only vehicle for raising new capital is by issuing bonds.

During the late 1900s, many Canadian mutual insurers issued shares and became stock insurance companies in order to be able to raise equity to compete with international insurers. This process is called **demutualization**.

Captive insurers are wholly-owned subsidiaries of non-insurance organizations. The primary function of a captive insurer is to insure the risk exposures of its parent and/or its parent's affiliates. There are several types of captive insurers:

- a **pure captive insurer** covers only the parent and companies the parent controls. This provides lower operating costs than a traditional insurer although the funds used to capitalize the insurance operation might be put to better use.
- a **group or association captive** has many parents. It spreads fixed costs among several entities and the risk sharing reduces volatility. **Canadian Universities Reciprocal Insurance Exchange (CURIE)** is the name for 44 universities who have banded together to pool and collectively insure their property, liability, and errors and omissions risks. It was formed in 1988 in response to rising premiums and decreasing liability coverage which was making liability rates per students escalate and more university activities uninsurable.

Consumer Protection

Consumers who have insurance policies in place are dependent on the insurer to be in business when a claim is made. Insurance companies do not fail frequently but when they do, they can leave insureds without coverage. There are four organizations that provide protection for consumers — two provide direct consumer protection, one helps consumers find the appropriate compensation plan, and one oversees insurance companies

- **Assuris formerly Canadian Life and Health Insurance Compensation Corporation (CompCorp)** [www.assuris.ca] is a federally- incorporated private company funded by the insurance industry to provide consumer protection. All federal and most provincial insurance companies are required to be members.
- **Property and Casualty Insurance Compensation Corporation (PACICC)** [www.pacicc.com] provides up to $250,000 per claim for claims left unpaid by a bankrupt insurer. It will also refund up to 70% of unexpired premiums. Most property and casualty insurers are members.
- **Canadian Consumer Protection for Financial Institution Failures (CCPFSI)** [www.financeprotection.ca] assists consumers in locating the appropriate compensation plan that provides protection for their savings, investments and insurance policies.
- **Financial Consumer Agency of Canada (FCAC)** [www.fcac-acfc.gc.ca] oversees consumer protection in the federally-regulated financial services sector. FCAC supervises financial institutions to ensure they comply with federal consumer protection measures. The Agency also monitors financial institutions (banks and federally incorporated trust, loan and insurance companies) to ensure they adhere to their voluntary codes and commitments. FCAC's mandate includes educating consumers about their financial rights and responsibilities. Agency operations are funded through assessments on the financial institutions it oversees.

The *Uniform Life Insurance Act* makes the nine common-law provinces uniform in their operations. Quebec, using civil law, is not included.

Types of Insurance

The following table provides a brief overview of general and life and health insurance products available for individuals and businesses which we will be looking at in later chapters.

Type	Personal lines	Commercial lines
Property and Liability	Homeowner's policy Automobile policy	Automobile insurance Building and personal property Burglary, robbery and theft insurance Business income insurance Casualty insurance Credit insurance Directors and officers liability Environmental liability Equipment breakdown (boiler and machinery insurance) Errors and omissions Fidelity and surety bonds Malpractice Insurance Product liability insurance Title insurance Transportation Insurance • Ocean marine originally only for ocean-going vessels and their cargo, now usually door-to-door • Inland marine covers carriers such as railroads, trucks inland ships and barges as well as bridges, tunnels, pipelines, power lines, radio and television communications equipment, and cellphone towers
Life	Individual policy	Group Policy Key-person insurance
Disability	Individual Policy	Group Policy
Critical Illness	Individual Policy	Not usually available
Long-term Care	Individual Policy	Not usually available
Health	Provincial and territorial governments and some private insurers (for example, Blue Cross)	Group Policy

Summary

There are many ways of categorizing risks, and these categories are useful to help ascertain the presence of a risk exposure and the likelihood of a loss. A peril is the cause of a loss while a hazard is something that increases the likelihood or probable severity of a loss. There are four different types of hazards: physical, moral, morale, and legal.

There are six steps in the risk management process and five main ways of handling risk. It is in the nature of insurance to pool fortuitous losses, transferring the risk from the insured to the insurer, who indemnifies the insured against future losses. Not every loss exposure is insurable. The principles of insurance include the principles of indemnity and subrogation, and insureds must have an insurable interest in the loss exposure, can expect the coverage to be reasonable with any exceptions being made clear, and are expected to provide complete and true information to the insurer.

Decision theory, minimax regret theory, expected value, pooling of losses and the law of large numbers all help us understand how insurers are able to determine the premium for various classes of insureds. This is explored further in Chapter 9 when the rationale for life insurance rates is presented.

The insurance industry is both a large industry and a highly regulated industry in Canada, and there are organizations whose function is to protect consumers in the event of an insurance company's failing to maintain solvency. The checks for solvency are laid out in Chapter 9.

Sources

Against the Gods. The Remarkable Story of Risk, Peter L. Bernstein, John Wiley & Sons, Inc., 1996, New York.

Facts 2008, Canadian Life and Health Insurance Association (CLHIA) [www.clhia.ca].

Facts 2008, Insurance Bureau of Canada (IBC) [www.ibc.ca].

Fundamentals of Risk and Insurance, 9th edition, Vaughan, E.J. and Vaughan, T., John Wiley and Sons, Inc., New York, 2003.

"Here's the lowdown on your losses", Ellen Roseman, *The Toronto Star*, January 14, 2009.

Primer on Insurance Compliance in Canada, Dale W. Scott, B. Com., LL.B., M.B.A., Senior Advisor, General Electric Company.

Principles of Risk Management and Insurance, 9th edition, George E. Rejda, Pearson Education, Inc., New York, 2004.

Statistics Canada [www.statcan.ca], *Quarterly Financial Statistics for Enterprises*, Product 61-008-XWE, First Quarter 2007, Vol. 18, No. 1.

Statistics Canada [www.statcan.ca], *Summary Tables in Canadian Statistics*, Product 61-008, Banking — Balance Sheet and Income Statement.

"What Happens if We're Wrong?", Peter L. Bernstein, *New York Times*, June 22, 2008. Peter L. Bernstein, a financial consultant and economic historian, is the editor of the *Economics & Portfolio Strategy* newsletter.

Application Case

Joanne, age 38, is a single mother with a 16-year-old son. She runs a public relations business from her home, where she has made a large, comfortable office in her basement. Mostly she meets clients at their offices but occasionally she invites clients to her home office. Her net income after business expenses is $63,000 a year — a nice living but not grand by any standard. Her ex-husband has moved to England. Instead of paying support, he paid off her mortgage before he left. In addition, he has agreed to finance their son's university education.

Joanne's friend, Jeremy, is also self-employed and has just been successfully sued by a client. Jeremy does not have insurance but since he had to pay only $9,000, he thinks he's fine without errors and omissions insurance. But his situation has led Joanne to make an appointment with Francesca, her financial planner to discuss her insurance needs.

A. Joanne asks, "**What is risk?**"

Francesca replies, "There are many definitions of risk, running from a hazard or danger to the chance of being wrong about our expectations, sometimes wrong in a good way. For insurance purposes, we will define risk as an uncertainty about the occurrence of a loss" (Page 7).

B. "Are there different **kinds of risk**?"

Francesca responds with the following list and explains, "The purpose of the list is to widen your view so that you are better able to recognize risks" (Page 7).

1. **Exogenous and endogenous** are risks over which we have no control and risks that are dependent on our actions.

2. **Objective and Subjective** are risks that can be determined using hard data as opposed to risks that are based on personal evaluations.

3. **Pure risks** have only a loss or no loss, while **speculative risks** can have an upside. Pure risks for

    (a) individuals include property with both direct and indirect losses, personal and liability

    (b) businesses are the same as for individuals plus financial (exchange rate and interest rate risk), credit risk, operational risk, strategic risk, and risk to reputation.

4. **Dynamic and Static** risks are or are not connected to changes in the economy.

5. **Fundamental and Particular** risks affect a large group of people or only individuals.

6. **Social and Private Insurance** cover some risks and are either required by governments or are purchased by individuals.

Now Joanne asks for an espresso — she's getting a headache from all these definitions and a strong coffee is in order. Francesca gets her the coffee and tells her to relax, that these definitions are just to help recognize various risks since the worst thing she could do is fail to recognize a risk because then she wouldn't be able to deal with it.

C. Joanne wants to know if it matters **what caused the loss** and are there things that increase the probability of a loss (Page 11).

"Losses are caused by **perils,** while **hazards** increase the likelihood or severity of losses. There are four types of hazards: physical, moral, morale, and legal," replies Francesca.

D. Jeremy thinks that insurance, except for liability on his car and home insurance, is for people with no nerve — it's just a **form of gambling** and he'd rather take his chances without paying the premiums. Can Francesca address this (Page 12)?

"Insurance transfers an existing risk to an insurance company while gambling creates a new risk."

E. Joanne takes a deep breath and asks how she can ever get on top of all this — it sounds so complicated. Francesca assures her there is a **standard approach to risk management**. In fact, there are six steps (Page 13).
   1. Determine your objectives.
   2. Identify your risks.
   3. Evaluate them — are they critical, material, minor, or insurable?
   4. Consider the options and choose the appropriate technique for handling them (more on this in a minute).
   5. Implement your plan.
   6. Evaluate and review your plan on a regular basis.

F. Joanne is ready to ask for another coffee but is afraid she might start shaking so she doesn't. She asks how she will ever be able to know the options and choose the **"appropriate"** technique? Francesca reassures her that there are standard ways of going at this also (Page 15).
   1. risk avoidance
   2. loss control:
      (a) reduction (severity)
      (b) prevention (frequency)
   3. retention
   4. non-insurance transfers such as incorporating a business, hedging financial risks, and hold-harmless clauses, and
   5. Transferring risk using insurance.

G. Joanne says: "How can insurance companies afford to pay out such huge payments? I read in the paper recently that the 9/11 tally came to $20 billion. I realize that insurance companies sometimes charge high premiums but how on earth do they ever figure out how much to charge?"

"Well," Francesca replies, "let's take this in small steps. Let's assume you have a $30,000 car and the collision coverage costs $400. Should you insure it? I realize the decision is obvious but there is actually some theory behind it."
   1. If we were to use **decision theory**, we would multiply the probability of a loss against the amount of the loss to come up with the **expected value** for either insuring it or not. For now we will talk only about the **pure premium** without the **loading costs** that cover all the expenses and are added to arrive at the **gross premium** (Page 17).
   2. Then again, using something called the **minimax regret theory**, we would want to minimize our maximum possible regret. Here we can use Pascal's Wager about how one should conduct oneself assuming God might exist (Page 17).
   3. Now let's classify risk by looking at two drivers — Alice and Joe. Joe is a good driver, Alice isn't. Insurance companies put them into different classes and, using historical data, they estimate how much they will have to payout for each of them. That is called the **Expected Value**. They can also have an idea of how accurate their prediction is by calculating the **Standard Deviation**" (Page 19).

4. If we add more drivers to each of their risk classes, we see that the overall expected payout for each class remains the same but the standard deviation drops, indicating less variability in the expected payout. This example illustrates both the pooling of losses doctrine and the law of large numbers that make it possible for insurers to set premiums with some assurance that they will be reasonably accurate.

H. Joanne asks, "Yes, but why is it so much cheaper to insure my house than my car when my house is worth so much more than my car?"

Francesca replies, "Let's look at what conclusion we can draw from these examples" (Page 21).

1. Don't risk more than you can afford to lose.
2. Don't risk a lot for a little.
3. The best buys on insurance cover those losses that are least likely to happen. You are far more likely to have a complete loss on your car than on your house. Even a small loss on your car is more likely than on your house.

I. Francesca continues, "Now let's look at the industry itself."

1. We'll start with a brief overview of how insurance is regulated at the provincial and federal levels. Federally, the Office of the Superintendent of Financial Institutions (OSFI) regulates and supervises federally regulated insurance companies. Every province and territory has its own regulator for provincially regulated insurance companies (Page 23).
2. Table 1.2 shows the size of the Finance and Insurance Industries in the context of all twenty-two industries in Canada while Table 1.3 looks more closely at this sector (Page 25).
3. There are two basic types of insurance companies — Property and Casualty (P & C) and Life and Health. Tables 1.4 to 1.7 show some income and asset information for these two sectors while Table 1.8 lists the top five natural disasters since 1992 in terms of insurance claims (Page 26).
4. And, finally, there are two types of ownership of insurance companies: stock insurers, and mutual insurers" (Page 27).
5. Captive insurers are a special kind of insurance company owned by a non-insurance organization to provide insurance only to a one organization or a group of organizations.

J. "**Consumer protection** is provided by the following organizations:

1. Assuris, formerly Canadian Life and Health Insurance Compensation Corporation (CompCorp) protects policyholders on the life and health side should a life insurer fail,
2. Property and Casualty Insurance Compensation Corporation (PACICC) protects policyholders in case a P&C insurer fails,
3. Canadian Consumer Protection for Financial Institution Failures (CCPFSI) assists consumers in locating the appropriate compensation plan, and
4. Financial Consumer Agency of Canada (FCAC) oversees consumer protection in the federally-regulated financial services sector.

K. Joanne says she didn't realize it was so structured and so complicated. Can Francesca give her an idea of the types of insurance available for individuals and for companies? Francesca answers that, while this list isn't exhaustive, it covers the **major types** (Page 28).

L. Francesca asks Joanne if she can guess from the list of insurance types what type of insurance she would need for the following types of risk exposures:

1. Joanne is killed in an auto accident while on the way to a client's office.
2. Joanne comes down with Lymes disease. She cannot work at all for six months and then can work only part-time for several more months.
3. Joanne's son comes down with Lymes disease and
   (a) she works part-time for a year to look after him, or
   (b) she hires someone to look after him.
4. Joanne loses a major client. Can she collect employment insurance benefits?

5. A client comes to her office and slips on the front stairs. The client has to have several months of physiotherapy, which is not covered by her provincial health plan.

Concept Questions

You have passed the Certified Financial Planner (CFP) exam and work for Francesca acquiring the two years work experience you need to receive the CFP designation. Jeremy, Joanne's friend, wants to meet with you because the hourly rate for you is a lot less than for Francesca and he is not yet convinced that this is a useful exercise. He asks you the following questions:

1. Define *risk* and explain how it relates to insurance.

2. Does the concept of the risk/return tradeoff mean that you will always get a higher return if you accept more risk in an investment?

3. Indicate if the following risks are exogenous or endogenous:
   (a) An earthquake
   (b) Driving while intoxicated
   (c) A flood
   (d) Walking into a final exam after staying up all night to study.

4. Does using a mean and standard deviation to evaluate investments always result in an accurate measure of risk?

5. What is the limitation of a subjective risk?

6. Explain why insurance companies use inductive reasoning.

7. Explain the difference between a pure risk and speculative risk.

8. What are the three categories of pure risk for individuals?

9. Maple Leaf Foods has recently had a bad run that has resulted from people getting sick with listeria. What kind of business risk does this present for the company?

10. Is the recent market turmoil, in both the housing market and the investing market, a dynamic risk or a static risk?

11. Is the possibility that the government of a nation can be overthrown by a foreign army an example of a fundamental risk or a particular risk?

12. What is social insurance? What does it include?

13. Are Old Age Security pensions and Guaranteed Income Supplement pensions considered to be social insurance?

14. Explain the difference between a hazard and a peril.

15. Explain the difference between a morale and a moral hazard.

16. What are the six steps involved in the risk management process?

17. The beloved and deceased Roy Orbison was giving an interview in England, saying that his house was indestructible because it was built out concrete and steel. However, the doors opened inward and when a fire started at the same time that he was giving the interview, his parents, who were babysitting, couldn't get the doors to open. The house burned down and two of his three young sons died. What part of the risk management process did Roy fail to assess accurately?

18. Explain the difference between the maximum possible loss and the maximum probable loss?

19. Explain what is meant by self-insuring.

20. Provide the risk management tool for each of the following examples.
    (a) Jan and her husband, Carl, both smoke but always step outside for their smoke to avoid providing their children with second-hand smoke.
    (b) Nonetheless, Jan allows herself only five cigarettes a day.
    (c) Carl smokes his little heart out, figuring he'll go when his time has come.
    (d) When Jan started her marketing company, she elected to incorporate even though she had to pledge some of her personal assets to get a bank loan.
    (e) When her business reached $500,000 in gross billings, Jan treated herself to a very, very nice Swiss watch which, in reality, she could ill afford to lose. What can she do other than giving up the watch?

21. When deciding whether to insure or retain a risk, why does the expected value method always conclude that retaining the risk is a better solution? How is the pure premium calculated?

22. Which is more important when evaluating a loss that might be insured — the severity of the loss or the probability that it will occur?

23. What are the names of the theories that explain why the more bad risks in a category, the cheaper the insurance?

24. Which of the three conclusions about risk management tells you that it is foolhardy to decide to insure your house for only enough to cover off the co-insurance requirement?

25. What is prudent regulation, and what is its purpose?

26. What is the name of the federal regulator for insurance?

27. For which province or territory is there no insurance regulator?

28. Which is the largest industry in Canada by
    (a) Assets?
    (b) Operating Revenue?
    (c) Operating Profit Margin?

29. Of the five sectors in "Finance and Insurance Industries", which is the second largest by:
    (a) Assets?
    (b) Revenue?
    (c) Net profit before extraordinary gains?
    (d) ROA?
    (d) ROE?

30. Where in Canada is it most dangerous to live in terms of natural disasters?

31. Which type of insurance company pays dividends that are only a refund of premiums?

32. What type of insurer is CURIE?

33. Which association would have protected policyholders when Confederation Life went bankrupt in 1994?

Application Questions

34. Robert and Amy are both in Las Vegas gambling with their hard-earned savings in hopes of winning millions. Assume that at the Casino they are in, there is 80% chance of loss at the roulette table. Explain how it is possible that the objective risk for both of them be different than 80% even though the chance of loss is identical if they choose to play roulette.

35. Identify each of the following independent situations as pure or speculative risks:

(a) Sunny and Paul decide to open a family restaurant.
(b) A house on Lakeshore Boulevard in Toronto can be seriously damaged during any sort of flood.
(c) George purchases 1,000 shares of Nortel stock.
(d) Mary decides to drive to work on a stormy morning.
(e) A steel worker can be seriously injured if he or she falls while on the job.

36. Many people compare insurance to gambling. They feel that insurance is another form of gambling. Are they correct? Explain.

37. For each of the following situations indicate the best risk management technique for handling the risk:
    (a) The Deol family decides it's time to take a vacation to the Dominican Republic. However, they fear that their vacation could be ruined by a hurricane or a tropical storm, as the Dominican Republic is known for violent hurricanes and tropical storms at this time of year. What risk management technique would you recommend?
    (b) Showtime Rentals is a movie rental franchise that has numerous franchises around the city of Toronto and surrounding areas. Recently, the store has seen a significant decline in profitability as a lot of merchandise is disappearing off the shelves without being purchased. What risk management technique would be best for this situation?
    (c) Stephen and Monica de la Hoya own a massive stock portfolio valued at approximately $500 million Canadian. They are worried that their stock portfolio, which is invested heavily in various foreign industries, could experience significant decline in value if exchange rates move significantly. What risk management technique is recommended for this situation?
    (d) Jason, the sole breadwinner in his family, works as a police officer in the increasingly deadly streets of Toronto. He does not want his family to suffer financial difficulties if he were to die on the job. What risk management technique is appropriate?
    (e) Helen loves her new vacation home in British Columbia. After purchasing her home she learned that it lies on a tectonic plate that will one day be responsible for a massive earthquake. She also learned that her homeowners' insurance does not cover earthquakes. What risk management techniques are available to her?

38. Nicole recently purchased a new home which cost her $350,000. She has installed a home security system and has fire extinguishers all over her home. She feels that the precautions she has taken to protect her home may be enough, and she is seriously considering not purchasing home insurance. The home insurance premium will cost $2,000 and the insurance company estimates that there is a 0.5% chance that the home will be totally destroyed.
    (a) Using decision theory, calculate the expected value of her two options: insuring the risk or retaining the risk. Which one would you choose using this method? (Retain the risk)
    (b) Using the minimax regret strategy, which alternative would Nicole choose? (Insurance)

39. Larry, who is accident-prone, falls in a risk category with an expected value of $3,200 and a standard deviation of $1,200. When Michelle, who is also accident-prone, is added to his risk class, would you expect the standard deviation to be $2,000 or $900 and why?

40. Describe the two ways insurance companies are organized in Canada.

Backdrop to Insurance
and Insurance Law

Learning Objectives

After completing this chapter, students will:

A. Know the nature of insurance, be able to recognize an insurable risk, and understand the four principles of insurance.

B. Be able to identify the different parts of an insurance contract and see how the rules of contract law apply to the insurance industry.

C. Have first-hand knowledge of a life insurance policy as a contract.

D. Be familiar with the fundamental elements of negligence, which is the basis for liability insurance and is enforced through tort law.

Introduction

Insurance has been around for about 4,000 years, and the basic characteristics have not changed a great deal since the fundamental benefits of insurance have not changed in that time. The principles have become refined over the years to ensure that one of the basic tenets — that of utmost good faith — is operable for both the insured and the insurer.

In Chapter 1, we looked at the first of two fundamental principles that explain how insurance works, that of the Law of Large Numbers. In this chapter, we look at the second — that *an insurance policy is a contract*. In the history of insurance that follows, we see that wealthy men would sign their name under the amount of risk they were willing to take, underwriting the risk and guaranteeing the amount of the shipment they were willing to take. In signing, they created a legal contract. Since insurance policies are contracts, they fall under **contract law** and we will look at the elements of contract law.

Tort law applies to private individuals for wrongs done to them by other people and it affects insurance companies as many potential wrongs can be covered by an insurance contract. This leads to negligence, which is the failure to exercise a reasonable standard of care when it leads to bodily harm of others or damage to their property.

Insurance

A Brief History

Insurance as a field dates back to 2100 B.C.E. in Babylonia whereby the trader (owner) of a caravan would take out a loan to finance the expedition. If the caravan didn't arrive due to robbery, bad weather or breakdown, the owner did not have to repay the loan. If it did arrive, the owner repaid with interest. The Code of Hammurabi in 1800 B.C.E.. extended this to ships. In 100 B.C.E., Romans developed burial clubs, which paid funeral expenses for members and, later, payments to their survivors.

The medieval era (as early as the 10th century) saw the establishment of **guilds** — groups of individuals with common goals. **Merchant guilds** were for those involved in long-distance commerce and local wholesale trade; **craft guilds** were for those in particular trades, such as bakers, brewers, and butchers; **guilds of manufacturers** were for those who made durable goods, such as textiles, military equipment, and metal ware, and these were guilds who sold skills and services such as clerks, teamsters and entertainers. Functioning essentially as trade unions whose goals were to protect the good quality of their work, they also looked out for the welfare of their members by protecting them from losses due to fire and shipwrecks, and paying ransoms to pirates as well as funeral expenses and support in times of sickness and poverty. In 1063, the Amalfi Sea Code reimbursed merchants whose ships were lost. The reimbursement came from a pool to which all members contributed.

The first actual insurance policy was signed in Genoa, Italy, in 1347. Individuals signed their names and, under the name, the amount of risk they were willing to assume — hence the term **underwriter**. Beginning in 1693, merchants, ship owners, and underwriters met at Lloyd's Coffee House in London, England, to arrange insurance contracts. This endeavour grew into Lloyd's of London, one of the first modern insurance companies. Also in 1693 the astronomer Edmond Halley created the first **mortality tables** (tables that show death rates by age), using statistical laws of mortality and the principle of compound interest. He used the same rate for all ages. In 1756, Joseph Dodson scaled the premium rates to age.

The first stock insurance companies, insurance companies with shareholders, were set up in England in 1720 and in the United States in 1735. The great New York fire of 1835 called attention to the need for adequate **reserves** (funds set aside for a special purpose) to meet unexpectedly high losses. The great Chicago fire of 1871 reinforced this need and led to the idea of **reinsurance** — more than one insurance company covering a policy to spread the risk among several insurance companies. The Canada Life Assurance Company, Canada's first insurance company, was set up in 1843 in Hamilton, Ontario. It was also a stock insurance company.

The *Workers' Compensation Act of 1897* in Britain required employers to insure their employees against accidents at work. In the 19th century, many fraternal societies, such as the modern-day Kiwanis Club, Lions Club, and Rotary Club, were created to provide low-cost life and health insurance for their members. And so it went. Farmers wanted crop insurance. Depositors wanted deposit insurance. Travellers wanted travel insurance.

So let's take a look at this business of insurance.

Basic Characteristics

Insurance is a way of handling a great many, but not all, risk exposures. The axioms of insurance include the following:

1. **Pooling or sharing of losses.** Pooling is combining one's risk exposure with others who have similar risks to distribute the risk among the group. This presupposes that future losses of the group can be predicted with some degree of accuracy.

2. **Losses must be fortuitous.** The losses must be accidental, not deliberate.

3. **Transfer of pure risks.** Only pure risk is transferred from the insured to the insurer.

4. **Indemnification of losses.** Insurers agree to indemnify insureds for losses. **To indemnify** means to restore a loss in whole or in part by payment, repair, or replacement without the insured making a profit from the loss. The losses might be a house and contents in case of a fire, income in case of accident or illness, lost future income in case of death, and legal obligations in case of a lost lawsuit. The **remedy of rescission** (from "rescinding" to annul, repeal, cancel) means the insurance will put the injured party back into the position the insured would have been in had there been no loss.

Benefits and Costs to Society
Benefits

- **Indemnification for loss.** The insured does not have to bear the financial consequences for major insurable losses.

- **Less worry and fear**. Because people are insured, they do not have to worry about and prepare for major losses.
- **Source of investment funds**. Insurance companies have large reserves of funds to pay out future losses. These funds are a major source of investment funds for the investment community, which we will look further at this later in this book.
- **Loss prevention**. Insurance companies play an active role in developing programs to minimize losses. These programs include fire prevention, preventing theft and arson, and reducing work-related disabilities.
- **Enhancement of credit**. Because people have insurance coverage for major loss exposures, they can more easily obtain credit. In fact, a homeowner cannot get a residential mortgage from a financial institution without showing proof of insurance coverage.

Costs

- **Cost of doing business**. Insurance premiums increase costs for the insured. In addition to the pure premium, the premiums have to cover the costs of insurance operations and profits. On the other hand, insurance companies also provide jobs to thousands of employees.
- **Fraudulent and inflated claims**. Claims for losses not actually incurred increases the cost to everyone who pays insurance premiums. Inflated claims show up as malingering after an illness while collecting disability, claiming for losses after a fire or break-in that did not actually happen, and as additional legal costs resulting from lawsuits that are made because the plaintiff knows the defendant is insured.

Insurable Risk

Can all risks be insured by private insurers or do some risks have to be left to government with deeper pockets? The basic requirements of an **insurable risk** are as follows:

1. **Large number of exposure units**. There have to enough insureds to be able to have a large enough pool of subscribers to spread the risk among them.
2. **Accidental and unintentional loss**. The losses have to be fortuitous, that is, they can't have happened deliberately. This is one of the reasons that self-employed people in Canada do not pay employment insurance premiums — self-employed people are the only ones who could lay themselves off, either outright or through being unable to find enough work. If self-employed people could collect employment insurance, they might lose a large incentive to find work.
3. **Determinable and measurable loss**. If the size of the loss cannot be predicted, there is no basis for determining the appropriate premium.
4. **No catastrophic loss**. Private companies cannot insure catastrophic losses. In the homeowners policy in Chapter 4, you will see that one of the **exclusions** (a peril not covered by the policy) is loss arising from war.
5. **Calculable chance of loss**. The insurer must be able to calculate the chance of loss. If tornados almost never hit Toronto, it is not possible to calculate the probability of a tornado hitting Toronto. This is why governments provide disaster relief where unexpected natural disasters occur since these types of losses are seldom insurable.
6. **Economically feasible premium**. The premium has to be affordable. It might be high but has to be cost-effective relative to the size of the loss. Would you insure the loss of a $60 watch? No, you wouldn't. By the time the insurance company added its mark-up to cover its operating costs and profits, the premium would be ridiculously high relative to the size of the loss exposure.

Let's compare the insurability of the risk in war in Canada with the risk of an oil pipeline breaking.

	War in Canada	Oil Pipeline Breaking
Large number of exposure units	• Yes	• Yes
Accidental and unintentional loss	• No	• Yes
Determinable and measurable loss	• No	• Yes
No catastrophic loss	• Losses could be catastrophic	• Losses could be large but would not be catastrophic
Calculable chance of loss	• No	• Yes
Economically feasible premium	• Cannot be determined	• Yes

Principles of Insurance

There are five basic principles that are reflected in all insurance contracts:

1. Principle of Indemnity
2. Insurable Interest
3. Reasonable Expectations
4. Subrogation
5. Utmost Good Faith

1. Principle of Indemnity

This principle states that the insured should not profit from the covered loss but should be restored to approximately the same financial position that existed prior to the loss. There are some exceptions to this principle:

(a) In a **valued policy,** the insured and insurer agree on the value of something, like a piece of jewelry or a painting, and that is the amount that is paid if it is lost or damaged.
(b) **Replacement cost** insurance on a home and contents will replace the lost or damaged item with a new one, not one that reflects the depreciated or used value.
(c) **Life insurance** policies pay the face value, which is based on the amount purchased at the inception of the policy. While we can calculate the present value of an individual's expected future earnings, there is no way to calculate the intrinsic value of a human life.

Further, a person can buy as much life insurance as he or she is prepared to pay for.

2. Insurable Interest

The person who takes out the policy must lose financially if a loss occurs, or must incur some other kind of harm if the loss takes place. In other words, the insured must have some kind of financial investment in whatever or whomever is insured. This requirement exists for several reasons:

(a) **To prevent gambling.** Without this, someone might think you are a terrible driver of your very expensive car and be willing to bet the cost of a few years' car insurance premiums that you will have a serious accident.
(b) **To reduce moral hazard.** Without this, someone might first take out an insurance policy on your life and then murder you to collect the proceeds.
(c) **Must be able to measure the loss.** The insurance company has to know that there is a limit on what it might have to pay out for any given loss exposure. Otherwise, if someone is a poor driver, each person in a group of friends could take out a car insurance policy on the car and just sit back and wait to collect. If the car in question is old and not worth much, the insurance company might be rather surprised to find itself paying out several thousand dollars for it. Even if several insurance companies are involved, should they really be paying out several thousand dollars for a car that might be worth $1,500?

In **property insurance** the insurable interest has to exist at the *time of the loss* while in **life insurance**, it must exist at the *time the policy is taken out*, not at the date of death.

3. Reasonable Expectations

The insured is entitled to the coverage he or she reasonably expects the policy to provide, and, to be effective, exclusions or qualifications must be conspicuous, plain, and clear. There should be no surprises later. That is why it is important to read your policy carefully to know what is and is not covered.

4. Subrogation

The insurer (the second party to the insurance contract) will pay the insured (the first party) for a loss caused by a third party and the insurer is entitled to recover the loss from a negligent third party (the third party is negligent by definition by virtue of having caused the loss). The goal of this principle is to

(a) prevent the insured collecting twice — once from the insurance company and once from the negligent third party;

(b) hold the guilty person responsible for the loss; and

(c) hold down insurance rates — if the insurance company who pays for the loss can recover some its cost from a third party, it does not have to reflect this amount in its premiums.

There are **five corollaries** to this principle:

1. The insurer can recover only the amount paid out, not more.
2. The insured cannot impair the insurer's rights by, for instance, making a deal with the third party.
3. The insurer can waive its rights to recover — it is not obligated to recover its loss.
4. This principle does not apply to life insurance and most individual health insurance contracts.
5. The insurer cannot subrogate its own insureds — it cannot pay an insured's losses and then go after the same insured to recover the amount paid out.

5. Utmost Good Faith

A higher degree of honesty is imposed on the parties to an insurance contract than to other contracts. **Good faith** (*bona fida*) means there is an absence of intent to take advantage or defraud. **Utmost good faith** (*uberrimae fidei*) means the insurer must rely on the insured to have provided true, complete information. The insurance company may require proof of certain things from you, but it operates on the assumption that you have told the truth and that you do not have fraud as your intent.

Contracts and Contract Law

Insurance policies are contracts and are dealt with under contract law. In Canada, there are two systems of laws:

1. **Civil Law** which has a comprehensive statement of rules that are often framed as broad, general principles. Called the **Civil Code** in Quebec, this system dates back to ancient Rome and is used also in France. In a dispute, the courts look first to the Code and then to prior decisions for consistency.

2. **Common Law** is used in the rest of Canada and the United States. It was developed in England, where it is called **judge-made law** because it is a system of rules based on precedents and there is no "code" or "legislation". It is based on laws but when the law is not clear, the

judge makes a decision based on prior decision or precedents. If there is no precedent, the court will find itself in the position of making a precedent.

The Law in Canada

There are two basic categories of laws in Canada:

1. **Public Law** deals with the relationship between individuals and the state or between jurisdictions, for example between federal, provincial and municipal governments. It deals with **public wrongs** — a violation of the rights of society as a whole. The three areas of public law are as follows:
   (a) **Criminal Law** — if someone breaks a criminal law, the state will prosecute the individual.
   (b) **Administrative Law** — the body of law that ensures that governments and government officials deal with citizens in a way that is both lawful and fair. It covers a range from dealings with Canada Revenue Agency (and the *Income Tax Act*) to applying for a municipal building permit. It includes laws such as the Employment Insurance Law, the *Broadcasting Act*, the *Canadian Radio-Television and Telecommunications (CRTC) Act*, the *Canada Transportation Act*, and the Immigration Law.
   (c) **Constitutional Law** — defines both the powers and the limits of those powers that different levels of government can exercise. Canada does not have a constitution per se (as the United States does), but the *Constitution Act*, 1982 defines the Constitution of Canada as the *Canada Act*, its schedules and amendments. The *Canada Act* includes in part:
      i. Canadian Charter of Rights and Freedom, which defines fundamental freedoms:
         • conscience and religion
         • thought, belief, opinion and expression, including freedom of the press and other media of communication
         • peaceful assembly
         • association
         • democratic rights, mobility rights, legal rights, equality rights, official language, etc.
      ii. Rights of Aboriginal Peoples of Canada
      iii. Equalization and Regional Disparities

2. **Private Law** deals with relationships between individuals, that is, with **private wrongs** — a violation of the rights of an individual as opposed to the public at large. Private Law is used primarily to settle disputes. It deals with property ownership, contracts, the rights and obligations of family members (**Family Law**), and damage to one's person or property caused by another (**Tort Law**). People who violate private laws are usually required to pay compensation or their property or salary might be seized. Private law covers private disputes called **civil suits** such as when a person who has lost his or her job sues for wrongful dismissal.

Contract Law

The area of insurance utilizes contract law and tort law. **Contract law** is based on several Latin legal principles, the most important of which is *consensus ad idem*, meaning a meeting of the minds between the parties or, in other words, a clear understanding, offering and acceptance of each participant's contribution. From the moment of *consensus ad idem*, a contract is formed and is enforceable by the courts.

A contract requires an agreement between the parties, but not all agreements are contracts. Non-business, religious, family, household, and charitable agreements are not always contracts. In fact, there is a common law presumption against such agreements being contracts, although this presumption can be rebutted. An example of family agreements not being construed as being contracts arose in Canada several decades ago. At the time, there were no laws giving common-law spouses any rights to their spouses' property even if they had been living together for a long time and both spouses had contributed to the growth of those assets. Rather than interpret a contract out of the situation, the Canadian courts preferred using another mechanism, that of **unjust enrichment**, to resolve the unfairness. Conversely, where an agreement issues from a commercial relationship, it will be presumed to be a contract.

Contract law is part of private law because it does not involve or bind the state or persons that are not parties to the contract. It is a miniature legal system that people establish between themselves; the contract becomes binding upon them as a sort of private and self-imposed law. Thus, contracts are voluntary and require an "exercise of the will of the parties".

Elements of a Valid Contract

For a contract to be legally enforceable, several elements must be present:

A. Offer and Acceptance
B. Consideration
C. Legal Objective
D. Competent Parties
E. Intention to Create a Legal Relationship

A. Offer and Acceptance

Each contract starts with an **offer,** which is a promise made by one person, the **offeror**, the one making the offer, to do something when requested to do so by another person, the **offeree**, the one receiving the offer. An offer can also be defined as a promise by one party to undertake an obligation, subject to **acceptance** by the other party. A mere statement of a person's intention, or a declaration of his or her willingness to enter into negotiations, is not an offer and cannot be accepted in order to form a valid contract. A **valid offer** includes the price and completion date. An offer must be a clear, unequivocal, and in direct approach to another party to contract. For this reason, advertisements, catalogues, or store flyers are not offers; nor is a "for sale" sign on a used car or a house. The law calls these **invitations to treat** — essentially invitations to the general public to make an offer on a particular item.

An offer, once made, can be revoked before acceptance unless it is under **seal** (a wax seal that formally creates a binding contract that does not require payment for completion). A seal is generally an impression stamped or embossed on paper to authenticate a document or attest to a signature, such as a corporate or notary seal. Some jurisdictions require certain documents, such as deeds and leases, to be under seal.

An offer can also expire if a deadline for acceptance passes. If there is no specified deadline, then the offer expires in a **reasonable time**, depending on the subject matter of the contract. For perishable goods, such as food, a reasonable time would likely be a matter of days. The reasonable time would be longer where the subject matter of the contract is a building.

B. Consideration

One of the other important elements of contract law is the requirement of **consideration**, which may be defined as "some right, interest, profit or benefit accruing to the one party or some forbearance, detriment, loss or responsibility given, suffered or undertaken by the other."[1] More simply, consideration is the price to be paid as part of the formation of a contract, something of value given in return for the promise of performance. Consideration is usually, but not necessarily, money — any discernible detriment to one of the parties could be that party's consideration. A contract differs from a gift. This explains why you sometimes hear of very expensive objects being sold for $1; this is done to ensure that what is essentially a gift comes with the legal protection of con-

---

1   Duhaime.org, (www.duhaime.org/LegalDictionary/c/consideration.aspx), August 10, 2010

tract law. Under contract law, there is no contract if there is no consideration. Or consider the possibility that you quit your job because you have a written job offer from another employer, which you have accepted, also in writing. When you arrive, you find the new employer has changed its mind and you don't have a job. What consideration did you give to this contract? Your old job. You had a valid contract.

C. Legal Objective

For a contract to be binding, the purpose of the contract must be legal. A contract for stolen goods is not considered a binding contract and would be considered unenforceable. Likewise, any contract that engages in illegal activity is not enforceable. In addition, the objective must not be a **restraint of trade** — an action that reduces another person's ability to compete fairly in the marketplace.

D. Competent Parties

A legal contract involves a **meeting of the minds**. For this, all parties must be capable of consent. Contracts are made by individuals. Corporations are considered to be an **artificial person** — a legal entity having legal rights and duties — and can make contracts as long as the contracts are within the scope of their stated purpose. This is why many companies make sure their incorporation documents are very generally worded regarding their stated purpose to prevent any restriction on their ability to make contracts.

Void and Voidable

A contract can sometimes be deemed **void** or **voidable**:

- A contract that is void is not enforceable by either party.
- A contract that is voidable may be set aside by one of the parties but is binding unless the party with the right to void it decides to do so.

There are some groups of people who merit special treatment:

1. **Minor children** can void a contract but the other party cannot. A minor child is someone who has not yet reached the **age of majority**, which is 18 or 19, depending on the province or territory. Children under this age can cancel the contract by advising the other party in writing. For example, Derek signs up for a book club, paying $1 plus shipping and handling and receives the first four books. The agreement requires him to buy one book a month for three years. Since Derek is only 17, he can cancel the agreement by informing the other party in writing. If he does so, Derek has **repudiated the contract** — he has informed the other party and the contract will be disregarded. If Derek does not repudiate the contract and **ratifies** (confirms) it by buying books after he reaches the age of majority, he is then bound to it. One exception is a contract for necessities of life — a parent who is under the age of majority has an obligation to provide the **necessities of life** (food, clothing, shelter, medical care, and education) to his or her child. In addition, a minor can buy an insurance policy at age 16.

2. **Mentally incompetent** or **incapacitated people** can void a contract but the other party cannot if the other party knew or should have known about the mental incompetency under the circumstances. A drunk person is mentally incapacitated, lacks the ability to consent to a contract and has the option of voiding a contract signed while intoxicated, providing it is done at the earliest opportunity upon sobriety. Again, an exception is made for contracts for the delivery of necessities of life, for which even a mentally incompetent person is liable.

3. A **bankrupt person** — a person who is insolvent and, thus, unable to pay debts as they are due — is prohibited from entering into contracts until the courts have discharged the debtor and cancelled any unpaid debts. An exception is providing the necessities of life for the

debtor and his or her family, which means a bankrupt person can, for instance, enter into a lease or rental agreement for accommodation.

4. An **enemy alien** is a person whose residence or business is located in enemy territory during war or other hostilities that are damaging to the public interest. An enemy alien is not allowed to enter into contracts. This is why Americans cannot legally travel to Cuba while Canadians can.[2] Canadians can buy cigars from Cuba while living in Canada, but people in the United States cannot buy Cuban cigars.

E. Intention to Create a Legal Relationship

Both parties to the contract must have the intention to willingly carry out the terms and conditions of the contract. However, a number of things might make the contract **voidable or unenforceable**:

1. Mistake
2. Misrepresentation
3. Concealment
4. Warranty
5. Duress
6. Undue Influence

1. Mistake

A contract requires a true and complete meeting of the minds, what Roman law called a *consensus ad idem*. If one or both parties are inadvertently mistaken about an element of the contract, then there is no *consensus ad idem* and the contract *may* be voidable depending on the kind of mistake or misunderstanding. It does not include bad judgment. Common law has tried to develop a fairly sophisticated set of rules for dealing with mistakes. Unfortunately, the final determination of what those rules are is often up in the air, moving with the changing currents of the courts.

(a) In **common mistake**, both parties make the same mistake. Each knows the intention of the other and accepts it but each is mistaken about some underlying and fundamental fact. When both parties are mistaken on a basic and fundamental element of the contract, the contract is void from the start if the mistake is of such significance that, in the words of English case law, it is a "false and fundamental assumption" of the contract. For example, Darlene agreed to sell her three-year-old Gucci handbag to Stella for $500 — a steal since it now sells for $2,500. The handbag had been used only a few times. What neither knew at the time was that the handbag was a knock-off and that Darlene had overpaid when she bought it. The mistake was discovered when Darlene took it to a shop to have a minor repair done. The item agreed upon had never existed and the contract is void.

(b) In **mutual mistake**, both parties are mistaken about the same material fact. They both make a mistake but each party's mistake is different and they are at cross purposes, that is, they cannot come to agreement. For example, Larry hired Lucy to write a proposal and said he would pay her $750, saying it would take a couple of days to write. Lucy thought he meant $750 a day, as $375 a day is far below Lucy's usual billing rate and, since Larry had hired

---

2   On February 7, 1962, the United States imposed a commercial, economic, and financial embargo on the Castro government in Cuba after the communist Castro government expropriated the property of American citizens and corporations. The embargo limits Americans from conducting business with Cuba and is still in effect. It is the most enduring trade embargo in modern history. The embargo was liberalized in 2000 to allow the American export to Cuba of some agricultural and medical products, and the United States is currently the seventh largest exporter to Cuba. Americans can travel to Cuba only with a special licence. American imports from Cuba are still restricted, including cigars. Cuban cigars are considered by cigar aficionados to be the best in the world. Recently, there has been talk of lifting the embargo even further.

her before, he would know that. This is a mutual mistake since there never was a true meeting of minds and the contract is not enforceable by either party.

(c) In **unilateral mistake** only one of the parties is mistaken. If the other party is aware of the misperception or should have been aware of the mistake, the contract may not be enforceable, even if the enlightened party did not cause the mistake. For example, Joanne agreed verbally to sell her friend Denny her grand piano for $10,000. However, when she sent him an e-mail confirming it, she wrote $100.00 by mistake. This contract would be voidable at Joanne's option and Denny cannot make her sell the piano for $100.

Rectification can correct a mistake. If, between the parties, the terms are clear enough, but there has been a drafting error that was not caught before signature, then there is a separate judicial procedure called rectification that allows the contract to be amended into the terms that were intended from the beginning of the contract. Joanne and the buyer in the prior example could agree to change the contract to $10,000.

2. Misrepresentation

Misrepresentation occurs when one of the parties to a contract made a wrong statement about some material element of the contract and, because of this statement, the other party entered into the contract. Contract common law treats **fraudulent misrepresentation** differently from **innocent misrepresentation**. Knowingly misrepresenting something and misrepresenting it by mistake are two different issues. The degree of the misrepresentation will determine whether the contract will be considered void or voidable and if any compensation to either party should ensue.

(a) **Fraudulent misrepresentation** occurs, for example, if you state that you were born in 1957 when you were in fact born in 1947. Botox may be able to make this seem reasonable but this contract is voidable at the option of the insurance company since you lied about your age. The same is true if you lie and say you are a non-smoker when, in fact, you smoke. The insurance company can cancel the policy if the lie is discovered before death. If you die, the insurance company can refuse to pay the death benefit and simply refund your premiums — it is not obligated to pay out the face value of the policy.

(b) **Innocent misrepresentation** occurs if you mistakenly say you are 57 when you are in fact 58. If you die, the insurance company can recalculate the correct premiums and deduct the difference from the face value when it pays the face value of the policy to the beneficiary.

Negligent misrepresentation is discussed later in this chapter under "Negligence".

3. Concealment

Concealment is wilful hiding of a relevant fact that invalidates the contract. For instance, if Marcia has a marijuana-growing operation in her attic and it causes a fire, the insurance company will not be required to pay the damages. (This is now stated in most homeowners' policies but didn't used to be.) The insurance company cannot be expected to ask specifically about this and not telling them is concealment. There is also an example of a man who changed his last name to hide his criminal record. When he was murdered seven months later, the insurer did not have to pay the life insurance claim as his criminal history was deemed a material fact. Had he died of a heart attack, the insurer would have had to pay.

4. Warranty

Warranty is a statement that is part of the contract and is guaranteed to be true in all respects. If you declare that your business has a fire alarm system with a battery backup and so can never fail, a power outage at the same time the batteries die could invalidate the insurance policy.

5. Duress

Duress is using coercion and intimidation to force another party into a contract. This contract is voidable at the option of the innocent party.

6. Undue Influence

Undue influence occurs when a person in a dominant position deprives another person of an independent decision. It is voidable at the option of the victim.

Discharge of a Contract

A **discharged contract** is the end of the rights and obligations of a contract — both parties are freed from their contractual obligation. Contracts can be discharged by:

1. **Performance** — both parties have done what they agreed to do in the contract.
2. **Agreement** — both parties agree not to continue the contract. For example, Maryann has a client she dislikes intensely. The meetings are torture for both of them. Even though they have a one-year contract, the relationship is so unproductive that both parties agree to end the contract after six months. They both sign the waiver Maryann has drawn up. A **waiver** is an agreement to not continue with a contract that already exists.
3. **Frustration** — the inability to complete a contract due to circumstances beyond the control of the contracting parties. For example, a singer cancels a concert due to illness.
4. **Breach of contract** — wrongful non-performance, meaning one party to a contract fails to perform an obligation that is part of the contract. There are two possible remedies for this:
   (a) **Damages** are court-awarded money paid to an injured party to compensate for a legal wrong committed against the injured party. A **legal wrong** is a violation of a person's legal rights, or a failure to perform a legal duty owed to a certain person or to society as a whole. For example, Jane hires a painter to paint her office, which is closed for three weeks in August so she and her staff can go on vacation. When she returns, the office has not been painted and Jane has to rent space from the office down the hall while her office is being painted. She sues and wins the amount she has to pay in extra rent.
   (b) **Injunction** is a legal order to stop one party from acting in a particular manner — to stop one party from breaching the terms of a contract. For example, Karen has a contract to be the exclusive Canadian distributor for Beautiful-Me cosmetics. She imports the cosmetics, marks them up 25%, and sells them from her website. Imagine her surprise when a discount store in her city starts selling Beautiful-Me for 5% above Karen's cost price. Since Karen has a contract to be the exclusive Canadian distributor, she gets an injunction to stop her supplier from selling to anyone else in Canada and to prevent someone in another country from buying the product and shipping it into Canada.

Estoppel prevents one party from denying a fact he has already confirmed or accepted by his own actions. For example, if Alex consistently pays his monthly insurance premium a couple of days late, the insurer cannot claim his policy is not in effect if he dies the day after the premium is due.

Insurance Contracts

Insurance policies are contracts with some special features:

Insurance Contracts	Financial Planning Contracts
Aleatory	Commutative
Adhesion	Bargaining
Unilateral	Bilateral

Aleatory versus Commutative

In **aleatory contracts**, the dollar amounts exchanged may not be equal but depend on an uncertain event. Insurance contracts are aleatory. In **commutative contracts**, each party gives up goods and services of theoretically equal value. For example, payments made for legal or accounting services equal the value of the services.

Bargaining versus Adhesion

In **bargaining contracts**, the applicant can make counter-proposals or ask for changes. In **adhesion contracts**, the applicant must accept the entire contract, including terms and conditions — there is no bargaining. Insurance policies are contracts of adhesion even though there can be negotiations about the coverage and terms.

Unilateral versus Bilateral

In a **unilateral contract**, only one party makes a legally enforceable promise. Insurance contracts are unilateral and there is agreement to exchange an act (paying the premium) for a promise (to be compensated if one experiences an insured loss). It is unilateral because the insured can cancel the contract by not paying the premiums and, as long as the premium is paid, the insured has fulfilled his or her part of the bargain and has not breached the contract. However, the insurer cannot cancel the policy before the end of the policy term.

In **bilateral contracts**, each party makes a legally enforceable promise. For example, if you work, you get paid and if the payment stops, you don't have to work. Conversely, your employer must continue to pay you as long as you continue to do your job. If you stop working, the employer can stop paying.

Insurance policies are also **contracts of indemnity**, which compensate for the loss or damage to the insured while not allowing the insured to make a profit. While this is true of most insurance contracts, life insurance contracts are not contracts of indemnity — when the insured dies, the insurer pays the face value.

Insurance policies are also **personal contracts,** where the owner is insured, not the property. The contract is between the insurer and the insured and, thus, cannot be assigned to someone else including a financial institution as collateral on a loan without the insurer's consent for property insurance although life insurance can freely be assigned since assignment does not change the risk.

Parts of an Insurance Policy

The basic parts are as follows:

1. Declarations
2. Definitions
3. Insuring Agreement
4. Exclusions and Restrictions
5. Conditions
6. Miscellaneous Provisions

In addition there may be the following:

7. Endorsements and Riders
8. Deductibles
9. Co-insurance Requirement

1. Declarations

Declarations in an insurance contract identify and give information about what exposures are to be covered and for how much, who is insured, the premium, deductibles under that contract, and the term — the period the policy is in effect. The risk exposure might be a car (automobile insurance), monthly income (disability insurance), or a person's life (life insurance). The declarations of a life insurance contract identify things such as the names of the insured, their age, whether they are a smoker or non-smoker, their address, the policy number, etc. Declarations are usually found on the first page of the insurance contract or as an insert to that policy.

2. Definitions

The **definitions** within an insurance contract are typically identified with quotation marks. These definitions identify things such as "we", "our", "you", and "yours" when identifying the insured or the insurer. These definitions are then used continuously throughout the insurance contract.

3. Insuring Agreement

Insuring agreement is an agreement that constitutes a promise by the insurer to pay a specified sum upon the occurrence of a specified event in return for premiums paid by the insured. It is the part of the insurance contract that summarizes the promises of the insurer, detailing what is covered, subject to limitations, exclusions, and conditions. It also contains an **entire-contract clause**, stating that the policy and attached application constitute the entire contract between the parties. In property and liability insurance, there are two kinds of coverage available:

(a) **Named perils coverage** identifies which perils are covered under the insurance contract. For example, if lightning damage is not named as one of the perils in the insurance agreement, then any damage from a lightning strike will not be covered — only losses from the named perils are covered under the insurance policy.

(b) **All risks coverage** covers all losses except specific perils that are named and excluded. If not specifically excluded, losses from all perils are covered under the insurance contract.

Contracts are usually **written** but can also be based on a **verbal** agreement. However, the **parol evidence rule** states oral terms agreed to but not included in the written contract cannot be added later. This prevents contradictions in the contract.

4. Exclusions and Restrictions

These are the specific conditions or circumstances listed in the policy for which the policy will not provide **benefit payments**. As mentioned, an "all risks" property insurance agreement may include specific exclusions that have to be mentioned in the contract. These **exclusions** may include the following:

(a) **Excluded perils,** which may include natural disasters such as earthquakes or floods. Most insurance contracts exclude losses from acts of war which leads to some debate in these times of terrorism and terrorist acts.

(b) **Excluded losses** may be included in an insurance contract. For example, a homeowner's insurance contract may exclude losses to an automobile. Other types of losses that may be excluded are those that arise from the insured's unwillingness to protect his or her property from further damage after a loss has occurred.

(c) **Excluded property** may also be included in an insurance contract. For example, automobile insurance may exclude certain property, such as that which is added for the purpose of modifying the car.

Restrictions might include no sky-diving for a disability policy or the suicide clause in a life insurance policy that states that the insurer will not pay the face value to the beneficiary if the insured commits suicide within two years of the inception of the policy.

5. Conditions

Conditions are provisions stated in an insurance contract that express the rights and duties of the insured, or the rights and duties of the insurer. These conditions are clearly stated in the insurance contract and outline what the insured's duties are in order to keep the insurance coverage in place. Typical duties have to do with the insured's duties after a loss, with cancellation provisions, and with the insurance company's right to inspect damaged property. If the duties or provisions outlined are not met by the insured, the insurer may decline to pay the claim.

6. Miscellaneous Provisions

Certain insurance contracts may contain miscellaneous **provisions** that apply to that specific policy. These provisions may include such things as grace periods, reinstatement requirements for policies cancelled due to missed premiums, misstatement of smoking status, and other things that may affect the contract.

7. Endorsements and Riders

Endorsements and riders are amendments to a policy that alter the provisions of the contract. They add, delete, or modify provisions in the original contract. They are usually an additional piece of paper, not a part of the original insurance policy and which, when attached to the original insurance policy, become a legal part of that contract. **Endorsements** apply to property and liability insurance while **riders** are used in reference to life and health insurance. For instance, you might have an endorsement on your home insurance policy to cover your $25,000 diamond ring or you might add a rider on a life insurance policy that provides monthly income in the event of a disability.

8. Deductibles

A **deductible** is the amount a policyholder agrees to pay per claim, per accident or per year toward the total amount of an insured loss. Deductibles have several purposes. They:

(a)   provide a way of eliminating small claims by the insured,
(b)   reduce the amount of the premium — the higher the deductible the lower the premium, and
(c)   reduce false and inflated claims — moral and morale hazards.

Auto and home insurance policies have standard deductibles of $500 or $1,000, usually deducted from each claim even if there is more than one claim in a year. Group health insurance policies usually have an annual deducible of $25 or $50 which is deducted from the first claim that is submitted to the insurer in each calendar year.

9. Co-insurance Requirement

Co-insurance is a clause that appears in contracts that serves a risk-sharing purpose. In property insurance, the co-insurance clause states the insured will share in losses to the extent that the property is underinsured at the time of loss. In medical insurance, the insured person and the insurer sometimes share certain covered procedures under a policy in a specified ratio (80 percent by the insurer and 20 percent by the insured for example). A health insurance policy having an 80 percent co-insurance clause means that, for a claim of $100, the insurer will reimburse you $80, leaving you responsible for the remaining $20. Again, the intent is to allocate the risk between the insurer and the insured.

Sample Term Life Policy

An insurance policy is simply a contract between two parties — the insured and the insurer. In a life insurance contract, the insurer agrees to pay the insured's beneficiaries a predetermined lump-sum payment in the event of the insured's death. In return, the insured agrees to pay the insurer a monthly premium. The term life insurance policy that follows exemplifies this simple contractual arrangement.

Term insurance provides life insurance coverage with no savings component for a specific period of time and is the most straightforward type of insurance policy possible. The policy even spells out what constitutes the contract between the insurer and the owner of the policy.

Elements of a Valid Contract
Offer and Acceptance

In an insurance contract, the offer is made by the individual who wants to buy insurance protection. When insurance agents solicit insurance applications, they are simply "inviting" prospective insurance buyers to make the insurer an offer for protection. The insurer can then accept or decline the offer, the offer being the application for benefits. In a life insurance contract, the insurer will accept the applicant's offer after receiving a satisfactory medical or examination of the applicant's medical history. The insurer's underwriters review the application and the medical both to further assess whether they will accept or decline the offer and also to determine the premium if they are going to accept the offer.

Consideration

A life insurance policy is not valid and in effect until the insurer has received the first premium.

Legal Objective

Only someone who has an insurable interest in the insured can take out a life insurance policy on them — a spouse, child, parent, business partner, or employer — someone who stands to lose financially should the insured die a premature death.

Competent Parties

A child must be at least 16 years old to take out an insurance policy. The insurer must be licensed to carry on business in the jurisdiction in which it operates.

Intention to Create a Legal Relationship

Both parties have agreed to this policy which even makes some allowances for small mistakes (but not for fraudulent misrepresentations).

In addition, the following apply to this policy:

- is an **aleatory contract** whereby the insurer agrees to pay the beneficiary a stated sum of money if the insured dies within the term of the policy. In return, the insured agrees to pay the premiums.
- It is a **contract of adhesion**. The only permitted "changes" referred to in the policy are riders that enhance the coverage and also increase the cost. Possible riders, covered in Chapter 8, include:
  - **disability waiver** benefit, which waives the premium while the insured is disabled;
  - **renewable** at the end of the term, usually with evidence of insurability which means another medical;
  - **guaranteed renewable** at the end of the term without evidence of insurability; and
  - **convertible** to a permanent life insurance policy, such as whole life insurance, which has a savings component.
- It is a **unilateral contract** — the insurer cannot cancel this contract while it is in force unless the insured lied on the application; however, the insured can cancel at any time or by not paying the premiums.

The Policy
Policy Declarations

In this policy, **you** and **your** are the owner[3] of the policy.

We, **us**, and **our** refers the life insurance company.

Your policy number is:	123-456-789
Your policy date is:	October 15, 2009
The owner or holder is:	Marian Duckworth
The insured person is:	Joseph Duckworth, male, born June 5, 1979
Risk classification:	Non-smoker
Death benefit:	$400,000
Beneficiary:	Marian Duckworth unless changed in writing by Marian Duckworth (the owner)
Policy ends on:	October 15, 2029
Premium:	$xxx a month

This is a non-participating[4] policy

Definitions

Age at the policy date or a policy anniversary is the age on the birthday nearest to the policy date or anniversary.

Face amount is the amount of insurance purchased under the basic policy and does not include any amount purchased under a supplementary rider.

Issue date is the date we, the insurer, prepared the policy and can be used to contest the policy under the suicide or incontestability provisions. It is the first day of the insurance coverage.

The Contract

Your contract includes

- the application and evidence of insurability,
- the policy,
- any documents attached to this policy,
- any applications for reinstatement, and
- any amendments agreed to in writing.

Only our president or one of our vice-presidents can agree to any changes in the policy, and then only in writing.

Premiums and Reinstatement

Premiums are paid monthly in Canadian funds and are due in advance as shown on the premium schedule.

---

3   The owner and the insured might be the same person.
4   All term life insurance policies are non-participating — they do not pay "dividends" out of premium profits.

For each premium, there is a 31-day **grace period** during which your policy remains in force. If the premium has not been received within the grace period, the policy will lapse, that is, it will have ended.

You can **reinstate** the policy, that is, put your policy back into effect, within two years if the insured person is still alive. To reinstate your policy, you must

- apply for reinstatement within two years of the policy's ending,
- provide new evidence of insurability that is satisfactory to us, and
- pay all overdue premiums with compound interest at a rate we set.

Your Right to Cancel This Policy

You may cancel this policy at any time by notifying us in writing. The cancellation is binding on you and any beneficiaries whether they are revocable or irrevokable.

Death Benefit

The death benefit will be paid to the designated beneficiary when we receive evidence of the insured's death. This benefit may be

- increased by any riders attached to this policy, or
- decreased by any unpaid premium.

Suicide

We will not pay the death benefit if the insured takes his or her own life, whether sane or insane, within two years of the issue date or any reinstatement date. We will refund to the beneficiary the premiums received since the issue date or reinstatement date.

Misstatement of Age and Sex

If the age or sex has been misstated, any amount payable will be increased or decreased to reflect the premium that should have been paid for the correct age and sex.

Beneficiary

The beneficiary is designated in the application and can be changed by notifying us in writing. If the beneficiary is irrevokable, the beneficiary must provide written consent.

If the beneficiary is not alive when the insured dies, the death benefit will be paid to the insured's estate.

Incontestability

We cannot contest this policy after it has been in force for two years except

- if it has been reinstated for less than two years,

- we can contest at any time with respect to fraud or any material fact that was not disclosed on the application including misstatement of age.

Claims of Creditors

To the extent permitted by law, benefits payable will not be subject to any claims of creditors of the insured or beneficiary.

Assignment

You can assign the policy. It is binding on us when we receive written notice. We are not responsible for its validity. You should file the assignment with us in duplicate and we will return a copy to you.

Added Note on Assignments

There are two types of assignment — full assignment and limited assignment. When a policy is **fully assigned** to a third party, the third party becomes the new owner of the insurance contract. The new owner is responsible for all the contractual obligations of the policy, including the premium, and can change and designate a new beneficiary.

A **limited or partial assignment** gives a third party temporary control of the policy. Policy ownership does not change on a partial assignment meaning the original policyholder is still obligated to pay the premium. However, on a partial assignment, the third party to the contract becomes the new beneficiary and has recourse against the policyholder if the policy is terminated without their consent. For example, a life insurance policy can be assigned to a third party to guarantee payment in the event of death. The most common is mortgage insurance, which is simply term life insurance purchased usually for the term of the mortgage. In addition, sometimes banks will not give out a loan unless the borrower can guarantee repayment. For mortgages and these types of loans, an insurance policy is purchased by the borrower and then assigned to a third party, the lender, who does not own the policy but does become the primary beneficiary should the borrower die before the loan is repaid.

Negligence and Tort Law

Negligence is the failure to exercise the standard of care required by law to protect others from an unreasonable risk of harm, thereby increasing the risk of bodily harm to them or damage to their property. **Standard of care** is the care required of a reasonably prudent person. Someone who has failed to exercise the required standard of care could be sued and held responsible for the injury or damage.

Elements of Negligence

There are four requirements that have to be met in order for an act to be considered negligent:

1. The existence of a **legal duty of care** — a legal duty to protect others from harm. In its absence, there is a legal wrong. For example, people have a legal duty to stop for red lights and to shovel their walk after a snowstorm.
2. A **failure to perform that duty** by an act (a **positive act**) or a failure to act (a **negative act**). Driving the speed limit in a bad snowstorm or cutting in and out of heavy traffic qualify as positive acts that a reasonably prudent person would not do. Not repairing faulty brakes qualifies as a failure to act.
3. The claimant suffers **damages** to his or her property and/or bodily **injury** or death and can be awarded
   • **special damages** for losses that can be determined and documented;
   • **general damages** for losses that cannot be determined and documented, for example, for pain and suffering or the loss of the companionship of a spouse; and
   • **punitive damages**, whose purpose is to punish and to be a deterrent. In Canada, these tend to be modest and rare.
4. A **proximate cause** relationship must exist, that is, there must be an unbroken chain of events between the negligent act and the infliction of damages.

For example, Theresa and Cindy come out of a movie theatre on a bitterly cold and somewhat snowy Saturday night. They haven't seen each other for a while and so they have a coffee after the movie and chat for a couple of hours. They came in separate cars and both cars are covered in frost when they leave the movie complex. Theresa is so cold she doesn't take the time to fully scrape the windshield and slowly starts for home. Five minutes later, a woman who is walking her dog crosses the street at a corner and slips and falls. Theresa doesn't see her right away because her windshield is not yet clear. She runs over the woman's leg. Is this a negligent act on the part of Theresa? Yes.

1. A reasonably prudent person would have cleared the windshield before starting off.
2. She failed to clear the windshield.
3. The woman on the street was injured.
4. Had Theresa cleared the windshield, she would have seen the woman in time to stop.

Defence against Negligence

There are four possible defences against negligence:

1. **Contributory Negligence.** The injured person's conduct falls below the standard of care required for his or her own protection and this conduct contributed to the injury; thus, the injured party cannot collect damages. Theresa might argue that, given the weather, the woman should have seen her coming and waited to make sure that Theresa was able to stop in time.
2. **Comparative Negligence.** Both the injured and the injuring share the damages when both contributed to the injury. The laws in different jurisdictions are not consistent on this so the rules are contradictory. However, essentially, the amount of compensation the victim can collect is proportional to the degree of fault of each party, which is decided by the courts. The rules are:
   (a) **Pure Rule** — the participation is proportional. So if Theresa is 66% responsible, the victim can collect 66% of the damages awarded.
   (b) **49% Rule** — The victim must be 49% or less at fault to be able to collect.
   (c) **50% Rule** — The victim can collect only if his or her negligence is not greater than the negligence of the other party.
3. **Last Clear Chance Rule.** The injured can recover damages if the injuring party had a last clear chance to avoid the accident but failed to do so. Theresa cannot claim the woman acted negligently if she, Theresa, could have stopped but didn't.
4. **Assumption of Risk.** A person who understands and recognizes the danger inherent in a particular activity cannot recover damages if injured. Theresa might argue that, given the

weather, the woman shouldn't have been out walking her dog or that if she had to walk her dog, she should have just gone around the block and avoided crossing the street!

Imputed Negligence

Under some conditions, the negligence of one party can be imputed (attributed or assigned) to another.

1. **Employee–Employer Relationship**. An employer can be held liable for negligent acts of employees who are acting on the employer's behalf. There are two requirements:
   (a) The worker must be an employee, not contracted.
   (b) The employee must be acting within the scope of employment, not driving a company car on personal business. For example, if Theresa is an employee for a large company that provides her with a company car, which she is permitted to use on weekends, the employer would not be liable since she was on personal business.
2. **Vicarious Liability**. A motorist's negligence is imputed to the vehicle's owner. For example, if Theresa lends her own car (now not a company car) to her *colleague*, Joe, and he causes an accident, Theresa is liable.
3. The **Family Purpose Doctrine**. This states that the owner of a car can be held responsible for the negligence of immediate family members while the family member is driving the car. For example, if Theresa lends her own car (still not a company car) to her *brother*, Joe, and he causes an accident, Theresa is liable.
4. **Joint Business Ventures and Partnerships**. Both are liable, that is, both can be held liable if one member of the joint venture or partnership causes an accident while working.
5. The **Dram Shop Law**. This states that people who sell liquor are liable if someone drinks too much and gets into an accident while driving home. In Ontario a few years ago, the owner of a restaurant and a company were both held responsible when a woman drank far too much at the company Christmas party and was in a one-car accident on the way home. The company president had insisted she not drive and offered to either drive her or call a cab but the woman refused. After the accident, she sued and won. She argued that the party, which started at mid-afternoon, was on company time and that, therefore, she was a victim since she was obligated to be at the party.

   More recently, in 2008, 16 people were charged under the *Liquor Licence Act* in Bracebridge, Ontario, after three young men drowned in a car accident after they and another person who escaped from the car consumed 31 drinks for lunch. Both alcohol and speed contributed to the accident in which the car broke through a guardrail and became submerged in a lake. Two people who are no longer with the club but whose names are still on the liquor licence have since had the charges dismissed. The other 14 charged include officers, directors, two servers, and a food and beverage manager.
6. **Res ipsa loquitur**. This means "the thing speaks for itself". There is a presumption of negligence because the event happened. For example, if a dentist takes out the wrong tooth or a surgeon amputates the wrong leg, the dentist and doctor are both, by definition, guilty of negligence. There are three criteria which must be met:
   (a) The event doesn't usually happen without negligence.
   (b) The injuring party had exclusive control over the event happening.
   (c) The injured did not contribute to the injury.

Tort Law

Tort law was established to compensate private individuals for the wrongs caused by others. A **tort** is a civil (personal) wrong or injury arising out of an act or failure to act that is independent of any contract, and for which an action for damages may be brought, that is, for which the victim can sue.

Fault must be established as the basis for liability. Fault is defined as inexcusable conduct that intentionally or carelessly causes harm to another person or their property. Negligence (and therefore fault) must be present, that is, a **duty of care** was owed and was lacking, and this caused the injury.

In addition, **professional liability** can arise because professionals are presumed to have **expertise**, specialized knowledge, and skills. Professionals also have a **fiduciary duty**, the duty to be trustworthy, to conduct oneself beyond reproach. **Negligent misrepresentation** is carelessness in providing specialized information or advice that knowingly misleads or conceals relevant information. For example, Rodney sells auto insurance. Marcia comes in. She is in the process of buying her first car and does not have a lot of money. To help her save money, Rodney assures her that the minimum required liability insurance in her province of $200,000 is adequate. One evening, Marcia is driving home from work. She is very tired because she has been putting in 10-hour workdays for the past several weeks. She hits another car, causing serious damage to the driver. The other driver sues for pain and suffering as he will have back pain for the rest of his life. Marcia is found guilty of negligence and the other driver is awarded $500,000. Marcia is now in a position to sue Rodney, who gave her bad advice. Rodney has the expertise, but he failed to exercise his fiduciary duty, and thus he acted carelessly.

Negligence — Special Cases

There are special instances of negligence that illustrate the complexity and possible extent of negligence.

Absolute and Strict Liability

There is a small difference between **absolute** and **strict liability**. In both, the person is guilty by definition, that is, the accused person is responsible for the action or neglect that caused the offence. Liability is imposed without the presence or proof of negligence or fault. In both absolute and strict liability, there is no need to prove **mens rea,** which is the intent, knowledge, or recklessness in committing the offence. The difference between them is that there is no defence for **absolute liability** while in **strict liability**, the defence of due diligence is available.

In some jurisdictions, dog owners are **absolutely liable** if their pet injures someone, regardless of the dog's past history. However, sometimes injuries from dogs are a matter of **strict liability** and the plaintiff must prove negligence; that is, the dog owner knew his or her dog was dangerous that perhaps it attacked someone before, but the owner failed to take precautions. The dog owner isn't usually held liable if it can be proven that the victim was either trespassing or provoking the dog.

Distinctions are made between the liability of owners of domestic animals and wild animals. Let's look at the case that occurred at the African Lion Safari, near Hamilton, Ontario, a few years ago.

> A former exotic dancer and her ex-boyfriend who were mauled by a Bengal tiger nearly nine years ago have been awarded more than $2.5-million from African Lion Safari.
>
> Madam Justice Jean MacFarland yesterday rejected claims that David Balac, 31, and Jennifer-Anne Cowles, 28, ignored posted signs at the game park warning visitors not to feed the animals and to keep their car windows rolled up.
>
> Judge MacFarland found the Rockton, Ont. Park strictly liable and awarded Mr. Balac $1.7-million and Ms. Cowles $813,000.
>
> "There is no question ... that tigers are dangerous, unpredictable, wild, predators. Persons who display such animals in out-of-control settlings should, in my view, be held strictly liable for any damage resulting from such a display," the Superior Court judge said.
>
> The judge accepted the couple's testimony that their vehicle's automatic windows were closed prior to the attack and were likely lowered inadvertently by Mr. Balac after a tiger butted against the car.
>
> ... the incident caused Mr. Balac, who had been an accomplished accordion player and an outgoing Sheridan College student, to turn into an unemployable recluse ... the disfiguring scars and anxiety Ms. Cowles suffered ... ended her career as an exotic dancer ... the single mother of two boys did manage to get a job...
>
> *Globe and Mail,* January 28, 2005.

In his ruling for the plaintiffs, the Judge stated:

... For damage resulting from the act of a wild animal, the defendant is strictly liable, without proof of negligence or other wrongful conduct, and without the necessity of proving that the defendant was aware of the dangerous character of the particular animal that caused the harm ... If the animal is [domestic], one that ordinarily did not cause the kind of harm that is involved, the common law requires that the particular animal concerned have the dangerous or mischievous propensity to commit the harm or damage that ir inflicted, and that the defendant knew of such propensity or characteristics of the animal.

... Sometimes it has been suggested that liability is absolute, where the animal is wild or a domestic animal known to be dangerous. This cannot be accurate, because it is clear that there are limits upon the liability of the defendant, for example, contributory negligence on the part of the plaintiff, voluntary assumption of risk or consent, the act of a stranger, or an act of God. Hence, liability although strict in the sense of without proof of negligence, is not absolute, which could mean that it would be imposed whatsoever the circumstances, as long as the animal caused harm.

Cowles v. *Balac, 2005 Canadian*
Legal Information Institute (CanLII) 2038 (ON S.C.)

Charities

Charities used to be immune from being held liable but are now no longer immune.

Governments

Sovereign immunity means that governments cannot be sued because "the king can do no wrong". However, this has been modified over the years, and now governments can be held liable if they are negligent in the performance of a proprietary function. Proprietary functions of governments include operation of water plants, hydro generators, transportation and telephone systems, and municipal auditoriums.

Parents and Children

Children who have attained the **age of reason** (7 and older) are responsible for their own actions except

- if the child uses a dangerous weapon to injure someone, the parent can be held responsible because the child had access to the dangerous weapon.
- if the child is acting as an agent for the parent.
- under **family purpose doctrine**, a parent is liable if a minor child operates a family car.
- in some places, parents are liable for the wilful and malicious acts of their children. We will revisit this one in Chapter 4, "Homeowners' Policy".

Property Owners

There are several categories of people who go onto the property of other people and the **degree of care** required for each category is different.

1. A **Trespasser** is a person who enters or remains on the owner's property without the owner's permission or consent. The owner has a **duty of** *slight* care — the owner cannot deliberately injure the trespasser or a set a trap that can cause injury to the trespasser.
2. A **Licensee** enters or remains on the premises with the occupant's expressed or implied permission but provides no economic benefit to the occupant, for example, door-to-door salespersons, charity solicitors, police officers and firefighters when they are doing their job, hunters who are not paying to hunt, and social guests in most jurisdictions (in some jurisdictions, social guests are invitees). They must take the premises as it comes. The owner is required to warn them of unsafe conditions or activity but has no obligation to inspect to find danger.
3. An **Invitee** is someone invited onto the premises for the benefit of the occupant or to further the use to which the occupant is putting the premises. This category includes customers in a store, mail carriers, churchgoers, people in a railway station, students in a school, service per-

sonnel coming to make repairs, theatregoers, delivery people, garbage collectors, people who are paying to hunt or fish, and people buying firewood or a Christmas tree. The occupant must inspect the premises and eliminate any dangerous conditions that are found. There is a special category for children. An **attractive nuisance** is a condition that can attract and injure children, such as a construction site with machinery that is left unattended at night. Children are considered to be **licensees, not trespassers** because they cannot recognize danger. The owner must keep the premises safe and take ordinary care to protect the children from harm. As a result, the machinery must be fenced in so children cannot get at it.

Summary

Insurance has been around for 4,000 years to provide its many benefits to society. While insurance policies have become refined over the years, the basic characteristics have not changed greatly during this time. Not all risks can be insured, and the five basic principles of insurance are aimed at ensuring that the expectations of both the insured and the insurer are met when they enter into an insurance contract. Insurance policies are contracts and contain of all the elements of contracts as established by Contract Law although insurance policies have some additional features that are unique to them. A term life insurance policy is an example of an insurance contract at its most basic. The area of negligence — the failure to do what a reasonably prudent person would do — takes us into the area of tort law, which covers the compensation of private individuals for wrongs committed against them.

Sources

Fundamentals of Risk and Insurance, 9th edition, Vaughan, E.J. and Vaughan, T., John Wiley and Sons, Inc., New York, 2003.

Principles of Risk Management and Insurance, 9th edition, George E. Rejda, Pearson Education, Inc., New York, 2004.

Risk Management and Insurance, Canadian Edition, Harrington, S.E. and Niehaus, G.R., adapted by Kleffner, A.E. and Nielson, N.L., McGraw-Hill Ryerson Ltd, Toronto, 1999.

Application Case

Joanne arrives once again to meet with Francesca, who promptly asks her if she would like an espresso. Indeed, she does. "Is there is anything else about insurance you would like to know before we begin on some basics of law that are behind all insurance contracts?" Francesca asks.

A. Joanne wants to know if insurance is a new concept.

"Not at all," replies Francesca. It has been around for about 4,000 years for caravans and ships where losses tended to be large and total. In addition (Page 38):

1. guilds in medieval times were essentially trade unions that looked after other guild members who were in the same line of work;
2. the first actual insurance policy was written in Italy in the 14th Century; and
3. mortality tables, which we talk about in Chapter 9, were created in the late 17th century.

B. Joanne wants to know if there is a definition of *insurance*, and if it has a particular essence. Francesca tells her that there are **four basic characteristics of insurance** (Page 39):

1. Pooling (sharing) of losses
2. Fortuitous losses
3. Transfer of pure risk
4. Indemnification for losses

C. Joanne is starting to feel better. Indeed, insurance is beginning to seem comprehensible. She also thinks Jeremy might be wise to have a session with Francesca so she asks, "What are the **benefits and costs of insurance** to society as a whole?"

Francesca replies:

1. The benefits are (Page 39)
   (a) indemnification for losses,
   (b) less fear and worry,
   (c) source of investment funds for the insurer,
   (d) loss prevention, and
   (e) enhancement of credit.
2. The costs are
   (a) that it increases the cost of doing business, and
   (b) fraudulent and inflated claims that increase the costs for everyone.

D. Now Joanne wants to know if everything can be insured. It doesn't seem likely but what are the **criteria** for knowing if something can be insured? Francesca again replies (Page 40):

1. Large number of exposure units
2. Accidental and unintentional loss
3. Determinable and measurable loss
4. No catastrophic losses
5. Calculable chance of loss
6. An economically feasible premium

E. Joanne now wants to know the rationale behind insurance. Francesca points out that all insurance policies are contracts that adhere to these **principles** (Page 41):

1. Principle of Indemnity
2. Insurable interest
   (a) property — at time of loss
   (b) life — at time policy is taken out
3. Reasonable expectations
4. Subrogation
5. Utmost good faith

F. Joanne sighs. "OK. What do I need to know about insurance policies?" Francesca replies, "Well, all insurance policies are contracts and if you want to understand your insurance policies, you need to know something about the law in Canada." (Page 38)

1. First, there are two systems of laws in Canada
   (a) **Civil law** in Quebec, which is a comprehensive statement of rules, and
   (b) **Common law,** which is built on precedence and, as a result, has no underlying code, per se.
2. **Public law** deals with interactions between government and individuals or between jurisdictions, and it covers (Page 43)
   (a) criminal law,
   (b) administration law, and
   (c) constitutional law.
3. **Private law** deals with relationships between individuals or private wrongs and is dealt with by, for instance, Family Law and Tort Law.
4. Insurance is covered under both Contract Law and Tort Law which deals with damage caused by one person to another person or to that person's property. We will mostly be concerned with Contract Law, which is the foundation for insurance policies.

G. "OK," Joanne says, thinking about asking for another espresso. She decides to wait for a bit. "What about contracts? Can you just hit the high spots on this one?"

"No problem," Francesca answers. The **basic elements of a contract are** as follows:

1. Offer and acceptance (Page 44)
2. Consideration

3. Legal objective
4. Competent parties
5. Intention to create a legal relationship

There are several things that can potentially invalidate a contract, making it void or voidable:
  (a) Mistake:
      i. common, where both parties make the same mistake
      ii. mutual, where both parties make a mistake about a material fact but they make different mistakes
      iii. unilateral, where only one of the parties is mistaken.
  (b) Rectification, which means the contract can be amended to make it valid
  (c) Misrepresentation, both fraudulent and innocent
  (d) Concealment
  (e) Warranty
  (f) Duress
  (g) Undue influence

H. "So how do you know a **contract is finished**?" asks Joanne.
  1. Performance (Page 48)
  2. Agreement
  3. Frustration — something gets in the way
  4. Breach of contract where one party does not fulfil its contractual obligations. This can be rectified by
  (a) payment of damages, or
  (b) an injunction.

I. Francesca takes the lead now. "I need to fill you in on **a few more basic concepts** about types of contracts which distinguishes insurance contracts from many other types of contracts," she says (Pages 48–49).
  1. **Aleatory** contracts like insurance policies where the dollar value exchanged is unequal and depend on some uncertain event versus **commutative**, where the goods or services delivered equals the payment.
  2. **Bargaining** contracts which you can negotiate the terms and contracts of **adhesion**, where one party has to just accept the terms offered and cannot eliminate certain paragraphs in the contract.
  3. **Unilateral** contracts, where only the insurer has made an enforceable commitment, versus **bilateral** where both parties have made a legally enforceable commitment.
  4. In addition, insurance contracts are **contracts of indemnity** and the insured is not supposed to make a profit. Furthermore, insurance policies are **personal contracts** which means the owner of the property is insured, not the property itself, and the policy cannot be transferred to someone else without the insurer's consent.

J. Joanne is seriously drooping now so Francesca suggests a short break while she makes an espresso for both of them. "Now let's look briefly at the **various parts of an insurance policy**," she says after setting down the coffees. The basic parts are as follows (Page 49):
  1. Declarations — what is covered, how much, who is insured, the premium, the deductible, and the length of the policy.
  2. Definitions used throughout the policy.
  3. Insuring agreement which specifies the details of the insurer's promise.
  4. Exclusions and restrictions that put limits on the coverage.
  5. Conditions that outline the duties and obligations of both the insured and the insurer.
  6. Miscellaneous Provisions, which might include, for instance, a grace period for late premium payments.

In addition, there may be the following:
  7. Endorsements and riders that add to the coverage.

8. Deductibles which are the amounts the insured has to pay.

9. Co-insurance requirement that outlines any risk-sharing provision over and above the deductible.

K. "Let's have a look at a real insurance policy to make sure you understand that this is just a contract. In a term life insurance policy, it is clear when the insurer has to pay — when the insured dies. The policies we will look at in the future are longer and more complex":

1. Auto policies in Chapter 3 have to deal with bodily injury, whose fault the loss is, and the extent of the damage.

2. Homeowners policies in Chapter 4 have many exclusions based on both the level of coverage and also the cause of the loss. For instance, losses caused by natural disasters are not covered.

3. Commercial insurance in Chapter 5 addresses the many potential losses that commercial operations face due to their particular line of work as well as many losses that individuals do not face.

4. Health insurance in Chapter 6 in Canada is first and foremost governed by the *Canada Health Act*, which governs provincial health plans. Private insurance is available to fill in the many gaps left by provincial plans.

5. Loss of income in Chapter 7 covers government-mandated plans at your place of employment as well as other government and private plans that cover you if you cannot earn your regular income.

6. Life insurance in Chapter 8 explains policies that offer more than just life insurance protection.

"So you see, understanding a basic insurance policy is to understand that all insurance policies, no matter how complex, are just contacts."

L. "Is that it? Contract Law? We're done?" asks Joanne.

"Not quite," Francesca replies. "Let's have a quick look at **negligence** because it is the reason we need to have **liability insurance** and it takes us into the realm of **Tort Law**". There are four requirements before an act can be considered negligent (Pages 55–56):

1. Legal duty of care
2. Failure to perform that duty
3. Victim suffers damage or injury
4. Proximate (adjacent, near) cause between the negligent act and the damage or injury

M. "That sounds pretty black and white. What if you are only partly guilty?" asks Joanne.

"Well, " Francesca replies, "there are several **defences against negligence** (Page 56):

1. Contributory negligence, where the injured person's conduct contributed to the loss
2. Comparative negligence, where both the injured party and the injury party must share responsibility for any damages
3. Last clear chance rule, if the injuring party could have prevented the loss but failed to do so
4. Assumption of risk, meaning the injured party knew the risk and accepted it

N. "And," Francesca continues, "sometimes someone is guilty by definition. This is called **imputed negligence**" and it occurs in the following: (Page 57)

1. Employee-employer relationship
2. Vicarious liability
3. Family purpose doctrine
4. Joint business ventures and partnerships
5. Dram Shop Laws
6. *Res ipsa loquitur* — the thing speaks for itself.

O. "So what does **tort law** have to do with this?" Joanne asks. "Tort law is how private law deals with negligence" (Page 57):

1. First of all, fault has to be established.

2. Negligence has to have been present.

3. Note that professional liability arises because the person has the expertise and a fiduciary duty to conduct oneself impeccably. Failing to fulfil that duty can result in negligent misrepresentation.

P. "We're nearly there," says Francesca. "Just a few more things having to do with somewhat special cases of negligence":
1. Absolute and strict liability (Page 58)
2. Charities
3. Governments
4. Parents and children
5. Property owners: (Page 59)
   (a) Trespasser
   (b) Licensee
   (c) Invitee
6. Special category for children (attractive nuisance)

Concept Questions

1. What is the name given in the medieval era to groups of people, like bakers and weavers, who formed an association?

2. Explain how insurance provides a society with
   (a) a source of investment funds.
   (b) indemnification for a loss
   (c) less fear and worry
   (d) enhancement of credit
   (e) loss prevention

3. Explain how insurance hurts societies by
   (a) increasing the cost of doing business, and
   (b) fraudulent and inflated claims.

4. List the six characteristics of an insurable risk.

5. What does it mean to indemnify someone?

6. Give three reasons why insurance companies require that an insured have an insurable interest in the insurance contract.

7. What are the three purposes of the principle of subrogation.

8. Explain the difference between Common Law and Civil Law.

9. Income tax fraud is covered under which form of public law in Canada?

10. What are the types of law that apply to the insurance industry?

11. List the elements of a valid contract.

12. Amany owns an internet service company and is contacted by Joe, who is interested in purchasing internet service from her company on a monthly basis. Identify the offeror and the offeree.

13. Andre tells his neighbour that he agrees to talk to his neighbour about fixing their shared fence. Does this qualify as a contract? Why or why not?

14. Sunny is addicted to television. A friend of his tells him that he can get Sunny an illegal cable hook up for only $200. Sunny agrees and pays his "friend" the money. His friend never does the job. Can Sunny sue his friend and recover his $200? Why or why not?

15. Sharena, 13, loves comic books and has signed up for an online comic book subscription. The subscription will send a bill to her home every month based on the amount of material that she has read off the website. Sharena's father is enraged when Sharena tells him that she has signed up for the subscription. Can Sharena cancel the contract without having to pay for the material that she has already read?

16. Jason is a used car dealer who has an alcohol addiction. One day while working on the lot, he has several stiff drinks with his buddy Andy. Andy, who is really drunk, decides that he will purchase a 2002 Audi A4 today from Jason. Andy cannot afford the car. Can Andy back out of the contract once he sobers up or is he stuck with his stupid alcohol-induced decision?

17. Why can Canadians legally buy Cuban cigars but Americans cannot?

18. Andrea sells carpets and sells Dalton a dark blue chair. However, when the chair is delivered, Dalton discovers that the chair is actually black.
    (a) What kind of mistake is this?
    (b) What if Andrea knew it was black and was hoping that Dalton wouldn't be able to tell the difference?

19. Ruben is a very overweight singer. One day on stage he dies of a heart attack. Ruben had purchased life insurance a year ago. On the insurance contract he lied about his age to obtain a lower rate. If he had told the truth, the premium he would pay would have cost him an extra $200 a year. What will happen to his settlement?

20. Justin owns a home improvement company. He has a client whose basement he is renovating. Justin and his client have a horrible relationship and Justin can't stand him. His client is always looking over his shoulder and telling him how to do his job. One day Justin and his client have a huge argument and Justin decides that the money he is making on this particular project is not worth it and he wants to stop. What can Justin do to get out of the contract without being sued for not completing his job?

21. When agreeing to the terms and conditions of his computer use at Ryerson University, is Reza signing a contract of adhesion or a bargaining contract?

22. Stella's homeowners insurance policy covers her for everything except a list of perils. What type of insuring agreement is this?

23. Joe's disability policy has added coverage for automatic inflation protection. Is this a rider or an endorsement?

24. List three purposes that deductibles serve.

25. In property insurance, what is the purpose of a co-insurance clause?

26. Using the sample term insurance policy, what do the following mean?
    (a) 31-day grace period
    (b) Suicide clause
    (c) Incontestability

27. What are the four elements of negligence?

28. Can a seat belt ticket be classified as a method of extracting punitive damages by the police? (Note, this ticket is under public law, but answer it as if it were part of private law.)

29. Carlos jaywalks across a busy street while he is high, is struck by a car, and is seriously hurt. What defence against negligence can the driver use to avoid having to pay the full amount of Carlos's injuries
    (a) if the driver is not paying attention to the road?
    (b) if the driver is paying attention?

30. If Paul lends his girlfriend his car and she smashes it into a streetcar, who is liable for the damages to the streetcar? Why?

31. Under which negligence concept is Paul liable if his son steals his car and smashes it through a store window?

32. Vic has opened a new bar, and to draw a crowd he has a fear-no-beer night. All domestic beer will cost only $2 a bottle, $4 a pint, and $8 a pitcher. One night his bar is visited by a bunch of drunken college students who gladly take advantage of his generous prices. If one of the students drives home and hits someone, are Vic and his business liable, and under what negligence concept would this fall?

33. What is the purpose of tort law?

34. Which has a more strict interpretation of liability — absolute liability or strict liability?

35. What is the difference between a licencee and an invitee? Is a child who stumbles onto a person's property without permission to use a swimming pool a trespasser or an invitee?

Application Questions

36. In each of the following situations, indicate which basic characteristic of insurance is violated.
    (a) Bill's carpet business is failing. He is having trouble meeting his weekly budget requirements as his expenses continue to outstrip his revenues. He decides he will burn down the building and collect on his building insurance.
    (b) Bill from the previous example is the son-in-law of the president of a large insurance company. He wants to make an agreement with his father-in-law to have the insurance company provide him with revenue insurance — the insurance company would pay a guaranteed amount of money to Bill every time his business was experiencing hard times.
    (c) Paul has his car broken into while he is parked at a GO transit parking lot. His stereo system, which had a value of $400, was stolen from his car. Paul decides he can use this opportunity to finally get the stereo system he wants. He lies on his claim form and somehow fools the insurance company to pay him $800 for his stereo.

37. Using the characteristics of an insurable risk, compare how the risk of theft compares with the risk of a hurricane.

38. Steve, the owner of a large collection of vintage baseball cards, feels that one day his cards will be worth at least $1,500. Currently, they are worth $1,000. He meets with his insurance company and after significant time negotiating with his insurer, the company agrees to insure his collection for $1,500. What type of insurance policy does he have?

39. Angela purchased her Honda Civic two years ago at a cost of $12,000. Since her purchase, the car has depreciated 30%. If she gets into a car accident today, how much will she receive from the insurance company, according to the principle of indemnity?

40. Mike is involved in horrific car accident with Harold, who is uninsured. Harold ran a red light and slammed into Mike's minivan. Mike has been injured severely and his insurance company pays out $200,000 for his therapy, which is not covered under his province's public health care. The insurance company then decides to recover its losses from Harold by launch-

ing a lawsuit against him. What insurance term best describes what Mike's insurance company is doing?

41. Having two competent parties is an essential requirement when signing a contract. What other essential variables are needed to create a valid contract?

42. Ryerson University is looking to build a new building for its nursing students. It enters into a construction contract with Construct Co. The company is paid $2,000,000 to begin work as of April 30th 2007. It is now September 2007 and nothing has been done at all. What can Ryerson do to get Construct Co. to either begin working or forfeit the contract to a firm that wishes to complete it?

43. Mr. Legend loves to collect vintage hockey jerseys. He keeps his expensive collection in his home, locked in a safe. One day while talking to his son, a university student taking a risk management and insurance class, he is made aware of the fact that his home insurance does not adequately compensate him for any losses to his extensive jersey collection, which is valued at approximately $50,000. How can Mr. Legend insure that his personal property will be adequately covered by his home insurance policy?

44. For each of the following independent situations, identify whether negligence can be established by using the four criteria that need to present.
    (a) Ronald, a paper boy, slips and falls on Phil's icy, snow-covered driveway.
    (b) John is on vacation at a ski resort in British Columbia. He decides to impress his girlfriend by going off the steepest slope available. He has a horrible fall and breaks his neck. Was the ski resort negligent?
    (c) During a chemical spill in Lake Ontario, the water supply is seriously contaminated. The government immediately shuts off all water going out of the lake for public consumption. The government pays for replacement water while Lake Ontario's water is being cleansed. After a couple months, the government deems the water safe to drink. Soon, after, a large portion of the population get critically ill after drinking the water. Is the government negligent? Can it be sued?

45. Jacob is involved in a boating accident with his neighbour Mike. Damage to Mike's boat is estimated to be at $10,000 and Jacob is 52% at fault. The judge in the court case decides to use the pure rule to determine negligence. How much will Jacob have to pay Mike?

46. Harold is known as a daredevil among his friends. One day he decides to impress his friends by de-muzzling a neighbour's pitbull. He leaps over the fence, wrestles the dog down, and takes off the muzzle. The dog instantly attacks him and take a big chunk of flesh out of Harold's face. Who is legally responsible for Harold's injuries — Harold or the dog's owner? What is the name of the doctrine that covers this?

47. Janice owns a large farm on the outskirts of Mississauga, Ontario. She raises dairy cows and, in order to keep troublesome teenagers away from her cows, she has built a large fence around the farm. She also has several no-trespassing signs. One night she is awakened by the sound of laughter. She runs outside to see her precious cows being tipped over by a bunch of drunk teenagers. She runs inside and gets her shotgun and shoots one of teenagers in the arm. Janice figures that she is right to do so, as the fence and the sign are clear signals to keep the teenagers out. Is she correct?

48. Randy is six years old. While out playing one day, he wanders out of his mom's sight. He goes into a neighbour's unattended and unfenced backyard and begins using the play set. As he is coming down a slide, he injures himself badly. Who is legally responsible for his injuries?

Automobile Insurance

Learning Objectives

After completing this chapter, students will be able to:

A. Describe basic and optional coverages in all jurisdictions.

B. Identify the major parts of a personal automobile policy.

C. Use a policy to decide whether or not situations and events are covered.

D. Select the appropriate insurance coverage for a few situations.

Introduction

All provinces and territories require the owners of automobiles to carry basic insurance coverage. Quebec (for bodily injury only), British Columbia, Manitoba, and Saskatchewan have a government-run auto insurance industry for the basic, **mandatory coverage that is the minimum required coverage. In these provinces, no policies are issued for this mandatory coverage since everyone has the same basic policy. The insurance premium is paid at the same time licenses are renewed. Both optional coverage** and **excess coverage** over and above the basic, mandatory coverage is available in these provinces through either the Crown corporation or private insurers.

Legal Aspects

All three levels of government are involved in regulating the use of automobiles in Canada. The federal government, through the *Insurance Act of Canada*, has given the provinces and territories legislative power to manage their own automobile insurance industries. The federal *Insurance Act* was created to control and monitor insurance companies. The act also delegates legislation and regulation of the auto insurance industry for each jurisdiction to the individual provinces and territories. The act also outlines the mandatory automobile insurance coverage that an individual is required to hold.

The provincial and regulatory bodies are outlined in Chapter 9, Table 9.1: Insurance Regulators and Licensing Bodies. Each jurisdiction has a standardized automobile insurance policy that specifies the minimum standards of compulsory coverage. These regulatory bodies also control the type of coverage that private insurers sell to drivers, the rates they are allowed to charge and the type of medical benefits that people injured in/by automobile accidents are entitled to receive through insurance claims. They also oversee the wording and terminology used by private insurers in the policies.

Table 3.1   Government Regulation of Insurance

Federal Level	Provincial Level	Municipal Level
• **Criminal Code of Canada** has several sections covering various aspects, such as impaired driving, dangerous operation of a vehicle, failure to stop at the scene of an accident, criminally negligent operation of a vehicle, and theft.	• **Highway Traffic Acts** set out laws relating to speed limits, age restrictions on driving, testing requirements, different license classes (M1, G, L, etc.), seatbelt requirements, and defines who has the right of way.	• Creates and sets laws for parking and crosswalks.

Table 3.1   Continued

Federal Level	Provincial Level	Municipal Level
• Convictions for violations affect premiums and coverage.	• Convictions for violations affect premiums and coverage.	• Convictions for violations do not affect premiums and coverage. However, municipal governments can impound vehicles and give fines that must be paid to renew a driving licence.
• Responsible for the *Insurance Act*.	• Sets rate guidelines and coverage requirements.	

Types of Coverage

The Statutory Conditions and standard policies in each jurisdiction ensure that coverage is the same for all insureds in that jurisdiction. The wording of these policies varies from province to province, but many provisions are similar.

We are covering only an auto policy and there is similar personal coverage for motorcycles, motor homes, trailers and camper units, off-road vehicles, motorized snow vehicles, and historic vehicles.

Compulsory Coverage

All provinces and territories require all drivers to have auto insurance and to have the following coverages:

- **Third-Party Liability** provides coverage of up to $200,000 ($500,000 in Nova Scotia, $50,000 in Quebec) to pay other people to whom the insured can be legally liable for bodily injury and/or damage to the property of others.
- **Accident Benefits** provide compensation, regardless of fault, for insured persons (the driver, the driver's passengers, and pedestrians) injured or killed in an auto accident for all provinces and territories except Newfoundland and Labrador, where Accident Benefits are provided through the provincial health care plan.
- **Uninsured Automobile** provides the same amount of coverage as third-party liability if a person is in an accident with an *uninsured* or *unidentified (hit-and-run)* auto to compensate the victim for the amount he or she would be entitled to receive from an uninsured or unidentified motorist. If the victim is not covered by an insurance policy, several jurisdictions have a Motor Vehicle Accident Claim Funds or Unsatisfied Judgment Fund (Table 3.11) to compensate the injured party.
- **Direct Compensation — Property Damage** in the four provinces having **no-fault insurance** covers physical damage to the vehicle and loss of use of the vehicle caused by another driver. In B.C. and Ontario, direct compensation covers only to the degree to which the insured is not at fault. Manitoba, Saskatchewan, B.C., and Quebec for bodily injury only have government-run insurance plans for mandatory coverage. In Manitoba and Saskatchewan All-perils Coverage for damage to the vehicle regardless of fault is part of the basic auto policy and is, therefore, mandatory.

Occasionally, it is suggested that the mandatory Accident Benefits Coverage should be optional if the driver already has coverage at work. This would reduce premiums for those drivers but would likely increase the cost to other drivers. The argument is that since these drivers already have coverage at work, they are unlikely to use the Accident Benefits Coverage in their auto policy, meaning these drivers are in effect, subsidizing other drivers.

Optional Coverage

Over and above the mandatory minimums, insureds can get coverage for the following:

- **Loss or damage to one's own vehicle**. In B.C. and Ontario, no-fault insurance covers damage to the owner's own vehicle to the degree to which the driver is not at fault. In Saskatchewan, optional insurance is available to lower the $700 deductible.
- **Excess coverage:**
  - **Additional liability** coverage over the mandatory minimum (many brokers and agents recommend $1,000,000 or even $2,000,000 liability coverage),
  - **Additional accident benefits**, and
  - **Additional loss and theft coverage**.

Table 3.2   Summary of Automobile Insurance Policies

	Mandatory Coverage		Direct Compensation for Property Damage**	Bodily Injuries: Right to Sue for	
	Private Insurers	Government-run*		Pain & Suffering	Economic Loss in Excess of No-fault Benefits***
AB	Private		No	Yes $4,144 max for minor injuries	Yes
BC		Government	No	Yes	Yes
MB		Government	No	No	No
NB	Private		Yes	Yes $2,500 max for minor injuries	Yes
NL	Private		No	Yes $2,500 Deductible	Yes
NT	Private		No	Yes $2,500 max for minor injuries	Yes
NS	Private		No	Yes $2,500 max for minor injuries	Yes
NU	Private		No	Yes	Yes
ON	Private		Yes	Yes with Verbal Threshold & $30,000 Deductible	Yes with conditions
PE	Private		No	Yes $2,500 max for minor injuries	Yes
QC	Private for Property Damage	Government for Bodily Injury	Yes	No	No
SK		Government	No	No	Yes with limitations
SK		Government	No	Yes with $5,000 deductible	Yes
YT	Private		No	Yes	Yes

*   In all government-run systems, the government administers the basic, mandatory portion and competes with private insurers for optional and excess coverage.

** All government-run plans provide direct compensation for mandatory coverage since there is only one insurer.

*** Everyone involved in an automobile accident is entitled to basic Accident Benefits regardless of fault.

Source: Insurance Bureau of Canada [www.ibc.ca], *2009 Facts*.

Table 3.3 Basic, Mandatory Coverage

	Name of Policy or Plan	Third-Party Liability	Accident Benefits	Uninsured and Unidentified Motorist / Automobile	Your Own Vehicle*
AB	• Standard Automobile Policy (**S.P.F. No. 1**)	• Section A	• Sections B-1, B-2	• Section B-3	
BC	• Autoplan	• Part I	• Part 1	• Part 1	• Inverse liability**
MB	• Autopac	• Basic	• Basic	• Basic	• All-perils coverage
NB	• S.P.F. No. 1	• Section A	• Section B	• Section D	
NL	• S.P.F. No. 1	• Section A	• Section B	• Section D***	
NS	• S.P.F. No. 1	• Section A	• Section B	• Section D	
NT, NU	• S.P.F. No. 1	• Section A	• Sections B-1, B-2	• Section B-3	
ON	• Ontario Automobile Policy (**OAP 1**)	• Section 3	• Section 4	• Section 5	• Section 6**
PE	• S.P.F. No. 1	• Section A	• Section B	• Section D	
QC	• Société de l'assurance automobile du Québec (**SAAQ**) Q.P.F. No.1	• Section A — Civil Liability (private insurers)	• No-fault (SAAQ)	• Fonds d'indemnisation (SAAQ)	
SK	• Saskatchewan Government Insurance (**SGI**)	• Part IV — Liability	• Part II — Injury Payments	• Part V — Family Security	• All-perils coverage with $700 deductible
YT	• S.P.F. No. 1	• Section A	• Sections B-1, B-2	• Section B-3	

* These coverages are described in the sections on Direct Compensation and Optional Property Loss or Damage Coverage.

** Covers to the degree to which you are **not** at fault.

*** In Newfoundland and Labrador, Accident Benefits coverage, S.P.F. No. 1, Section B — Accident Benefits, Subsection 1 — Medical, Rehabilitation and Funeral Expenses, is provided through the *Newfoundland Medical Care Insurance Act*, which governs Medical Care Plan (MCP), the provincial health care plan.

Table 3.4 Optional and Excess Coverage

	Policy or Plan	Optional for Your Own Vehicle	Provided by
AB	S.P.F. No. 1	Section C — Loss or Damage to Insured Automobile	Private insurers
BC	Autoplan ICBC	Collision, comprehensive, or specified perils coverage	Private insurers & Autoplan
MB	Autopac	Collision, comprehensive, or specified perils coverage	Private insurers & Autopac
NB	S.P.F. No. 1	Section C — Loss or Damage to Insured Automobile	Private insurers
NL	S.P.F. No. 1	Section C — Loss or Damage to Insured Automobile	Private insurers
NS	S.P.F. No. 1	Section C — Loss or Damage to Insured Automobile	Private insurers
NT, NU	S.P.F. No. 1	Section C — Loss or Damage to Insured Automobile	Private insurers
ON	OAP 1	Section 7 — Loss or Damage Coverages (Optional)	Private insurers
PE	S.P.F. No. 1	Section C — Loss or Damage to Insured Automobile	Private insurers
QC	SAAQ	Section B1, B2	B3 and B4 — Loss of or Damage to Insured Automobile
SK	SGI	Part III — Damage to Your Auto	Private insurers & SGI
YT	S.P.F. No. 1	Section C — Loss or Damage to Insured Automobile	Private insurers

Legal Principles

The following three legal principles are relevant to this discussion of auto insurance.

1. Absolute Liability

A person injured or killed by your vehicle (third parties) have the right to collect from your insurance company even if coverage is denied to you because you have violated the terms of the contract. If you violate the terms of the contract, your property is not covered. However, third parties who suffer loss or damage caused by you are still covered by your insurance policy under the absolute liability doctrine. Furthermore, the insurer has the right to be reimbursed by you for any monies paid to third parties for property damage, bodily injury, or death. This doctrine holds true in all jurisdictions for medical benefits coverage. That is for anyone injured or killed by your vehicle.

EXAMPLE 1 You've had several drinks with friends but stopped drinking a couple of hours ago and believe you are not "impaired". You hit a pedestrian who ran out to catch a bus. The pedestrian has serious injuries and requires several months of physiotherapy, which is covered by Accident Benefits Coverage. Your blood alcohol level is 85 mg, which is over the legal limit of 80 mg. You will be charged and undoubtedly convicted of impaired driving.

The insurance company will pay for the pedestrian's treatment and has the right to be reimbursed by you since you have been convicted of impaired driving. Your own injuries will also be covered. Any damages your car sustains that would normally be covered by your policy will not be covered because you will be convicted for impaired driving under the Criminal Code of Canada.

2. Negligence

Third-party liability covers damage or injury to an innocent third party caused by your negligent operation of a motor vehicle — negligent in that you caused the accident. Negligence was discussed in the prior chapter. To be negligent is to fail to do what a reasonable and prudent person would do, or not do what such a person would do; the negligent act causes property damage, bodily injury, and/or death.

EXAMPLE 2 You are driving home, tired, after work. As you are talking on your cell phone, you hit a pedestrian, who ran out to catch a bus. The pedestrian has serious injuries and requires several months of physiotherapy, which is covered in Accident Benefits Coverage. You were driving at the speed limit and were will not be charged with any criminal act.

You are negligent in that you were distracted by talking on the phone while driving (assuming your province does not have a law against using a cell phone while driving). All your coverage is in place since you were merely negligent, not criminally negligent.

3. Subrogation

New Brunswick, Ontario, Saskatchewan, and Quebec for bodily injury have no-fault or direct compensation insurance, which means that each person collects from his or her own insurance company and the victim's insurer cannot try to get compensation from the at-fault driver's insurer. These provinces have removed the right of subrogation — the right to collect the claim paid from the insurer of the at-fault driver. The exact policy wording is given in Optional Property Loss or Damage Coverage later in this chapter.

EXAMPLE 3   You live in a province with no-fault insurance. You are driving home, tired, after work. As you slow down for a red light, you hit a pedestrian, who ran out to catch a bus. The pedestrian has serious injuries and requires several months of physiotherapy, which is covered in Accident Benefits Coverage. In addition, in attempting to avoid the pedestrian, you swerve and hit another car.

Your insurer will pay for the pedestrian's medical costs as well as any medical costs you might incur and for any repairs to your car. The other motorist's insurer will pay for repairs to the car you hit.

If you live in a province without no-fault, the other motorist's insurer has the right of subrogation — to be compensated by your insurance company for the costs of repairing the other car.

The Automobile Policy as a Contract

An automobile policy is a contract that lays out in great detail what the insurer, the second party to the contract, will and will not pay for under what circumstances, terms, and conditions. We will go through aspects of the policies after the next section.

Determining the Premium

Many factors contribute to the amount of your insurance premium in most jurisdictions:

1. Probability of a loss:
   • Age, gender, and marital status
   • Driving record
   • Driver training
   • Number of years licensed
   • Number of claims
   • Number of at-fault accidents
   • Make and model of car
   • Location — urban or rural
   • Vehicle use and how much you drive
   • Number of other operators
2. Particular risk
3. Size of the deductible
4. Coverage — the amount of excess and optional coverage
5. Taxes on the premiums

Probability of a Loss

As discussed in the prior chapter, insurance premiums are based on probabilities, and auto insurance is no different. Policy owners are categorized based on historical data and information in regard to the likelihood they will experience a loss.

Age, Gender, and Marital Status

Since young, single males have, as a group, higher rates of auto accidents, their premiums are higher than those of someone with a similar driving record who is older, married, and female. Is this fair to the individual driver? Perhaps not (and some jurisdictions have new laws to reflect this). However, insurance companies have no way to predict exactly who will experience a loss so they depend on historical data. If you cause an accident, either a single-car accident or one involving another vehicle, the insurer now has specific information about you and your rates will likely increase.

Driver Training

Completing recognized driver training can reduce premiums for newly licensed drivers.

Driving Record

In the prior chapter we looked at Alice and Joe and their probabilities for having an accident. With her driving record after only a few years of driving, Alice will undoubtedly pay more for insurance than Joe.

Number of Years Licensed

More experienced drivers tend to have fewer accidents than newly licenced drivers.

Number of Claims

Insurance is designed to protect against catastrophic losses, and insurers are often less concerned with the *size* of the claim and more concerned about the *number* of claims. Filing two or three claims in a few years will increase premiums dramatically and may even get you cut off. Calling an insurance company to ask a question about a minor accident you have caused means you have reported the accident and will affect your auto premium (but not a home insurance premium) even if you do not make a claim.

Number of At-fault Accidents

If the policy does not provide any accident forgiveness (often provided for the first accident in a given number of years), your premiums can increase by 100% or more.

Make and Model of Car

Some vehicles are more at risk for an insurance claim. These are vehicles that are the least safe, more prone to damage and more likely to be stolen.

The **Vehicle Information Centre of Canada (VICC)** is a division of **Insurance Information Centre of Canada (IICC)** which is, in turn, part of the **Insurance Bureau of Canada (IBC)** [www.ibc.ca].

- IBC is the national trade association of non-government property and casualty insurers, the private companies that insure cars, homes, and businesses in Canada. Its members are insurance companies.
- IICC collects, validates, and analyses insurance-rated data and publishes reports.
- VICC has developed the **Canadian Loss Experience Automobile Rating (CLEAR)** system which tracks actual performance of makes and models of cars and publishes the results on its website (through the IBC website).

In the theft portion of the premium, the most at-risk vehicles are rated between 2.5 and 4 times the average cost of $48 of insuring a vehicle, that is, the cost for these vehicles is $120 to $200 for the comprehensive portion of the policy (that covers theft claims). CLEAR FAQ (frequently asked questions) states that in a province that has no-fault insurance, CLEAR could affect as much as 80% of the premium, while in other provinces CLEAR impacts about half of the premium. The CLEAR system does not change the total premiums charged by insurance companies — it merely redistributes the existing premiums, rewarding those policyholders who buy cars that are less likely to incur losses.

In July 2005, the **Consumers' Association of Canada (CAC)** released a report stating that government-run premiums in B.C. are significantly lower than in privately run Alberta and Ontario. This report was criticized by the Insurance Bureau of Canada for (1) not shopping around for the lowest premium and for (2) not taking a weighted average based on market share but taking a simple average. The average costs quoted were as follows:

Table 3.5   Quotes for Government-run Insurers versus Private Insurers, 2005

	Canadian Consumer Association		Insurance Bureau of Canada	
B.C.	$1,325	100%	$1,096	100%
Alberta	$1,715	129%	$1,076	98%
Ontario	$2,384	180%	$1,279	117%

Source: Adapted from National Study of Automobile Insurance Rates, July 7, 2005, www.consumer.ca.

IBC further claims that Ontario's higher rates can be explained by higher density of traffic in Ontario as well as more generous no-fault benefits. In addition, some 460,000 drivers in Ontario, or 5.8% of all drivers, *do not carry insurance even though it is mandatory*. This increases premiums for the other 7.5 million drivers who are insured.

Location

Where you live affects your premiums. While there are more fatalities for accidents in rural settings due to higher speed on highways and rural roads, there are far fewer accidents outside of the city. As a result, a person living in a large urban centre will face much higher premiums than someone who lives in a rural community — a small town or in the country. Furthermore, some areas of urban centres are considered to be more high-risk than others. As a result, in large cities rates can change by moving across the street since rates for people living in the suburbs who commute to work are higher than rates for people who live in the city.

Vehicle Use and How Much You Drive

Drivers who use their cars for pleasure driving only and who do not drive to work pay lower premiums since they both drive less frequently and drive less in heavy traffic.

Number of Operators

The more people who regularly drive the vehicle, the higher the premium.

Particular Risk

Some insurers have very high rates for a certain class of drivers because they prefer not to have a lot of policyholders in a particular risk category — they set high rates to both discourage policyholders and also to compensate themselves for taking on policies in certain categories. The **Financial Services Commission of Ontario (FSCO)** has a website that allows you to get sample quotes for four different profiles for several cities in Ontario and for all insurance companies operating in Ontario ([www.autoinsurance.gov.on.ca], Consumer Information, Educational Auto Rate Tutorial). Using these quotes, Table 3.6 notes the highest and lowest possible rates for Hamilton, Ontario, and Ottawa (from a list of 57 insurers).

Table 3.6   Premiums for Two Metropolitan Areas

	Ottawa		Hamilton	
• 2006 population of city (metropolitan area)	812,129 (1,130,761)		504,559 (692,911)	
• Age 70, licensed 50 years, pleasure only, $1,000,000 liability	$ 633	$ 2,199	$ 738	$ 3,467
• Male, age 19, licensed 3 years, commute, $500,000 liability	$1,953	$10,707	$4,411	$15,137
• Female, age 23, licensed 6 years, 1 chargeable accident, drive to work, $500,000 liability	$1,238	$10,534	$2,355	$14,520
• Couple, age 39 and 40, drive to work, $1,000,000 liability	$1,680	$ 5,260	$1,665	$ 7,812

Source: Adapted from Financial Services of Ontario website, (www.autoinsurance.gov.on.ca)

Why is Hamilton consistently more expensive than Ottawa? We can only speculate that it might have to do with a greater RCMP presence in Ottawa or perhaps it is related to heavier transport traffic around Hamilton on its way to and from the American border. For whatever reason, there is a great variety in insurance premiums. It definitely pays to shop around.

Size of the Deductible

The deductible is the first amount of loss and is usually a dollar amount (say $500) and it is paid by the insured. The size of the deductible also has an effect on the premium — increasing the deductible from $300 to $500 can reduce the premium by as much as 10%. Raising it to $1,000 will reduce the premium even more. This decreasing premium for an increasing deductible can also be weighed against the effect of filing a claim for $1,000 or even $1,500. While these amounts might feel catastrophic at the time, a true catastrophic loss is more like a $1 million liability from a lawsuit or the total loss of the vehicle. Also, a few small claims will increase your premium so the reduction in premiums that comes with a higher deductible may more than offset any damage not covered by a higher deductible.

Coverage

The coverage also affects premiums — more or better coverage increases the premium. Again, insurance is meant to cover catastrophic losses. While you must be sure to have adequate liability insurance, you should question carrying collision (the coverage for damage to your own vehicle itself when you are at fault) on older cars. Some insurers automatically remove the collision coverage once a car is ten years old. Some people take off the collision coverage as soon as the car is paid for figuring that if they can pay for the car once, they could pay for it again. Then again, the collision coverage on an old car may not be very high if the car doesn't have much value.

The *Insurance Act* requires auto insurance to provide Accident Benefits to *everyone* involved in an accident with a motor vehicle whether or not they are the legal owner of the car or if they even own a car. This is a way of shifting some of the burden for health care costs to both the private sector for those jurisdictions having private insurance coverage or to another public sector for those jurisdictions having government auto insurance.

Taxes on Premiums

Studies comparing auto insurance premiums in different jurisdictions do not include taxes. As you can see from the following table, some jurisdictions add a considerable amount of taxes to the premium.

The following table provides premiums, information on injuries and fatalities (died within 30 days of the accident except in Quebec where it is 8 days). The taxes are charged to the insurance companies like income taxes and are not necessarily charged to the insureds directly.

Table 3.7 Auto Premiums, Casualty Rates and Premium, Sales and Fire Tax Rates

	2007 Average Premiums**			2006 Casualty Rates*		2007 Insurance Premium Tax				2007 Fire Tax
	Premium	Registration Fee	Total	Fatalities	Injuries		Including Auto and/or Property	Excluding Auto and/or Property	Sales Tax	
Canada	$1,122	$ 322	$1,444	8.9	612.3					
AB	$1,526	$ 125	$1,651	10.6	570.7		3.00%			
BC	$ 705	$1,046	$1,751	13.9	860.6	Auto & Property	4.40%			
BC								4.00%		
MB	$ 895	$562	$1,457	10.3	729.1		3.00%			1.25%
NB	$1,113	$115	$1,228	13.6	452.1		3.00%			1.00%
NL	$1,136	$207	$1,343	9.8	501.3		4.00%		15.00%	
NS	$1,022	$ 86	$1,108	7.1	470.8		4.00%			1.25%
NT	$ 867	$ 90	$ 957	5.4	294.3		3.00%			1.00%
NU	$ 294	$ 107	$ 401	Not available			3.00%			1.00%
ON	$1,577	$ 93	$1,670	6.1	527.5	Auto	3.00%			
ON								3.00%	8.00%	
PE	$1,018	$ 123	$1,141	12.8	803.6		3.50%			1.00%
QC	$ 680	$ 287	$ 967	10.6	711.1	Auto	3.35%		5.00%	
QC								3.35%	9.00%	
SK	$ 171	$1,111	$1,282	13.2	610.7	Auto	5.00%			
SK								4.00%		
YT	$1,088	$ 70	$1,158	12.3	434.5		2.00%			1.00%

* Fatalities and injuries per billion vehicle kilometres.
** Jurisdictions that have public insurance tend to include the cost of mandatory insurance in The Registration Fee and optional coverage is included in the Premium. Nunavut has hardly any cars, so these rates are mostly for snowmobiles and all-terrain vehicles, so these rates are pretty much meaningless when compared to the rest of the country.

Sources: Statistics Canada, Household Spending, Transportation = Private and Public Vehicle Insurance premiums, Average Expenditures, Table 203-007, Transport Canada using Statistics Canada, Catalogue No. 53-223-XIE, Canadian Vehicle Survey, Insurance Bureau of Canada, *Facts 2009* for taxes.

Factors that Do Not Affect Premiums

Some factors are not allowed to be used to determine premiums and these factors can vary a great deal by jurisdiction. The following for Ontario and Saskatchewan illustrate the great differences in what is not allowed to be used in setting premiums.

Ontario   *(Private Insurance)*

The Financial Services Commission of Ontario (FSCO) states that insurance companies *cannot* use the following to *determine premiums*:
• Credit history

- Bankruptcy
- Employment status
- Whether you own a credit card
- How long you have lived in your current home
- Not-at-fault-accidents
- Whether your vehicle is owned or leased
- Whether there was a period of time when you had no automobile coverage

Saskatchewan   *(Public Insurance)*

Our philosophy is that all drivers should be treated equally unless their driving records show they are a greater risk for causing a collision. That means we don't use a driver's age, gender or where they live to determine a cost for their auto insurance.

Getting Insurance Coverage — Underwriting Rules

Underwriting rules are used by insurance companies to assess the probability and size of a loss based on analysis of historical information. The rules are different for each insurance company and determine whether or not you can get or renew your insurance coverage with a particular company. These rules commonly *include* the following:

- Number of at-fault accidents
- Number of moving violations
- Number of times coverage was cancelled for failing to pay premiums
- Providing incorrect or incomplete information in the past

Underwriting rules may *not* include certain rules that are discriminatory although they *can* charge premiums that are prohibitive. Unacceptable rules are rules that deny coverage based on:

- Whether you are newly licensed or a driver new to Canada
- Age, sex, and marital status
- Religion, race, nationality, or ethnicity
- Where you live or the location of the vehicle.

Some jurisdictions have enacted additional prohibitions that shape underwriting rules. For instance, Nova Scotia and Newfoundland and Labrador have recently passed legislation that makes it easier for drivers/owners to get auto insurance.

Nova Scotia   *(Government of Nova Scotia, Department of Finance, Auto Insurance Highlights, October, 2003)*

Effective August 1, 2003, insurers may *not refuse to issue or renew* auto insurance for an existing or potential customer on any of the following grounds:
- Age
- Gender
- Marital status
- Age of vehicle
- Previous coverage by Facility Association
- A previous refusal of insurance coverage, previous not-at-fault accidents
- Making a late payment
- A lapse in auto insurance coverage less than two years long

Newfoundland and Labrador   *(Government of Newfoundland and Labrador, Department of Government Services, Financial Services Regulation Division, St. John's, NL, May 2005, "What Auto Insurance Reform Means to You".)*

In 2005, Newfoundland implemented insurance reforms with the result that premiums for young drivers dropped, premiums for drivers over age 55 remained about the same due to senior's discounts and premiums for those in-between increased. Insurers must now use one base rate and increases are reflected only on the insured's driving record. An insurance company is no longer able to *refuse coverage or rate individuals* solely based on:
- Not at-fault accidents and claims,
- Minor damage where no claim is paid,

- Non-sufficient funds (NSF) cheques,
- Another company refusing to insure the individual, and
- Lapse in coverage with some exceptions.

A company in Newfoundland and Labrador can no longer *refuse coverage* based on:
- Age, gender or marital status,
- Age of vehicle (may request an inspection after eight years),
- Not having other policies with the company, known as **tied selling**, and
- The individual currently being in the Facility Association.

Insurers of Last Resort

Most jurisdictions have **facilities associations,** which are the insurers of last resort. Since auto insurance is compulsory, they will provide insurance when no private insurer will. The insurer provides the insured with an **inter-province motor vehicle liability insurance certificate,** which is evidence of insurance and is honoured across Canada. By law, it must be carried at all times.

Direct Compensation or No-Fault Insurance

New Brunswick, Quebec, and Ontario have mandatory **direct compensation**, also referred to as **no-fault insurance**. It means each policyholder collects from his or her own insurance company regardless of who is at fault. The purpose of no-fault insurance is to speed up the collection process for the injured parties. The question of who is at fault is still very relevant — the party who is at fault will probably experience an increase in premiums. Quebec has a Fault Determination Chart while both New Brunswick and Ontario have Fault Determination Rules.

Saskatchewan has two plans — a no-fault plan that the policyholder can opt out of in favour of the tort system. It is direct compensation for mandatory coverage only because, as a government-run system for mandatory coverage, there is only one insurer.

Ontario Fault Determination Rules *(Ontario Insurance Act, R.R.O. 1990, Regulation 668)*

There are several rules some of which are:

3. The degree of fault of an insured is determined without references to,
   (a) the circumstances in which the incident occurs, including weather conditions, road conditions, visibility or the actions of pedestrians;
6. (1) this section applies when automobile "A" is struck from the rear by automobile "B", and both automobiles are travelling in the same direction and in the same lane.
   (2) If automobile "A" is stopped or is in forward motion, the driver of automobile "A" is not at fault and the driver of automobile "B" is 100 per cent at fault for the accident.
   (3) If automobile "A" is turning, either to the right or to the left, in order to enter a side road, private road or driveway, the driver of automobile "A" is not at fault and the driver of automobile "B" is 100 per cent at fault for the incident.
   (4) If automobile "A" is in forward motion and is entering a parking space on either the right or left side of the road, the driver of automobile "A" is not at fault and the driver of automobile "B" is 100 per cent at fault for the incident.

Pure no-fault insurance often comes at a price — the insured is compensated more quickly since it isn't necessary to go to court but he or she usually cannot sue.

Types of No-fault Plans

There is one pure no-fault plan and three modified no-fault plans; all four are in place in Canada.

Pure No-fault System

Lawsuits are not permitted. Quebec and Manitoba have pure no-fault systems. In Quebec, bodily injury is **government-run** while property damage coverage is provided by private insurers. Manitoba auto insurance is government-run for the mandatory coverage, and government and private insurers compete for the optional coverage.

Modified No-fault Plan

These plans permit lawsuits if a certain threshold (minimum) of damage or injury is met. There are two possible thresholds:

- A **monetary threshold** — if the claim is less than this amount, the injured person cannot sue.
- A **verbal threshold** for serious cases only — plaintiffs must prove that their injuries are serious and permanent.
  - In Ontario, lawsuits for pain and suffering are allowed only if the injured person dies or sustains permanent serious disfigurement and/or impaired physical, mental, or psychological functioning. The court assesses the damages and there is a $30,000 deductible or $15,000 if it is a *Family Law Act* claim.

Add-on Plan

The benefits are paid on a no-fault basis and the injured person also has the right to sue. This is the case in New Brunswick.

Choice No-fault Plan

Policyholders can choose between a cheaper no-fault insurance plan with no right to sue for personal injury or they can opt out and elect the **tort system** and retain the right to sue for compensation for injuries that are a result of negligence. This is the case in Saskatchewan, where the tort system provides *much* lower medical benefits but permits the injured party to sue the at-fault driver (who will be covered by his or her third-party liability insurance).

The Insurance Policy

Since automobile insurance coverage is mandatory in all provinces and territories, the policy itself is legislated. However, because requirements are different in each jurisdiction, the policies are also different although much of the same material is covered. We will use actual policy wordings primarily from S.P.F. No.1 used by several jurisdictions: British Columbia and Manitoba, who both have government-run auto insurance; and Ontario, which has no-fault insurance.

It is important to know what the coverage is in your own province and where to find it since insureds are often covered when they don't know they are and, conversely, are not covered when they think they are. We will use actual policy wordings from several policies to illustrate the coverages in order to encourage an in-depth reading of the policy for your own province.

Overview of All Policies

All provinces and territories have a standard auto policy for their jurisdictions. There are six standard policies called **Standard Policy Form (S.P.F.) No. X**:

- **S.P.F. No. 1 Automobile Policy** for owners of automobiles.
- **S.P.F. No. 2 Drivers Automobile Policy** provides additional liability coverage for people who drive vehicles they don't own and do not have their own insurance that could extend to another vehicle. This can include limousine drivers and taxi drivers. It is not required in Ontario and Quebec, where coverage is provided in their version of S.P.F. No. 1.
- **S.P.F. No. 4 Garage Policy** for owned, non-owned, and customer's automobiles.
- **S.P.F. No. 6 Non-owned Automobile** provides coverage for damage to a vehicle for drivers who do not own the auto but who have the auto in their care and have agreed to be responsible for any

damage for which they may be found legally liable. This would apply to a rented vehicle but not to a "temporary substitute vehicle", which is covered under S.P.F. No. 1 (and is defined below).
- **S.P.F. No. 7 Excess Automobile Liability** in connection with No. 1, 2, 4, and 6 for drivers of rented or leased vehicles.
- **S.P.F. No. 8 Lessors Contingent Automobile Policy** for businesses that lease vehicles long-term.

Most provinces and territories use S.P.F. No. 1 except those having government plans and Ontario and Quebec, which have developed their own policies.

Declarations: Introduction

The following excerpts of policies or government plans provide information on who is covered, what is the coverage, and how much the coverage is.

The Ontario policy begins by telling policyholders that the policy is a contract but that you have coverage only if it is shown on the Certificate of Automobile Insurance which details the coverage for each section of coverage as well as the cost for each coverage.

This Policy Is Part of a Contract   (*Ontario OAP Section 1.1*)

This policy is part of a contract between you and us. The contract includes three documents:
- A completed and signed Application for Automobile Insurance,
- A Certificate of Automobile Insurance, and
- This policy.

Under the contract, we agree to provide you with the insurance that is summarized on your Certificate of Automobile Insurance, and for which you have agreed to pay a premium.

> You only have a particular coverage for a specific automobile if your Certificate of Automobile Insurance shows a premium for it or shows the coverage is provided at no cost.

Where You Are Covered   (*B.C. Autoplan fine print*)

Basic Autoplan coverage applies only in Canada and the U.S.A. (including Hawaii and Alaska). Your coverage does not extend to Mexico or any other country. Some individual coverages have specific geographic restrictions; read the detailed descriptions in this brochure for more information.

> If you fail to meet your responsibilities, claims under this policy, with the exception of certain Accident Benefits, may be denied.

Your Responsibilities   (*Ontario OAP Section 1.4*)

By accepting this contract you agree to the following conditions.

1.4.1 You agree to notify us promptly in writing of any significant change of which you are aware in your status as a driver, owner or lessee of a described automobile. You also agree to let us know of any change that might increase the risk of an incident or affect our willingness to insure you at current rates.

You must promptly tell us of any change in information supplied in your original application for insurance, such as additional drivers, or a change in the way a described automobile is used.

This last clause can be particularly important if the driver modifies the car — by "upgrading" the engine, for instance. Failing to notify the insurance company of such a change can void the policy.

And you must notify the insurance company within *seven days* of any incidents that you report to the police or for which you are going to make a claim or, again, the policy can be voided at the insurer's option.

1.4.4 You agree to inform us in writing of any incident involving the automobile that must be reported to the police under the *Highway Traffic Act* or for which you intend to make a claim under this policy. You must notify us within seven days of the incident or, if unable, as soon as possible after that.

Warning — Offences *(Ontario OAP 1.5 Where to Make A Claim and Who May Make It)*

It is an offence under the **Insurance Act** to knowingly make a false or misleading statement or representation to an insurer in connection with the person's entitlement to a benefit under a contract of insurance, or to wilfully fail to inform the insurer of a material change in circumstances within 14 days, in connection with such entitlement. The offence is punishable on conviction by a maximum fine of $100,000 for the first offence and a maximum fine of $200,000 for any subsequent conviction.

It is an offence under the **federal** *Criminal Code* for anyone to knowingly make or use a false document with the intent it be acted on as genuine and the offence is punishable, on conviction, by a maximum of 10 years imprisonment.

It is an offence under the **federal** *Criminal Code* for anyone, by deceit, falsehood, or other dishonest act, to defraud or to attempt to defraud an insurance company. The offence is punishable, on conviction, by a maximum of 10 years imprisonment for cases involving an amount over $5,000 or otherwise a maximum of 2 years imprisonment.

Who Is Covered

The person who insured the auto is covered as well as anyone driving the car with the owner's permission with the following exceptions.

Excluded Drivers and Driving without Permission
(Ontario OAP Section 1.8.2)

Except for certain **Accident Benefits** coverage, there is no coverage (including coverage for occupants) under this policy if the automobile is used or operated by a person in possession of the automobile without the owner's consent or is driven by a person named as an *excluded driver* of the automobile.

Except for certain **Accident Benefits** coverage, there is no coverage under this policy for an *occupant* of an automobile used or operated by a person in possession of the automobile *without the owner's consent*.

The Ontario policy also specifies that coverage does not extend to the following:

• Vehicles rented or leased to someone else *(OAP 1.8.3)*,
• People who sell, repair, maintain, stores, services or parks autos *(OAP 1.8.4)*, and
• Losses that result from wars *(OAP 1.8.5)*.

When Not Covered

The following is a summary of exclusions, that is, circumstances under which the owner is not covered. Notice that it refers to the driver who can be the owner or someone else to whom the auto has been lent.

Table 3.8   Policy Exclusions / When Not Covered

	B.C.	S.P.F. No. 1	Manitoba	Ontario
• The driver was not qualified, not a licenced driver or the driver's licence had been suspended (not authorized by law to drive) or couldn't the driver couldn't drive because of a court order.	✓	✓	✓	✓
• The driver was impaired by alcohol, drugs, or other intoxicating substance at the time of the crash.	✓	✓	✓	✓
• The automobile was used in a race or speed test.		✓	✓	✓
• The automobile was used for illegal trade or transportation.		✓	✓	✓
• The driver was convicted of				
• causing bodily harm or death by criminal negligence.				
• dangerous operation of vehicle.		✓		✓
• failure to stop at the scene of an accident.		✓		✓
• impaired driving or having a blood alcohol level over .08% at the time of the accident or of refusing to take a breathalyser test.		✓	✓	✓
• An unregistered trailer was attached to the vehicle when the law requires the trailer to be registered.			✓	
• The accident occurred when fleeing from the police.	✓		✓	
• Vehicle use is different from the use declared on the application — it was improperly rated.	✓		✓	
• The claimant won't identify the driver at the time of the loss or damage.			✓	
• You were outside Canada and the U.S.	✓			
• The crash resulted from avoiding the police or using a vehicle for any illicit or illegal purpose.	✓			
• You present a fraudulent or exaggerated claim.	✓			
• The vehicle was deliberately used to cause loss or damage.	✓			
• Your claim results from acts of war, rebellion, insurrection, or a nuclear energy hazard.		✓		

Sources: Exclusions *(Manitoba Autopac, page 41)*
Fine Print *(B.C. Basic Autoplan, page 3)*
Your Responsibilities *(Ontario OAP 1.4 Your Responsibilities, 7.2.2 Illegal Use)*
Exclusions *(Alberta S.P.F. No. 1, General Provisions, Definitions and Exclusions, page 11)*

General Exclusion   *(Ontario OAP Section 1.8.1)*

Except for certain **Accident Benefits** coverage, there is no coverage under this policy if:
• The automobile is used to carry explosives or radioactive material; or
• The automobile is used as a taxicab, bus, a sightseeing conveyance or to carry paying passengers.
  However, we don't consider the following as situations involving carrying paying passengers:
  • Giving a ride to someone in return for a ride,
  • Sharing the cost of an occasional trip with others in the automobile,
  • Carrying a domestic worker hired by you or your spouse,
  • Occasionally carrying children to or from school activities that are conducted within the educational program,
  • Carrying current or prospective clients and customers, or
  • Reimbursing volunteer drivers for their reasonable driving expenses, including gas, vehicle wear and tear and meals.

Cancelling Your Insurance

You can cancel your insurance at any time and pay the minimum premium shown on the Certificate of Insurance. The insurance company can cancel the policy for non-payment of premiums.

- If you pay the premium and administration fee within a specified time limit, the policy will not be cancelled.
- Once cancelled, the insurance company does not have to accept the late payment and keep the policy in force.

When We Cancel   (*Ontario OAP Section 1.7.2*)

Where your policy has been in effect for more than 60 days, we may only cancel your policy for one of the following reasons:
- Non-payment of premium,
- You have given false particulars of the automobile,
- You have knowingly misrepresented or failed to disclose information that you were required to provide in the application for automobile insurance, or
- The risk has changed materially.

Which Automobiles Are Covered

Policies cover the "described automobile" (the one shown on the Certificate of Automobile Insurance). In most, but not all jurisdictions, coverage is expanded to include the "the automobile", "newly acquired automobiles", "temporary substitute vehicles", as well as "other automobiles" and "trailers".

The Automobile   (*Ontario OAP Definitions and OAP Section 2.2*)

- A described automobile,
- A newly acquired automobile:
  - Replacement auto,
  - Additional auto (covered with conditions)
- A temporary substitute automobile,
- Other automobiles driven by you, or driven by your spouse who lives with you, are covered for liability, accident, uninsured automobile and direct compensation. They are also covered for optional Loss or Damage with conditions (depending on the level of coverage), and
- Trailers, in certain circumstances.

Newly Acquired Automobiles   (*Ontario OAP Section 2.2.1*)

A newly acquired automobile is an automobile or trailer that you acquire as owner and that is not covered under any other policy. It can be either a replacement or an additional automobile. The replacement automobile will have the same coverage as the described automobile it replaces. We will cover an additional automobile as long as:
- We insure all automobiles you own, and
- Any claim you make for the additional automobile is made against a coverage we provide for **all** your other automobiles.

Your newly acquired automobile(s) will be insured as long as you inform us within 14 days from the time of delivery and pay any additional premium required.

We may inspect the newly acquired vehicle and its equipment at any reasonable time.

Special Condition: Coverage is not extended to a newly acquired automobile if you are in the business of selling automobiles.

Temporary Substitute Automobile   (*Ontario OAP Section 2.2.2*)

A temporary substitute automobile is an automobile that is temporarily used while a described automobile is out of service. The described automobile must not be in use by anyone insured by this policy, because of its breakdown, repair, servicing, theft, sale or destruction.

Special Condition: A temporary substitute automobile cannot be owned by you or by anyone living in the same dwelling as you.

In Ontario, rental of a temporary substitute vehicle is part of the mandatory coverage. However, this coverage is optional in Manitoba and B.C. and, even then, has restrictions.

Auto Loss of Use   (*Manitoba Autopac, Optional Coverage, Page 47*)

If you rely on your vehicle daily, extra *Auto Loss of Use* can make your life easier. It covers the cost of replacement transportation if your vehicle can't be driven because it was stolen or damaged accidentally regardless of fault.

Coverage applies to rentals from a company whose business is renting vehicles. It does not apply to rentals from friends, family or other private persons.

Loss of Use Coverage   (*B.C. Autoplan, Part III, RoadsidePlus Optional Coverage*)

If you make a claim under your Autoplan Collision, Comprehensive or Specified Perils insurance and cannot drive the RoadsidePlus insured vehicle, Loss of Use coverage reimburses you for the cost of renting a substitute vehicle, hiring taxis or using public transportation. This includes a replacement vehicle but will be limited to one that is of a make and model specified by ICBC and similar in size to what you own.

Please note: If you do not carry the corresponding Autoplan Collision, Comprehensive or Specified Perils coverage, the RoadsidePlus Loss of Use coverage will not apply. There would also be no coverage for loss of use if the damage to your vehicle is less than your deductible, or if you elect not to make a claim.

If you were not at fault for the motor vehicle crash, you may be entitled to a substitute vehicle as part of your claim against the at-fault motorist. However, it can take time for the issue of fault to be resolved. RoadsidePlus Loss of Use coverage allows you to get substitute transportation immediately. It also covers loss of use from claims where you are at fault, or for Comprehensive and Specified Perils claims which otherwise only include Loss of Use coverage when your vehicle has been stolen.

Other Automobiles   (*Ontario OAP Section 2.2.3*)

Automobiles, other than a described automobile, are also covered when driven by you, or driven by your spouse who lives with you.

Trailers   (*Ontario OAP Section 2.2.4*)

Any trailer used in connection with the automobile is insured for the following coverages:
• Liability,
• Accident Benefits, and
• Uninsured Automobile.

Special Conditions: Any trailer you own and that is not described in this policy is also covered for **Direct Compensation - Property Damage** Coverage under the following conditions:
• If it is attached to an automobile with a manufacturer's gross vehicle weight rating of not more than 4,500 kilograms, or if not attached, it is normally used with an automobile with a manufacturer's gross vehicle weight rating of not more than 4,500 kilograms.
• It is not designed or used for living in, to carry passengers, or for commercial purposes.

Rented or Leased Automobile   (*Ontario OAP Section 1.8.3*)

Except for certain **Accident Benefits** coverage, there is no coverage under this policy if the automobile is rented or leased to another. **However**, if an insured person is using the automobile for an employer's business and is paid for using it, we won't consider that renting or leasing.

Third-Party Liability

Third-party liability covers the insured when he or she is sued and found responsible for loss or damage to the property of others and/or bodily harm or death. Most policies include a provision that any loss or damage to property carried in or upon the auto or to property owned or rented by, or in the care, custody, or control of any person insured is not covered in *this* section (*S.P.F. No. 1, Section A*).

Basic Third-Party Liability Coverage   *(Manitoba Autopac, Page 60)*

Basic (that is, mandatory minimum) third-party liability coverage provides you with up to $200,000 of coverage for claims made against you from others:
• Whose property your vehicle or a vehicle you were driving with the owner's permission may have damaged, and
• Whose injuries your vehicle may have caused, in an accident outside Manitoba.

What We Cover   *(Ontario OAP Section 3.3)*

You or other insured persons may be legally responsible for the bodily injury to, or death of others, or for damage to the property of others as a result of owning, using or operating the automobile. In that case, we will make any payment on your or other insured persons' behalf that the law requires, up to the limits of the policy.

The policy includes a provision that states the insurance company is authorized to act on your behalf in a lawsuit and that they will provide a defence and pay all legal costs that are a result of this lawsuit. Furthermore, they can settle out of court if they so choose:

If Someone Sues You   *(Ontario OAP 3.3.1)*

If there is a judgment against you or other insured persons, we will pay any post-judgment interest owed on that part of the amount the court orders that falls within the liability limits of your policy.
We reserve the right to investigate, negotiate and settle any claim out of court if we choose.

> If you are sued for more than the limits of your policy, you may wish to hire, at your cost, your own lawyer to protect yourself against the additional risk.

All provinces and territories have a mandatory minimum amount of third-party liability coverage. Many people also carry excess liability insurance to provide coverage up to $1 million or even $2 million.

Table 3.9   Mandatory Minimum Required Coverage for Third-Party Liability

	Total ($)	Property Maximum ($)	(a)
AB	200,000	10,000	
BC	200,000	20,000	
MB	200,000	20,000	
NB	200,000	20,000	
NL	200,000	20,000	
NT	200,000	10,000	
NS	500,000		(b)
NU	200,000	10,000	
ON	200,000	10,000	
PE	200,000	10,000	
QC	50,000	50,000	(c)
SK	200,000	10,000	
YT	200,000	10,000	

(a) If the liability for *both* property and body damage reaches the total minimum required amount, the maximum payment for property damage is capped as shown. If the liability is for either bodily injury or property damage, the coverage is for the maximum liability amounts.
(b) In Nova Scotia the mandatory liability limit in total for both property and bodily injury is $500,000.
(c) The province of Quebec has a pure no-fault system. Government insurance covers injuries to people and private insurers cover property damage. In Quebec, the victim of an at-fault accident is not allowed to sue for pain and suffering, medical expenses, and economic losses.
Quebec requires that you carry a minimum of $50,000 in property damage insurance. This insurance is not provided by the government insurance company but must be obtained through a private insurance company.

How Much We Will Pay   *(Ontario OAP Section 3.3.2)*

The most we will pay on your behalf and on behalf of all other insured persons insured by this Section, for any one incident (over and above legal costs and post-judgment interest) will be determined by the extent of your coverage.

> **OAP Example**
>
> You are sued for injuries suffered by another person in an accident that you are legally responsible for. We will hire lawyers at our expense and cover all costs of your defence in court.
>
> The court orders you to pay $10,000 in costs and $600,000 to cover losses. Your liability limit is $500,000.
>
> We will cover the $10,000 in costs, and $500,000 of the judgment. We will also pay any interest owed on that amount from the day of the judgment. You will be responsible for the remaining $100,000 of the judgment and any interest owed on that.

Outside the Province or Your Residence   *(Ontario OAP Section 3.3.3)*

If the incident happens in a jurisdiction covered by this policy in which the minimum liability coverage required is higher than the limit shown on the Certificate of Automobile Insurance, we will honour the higher amount. We also agree not to use any legal defence that would not be available if the policy had been issued in that jurisdiction.

> **OAP Example**
>
> You have an accident in a province where the minimum liability coverage required is $500,000. Even though you are only carrying $200,000 worth of liability insurance, we will pay up to $500,000.

Right of Subrogation

As stated earlier, the doctrine of subrogation applies and is explicitly stated in the policies.

Agreements of Insured   *(Alberta S.P.F. No. 1, Section A — Third Party Liability)*

Where indemnity is provided by this section, every person insured by this Policy: (b) shall *reimburse the Insurer, upon demand*, in the amount which the Insurer has paid by reason of the provisions of any statute relating to automobile insurance and which the insurer would not otherwise be liable to pay under this Policy.

Your and Other Insured Persons' Responsibilities   *(Ontario OAP Section 3.4)*

We may, on occasion, be required by law to make payments, even though we are not otherwise liable for them under this policy. If so, you or other insured persons will have to *reimburse us upon demand* for those payments.

Limitations On Your Third-Party Liability Coverage

Damage to property not covered in this section includes property

- carried in or on the auto;
- in the insured's care, custody, or control whether owned or rented;
- damage resulting from contamination; and
- damage resulting from nuclear hazards.

Accident Benefits Coverage

Basic accident benefits coverage is mandatory in all jurisdictions except Newfoundland and Labrador. **Excess coverage** provides additional dollar maximums and indexation.

Who Is Covered?

Basic mandatory coverage applies to any person who is injured or killed and is not covered by his or her own auto insurance policy or any other auto insurance policy. This includes the named insured, the driver, passengers and pedestrians. In some jurisdictions, there is an exclusion

• if the accident was a result of suicide or a suicide attempt, or
• if the injured or deceased person, is covered by Workers Compensation payments.

Although there can be some limits to the coverage, insurers *must* pay accident benefits for *everyone* involved in the accident even if the property damage is voided as outlined in Table 3.8. In this sense, Accident Benefits is no-fault coverage — even if the insurance would otherwise be avoided, the insurer must pay accident benefits and can then demand to be reimbursed by the insured (absolute liability). In addition, there are times when the coverage can be limited.

Limitations on Your Coverage *(Ontario OAP 1 Section 4.4)*

You or other insured persons are not entitled to the Income Replacement Benefit, Non-Earner Benefit or Compensation for Other Expenses if you or they:
• Knew, or should reasonably have known, that they were operating an automobile without insurance;
• Were driving an automobile while not authorized by law to drive;
• Were driving an automobile which they were specifically excluded from driving under this policy;
• Knowingly operated, or should reasonably have known that the automobile was operated, without the owner's consent;
• Made or knew about a material misrepresentation that induced us to issue this policy;
• Intentionally failed to notify us of any significant changes as required under Section 1.4.1; or
• Were convicted of a criminal offence involving the operation of an automobile.

Mandatory Accident Benefits

Several benefits are paid under accident benefits and they vary greatly by jurisdiction, as shown in Table 3.10. Accident benefits can include the following:

• **Income replacement** compensates for lost income due to injuries from an accident.
• **Non-earner benefit** is paid if the injured person is not entitled to Income Replacement or Caregiver Benefits.
• **Caregiver benefit** provides compensation if the injured person cannot continue to be the main caregiver for a member of the household who requires care.
• **Medical benefit** pays for all reasonable and necessary medical expenses, such as occupational therapy, physiotherapy, medication, wheelchairs, prostheses, and transportation to and from treatment.
• **Rehabilitation benefit** pays for measures to help the person go back to work, including employment counseling, life skills training, and vocational or academic training.
• **Case manager services** for those who sustained a catastrophic injury.
• **Attendant care benefit** pays for an aide, an attendant, or a long-term care facility.
• Other expenses:
  • **Lost educational expenses** if the injured person was enrolled in school and cannot continue the program.
  • **Housekeeping and home maintenance** if the injured person is no longer able to perform these services.
  • Damages to clothing, glasses, hearing aids, etc., as a result of the accident.

Table 3.10   Minimum Mandatory Accident Benefits

	Income Replacement	Non-Earner	Caregiver	Medical, Rehabilitation
AB	• 80% of average **before-tax** wages up to $400/week for 104 weeks.		• Included in medical.	• $50,000 per person.
BC	• If temporary: 75% of **before tax** weekly pay up to a maximum of $300/week. If complete and permanent disability: payments for life.	• $145 for homemaker to hire someone to do their tasks as long as they are disabled.	• Included in medical.	• $150,000 per person.
MB	• **90% of after-tax** weekly pay while unable to work to a maximum before-tax income of $69,000. Adjusted annually for inflation. Begins 180 days after injury.	• If can prove you would have held employment during the first 180 days, you'll be entitled to income replacement based on that job. Same coverage as if you had a job.	• No limit.	• No limit.
NB	• $250/week for up to 104 weeks.	• $100 a week for 52 weeks for adults.	• N/A	• $50,000 including rehabilitation for up to four years.
NL	• N/A — not mandatory.	• N/A	• N/A	• N/A
NS	• If temporary: $140/week up to 104 weeks.	• If permanent: for life.	• $70/week for 12 weeks maximum if unable to preform normal tasks.	• Included in medical.
NT, NU	• 80% of gross wages to a maximum of $140/week. If temporary up to 104 weeks. If permanent for lifetime.	• Housekeeper: $100/week for up to 12 weeks.		• $25,000 a person.
ON	• 80% of **after-tax** wages up to $400/week for 104 weeks.	• $185/week for 104 weeks. Then $320 a week if a student or graduated in the previous year and not yet working in field related to education.	• Up to $72,000. If classified as catastrophic — $1 million.	• $100,000. If classified as catastrophic — up to $1 million.
PE	• $140/week up to 104 weeks if you are temporarily disabled. And for a lifetime if you are permanently disabled.	• $70 a week for a maximum of 12 weeks if your injury prevents you from performing normal tasks.	• Included in medical.	• $25,000 per person.
QC	• 90% of net income up to $60,500 gross annual income.	• $4,487/elementary school year lost, $8,231/secondary and post-secondary school year lost. Post secondary the maximum $16,231/year. Nothing, non-earners who are not students.	• Up to $749/week if requires continuous care.	• Provides a list of coverages.

Table 3.10 Continued

	Income Replacement	Non-Earner	Caregiver	Medical, Rehabilitation
SK	• **No-fault (is default and most common).** Up to 90% of after-tax wages up to gross income of $63,043. Indexed annually. If disabled: $192,594 for catastrophic injury $157,687 for non-catastrophic injury.	• After 180 days, non-earners receive minimum wage and students receive $17,112 for each year of school missed.	• $37,648/year.	• $5,502,680
SK	• **Tort system** Income replacement ($16,796 per year up to $8,398 for partial disability from employment lasting up to 104 weeks). If you are disabled you can receive a maximum of $139,853 for a catastrophic injury and $10,758 for a non-catastrophic injury.			• Medical: $21,506. $161,369 for catastrophic injury.
YT	• 80% of gross wages to a maximum of $300/week for 104 weeks for both temporary and permanent disability.	• Housekeeper: $100/week for up to 26 weeks.		• $10,000 a person.

In addition, accident benefits covers the following:

• A **death benefit** for anyone killed. This benefit often depends on the number of dependants and the status of the person in the family (father earning income or child not earning income, for instance) or the income of the deceased before the accident. It can also be a flat rate.
• **Funeral expenses,** ranging from low of $1,000 in Nova Scotia, Northwest Territories, Nunavut, and PEI to $8,254 in Saskatchewan.

Uninsured and Unidentified Motorist/Driver/Automobile Coverage

Uninsured automobile coverage is mandatory and provides coverage in most jurisdictions for

• costs related to injury or death resulting from an accident with an uninsured or unidentified (hit-and-run) driver, and
• damage to your vehicle only for identified, uninsured drivers, sometimes with a maximum. Damages over any maximum would be covered under property damage coverage.

An **uninsured** driver or owner does not have third-party liability insurance to cover court-awarded damages (damages that the plaintiff has a "legal right to recover") for bodily injury or property damage when the uninsured is at fault. An **unidentified** driver or owner cannot be determined. (*Alberta, S.P.F. No. 1, Section 3 (2) and (3), B.C. Autoplan, Part I — 4, Ontario OAP 5.1.2 and 5.1.3*).

• In B.C., this coverage is also available to all B.C. residents, even if they do not own and insure a vehicle (*B.C. Autoplan, Page 8*).
• Manitoba's Basic Autopac includes all-perils coverage for damage to the vehicle and permanently attached equipment to a maximum of $50,000 (*Manitoba Autopac, Page 37*). All-perils coverage is the most narrowly defined coverage for loss or damage to the insured's automobile. As a result of the all-perils coverage, Autopac does not specifically mention an accident with an uninsured automobile.

Some provinces have **Motor Vehicle Accident Claim Funds (MVAC)** (also known as **Unsatisfied Judgment Fund**) which provide statutory accident benefits, as well as compensation for personal injury or property damage for victims of motor vehicle accidents with an uninsured or unidentified (hit-and-run) driver or a stolen vehicle if the victim does not have auto insurance coverage. Where legally possible, they also recover funds from uninsured owners and drivers paid out on their behalf.

Table 3.11 Summary of Unidentified and Uninsured Automobile Coverage

Jurisdiction	Uninsured and Identified			Unidentified — Hit and Run			MVAC/ Unsatisfied Judgment Fund
	Bodily Injury	Death	Property Damage	Bodily Injury	Death	Property Damage	
AB	Yes	Yes	No	Yes	Yes	No	Yes
BC	Yes	Yes	No	Yes	Yes	No	Yes
MB	Yes	Yes	No	Yes	Yes	No	Yes. Covered by PIPP*
NB	Yes	Yes	Yes	Yes	Yes	Yes	Yes
NL			Yes	Yes	Yes	No	Yes
NT			Yes	Yes	Yes	No	No
NS	Yes	Yes	Yes	Yes	Yes	Yes	Yes
NU			Yes	Yes	Yes	No	No
ON	Yes	Yes	Yes up to $25,000	Yes	Yes	No	Yes
PE	Yes	Yes	Yes	Yes	Yes	Yes	Yes
QC	Yes	Yes	Yes up to $50,000	Yes	Yes	Yes up to $50,000	Yes**
SK			Yes			Yes	Yes
YT	Not mandatory			Not mandatory			No

* PIPP, Personal Injury Protection Plan, is part of Autopac and compensates people from Manitoba for injuries or death caused by an automobile no matter who is at fault. It covers accidents in Canada and the U.S.

** In Quebec, the Unsatisfied Judgment Recovery Fund has been replaced by the "Régie de l'assurance automobile du Québec".

Claims for Bodily Injury or Death

Who Is Covered? *(Ontario OAP, Section 5.3.1)*

The following are insured persons for bodily injury or death:
* Any person who is an occupant of the automobile
* You, your spouse, and any dependent relative of you or your spouse,
  * when an occupant of an uninsured automobile, or
  * when not in an automobile, streetcar or railway vehicle if hit by an unidentified or uninsured automobile.

In Ontario,

* the insurance company must receive notice of a claim for an uninsured automobile within 30 days of the accident, and
* an accident involving an unidentified automobile must be reported to the police with 24 hours.

In addition, coverage does not apply to a dependent relative who owns an insured automobile or is an occupant of his/her own uninsured automobile. The insurer can request medical or psychological examinations at reasonable intervals at the insurer's expense.

Claims for Property Damage

Who Is Covered (Ontario OAP Section 5.4.1)

In a claim for damage to the automobile, the owner of the automobile is covered for damage.
   In a claim for damage to the contents of the automobile, the owner of the contents is covered for damage.

Several conditions apply to this (and other) coverage:
- The insured must notify the insurer of the accident within seven days for property damage, or 30 days for bodily injury or death with details of the accident.
- The insured must try to protect the auto from further damage.
- No repairs can be made without the insurer's written consent or inspection.
- The insured must allow the insurer to copy all reports that pertain to the accident.
- The insured must permit an inspection.
- The insured must complete a statutory declaration within 90 days that describes what happened with details of the loss and who was affected.
- The insurer will not be left to dispose of the auto unless they agree to do so.

How Much We Will Pay (Ontario OAP Section 5.4.4)

We will pay the lower of the following:
- The cost to repair the loss or damage, less the deductible; or
- The actual cash value of the automobile at the time it was damaged, less the deductible.

OAP Example

Your car is four years old and is hit on the front left side by an identified but uninsured automobile. The damaged part of the body of your car is repaired. We will pay the cost of the repairs, less the $300 deductible, including new paint for the damaged part of your automobile. If you want the entire car repainted, you will have to pay the cost of painting the rest of the car.

Claims for Both Bodily Injury and Property Damage

In most jurisdictions, if property damage is covered the coverage is divided between property damage and bodily injury in the same way that third-party liability is allocated.

   In Alberta, where this coverage applies only to bodily injury or death, for claims for property damage the injured party has to apply to MVAC to recover amounts awarded but that the plaintiff cannot collect. For bodily injury, the Alberta policy is second payor to any payment from an unsatisfied judgment fund in Canada and the United States.

Ontario (OAP, Section 5.5)

An accident may result in a valid claim for both bodily injury or death and for damage to the automobile or its contents. In that case, payments for bodily injury and death have priority on 95% of the total amount payable. Payment for damage to the automobile or contents will have priority on 5%.

OAP Example

An accident in Ontario for which an identified but uninsured driver is responsible destroys your $20,000 car, and results in injuries to you and your spouse, totaling $350,000.
   We will not pay more than the minimum liability limit of $200,000. Of that money, 95%, or $190,000, will go toward payment for bodily injury. The remaining 5%, or $10,000, will apply to the loss of your car.

Maximum Amount of Coverage

In most jurisdictions, the maximum amount of coverage is the amount of compulsory third-party liability coverage in the province or territory where the accident happened.

Payments Limits *(Ontario OAP Section 5.7.1)*

We will not pay more than the minimum limits for automobile liability insurance in the jurisdiction in which the accident happens. This amount applies regardless of the number of persons injured or killed, or the damage to the automobile and contents. In no event will we pay more than the minimum liability limits required in Ontario.

> **OAP Example**
> You are travelling in a car outside Ontario when you are injured in an accident for which an uninsured driver is responsible. The minimum liability limit in that jurisdiction is $100,000. Your injuries are serious and are assessed at $300,000 or more. We will pay no more than $100,000.

Alberta *(S.P.F. No. 1, Section B, Subsection 3)*

(1) The insurers shall not be liable under this subsection,
   (c) for any amount in excess of the minimum limit(s) for automobile bodily injury liability insurance applicable in the jurisdiction in which the accident occurs regardless of the number of persons so injured or killed ...

Manitoba

In Manitoba, the owner pays the deductible and the car is covered up to $50,000 by basic all-perils coverage *(Autopac, Page 39)*... If the driver can identify the person who did the hit Autopac will try to get the deductible back for you *(Autopac, Page 43)*.

B.C. Autoplan covers the victim where there is no MVAC or Unsatisfied Judgment Fund.

B.C. *(Autoplan, Part I — Basic Autoplan Insurance, 4. Protection Against Hit-and-Run and Uninsured Motorist)*

Some Canadian provinces have special funds, Motor Vehicle Accident Claim Funds (MVAC) or Unsatisfied Judgment Funds, set up to pay for uninsured or unidentified motorist bodily injury claims. Some funds cover injury only while others may also pay for property damage subject to a deductible.

However, since the Yukon, Northwest and Nunavut territories, and most U.S.A. states, do not have such funds, Basic Autoplan also covers you if you are injured or killed in a crash on a highway in any of these jurisdictions if the crash is caused by a hit-and-run driver or one who is uninsured. The coverage is limited to the equivalent of whatever compulsory Third Party Liability limit applies in the jurisdiction where the crash occurred, or $200,000, whichever is less. This coverage does not include damage to your vehicle.

Property damage not covered by this coverage is covered under property damage coverage, which is optional in most jurisdictions but is included in basic coverage in some jurisdictions (Table 3.11).

B.C. Underinsured Motorist Protection

B.C. is unique in providing specific protection against *underinsured* at-fault drivers and owners. In all jurisdictions, the maximum payment for uninsured and unidentified owners and drivers is the third-party liability limit in the jurisdiction where the accident happened regardless of how much third-party liability insurance the victim has. However, B.C. provides up to $1 million of coverage if the accident happened in B.C. and the at-fault driver is insured but does not have enough third-party liability insurance to pay the entire award.

B.C. *(Autoplan, Part I — Basic Autoplan Insurance, 3. Underinsured Motorist Protection)*

In B.C., Basic Autoplan also provides *Underinsured* Motorist Protection that pays to a maximum of $1 million per person. It provides coverage when the at-fault, other driver does not have enough third party liability insurance to cover the court-awarded damages.

It covers Autoplan holders and members of their household as long as the Autoplan holder has a valid B.C. driver's licence. Furthermore, people who don't have a license, own a vehicle or live in a household with a person that has Autoplan can still buy this coverage. It covers these people when they are:

• Injured or killed while driving or while a passenger in the insured or someone else's vehicle, or
• Injured or killed while a pedestrian or cyclist.

It does not pay if the vehicle is unlicensed, being driven without the owner's permission and in a few other circumstances.

Direct Compensation — Property Damage Coverage

Direct compensation covers the owner for loss or damage to the automobile and its contents to the degree to which the driver was not at fault in an accident involving at least one other automobile. The owner collects from his or her own insurance company. New Brunswick, Ontario, and Quebec have direct compensation, but Ontario is the only province that spells out the requirements in its policy.

Ontario *(Ontario OAP Section 6).*

Introduction *(OAP 6.1)*

This Section of your policy covers damage to the automobile and certain trailers not shown on the Certificate of Automobile Insurance, their equipment, contents, and loss of use of the automobile or contents caused by another person's use or operation of an automobile in Ontario.

The coverage under this Section applies only if the accident takes place in Ontario and at least one other automobile involved is insured under a motor vehicle liability policy. The policy covering the other automobile must be issued by an insurance company licensed in Ontario, or one that has filed with the Financial Services Commission of Ontario to provide this coverage.

It is called direct compensation because you will collect from us, your insurance company, even though you, or anyone else using or operating the automobile with your consent, were not entirely at fault for the accident.

What We Will Cover *(OAP 6.2)*

We will pay the cost of damage to the automobile, its equipment, contents and for loss of use of the automobile or contents arising from an accident for which another person would have been legally responsible in the absence of section 263 of the *Insurance Act* (Ontario). Section 263 takes away your right to sue the other person for these losses. We will pay no more to repair or replace the automobile or property than its actual cash value at the time it was damaged, less the applicable percentage of the deductible shown on your Certificate of Automobile Insurance.

If a part needed to repair the automobile is no longer available, we will pay an amount equal to the manufacturer's latest list price for the part.

Note: You should be aware that this coverage does not apply if the automobile is described in another motor vehicle liability policy.

OAP Example

You are driving a friend's car. That car is described in your friend's motor vehicle liability policy. You have an accident for which you are not at fault.

Your friend will claim under the direct compensation property damage provisions of his or her motor vehicle liability policy for the loss.

We will not pay for damage to, or loss of use of, contents that are being carried for reward.

Who Is Covered *(OAP 6.3)*

In a claim for damage to the automobile, the owner of the automobile is covered for damage.

In a claim for damage to the contents of the automobile, the owner of the contents is covered for damage.

How Much We Will Pay *(OAP 6.4)*

Determining Fault *(OAP 6.4.1)*

The amount we pay under this Section of your policy will be determined by the degree to which you or the driver were not at fault in the accident.

Responsibility for an accident is determined by the *Insurance Act* (Ontario) and the *Fault Determination Rules*. These may find you or the driver wholly or partially responsible.

The degree of responsibility is expressed as a percentage.

The Deductible *(OAP 6.4.2)*

The deductible applies.

EXAMPLE 4 Your car has an actual cash value of $20,000 and the deductible is $500 for direct compensation. You are in an accident with another vehicle and your car is a write-off. You have only mandatory coverage.

Your degree of fault:	100% Not At Fault	25% At Fault	90% At Fault
Insurer pays under direct compensation	19,500	14,625 *(20,000 – 500) x 75%*	1,950
You pay:			
• The deductible on the direct compensation portion	500	375 *(500 x 75%)*	50
• The rest of the direct compensation deductible	0	125 *(500 x 25%)*	450
	500	500	500
• With no optional vehicle coverage, the at-fault portion	0	4,875 *(20,000 – 500) x 25%*	17,550
You pay in total	500	5,375	18,050

The same applies to the autos contents including rented equipment.

EXAMPLE 5 Your car has an actual cash value of $20,000 and the deductible is $500 for direct compensation. In addition, you have full optional coverage on the car and its contents with a $300 deductible.

Your degree of fault:	100% Not At Fault	25% At Fault	90% At Fault
Under direct compensation, insurer pays	19,500	14,625 *(20,000 – 500) x 75%*	1,950
Optional vehicle coverage pays	0	4,925 *(20,000 – 300) x 25%*	17,730
Insurer pays in total	19,500	19,550	19,680
You pay the direct compensation deductible	500	375 *(500 x 75%)*	50
You pay the optional loss or damage deductible	0	75 *(300 x 25%)*	270
You pay in total	500	450	320

B.C. — Inverse Liability *(B.C. Part — Basic Autoplan Insurance, 5. Inverse Liability Coverage)*

The portion paid in Ontario by direct compensation is paid in B.C. by inverse liability coverage.

Under inverse liability, B.C. Autoplan covers that portion of a loss that is not your fault but that you cannot sue, presumably because the state or province has no fault where you cannot sue. So if you are 25% at fault and have an accident in Ontario where you cannot sue, the B.C. Basic Autoplan policy will compensate you for the 75% that you cannot collect. The 25% that is your fault can be collected if you have optional collision coverage.

Manitoba

Manitoba's basic Autopac includes all-perils coverage, which is optional in Ontario and will be described in the next section. While all-perils coverage contains the usual limitations, it pays for loss or damage to the auto and permanently attached equipment without regard to fault. In addition, all-perils covers one-car accidents whereas direct compensation in Ontario and inverse liability in Manitoba cover property loss or damage that involves at least one other vehicle. Being at fault in Manitoba affects the amount of the deductible. Saskatchewan also has All-perils coverage but with a $700 deductible.

Optional Property Loss or Damage Coverage

In most provinces and territories, coverage for damage to your own vehicle is optional:

- In Ontario and B.C., this section covers damage to your vehicle to the degree to which you are at fault in an accident.
- B.C. Autoplan does not cover contents.
- Saskatchewan's basic plan include all-perils (collision and comprehensive) and does not mention fault. The deductible is $700 and optional insurance provides a lower deductible.
- Manitoba's mandatory all-perils coverage does not include contents or a temporary substitute vehicle, which are provided by optional coverages.

Most policies state that you have this coverage only if the Certificate of Automobile Insurance shows a premium.

Introduction *(OAP 7.1)*

Coverage for Loss of or Damage to Your Automobile *(OAP 7.1.1)*

We agree to pay for direct and accidental loss of, or damage to, a described automobile and its equipment caused by a peril such as fire, theft, or collision if the automobile is insured against these perils.

By direct loss or damage we mean loss or damage resulting directly from a peril for which coverage has been purchased.

This Section applies only to the extent that a claim for damage to an automobile and its equipment would not be covered by Section 6, Direct Compensation — Property Damage Coverage of a motor vehicle liability policy.

We may inspect the described vehicle and its equipment at any reasonable time. If you do not co-operate with any reasonable arrangements for inspection, your coverages under this Section may be cancelled and any claims under this Section may be denied.

> Your Loss or Damage Coverages may apply to types of automobiles other than described automobiles. See Section 2 for details and additional conditions.

Coverage Options

The following coverages are described in the following:

- S.P.F. No.1 Section C — Loss of or Damage to Insured Automobile for several provinces and territories
- Ontario OAP Section 7.1.2
- B.C. Autoplan Part II Optional Auto Plan Insurance

Specified Perils

This coverage covers for losses caused by the following:

- Earthquake
- Explosion
- Falling or forced landing of aircraft or parts of aircraft

- Fire
- Hail
- Lightening
- Riot or civil disturbance
- Rising water
- The stranding, sinking, burning, derailment, or collision of any kind of transport in or upon which a described automobile is being carried on land or water
- Theft or attempted theft, windstorm

Comprehensive

This coverage pays for losses other than those covered by collision or upset, including the following:

- Perils listed under Specified Perils
- Falling or flying objects
- Missiles
- Vandalism

Collision or Upset

This coverage pays when a described automobile is involved in a collision with another object or tips over. *Object* includes the following:

- Another automobile that is attached to the automobile
- Any object in or on the ground
- The surface of the ground

All Perils

This coverage combines the coverages of Collision or Upset and Comprehensive, including, in Ontario,

- loss or damage caused if a person living in the insured's household steals a described automobile, and
- if an employee who drives or uses, services, or repairs a described automobile, steals it.

Loss or Damage Not Covered *(S.P.F. No. 1 Section C Exclusions, Manitoba Autoplan, Part II, Ontario OAP Section 7.2.1)*

Generally, the following losses are not covered unless the loss is a result of a covered peril
- Change in ownership that is agreed to even if trickery or fraud was involved,
- Engine failure,
- Mechanical breakdown,
- Radioactive contamination,
- The car was repossessed,
- The contents of automobiles and trailers, other than their equipment,
- The result of illegal disposal, and
- Tires.

Loss or damage caused by illegal use (Table 3.8) is not covered by Optional Coverages.

Certain Thefts Not Covered *(S.P.F. No. 1 Section C Exclusions (2), Ontario OAP 7.2.3)*
We won't pay under either the Comprehensive or Specified Perils coverages for loss or damage caused when a person who lives in your household steals the automobile.

We also won't pay under these coverages for loss or damage caused when an employee of yours steals the automobile and the employee's duties include driving, maintaining or repairing the automobile. This applies at any time, and not simply during working hours.

> **OAP Example**
> We will not pay for a tire blow-out in normal driving, but if the tire is destroyed in a collision and you have Collision or Upset Coverage, we will cover that loss up to the value of your tire at the time of the incident.

> **OAP Example**
> Late one evening at a party, you sell your car to a stranger in return for a cheque. A week later the cheque bounces. We will not cover the loss.

Subrogation

Subrogation was described in "Legal Principles" on page 74. This is how it appears in a policy:

Foregoing Our Right to Recover   *(Ontario OAP 7.4.2)*

If someone else is using a described automobile with your permission when an insured loss occurs, we will pay for the resulting claim. We will also forego our right to recover the money from that person.

However, we will keep the right to recover payment:
- If the person has the automobile in connection with the business of selling, repairing, maintaining, storing, servicing or parking automobiles; or
- If the person using the automobile violates any condition of this policy, or operates it in circumstances referred to in 7.2.2 (Illegal Use).

> **OAP Examples**
> 1. You allow a friend to use your car and she runs into a fire hydrant and damages the car. We will pay for repairs and will not sue her to recover the money.
> 2. You hand over your car to a parking attendant or garage employee. He scratches the side while parking it. We will pay for repairs and recover from the garage owners because they had your automobile in connection with their business.
> 3. You allow a friend to use your car. Later, without your knowledge, he drives it while impaired by alcohol and hits a tree. We will pay for the repairs to the car, but we will recover from your friend. Driving while impaired is illegal and a violation of the terms of this policy.

Disputing the Settlement   *(S.P.F. No. 1 Statutory Conditions (8) In Case of Disagreement, Ontario OAP 7.8 Settling a Claim)*

If you disagree with us over the value of the vehicle or equipment or the nature amount or costs of any repairs, the issue can be submitted for an appraisal under the *Insurance Act,* if you and we agree on this process. You and we will each appoint an appraiser, who will either agree on the award or, if they disagree, will appoint an umpire to decide as between their respective positions.

Statutory Conditions

The *Insurance Act* for each jurisdiction mandates certain coverages. These coverages or statutory conditions are the foundation for the policies and, in some jurisdictions, are included at the end of the policy.

Summary

An automobile policy is a contract between the insured and the insurer. As a contract, it spells out the responsibilities and rights of each party. Some coverage is mandatory while other coverage is optional. For example, in most jurisdictions a driver is not required to have coverage for damage or loss to his or her own vehicle but is required to have this coverage for losses to third parties. Four provinces have direct compensation (no-fault) insurance, and four provinces have government-run coverage for the mandatory part of auto insurance coverage. Three of these provinces do not permit lawsuits.

An auto policy is a contract and, as such, it spells out the rules and requirements. Without a thorough reading of the policy and *all* its sections, the insured cannot know whether or not something is covered and why it is or is not covered.

Many factors affect the amount of the premium, the most predictable being the driving record of the insured. However, many other factors come into play, some of them surprising — where you live, the make and model of your car and, while the price of the car obviously matters, even more important is how at-risk it is to incur a loss.

Sources

Alberta, S.P.F. No. 1 [www.finance/alberta.ca]
British Columbia, Insurance Corporation of British Columbia (ICBC), Autoplan [www.icbc.com/insurance]
Manitoba Public Insurance (MPI), Policy Guide [www.mpi.mb.ca]
New Brunswick, S.P.F. No. 1 [www.gnb.ca]
Newfoundland and Labrador, S.P.F. No. 1 [http://assembly.nl.ca]
Northwest Territories, S.P.F. No. 1 [www.justice.gov.nt.ca]
Nova Scotia, S.P.F. No. 1 [www.gov.ns.ca/finance]
Nunavut, S.P.F. No. 1 [www.gov.nu.ca]
Ontario, Ontario Auto Policy [www.fsco.gov.on.ca/insurance/auto/OAP.asp]
Prince Edward Island, S.P.F. No. 1 [www.gov.pe.ca]
Quebec, The Société de l'assurance automobile du Québec (SAAQ) [www.saaq.gouv.ca]
Saskatchewan Government Insurance (SGI) [www.sgi.sk.ca]
Yukon, S.P.F. No. 1 [www.gov.yk.ca]

Application Case

By now Francesca knows to have the espresso machine warmed up — Joanne is keen enough to understand insurance but is easily overwhelmed by the details. Joanne arrives, gets her espresso and says, "OK. I'm ready. Take me through auto insurance. I don't want all the details — just tell me what the policies are about." Francesca replies, "Insurance policies are contracts and all the details make it clear exactly what is covered and, in what circumstances, something might not be covered. Let's go through the major parts of policies, looking at a few details as we go".

Legal Aspects

A. "But before we do that," says Francesca, "Do you have any questions about the **legal aspects** of auto insurance"?

1. Joanne asks, "What laws are applicable to auto insurance?" Francesca replies, "Three levels of government have laws and by-laws about operating an auto" (Table 3.1).
2. "What's this about government-run insurance and private insurers? It all seems so confusing. Can you give me the **big picture** about the differences in the provinces and territories?" So Francesca shows her the summary (Table 3.2).
3. Joanne then asks, "I know people who seem to pay a lot less than I do. I trust my broker and assume she is providing me with both the cheapest and best coverage I need.

What's going on?" Francesca replies, "Some coverage is required (mandatory or compulsory) and some is optional (Page 71).

    (a) **Required coverage** (Table 3.3):
- Third party liability
- Accident benefits (except in Newfoundland and Labrador)
- Uninsured auto coverage
- Direct compensation (no-fault) in those provinces that have no-fault insurance

    (b) **Optional or excess** (more than the required) coverage (Table 3.4):
- Loss or damage to your own vehicle
- Additional liability
- Additional accident benefits.

You'll see that a number of provinces and territories use S.P.F. No. 1 (Standard Policy Form No. 1). I want to point out that all these S.P.F. No. 1 policies do not provide identical coverage. The coverages that are the same use the exact same wording but there are differences. For instance, the Newfoundland policy contains Accident Benefits in Section B but it merely refers to the Newfoundland Health Plan which is why Accident Benefits are not mandatory in Newfoundland and Labrador for auto insurance. This is different from all the other Section Bs for S.P.F. No. 1."

    "Yikes! This looks really confusing. How am I supposed to remember all this?"

    "Don't worry," Francesca replies, "It's not so bad. You'll see. Details vary in some provinces but the concepts are pretty consistent. Where do you want to start?"

4. "I've heard that, if you are convicted of impaired driving, your insurance is voided. What else should I know about the legal aspects of insurance?"

    Francesca replies, "Three **legal principles**, two of which we have already discussed in earlier chapters, are particularly applicable to auto insurance" (Page 74):

    (a) Absolute liability
    (b) Negligence
    (c) Subrogation

"Let's look at some examples so you can understand how these concepts apply to auto insurance". (Examples 1, 2, and 3).

5. "What else do I need to know on a general level?" asks Joanne. Francesca replies, "We have to always remember that an auto insurance policy is a **contract** and that it stipulates the rights and obligations of both parties to the contract — the insured and the insurer. We'll look at this in more detail in a minute" (Page 75).

Determining the Premium

B. Joanne asks about the **factors that affect the amount of the premium**. Francesca responds that these are some of factors in most provinces and territories:

    1. Probability of a loss based on assumptions about certain classes of drivers (Page 75):
        (a) Age, gender and marital status
        (b) Driving record
        (c) Driver training
        (d) Number of years licensed
        (e) Number of claims is even more important than the size of the claims
        (f) Number of at-fault accidents
        (g) Make and model of car — Canadian Loss Experience Automobile Rating (CLEAR) rates cars that are less safe, more prone to damage and more likely to be stolen,

            "There is some speculation that government-run plans are cheaper than plans where private insurers provide the coverage. The Insurance Bureau of Canada disputes this claim but let's look at some data provided by both IBC and the Consumers' Association of Canada (Table 3.5).

        (h) Location — urban or rural — and, moreover, it can vary block by block in the city

    (i)   Vehicle use and how much you drive

    (j)   Number of other operators

2. Particular risk meaning insurers may have very high rates for certain classes of drivers because they don't want to insure them (Table 3.6).

3. Size of the deductible.

4. Coverage — the amount of excess and optional coverage.

5. Taxes on the premiums. Insurance companies pay insurance premium taxes that they do not necessarily charge consumers directly. Let's look at some premiums, casualty rates and taxes. I don't know about you, but I can't see any particular pattern" (Table 3.7).

6. Francesca continues, "It varies a lot by jurisdiction but there are a number of things that the insurance companies **cannot use** to determine premiums although Saskatchewan has decided to throw out the driver's age, gender or where they live."

    (a)   "In Ontario, insurers cannot use the following" (Page 79):

        i.   credit history

        ii.   bankruptcy

        iii.   employment status

        iv.   whether the insured owns a credit card

        v.   how long the insured has lived in his or her current home

        vi.   not-at-fault-accidents

        vii.   whether the insured's vehicle is owned or leased

        viii.   whether there was a period of time when the insured had no automobile coverage

    (b)   "What do they usually **include** to determine the premium?"

        i.   Number of at-fault accidents,

        ii.   Number of moving violations,

        iii.   Number of times coverage was cancelled for failing to pay premiums, and

        iv.   Providing incorrect or incomplete information in the past.

    (c)   "Insurance companies cannot use rules that discriminate but they can charge higher premiums. However, they **cannot deny coverage** based on the following:"

        i.   Whether you are newly licensed or a driver new to Canada

        ii.   Age, sex, and marital status

        iii.   Religion, race, nationality or ethnicity

        iv.   Where you live or the location of the vehicle

Again, Nova Scotia and Newfoundland and Labrador have thrown some of the traditional rules out the window. In addition, there are **Facilities Associations** who are insurers of last resort — for those people whose driving record is so bad they can't get insurance anywhere else" (Page 81).

C. "What is **no-fault insurance**? My friend, Dan, caused an accident and his rates went up a lot. Doesn't no-fault mean it doesn't matter whose fault it is?

1. "No-fault insurance is a bit of a misnomer. It is actually called **Direct Compensation** and means you collect from your own insurer. Fault matters — your premiums will likely go up if you cause an accident. There are several types of no-fault and there is at least one example of each type operating in Canada" (Pages 81–82):

    (a)   **Pure no-fault** systems do not allow lawsuits (Quebec and Manitoba).

    (b)   **Modified no-fault** plans permit lawsuits for serious injuries so there is a threshold (Ontario).

    (c)   **Add-on** plans pay on a no-fault basis and also permit law suits (New Brunswick).

    (d)   **Choice no-fault** gives policyholders the right to direct compensation without the right to sue or they can opt out of the no-fault system, elect the tort system, and sue (Saskatchewan).

2. "Many people find their rates went up after a not-at-fault accident. This reflects a general rate increase and those who have had no accidents will experience the same increase."

The Insurance Policy

D. "Now that we have looked at some of the issues, let's look at some specifics in various policies. You never know, your son might decide to move to another province and he should likely know what some fundamental differences are. As I said earlier, this will be just an overview highlighting a few things that might surprise you."

  1. "All vehicle policies are based on a standard format called a Standard Policy Form (S.P.F.) although five provinces have written their own rules to the extent that they don't even refer to the S.P.F. format. We saw this in Tables 3.3 and 3.4. We are going to concern ourselves only with one form, S.P.F. No. 1, which covers auto policies for the owner of the vehicle. There are other forms for garage-owners and people who lease cars long-term (Page 82). The Ontario policy has a lot of examples and high-lighted warnings that no other policy has, so let's look at some of them as they come up."

  2. "The policy is a contract so it starts with the Declarations, an Introduction that spells out the basic rules like where coverage is in place (Canada and the United States), and the rules you must follow to keep your coverage. These rules include the following":

  (a) **Who** is covered and who is not covered by the policy.

  (b) What situations might **invalidate the policy** such as using the care in a speed race or to transport something illegally. Read this carefully. It's important. You'll notice that a lot of the situations are the same but some jurisdictions have special prohibitions (Table 3.8).

  3. "It spells out how your insurance can be cancelled. Notice in particular that the insurance company can cancel if the risk changes materially. Have three, minor, at-fault accidents in a short while and you could find yourself without insurance" (Pages 86–86).

  4. "Notice also the broad definition of automobile such as, 'Temporary Substitute Vehicle' which covers you if you are driving a rental because your car is in for repairs. Notice also, this definition does **not** include when you are on vacation" (Page 86).

E. "Let's move on to third-party liability, which covers you when you cause physical damage to the property of others or cause them bodily injury or death. Most jurisdictions have a minimum required third-party liability coverage of $200,000 but for most of us, much more is needed. It wouldn't be all that difficult to fall asleep and, assuming you survive, cause an accident for which the courts award the third party a settlement of several hundred thousand or even a million dollars" (Table 3.9).

  1. "Notice also that, if you have only the minimum required coverage (which is the coverage for *this* section), the insurance company will pay only the minimum required coverage in the jurisdiction **where the accident happened**" (Page 89).

  2. "Notice also that, if you have done something that invalidates the policy, the insurance company will pay any amount the courts award the third party up to the limits of your coverage but, and this is a big but, has the right to come back to you to collect the money it paid out. This is **subrogation** in action" (Page 89).

F. "**Accident Benefits Coverage** spells out the medical and income replacement benefits available to people insured by this policy."

  1. "Notice that *everyone* injured by the vehicle covered by this policy has a right to *basic* accident benefits. This is no-fault accident benefits in every province and territory. And, believe it or not, it includes someone who steals your car" (Page 90).

  2. "Also, *some benefits* are disallowed if the person in question knew the auto was not insured, had lost his/her licence, was an excluded driver, was driving without the owner's consent, etc" (Page 90).

  3. "There is a list of **mandatory accident benefits**. I cannot recommend strongly enough that you should buy optional excess insurance. As you see in Table 3.10, the minimum benefits can be quite meager. I know no one wants to tempt fate by having extra coverage but, should the second worst happen — the worst being death — you don't want to

find yourself disabled for life without any money. We'll talk about disability insurance in a later meeting, but don't stint on coverage here either. It can pay rehabilitation expense, can help you with you education if you need to be retrained, can provide housekeeping help if you need it, caregivers if you need them, etc. I'm prepared to go as far as to say that if you can't properly insure your car, you shouldn't have one." (Table 3.10)

4. "Minimum accident benefits also include a **death benefit** for anyone who is killed as well as some amount for **funeral expenses**."

G. "**Uninsured automobile coverage** outlines the coverage you and others covered by this policy have for damage to your property and for bodily injury or death if it was caused by an **uninsured** or **unidentified (hit and run)** driver even if you are not in your car."

1. "Several jurisdictions, shown in Table 3.11, have a **Motor Vehicle Accident Claim Fund (MVAC)**, also known as an **Unsatisfied Judgment Fund**, that pays if there is no insurance to cover the loss. In Alberta, for instance, insurance covers only bodily injury or death and MVAC pays for property damage. I remember a newspaper story many years ago about two little old Italian widows, crossing St. Clair Ave on their way home from church one Sunday morning. They were hit by a hit-and-run driver. One was killed and the other was severely injured. Neither one drove so neither was covered by an insurance policy. This is where MVAC would step in to compensate."

2. "There is a maximum amount the insurer will pay without a lawsuit" (Page 94).

3. "In addition, in many jurisdictions the maximum is divided between property damage and bodily injury or death according to a formula."

4. "The maximum under this section is the third-party liability limits in the jurisdiction where the accident happened."

5. "It is worth noting that B.C. has a specific section to cover **underinsured drivers**. What if the courts award you a million dollars and the driver is unemployed with no assets was driving an old heap, insured but only for the mandatory minimum of $200,000? B.C. deals with this in its basic Autoplan policy" (Page 95).

H. "**Direct Compensation — Property Damage Coverage** outlines what you can collect for damage to your property, including your car, if you are either entirely not at fault or partially not at fault for a loss caused by an accident with at least one other vehicle. This is the "no-fault" section for provinces having direct compensation — you are compensated by your insurer even though you are not at fault" (Page 96).

1. "Notice that the Ontario policy OAP 6.2 states that you cannot sue for these damages."

2. "You cannot collect *under this section* for that portion of the loss that was your fault. Let's look at a couple of examples so you can see how it works."

3. "B.C. has the same coverage but it is called **Inverse Liability** there. And Manitoba and Saskatchewan don't need it because their basic policies are All-perils policies which we'll talk about in a minute."

I. "**Loss or Damage Coverages (Optional)** outlines coverage for loss or damage to your property. This applies in no-fault jurisdictions, both when you were at fault and when another driver was not involved in jurisdictions."

1. "There are four levels of coverage":
   (a) **Specified-perils** pays if the loss is caused by a list of specific perils.
   (b) **Comprehensive** pays for the specified perils list of perils as well as when your car is hit by a flying object or is vandalized.
   (c) **Collision or Upset** pays if you run into something or drive off the road ("tips over").
   (d) **All Perils** coverage pays for almost everything. All of the other three, including, you'll notice, if your spouse, child or chauffeur steals it. O.K. it's a little more specific than that but that is the idea.

2. "Some things are not covered, such as car repairs, if the car is repossessed or driven off a cliff on purpose to collect the insurance. And the list that negates the policy shown in Table 3.8 applies here, too" (Page 99).
3. "And there is, in the Ontario policy, a short list of further exclusions for Comprehensive and specified perils coverage, namely
   (a) if your spouse or child who lives with you steals it, or
   (b) an employee who drives, uses, services or repairs your car."
4. And the circumstances that maintain the right to subrogation are given, namely
   (a) if your car is being serviced or parked, or
   (b) if it is used for an illegal purpose" (Page 100).

Concept Questions

1. Which jurisdiction does "failure to stop at the scene of an accident" fall under? Will a conviction affect your premiums?

2. In most jurisdictions, is it mandatory to have coverage for loss of or damage to
   (a) your own vehicle?
   (b) the property of other people?

3. Which is the only province having direct compensation that does not allow any lawsuits for bodily injury?

4. Which provinces do not use S.P.F. No. 1?

5. Which four provinces have mandatory coverage for your own automobile to some extent?

6. In provinces and territories using S.P.F. No. 1, in which section is "optional coverage for your own vehicle" covered?

7. If a person is driving while his or her licence is suspended and hits a pedestrian, according to absolute liability which of the following is true about collecting from the insurer?
   (a) No one will collect.
   (b) Both will collect.
   (c) Only the pedestrian will collect.
   (d) Only the driver will collect.

8. If you are negligent and cause an accident by, for instance, talking on your cell phone, will your car still be covered for property damage? Why or why not? What assumption must you make about cell phone use while driving?

9. If you live in a province that has no-fault insurance and you cause an accident, does your insurance company have the right of subrogation?

10. Everything else being equal and making no judgments about apparent fairness, which of the following in each pair is likely to have the lower insurance premium?
    (a) A man age 25 or a man age 55?
    (b) A woman who has made three small claims in the past year or a woman who has made one large claim?
    (c) A driver in Ottawa or a driver in Nanaimo, B.C.?
    (d) A man with a $300 deductible or a man with a $1,000 deductible?
    (e) A driver with an eight-year-old car insured with or without damage to the car itself?

11. If Joe is unemployed in Ontario, can this be used to charge him a higher auto insurance premium?

12. In Saskatchewan, are premiums for young men calculated the same way as in Ontario? What's the difference?

13. Is it legal to deny coverage to an experienced driver based on race?

14. Insurance coverage is mandatory. If no private insurer will insure you due to your driving record, how can you get insurance?

15. Jenny was driving home on a dark and stormy night. Her wipers were on top speed and she was not tailgating. Suddenly the person in front of her slammed on his breaks and she ran into him. According to Ontario's Fault Determination Rules, who is the at-fault driver, Jenny or the driver of the car in front of her?

16. Which provinces have a(n):
    (a) pure no-fault system?
    (b) modified no-fault plan?
    (c) add-on plan?
    (d) choice no-fault plan?

Concept and Application Questions
The Insurance Policy
Introduction

17. If you own a garage and you repair cars, under which S.P.F. form will you be insured?

For all of the following questions, except where indicated, state *exactly* which section it states that the loss is or is not covered.

18. Are you covered if you drive your car in
    (a) a province other than the one you live in?
    (b) New York City?
    (c) Mexico City?

19. Vic, a resident of Windsor, Ontario, is in Detroit to attend the Detroit auto show. Once he crosses the border into the United States, Vic gets into a minor accident with an American motorist. Is he covered?

20. George specifically listed his son, Randy, as an excluded driver because Randy has such a terrible driving record. Even though Randy is excluded, he takes the car with George's permission and gets into an accident and is badly injured. The car is a write-off. Will the policy pay anything? If yes, which benefits will it pay? Why or why not?

21. Your cousin, Jane, has had her licence suspended and you allow her to borrow your car. Is the coverage in place? Why or why not?

22. You race your car late at night on fairly deserted suburban streets. Is it covered?

23. On his way back from Detroit, Vic decides to smuggle some illegal drugs back into Canada for sale. Once he has crossed the border into Canada, his brakes fail and he smashes into a parked police cruiser. The police recover the illegal drugs from Vic's badly damaged car. Is Vic's car covered?

24. Bill recently lost his job, and is unable to pay the monthly payments on his minivan. He decides a good way to cover his monthly payments would be to use his van as a taxicab on weekends. While out one weekend driving his customers to their destinations, he is involved in an accident with another cab driver. Is he covered in Ontario?

25. You are single and own one car, which is insured. Under which definition of *automobile* are the following insured?
    (a) Your own car.
    (b) You trade in your car and buy a new car.
    (c) Your car is in for repairs for a week so you rent another car.
    (d) You borrow your friend's van for a quick run to Canadian Tire.

26. Paul is the proud owner of a brand new Dodge Charger. Paul purchases only the insurance coverage required by law. For each of the following situations, use the sections provided to explain if Paul is covered by *his* auto policy.
    (a) After driving his new Charger around for a couple of months he gets bored with it, decides to trade it in, and purchases an H3 Hummer. After receiving his new H3 Paul realizes that he must notify his insurance company of the change of vehicle. On his way home from the dealership he swerves to avoid a dog and crashes his brand-new Hummer into oncoming traffic.
    (b) While Paul's Hummer is in the shop, he asks if he can borrow his friend Nathan's car. While stuck in traffic, Paul falls asleep at the wheel and smashes into the stopped car in front of him causing $7,000 damage to Nathan's car and $11,000 to the other driver's car.
    (c) Paul's' wife hates using public transit and refuses to take the bus. She decides to borrow her sister's minivan. While she is driving to the mall, she is distracted by a ringing cell phone and takes her eyes off the road. She jumps the curve and smashes into a brick wall.
    (d) Paul decides it's time to move from Toronto to Burlington as he feels Toronto traffic is too congested. He has had his Hummer repaired and has attached a small trailer he owns to haul his couch to his new home. On the highway to Burlington, Paul's Hummer goes over a large pothole and the trailer detaches and slams into the car behind it. The driver is badly injured and decides to take legal action.

27. Nav, a Toronto resident, attends school in New York City. While he is at school he decides he can make some extra money by renting out his Nissan Pathfinder to his friend Shawn. Shawn has no insurance of his own and is involved in an accident while driving the rented Pathfinder. Is the car covered?

Ontario OAP Only

28. Your auto policy covers June 1 to May 31. The last time you paid, it was $2,400. If you cancel the policy as of December 1, which of the following is the amount of refund can you expect?
    (a) $1,200
    (b) Less than $1,200
    (c) More than $1,200
    (d) $0

29. Sharleen owns two automobiles and has insured them under two separate policies. Policy A has a liability limit of $400,000 and Policy B has a liability limit of $300,000. While out visiting her boyfriend in Mississauga she is driving his uninsured car. She ends up getting into an accident.
    (a) Calculate the maximum amounts that both policies will pay out to cover her liabilities. (A: 228,560, B: 171,440)
    (b) What is the total maximum amount of liability coverage that she will be able to receive. ($400,000)

Third-Party Liability

30. Jacob decides that he will use his pickup truck to help his friend Janine move to her new apartment. Janine prefers using professional movers, but Jacob convinces her that he can do the same job for free. While transporting Janine's big-screen television to her new apartment, the flat-bed's door opens, and the television falls out and lands on the road. The television is smashed to pieces. Upon closer inspection of the flat-bed's door it becomes clear to both Jacob and Janine that Jacob failed to properly lock the door. Janine is enraged and sues Jacob, and wins a judgment against Jacob for $2,500. Will Jacob's auto insurance cover his liability losses?

31. On his way home from work one stormy night, Bob's car skids and slams into an old lady walking with her grandson. The old lady and her grandson are hurt critically. The families sue Bob for $300,000, and the courts order him to pay out this amount. In addition, the court orders Bob to pay an additional $15,000 in court costs. Bob's maximum liability coverage is $300,000. How much will Bob's insurance pay on his behalf? ($315,000)

Accident Benefits Coverage

32. Tatiana has never driven an automobile in her life, as she has always been chauffeured everywhere by friends and family. One night, after leaving a popular Toronto club, she gets into a car with a friend who agrees to drive her home. On the way home a drunk driver hits them and Tatiana is critically injured. Tatiana recovers from her injuries but the doctors say that she will be paralysed all her life and will not be able to take on any sort of occupation.
    (a) Will her friend's auto insurance pay Tatiana accident benefits even though she is not specifically named an insured on his policy? (Yes)
    (b) If her friend does not have insurance, will the drunk driver's insurer cover it? (Yes)

33. For each of the following independent situations, indicate if the individual is entitled to receive any compensation and, if yes, which type of compensation the insured is qualified to receive.
    (a) Richard works nights at an automotive supplies warehouse. He is paid on an hourly basis. He recently missed a couple months due to injuries he suffered in an accident he had in his automobile.
    (b) Carmine has lost his ability to take care of his disabled son for at least three months until his injuries from his auto accident heal. As a result, he has hired a live-in caregiver who charges $400 a week.
    (c) Jason was taking his sick dog, Fluffy, to the veterinarian. On his way there he was hit by a driver who ran a red light. Jason was okay, but poor Fluffy was killed. Jason has been emotionally distraught ever since the accident and has trouble eating and sleeping.
    (d) Rick was severely injured in an auto accident and is unable to walk or live alone. His insurance is paying for his rehabilitation but, since he cannot live alone, he has had to move in with his father. Is his father entitled to any benefits?

Ontario OAP Only

34. Sharon ran a red light and hit another car. The occupants of the other car had only minor injuries but Sharon's injuries require several months of therapy. Because she ran the light, she has been convicted of careless driving. Is she entitled to receive the Income Replacement Benefit? Why or why not?

Uninsured Automobile Coverage

35. Your Aunt Hilda has never owned or driven a car. She is injured by a hit-and-run driver and requires several months of rehabilitation not covered by the provincial insurance plan. Where can she find compensation?

36. For each of the following independent situations, indicate whether the individual is insured for his or her losses.
    (a) Jason has auto insurance, but today he decides to walk to his girlfriend's house and is hit by a car at a pedestrian crosswalk. The car fails to remain at the scene of the accident and none of the witnesses are able to make out the licence plate. Unfortunately for Jason, the provincial health insurance in his province has been privatized and he is unable to receive free medical care from a hospital. Jason needs to have his broken hip replaced and cannot afford the surgery.
    (b) Gilberto works as a delivery driver for Chang delivery services. He makes a fairly good salary, and owns a vintage Chevrolet Corvette, which he has recently insured. While out driving to deliver a parcel he is hit by a large truck and knocked into a ditch. The driver of the truck fails to remain at the scene and Gilberto is seriously hurt. Will the *company's* auto insurance cover Gilberto's injuries?
    (c) Mike is involved in an accident in which the other driver has no insurance. Mike is okay, but his brand new stereo system has been destroyed and his car has $18,000 of damage. Would Mike be covered if the driver flees the scene?
    (d) Mark was the victim of a hit-and-run. His motorcycle has been damaged but he feels it can still be driven. Mark has made an uninsured driver claim with his insurance company but decides not to tow the bike to his mechanic. Instead, he decides to ride it there. On his way to the mechanic, the bike's front tire detaches, causing Mark to crash and cause further damage to the bike. Assume his motorcycle coverage is the same as the OAP. Is all the damage covered?

37. Kathleen and her husband are out driving their brand new BMW when a tailgating SUV driver hits them from behind. The SUV driver does not have insurance. The accident causes significant damage to Kathleen's BMW and results in serious whiplash for both Kathleen and her husband. The damage to the car results in $20,000 worth of damage, and both their medical and therapy bills results in $250,000 of charges. Assume whiplash injuries are no longer covered under a provincial health insurance plan. How much will the insurance company pay out for bodily injuries and for damage to their car if the accident happened in PEI?

38. Mohamed, a resident of Ontario, is, while driving to Atlanta to visit his sister, hit by an identified driver who lacks insurance. Mohamed has the minimum required insurance of $200,000. His bodily injuries amount to $400,000. However, the jurisdiction in which the accident occurs has a minimum liability limit of $100,000. How much will his insurance company pay him for his injuries?

Direct Compensation — Property Damage Coverage
Ontario OAP for All Questions

39. Petra is putting herself through school by working nights as a waitress. Her old car is worth about $5,000. Because she is so short of money, she has only the mandatory insurance. One day, after work, she is driving home on icy roads. The car skids and incurs $2,000 of damage when it hits a bridge. How much can she collect from her insurance company under Direct Compensation?

40. Ted, a resident of Brampton, Ontario, is involved in a minor accident in a parking lot. The car behind him accidentally backs into him and smashes his brake lights and back bumper. Will he collect from the culprit's insurance company?

41. Janet occasionally borrows her mom's car to go out on Saturday evenings. One night Janet gets very drunk and asks her sober friend, Mary, to drive her home. Mary is involved in a minor accident in which the back end of the car is damaged. Is Janet's mother covered for the damages that have occurred to the vehicle?

42. In each of the following situations, indicate how much Satnam will receive from his insurance company if he has no optional coverage.
    (a) Satnam is involved in an accident and the police determine that he is totally innocent. His car has been completely destroyed, but luckily he survives without injury. At the time of the accident, his car has a cash value of $20,000 and his deductible is $300. How much will he receive for his destroyed car? ($19,700)
    (b) Satnam is involved in an accident that completely destroys his car. It is determined he is 25% responsible. The cash value of his car at the time of the accident is $20,000 and his deductible is $400. How much will Satnam receive from his insurance company? ($14,700)
    (c) For the Super Bowl, Satnam rented a flat screen television worth $4,000. Transporting it home, he is involved in an accident for which he is deemed 25% responsible. His deductible is $300. ($2,775)
    (d) Satnam is in an accident in which he sustains $150 damage to his car and $200 damage to the contents of his car. His deductible is $300. ($50)

Optional Property Loss or Damage Coverages

43. Oscar is on his way to visit family in Woodstock, Ontario, when a tire blows out because he didn't notice the tire's low pressure.
    (a) Will his optional loss or damage coverage cover the cost of replacing the tire?
    (b) What if the tire was ruined due to an accident and he had Comprehensive coverage?

44. Sandra loves taking long road trips with her seven-year-old son. To help her stay awake and to pass the time, she listens to her vast CD collection that she stores in her car. On her last road trip her little son damaged her CDs. The damaged CDs were valued at $750 dollars. If she has a $300 deductible, how much will Sandra receive for these CDs? ($0)

45. Mindy attends school in downtown Toronto. The cost of parking is very expensive, especially for a student on a tight budget. Mindy usually parks her car at a lot near her school that charges eight dollars a day. The particular parking lot that Mindy chooses requires that all patrons leave their keys at the lot, so that their car can be moved around to allow other cars to leave and enter the lot. One day Mindy goes to pick up her car and notices her side door is severely dented. Mindy owns optional collision coverage along with her automobile insurance. Will her insurance company compensate Mindy, or is she stuck looking to recover damages from the company that owns the parking lot?

Ontario OAP

46. Raymond's car has a cash value of $15,000, his direct compensation deductible is $300, and his optional collision coverage deductible is $400. Raymond is involved in an accident that destroys his car. He is 25% responsible. Raymond has the optional collision coverage along with the standard mandatory auto insurance required in Ontario. How much in total will Raymond receive from the insurance company under both Section 6, Direct Compensation, and Section 7, Loss or Damage Coverage? ($14,675)

Homeowners Insurance

Learning Objectives

After completing this chapter, students will be able to:

A. Outline the major issues in homeowners insurance.

B. Identify the major parts of a homeowners policy.

C. Describe coverages and exclusions.

D. Use the policy to know whether or not certain types of losses are covered.

E. Select appropriate coverage for different situations.

Introduction

For many of us, our home is the single largest investment we will make with the possible exception of retirement savings. For each dollar of property damage coverage, the cost of insuring a home is much less than the cost of insuring an automobile because, as we saw in Chapter 1, the probability of a major loss is far less for a home than for an auto. Unlike auto insurance, there is no standard homeowners policy — they vary from insurer to insurer. The sample policy used in this chapter is an example of wording you *may* find in a policy.

There are three levels of coverage for home insurance:

• **Basic coverage** is a **named perils** policy — only those perils listed, such as fire, falling objects, and vandalism are covered. This is the cheapest and the most risky of the three. A Basic Policy is also called a Standard Policy.

• **Broad coverage** provides all-risks coverage on the buildings and named perils coverage on the contents.

• **Comprehensive coverage** covers the buildings and contents for **all-risks** that are not specifically excluded. It is the most expensive of the three and provides the most complete coverage.

The Policy as a Contract

A homeowners policy is a contract and establishes the terms of the contract including

• that it is an agreement between legally competent parties;
• the consideration, that is, the amount of the premium;
• the intent to do something that is legal;
• the details of exactly what losses are covered and for how much they are covered; and
• the period of time covered by the contract.

The policy must contain certain statutory conditions which, in our sample policy, are included in Section III. Losses covered are either

• **Direct losses** — damage to or destruction of the building and personal property, or loss of property if theft is also covered; or

• **Indirect losses** — for example, loss of rental income from a tenant or the need to rent other living accommodations while the home is being repaired.

The policy covers the **four principles of insurance** covered earlier:

1. **Indemnity** — the insured is returned to the same financial position as before the loss, without making a profit. This financial position is defined using one of the following:
   (a) **Actual cash value** of the market value. It provides compensation to replace what was there in the actual condition it was in at the time of the loss. It is *replacement cost less any depreciation* arising from its age, use, fair market value, and/or obsolescence. This can also be called its **replacement value,**
   (b) **Replacement cost**, which is the cost to replace what was there without deducting depreciation, that is, to replace it in new condition, and
   (c) **Guaranteed replacement cost**, which is the same as replacement cost but payment is not limited to the amount of the insurance coverage.
2. **Insurable interest** — only the homeowner(s) can insure the property.
3. **Subrogation** — the insurer will pay the insured the amount of the loss and is entitled to recover from a negligent third party who is not the insured, that is, the insurer pays the injured party and then has the right to recover this amount from the person who caused the loss.
4. **Reasonable expectations** — the insured is covered for anything that he or she can reasonably expect to be covered for and any exclusions must be specified.

The contract also specifies anything excluded from the coverage, what property of other people is covered, what the insured is required to do in the event of a loss, as well any **coinsurance** requirements.

Coinsurance

Coinsurance for a *homeowners policy* is the requirement that the property be insured for a minimum amount if the insured is to collect the full amount of a loss. The insurer's goal is to make sure that a home is not deliberately underinsured. Since a complete loss is unlikely to happen, the insured might be tempted to deliberately underinsure in order to reduce the premiums. The insured value is the cost to clean up the site and rebuild the house, not its market value and not including the value of the land.

Often the coinsurance requirement is that the home be insured for at least 80% of the replacement cost and, if the coinsurance requirement is met, the insurer will pay the full amount of the loss even if it is more than the amount of the coverage (which amounts to Guaranteed Replacement Cost). The coinsurance requirement varies from 80% to as high as 100%.

If the coinsurance requirement is not met, the insurer will pay either the actual cash value or a percentage of the replacement cost as shown in the examples on the following pages.

Cost to Repair or Rebuild

Typically, homeowners policies specify two types of coverage although a few other types can also occur. The type of coverage is important because it spells out how much the insurer is obligated to pay should the homeowner incur a loss. Some by-laws prohibit the owner from re-building the structure if the damage is more than 75% of the assessed value. In this case, the homeowner must tear down the structure and build a new one. Homeowner policies pay the cost to repair or rebuild and generally do not pay more than the actual cash value if you do not repair or rebuild.

Guaranteed Replacement Cost

This pays the full cost to repair or replace the home and contents with similar quality materials even if it is more than the **policy limit** (the amount of insurance required) *as long as the home was "properly insured" meaning 100% insured* at the last assessment. This is shown in the sample policy which follows, (see "Basis of Claims Settlement, Guaranteed Replacement Cost on Dwelling Buildings" on page 16). Even this coverage does not pay for upgrades such as better quality windows. If the home was not properly insured at the time of a loss, that is, it was insured for less than 100%, the homeowner usually receives the lesser of the amount of the loss and the **limits of insurance** (the amount of the coverage) to a maximum of the **actual cash value** (the replacement cost less any depreciation and obsolescence).

Replacement coverage pays the replacement cost without depreciation but only up to the limits of the policy while **extended replacement coverage** pays the cost to rebuild up to a stated percentage over the insured amount.

Actual Cash Value

This valuation pays the cost to put the home back to the condition it was in at the time of the loss — the replacement cost minus depreciation or wear and tear. The result is that a homeowner can replace 30-year-old windows only with similar 30-year-old windows. Of course, the homeowner buys new windows but the amount the insurer pays is less than the cost of the new windows since the old windows had been subjected to wear and tear for 30 years. The same goes for the roof, insulation, floors, walls, kitchen cupboards, and bathroom fixtures. The same distinction applies to the contents — actual cash value pays only the fair market value, which means the insured gets only enough to replace an old couch with another old couch.

Coinsurance Calculation

If the homeowner has guaranteed replacement cost coverage but the coinsurance requirement is not met, the most frequently used formula for the amount collected using a 80% coinsurance requirement is

$$\left(\frac{\text{Amount of Insurance}}{80\% \times \text{Replacement Value}}\right) \times \text{Amount of Loss}$$

Example 1 uses an 80% coinsurance requirement with the result that the insurer will pay out the full amount of a partial loss if the coverage is at least 80% while **Example 2** uses a 100% coinsurance requirement.

EXAMPLE 1   Susan's home had a fair market value of $650,000 at the time she had a major fire. The replacement cost of her home was $300,000 and it cost $100,000 to repair her house. (In this example, we will ignore the contents.)

The home was fully covered when she bought it but she did not increase the coverage over the years to reflect increases in construction costs. Moreover, her insurer did not automatically increase her coverage every year to reflect this increase in costs. The following table shows how much she would receive from her insurer for various levels of coverage.

	Replacement value of house at the time of the loss		$300,000
	Coinsurance requirement		**80%**
	Minimum amount of insurance required		$240,000 ($300,000 x 80%)
	Amount of loss		$100,000

	Amount of insurance	Amount recovered*	Calculation
1.	$300,000	$100,000	$\left(\frac{300,000}{300,000}\right)$ = 100% = more than required
2.	$270,000	$100,000	$\left(\frac{270,000}{300,000}\right)$ = 90% = more than required
3.	$240,000	$100,000	$\left(\frac{240,000}{300,000}\right)$ = 80% = minimum required
4.	$200,000	$83,333	$\left(\frac{200,000}{300,000}\right)$ = 66.67% = less than required
			$83,333 = \left(\frac{200,000}{0.8 \times 300,000}\right) \times \$100,000$

* Amount recovered is *before* the deductible.

With an 80% coinsurance requirement, without guaranteed replacement cost and with $300,000 of coverage, her insurer would pay her a maximum of $300,000 should her house be completely destroyed and the cost to rebuild is more than $300,0000.

EXAMPLE 2 Susan has a different insurer who pro-rates the payout if her coverage is less than 100%.

Replacement value of house at the time of the loss		$300,000
Coinsurance requirement		**100%**
Minimum amount of insurance required		**$300,000**
Amount of loss		$100,000

	Amount of insurance	Amount recovered*	Calculation	
1.	$300,000	$100,000	$\left(\dfrac{300,000}{300,000}\right)$	= 100% = more than required
2.	$270,000	$90,000	$\left(\dfrac{270,000}{300,000}\right)$	= 90% = more than required
3.	$240,000	$80,000	$\left(\dfrac{240,000}{300,000}\right)$	= 80% = minimum required
4.	$200,000	$66,667	$\left(\dfrac{200,000}{300,000}\right)$	= 66.67% = less than required

* Amount recovered is *before* the deductible.

If Susan's house is completely destroyed and she is fully insured, that is, she is 100% insured and has guaranteed replacement cost insurance, the insurer will pay the entire cost to rebuild it even if it costs more than $300,000.

Conclusion

Read your policy very carefully. Houses are infrequently completely destroyed but it does happen. In an earlier chapter, we discussed risk classification. One of the conclusions was *don't risk more than you can afford to lose*. It may be tempting to not insure for the full value but is it really worth the risk given the cost savings? In Example 2, if the premium is $900 for $300,000 of insurance and, hence, $600 for $200,000 of insurance, one should ask whether it worth a savings of $300 a year to risk $33,333 ($100,000 – 66,667) for a loss that isn't even a total loss? If the loss were a complete loss, the insurer would pay $200,000 ($300,000 × 66.67%) and the insured would have to pay the other $100,000 in order to save $300 a year.

In addition, most insurance companies will not allow you to deliberately underinsure. When you first sign up with an insurance company, it will do drive-by inspections at a minimum and sometimes the insurer sends an inspector to do a full inspection. Insurers are not required by law to provide you with insurance, and most would pass up the opportunity to do business with you if you attempted to underinsure your house by a significant amount.

Insurers also do not want houses overinsured — this would provide an incentive for arson (morale hazard) and would also violate the principle of indemnity. Most insurance companies automatically increase the coverage annually to reflect increases in construction costs. However, you can unwittingly find yourself underinsured if you do a major renovation and forget to call your insurer.

Health and Commercial Insurance

In commercial insurance, the 80% co-insurance requirement usually means that, after the deductible which the insured pays, the cost is shared on an 80%/20% basis — the insurer pays 80% while the insured pays 20% (plus the deductible). This will be addressed further in Chapter 5.

In health insurance, for instance dental coverage in a group policy at work, there may be 65% coverage on certain types of claims and 100% on other types. The premiums increase in order to get 90% or 100% coverage.

Calculating the Premium

Many factors influence both your eligibility for insurance and the amount of the premium, including the following:

- Type of structure — brick or frame
- Detached, semi-detached or row house
- Proximity to a fire hydrant and/or fire station
- Whether it is owner-occupied or rented
- Type of heat — natural gas, oil or electricity
- Size of the deducible
- Your history with the insurance company
- Your credit history. It is a recent and controversial development that insurers use your credit history as a factor in determining the amount of your premium. Insurers maintain that credit history has a good, although unreliable, ability to predict behaviour, that is, people with a poor credit rating are more likely to incur a loss and make a claim.

Some insurers also offer **discounts** for the following:

- Having both a home and auto policy with one insurer
- Improving security with smoke detectors, carbon monoxide detectors, monitored burglar alarm systems and dead-bolt locks
- Having an affinity with an association
- Being claims-free for several years
- Being loyal — staying with the same insurer for a number of years
- Being a non-smoking household

Redlining

It can be argued that credit scoring is a form of **redlining** — denying coverage in certain areas based on geographical location. It is illegal for insurance companies to deny coverage to, for instance, poor people or people of a certain race. (Other financial institutions are also not allowed to redline — to deny mortgages, for instance, to lower-income families). But the line between redlining and underwriting can be a very fine one, and, while redlining is illegal, it is used in a modified form — insurers may decide to accept only a certain number of policies in a high-risk area. For instance, if you live downtown in an older part of the city, especially in a semi-detached or row house, where the streets are quite narrow and, perhaps, somewhat winding, you may not be able to get insurance from a company that provides it for a neighbour or even for a few neighbours. This will likely be viewed as a high-risk area in that the houses are often frame and close together. The narrow streets can make it difficult for a firetruck to arrive. As a result, while insurers will provide insurance for a few houses, they will limit the number they will insure in that neighbourhood.

Coverage of Personal Property (Contents of Your Dwelling)

Typically, the contents of your home are valued at 60% of the value of the building. You may want to review this to ensure you are adequately covered. However, depending on your lifestyle compared to the cost of rebuilding the house you live in, your overall contents may exceed this 60%. This would be particularly true for homes in downtown urban centres where the market value of the land and building is far above the cost to rebuild. Coverage for particular items can be added using an endorsement to the policy. In addition, the coverage on contents can be increased to reflect the true value.

You also need to document and value your contents. To value them, you can make a list of the contents of each room, adding the estimated replacement cost or actual cost and the year they were purchased. Some insurance companies provide a blank form for this. You can photograph your contents, including the contents of drawers and cabinets and keep this record someplace other than your home (where it could be destroyed in the event of a complete loss of your home). You can also photograph any special features in your home, such as 11-inch baseboards and wide trim in older homes, hardwood floors, antique fixtures in bathrooms, special light fixtures, and other expensive-to-replace features that you would want to replace should you suffer a complete loss of your home.

Many policies now include a maximum loss amount called the **limit of liability** so that in the event of a total loss, the insurer will pay a lump sum maximum for the home and its contents.

Endorsements

An endorsement is an amendment to the original policy that adds, subtracts, or alters coverage. A **floater** is an endorsement for property that moves from location to location. Endorsements are often added for items that are not adequately covered in the policy. You might have an endorsement for:

- personal articles such as jewelry, furs, stamp (**philatelic property**) and coin (**numismatic property**) collections, musical instruments, cameras, silverware, golf equipment, and firearms;
- fine art; and
- outboard motors and boats.

Many of the items on these riders will be on a **valued basis** — after being appraised, the insured and insurer agree on its value. If the item is lost, stolen, or destroyed, the insured does not have to prove its value when submitting a claim.

Some types of coverage are excluded from even comprehensive coverage. Exclusions can include losses from floods, wars, earthquakes, furnace oil spills, and sewer back-ups. Coverage can often be obtained separately. More recent exclusions for damage due to marijuana-growing operations and for mould cannot be insured.

Homeowners Policies

Homeowners policies are **not** exactly the same in all provinces and territories since they are not mandatory like auto insurance. They are, however, similar and have many standard features. **Section I** covers your home and contents, **Section II** covers liability coverage, and **Section III** covers the conditions that apply to the policy. Every policy begins with a declaration page that outlines your coverage.

The following sample homeowners policy is a comprehensive policy. There are three levels of coverage that will be discussed further, after Section III. The three levels are as follows:

	Building	Contents
Comprehensive	All risks	All risks
Broad	All risks	Named perils
Basic	Named perils	Named perils

The basic plan is the cheapest since the coverage is more limited than in the comprehensive policy. Policies vary by insurance company and type of coverage, not by province. Many features are the same in all policies but everyone should take the time to read his or her policy carefully at the time the policy is taken out. At each renewal, you should review your policy to see if there any major changes although a good broker or agent will advise you of any significant changes.

The **declarations page** includes each of the following:
- Name and address of insured
- Insurance period covered
- Location of insured property
- Property covered
- Amount of each coverage
- Cost of each coverage
- Amount and cost of endorsements
- Any applicable surcharges or discounts
- Amount of deductible

Policy Wordings[1]

These forms describe information that is unique to your insurance policy. Together with the declaration page(s), these represent the legal contract of indemnity that exists between you and us. All of the coverages outlined in the policy are part of this Comprehensive Policy. That is, the homeowner gets all these coverages and does not get to pick and choose which coverages to have.

Homeowners Comprehensive Package

Your Homeowners Comprehensive Package Form Policy is written in plain language so that you may properly understand the protection you have purchased. The policy consists of these wordings, the declaration page(s) which contains information that is unique to your insurance policy and other forms that may need to be attached to complete your package coverage. Together, these represent the legal contract of indemnity that exists between you and us.

Insuring Agreement

We provide the insurance described in this policy in return for payment of the premium and subject to the terms and conditions set out.

Insurance cannot be a source of profit. It is only designed to indemnify you against actual losses incurred by you or for which you are liable.

Only losses or claims that occur within the policy term shown on the Declarations will be covered under this policy. In no case will we entertain any loss or claim that occurred or was in progress prior to the policy period inception date or after the policy period expiry date shown on the Declarations.

All amounts of insurance, premiums, and other amounts as expressed in this policy are in Canadian currency.

The declarations form an integral part of this policy and summarize the coverage you have selected and the premiums and limits that apply to them. Among other things, the Declarations identify the policyholder and the policy term.

---

1   The following policy is representative of what a prospective policy-holder might receive from an insurance company. While the exact wording may vary from company to company, it is representative what he or she can expect to receive.

This form consists of three sections:

- Section I describes the insurance for your property.
- Section II describes the insurance for your legal liability to others because of bodily injury and property damage.
- Section III provide general policy provisions as well as Statutory Conditions.

This policy applies to losses under Section I and III, or bodily injury or property damage under Section II, which occurs during the policy period.

If a Broadening of Coverage occurs during the term of this policy, you will automatically benefit from the improved coverage at no additional cost to you. In addition, any loss or damage that is covered by another of our homeowners policy forms that is less broad than this policy form is also insured hereunder.

Section I — Insurance on Your Property
Definitions

Business means any full-time or part-time activity of any kind undertaken for financial gain, and includes a trade, profession, or occupation and the storage of merchandise.

Business Property means property used in any full-time, part-time, or occasional activity of any kind undertaken for financial gain.

Civil Authority means any person acting under the authority of the Governor-General-in-Council of Canada or the Lieutenant-Governor-in-Council of a province, and/or any person acting with authority under a federal, provincial, or territorial legislation with respect to the protection of persons and property in the event of an emergency.

Domestic Appliance means a device or apparatus for personal use on the premises for containing, heating, chilling or dispensing water.

Dwelling means the building described in the Declarations occupied by you as a private residence.

Fungi includes, but is not limited to, any form or type of mould, yeast, mushroom, or mildew whether or not allergenic, pathogenic, or toxigenic, and any substance, vapour, or gas produced by, emitted from, or arising out of any fungi or spore(s) or resultant mycotoxins, allergens, or pathogens.

Ground Water means water in the soil beneath the surface of the ground, including but not limited to water in wells and in underground streams, and percolating waters.

Premises means the land, buildings, and related structures contained within the lot lines on which the dwelling is situated.

Residence Employee means a person employed by you to perform duties in connection with the maintenance or use of the insured premises. This includes persons who perform household or domestic services or duties of a similar nature for you.

This does *not include*[2] persons while performing duties in connection with your business.

Single limit of insurance is the maximum amount we will pay under one or more coverages provided under Section I in respect of one accident or occurrence unless otherwise stated.

Specified Perils means the following, subject to the exclusions and conditions in this policy:

1. Fire.
2. Lightning.
3. Explosion of coal, natural or manufactured gas.
4. Smoke due to a sudden, unusual, and faulty operation of a fireplace, or of any heating or cooking unit in or on the premises.
5. Falling object that strikes the exterior of the building.
6. Impact by aircraft or land vehicle.
7. Riot.
8. Vandalism or malicious acts, *not including* loss or damage caused by theft or attempted theft.
9. Water damage meaning damage caused by
   (a) the sudden and accidental escape of water from a watermain;
   (b) the sudden and accidental escape of water or steam from within a plumbing, heating, sprinkler, air conditioning system, or domestic appliance, which is located inside your dwelling;
   (c) the sudden and accidental escape of water from a domestic appliance located outside your dwelling (however, such damage is not covered when the escape of water is caused by freezing);
   (d) water which enters through an opening that has been created suddenly and accidentally by an Insured Peril.
10. Windstorm or hail, including loss or damage caused by weight of ice, snow, or sleet.
11. Transportation, meaning loss or damage caused by collision, upset, overturn, derailment, stranding, or sinking of any motorized vehicle or attached trailer in which the insured property is being carried. This would also apply to any conveyance of a common carrier, but does *not include* loss or damage to property in a vacation or home trailer which you own or any watercraft, their furnishings, equipment, or motors.

Spore(s) includes, but is not limited to, any reproductive particle or microscopic fragment produced by, emitted from, or arising out of any fungi.

Surface Waters means water on the surface of the ground where water does not usually accumulate in ordinary watercourses, lakes, or ponds.

Terrorism means an ideologically motivated unlawful act or acts, including but not limited to the use of violence or force or threat of violence or force committed by

---

2   Italics have been added throughout to highlight items that are not covered.

or on behalf of any group(s), organization(s), or government(s) for the purpose of influencing any government and/or instilling fear in the public or a section of the public.

Under Construction means any work resulting in any improvement, extension or addition to the dwelling when the work involves the piercing of an exterior wall or the roof for more than 24 hours.

Vacant means that all occupants have moved out with no intention of returning regardless of the presence of furnishings or in the case of a newly constructed house, no occupant has yet taken up residence.

Watermain means a pipe forming part of a water distribution system which conveys consumable water but not wastewater.

We or **us** mean the company providing this insurance.

You or **your** means the person(s) named in the Declarations and, while living in the same household, his or her spouse, the relatives of either, or any person under 21 in their care. This also includes any full-time student at college or university who is dependent on the named insured or spouse of the named insured. Spouse means either of a man and a woman who are married to each other or who have together entered into a marriage that is voidable or void or either of two persons who are living together in a conjugal relationship outside marriage and have so lived together continuously for a period of 3 years or, if they are the natural or adoptive parents of a child, for a period of 1 year.

   Only the person(s) named in the Declarations may take legal action against us.

Coverage A — Principal Dwelling
We insure the following:
1. The principal dwelling and attached structures.
2. Permanently installed outdoor equipment on the premises.
3. Outdoor swimming pool and attached equipment on the premises.
4. Materials and supplies located on or adjacent to the premises intended for use in construction, alteration, or repair of your dwelling or private structures on the premises. We insure against the peril of theft only while your dwelling is completed and ready to be occupied.

Tear Out
If any walls, ceilings, or other parts of insured buildings or structures must be torn apart before water damage from a plumbing, heating, air conditioning, sprinkler system, domestic appliance, waterbed, or aquarium can be repaired, we will pay the cost of such repairs, unless damage to such system or appliance is otherwise excluded.

   The cost of tearing out and replacing property to repair damage to outdoor swimming pools, public watermains, or sewers is *not insured*.

Building Fixtures and Fittings

You may apply up to **10%** of the limit of liability on your dwelling building to insure building fixtures and fittings temporarily removed from the premises for repair or seasonal storage.

Coverage B — Additional Buildings

We insure structures or buildings separated from the dwelling by a clear space on your premises but *not insured* under Coverage A[3]. If they are connected to the dwelling by a fence, utility line, or similar connection only, they are considered to be detached structures. If there is more than one detached structure or building, the available insurance under Coverage B will be proportioned among them, based on their relative replacement cost or actual cash value, depending upon your election under Basis of Claims Settlement.

If there are no detached structures for which the combined replacement cost values for all such structures exceeds $500, the limit of insurance for Coverage B shall be added to the limit of insurance for Coverage A or C. The sum of the two shall be the new limit of insurance applicable to Coverage A Dwelling, or Coverage C Personal Property, at your option.

Coverage C — Personal Property

1. We insure the **contents of your dwelling and other personal property** you own, wear or use while on your premises which is usual to the ownership or maintenance of a dwelling.

   If you wish, we will include personal property of others while it is on that portion of your premises which you occupy but we do *not insure* property of roomers or boarders who are not related to you.

   We do *not insure* loss or damage to motorized vehicles, trailers, camper units, truck caps, and aircraft or their equipment, except that we do insure lawn mowers, other gardening equipment, snow blowers, motorized wheelchairs or wheelchair-scooters, and watercraft. The word "equipment" includes audio, visual, recording or transmitting equipment designed to be specifically powered by the electrical system of a motor vehicle or aircraft.

2. We insure your personal property while it is **temporarily away from your premises**, anywhere in the world. If you wish, we will include personal property belonging to others while it is in your possession or belonging to a residence employee travelling with or for you.

   We do *not insure* personal property that is kept at another of your premises or portion thereof that is not stated in this policy, whether you own, rent, or occupy it.

---

3   Often, a structure such as a garage will automatically be covered for 10% of the value of the principal dwelling. This coverage can be increased.

124

3. The personal property of a **student**, who is insured by this policy but is temporarily residing away from home for the purpose of attending a school, college, or university, is insured at the student's residence for an amount not exceeding $7,000.

4. We insure the personal property of your father and/or mother or your spouse's father and/or mother who are living in a **nursing home or a home for the aged**, but who are in your legal custody, for an amount not exceeding $2,500.

5. If you are **moving** your personal property from your principal residence to a new location in Canada, which you intend to occupy as your new principal residence, your limit of insurance on personal property may be apportioned among and applied at your present principal residence, your new one, and in transit between them. This extension comes into effect on the day that you actually commence the physical transfer of your personal property from the old premises to the new premises, and terminates 30 consecutive days afterwards or on any termination of the policy, whichever occurs first.

6. We insure your personal property damaged by **change of temperature** resulting from physical damage to your dwelling or equipment by an insured peril. This applies only to personal property kept in the dwelling.

Personal property **stored in a warehouse** is insured for a period of 30 days only, from the date the property was first stored. We will continue coverage beyond that date for the peril of theft only.

We do *not insure* losses or increased costs of repair due to the operation of any law regulating the zoning, demolition, repair, or construction of buildings and their related services.

Special Limits of Insurance
We insure the following:

1. Books, tools, and instruments pertaining to a business profession or occupation for an amount up to $2,500 in all, but only while on your premises.

2. Securities, books of account, deeds, evidences of debt or title, letters of credit, notes other than bank notes, manuscripts, passports, tickets, and documents or other evidence to establish ownership or the right or claim to benefit, for an amount up to $5,000 in all.

3. Money or bullion up to $500 in all.

4. Garden type tractors and personal snow removal equipment, including attachments and accessories up to $10,000 in all.

5. Watercraft, their trailers, furnishings, equipment, accessories, and motors up to $2,000 in all. Loss or damage from windstorm or hail is insured only if they were inside a fully enclosed building. Canoes and rowboats are also insured while in the open.

6. Spare automobile parts up to $1,000 in all. The maximum is $250 for any one item.

7. Animals, birds, or fish up to $2,500 in all but *excluding* loss by theft or mysterious disappearance.

The following special limits of insurance do *not apply* to any claim caused by a specified peril.

8. Jewelry, watches, gems, fur garments, and garments trimmed with fur up to $6,000 in all.

9. Numismatic property (such as coin collections) up to $500 in all.

10. Stamps and philatelic property (such as stamp collections) up to $2,000 in all.

11. Silverware, silver-plated ware, goldware, gold-plated ware, and pewterware up to $10,000 in all.

12. Any one bicycle, tricycle, or unicycle up to $1,000 per item, inclusive of equipment and accessories.

13. Collectibles, meaning specifically sports cards, sports memorabilia, and comic book collections, up to $2,500 in all. The maximum is $250 for any one item.

Limitation of Coverage — Business Use of Premises

You are *not insured* for loss or damage occurring on premises used in whole or in part for business purposes, unless the business use is stated in the Declarations.

However, the following incidental business uses by you are permitted without being stated in the Declarations:

1. School, if not more than three students involved at any one time.
2. Babysitting or daycare, if not more than three children involved at any one time.
3. Storage of merchandise not exceeding $2,500 in value.

Coverage D — Loss of Use

The amount of insurance for Coverage D is the total amount for any one or a combination of the following coverages. The periods of time stated below are not limited by the expiration of the policy.

1. Additional Living Expenses

If an insured peril makes your dwelling unfit for occupancy, or you have to move out while repairs are being made, we insure any necessary increase in living expenses, including moving expenses incurred by you, so that your household can maintain its normal standard of living. Payment shall be for the reasonable time required to repair or rebuild your dwelling or, if you permanently relocate, the reasonable time required for your household to settle elsewhere.

2. Fair Rental Value

If an Insured Peril makes that part of the dwelling or detached private structures rented to others or held for rental by you unfit for occupancy, we insure its fair rental value. Payment shall be for the reasonable time required to repair or replace that part of the dwelling or detached private structures rented or held for rental. Fair rental value shall *not include* any expense that does not continue while that part of the dwelling or detached private structures rented or held for rental is unfit for occupancy.

If a civil authority prohibits access to your dwelling as a direct result of damage to neighbouring premises by an insured peril under this form, we insure any resulting additional living expense and fair rental value loss for a period not exceeding two weeks.

We do *not insure* the cancellation of a lease or agreement.

Insured Perils

You are insured against all risks of direct physical loss or damage subject to the exclusions and conditions in this form.

Exclusions — Loss or Damage Not Insured

We do not insure the following:

1. Buildings or structures used in whole or in part for business or farming purposes or business property pertaining to a business actually conducted on the residence premises, or business property away from the residence premises, unless stated in the Declarations.
2. Retaining walls, except for fire, lightning, impact by land vehicle or aircraft, or vandalism and malicious acts.
3. Sporting equipment where the loss or damage is due to its use.
4. Contact lenses unless the loss or damage is caused by a specified peril, watercraft, or aircraft, or theft or attempted theft.
5. Animals, birds, or fish unless the loss or damage is caused by a specified peril, but *not* by impact by aircraft or land vehicle.
6. Property at any fairground, exhibition, or exposition for the purpose of exhibition.
7. Any property illegally acquired, used, kept, stored, imported, or transported, or any property subject to forfeiture.
8. Property of roomers or boarders.
9. Securities, books of account, deeds, evidences of debt or title, letters of credit, notes other than bank notes, manuscripts, passports, tickets, and documents or other evidence to establish ownership or the right or claim to a benefit, other than as provided and limited under special limits of insurance.
10. Any property lawfully seized or confiscated unless such property is destroyed to prevent the spread of fire.
11. Losses or increased costs of repair due to operation of any law or by-law regulating the zoning, demolition, repair, or construction of building and their related services.

12. Marring or scratching of any property or breakage of any fragile or brittle articles unless caused by a specified peril, watercraft, or aircraft, or theft or attempted theft.
13. Wear and tear, deterioration, defect, design fault or mechanical breakdown, rust or corrosion, extremes of temperature, wet or dry rot, fungi or spores, and contamination except that resulting damage by an insured peril is covered.
14. Inherent vice or latent defect.
15. The cost of making good faulty material or workmanship or any damage that occurs due to any fault in design except that resulting damage by an insured peril is covered.
16. Against loss or damage caused directly or indirectly by the failure of any computer or other equipment, including embedded microchips, computer program or software to correctly read, recognize, process, distinguish, interpret, or accept any date, time, or combined date/time data or data field. Such failure shall include any error in original or modified data entry or programming. This exclusion does *not apply* to any loss caused by a specified peril.
17. Data, or loss or damage caused directly or indirectly by data problem. However, if loss or damage caused by data problem results in the occurrence of further loss of or damage to property insured that is directly caused by fire, explosion, smoke, water damage, all as described specified perils, this exclusion shall *not apply* to such resulting loss or damage.

We do not insure loss or damage that occurs as follows:
18. Resulting directly from settling, expansion, contraction, moving, bulging, buckling or cracking of pavements, patios, foundations, walls, floors, roofs or ceilings, except resulting damage to building glass.
19. Occurring after your dwelling has, to your knowledge, become vacant.
20. Caused directly or indirectly by:
    (a) any nuclear incident as defined in the Nuclear Liability Act or any other nuclear liability act, law, or statue, or any law amendatory thereof or nuclear explosion, except for ensuing loss or damage which results directly from fire, lightning, or explosion of coal, natural, or manufactured gas;
    (b) contamination by radioactive material.
21. Caused by war, invasion, act of a foreign enemy, hostilities, civil war, rebellion, revolution, insurrection or military power.
22. Arising from or resulting from, caused directly or indirectly, in whole or in part, by terrorism or by any activity or decision of a government agency or other entity to prevent, respond to, or terminate terrorism except for ensuing loss or damage which results directly from fire or explosion, as described in specified perils. Such loss or damage is excluded regardless of any other cause or event that contributes concurrently or in any sequence to the loss or damage.
23. Resulting from an intentional or criminal act or failure to act by:
    (a) any person insured by this policy; or
    (b) any other person at the direction of any person insured by this policy;

    (c) any tenant, tenant's guests, boarders, employee, or any member of the tenant's household whether you have any knowledge of these activities or not.

24. Any damage arising directly or indirectly from the growing, manufacturing, processing or storing by anyone of any drug, narcotic, or illegal substances or items of any kind the possession of which constitutes a criminal offence. This includes any alteration of the premises to facilitate such activity whether or not you have any knowledge of such activity.

25. To personal property undergoing any process or while being worked on, where the damage results from such process or work, but resulting damage to other property is insured.

26. Caused directly by animals owned by or in the care, custody, or control of anyone included in the definition of "you" and "your".

27. Caused by continuous or repeated seepage or leakage of water or steam from within a plumbing, heating, sprinkler, or air conditioning system, or domestic appliance, including but not limited to a waterbed, aquarium.

28. Caused by birds, vermin, racoons, skunks, rodents, bats or insects, except resultant damage and loss or damage to building glass caused by birds.

29. Caused by smoke from agricultural smudging or industrial operations.

30. Resulting directly from earth movement, meaning any loss caused by, resulting from, contributed to, or aggravated by, earthquake, snowslide, landslide, mudflow, earth sinking, rising, or shifting, unless fire, explosion, or breakage of glass or safety glazing material which is part of a building, storm door, or storm window ensues and then we will pay only the resulting loss.

31. Caused by theft or attempted theft by any tenant, tenant's guest, any boarder of yours, employee or member of the tenant's household if the part of the dwelling containing the property insured, normally occupied by you, is rented to others.

32. Caused by vandalism or malicious acts or glass breakage occurring while your dwelling is under construction or vacant even if permission for construction or vacancy has been given by us.

33. Resulting from a change in ownership of property that is agreed to even if that change was brought about by trickery or fraud.

34. Caused by or resulting from contamination or pollution, or the release, discharge or dispersal of contaminants or pollutants, *unless* the loss or damage is caused by the bursting or overflowing of your domestic fixed fuel oil tank, apparatus, or pipes.

35. Caused by theft or attempted theft of property in or from a dwelling under construction, or of materials and supplies for use in the construction, unless the dwelling is completed and ready to be occupied.

36. Caused by flood, surface water, spray, waves, tides, tidal waves, ice, or waterborne objects, all whether driven by wind or not, *unless* the loss or damage resulted from the escape of water from a public watermain, swimming pool or equipment attached.

37. Caused by water *unless* the loss or damage resulted from
    (a) the sudden and accidental escape of water from a watermain;

    (b) the sudden and accidental escape of water or steam from within a plumbing, heating, sprinkler, air conditioning system or domestic appliance, which is located inside your dwelling;

    (c) the sudden and accidental escape of water from a domestic appliance located outside your dwelling (however, such damage is not covered when the escape of water is caused by freezing);

    (d) water which enters through an opening which has been created suddenly and accidentally by a specified peril other than water damage;

    (e) the backing up or escape of water from an eavestrough or downspout, or by the melting of ice or snow on the roof of the building, provided the water has not entered the ground and seeped through a basement or foundation wall.

We do not insure loss or damage that occurs as follows:

38. Caused by continuous or repeated seepage of water.
39. Caused by the backing up or escape of water from a sewer, sump or septic tank.
40. Caused by groundwater or rising of the water table.
41. Caused by surface waters, unless the water escapes as described in 38, above.
42. To a watermain.
43. To a system or appliance from which the water escaped.
44. Caused by shoreline ice build-up or by water-borne ice or other objects, all whether driven by wind or not.
45. Occurring while the building is under construction or vacant even if we have given permission for construction or vacancy.
46. Caused by freezing of any part of a plumbing, heating, sprinkler, air conditioning system or domestic appliance unless within a portion of your dwelling heated during the usual heating session.
47. Caused by freezing during the usual heating season within a heated portion of your dwelling if you have been away from your premises more than 4 consecutive days; but you will still be insured if you had taken any of the following precautions:
    - arranged for a competent person to enter your dwelling each day you were away to ensure that heating was being maintained, or
    - if your heating system is connected by a monitored heating alarm to a station providing 24-hour service, or
    - if you had shut off the water supply and had drained all the pipes and appliances.

Additional Coverages

In addition to your property coverages, your policy provides some additional special coverage features.

Credit Card,[4] Automated Teller Card, Forgery, and Counterfeit Money Coverage

We will pay for the following:

1. Your legal obligation to pay because of the theft or unauthorized use of credit cards issued to you or registered in your name provided you have complied with all of the conditions under which the card was issued.
2. Loss caused by the theft of your automated teller card provided you have complied with all of the conditions under which the card was issued.
3. Loss to you caused by forgery or alteration of cheques, drafts or other negotiable instruments.
4. Loss by your acceptance in good faith of counterfeit Canadian or United States paper currency. We do not recover loss caused by the use of your credit card or automated teller card by a resident of your household or by a person to whom the card has been entrusted.

The most we will pay under this coverage during the term of this policy is $5,000.

This coverage is *not* subject to a deductible.

Debris & Protective Removal

The amounts of insurance include the cost of removing debris of the property insured as a result of the occurrence of an insured event.

If the amount payable for loss, including expense for debris removal, is greater than the Limit of Liability, an additional 5% of that amount will be available to cover debris removal expense.

If you must remove insured property from your premises to protect it from loss or damage that is covered by this policy, it is insured for 90 days or until your policy term ends — whichever happens first. The amount of insurance will be divided in the proportion that the value of the property removed bears to the value of all property at the time of loss.

You may also apply up to 10% of the amount of insurance on your dwelling building to insure building fixtures and fittings that are temporarily removed from your premises for repair or seasonal storage.

Fire Department Charges

If a fire department attends your premises in response to the occurrence of an insured event, you may be billed for these services. If this happens, your policy will pay for such expenses which are *not* subject to a deductible.

---

4   A **credit card** allows you to either a) charge something and pay for it later, or b) withdraw cash and charge it to your credit card. A **debit card** allows you to pay for something and the funds are immediately withdrawn from your account. An automated teller card allows you to access your account using an **automated teller machine** (ATM). *These functions may be on one, two or three cards but they are three separate functions and, for the purposes of this policy, three separate cards.*

Frozen Food Protection

You are insured for loss or damage by spoilage to food contained in any home freezer within your premises resulting from

1. mechanical or electrical breakdown of the freezer, or
2. failure or interruption of an outside power supply.

When a breakdown or power interruption happens, you must take all reasonable steps to save or preserve the food from spoilage, and we will pay for any reasonable extra expenses you incur in doing so.

This coverage includes the freezer unit when damage is due to food spoilage as well as the food. We will *not pay* for loss caused by

1. inherent vice or natural spoilage;
2. accidental or deliberate manual disconnection of the power supply within your dwelling. The deductible applies to this coverage.

Inflation Guard

Your policy includes an inflation index. We will increase the limits of insurance stated in the Declarations as applicable to Coverages A, B, C, and D by the Building Inflation Rate % (BIR) at regular intervals.

- 2 months after inception — increased to ¼ of the BIR
- 5 months after inception — increased to ½ of the BIR
- 8 months after inception — increased to ¾ of the of BIR
- 11 months after inception — increased to the full BIR

If you request a change in the amount of insurance during the policy term, we will treat the effective date of that change as the inception date for purpose of this feature.

Lock Replacement

If your exterior door keys are stolen, your policy provides up to $500 to re-key your locks or to replace them if it is not possible to re-key them. If your exterior door keys are lost, we will pay 50% of the cost, up to $500, to re-key your locks or to replace them if it is not possible to re-key them. You must notify us within 72 hours of the discovery of the keys being lost.

This coverage is *not* subject to a deductible.

Mass Evacuation

We will pay any necessary and reasonable increase in living expense to a maximum of $2,500 incurred by you while access to the residence premises is prohibited by order of civil authority, but only when such order is given for a mass evacuation as a direct result of a sudden and accidental event.

You are insured for a period not exceeding 30 days from the date of the order of evacuation. You are *not insured* for any claim arising from evacuation resulting from the following:

1. Flood,[5] meaning waves, tides, tidal waves, and the rising of, or the breaking out of the overflow of, any body of water, whether natural or man-made.
2. Earthquake, unless the earthquake peril is added to this policy by a Section III form.
3. Caused directly or indirectly, in whole or in part, by terrorism or by any activity or decision of a government agency or other entity to prevent, respond to a claim, or terminate terrorism except for ensuing loss or damage that results directly from fire or explosion, as described in specified perils. Such loss or damage is excluded regardless of any other cause or event that contributes concurrently or in any sequence to the loss or damage.
4. War, invasion, act of a foreign enemy, hostilities, civil war, rebellion, revolution, insurrection, or military power.
5. Nuclear incident as defined in the Nuclear Liability Act, nuclear explosion, or contamination by radioactive material.

This $2,500 coverage will be provided as part of the limits specified in the Declarations for Coverage D — Additional Living Expense/Fair Rental Value.

We do *not insure* the cancellation of a lease or agreement.

Mortgage Rate Protector

You may use this no-deductible feature after a total loss to your dwelling. A total loss is one equal to at least the amount specified in the Declarations. It must also be a loss for which you are covered.

Your bank or lending institution may have the right to "call in" your mortgage after a loss. If a new mortgage at a higher, competitive rate of interest is obtained, we will pay, in addition to the policy limits, the difference between the old and new rates on the balance of your outstanding mortgage.

We will pay each month. We will only pay for the duration period of your old mortgage until its expiry. We will cease to pay if title or interest in your premises is relinquished.

We will also pay for fees charged by a lawyer to obtain the new mortgage. We will *not pay* for other costs, such as judgments or service charges.

Outdoor Greenery

You may apply up to 5% in all of the amount of insurance on your dwelling building to trees, plants, shrubs, and lawns on your premises. We will *not pay* more than $1,000 for any one tree, plant, or shrub, including the cost of removing its debris.

We insure these items against loss caused by fire, theft, lightning, explosion, impact by aircraft or land vehicle, riot, vandalism, and malicious acts. We do *not insure* items or lawns grown for commercial purposes.

---

5   In 2005, Hurricane Katrina caused mass evacuation, which is *not* covered by homeowners policies in the United States, where hurricanes are common. In addition, the evacuation was caused by flooding, which is usually not a covered peril.

The deductible applies to this coverage.

Permissions Granted

You have our permission under the terms and conditions of this policy to

1. make alterations, additions, and repairs to the dwelling building that you occupy (you may, however, need to request an increase in your limits of insurance).
2. keep and use reasonable and normal quantities of fuel oil, L.P.G. gasoline, benzene, naphtha, or other similar materials.

Personal Records Stored in a Personal Computer

We will pay up to $3,000 to recreate personal records stored in a home computer located on your residence premises if the loss of those records is caused by a covered peril. This coverage does *not apply* to business records stored in the personal computer.

The deductible applies to this coverage.

Reward Coverage

We will pay up to $1,000 to any individual or organization for information leading to the arrest and conviction of any person(s) for arson or theft of any covered personal property from you.

Safety Deposit Box

We will pay up to $10,000 for loss or damage to your personal property while contained in a bank (or trust company) safety deposit box caused by any of the insured perils which apply to Coverage C, Personal Property.

The deductible applies to this coverage.

Basis of Claims Settlement

We will pay for insured loss or damage up to your financial interest in the property, but not exceeding the applicable amount(s) of insurance for any loss or damage arising out of one occurrence.

Any payments made for loss or damage shall not reduce the amounts of insurance provided by this policy.

Deductible

We insure the amount by which the loss or damage caused by any of the insured perils exceeds the amount of the deductible in any one occurrence.

If your claim involves personal property on which the special limits of insurance apply, the limitations apply to losses exceeding the deductible amount.

Your Principal Residence and Other Buildings

If you decide to repair or replace the damaged or destroyed building(s) we will pay the lesser of

- the cost to repair the property with materials of similar kind and quality, or
- the cost to replace the damaged or destroyed property with materials of similar kind or quality without deduction for depreciation, or
- the applicable limit of insurance.

But we will *not pay* more than the actual cash value of the loss or damage

- if the building(s) is (are) not repaired or replaced,
- if repair or replacement is not effected as soon as reasonably possible,
- if replacement of the building(s) does not take place on the same site,
- if the building(s) is (are) not returned to the same use or occupancy as existed immediately prior to the loss or damage.

If you decide not to repair or replace the damaged or destroyed building(s) we will pay the actual cash value of the damage at the date of the occurrence.

When determining the amount payable under Basis of Claim Settlement for any insured loss or damage, in no event will we include payment for losses or increased costs of repair or replacement due to the operation of any law requiring the zoning, demolition, repair, or construction of buildings and their related services.

Guaranteed Replacement Cost on Dwelling Buildings

If Guaranteed Replacement cost is indicated in the Declarations, we will pay the full cost of repairs or replacement even if it is more than the amount of insurance for Coverage A, provided the following conditions are met:

1. The amount of insurance for Coverage A shown on the Coverage Summary page on:
   - the inception date of the policy, or
   - the most recent renewal date, or
   - the increased amount under the inflation protection coverage on the date the increase took effect

   was not less than 100% of the cost to replace the dwelling building, as determined by a valuation guide acceptable to us;
2. The amount of insurance applicable to Coverage A has not been reduced below the amount determined by the valuation guide.
3. You notified us within 30 days of the start of the work if any addition, extension, or improvement has been made to your dwelling that would increase the replacement cost by 5% or more. This requirement does *not apply* if such additions, extensions, or other improvements do not exceed $5,000 in total during the policy term.

If you do not repair or replace, we will pay the actual cash value of the damage on the date of occurrence. In determining the cost of repairs or replacement, we will *not pay* or include the increased costs of repair or replacement due to the operation of any law regulating the zoning, demolition, repair or construction of buildings and their related services.

If any guaranteed replacement cost provisions under the Basis of Claims settlement are not met, this will result in the loss of any single limit coverage available.

Personal Property

We will pay the actual cash value of the loss or damage to personal property covered under Section I up to the applicable amount of insurance.

For records, other than computer records, including books of account, drawings, or card index systems, we will pay the cost of blank books, pages, cards, or other materials plus the cost of actually transcribing or copying the records.

If "Replacement Cost — Personal Property" is shown in the Declarations as an additional coverage for this location, we will pay on the basis of replacement cost, provided that

1. the property at the time of loss was useable for its original purpose, and
2. you repair or replace the property promptly.

Otherwise, the basis of claim payment will be Actual Cash Value.

"**Replacement cost**" means the cost, at the time of loss, of repairs or replacement (whichever is lower), with new property of similar kind and quality, without deduction for depreciation, up to the applicable amount of insurance.

Replacement cost does *not apply* to the following:

1. Antiques, fine arts, paintings and statuary.
2. Articles that, because of their inherent nature, cannot be replaced with new articles.
3. Articles for which their age or history contribute substantially to their value such as memorabilia, souvenirs and collectors' items. You may choose payment on an actual cash value basis initially.

You may make a subsequent claim on a replacement cost basis but no later than 180 days after the date of loss or damage.

Actual Cash Value

Whenever the words *actual cash value* are used in this policy, settlement of a claim will take into account such things as the cost of replacement less any depreciation, and in determining depreciation we will consider the condition immediately before the damage, the resale value, and the normal life expectancy.

Insurance Under More than One Policy

If you have insurance on specifically described property, this policy will be considered excess insurance and we will *not pay* any loss or claim until the amount of such other insurance is used up.

In all other cases, we will pay our ratable proportion of the loss or claim under this policy.

Conditions

The following conditions apply to the coverage provided under Section I of this policy.

No Benefit to Bailee

It is warranted by you that this insurance shall in no way be directly or indirectly to the benefit of any carrier or other bailee.

Notice to Authorities

Where the loss is due to or appears to be due to theft, burglary, robbery, malicious mischief, or disappearance of insured property, you must give immediate notice thereof to the police or other authorities having jurisdiction.

Pairs, Sets, and Parts

In the case of loss of or damage to any part of the insured property whether scheduled or unscheduled, consisting, when complete for use, of several parts, the insurer is not liable for more than the insured value of the part lost or damaged, including the cost of installation.

Subrogation[6]

Once we have made any payment or have assumed any liability for making such payment, we shall inherit or be subrogated to all the rights of recovery that you might have had against any person and are entitled under the law to bring action in your name to enforce such rights.

If such action on our part does not fully indemnify both you and us, the amount that we do recover will be divided between you and us in the proportions in which the loss or damage has been borne by each of us, respectively. The amounts so available for distribution shall be net of the costs of effecting the recovery.

Sue and Labour

In the event that any property insured under this policy is damaged or destroyed, it is your duty to take all reasonable steps that might be available to you to bring about recovery of such property. We will contribute on a proportionate basis towards any reasonable and proper expenses in accordance with our respective interest in the property insured.

---

6   If someone causes your house to be destroyed and you sue and are awarded a settlement, the insurer can collect a portion of your award so you do not profit from the loss.

Section II — Insurance on Your Liability to Others

In the event you have, under another policy or policies issued by us, liability insurance that applies to a loss or claim, then under no circumstances will we pay in total more than the highest of the liability limits stated on the Declaration Pages of all such policies issued by us.

Definitions

Bodily injury means bodily injury, sickness, disease, disability, shock, mental anguish, mental injury or resulting death.

Business means any continuous or regular pursuit undertaken for financial gain including a trade, profession, or occupation.

Business property means property on which a business is conducted, property rented in whole or in part to others, or held for rental.

Business pursuits means any full-time, part-time or occasional activity of any kind undertaken for financial gain, and includes a trade, profession or occupation.

Business premises means premises on which a business pursuit is conducted, and premises rented in whole or in part to others, or held for rental.

Legal liability means responsibility which courts recognize and enforce between persons who sue one another.

Premises in this Section means all premises where the person(s) named as Insured in the Declarations, or his or her spouse, maintains a residence. It also includes the following:
1. Other seasonal and residential premises specified in the Declarations except business property and farms.
2. Individual or family cemetery plots or burial vaults.
3. Vacant land in Canada you own or rent, *excluding* farm land.
4. Land in Canada where an independent contractor is building a one- or two-family residence to be occupied by you.
5. premises in Canada you are using or where you are temporarily residing if you do not own such premises;
6. a swimming pool on your premises. **Property damage** means damage to, or destruction of, or loss of use of tangible property.

Residence employee and **employee** in this section have the same meaning as **residence employee** in Section I.

Voluntary payments are paid without your being legally liable.

We or **us** in this section have the same meanings as in Section I.

Weekly indemnity means two-thirds of your employee's weekly wage at the date of the accident, but we will *not pay* more than $100 per week.

You or **your** in this section have the same meanings as in Section I. In addition, the following persons are insured:

1. Any person or organization legally liable for damages caused by a watercraft or animal owned by you, and to which this insurance applies. This does *not include* anyone using or having custody of the watercraft or animal in the course of any business or without the owner's permission.
2. A residence employee while performing duties in connection with the ownership, use, or operation of motorized vehicles and trailers for which coverage is provided in this form.
3. Your legal representative having temporary custody of the insured premises, if you die while insured by this form, for legal liability arising out of the insured premises.
4. Any person who is insured by this form at the time of your death and who continues residing on the insured premises. All other definitions mentioned in Section I have the same meaning in Section II.

Coverages

This insurance applies only to accidents or occurrences that take place during the period this policy is in force.

The amounts of insurance are shown in the Declarations. Each person insured is a separate insured but this does not increase the limit of insurance.

Coverage E — Legal Liability

We will pay all sums that you become legally liable to pay as compensatory damages because of unintentional bodily injury or property damage.

The limits of insurance are shown in the Declarations and are the maximum we will pay, under one or more sections of Coverage E, for all compensatory damages in respect of one accident or occurrence other than as provided under defence, settlement, and supplementary payments.

You are insured for claims made against you arising from the following:

1. Personal Liability

Personal liability is legal liability arising out of your personal actions anywhere in the world.

You are *not insured* for claims made against you arising from:

(a) The ownership, use, or operation of any motorized vehicle, trailer, watercraft, or farm equipment, except those shown under items 1, 2, and 3 of "motorized vehicles — vehicles you own", or those for which coverage is shown in the Declarations.
(b) Damage to property you own, use, occupy, rent, or lease.
(c) Damage to property in your care, custody, or control.
(d) Damage to personal property or fixtures as a result of work done on them by you or anyone on your behalf.
(e) Bodily injury to you or to any person residing in your household other than a residence employee.

2. Premises Liability

Premises liability is legal liability arising out of your ownership, use, or occupancy of the premises defined in Section II. This insurance also applies if you assume, by a written contract, the legal liability of other persons in relation to your premises.

You are *not insured* for claims made against you arising from the following:
(a) Damage to property you own, use, occupy, or rent or lease from others.
(b) Damage to property in your care, custody, or control.
(c) Damage to personal property or fixtures as a result of work done on them by you or anyone on your behalf.
(d) Bodily injury to you or to any person residing in your household other than a residence employee.

3. Tenant's Legal Liability

Tenant's legal liability is legal liability for property damage to premises of others or the contents contained therein belonging to others, which you are using, renting, or have in your custody or control, provided such property damage is caused by fire, explosion, water escape including escape of water from a waterbed or aquarium, or smoke, all as defined or limited in Section I.

You are *not insured* for liability you have assumed by contract unless your legal liability would have applied even if no contract had been in force.

4. Employer's Liability

Employer's liability is legal liability for bodily injury to residence employees arising out of and in the course of their employment by you.

You are *not insured* for claims made against you resulting from the ownership, use, or operation of aircraft while being operated or maintained by your employee.

You are *not insured* for liability imposed upon or assumed by you under any Workers' Compensation Statute.

You are *not insured* for any claim for loss, cost, or expenses arising out of:
(a) The actual or alleged failure, malfunction, or inadequacy of any computer or other equipment, including embedded microchips, computer program or software to correctly read, recognize, process, distinguish, interpret, or accept any date, time, or combined date/time data or data field. Such failure shall include any error in original or modified data entry or programming.
(b) Any advice, consultation, design, evaluation, inspection, installation, maintenance, repair, replacement or supervision provided or done by you or for you to determine, rectify, or test for any potential or actual problems described in paragraph (a) of this exclusion.

Defence, Settlement Supplementary Payments

We will defend you against any suit that makes claims against you for which you are insured under Coverage E and that alleges bodily injury or property damage and seeks compensatory damages, even if it is groundless, false, or fraudulent. We reserve the right to investigate, negotiate, and settle any claim or suit if we decide this is appropriate. In addition to the limit of insurance under Coverage E, we will pay:

1. All expenses that we incur.
2. All costs charged against you in any suit insured under Coverage E.
3. Any interest accruing after judgement on that part of the judgment that is within the limit of insurance of Coverage E.
4. Premiums for appeal bonds required in any insured lawsuit involving you and bonds to release any property that is being held as security, up to the limit of insurance, but we are not obligated to apply for or provide these bonds.
5. Expenses that you have incurred for emergency medical or surgical treatment to others following an accident or occurrence insured by this form.
6. Reasonable expenses, except loss of earnings, which you incur at our request.

Coverage F — Voluntary Medical Payments

We will pay reasonable expenses incurred within one year of the date of the accident, if you unintentionally injure another person or if that person is accidentally injured on your premises. This coverage is available even though you are not legally liable. Medical expenses include surgical, dental, hospital, nursing, ambulance service, and funeral expenses. Medical expenses for residence employees are insured.

The amount of insurance shown in the Declarations is the maximum amount we will pay for each person in respect of one accident or occurrence.

We will *not pay*

- expenses covered by any medical, dental, surgical, or hospitalization plan or law, or under any other insurance contract;
- medical expenses or those of persons residing with you, other than residence employees;
- medical expenses of any person covered by any Workers' Compensation Statute.

You are *not insured* for claims arising out of the ownership, use, or operation of any motorized vehicle, trailer or watercraft, except those for which coverage is shown in this policy.

You shall arrange for the injured person, if requested, to

1. give us, as soon as possible, written proof of claim, under oath if required;
2. submit to physical examination at our expense by doctors we select as often as we may reasonably require;
3. authorize us to obtain medical and other records. Proofs and authorizations may be given by someone acting on behalf of the injured person.

Coverage G — Voluntary Property Payments

We will pay for unintentional direct damage you cause to property even though you are not legally liable. You may also use this coverage to reimburse others for direct property damage caused intentionally by anyone included in the definition of *you* or *your* of Section II of this form, 12 years of age or under.

You are *not insured* for claims

1. resulting from the ownership, use, or operation of any motorized vehicle, trailer, or watercraft, except those for which coverage is provided by this form;
2. for property you or your tenants own or rent;
3. insured under Section I;
4. caused by the loss of use, disappearance or theft of property.

Basis of Payment

We will pay whichever is the least of the following:

1. The actual cash value of the property at the time of loss.
2. What it would cost to repair or replace the property with materials of similar quality at the time of loss.
3. The amount shown in the Declarations.

We may pay for the loss in money or may repair or replace the property, and may settle any claim for loss of property either with you or the owner of the property. We may take over any salvage if we wish.

Within 60 days after the loss, you must submit to us (under oath if required) a Proof of Loss Form containing the following information:

1. The amount, place, time and cause of loss.
2. The interest of all persons in the property affected.
3. The actual cash value of the property at the time of loss. If necessary, you must help us verify the damage.

Coverage H — Voluntary Compensation for Residence Employees

We offer to pay the benefits described below if your employee is injured or dies accidentally while working for you, even though you are not legally liable.

If your employee does not accept these benefits or sues you, we may withdraw our offer, but this will not affect your legal liability insurance.

An employee who accepts these benefits must sign a release giving up any right to sue you. We have the right to recover from anyone, other than you, who is responsible for the employee's injury or death.

An injured employee will, if requested

1. submit to physical examination at our expense by doctors we select as often as we may reasonably require;
2. authorize us to obtain medical and other records; in case of death, we can require an autopsy before we make payment.

We will *not pay* benefits

1. unless your employee was actually performing duties for you when the accident happened;
2. for any hernia injury;

3. for injury or death caused by war, invasion, act of a foreign enemy, hostilities, civil war, rebellion, revolution, insurrection, or military power.

Schedule of Benefits

1. Loss of Life

If your employee dies from injuries received in the accident within the following 26 weeks we will pay

(a) to those wholly dependent upon him or her, a total of one hundred times the weekly indemnity in addition to any benefit for Temporary Total Disability paid up to the date of death;

(b) actual funeral expenses up to $500.

2. Temporary Total Disability

If your employee temporarily becomes totally disabled from injuries received in the accident within the following 14 days and cannot work at any job, we will pay weekly indemnity up to 26 weeks while such disability continues. We will *not pay* for the first seven days unless the disability lasts for six weeks or more.

3. Permanent Total Disability

If your employee becomes permanently and totally disabled from injuries received in the accident within the following 26 weeks and cannot work at any job, we will pay weekly indemnity for 100 weeks in addition to benefits provided under temporary total disability.

4. Injury Benefits

If, as a result of the accident, your employee suffers the loss of, or permanent loss of use of any of the following within 26 weeks of the accident, we will pay weekly indemnity for the number of weeks shown.

These benefits will be paid in addition to temporary total disability benefits but no others and for not more than 100 times the weekly indemnity.

For Loss of:	Number of Weeks	For Loss of:	Number of Weeks
A. One or more of the following:		C. One eye	50
Hand	100	OR	
Arm	100	Both eyes	100
Foot	100		
Leg	100		
B. One finger or toe	20	D. Hearing of one ear	25
OR		OR	
More than one finger or toe	50	Hearing of both ears	100

5. Medical Expenses

If, as a result of the accident, your employee incurs medical expenses including surgical, dental, hospital, nursing, and ambulance expenses within the following 26 weeks, we will pay up to a maximum of $1,000 in addition to all other benefits.

We will pay for the cost of supplying or renewing artificial limbs or braces, made necessary by the accident, for up to 52 weeks after the accident, subject to a maximum of $5,000.

We do *not insure* you for costs recoverable from other insurance plans.

Special Limitations
Watercraft
Watercraft You Own
You are insured against claims for bodily injury to or damage to the property of others, arising out of your ownership, use or operation of watercraft equipped with an outboard motor or motors of not more than 19 kW (25hp) in total when used with or on a single watercraft. You are also insured if your watercraft has an inboard or an inboard-outboard motor of not more than 38 kW (50 hp) or for any other type of watercraft not more than 8 metres (26 feet) in length.

If you own any motors or watercraft larger than those stated above, you are insured only if they are shown on the policy. If they are acquired after the effective date of this policy, you will be insured automatically for a period of 30 days only from the date of their acquisition, or until expiry of the policy, whichever comes first.

Watercraft You Do Not Own
You are insured against claims for bodily injury to or damage to the property of others, arising out of your use or operation of watercraft that you do not own, provided

1. the watercraft is being used or operated with the owner's consent;
2. the watercraft is not owned by anyone included in the definition *you* or *your* in Section II of this form; you are *not insured* for damage to the watercraft itself.

Regardless of whether you own or do not own a watercraft for which third-party liability coverage is provided above, there is no coverage here

1. if you use the watercraft for carrying passengers for compensation or hire;
2. in any race or speed test;
3. if you rent or lease it to others;
4. if you use it for business purposes;
5. if you use or operate it without the owner's consent if you are not the owner.

Motorized Vehicles
Vehicles You Own
You are insured against claims for bodily injury to or damage to the property of others, arising out of your ownership, use, or operation of the following, including their trailers or attachments:

1. Self-propelled lawn mowers, snow blowers, garden-type tractors of not more than 19 kW (25 hp) used or operated mainly on your property.
2. Motorized golf carts while in use on a golf course.
3. Motorized wheelchairs (including motorized scooters having more than two wheels and specifically designed for the carriage of a person who has a physical disability).

Vehicles You Do Not Own

You are insured against claims for bodily injury to or damage to the property of others, arising out of your use or operation of any self-propelled land vehicle, amphibious vehicle, or air cushion vehicle, including their trailers, that you do not own, provided that

1. the vehicle is not licensed and is designed primarily for recreational use off public roads;
2. the vehicle is being used or operated with the owner's consent;
3. the vehicle is not owned by anyone included in the definition of *you* or *your* in Section II of this form.

You are *not insured* for damage to the vehicle itself.

Regardless of whether you own or do not own a motorized vehicle for which third-party liability coverage is provided above, there is *no coverage* here

1. if you use the motor vehicle(s) for carrying passengers for compensation or hire;
2. in any race or speed test;
3. if you rent or lease it/them to others;
4. if you use it for business purposes;
5. if you use or operate it without the owner's consent if you are not the owner.

There is also *no coverage* here for liability arising out of the ownership, use, or operation of any motorized vehicle or trailer or part thereof except as mentioned here.

Trailers

You are insured against claims for bodily injury to or damage to the property of others, arising out of your ownership, use, or operation of any trailer or its equipment, provided that such trailer is not being towed by, attached to, or carried on a motorized vehicle.

Business Pursuits and Business Property

You are insured against claims for bodily injury to or damage to the property of others, arising out of the following:

1. Your work for someone else as a sales representative, collector, messenger or office employee, provided that the claim does not involve injury to a fellow employee.
2. Your work for someone else as a teacher or educator, provided that the claim does not involve physical disciplinary action to a student or injury to a fellow employee.
3. The temporary or part-time business pursuits of an insured person under the age of 21 years.
4. Activities during the course of a business pursuit that are usually considered to be personal activities.

5. The occasional rental of your residence to others; rental to others of a one- or two-family dwelling usually occupied in part by you as a residence, provided no family unit includes more than two roomers or boarders.

6. The rental to others of not more than three car spaces or stalls in garages or stables. Claims arising from the rental of residential buildings containing not more than six dwelling units are insured only if the properties or operations are stated in the Declarations.

Loss or Damage Not Insured

You are *not insured* against claims for bodily injury to or damage to the property of others, arising from the following:

1. War, invasion, act of a foreign enemy, hostilities, civil war, rebellion, revolution, insurrection or military power.

2. Caused directly or indirectly, in whole or in part, by terrorism or by any activity or decision of a government agency or other entity to prevent, respond to, or terminate terrorism except for ensuing loss or damage that results directly from fire or explosion, as described in specified perils. Such loss or damage is excluded regardless of any other cause or event that contributes concurrently or in any sequence to the loss or damage.

3. Bodily injury or property damage caused directly or indirectly by:
   (a) any nuclear incident as defined in the Nuclear Liability Act or any other nuclear liability act, law or statute, or any law amendatory thereof or nuclear explosion, except for ensuing loss or damage that results directly from fire, lightning, or explosion of coal, natural or manufactured gas; or
   (b) contamination by radioactive material.

4. Your business or any business use of your premises except as specified in this policy;

5. The rendering or failure to render any professional service;

6. Caused intentionally by you, at your direction, or by or through any criminal act or failure to act by
   (a) any person insured by this policy; or
   (b) any other person at the direction of any person insured by this policy.

7. The ownership, use or operation of any aircraft or premises used as an airport or landing strip, and all necessary or incidental operations.

8. The ownership, use or operation of any motorized vehicle, trailer, or watercraft except those for which coverage is provided in this form.

9. The transmission of communicable disease by any person insured by this policy.

10. Abuse or molestation, meaning any form of actual or threatened sexual, physical, psychological, mental and/or emotional abuse, molestation, or harassment, including corporal punishment, directly or indirectly
    (a) by any person or named insured who is insured by this policy;
    (b) by any person or named insured who is insured by this policy having knowledge of such an activity taking place;

      (c) by any person or named insured who is insured by this policy failing to prevent such activity from taking place;

      (d) by at the direction of any person or any named insured who is insured by this policy.

11.   (a) "Bodily injury" or "property damage" arising out of the actual, alleged, or threatened discharge, dispersal, release or escape of pollutants

          i. at or from premises owned, rented, or occupied by an insured;

          ii. at or from any site or location used by or for an insured or others for the handling, storage, disposal, processing, or treatment of waste;

          iii. which are at any time transported, handled, stored, treated, disposed of, or processed as waste by or for an insured or for any person or organization for whom the insured may be legally responsible; or

          iv. at or from any site or location on which an insured or any contractors or subcontractors working directly or indirectly on behalf of an Insured are performing operations

              (1) if the pollutants are brought on or to the site or location in connection with such operations; or

              (2) if the operations are to test for, monitor, clean up, remove, contain, treat, detoxify, or neutralize the pollutants.

    (b) Any loss, cost, or expense arising out of any governmental direction or request that an insured test for, monitor, clean up, remove, contain, treat, detoxify, or neutralize pollutants.

Pollutants mean any solid, liquid, gaseous, or thermal irritant or contaminant including smoke, vapour, soot, fumes, acids, alkalis, chemicals, and waste. Waste includes materials to be recycled, reconditioned, or reclaimed.

Sub-paragraphs (I) and (iv.)(1) of paragraph (a) of this exclusion do *not apply* to "bodily injury" or "property damage" caused by heat, smoke, or fumes from a hostile fire. As used in this exclusion, a "hostile fire" means one that becomes uncontrollable or breaks out from where it was intended to be.

12. Any type of discrimination, including discrimination due to sex, age, or marital status, colour, race, creed, or national origin.

13. Punitive or exemplary damages, meaning that part of any award by a court that is in excess of compensatory damages and is stated or intended to be a punishment to you.

Section III — Conditions
General Policy Conditions

The following conditions apply to all sections of this policy including any riders or endorsements.

Notice of Accident or Occurrence

When an accident or occurrence takes place, you must promptly give us notice (in writing if required). The notice must include

1. your name and policy number;
2. the time, place, and circumstances of the accident;
3. the names and addresses of witnesses and potential claimants.

Co-operation

You are required to

1. help us obtain witnesses, information, and evidence about the accident and co-operate with us in any legal actions if we ask you;
2. immediately send us everything received in writing concerning the claim, including legal documents.

Unauthorized Settlements — Coverage E

You shall not, except at your cost, voluntarily make any payment, assume any obligations, or incur expenses, other than first aid expenses necessary at the time of accident.

Action Against Us — Coverage E

You shall not bring suit against us until you have fully complied with all the terms of this policy, nor until the amount of your obligation to pay has been finally determined, either by judgment against you or by an agreement that has our consent.

Action Against Us — Coverages F and G

You shall not bring suit against us until you have fully complied with all the terms of this policy, nor until 60 days after the required Proof of Loss Form has been filed with us.

Insurance Under More than One Policy

If you have other insurance that applies to a loss or claim, or would have applied if this policy did not exist, this policy will be considered excess insurance and we will *not pay* any loss or claim until the amount of such other insurance is used up.

Waiver

We shall not be deemed to have waived any term or condition of this policy in whole or in part, unless our waiver is clearly stated and in writing, and is signed by a person authorized to do so. In addition, neither we nor you may be lawfully considered to have waived any term or condition of this policy by any act relating to the appraisal of the amount of a claim, the delivery or completion of proof, or the investigation of or adjustment of any claim under the policy.

Examination Under Oath

In the event of a loss, each of you is required, after submission of the Proof of Loss, to submit to examination under oath and produce for examination all documents in your possession or control that relate to the application for insurance and

Proof of Loss and you shall permit extracts and copies thereof to be made, all at such reasonable place and time as is designated by the insurer or its representative.

Conditions Required by Law

With respect to Section II — Liability Coverage, including Voluntary Compensation for Residence Employees Endorsement when added, Statutory Conditions 1, 3, 4, 5, and 15 only apply. Otherwise, all of the conditions set forth under the titles Statutory Conditions and Additional Conditions apply with respect to all of the perils insured by this policy except as these conditions may be modified or supplemented by the forms and endorsements included herein or attached.

Statutory Conditions *(Applicable in Common Law Jurisdictions)*

The "Statutory Conditions" set out in this policy are renamed "Policy Conditions" and now apply, as modified or supplemented in forms or endorsements attached to this policy, as "Policy Conditions" to all coverages and all perils (including fire) insured by this policy.

Misrepresentation

If a person applying for insurance falsely describes the property to the prejudice of the insurer, or misrepresents or fraudulently omits to communicate any circumstance that is material to be made known to the insurer in order to enable it to judge of the risk to be undertaken, the contract is void as to any property in relation to which the misrepresentation or omission is material.

Property of Others

Unless otherwise specifically stated in the contract, the insurer is not liable for loss or damage to property owned by any person other than the insured, unless the interest of the Insured therein is stated in the contract.

Change of Interest

The insurer is liable for loss or damage occurring after an authorized assignment under the *Bankruptcy Act* (Canada) or change of title by succession, by operation of law, or by death.

Material Change

Any change material to the risk and within the control and knowledge of the insured avoids the contract as to the part affected thereby, unless the change is promptly notified in writing to the Insurer or its local agent, and the insurer when so notified may return the unearned portion, if any, of the premium paid and cancel the contract, or may notify the insured in writing that, if the Insured desires the contract to continue in force, the insured must, within 15 days of the receipt of the notice, pay to the insurer an additional premium, and in default of such a payment the contract is no longer in force and the insurer shall return the unearned portion, if any, of the premium paid.

Termination

(1) This contract may be terminated

    (a) by the insurer giving to the insured 15 days' notice of termination by registered mail or five days' written notice of termination personally delivered;

    (b) by the insured at any time on request.

(2) Where this contract is terminated by the Insurer,

    (a) the insurer shall refund the excess of premium actually paid by the insured over the proportionate premium for the expired time, but in no event shall the proportionate premium for the expired time be deemed to be less than any minimum retained premium specified; and

    (b) the refund shall accompany the notice unless the premium is subject to adjustment or determination as to amount, in which case the refund shall be made as soon as practicable.

(3) Where this contract is terminated by the insured, the insurer shall refund as soon as practicable the excess of the premium actually paid by the insured over the short rate premium for the expired time, but in no event shall the short rate premium for the expired time be deemed to be less than any minimum retained premium specified.

(4) The refund may be made by money, postal or express company money order, or cheque payable at par.

(5) The 15 days mentioned in clause 1(a) of this condition commences to run on the day following the receipt of the registered letter at the post office to which it is addressed.

Requirements After Loss

(2) Upon the occurrence of any loss of or damage to the insured property, the insured shall, if the loss or damage is covered by the contract, in addition to observing the requirements of conditions 9, 10, and 11,

    (a) forthwith give notice thereof in writing to the insurer;

    (b) deliver as soon as practicable to the insurer a proof of loss verified by a statutory declaration

        i. giving a complete inventory of the destroyed and damaged property and showing in detail quantities, cost, actual cash value and particulars of amount of loss claimed,

        ii. stating when the loss occurred, and if caused by fire or explosion due to ignition, how the fire or explosion originated, so far as the Insured knows or believes,

        iii. stating that the loss did not occur through any wilful act or neglect or the procurement, means or connivance of the insured,

        iv. showing the amount of other insurances and the names of other insurers,

        v. showing the interest of the insured and of all others in the property with particulars of all liens, encumbrances and other charges upon the property,

        vi. showing any changes in title, use, occupation, location, possession or exposures of the property since the issue of the contract,

        vii. showing the place where the property insured was at the time of loss.

(c) if required, give a complete inventory of undamaged property and show-ing in detail quantities, cost, actual cash value;

(d) if required and if practicable, produce books of account, warehouse re-ceipts and stock lists, and furnish invoices and other vouchers verified by statutory declaration, and furnish a copy of the written portion of any other contract.

(3) The evidence furnished under clauses (c) and (d) of subparagraph (2) of the condition shall not be considered proofs of loss within the meaning of condi-tions 9 and 10.

Fraud

4. Any fraud or wilfully false statement in a statutory declaration in relation to any of the above particulars vitiates the claim of the person making the declaration.

Who May Give Notice and Proof

5. Notice of loss may be given and proof of loss may be made by the agent of the insured named in the contract in case of absence or inability of the in-sured to give the notice or make the proof, and absence or inability being satisfactorily accounted for, or in the like case, or if the insured refuses to do so, by a person to whom any part of the insurance money is payable.

Salvage

6. (a) The insured, in the event of any loss or damage to any property insured under the contract, shall take all reasonable steps to prevent further damage to such property so damaged and to prevent damage to other property insured hereunder including, if necessary, its removal to pre-vent damage or further damage thereto.

(b) The insurer shall contribute pro rata towards any reasonable and proper expenses in connection with steps taken by the insured and required un-der sub-condition (a) of this condition according to the respective inter-ests of the parties.

Entry, Control, Abandonment

7. After loss or damage to insured property, the insurer has an immediate right of access and entry by accredited agents sufficient to enable them to survey and examine the property, and to make an estimate of the loss or damage, and, after the insured has secured the property, a further right of access and entry sufficient to enable them to make appraisement or particular estimate of the loss or damage, but the Insurer is not entitled to the control or pos-session of the insured property, and without the consent of the insurer there can be no abandonment to it of insured property.

Appraisal

8. In the event of disagreement as to the value of the property insured, the property saved or the amount of the loss, those questions shall be determined

151

by appraisal as provided under The Insurance Act before there can be any recovery under this contract whether the right to recover on the contract is disputed or not, and independently of all other questions. There shall be no right to an appraisal until a specific demand therefore is made in writing and until after proof of loss has been delivered.

When Loss Payable

9. The loss is payable within 60 days after completion of the proof of loss, unless the contract provides for a shorter period.

Replacement

10. (a) The Insurer, instead of making payment, may repair, rebuild, or replace the property damaged or lost, giving written notice of its intention so to do within 30 days after receipt of the proofs of loss.

    (b) In that event the Insurer shall commence to so repair, rebuild, or replace the property within 45 days after receipt of the proofs of loss, and shall thereafter proceed with all due diligence to the completion thereof.

Action

11. Where permitted by law, every action or proceeding against the insurer for the recovery of a claim, under or by virtue of this contract, shall be absolutely barred unless commenced within one year* next after the loss or damage occurs, except in the provinces of British Columbia and Ontario.

    • In the province of British Columbia, the period of one year next shall commence from the furnishing of a reasonably sufficient proof of loss.

    • In the province of Ontario, the action shall be commenced within the time period prescribed by s. 4 of the Limitations Act 2002, S.O. 2002, Chapter 24, Schedule B.

    *Two years in the Yukon Territory and in the province of Manitoba.

Notice

12. Any written notice to the insurer may be delivered at, or sent by registered mail to, the chief agency or head office of the insurer in the province. Written notice may be given to the insured named in the contract by letter personally delivered to him or by registered mail addressed to him at his latest post office address as notified to the insurer. In this condition, the expression "registered" means registered in or outside Canada.

Comparison of "All-Risks" Coverage with "Named Perils"

The preceding policy is a comprehensive policy. Insured Perils in Section I states "You are insured against all risks of direct physical loss or damage subject to the exclusions and conditions of this policy". What perils would be covered by "named perils" coverage? We will use the list of "specified perils" from the comprehensive policy to compare coverage. This list of specified perils is used in the comprehensive policy to enumerate the exclusions, which are the same for all three policies.

	Building	Contents
Comprehensive	All risks	All risks
Broad	All risks	Named perils
Basic	Named perils	Named perils

Basic Policy	**Specified Perils from Comprehensive** *(used for exclusions*)*
You are insured against direct loss or damage caused by the following perils:	
1. Fire.	1. Fire.
2. Lightning.	2. Lightning.
3. Explosion of coal, natural or manufactured gas. *This peril does not include water hammer (prolonged vibration).*	3. Explosion of coal, natural or manufactured gas.
4. Smoke due to a sudden, unusual and faulty operation of any heating or cooking unit in or on the premises *but not smoke from fireplaces*;	4. Smoke due to a sudden, unusual, and faulty operation *of a fireplace*, or of any heating or cooking unit in or on the premises.
5. Falling objects which strikes the exterior of the building.	5. Falling object that strikes the exterior of the building.
6. Impact by aircraft or land vehicle. *This peril does not include any impact by a vehicle owned or operated by you or your employee.*	6. Impact by aircraft or land vehicle.
7. Riot.	7. Riot.
8. Vandalism or malicious acts, *not including* loss or damage caused by theft or attempted theft. *This peril does not include damage caused by you.*	8. Vandalism or malicious acts, *not including* loss or damage caused by theft or attempted theft.
9. Water damage ... same for both.	9. Water damage ... same for both.
10. Windstorm or hail: *Your personal property inside a building is covered only if the storm first creates an opening in the building and damage results coincidentally with the windstorm or hail. This peril does not cover:* (a) loss or damage due to waves, flood, waterborne objects or the weight or pressure or melting of ice or snow, whether driven by wind or not; (b) outdoor radio and/or T.V. antennae and satellite receivers.	10. Windstorm or hail including loss or damage caused by weight of ice, snow, or sleet.
11. Transportation ... same for both.	11. Transportation ... same for both.
The following are some of the additional perils that might be added to the named perils.	
12. *Glass breakage. Glass that forms part of your dwelling or private structures on your premises, including glass in storm windows and doors, is insured against accidental breakage.*	
13. *Theft including damage caused by theft or attempted theft: If "Theft Included" is stated on the Coverage Summary page, we insure theft including damage caused by theft or attempted theft.*	* This list of specified perils from the Definitions at the beginning of Section I in the comprehensive policy is used in the policy only to describe exceptions — See:
14. *Escape of fuel oil.*	• Loss or Damage *Not Insured*,
15. *Collapse including weight of ice, snow, and sleet.*	• Section I, page 127, and
16. *Electricity.*	• Section II, page 146.

Other Types of Home Insurance Coverage

Condominium Insurance

The condominium association has a master policy that covers the overall building and any common areas, such as lobbies, halls, and elevators as well as the bare walls in each unit.

Condo owners need to have homeowners insurance to cover upgrades (broadloom, kitchens, bathrooms, etc.), personal property (clothes, books, dishes, furniture, entertainment centres, etc.), liability insurance as outlined in Section II and additional living expenses should they have to move out while the unit is being rebuilt. It shouldn't be necessary to have insurance that supplements that of the condo association but it is available if the owners believe (and can support their belief) that the association is underinsured.

Mobile Homes

Mobile homes can be insured for named perils only. Replacement cost coverage is usually available for the contents but not for the mobile home itself. While it is attached to your car, it is covered under your auto policy whether it is being towed or just sitting in your driveway. Some mobile homes are installed on foundations and hooked up to water and sewage systems and may, as a result, qualify for conventional home insurance.

Mortgage Insurance

Mortgage insurance refers to two types of insurance: mortgage life insurance and mortgage default insurance.

1. Mortgage Life Insurance

This pays the outstanding mortgage in the event the mortgagor (the person who has borrowed the funds) dies. This type of insurance is also available to cover the mortgagor if he or she is unable to make mortgage payments due to an accident or illness. A quick quote from the Bank of Montreal website calculates the cost for a $200,000 mortgage with monthly payments of $1,079.32 and a 25–year amortization for a couple 30–35 years old at $38 a month ($456 a year) for the life insurance and $20.18 each a month ($484 year for both) for the accident and illness insurance for a total annual cost of $940.

This is a form of **reducing term life insurance** and is also a form of **group insurance** (both of these will be discussed further in the life and health insurance section). It is usually not transportable (from one mortgage to another meaning if you need this coverage later because you have bought a new home, the premium will be higher because you are older). Group insurance is usually cheaper than individual coverage. Since it is group insurance, acceptance is usually automatic and a medical examination may not be required. This coverage is usually available through the lender and the premiums can be added to your mortgage payments. The face value is paid to the mortgagee (the lender) if the mortgagor dies.

Instead of this type of insurance, you could just have sufficient term life insurance payable to a beneficiary. Having an individual term policy may be more expensive than having a group policy through the lender but as you pay down the principal, there is less and less mortgage liability to cover. With mortgage insurance, if you should die after making 208 or 69% of the 300 payments and the mortgage is now down to $95,000, the lender gets $200,000 and the survivor gets nothing. With a term policy, the beneficiary gets the $200,000, pays the outstanding mortgage of $95,000, and keeps $105,000.

2. Mortgage Default Insurance

Under the *Bank Act*, every mortgage from a bank or other federally regulated institution with a down payment of less than 20% must carry mortgage insurance. The purpose is to provide protection to lenders for people who can make regular mortgage payments but are not able to save a 20% down payment.

There are two sources of mortgage default insurance in Canada: **Canada Mortgage and Housing Corporation (CMHC)** [www.cmhc-schl.gc.ca], a federal Crown corporation, and **private American-based mortgage insurance companies,** of which only two remain — Genworth Financial Mortgage Insurance Company Canada, a subsidiary of GE Mortgage Insurance of Canada and AIG United Guaranty Mortgage Insurance Company Canada, an affiliate of United Guaranty Corporation. The federal government guarantees 100% of CMHC's mortgages and 90% of other insurance policies. As a result, lenders prefer CMHC, which has about 70% of the market share. Genworth has a significant portion of the other 30% because it took over the mortgage insurance portfolio of MICC (Mortgage Insurance Corporation of Canada), a private mortgage insurer, after MICC encountered financial difficulties in 1995.

As of October 15, 2008, CMHC requires that the buyer have a down payment of at least 5% and the amortization period cannot be longer than 35 years. Mortgages with no down payment and 40-year amortizations helped fuel the recent housing bubble where people were able to buy housing that they would otherwise have not been able to afford. The first 40-year amortizations were introduced in Canada in October 2006 by Genworth, and CMHC soon followed. Mortgages having down payments less than 5% with 40-year amortization periods are called **sub-prime.**

In 2007, CMHC earned premiums of $1.4 billion and its net claims were 22% of this (17% in 2006, 10% in 2005, 4% in 2004, 20% in 2003 and 17% in 2002). CMHC uses some of the excess to invest in housing projects with and without the provinces, territories, and the federal government and these investments generate a surplus in some years and a deficit in others.

CMHC insured mortgages can be used to

- rewrite an existing mortgage or to consolidate debts up to 90% of the market value,
- buy a home for up to 95% of the purchase price,
- construct a home up to 95% of the cost (with very specific guidelines),
- purchase a spouse's share in the event of a marriage breakup up to 90% of the value, and
- pay off existing mortgages and provide funds for improvements.

Cost of CMHC Mortgage Loan Insurance

The CMHC premium is calculated as a percentage of the loan and is based on the size of your down payment. Typically, it is added to the amount of the mortgage. The following rates are increased if the borrower chooses a portability and refinance option. There is also a premium refund for energy-efficient homes.

Loan-to-Value	Premium on Total Loan	
	Standard Premium	Self-Employed without 3rd Party Income Validation
Up to and including 65%	0.50%	0.80%
Up to and including 75%	0.65%	1.00%
Up to and including 80%	1.00%	1.64%
Up to and including 85%	1.75%	2.90%
Up to and including 90%	2.00%	4.75%
Up to and including 95%	2.75%	6.00%
90.01% to 95% — Non-Traditional Down Payment	2.90%	n/a

Extended Amortization Surcharges
- Greater than 25 years, up to and including 30 years: 0.20%
- Greater than 30 years, up to and including 35 years: 0.40%

Premiums in Ontario and Quebec are subject to provincial sales tax, which cannot be added to the loan amount.

Let's compare the total cost of borrowing for a $250,000 home. The base payment is a 20% down payment with a 25-year amortization. We will also assume the mortgage rate is the same for all options. In addition, for the sake of comparison, let's include a 0% down, 40-year amortization at the highest CMHC rate but without any premium for portability and refinancing even though this option is no longer available. The mortgage interest rate is 4.25%, compounded semi-annually or 0.35107% a month.

Down		Mortgage	CMHC rate	Total amount mortgaged	Amortization		Payment	Total		Increase over lowest
%	$				Years	Months		Payments	Interest	
20.00%	50,000	200,000		200,000	25	300	1,079.32	323,796	123,796	0
19.50%	48,750	201,250	1.00%	203,263	25	300	1,096.93	329,078	127,828	4,032
14.50%	36,250	213,750	1.95%	217,918	30	360	1,067.29	384,225	170,475	46,679
9.50%	23,750	226,250	2.40%	231,680	35	420	1,055.61	443,355	217,105	93,309
4.50%	11,250	238,750	3.15%	246,271	35	420	1,122.09	471,277	232,527	108,731
0.00%	0	250,000	3.30%	258,250	40	480	1,113.76	534,606	284,606	160,810

A longer amortization usually lowers the monthly cost but when the CMHC insurance premium is added to the mortgage, the cost sometimes increases (and we haven't used the highest possible CMHC premium). The other problem with starting with a 5% down, 35-year amortization is that, should you lose your job or suffer some other financial setback, there is nowhere to go as you are already at the maximum possible amortization.

Other Financial Assistance Available through CMHC

- **Homeowner Residential Rehabilitation Assistance Program (Homeowner RRAP)** is available to low-income homeowners for mandatory home repairs that will preserve the quality of affordable housing.
- **Residential Rehabilitation Assistance Program (RRAP) for Persons with Disabilities** provides financial assistance to allow homeowners and landlords to pay for modifications to make their property more accessible to people with disabilities.
- **Home Adaptations for Seniors' Independence (HASI)** helps finance minor home adaptations that help low-income seniors perform daily activities in their home independently and safely.
- Emergency Repair Program (ERP) provides financial assistance to low-income households in rural areas to make emergency repairs needed for the continued safe occupancy of their home.

CHMC also has a **Renovation Programs Pre-Application Tool** that provides information specific to geographic areas about eligibility for financial assistance through their renovation programs for low-income households.

Tenants Insurance

People who rent do not have to insure the building they live in but they are responsible for the following:

- Any damage they or their guests cause to the building, for example causing a fire in the kitchen which might result in a little fire damage and a lot of smoke damage to other apartments.
- Unintentional harm to visitors or damage or loss of the personal property of visitors.
- Loss or damage to their own personal property.
- Additional living expenses, such as hotel and meals, if you have to move out while your apartment is being repaired.

None of these losses or damage is covered by a landlord's policy. Tenants may have made improvements to the property, such as installing broadloom or building in cabinets. These also should be insured by the tenant as they may not be covered by the landlord's policy.

Title Insurance

Title insurance is relatively new to Canada, arriving when American title insurers saw an untapped market. Title insurance protects the owner of the property or the lender of money against any unknown defects (defects to a clear title) in the title to the property. In the United State, this insurance is mandatory in all states except Iowa, where it is banned because Iowa and many countries such as Canada, England, Australia, and New Zealand, use the Torrens System, whereby each parcel of land is given a unique number called a folio and a court or bureau of registration is in charge of maintaining the registry for each parcel. The U.S. has had inadequate deed registry systems with many privately held mortgages that were not always registered. Their system is dependent on tracking ownership, which can sometimes be difficult.

In Canada, when a survey is done (and a survey is neither mandatory nor automatic), the surveyor can contact the municipality to confirm that the property conforms to zoning and building by-laws to ensure, for instance, that the basement or third floor apartment is legal and built to code. The survey itself will reveal the existence of easements (the existence of a neighbour's sewer pipe running under your property for example), rights-of-way (to, for instance, reach a garage which is otherwise inaccessible), or encroachments (for instance, your neighbour's garage crosses onto your property line).

Title insurance tends to cover work order, zoning, and setback non-compliance, lack of pedestrian or vehicular access to the property, survey irregularities, forced removal of existing structures (that were, perhaps, constructed without a building permit and are not up to code), claims due to forgery or duress, and unregistered easements and rights-of-way. Typically, they exclude native land claims and environmental hazards (buy a former marijuana-grow operation and you're on your own). Title insurance can also protect you from fraud arising from false identities, forged documents, and the artificial inflation of property values if this might be a problem.

Policies are available for new and existing homeowners as well as for lenders in a residential mortgage. This also protects the bank and/or consumers against mistakes made in a title search. Generally, the two lawyers involved (for the buyer and the seller) will ensure that any outstanding claims will be cleaned up before closing.

Title insurance is most useful if you are buying a second home in another country, such as the U.S. or Mexico. In addition, home inspections may not find defects buried under floors or behind drywall. While the home inspectors would likely refund your fee, you could still be left with very costly repairs. In Canada, title insurance costs about $250 for a home valued up to $500,000 while in the U.S., it costs 0.5% — 1% of the mortgage amount — $1,000 to $2,000 for a $200,000 mortgage.

Mortgage Fraud

Mortgage fraud occurs most often, but not always, when the legal owner is absent from the house, either living at the cottage or in another country for several months of the year, or the home is rented out and the tenants perpetrate the fraud. The reason is that an innocent buyer would not buy a property from a fraudulent owner if the buyer could not see the house before buying it. The fraudulent seller has typically forged the deed to the property and registered the property in his or her own name. The fraudulent seller can also forge a discharge of an existing mortgage to borrow against a now-clear title. Unfortunately, it is up to the innocent owner to prove that a crime was committed.

The **Land Titles Act Fund** in each province will compensate the innocent owner after he or she proves there was fraud. However, *compensated* does not mean the owner will necessarily recover the property. This fund will compensate either the innocent owner or the financial institution but the innocent owner *cannot assume* that the courts will

• decide that the lender's mortgage is not valid, or
• "stay" (postpone) a foreclosure notice against the property.

The courts can, but do not have to, decide that the lender's mortgage is valid but that it must apply to the Fund for compensation. In this instance, the courts might also decide that the innocent owner must be the one to apply to the fund for compensation. Furthermore, the Land Titles Assurance Fund (as it is called in Ontario) is a fund of last resort, and the innocent owner or lender must pursue all other remedies before being entitled to compensation, which can be both time-consuming and expensive.

Mortgage insurance can cover this risk for a one-time premium of about $250 for a home valued at $500,000 or less. An additional one-time premium can also protect a homeowner from identity theft. Mortgage fraud is relatively rare and penalties against the fraudulent seller are getting stronger — if the person committing the fraud can be found. In addition, the fund compensates only financial losses, not lost time. From 2004 to 2007, a title insurer in B.C. turned down more than $8 million in business because it suspected fraud. For the first half of 2008, it had refused $3.5 million.

It is interesting that, in a case of credit card fraud, banks will allow a person to suspend payments until an investigation has taken place, but no such thing happens with mortgage fraud. Those of us who are not legal experts find it difficult to understand how

- a financial institution's mortgage can be deemed valid when it was based on fraudulent documents, and
- innocent owners can be left having to spend time and money to prove that they are the true owners of their home.

Identity Theft/Fraud

The **Office of the Privacy Commissioner of Canada (OPCC)** defines identity theft as the unauthorized collection and use of your personal information, usually for criminal purposes. Your name, date of birth, address, credit card, Social Insurance Number (SIN), and other personal identification numbers can be used to open credit card and bank accounts; redirect mail; establish cell phone service; rent vehicles, equipment, or accommodation; and even secure employment. If this happens, you could be left with the bills, charges, bad cheques, and taxes.

The **Financial Consumer Agency of Canada (FCAC)** states that "Identity fraud (or identity theft) occurs when your personal information is collected and used by someone identifying him/herself as you and making transactions or requests on your account(s). These transactions could include taking over your credit accounts, opening up new ones or accessing your bank accounts."

How to Avoid Identity Theft / Fraud

These two organizations advise the following:

Office of the Privacy Commissioner of Canada	Financial Consumer Agency of Canada
Sharing Personal Information • Minimize the risk. Be careful about sharing personal information or letting it circulate freely. • When you are asked to provide personal information, ask how it will be used, why it is needed, who will be sharing it, and how it will be safeguarded. • Give out no more than the minimum, and carry the least possible with you. • Be particularly careful about your SIN; it is an important key to your identity, especially in credit reports and computer databases. • Don't give your credit card number on the telephone, by electronic mail, or to a voice mailbox, unless you know the person with whom you're communicating or you initiated the communication yourself, and you know that the communication channel is secure.	• Be careful about sharing personal information and don't give out more than you need to. Only share your personal information with companies you know and trust. • Put other ID documents (SIN, birth certificate, passport) in a safe place. • Do not give out any personal information or a credit card number over the phone on unsolicited calls, even if the caller claims to be from a legitimate company. • In the same way, do not give out this information by e-mail as it is not a secure method of transmission.
The Internet • Take advantage of technologies that enhance your security and privacy when you use the Internet, such as digital signatures, data encryption, and "anonymizing" services.	• When on the Internet, make sure the website you are using is secure before transmitting personal information. • Ensure that your computer firewalls/spyware are up to date to protect personal information that might be stored.

Continued

Office of the Privacy Commissioner of Canada	Financial Consumer Agency of Canada
Credit Cards • Pay attention to your billing cycle. If credit card or utility bills fail to arrive, contact the companies to ensure that they have not been illicitly redirected. • Notify creditors immediately if your identification or credit cards are lost or stolen. • Access your credit report from a credit reporting agency once a year to ensure it's accurate and doesn't include debts or activities you haven't authorized or incurred.	• Carry a minimum number of credit cards and personal identification information with you. • When making a purchase, keep your card in sight, and make sure that the card returned to you is yours.
Banking and Other Information • Ask that your accounts require passwords before any inquiries or changes can be made, whenever possible. • Choose difficult passwords — not your mother's maiden name. Memorize them, change them often. Don't write them down and leave them in your wallet, or some equally obvious place. • Key in personal identification numbers privately when you use direct purchase terminals, bank machines, or telephones. • Find out if your cardholder agreement offers protection from credit card fraud; you may be able to avoid taking on the identity thief's debts. • Be careful what you throw out. Burn or shred personal financial information such as statements, credit card offers, receipts, insurance forms, etc. Insist that businesses you deal with do the same.	• When you receive a renewal or replacement for a document or certificate that contains identity information (such as your driver's licence or vehicle registration), make sure you destroy — preferably by shredding — the old one. • Shred documents with personal information (including your name and address). • Keep your wallet or purse out of reach — in public places, crowds, and while on public transportation. • Don't leave personal information lying around at home, in your vehicle, or at the office. • Lock your household mailbox if possible. If you are going to be away, arrange for a trusted neighbour to pick up your mail. You can also go to your local post office (with identification) and ask for Canada Post's hold mail service. There will be a charge for this service.

If You Have Been a Victim of Identity Theft

Office of the Privacy Commissioner of Canada	Financial Consumer Agency of Canada
• Take steps to undo the damage. Avoid "credit-repair" companies: there is usually nothing they can do, and some have been known to propose a solution — establishing credit under a new identity — that is itself fraudulent. • Document the steps you take and the expenses you incur to clear your name and re-establish your credit. • Cancel your credit cards and get new ones issued. Ask the creditors about accounts tampered with or opened fraudulently in your name. • Have your credit report annotated to reflect the identity theft. Do a follow-up check three months after to ensure that someone has not tried to use your identity again. • Close your bank accounts and open new ones. Insist on password-only access to them. • Get new bank machine and telephone calling cards, with new passwords or personal identification numbers. • In the case of passport theft, advise the Passport Office. • Contact Canada Post if you suspect that someone is diverting your mail. • Advise your telephone, cable, and utilities that someone using your name could try to open new accounts fraudulently. • Get a new driver's licence.	• Report it to your local police or to Phonebusters, a national anti-fraud call centre jointly operated by the Ontario Provincial Police and the Royal Canadian Mounted Police (toll-free phone is 1-888-495-8501; e-mail is info@phonebusters.com). • Contact your financial institution immediately. • Keep notes and all documentation, as this information may be required to assist with any investigation.

Contact Information

Office of the Privacy Commissioner of Canada	Financial Consumer Agency of Canada
• **Service Canada** if you suspect that your SIN has been compromised in some other way at Service Canada, Social Insurance Registration Office, P.O. Box 7000, Bathurst, New Brunswickt E2A 4T1. • Office of the Privacy Commissioner of Canada for information on your privacy rights, toll-free at 1-800-282-1376, or write The Office of the Privacy Commissioner, 112 Kent Street, Ottawa, ON K1A 1H3, www.privcom.gc.ca	• Financial Consumer Agency of Canada (FCAC) for information on your rights with regard to financial institutions at 1-866-461-3222 toll-free (TTY number is 613-947-7771, toll-free 1-866-914-6097) or by visiting their website at www.fcac.gc.ca. • Also check your bank's website.

On March 23, 2009, Justice Minister Rob Nicholson re-introduced legislation to clamp down on identity theft. The three new offences, subject to five-year maximum prison sentences, and are as follows:

• Obtaining and possessing information about someone's identity with the intent of using the information deceptively, dishonestly or fraudulently to commit a crime.
• Trafficking in identity information, that is, transferring or selling information knowing or not caring that its use might be criminal.
• Possessing or trafficking in illegal government-issued identity documents that contain information of another person.

The actual fraudulent or deceptive use of other people's identities is already part of the Criminal Code. Additional amendments would create new offences for the following:

• Fraudulently redirecting or causing a person's mail to be redirected.
• Having a counterfeit Canada Post mail key.
• Having tools for obtaining and copying debit and credit card information.

Costs of Buying a House

The CMHC website outlines the following up-front costs of buying a home:

• Mortgage loan insurance for high-ratio loans
• Appraisal fee might be require by the lending institution
• Deposit — usually 5% of the purchase price
• Down payment
• Inspection fee — perhaps $200 or more
• Land transfer tax
• Prepaid property taxes and utility bills
• Property insurance
• Survey
• Water quality inspection for wells
• Legal fees and disbursements — not less than $500, likely more
• Title insurance

And once you move in?

• Appliances if they don't come with the house
• Gardening and snow-clearing equipment
• Curtains, drapes, paint, flooring, etc.
• Hand tools
• Dehumidifier to control excess moisture (take a close look at the exclusions in the homeowners policy)

- Moving expenses
- Renovations and repairs
- Costs for utilities hookups.

Summary

Home insurance is designed to protect the homeowner from various perils — the depth of coverage depends on the policy chosen. However, no homeowners policy protects from all perils — even in the best comprehensive policy, some perils are excluded. Special provisions are possible for exceptional items that may not be adequately covered by standard coverage. Your home and its contents are covered for loss and/or damage both in the home and off-premises. In addition, your home is covered for loss or damage to others who visit your home for whatever reason. Your policy also covers some losses to other people's property due to your negligence.

There are many other types of home insurance available, including protection from mortgage fraud and identity theft. The Canada Mortgage and Housing Corporation provides protection to lenders in cases where the buyer has less than a 20% down payment but is considered credit-worthy enough to be able to make the mortgage payments.

Sources

Canada Housing and Mortgage Corporation (CMHC) [www.cmhc-schl.gc.ca]
Financial Consumer Agency of Canada (FCAC), Tips to Prevent Identity Fraud, [www.fcac.gc.ca]
Homeowners Comprehensive Policy, Pilot Insurance, 2005
Office of the Privacy Commissioner of Canada (OPCC), Identity Theft: What Is It and What You Can Do About It. [www.privcom.gc.ca]
Real Estate Title Fraud — Is Title Insurance the Answer? Bruce McKenna, Lang Michener LLP [www.langmichener.ca]

Application Case

Joanne didn't see this one coming! Yesterday could have been Friday the 13th except that it was Wednesday. Her cleaning lady fell while dusting the fan on her 11-foot ceiling. What is this going to cost? And who is going to clean while she is laid up? An elitist problem, perhaps, but a real one nonetheless. Then, to top it off, a courier slipped on the steps she didn't have time to shovel after the big snowfall Tuesday night. Is this covered? Did a condominium ever look so good?

Francesca rushes to make a latte — espresso, yes, but with milk to calm down Joanne. Then Francesca takes the lead.

A. "First of all, there are **three levels of coverage**. You have the best — comprehensive. The three types are:
   1. Basic,
   2. Broad, and
   3. Comprehensive" (Page 114).

B. "Your policy will cover you for both
   1. direct losses, and
   2. indirect losses" (Page 114).

C. "Home insurance policies adhere to the **four principles of insurance** (Page 115):
   1. Indemnity
   2. Insurable interest
   3. Subrogation
   4. Reasonable expectations

D. "I remember advising you to make sure your home was fully insured so you wouldn't run into problems with the **coinsurance requirement** down the road. Your insurer probably increases your coverage automatically each year to cover inflation and this means you don't have to remember to call them up to cover this off each year" (Page 115).

E. "I also remember advising you to buy the best and most expensive coverage in terms of what you can collect so you are not out of pocket for a lot of money if you have a large loss. The two types are
   1. guaranteed replacement cost, and
   2. actual cash value (Page 116).

F. Joanne is beginning to relax so Francesca asks her if she has any questions. "Yes," says Joanne, "what **determines my premium**? I have talked to some friends and their premiums are very much higher or lower than mine". Francesca tells her the factors (Page 118).

G. Francesca reminds her that she had a lot of problems getting insurance because her house is 120 years old in an old, downtown neighbourhood. This is a form of **redlining** that is legal while discriminating against homeowners based on their income or race is not. (Page 118)

H. "Yes, I remember," says Joanne. "I also remember getting **extra coverage on my contents** because when I costed my contents, using the standard 60% of the cost of rebuilding the house, I seemed to be underinsured. You know I really have a lot of books and, of course, the grand piano. Too bad I have so little time to read the books and play the piano. I got an **endorsement** for the antique harpsichord my grandfather left me" (Pages 118–119).

I. Seeing that Joanne has visibly relaxed, Francesca suggests they take a look at the policy itself. "Each year with your annual invoice, your agent or broker will send you the **Declarations Page** that outlines details about your coverage that are unique to your policy. They do not generally send the actual policy itself each year" (Page 120).

The Homeowners Comprehensive Policy

J. "Now let's have a look at Section I which outlines the coverage you have on your property. This section starts with a list of **definitions that** we won't go through in detail. However, pay attention to the list of specified perils. You have comprehensive coverage and in your policy, these perils are the basis for the **exclusions** — what is not covered — which comes later in the policy" (Pages 121–122).

K. "Your coverage starts with your **house — Coverage A — Principal Dwelling**" (Pages 123–124).

L. "Then it moves to **other buildings — Coverage B — Additional Buildings**. For most of us, this is the garage. It is generally covered for 10% of the value of the house. I know this seems silly since you have a plywood garage, as cute as it may be, but 10% is the standard coverage for it" (Page 124).

M. "Then is goes on to outline the coverage you have on the **contents** — your furniture, books, clothes, dishes and other stuff like that — **Coverage C — Personal Property**. We won't go through it now, but notice, just before the end of this section, that there are a few things that they do not insure" (Pages 124–125).

N. "Notice also that there are some **special limits** on some coverages. None of these applies to you right now, but you never know, something might apply to you in the future" (Page 125).

O. "And since your work out of your home, you need to pay particular attention to that part of your policy that says you are **not covered** for any losses that are a result of your **business** — if, for instance, a client came to your office and was somehow injured. That's why I recommended that you get business coverage for such a possibility" (Pages 126).

P. "The next section tells you what you can expect if your house suffers major damage and you have to **move out** for a few months — **Coverage D — Loss of Use**. You don't have a tenant just now but the day might come when you might get an office somewhere and decide to rent out what is now your office space. If you had to move out, your tenant would also. Could you live without the extra income? This section addresses that" (Page 126).

Q. "You have comprehensive coverage so you are covered for all losses regardless of the cause. Well, as it happens, not quite all. This policy is different from your auto policy in one major way. There is a long list of very specific **exclusions**. I know you are going to read all of this but I want you to note in particular the following list of exclusions:
   1. Property of your tenant (Page 127, #8)
   2. Terrorism (Page 128, #22)
   3. A constant water leak that you didn't fix in time to prevent damage (Page 129, #27)
   4. Racoons make a home in your attic (Page 129, #28)
   5. An earthquake (Page 129, #30)
   6. Flood (Page 129, #36)
   7. The heat goes off when you arc away on a week's vacation in the winter unless you have taken some required precautions. (Page 130, #47)

R. "But the good news is — you have some coverage you may not have realized you have, so of which is not subject to the deductible:
   1. If your credit card is stolen (Page 131).
   2. If you have to call the fire department and you are charged (Page 131).
   3. If the hydro goes out and you lose all the food in your freezer. However, the loss had better be substantial because you do not want to have a lot of small claims (Page 132).
   4. If you have to move out because of a general evacuation order. I know this sounds pretty unlikely but remember that train derailment in Mississauga in the late 1970s when all those people had to move out for three or four days because some toxic substance was released into the air? Well, you are covered for that cost" (Page 132).

S. "Section I, the coverage on your own property, finishes with the **Basis of Claims Settlement** section that tells you what you can expect to receive from your insurer if there is a loss to your house and property. You have **guaranteed replacement cost** coverage. What exactly does that mean and does it ever happen that you might not get the full cost of replacing your property?
   1. First, you should notice is that if you do not choose to rebuild or repair the buildings, you won't get the replacement cost. Remember that madman who was running around setting fires in people's garages? If you should decide that you could live with a parking pad, you would not collect the replacement cost — only the **actual cash value**. Since you have a plywood garage, that wouldn't amount to much (Page 134).
   2. You should also notice that you have to keep your coverage on the buildings at 100% of the replacement cost to be sure of receiving the full amount of any loss. If you do go ahead and renovate the kitchen, don't forget to call your insurer or your house will be underinsured.
   3. Notice also that your contents are not covered for guaranteed replacement cost but only **guaranteed cost** — up to the limits of your insurance but not over it.
      (a) Again, you would get only the actual cash value for anything that is not repaired or replaced.
      (b) You should get an endorsement for anything that would not readily be covered by replacement cost coverage. I'm thinking here of your grand piano" (Page 135).

T. "Now we're ready to move on to Section II and deal with your cleaning lady and the courier person. Again we start with a bunch of **definitions**. I'll leave those to you to read through later" (Page 138).

U. "Section II covers you if you or someone covered by this policy unintentionally cause bodily injury to other people not insured by this policy or damage to the property of other people. Notice it does not cover bodily harm to anyone covered by this policy. Nor does Section II cover damage to your own property. There are two basic types of coverage:

   1. **Coverage E — Legal Liability** covers you if you are **sued** and are required to pay compensatory damages. It covers the following (Pages 139–140):

     (a) Personal liability from your actions anywhere in the world

     (b) Premises liability covering all your "premises" as outlined in the definitions

     (c) Tenants legal liability, which covers you if you cause damage to someone's property that you have, for instance, borrowed or rented

     (d) Employers' liability for claims from residence employees, but not business employees.

   2. **Coverages F, G, and H — Voluntary Payments**, essentially cover the same things but you do not have to lose a lawsuit for the insurer to pay. Voluntary payments are payments your insurance company will make without anyone having to go to court."

     (a) **Coverage F — Voluntary Medical Payments** covers unintentional injury to other people (Page 141).

     (b) **Coverage G — Voluntary Property Payment** covers damage to other people's property caused by anyone covered by this policy, both

       i. unintentional damage caused by an adult, and

       ii. intentional damage caused by a child 12 years of age (Pages 141–142).

     (c) **Coverage H — Voluntary Compensation for Residence Employees**. This is where your cleaning lady fits. She can be compensated but there is no provision in here for you to hire another cleaning lady. After all, you won't be paying her — the insurance company can do that so you can hire a replacement if you can find one" (Page 142).

V. "The next section covers some **special limitations**:

   1. **Watercraft** — both those you own and those you don't own (Page 144)

   2. **Motorized vehicles** like a lawn mower or snow blower — both those you own and those you don't own (Page 145)

   3. **Trailers**

   4. **Some business activities**"

W. Joanne is visibly wilting but declines another espresso. Nothing is going to help at this point! Francesca can see that she'd better not go into too much detail — but there is still quite a bit. "With apologies," says Francesca, "the next section covers **loss and damage not insured**. I'll leave you to read this. Much of it is no surprise after the losses and damage not covered in Section 1" (Page 146).

X. "The last section of your policy, **Section III**, outlines the conditions of the policy. Since you know the auto policy, you are already familiar with the kind of thing in here. Some of the conditions are statutory, meaning they are required by law. I'll leave you to read this through later" (Page 147).

Y. "You have comprehensive coverage," Francesca reminds Joanne, "but if money ever becomes tight, you might be tempted to downgrade your coverage to save a few dollars. There is a brief comparison of a few of the **differences in coverage between a basic policy** which provides "named perils" coverage on your house and its contents **and** your **comprehensive coverage** which provides "all risks" coverage on both" (Page 153).

Z. "We won't go through the next part in detail which covers **other types of home insurance coverage**. Some of them don't apply to you just now while I'm sure you already have mortgage life insurance. After reading this, you may want to look into fraud insurance also since mortgage fraud has been getting quite a bit of press lately:

   1. Condominium insurance (Page 154)

2. Mobile homes
3. Mortgage insurance
   (a) Mortgage life insurance,
   (b) Mortgage default insurance and CMHC
4. Tenant's insurance for people who rent living space from someone else (Page 156),
5. Title insurance and mortgage fraud (Page 156)
6. Identity Theft or Fraud and what you can do to prevent it"

AA. "Last but not least, there is a short list of **costs** you can expect to run into **when you buy a home**. You already have a home but you might buy another one someday and forget what you encounter when you buy a home. It doesn't really have anything to do with insurance, but these costs can come as a surprise and can make you decide on a type of insurance coverage that does not really cover you as well as you would like if you weren't already drowning in unexpected expenses" (Page 160).

Concept Questions

1. List the three levels of home insurance coverage from the most risky to the least risky.

2. What are the two types of losses that a homeowners insurance policy can cover? Define, and provide an example.

3. List the four principles of insurance that underlie the entire insurance industry.

4. Define *indemnity*.

5. Briefly explain the difference between actual cash value, replacement cost, and guaranteed replacement cost.

6. Define *coinsurance* for property insurance and explain why insurance companies require it.

7. Explain why a person might consider under-insuring their home.

8. List the main factors insurance companies use to determine the amount of home insurance premium.

9. Insurance companies often offer discounts to homeowners. Name six reasons for a discount.

10. Explain what the term *endorsement* means in a home insurance contract, and to what it applies.

11. What does the term *floater* mean in the context of home insurance?

12. What information is found on the declaration page of the homeowners insurance policy?

Application Questions

13. Janice owns a house on Riverside Road in Windsor, Ontario. Her house backs up on the beautiful but heavily polluted Detroit River. One day during a massive storm, the Detroit River overflows and she is forced to evacuate her home. The bottom floor of her home is totally destroyed by the flooding. Janice decides that she can use this as an opportunity to take advantage of her insurance company. She deliberately lies and is able to fool the insurance company into giving her an extra $20,000 for the contents in her home. What principle of insurance has Janice violated?

14. Fernando's home insurance policy includes an 80% coinsurance clause and a 100% guaranteed replacement cost clause. He has just insured his home for $350,000, which has a value

of $500,000 when he purchased it a couple of weeks ago. While installing his natural gas oven, a pipe explodes, causing $200,000 worth of damage. How much will Fernando recover from his insurance company using
(a) the 80% coinsurance clause? ($175,000)
(b) the 100% guaranteed replacement cost clause? ($140,000)

15. Derek recently moved into his wonderful new house, which is, in fact, 90 years old. It is frame row house and the front and back are covered in the original insulbrick siding. He plans to replace the siding as well as the furnace as soon as he can find the money. His house is just like many others in his neighbourhood, so he asks several neighbours for the names of their insurance company so he can get the best price. Much to his surprise, none of the insurers is willing to cover him, saying they have enough houses insured in this high-risk neighbourhood. Is this legal?

16. Manuel has recently purchased a large plot of land in Woodbridge, Ontario. He is currently building a home on his property. His garage is partially complete, so Manuel decides he can store his John Deere lawnmower there. One night, a band of drunken teenagers stumble on to his property, steal his lawnmower, and drive off with it into the night. Is Manuel covered for the loss of his lawnmower?

17. Alex has an outdoor pool in his backyard. One day he wakes up to find a huge hole in the pool because someone had dropped a boulder into it, making a large hole in the pool floor and damaging some pipes leading into his home. A plumber tells him that the entire foundation of the pool needs to be torn out to repair the pipes. Will Alex be covered for all of the repairs?

18. Some weirdo is running around setting fire to garages in the lanes behind the semi-detached houses in Mark's neighbourhood. His garage is old but shields his car from the elements and he doesn't really care if it is a thing of beauty, which it certainly is not. Is his garage insured under his homeowners policy?

19. Patrick owns a house that is located on a lonely stretch of the Trans-Canada Highway in northern Ontario. To make some extra money, he rents out rooms in his house to motorists who need a place to sleep for the night. One night, Patrick falls asleep with a lit cigarette in his hand. The cigarette causes a small fire on the top floor of the home, destroying his room and the room of a "guest". The motorist, a total stranger, has his suitcases full of clothing and personal possessions destroyed. Will Patrick's homeowners insurance cover him for the cost of compensating the motorist for his destroyed processions?

20. On a vacation in New Zealand, Ozlem has her digital camera stolen from her hotel room. Will her homeowners insurance cover her loss?

21. Harold, 19, lives with his parents in Toronto. While he attends school in Halifax, he lives in an apartment by himself. As a parting gift, his parents buy him a new laptop, which costs them $4,500. One night while he is out with friends, his apartment is broken into and his laptop is stolen. Will his parent's homeowners policy cover the loss of his laptop?

22. Savita has legal custody of her 75-year-old mother-in-law, Rani. Savita cannot stand living with her mother-in-law and, while her husband is on assignment in Cambodia, she places her mother-in-law in a retirement home. While in the retirement home, an unethical worker steals Rani's prized $2,300 pearl necklace. Will Rani's losses be covered under Savita's homeowners insurance?

23. Randy is moving his office out of his garage and into a new suite in an office building in downtown Toronto. While moving the equipment out of his office and into his van, he drops his $5,000 office computer and destroys it. Is Randy covered for this loss?

24. Joanna's $25,000 fur coat is destroyed when her fiance's dog digs a nest in it to deliver her litter of puppies. Cute puppies, but goodbye coat. Joanna has no endorsements. How much will she receive from her insurer?

25. Scot runs a dog kennel on his property in Mississauga, Ontario. One day he leaves a young German shepherd unattended and the pup walks up to the house and chews a large hole on the back of his wooden home. Will Scot be reimbursed for the costs to repair the damages to his home?

26. While Sandra's home is being repaired for damages caused by a large forest fire, Sandra is forced to move into a hotel and eat all her meals at restaurants as she no longer has use of a kitchen. This has resulted in Sandra spending an extra $250 a day for her in expenses. Will her homeowners insurance cover these expenses?

27. Molson, Roman's pet poodle, is struck and killed by a car as he crosses a rural road that runs along his home. Will Roman's homeowners policy compensate Roman for the loss of his pet? Would he be covered if Molson had been struck by lightning?

28. Nav uses the basement of his house to grow marijuana for sale. One night while he is out at his girlfriend's house, an electrical fire starts in the basement, and his entire home is destroyed. Will Nav's insurance cover his loss?

29. Jorge has just bought a huge new house in Kingston Ontario. His master bedroom is at the top of a four-storey tower. One afternoon while taking a nap, Jorge is jolted awake by a large thud and the sound of breaking glass. He looks at his custom-made bedroom window to find a big crack and a smear of blood. Upon closer investigation he notices a dead sparrow at the bottom of the window. Does Jorge's home insurance cover the damage to his window?

30. Suzie has just bought a home along Canada's beautiful Pacific coast in British Columbia. One day as Suzie is out on her balcony enjoying her view of the Pacific Ocean, the earth begins to shake violently. Suzie's balcony collapses and, luckily for Suzie, she lands in her swimming pool. The earthquake is a violent one and causes serious structural damage to her home. Is Suzie covered for the damage?

31. Belinda bought a beautiful home in Mississauga that backs on to Lake Ontario. One day during a severe thunderstorm a huge wave hits her home, damaging the back end and flooding the first two floors of the home. Is Belinda covered for the damages?

32. Grace has ignored the leak in her roof for a number of years, as she is single and is away from home most of the year. One night as she is sleeping, the portion of the roof that has the leak collapses. Is Grace covered for the damage?

33. Jerry and his wife, Marsha, are celebrating New Year's in Cuba. While enjoying the tropical weather of Cuba, five days into their vacation, the below-zero temperatures cause the pipes in their Edmonton home to freeze and burst. When Jerry and Marsha come back, they realize what has happened. Are they covered by their homeowners insurance for the loss?

34. One night while out at a night club, Paul, who was very drunk, accidentally lost his wallet. In his wallet were his credit cards The next morning when he notices everything is gone, he calls his bank to check his credit card balance and notices that somebody had put $500 worth of hotel charges on it. Does Paul's homeowners insurance cover him?

35. Jason's homeowners policy has a $200 deductible. While trying to make fried chicken wings and french fries he sets his kitchen cupboards on fire, destroying them. He contacts the fire department and after they put out the fire they give him a bill for $300 for putting out the fire. Will his insurance company pay for his fire service bill? If so, how much?

36. Mary buys groceries for a large dinner party she is having in four days. She purchases frozen lobsters, crab claws, salmon fillets, seafood hors d'oeuvres and organic desserts costing her $750 in total as her guests love seafood and high-fat pastries. The morning of the dinner

party she notices that her freezer is not working, and all that expensive food has gone bad. Will her home insurance cover her losses?

37. Derek and his family and the neighbours were forced to spend two weeks in a hotel after a train derailed and spilled several thousand litres of toxic waste. As a result, Derek is out-of-pocket $2,900 although his normal grocery bill for the two weeks would have been $450. How much will his insurer compensate him?

38. Julie has paid $20,000 dollars to landscape her front yard and place an impressive garden there. One night she hears a bunch of teenagers laughing and the sound of a chainsaw. She runs out to see what is happening, only to find that six trees, each costing $2,000, have been chopped down. How much, if any, will her homeowners insurance cover?

39. Tarik's mountain bike was stolen from his home. He places signs offering a $1,000 reward to anyone who has information that will help the police find his bike. Some neighbourhood children step forward and help the police locate the culprit. Tarik asks the company that insures his home to pay the reward. Will the insurance company pay for this?

40. Grace wakes up one night find that her falling-down (but still functional) garage has been the victim of the local madman who is torching garages. As she understands it from her policy, the old garage is covered for the standard 10% of the replacement cost of her house, which is covered for $180,000 guaranteed replacement cost. She hires the local handyman to build her a new brick garage. How much will her insurer pay if the new garage costs
   (a) $15,000?
   (b) $25,000?

41. Rick is doing Richard a favour by walking his dog Gus while Richard is on vacation. Gus breaks free of his leash one day while walking and, for some unexplained reason, attacks a mail carrier. The mail carrier is badly hurt and decides to take legal action. Will Richard's homeowners insurance cover the liability to the mail carrier?

42. Curtis is holding on to some of his ex-girlfriend's furniture at his home while she is moving into her new home. Curtis accidentally knocks over an expensive vase that she hadn't picked up yet. She becomes enraged and sues Curtis for breaking her vase. Is Curtis covered for breaking the vase?

43. Tom's friend, George, gets drunk at a party and insists on standing on a barstool to sing homage to the Queen. He falls off the barstool and breaks his leg. The ambulance company sends Tom an invoice for $150.
   (a) Is the ambulance cost covered under Tom's homeowners insurance?
   (b) George's job requires him to drive around to stores checking inventory supplies. Since he can't drive, he has to take cabs all over Vancouver. Will Tom's homeowners policy cover George for his cab fares?

44. Jeffery, a butler in the Banks household, falls off a stepstool and lands face-first on the TV while trying to change the lightbulb in an awkwardly positioned light fixture. Jeffery has three teeth knocked out and requires extensive dental surgery to replace them and fix the damage to his gums. Is there any way Jeffrey can be compensated by Mr. Banks' homeowners insurance even though Mr. Banks is not legally responsible?

45. Jeffery, the butler from the above question, hurts his stomach muscles moving the couches while sweeping. The doctors tell him that he has a hernia. Is he eligible to receive anything from Mr. Banks' insurance?

46. While out boating at his cottage, James accidentally losses control of his 20 horsepower outboard motorboat and smashes into a sailboat, seriously hurting a number of people on the sailboat. Is his legal liability covered under his homeowners insurance?

47. Lenny was out golfing with co-workers. He was driving the rented motorized golf cart when he accidentally rolled it over while speeding around a corner. In the accident his co-worker Carl was seriously injured and decided to sue Lenny. Will Lenny's homeowners insurance cover Lenny's liability to Carl?

48. While on trial for his involvement in a car accident, Anthony lashes out at the judge in anger and, as punishment, he is fined an extra $700. Will his house insurance cover his additional costs?

49. Matthew's neighbour Damon slips and falls on Matthew's icy driveway. Damon claims to have hurt his back and wants to be compensated for it. Matthew figures it would be cheaper for all parties involved if he gives Damon a cash settlement of $1,000, assuming his insurance company will reimburse him for his efforts to go out of his way to resolve the issue. Is this true?

50. Monica is getting set to enjoy the fireplace in her new home with several friends. Unfortunately, after she lights it, smoke comes billowing out and they can't get it to stop for several minutes. The resulting smoke damage means she has to clean and repaint her entire first floor at a cost of $950. Is this covered if she has a
    (a) comprehensive policy?
    (b) basic policy?

51. Terry and Jane were four payments from the end of their mortgage when Jane died suddenly. They had mortgage insurance for the original value of their mortgage of $275,885. At the time of Jane's death, they owed the bank $2,885 on their mortgage. How much will Terry receive?

52. Connie is finally finishing her PhD. She has been in school for many years, having taken a few years off here and there to work in order to finance her education, travel a bit, and also acquire some rather nice furniture and other personal possessions. Fortunately she was not at home when the building she lives in burned to the ground. Equally fortunately, she had a backup of her thesis at her university. The replacement value of her lost possessions is about $35,000, including clothes, furniture, and her laptop. The actual cash value is about $9,000. How much will she be able to collect from her landlord's insurance policy?

53. Marty got an e-mail from his bank asking him to confirm his account number, account balance, and PIN. If Marty supplies this information, to what type of theft is he exposing himself?

5

Commercial Insurance

Learning Objectives

After completing this chapter, students will be able to:

A. Identify the significant risks for businesses and other organizations such as charities, churches, schools, and government agencies.

B. Explain the coverage provided by the various types of insurance policies.

C. Select the appropriate insurance coverage for diverse situations.

Introduction

Commercial insurance provides a more comprehensive version of the coverages found in automobile and homeowners insurance, and is sold to businesses and other non-personal enterprises because they face greater risk exposures than the average household. **General insurance** is the name given to all insurance except life and health and is often referred to as **Property and Casualty insurance** or **P&C**.

- **Property insurance** is first-party coverage providing protection against risks to the policyholder's own property. It covers risks such as fire, theft, or weather damage
- **Casualty insurance** is broadly defined as "third-party" coverage providing protection against losses that the policyholder may cause to others but has come to mean any coverage that is not related to life, marine or property. It includes but is not limited to the following:
  - Product liability insurance
  - Liquor liability insurance
  - Errors and omissions insurance
  - Directors and officers insurance
  - Malpractice insurance

Overview

Commercial insurance is bought by businesses and non-commercial organizations to protect themselves against possible loss or damage to their assets. Coverage varies from insurer to insurer and is based on the risk exposures the organization faces coupled with the level of protection it wants.

These organizations are exposed to a greater number of risks than an individual and these risks can negatively impact normal business operations. It is important to effectively manage the risks by first identifying the various risk exposures and then evaluating the potential loss. Once the risks have been identified and evaluated, the organization can decide how it wants to manage these risks. Commercial insurance is a cost-effective form of risk management that corporations and non-profits use to effectively limit the risk exposures that can arise from damage to their operations, from consumer lawsuits, as well as from their employees.

Types of Commercial Insurance
Commercial insurance falls into two main categories:

• Property insurance
• Liability insurance

Commercial Property Insurance
Commercial property insurance is used by organizations to protect property such as buildings, equipment, and machinery from loss or damage. The coverage offered by a commercial property insurance policy is comprehensive and can be structured to provide coverage to property owned by a firm but not located on its physical premises. For example, a construction company would structure its policy to provide coverage for machinery in the event it is damaged or suffers a loss when it is in use, but is not located on the company's premises.

There are a variety of risks that property is exposed to every day, and these risks can result in two types of losses:

• a *direct loss* resulting from a hazard or peril, and
• an *indirect loss*, which is contingent on an event or a repeated occurrence and is usually the result of a direct loss.

Commercial Liability Insurance
Commercial liability insurance is used by corporations and non-profits of all sizes to protect themselves against legal liability risks that might require them to financially compensate a third party as a result of a wrongful act, injury, or damage. These types of risks could significantly damage a firm's working capital, impairing its ability to cover payables, which is critical to its day-to-day operations. Prudent firms implement appropriate risk-management tools to minimize the financial impact that might arise from these risk exposures. Although liability can be broken down into numerous categories, we will use three broad classifications:

• General liability,
• Professional liability
• Employer liability

General Liability
General liability is defined as the legal liability that an enterprise faces when running its day-to-day operations. There are five defined areas of operations that are exposed to risk and for which a firm can be held legally liable. They are premises and operations, product, completed operations, contingent liability, and contractual liability.

Professional Liability
Professional liability arises from negligent acts, errors, omissions, and poor performance by employees when performing their professional duties. Professional liability insurance provides the firm — a corporation, non-profit organization, partnership, or sole proprietor — with coverage that is a result of litigation by unsatisfied clients and customers. There are many different forms of professional liability and, as a result, there are many different forms of insurance coverage that an organization can obtain to protect itself against those risks. For example, a large chartered bank that employs financial advisors can be held liable for the financial advice its employees provides to customers, even if the advice is contrary to bank policy.

Employer Liability

Employer liability covers the various risk exposures that an organization faces when it employs people to complete various tasks. One of the greatest liabilities that a firm is exposed to when it hires employees is their health and safety while they are on company premises or away on a site to complete a job. In addition, part of the employer's responsibility is to ensure that employees are treated equally and fairly. An employer must also ensure that employee duties are clearly defined and that employees are properly trained and adequately compensated for the work they do.

Fundamentals of Commercial Policies

Because the risk exposures are more complex and many companies have large financial resources enabling insureds to absorb larger losses than individuals can absorb, many aspects of commercial policies have evolved to provide more coverages and more options for the insured. These include the following:

- a broader definition of the occurrence — the cause of the harm or loss;
- choices as to the timing of the occurrence with respect to the coverage; and
- options for the deductible.

Occurrence

Commercial policies require that the loss or bodily harm be caused by an **occurrence** which includes the following:

- events that happen over a period of time, resulting in continuous or repeated exposure to essentially the same harmful conditions;
- an accident; or
- a series of accidents. An **accident** is an event that causes a loss and is sudden, unexpected, and unintended.

Bases of Paying Out

There are two bases for commercial liability policies to pay out:

1. **Occurrence polices** pay for losses that occurred during the policy period regardless of when the claim is filed. This type of policy is appropriate for a drug manufacturer who produces a drug whose harmful effects might not be know for some time after it is taken.
2. **Claims-made policies** pay for losses after a certain date (some specific time before the beginning of the policy period) but the claims are made during the policy period. This type is appropriate for an oil producer who is at risk for oil spills.

Deductible

The deductible in commercial insurance is the same as for personal insurance — it is an amount subtracted from the total payment. It also has the same purposes, which are to reduce

- small claims,
- premiums, and
- moral and morale hazard.

There are several types of deductibles in commercial insurance:

- **Aggregate deductible** — the firm pays all the losses for the year until the deductible limit is reached.
- **Straight deductible** or **per occurrence deductible** — the firm pays the deductible for each separate loss. On September 11, 2001, the first airplane hit the North Tower at 8:46 a.m. while the second plane hit the South Tower at 9:03 a.m. The buildings collapsed at 10:05 a.m. (South Tower) and 10:28 a.m. (North Tower). Was this one loss or two? With a per occurrence deductible, the

Exhibit 5-1 Financial Cost of 9/11

The financial cost of the attacks on the World Trade Centre was borne by insurance companies, various levels of the government and charities, organizations as diverse as insurance companies, workers compensation, unemployment insurance, disaster relief Medicaid, social security, the Office of the Victims of Crime, FEMA (Federal Emergency Management Agency) and charities such as the American Red Cross, Salvation Army, and the New York Firefighters Disaster Relief Fund.

The Rand Institute for Civil Justice [www.rand.org] produced a Research Brief entitled "Compensating Victims of 9/11" in 2004. The Abstract from the brief read as follows:

> A unique combination of insurance payments, government programs, and charitable distributions provided benefits to individuals and businesses affected by the 9/11 terrorist attacks. This research quantifies the benefits received by the various victim groups from each compensation mechanism. It examines how the benefits stack up against various measures of equity and assesses outcomes based in part on interviews with stakeholders in New York City. Issues are identified that policymakers should consider as they formulate policies for compensation and assistance in the event of a future attack.

The following table summarizes the financial losses as of September, 2003 for the attacks on the World Trade Centre as reported in the Rand's Research Brief.

Rand Institute: Estimates of Benefits by Type of Loss ($ millions)

	Insurance	Tort [a]	Government	Charity	Total
Personal injury [b]	2,090	0	8,010	1,310	11,410
Property damage [c]	7,970	0	910	80	8,960
Income loss	9,510	0	1,690	540	11,740
Revitalization	0	0	5,190	100	5,290
Unallocated [d]				650	650
	19,570	**0**	**15,800**	**2,680**	**38,050**

a At September 2003, no compensation had been awarded though the tort system, although some wrongful death and financial injury cases were still being pursued in the courts. Compensation through torts made the recipient ineligible for compensation from the Victim Compensation Fund.

b personal injury:
- Includes all citizens killed or seriously injured, not just those who died in attacks on the World Trade Centre.
- For government benefits, does not include the value of income tax and estate tax relief.
- For insurers does not include payments from private health insurance and employee-assistance plans.

c Property damage includes $40 million from the Residential Grant Program to compensate households for hardships after 9/11.

d Most of the unallocated funds are funds that had not been spent as of September 2003.

The costs may continue to the future. The *Terrorism Risk Insurance Act* (**TRIA**) was signed into law by President Bush on November 26, 2002 and is currently set to expire on December 31, 2014. It provides reinsurance coverage for the insurance companies after a declared terrorism event. Losses from the terrorist act must exceed $100 million as of 2007 and is triggered for an individual company when the deductible is 20% of premiums received the previous year. The industry as a whole must absorb $27.5 billion before federal assistance is available after which the government picks up 85% of the claims. The cap on annual assistance is $100 billion per year. The act is designed to encourage insurance companies to offer terrorism risk insurance by letting insurance companies keep the profits from the premiums and having the government assume the risk called "privatizing profit, socializing risk".

insurers preferred to call it two while the insureds preferred to call it one. The courts agreed with the insureds.

- **Franchise deductible** is found only in ocean marine insurance. It is either a dollar amount or a percentage of the loss and the entire loss is paid once the loss is greater than the deductible — a disappearing deductible.

The firm must decide how much risk to retain, either by

- having a high deductible,
- including a **stop-loss provision** that caps the amount the insured pays in total throughout the policy period; or
- **self-insuring**, which is a risk management technique whereby the firm retains part of the risk exposure and usually, but not always, has a fund set aside to cover losses — instead of insuring the risk, they retain the risk. Smaller losses are paid out of operations. A deductible is also called **self-insured retention**.

Coinsurance in Commercial Property Insurance

The coinsurance requirement on commercial property is not the same as the 80% rule for the homeowners property. As with one's home, most losses are partial losses as shown in the following table for commercial property losses.

Table 5.1 Size of Loss on Commercial Property

# of Losses	Loss as % of Replacement Cost
85%	20% or less
10%	21% to 49%
5%	50% or more
100%	

Commercial property owners are different from homeowners in two important ways:

- They often have buildings in several locations. While the probability of loss may be similar for most locations, the probability of a partial or total loss in all locations at the same time is virtually small.,
- Companies can afford to take more risk on all their properties combined.

As a result, an insured can elect to underinsure but will pay a higher premium for doing so and is expected to keep the amount of the coverage based on current replacement value. If the coverage is kept at replacement cost, the insurer will pay all losses up to the limits of the policy.

EXAMPLE 1   Marie owns a very successful chain of clothing stores and the buildings that house them. She insures 200 buildings worth $800,000 each — a total value of $160,000,000. Her insurer expects that one building will be totally destroyed and another five will experience partial losses averaging $80,000 each. Marie asks to see the calculation of the pure premium (without loading charges) assuming the buildings are either 100% insured or 80% insured.

	Losses		Losses Paid	
#	$	Total	100% Insured	80% Insured
1	800,000	800,000	800,000	640,000
5	80,000	400,000	400,000	400,000
		$1,200,000	$1,200,000	$1,040,000
Value of coverage			$160,000,000	$128,000,000
Pure premium			$0.7500	$0.8125
Calculation =	$\left(\dfrac{\text{Expected loss paid}}{\$\text{ coverage}}\right)$		$\left(\dfrac{1,200,000}{160,000,000}\right)$	$\left(\dfrac{1,040,000}{128,000,000}\right)$

Notice:

1. 80% coverage is more expensive per dollar of coverage although not by 20%. It is more expensive by only 8.3% (6.25¢ ÷ 75¢) although the payout for 80% is 13.3% ($160 ÷ $1,200) lower.
2. The insurer is paying 100% of the partial losses in both cases. This is because the insurer will pay 100% of the losses up to the face amount of the policy on each building as long as the insured keeps the buildings insured up to the agreed value — in these examples, either 100% or 80%. It is usual for the percentage to be 80% or 90% or 100%.

EXAMPLE 2   Success has gone to Marie's head and she has not had any serious losses so when the buildings increase in value by an average of 25%, she decides not to inform the insurance company although she has agreed to do so.

The following table shows the payout and the formula for the payout for the same losses if the buildings increased in replaccment value to $1,000,000 (from $800,000) but the coverage remains the same.

Actual coverage: Required Coverage:	$160,000,000 $200,000,000 *(100%)*	$128,000,000 $160,000,000 *(80%)*
Formula for Payout $\left(\dfrac{\$ \text{ insurance carried}}{\$ \text{ insurance required}}\right) \times \$ \text{ loss}$	$\left(\dfrac{160,000,000}{200,000,000}\right) \times 80\%$ coverage 20% underinsured (80% ÷ 100%)	$\left(\dfrac{128,000,000}{160,000,000}\right) \times 64\%$ coverage 20% underinsured (64% ÷ 80%)
Losses (Same as Example 1)	**Losses Paid**	
1 @ 800,000 = 800,000 5 @ 80,000 = 400,000 **$1,200,000**	800,000 x 80% = 640,000 400,000 x 80% = 320,000 1,200,000 x 80% = **$960,000**	640,000 x 80% = 512,000 400,000 x 80% = 320,000 1,040,000 x 80% = **$832,000**
Payments in Example 1 Payment when 20% underinsured Payment is decreased by: % decrease from fully insured	$1,200,000 960,000 $240,000 20% (240,000 ÷ 1,200,000)	$1,040,000 832,000 $208,000 20% (208,000 ÷ 1,040,000)

In both instances, the buildings were underinsured by 20% and, in both instances, the amount of the payments for the losses also decreased by 20%. This is because Marie is *required* to keep the coverage of 80%, 90%, or 100% to be based on the *current* replacement value. Since she did not do this, the amount of the loss reflects the extent to which the buildings were underinsured.

Another possible method for applying the coinsurance requirement in commercial insurance is to use this formula:

$$\left(\frac{\text{Amount of insurance}}{\text{Replacement value}}\right) \times 80\% \times \text{Amount of loss}$$

Again, the insured is willing to take some of the risk and can elect to underinsure. If the building is insured for 80% of its replacement cost, the premium could be less than 80% of the 100% coverage because whatever coverage she chooses, she will get only 80% of the loss even if she is insured for 100% of replacement cost.

EXAMPLE 3   Marie decides to shop around and speaks to another insurer who uses this other formula to apply the coinsurance requirement. She is now less concerned about the amount of the premium and interested more in the amount of coverage so the second insurer shows her what she would get for the same $1,200,000 loss using a different formula.

Amount of insurance		Amount recovered	Calculation
100%	$160,000,000	$960,000	$\left(\dfrac{160,000,000}{160,000,000}\right) \times 80\% \times 1,200,000$
80%	$128,000,000	$768,000	$\left(\dfrac{128,000,000}{160,000,000}\right) \times 80\% \times 1,200,000$

Maria decides she is not in the business of taking insurance risks and stays with the first insurer. Even though the premiums are significantly less for the second insurer, she doesn't like the size of the payouts.

Coinsurance for Indirect Losses

Indirect loss coverage such as extra expenses coverage to cover additional costs incurred as a result of a direct loss (for instance, renting other premises) can be purchased with a **coinsurance requirement,** which is based on the amount of time a firm would be shut down if it incurred a loss. The formula is as follows:

$$\left(\frac{\text{Net income}}{\text{All operating expenses for 12 months}}\right) \times y\%$$

where y% is how long the firm would be shut down.

If the firm might be shut down for more than a year, y might be 125%.

EXAMPLE 4   Marie expects net income for the current year of $150,000 per store, and she estimates it would take eight months to get up and running again if it were completely destroyed. As a result, the coinsurance requirement would be about 67%, meaning Marie would need to have $100,000 ($150,000 $\times$ 0.6667) of coverage. If a store were to be shut down for a year, she would buy $150,000 of extra expenses coverage for each.

Structure of Policy Coverage

There are many ways to structure commercial insurance coverage. However, before an organization looks at the structure of its commercial insurance policy, it must go through the risk management process which, as we covered in Chapter 1, involves the following:

1. Determining the objectives
2. Identifying the risks
3. Evaluating the potential losses
4. Considering the alternatives
5. Implementing the risk-management techniques
6. Performing ongoing evaluation and review

The biggest obstacle an organization faces in the risk-management process is not thoroughly going through the six steps. A business could inadvertently overstate or understate its objectives and miss large-risk exposures that leave it susceptible to large losses. An organization must clarify its objectives and identify all possible risks so it can accurately evaluate potential losses and decide which methods it will use to manage the risks.

P&C agents and brokers can be the insured's best friend. Brokers often specialize in certain types of organizations, and one appropriate for your organization can be found by asking an association, friendly competitors, bankers, and accountants. A broker with experience in the insured's business can help in the evaluation process and also can provide a warning if a certain business has certain requirements that will reduce the cost or even make the insurance coverage possible. Obvious items include monitored smoke detectors and sprinkler systems, but an art gallery or jewellery store, for instance, might require a certain type of burglar alarm system before insurance is even possible.

Once all the potential losses have been evaluated, the organization will determine which risk-management tools it wants to implement. The risk-management tools, again from Chapter 1, are as follows:

1. Risk avoidance, which is the oldest and most commonly used risk-management tool. Deciding not to operate in a specific geographical area or not to sell a certain product avoids risk exposures a business might face.
2. Loss control allows an organization to reduce the severity or frequency of a loss by, for instance, limiting the products sold or the hours of operations.
3. Retaining the risk is another common form of risk management that large corporations use to limit their expenditures. This is a form of self-insuring since the insured sets aside funds to pay out large future claims and pays smaller claims out of operating cash flows.
4. Sharing the risk is done by incorporating, hedging, and hold-harmless clauses.
5. Insuring the risk is used for large-risk exposures. Commercial policies can be custom tailored to meet the needs of the insured. Not only does the organization need to buy the right kind of insurance, it also needs to buy the right amount — don't risk more than you can afford to lose, but do not insure that which you can afford to lose.

Once the alternatives have been considered and evaluated, the organization can then implement the appropriate risk-management tools and continuously monitor and evaluate their effectiveness.

There are many ways an insurer can customize policies to meet the needs of the insured entity:

- Pure captives or group captives
- Various structures of the coverage itself:
  - Umbrella policies
  - Blanket insurance
  - Multiple-lines insurance

Captive Insurers

Captive insurers are insurance companies owned by a firm or firms. The insurer insures the firm and perhaps other non-related companies to capitalize on the principle of risk pooling. There are two types:

1. **Pure captives** insure only parents and parent's subsidiaries.
2. **Group captives** are insurers having many parents.

Structure of the Policy

Commercial coverage can be structured in many ways to help the insured obtain the broadest possible coverage at the least cost.

Umbrella Policies

Umbrella policies provide protection against a catastrophic lawsuit by providing broad blanket coverage to areas not covered by the underlying policy. **Excess insurance**, described in the auto policy for liability insurance, provides an additional dollar amount of coverage based on the underlying policy while the coverage of an **umbrella policy** goes beyond the scope of the underlying policy, providing coverage where there is no primary coverage at all (this is the same as the optional coverage in personal auto insurance). Many umbrella policies provide a very broad definition of personal injury such as mental anguish and injury, shock, discrimination, and/or humiliation. Typically they provide coverage anywhere in the world. Umbrella policies cover both of the following:

- Personal injury — bodily injury, libel, slander, defamation of character, invasion of privacy, wrongful eviction or detention, false arrest, false imprisonment, and malicious prosecution
- Property damage — physical damage to tangible property, including the loss of use of the damaged property.

Blanket Insurance

Blanket insurance provides coverage under a single limit for:

- Two or more items, for example, the building and it contents.
- Two or more locations, for example, Location A and Location B.
- A combination of items and/or locations.

Multiples-lines Insurance

Multiple-lines insurance covers property and casualty in one contract. It could provide insurance for property, general liability, business income, equipment breakdown, and crime. Examples for personal coverage are both auto policy and the homeowners policy, which cover several areas.

Commercial Property Insurance

Commercial property insurance covers damage and loss to property. A **loss** has occurred when something is entirely destroyed, damaged, or missing. Property risk is the risk of loss — either a **direct loss** (the loss of the property itself) or an **indirect** or **consequential loss** (added expenses that are incurred as a result of the direct loss). The loss can be reduced by the **salvage**, that portion not damaged, which reduces the amount of the claim.

Direct Losses

There are two categories of loss or damage:

1. Losses due to **perils**
2. Losses due to **dishonesty**

1. Direct Losses Due to Perils

The direct loss an organization might incur depends on the nature of its operations. As a result, there are many types of possible coverages, and no business will need all of the following, which fall under the heading of commercial property insurance. **Extended coverage** insurance provides protection against perils not covered by the basic policy, such as riots and civil commotion. **Specified perils** coverage covers the list of perils named while **open perils** provides coverage for every peril except for a list of exclusions.

1. **Building and Personal Property** covers direct losses from fire, windstorms, explosions and other perils on three insuring agreements:
   (a) **Real Property**:
       i. The **building(s), extensions and additions;**

     ii. **Permanently installed** fixtures and equipment; and

    iii. **Property improvements** to leased premises that cannot be removed if the firm moves out (carpeting, partitions, and walls).

(b) **Business Personal Property** of the insured:

     i. **Furniture and fixtures;**

    ii. **Inventory** (raw material, work-in-progress, finished goods, and goods in transit); and

    iii. **Machinery and equipment.**

(c) **Personal property of others** in the firm's temporary custody — primarily leased machinery, equipment and vehicles.

Coverage generally includes the following:
- **Debris removal.**
- **Preservation of property** (additional costs to preserve the property rather than just demolishing it).
- **Fire department charges.**
- **Pollutant clean up** and removal from land and water.
- **Additional building costs** due to changes in building codes.

Optional coverage deals with the following:
- **Valuable business records** that have to be restored.
- **Property off the premises** such as property at trade fairs or in storage.
- **Outdoor property** such as trees, fences, detached signs, and antennas.
- **Trailers of others** such as trucks that transportation firms may leave on the premises overnight.
- **Spoilage** of your own or another firm's perishable goods resulting from a power outage.

2. **Boiler and machinery** insurance protects against the physical damage and financial loss that results from the sudden and accidental breakdown of boilers, machinery, and equipment, including telephone systems, computer systems, refrigerating systems, air conditioning equipment, engines, pumps, pipes, compressors, blowers, electric motors, generators, and transformers. This coverage is also called **mechanical breakdown** or **equipment breakdown.**

    It is necessary because commercial property policies exclude breakdown of machinery and explosion of steam boilers. Coverage typically includes compensation for the physical damage, expediting costs to bring parts or equipment in by express transportation and business interruption losses. It might also include **business income and extra expenses** coverage. Other types of insurance (other than boiler and machinery) provide protection for indirect losses such as the following:

(a) Lost time and profit (**Business Interruption** coverage) if not included,

(b) Spoiled food if a freezer breaks down (**Consequential Damage** or **Refrigeration Interruption** coverage), and

(c) Added costs to keep the business going while the equipment is being repaired (**Extra Expenses** coverage).

Boiler and machinery insurance might also provide regular inspections by the insurer using trained engineers to look for weaknesses and defects that can be repaired before the machine breaks down.

3. **Accounts receivable** coverage provides protection for the following:

(a) Amounts owed to the insured from customers if the insured cannot collect as a direct result of loss or damage to receivable records.

(b) Interest charges on any loan needed to offset losses of amounts made uncollectible by the loss or damage.

(c) Any added collection expense in excess of normal made necessary by the loss or damage.

(d) Other expenses incurred to re-establish receivable records.

4. **Builders risk** insurance, also called **Course of Construction** for buildings under construction, provides fire insurance and optional coverage for risks like windstorms, floods, and earthquakes. Most policies are **broad form,** providing all-risk protection during construction, including coverage for fire and vandalism.

5. **Condominium association** insurance covers the building, equipment, common areas, and walls in each unit.

6. **Credit** insurance protects against customer insolvency and covers only abnormal losses. It is for manufacturers, wholesalers, and services organizations, not retailers.

7. **Crop (hail)** insurance covers damage to growing crops due to hail or other named perils.

8. **Glass** insurance covers plate-glass windows and doors, which are often excluded from building coverage. It is usually for full replacement cost and covers the expense of repairing frames, installing temporary plates, and boarding up openings.

9. **Marine** insurance covers means of transportation and communication as well as goods in transit. It is provided by marine insurers who can insure the following:
   (a) Imports and exports
   (b) Domestic shipments
   (c) The means of transportation and communication
   (d) Personal property floater risks
   (e) Commercial property floater risks

   There are two types of marine insurance:
   1. **Ocean marine** covers goods being transported over water and can include legal liability.
   2. **Inland marine** covers goods that are moveable or moving (being shipped on land, that is, domestic goods-in-transit) as well as bridges and tunnels.

Ocean Marine

The major types of Ocean Marine insurance are as follows:
1. **Cargo** insurance covers the goods being shipped if they are damaged or lost.
2. **Hull** insurance covers the ship and is usually written on an all-risks basis. It includes a collision liability clause (a **running down clause**) in case the ship collides with another ship or damages the cargo of another ship. It does not include injury to people.
3. **Protection and indemnity** insurance covers
   (a) damage to piers, docks, and the ship's cargo;
   (b) illness or injury to passengers and crew; and
   (c) fines and penalties.
4. **Freight** insurance covers loss of earnings to the ship's owners if goods are damaged or lost and are not delivered.

When goods are shipped by sea, there are three implied warranties:
1. The vessel is seaworthy.
2. The vessel will not deviate from its course.
3. The voyage is for legal purposes, for example, it is not carrying goods that are being smuggled.

Violation of any one of these can void the insurance if the insured was in a position to know about the deviation since the insured may not know which ship the cargo is on.

There are two ways of deciding who pays the loss:

- **General average** or **partial loss** (*average* means partial loss) is a loss incurred for the common good, in which case the loss is shared by all parties. For example, it might necessary to throw part of the cargo overboard to save the ship and crew. The loss must be necessary, voluntary, successful (the ship and crew were saved) and none of the participants caused the risk. The owner of the ship and the cargo share the loss in proportion to the total value of their interest. For example, if several tractors valued at $3 million have to be thrown overboard to save the rest of the cargo and the ship, the loss would be shared by the insurers of all the cargo and the ship as follows:

Value of		% of loss	Share of loss
Tractors	$3 million	3/30 = 10%	$300,000
Other Cargo	6 million	6/30 = 20%	600,000
Ship	21 million	21/30 = 70%	2,100,000
	$30 million		$3,000,000

- **Particular average** is a loss that falls on one party. The loss is not covered unless the loss was caused *only* by certain perils such as stranding, sinking, burning, or collision with another vessel. In other words, if the loss was caused by pirates taking over the ship to steal its cargo of gold chopsticks, the loss would not be covered. It is often written as a franchise loss such as 5% — if the loss is less than 5%, the insurer pays nothing but if the loss is more than 5%, the insurer pays the entire loss with no deductible.

Inland Marine

This covers articles in transit and also bridges and tunnels. The major types of inland marine insurance are as follows as follows:

1. **Bailee** coverage for property held by bailees — someone who has temporary possession of property that belongs to another for storage, repair, or servicing. This coverage is used by dry cleaners, jewellers, laundries, TV repair shops, furriers, and garages.
2. **Business floaters (inland marine floaters)**. A floater is a policy that provides broad and comprehensive protection on property that is frequently moved from one location to another. There are floaters for the following:
   (a) Mobile equipment and property, such as cranes, bulldozers and livestock.
   (b) Property of certain dealers like jewellers, furriers and dealers in diamonds, fine art, cameras, and musical instruments. These are also called **block policies** and they cover loss to the property of a merchant, wholesaler or manufacturer including the following:
      i. Property of others in the insured's care, custody, or control that might also covered under Bailee coverage;
      ii. Property on consignment, such as pieces of art at an auction house waiting for the auction to begin; and
      iii. Property sold but not delivered.
3. **Means of transportation** and **communication in a fixed location** are also insured under inland marine policies. This includes bridges, tunnels, piers, docks, wharves, pipelines, power transmission lines, and radio and television towers.

B. Direct Losses Due to Dishonesty

There are two types:

1. Theft by non-employees covered by crime insurance
2. Theft by employees covered by fidelity bonds

1. Crime Insurance for Non-employee Theft

There are three categories of theft covered by this type of insurance:

- **Theft**, which is any act of stealing property without force or violence.
- **Burglary**, which is theft using force to gain entry.

* **Robbery**, which is theft using threats of bodily harm or using violence to take property from a person.

Only direct losses are covered — indirect losses are not covered by crime insurance. The employer has a limited period of time called the **discovery period** to discover the loss. The covered losses are losses discovered

* during the policy period and up to 60 days after the policy ends,
* during the policy period and up to one year after the policy ends, or
* during the policy period but the crime occurred after the discovery period of the prior contract had ended.

The major types of coverage are as follows:

1. **Forgery or Alteration** insurance covers losses arising from forgery or alteration of cheques or any other negotiable instruments the firm has drawn up. This includes
   (a) cheques, drafts, or notes payable to a fictitious entity;
   (b) cheques, including payroll cheques, where the signature was forged; and
   (c) cheques whose amount was altered.
2. **Inside the premises** covers
   (a) Robbery or safe burglary of money and securities;
   (b) Robbery or safe burglary of property other than money and securities and it also covers robbery outside the premises if the property is in the care of a messenger; and
   (c) **Liability for guests' property**
      i. in a safe deposit box if the insured is legally liable, for instance, deposits in a hotel safe; and
      ii. on the premises, excluding vehicles.
3. **Outside the premises** insurance covers premises theft and robbery for property other than money and securities while in the care of a custodian.
4. **Computer fraud** insurance covers the theft of money, securities and property by computer fraud.
5. **Money orders and counterfeit currency** insurance covers the loss when a firm accepts counterfeit money without realizing it.

2. Fidelity Bonds for Employee Theft

Employees who are **bonded** are covered by this insurance. Employee dishonesty includes embezzlement (stealing money or other property) and unauthorized discounts. There are two types of coverage:
* **Blanket coverage** covers all employees.
* **Scheduled coverage** covers named individuals or positions.

The standard **exclusions** are:
* employees who were cancelled under prior insurance, and
* inventory shortages.

The insured must report all dishonest acts when they occur or the coverage on that person immediately ceases. If Alice steals $50 from the till and her employer lets her off with a warning, the coverage on Alice is immediately terminated.

Indirect or Consequential Losses

These are losses that are a result of a direct loss ss mentioned earlier under boiler and machinery insurance. The types of coverage are as follows:

1. **Business income** insurance, also called **business interruption** insurance, covers net income before taxes plus continuing expenses. These continuing expenses may exclude rank-and-file workers who would be out of work if the firm could not continue operations.

2. Spoiled food is covered if a freezer or refrigerator breaks down (**consequential damage** or **refrigeration interruption** coverage).
3. **Extra expenses** coverage pays if the insured has to, for example, rent other premises and install new telephones in order to be able to continue operating. There can also be extra expenses coverage for computers to compensate the firm for extra costs to recapture and re-enter lost information after the equipment is repaired or replaced. This is in addition to normal, ongoing day-to-day operations. This coverage can be purchased with a **coinsurance requirement**.
4. **Contingent business interruption** covers losses arising from damage to the property of others. For example, this coverage would indemnify the insured if there is a loss to a
   (a) major supplier of material (for a manufacturer) or merchandise (for a wholesaler or retailer),
   (b) major customer, or
   (c) neighbouring business that attracts business to the firm, for instance, a large department store in a mall might attract customers to other tenants in the mall.
5. **Leasehold Interest** insurance insures against the loss of a favourable location due to loss or damage of the premises.
6. **Rain insurance** covers the loss of business due to inclement weather. It is usually for outdoor events where attendance is dependent on the weather.

Commercial Liability Insurance

Liability insurance covers the liability a firm — a corporation, a partnership, a sole proprietorship, in both the public and private sectors — might have to financially compensate another party for a wrongful act, bodily injury, or damage to property. It is present in:

- tort law, which covers negligence;
- agreements including contracts; and
- the carrying out of a fiduciary duty.

Two aspects of liability have previously been discussed:

- **Vicarious liability** is the obligation of a principal, for example an employer, to pay for losses of a third party caused by the acts of an agent such as an employee.
- **Strict liability** is where those engaging in certain undertakings, such as hazardous practices like the industrial use of high explosives, are held responsible for injury without inquiry into fault.

Product liability is increasingly held to strict liability for makers of such varied items as foods, drugs, cosmetics, and automobiles.

General Liability

General liability covers **legal liability** arising out of business operations other than automobile, aviation accidents or employee injuries. There are five areas:

1. **Premises and operations coverage** addresses the need for a firm to keep the premises and the operations safe. It deals with injury to the public or damage to their property arising from the following:
   (a) **Ownership and maintenance of the premises** — liability due to a condition in or arising from the premises itself. For example, a wet floor in a store could cause someone to slip and fall.
   (b) **Conduct of business operations** — liability due to business operations. For example, McDonald's was successfully sued when a woman burned herself after she spilled an extremely hot cup of coffee on herself.

185

2. **Product liability** is the legal liability for products of manufacturers, wholesalers or retailers to people who incur bodily injuries or property damage from a defective product. It arises from the following:

    (a) **Negligence** — damage or injury that is a result of defective products.

    (b) **Breach of warranty** — the product does not do what it is intended to do. The warranty is implied when the product is purchased.

    (c) **Strict liability** — a manufacturing defect that causes injury or damage even when the product does what it is supposed to do. For example, a product catches fire due to a design modification.

3. **Completed operations** covers faulty work performed away from the premises after the work or operation is completed. This coverage is used by plumbers, electricians, and contractors for their own business operations and also for work they perform as installers.

4. **Contingent liability** arises from work done by independent contractors and covers the company who subcontracted the work.

5. **Contractual liability** covers situations where a business firm assumes a legal liability of another party in a written or oral contract. For example, a tenant assumes a legal liability when renting the entire building. A **hold-harmless clause** written into a contract releases one party from all legal liability such as when the owner of rented equipment is not held liable if the equipment causes a loss.

General liability coverage has many exclusions that are often covered by **comprehensive general liability** coverage. The **exclusions** can generally be covered by separate policies.

1. **Advertising injury** or **personal injury** or **personal and advertising injury** coverage deals with slander, libel, persecution, defamation of character, false arrest, detention or imprisonment (when, for example, a retailer wrongly accuses someone of shoplifting), malicious prosecution, violation of the right of privacy, and unlawful entry or eviction.

2. **Environmental liability** covers pollution from smoke, acid, fumes, toxic chemicals, waste materials, and underground storage tanks. The parties responsible are obligated to clean up and if they don't, the government can clean it up and sue the parties responsible for the pollution. Policies often distinguish between **gradual pollution,** which occurs over many years, and **sudden pollution**, for example, when in 1990 in Hagersville, Ontario, a tire fire polluted not only the air with smoke but also produced contaminated runoff.

3. **Fire legal liability** occurs when a fire causes a loss to another party's property. It is needed because there is generally a fire exclusion for property in the care, custody, or control of the insured when, for example, premises are rented. If a tenant or an employee of a tenant causes a fire, the landlord might seek to recover the damages from the tenant to avoid making an insurance claim.

4. **Liquor liability** arises from the **Dram shop law** that imputes negligence to an owner of a business that sells liquor should a customer, while intoxicated, cause injury or damage to another person or their property.

5. **Property in the insured's care, custody, or control** covers the property of others in the same way as stated in the homeowners policy.

Professional Liability

Professional liability insurance provides coverage for liability resulting from negligent acts, errors, or omissions in the performance of professional duties. The goal of managing these claims is to minimize

- the cost of the claims,
- the cost of settling the claims, and
- adverse publicity.

For these reasons, insurers often prefer to settle even though there is no admission of guilt. There are several types of professional liability:

1. **Errors and omissions (E&O)** insurance covers professional activities whose primary risk exposure is property damage, not bodily injury. It is used to cover activities such as banking, accounting, law, insurance, and real estate. **Law liability** insurance takes care of the particulars that affect lawyers and is also known as **legal malpractice** insurance because it looks after the law firm as a whole as well as the individual lawyers.

2. **Directors and officers (D&O)** insurance is a sort of errors and omissions policy for management. Errors and omissions is concerned with performance failures and negligence arising from products and services while directors and officers insurance is concerned with the performance and duties of management. Claims from stockholders, employees, and clients can be made against a firm and against the directors and officers of the organization who can be held personally responsible for acts of the company. As a result, most directors and officers will require protection from the organization rather than put their personal assets at stake. Directors and officers are subject to the duties of diligence, obedience, and loyalty, and can be sued for negligence in the performance of these duties. D&O liability insurance usually includes the following:
   (a) Conflicts of interest.
   (b) Libel, slander, and defamation of character.
   (c) Invasion of privacy.
   (d) Copyright infringement, misrepresentation of ideas, and unauthorized use of logos.
   (e) **Employment practices liability**. Over 50% of D&O claims are employment-practices related — wrongful termination, sexual harassment, wrongful discipline, failure to employ or promote, and discrimination due to race, sex, age, national origin, religion, disability, or sexual orientation.

3. **Malpractice** insurance provides coverage to medical practitioners such as dentists, doctors, nurses and mental health practitioners when they are sued for harm or injury to patients.

4. **Architects and engineers** liability arises out of bodily injury, death, and property damage due to design faults.

5. **General partners liability** or **limited partnership reimbursement** covers the management and fiduciary responsibilities of a general partner to a limited partnership. These responsibilities are similar to that of directors and officers to a corporation. Exposure occurs when general partners become the financial managers of a limited partnership. The directors and officers of corporate general partners share this type of exposure. Some causes of claims are as follows:
   (a) Untrue written or oral statements made by the general partners
   (b) Breach of fiduciary duty
   (c) Incomplete disclosure of facts
   (d) Omission or misleading statements in an offering memorandum
   (e) Selling of unregistered limited partnership interests
   (f) Conflict of interest
   (g) Failure to devote adequate time to the partnership
   (h) Failure to minimize risk factors that prove detrimental

Surety Bonds

A Surety Bond is a bond that provides monetary compensation if the bonded party fails to perform certain acts.[1] Surety bonds are included under professional liability because they guaranty the performance of the principal. There are three parties to the bond:

---

1   In *Roget's Thesaurus*, the entry for *surety* provides index listings for *belief, certainty, guarantor, pledge, safety, security* and *sureness* all of which give the sense of providing sureness. The definition for surety from *The New Collins Concise English Dictionary* is: "1. A person who assumes legal responsibility for the fulfilment of another's debt or obligation and himself becomes liable if the other defaults. 2. Security given against loss or damage or as a guarantee that an obligation will be met. 3. *Obs.* the quality or condition of being sure."

1. **Principal**, the party bonded, is the party who agrees to perform certain acts or fulfil certain obligations.
2. **Obligee** is the party who is reimbursed for damages if the principal fails to perform.
3. **Surety** is the party who agrees to answer for the debt, default, or obligation of another.

There are several types of surety bonds:

- **Auctioneer's bonds** guarantee the faithful accounting of sales proceeds by an auctioneer.
- **Contract bonds** guarantee that the principal will fulfill all contractual obligations.
  - **Bid bonds** guarantee the owner (obligee) that the party awarded a bid on a project will sign a contract and furnish a performance bond.
  - **Performance bonds** guarantee that work will be completed according to contract specifications,
  - **Payment bonds** guarantee that the bills for labour and materials will be paid by the contractor when due.
  - **Maintenance bonds** guarantee the workmanship will be good or defective materials will be replaced.
- **Insurance agent bonds** indemnify an insurer for any penalties that may result from the unlawful acts of agents.
- **Judicial bonds** guarantee that the party bonded, the principal, will fulfill certain obligations specified by law.
  - **Court bonds** protect one person (obligee) against loss in the event that the person bonded, the principal, does not prove that he/she is legally entitled to the remedy sought against the obligee:
    - **Attachment bonds** guarantee that if the court rules against the plaintive who has attached the property of the defendant in a lawsuit, the defendant will be reimbursed for damages as a result of having the property attached.
    - **Bail bonds** are forfeited if the bonded person fails to appear in court.
- **Federal surety bonds** guarantee that the bonded party will comply with federal standards.
- **Fiduciary bonds** cover people who are responsible for the property of others. They are used when an individual is legally in control or manages the property of others. The bond guarantees that the person will fulfill all required duties, provide an accounting, and make up any deficiencies in the fund. They are used by guardians of minor children, receivers or liquidators, and administrators of estates.

  These bonds provide coverage for losses that the insured becomes legally liable to pay because of a claim for a wrongful act as well as the defence costs. A **wrongful act** includes any violation of the responsibilities, obligations, and duties imposed on fiduciaries as well as acts, errors, or omissions in the performance of their duties as a plan administrator, and fraud and embezzlement.
  - Fiduciary bonds include a **pension trust bond** that covers administrators of pension funds. The plans covered are fairly broadly defined — any plan, fund, or program established or maintained for the purpose of providing employee benefits to its participants or beneficiaries. Under a **fiduciary liability policy**, the insured includes the sponsor organization, the plan, and any natural person in his/her capacity as fiduciary or administrator of the plan.
- **License and permit bonds** guarantee that the person bonded will comply with all laws and regulations that govern his or her activities.
- **Lost-instrument bonds** guarantee the obligee against loss if the original instrument (such as a stock certificate) turns up in the possession of another party.
- **Public official bonds** guarantee that public officials will faithfully perform their duties for the protection of the public.

Employer Liability

Employer liability covers employee injury, employment practices, and the liability risk from employees driving company vehicles.

1. **Employee injury.** In Canada, much of the responsibility for employee **health insurance** is legislated and will be covered in Chapter 6. Coverage for work-related injuries is provided by **Workers compensation** and is covered in Chapter 7.
2. **Employment practices** as described above in Directors and Officers coverage.
3. **Automobile liability** coverage is essentially the same for commercial vehicles as for personal automobiles. However, in some situations, the business auto policy does not extend coverage to employees and their family members and the employee must obtain personal coverage through special endorsements or policies. The situations are as follows:
   (a) The employer's permission for use of a company vehicle may not extend to employee vacation and other personal activities or to use of the vehicle by members of the employee's family.
   (b) Even if permission is granted for personal use of the vehicle, the business auto policy covers only vehicles owned, rented, or borrowed by the named insured. No coverage extends to vehicles rented or borrowed by an employee on a personal basis.

Individuals who drive a company-furnished vehicle must make other insurance arrangements to protect against these coverage gaps in the business auto policy. Four alternatives are available to cover the employee and the employee's family:

   (a) An **extended non-owned liability endorsement** expands a personal auto policy if the employee owns one or more personal vehicles in addition to operating a company-furnished car. This coverage provides liability and physical damage coverage for the operation of a vehicle furnished for the insured's regular use.
   (b) **Named non-owner coverage** covers individuals who do not own a personal vehicle.
   (c) An **Individual named insured endorsement** expands a business auto policy for individuals who operate their business as a proprietorship with all vehicles, both personal and business, titled in the business name. This coverage can include family members.
   (d) A **Drive-other-car endorsement** can be added to a business auto policy. It can include listed individuals and their spouses and possibly all family members as insureds for the operation of automobiles hired or borrowed by the listed person. This endorsement is used when the scheduled individual is not the named insured.

Other Areas of Liability

We have not covered all possible scenarios that produce a risk exposure since, to do so, would require an exhaustive list of operations for businesses and non-profit organizations. These might include things like the following:

- Holding a 100-year celebration for a charity. The organization rents a restaurant for the evening and provides hors d'oeuvres, mini-burgers, and dessert. Should it also supply wine and liquor so as not to seem cheap? If an organization provides free liquor and wine, it must also provide taxi fare at the end of the evening. Does a cash bar sounds like a good idea?
- Holding a company picnic at the local park where you supply food, wine, beer (we've already covered that), and canoes. Might some employees decide to have a ballgame? Will there be fireworks at dusk? All of these things might require a permit, but they also might require special liability insurance, signed waivers, and extra supervision for the children.
- Hiring unpaid interns. Since they are unpaid, are they covered by all the normal coverages?
- Using volunteers either on a regular basis or for a special event. Do you do a police check on all of them or is that over the top? Since they aren't paid, again are they covered for injury to themselves and others, for property damage, or for theft should they decide to pursue a life of crime? In addition, this chapter deals only with property and casualty insurance so we haven't look at key-person insurance (life insurance, whose death or disability would result in a financial loss for the organization) and life, health, and disability insurance for employees, which will be covered in the following chapters.

Again, your agent or broker can be your best friend, particularly for small organizations who do not have a risk-management specialist on staff in helping to ensure that all risk exposures have been recognized, evaluated, and managed.

Summary

Commercial coverage is the same, in principle, as the coverage under the personal automobile policy and the homeowners policy. However, because commercial and non-profit) activities are more complex than personal activities, the coverage is much more complex. Like the policies covered earlier, coverage is divided into two main categories — property and liability. This chapter does not name all possible insurance coverage available, but it does provide a survey of only major coverages.

Application Case

Joanne arrives, grateful for the waiting espresso. Francesca has warned her that this meeting will be full of definitions, many of whose meaning will be obvious. Nonetheless, while it will not be a long meeting, it will be overwhelming in the level of detail.

"Do you have any questions you'd specifically like answered?" asks Francesca.

A. "Yes," says Joanne, "I've heard this term **property and casualty — P&C**. What is this about?" Francesca replies, "The earliest forms of insurers were marine, life, and fire. Property insurance covered possible losses to one's own property, principally from fire in the beginning. Casualty insurers began later and wrote insurance to cover accidents involving third parties — first to railroad passengers and then to travelers. These specialty insurers who did not write fire, marine, and life insurance tended to cover accidents or casualties and they soon expanded to cover liabilities arising from boiler explosions, and then liabilities to third parties for employers, elevators, public utilities and autos. As a result, general insurance is also called Property and Casualty or P&C" (Page 172).

B. "Does commercial insurance cover only businesses?" Joanne asks.

Francesca replies, "No. Commercial insurance is the name for insurance coverage for all organizations — businesses and non-profits like charities, churches, schools, and government offices. It even covers volunteer organizations like search-and-rescue operations for ski resorts" (Page 172).

C. "What kinds of commercial property insurance are there?" Joanne asks. "I know I have errors and omissions insurance and some other coverages but basically I just let my broker tell me what I need."

Francesca replies, "Well you got your broker from a colleague who is also self-employed so the broker knew your business when you came calling. Basically, commercial insurance covers the same kinds of things covered by homeowners' and auto insurance. Remember the sections they contained? Well, those sections reflect different kinds of coverages. Basically, there is the following:

1. **Property insurance** for your own property.
2. **Liability insurance** for loss or injury to others who are called third parties. This can be broken down into:
   (a) **general liability** that covers things like people slipping in a store and being injured by a company's product;
   (b) **professional liability** that covers risks inherent in the job like malpractice for doctors, errors and omission for accountants; and

(c) **employer liability** that covers employee injury, employment practices, and liability for employees who drive company cars and use them on weekend and on vacation" (Page 173).

D. "And what about the **deductible**? Does is work the same way as it does for my house and car?" asks Joanne.
1. "Well, no. But first you need to know that commercial polices can **pay out** differently than personal policies. They pay out based on the following:
(a) **Occurrences** — losses during the policy period regardless of when they were reported.
(b) **Claims-made** — basically for claims made during the policy period regardless of when the loss occurred" (Page 174).
2. "And the deductibles can be different also:
(a) **Aggregate** — the firm pays everything until the deductible limit is reached.
(b) **Straight or per occurrence** meaning a deductible is applied to each claim.
(c) **Franchise deductible** is found only in marine insurance" (Page 175).

E. "And speaking of deductible, 9/11 was interesting because the two planes crashed into the towers at 8:46 a.m. and 9:30 a.m. and the towers fell at 10:05 a.m. and 10:28 a.m. The insurers tried to argue that they were two separate events so there would be two deductibles but the courts decided that it was one act of terrorism.

Don't neglect to look at Exhibit 5-1, which outlines some details about the costs of 9/11. You may not realize it but insurance companies bore the brunt of only about half of the costs. We tend to think only of the buildings falling down when we think of the loss but about half of the insurers' payouts were for business interruption expenses ($10.5 billion) while the two buildings cost insurers $3.6 billion and other commercial property cost $5.4 billion. And these numbers do not include the costs of the four airplanes that were destroyed" (Exhibit 5-1).

F. "**Coinsurance** works differently for commercial insurance. The insured can elect to insure for less than 100% of the replacement cost but must keep the coverage up-to-date, that is, an insured can cover only 80% or 90% but that must be based on the current replacement cost. And if this is not the case, the amount of the loss that is covered reflects the amount by which the buildings are underinsured" (Page 176).
1. "Let's look at the examples for direct losses first."
2. "Now let's look at indirect losses. If your premises are damaged, you might have to rent alternative premises for a few months at extra cost. The co-insurance requirement here is based on the time you expect you would have to have the extra expenses.

$$\left(\frac{\text{Net income}}{\text{All operating expenses for 12 months}} \right) \times y$$

where y% is how long the firm would be shut down."

G. One thing I do need to emphasize is the need for organizations of all sizes to make sure they have consciously gone through the **risk management process** to make sure they have recognized all possible risk exposures. Once again the steps are as follows:
1. Determining the objectives
2. Identifying the risks
3. Evaluating the potential losses
4. Considering the alternatives
5. Implement the risk management techniques
6. Performing ongoing evaluation and review" (Page 178).

H. "And, as a reminder, the **risk management tools** are as follows:
1. Risk avoidance.
2. Loss control to reduce the severity or frequency of a loss.

3. Retaining the risk or self insuring.

4. Sharing the risk — incorporating, hedging and hold-harmless clauses.

5. Insuring the risk which is used for large risk exposures — Don't risk more than you can afford to lose, but do not insure that which you can afford to lose."

I. "The other thing you need to know is that there is flexibility in commercial policies, as follows:

1. Pure **captives** or group captives.

2. Various structures to the coverage itself:

   (a) **Umbrella policies** provide broader coverage to areas not covered by the underlying policy. They cover both personal injury and property damage.

   (b) **Blanket insurance** provides coverage under a single limit for two or more items, two or more locations, or a combination of items/locations.

   (c) **Multiple-lines insurance,** which covers property and casualty in one contract.

J. "I have business coverage since I have an office in my home," says Joanne. "It seemed pretty straight-forward to get. I just called my broker and she set it up. So why are you warning me about the complexity of commercial coverage?"

Francesca replies, "Well, I remind you. Since you got her name from a colleague, she already knew your business and what you would need. It's not so much that commercial insurance is complex as it is extensive and tends to be very specific. We're not going to talk about every single kind of coverage available — it can get quite narrowly defined depending on what business you are in."

1. "Commercial **property** insurance (Pages 180–185) covers the following:

   (a) **Direct losses**

      i. **Losses due to perils** due to property damage to your own and other people's property and bodily injury to non-employees (Pages 180–183).

      ii, **Losses due to dishonesty**, both by employees and non-employees (Pages 183–184).

   (b) **Indirect or consequential losses,** which are a result of a direct loss. Essentially this covers the following:

      i. Loss of business profits, and

      ii. Extra expenses a firm might have to incur to keep operating while repairing the direct loss. (Pages 184–185)

2. Commercial **liability** insurance (Pages 185–190) is categorized many different ways by different people but we'll look at it this way:

   (a) **General liability** arising from your operations, premises, and products (Pages 185–186).

   (b) **Professional liability,** which covers negligence, errors and omissions in the performance of professional activities (Pages 186–187).

      i. **Surety bonds** are a special type of liability insurance that covers the insured in case the other party to a contract does not meet the expected standard or fails to perform a certain act (Page 187).

   (c) **Employer liability,** which arise from the firm as an employer. Essentially it covers employee health and accident liabilities as well as liabilities originating from employment practices (Pages 188–189)."

Concept Questions

1. What are the two basic categories of commercial general insurance?

2. What are the three categories of commercial liability insurance?

3. What are the two bases for commercial polices to pay losses?

4. How does the concept of the deductible in commercial insurance differ from its manifestation in personal insurance?

5. What is the difference between an aggregate deductible and a straight deductible?

6. A deductible is not a type of self-insurance because the firm does not retain any of the loss. Do you agree with the statement? If not, correct it to make it correct.

7. What percentage of the total loss of 9/11 did insurers pay? Charities? (Answers: 51.4%, 7.0%)

8. If there is another large terrorist attack in the United States, what percent of the claims will the government pick up after insurers pay the first $27.5 billion? What is the annual maximum the government will pay?

9. List the six steps in the risk-management process.

10. List five risk-management tools.

11. Describe the difference between pure captive and group captives.

12. What is the different between excess insurance and an umbrella policy?

13. Justin wants to have a total of $1 million of coverage on his building and $1 million on his contents for a total of $1 million. What kind of policy will provide him with this coverage?

14. Does the auto policy qualify as multiple-lines insurance? Why or why not?

15. What are the two categories of loss or damage?

16. Jasmine is worried that any damage to the welding machine her company uses to manufacture auto parts would cause her to shut down operations for a significant period, resulting in a loss of profit. Can Jasmine purchase any insurance to cover her exposure? If so, what kind?

17. List all the loss exposures that are covered under accounts receivable insurance.

18. List the types of ocean marine insurance.

19. List the three warrantees that are implied when shipping goods by sea?

20. What is a bailee? What type of business would be interested in using one?

21. If Construct Co. wishes to insure its fleet of bulldozers from damage, what type of inland marine insurance would it use?

22. What are the three categories of theft, and what is the difference?

23. Compare and contrast inside the premises theft coverage with outside the premises non-employee theft coverage.

24. What are the standard exclusions under fidelity insurance?

25. Describe the purpose of contingent business interruption.

26. List the three sources of product liability.

27. Define a hold harmless clause, and describe a situation in which it would be useful.

28. What is advertising injury? What are its other names?

29. What are the three goals of professional liability insurance?

30. What is director and officers insurance? What type of losses does it cover?

31. Name and describe the parties to a surety bond.

32. List and describe four alternatives to solving the gaps in commercial automobile insurance when the auto is used personally.

Application Questions

33. Stanley owns a private firm that manufactures diet pills. The diet pills incorporate cutting-edge ingredients and scientific processes. He wishes to protect his firm from any possible future lawsuits. What type of commercial insurance policy is best for his company? Why?

34. A firm has a commercial automobile insurance policy that pays for losses to its automobiles. The deducible on the policy is $2,000. Over the course of the year the company suffers three losses of $500, $1,500, and $600.
    (a) If the aggregate deductible is used, how much will the firm receive from the insurance company? ($600)
    (b) If a straight deductible is used? ($0)

35. If Marie in Example 1 has 90% coverage, how much does she collect on the $1,200,000 loss if she has 90% coverage and is
    (a) fully insured? (Answer: $1,120,000)
    (b) covered for $180 million when the atcual cost is $200 million (Answer: $1,008,000)

36. If Marie's contractor tells her it would take six months to get a store up and running after a fire, how much Extra Expenses coverage should she have for each store? (Answer: $75,000)

37. Simon makes component parts for mattress manufacturers. He cannot afford to have his equipment down for long periods. What type of insurance will he have?

38. For each of the following situations, indicate which type of ocean marine insurance would have been most appropriate.
    (a) A Petri Canada oil freighter sailing through the Bermuda triangle encounters a serious storm. During the storm the ship's cargo is washed into the sea.
    (b) Due to rough waters, the crew of the *Iceberg* have to throw some cargo overboard. The abandoned cargo costs *Iceberg* approximately $20,000 in lost earnings.
    (c) Crab King, a crab fishing firm, often has its workers seriously injured while on dangerous crab fishing expeditions into the North Atlantic.
    (d) While trying to dock its oil tanker on an offshore oil rig near Newfoundland, the captain of a fully loaded Petri Canada vessel loses control and crashes into the oil rig, seriously damaging the hull and leaking thousands of litres of oil stored in the hull into the Atlantic Ocean.

39. Arthur wishes to export Canadian maple syrup to Spain. He decides to use a discount shipping company a friend of a friend told him about. Arthur decides that he will purchase cargo insurance for his bulk shipment of maple syrup. The shipping company claims that the trip will be non-stop from Toronto to a port in Spain. However, once the ship is en route, the captain makes a detour to Boston to pick up some cocaine. While leaving Boston Harbor, the ship is boarded by American customs, impounded, and taken back to shore. Will Arthur's cargo insurance cover him for his impounded cargo?

40. While transporting a shipment of automobiles valued at $1,000,000 for Ed's BMW from Germany to Montreal, the brand new vessel, valued at $81 million begins to sink. In order to save the ship and the crew, much of the cargo is thrown overboard. The estimated loss is $700,000. How much of the loss will each party assume using the general average method of calculating losses? (Answer: $691,463, 8,537)

41. For each of the following situations, indicate what type of non-employee theft coverage would apply.

(a) Jacob Jewellers is robbed by four masked bandits who steal a collection of very valuable Rolex watches.

(b) The local Try-N-Save discount electronics store issues a refund cheque to Beth for $500 for a defective MP3 player. Beth, angered that she is not paid in cash, decides to get back at Try-N-Save and she electronically doctors the amount of the cheque so it now reads $5,000. What type of insurance would cover Try-N-Save?

(c) Jacob Jewellers decides to move his store to a less crime-prone neighbourhood. He loads up what is left of his inventory with a moving company that specializes in moving highly valued inventory. During the move, the moving van is looted by gun-waving thugs and all Jacob's remaining inventory is gone.

(d) Hackers crack into the BNO on-line banking accounts of customers. They illegally transfer the hard-earned balances in the savings accounts of BNO customers into their illegal accounts overseas.

(e) Joanna has a customer pay for a large bar tab at her restaurant with fake $100 bills. She realizes this after the customer is long gone.

42. Ana is caught stealing merchandise from the retail clothing outlet she works at. Her boss, Mike, decides to let her off by deducting from her pay the value of the merchandise that she tried to steal. But he also decides to keep her on. However, later in the day he tells the insurance company what happens and how he has decided to fix the situation. A week later, Ana runs off, never to be found, with $1,500 of cash from the till. Will the insurance company cover the loss due to theft?

43. Marcia's hat store was doing extremely well before the coat store next door closed for six months due to a fire. What kind of insurance should she have to keep her in business until the coat store opens up again?

44. Secure Tech designs bullet-proof vests for police officers and other security officials. Recently it has come under fire because officers have been dying from bullet wounds to the chest while wearing the vests. What form of product liability is this? Support your argument.

45. For each of the following situations, indicate what type of liability insurance would be best.
(a) A week after fixing a leaky plumbing connection, the pipe bursts and floods a customer's home. It is determined that the plumber actually did not secure the pipe properly, thus leading to the breakage.

(b) The Daimler Chrysler plant in Brampton, Ontario, subcontracts the building of brakes for all of its vehicles to a small brakes manufacturing plant in Brampton. Recently Daimler Chrysler has been named as the defendant in hundreds of civil lawsuits in Canada, where customers suffered serious injury due to faulty brakes.

(c) Daimler Chrysler has been informed that a large batch of its Chrysler 300 have been inexplicably catching fire and seriously burning their customers.

46. Moe is throwing a bachelor party for his friend, Lenny, at his bar, Moe's Tavern. Moe has been providing drinks at half price to everyone who is at the party. After a night of drinking at the party, Carl, a close friend of Lenny, decides to drive home. On his way home he jumps a curve and kills local millionaire Monty Burns. Who is liable for the death? What legal principle qualifies this person as guilty?

47. For each of the following situations, indicate which type of professional liability is present.
(a) While closing the sale of a million-dollar-home in Mississauga, Sundeep, who is a real estate agent, forgets to do the title search on the property that he was contracted to do.

(b) Paul, a recently graduated civil engineer from Ryerson University, has just landed a job with a construction company that does large-scale welfare housing construction for the Ontario government. Paul is responsible for designing a new block of homes that will replace some old unsafe homes located in Toronto. Paul forgets to double-check his calculations in his specifications before authorizing the homes be built according to his plan. There is a strong possibility that he made an error that could lead to serious bodily harm to the tenants of those homes.

(c) A plastic surgeon accidentally gives a patient breast reduction surgery when he was supposed to give her breast enhancement surgery.

(d) Martin is vice-president of human resources at a small brewery in Quebec and he has a particular prejudice against applicants who are French speaking. He is caught by some francophone workers making prejudicial remarks about numerous francophones. The employees decide to sue him, the company, and the board of directors.

48. For each situation, indicate what type of surety bond is required.

(a) A Canadian firm successfully bids on a contract to replace all the water treatment equipment at all the water sanitization facilities in New Orleans.

(b) The City of New Orleans requires that the water sanitization facilities be equipped with water pumps that are in excess of 125 horsepower.

(c) The city is worried that after the equipment has been installed it will require frequent servicing.

(d) The Canadian firm is worried that it may not get paid by the city of New Orleans in a timely fashion, as the city is already heavily indebted.

(e) U.S. federal law requires that the pumps installed must be able to pump water continuously at a minimum speed of 100 horsepower. If not, the federal government can step in and shut down the water treatment facility.

(f) Before Virginia could begin work for Latino Life Insurance Company, she had to be bonded. What type of bond is this?

Health Care

Learning Objectives

After completing this chapter, students will be able to:

A. Know the ways health care risk is insured in Canada.

B. Understand the philosophy behind "universal health care", which is the foundation for the *Canada Health Act*.

C. Be aware of what is covered and what is excluded in provincial and territorial health care plans.

D. See how the gaps in provincial and territorial coverage are met by supplementary health care plans.

Introduction

This chapter is the first of three that addresses **life and health risks**. These risks are addressed by

- health care plans for the provinces and territories,
- income protection plans,
- life insurance, and
- retirement plans, which are not covered in this textbook.

There are three sources of health care benefits which are summarized in Table 6.1:

1. Government plans
2. Group plans through employers or associations
3. Individual plans

Table 6.1   Coverage for Life and Health Risks

Risk	Sources of coverage		
	Government Plans	Plans Through Employers or Associations	Individual Plans
Health Care (Chapter 6)	• Provincial and Territorial Health Plans	• Group insurance	• Individual plans such as Blue Cross • Travel insurance • Long-term care insurance
Income Protection (Chapter 7)	• Workers' Compensation • Employment Insurance • Canada Pension Plan disability benefits	• Group disability insurance	• Disability insurance • Critical Illness insurance

Life Insurance (Chapter 8)	• Canada Pension Plan death benefit (maximum $2,500)	• Group life insurance
		• Key person insurance
			• Individual politics:
			  • Term
			  • Whole life
			  • Universal life
			  • Segregated funds

Table 6.1   Continued

Risk	Sources of coverage		
	Government Plans	Plans Through Employers or Associations	Individual Plans
Retirement Income	• Canada Pension Plan retirement benefits • Old Age Security Program which includes Old Age Security Pension (OAS) and Guaranteed Income Supplement (GIS)	• Registered Pension Plans (RPP) • Deferred Profit Sharing Plans (DPSP) • Supplementary Retirement Account (SRA)	• Registered Retirement Savings Plans (RRSP) • Individual Pension Plans (IPP)

Government Health Insurance Plans

Medicare in Canada developed over several decades and while there are now many problems with the system, Canadians have the benefit of **universal health care** — health care coverage available to al residents of a province or territory.

Background

T.C. (Tommy) Douglas (1904–1986) is known as the father of medicare. Born in Scotland, his family immigrated in 1910 and settled in Winnipeg, went back to Scotland for the First World War, and returned in 1919. In 1911, Douglas came close to having a leg amputated due to a bone infection since his family could not afford a specialist. However, a surgeon offered to operate for free if his students could attend the surgery, thus saving his leg and perhaps his life. This is said to be the formation of his dream of universal health care.

Douglas went to Saskatchewan in 1930 as the minister for Calvary Baptist Church. From 1935 to 1944, he was the Member of Parliament for the federal Co-operative Commonwealth Federation (CCF), which was formed in 1932. As leader of the provincial CCF, he was premier of Saskatchewan from 1944 to 1961. In 1961, the federal CCF joined with the Canadian Labour Congress (CLC) to create a new national party, New Democratic Party (NDP), and Douglas was its leader from 1961 to 1971.

Hospital Insurance Plans

By the 1920s, Saskatchewan was providing treatment and free hospitalization for tuberculosis patients. Under Douglas, the Saskatchewan CCF passed the *Saskatchewan Hospitalization Act* to provide free hospital care (universal hospital care) in 1946. Limited provincial hospital insurance plans followed in B.C. in 1949 and Alberta in 1950.

In 1957, the federal *Hospital Insurance and Diagnostic Services (HIDS) Act* funded 50% of the cost for any jurisdiction that adopted a universal hospital insurance plan. As a result, the Saskatchewan plan was revised to come under the cost-sharing program and, between 1958 and 1961, all other jurisdictions introduced hospital insurance plans. The *HIDS Act* contained five conditions that are also the requirements of the current *Canada Health Act*: public administration, comprehensiveness, universality, portability, and accessibility.

Health Care Plans

The Saskatchewan NDP party set up a universal health care plan in 1962. Doctors went on strike for 23 days, revisions were made to the plan and, by 1965, most Saskatchewan doctors supported the plan. In 1961 the federal Conservative party under John Diefenbaker created a **Royal Commis-**

sion on Health Services, led by Supreme Court Justice Emmett Hall. In 1964, his report, the **Hall Report**, recommended a national health care plan — a joint federal/provincial system to cover the costs of preventative health care services and hospital care for everyone.

In 1966, the federal Liberals under Lester Pearson introduced the *Medical Care Act of 1966*, which came into effect on July 1, 1968, again paying 50%. In 1977, the federal Liberals under Pierre Trudeau replaced 50–50 funding with block funding. Saskatchewan and B.C. were the first to create health insurance plans in 1968 and all the others joined, ending with Yukon in 1972.

There was not then and is not now a Canadian health care system since all jurisdictions developed their own plans. Hospitals are mostly non-profit while lab services are often provided by private corporations who operate under a Schedule of Benefits that defines costs. Most medical doctors operate small, independent businesses operating alone or in small groups on a fee-for-service basis. Since 2000, medical doctors can incorporate, which they do for tax reasons. It is a public system but not a national system, such as the **National Health Service (NHS)** in the United Kingdom.

During the 1970s, federal requirements and funding both decreased. Provinces and territories started charging user fees and allowing extra billing or, in the case of Ontario, paid 90% of the Schedule of Benefits amount in order to fund increasing medical costs. In 1980, the **Health Services Review**, again under Emmett Hall, recommended putting an end to user fees and extra billing. In 1984, the federal government passed the *Canada Health Act* **(CHA)**, which mandated five criteria for the health plans and banned extra billing and user fees.

Canada Health Act (CHA) — Provincial and Territorial Health Plans

The *Canada Health Act* is Canada's federal health insurance legislation. The act sets out the primary objective of Canadian health care policy:

> *"... to protect, promote and restore the physical and mental well-being of residents of Canada and to facilitate reasonable access to health services without financial or other barriers."*

Our system is based on the principle of "universal health care" for residents of provinces and territories, comes under provincial jurisdiction, and is based on the *Canada Health Act* (Health Canada www.hc-sc.gc.ca) that sets out the minimum criteria the provinces and territories must meet:

1. **Public Administration**. The plan must be administered and operated on a non-profit basis by a public authority accountable to the provincial or territorial government.
2. **Comprehensiveness**. The plan must be comprehensive — it must cover all health services provided by hospitals, physicians, or dentists (i.e., surgical-dental services that require a hospital setting) and, where the law of the jurisdiction so permits, similar or additional services rendered by other health care practitioners.
3. **Universality**. All of the province or territory's residents must be covered by the plan based on uniform terms and conditions. Provinces and territories generally require that residents register with the plans to establish entitlement, usually as evidenced by having a valid health card. Newcomers to Canada, such as landed immigrants or Canadians returning from other countries to live in Canada, may be subject to a waiting period not to exceed three months as set by a province or territory before they are entitled to receive insured health services.
4. **Portability**. Coverage must be portable from one province to another, i.e., you are never not covered while in Canada. The waiting period from province-to-province must not exceed three months. In addition, the following applies:
   (a) Residents temporarily absent from their home province or territory or from Canada must continue to be covered for insured health services during their absence.
      i. This does not entitle a person to seek services in another province, territory, or country.
      ii. It is intended to permit a person to receive necessary services in relation to an urgent or emergency need when absent from Canada temporarily, such as on business or vacation.

(b) While temporarily absent in another province or territory, insured services are paid at the **host province's** rate — the rate in the jurisdiction where the patient needs treatment.

(c) While temporarily out of the country, insured services are to be paid at the **home** province's rate — the rate where the patient normally lives. (*Note: This is where the problem arises when travelling in, for instance, the United States, where the costs are significantly higher.*)

(d) Prior approval by the health care insurance plan in a person's home province or territory may also be required before coverage is extended for elective (non-emergency) services to a resident while temporarily absent from his or her province or territory. This means that if someone goes to the United States for a hip replacement, for instance, he or she needs prior approval from the home province's plan, which may reimburse either the home province's rate or the full cost.

5. **Accessibility**. The same services must be provided for all residents in a province or territory so that insured persons have reasonable access to insured hospital, medical, and surgical-dental services on uniform terms and conditions, unprecluded or unimpeded, either directly or indirectly, by charges (user charges or extra-billing) or other means (e.g., discrimination on the basis of age, health status, or financial circumstances). In addition, health care insurance plans of the province or territory must provide:

    (a) reasonable compensation to physicians and dentists for all the insured health services they provide, and

    (b) payment to hospitals to cover the cost of insured health services.

Reasonable access in terms of physical availability of **medically necessary** services has been interpreted under the Act using the "where and as available" rule. Thus, residents of a province or territory are entitled to have access on uniform terms and conditions to insured health services at the setting *where* the services are provided and *as* the services are available in that setting.

What Is Covered

The *Canada Health Act* prescribes the two services — extended health care and insured health — to be included in a provincial or territorial plan and provided to residents of the jurisdiction.

Extended Health Care Services

These services are:

- nursing home intermediate care service,
- adult residential care service,
- home care service, and
- ambulatory health care service.

Insured Health Services

This means hospital services, physician services, and surgical-dental services provided to insured persons, but does not include any health services that a person is entitled to and eligible for under any other act of Parliament and provincial Workers' Compensation.

1. **Hospital services** means any of the following services provided to in-patients or out-patients at a hospital, if the services are medically necessary, for the purpose of maintaining health, preventing disease, or diagnosing or treating an injury, illness, or disability, namely
    - accommodation and meals at the standard or public ward level and preferred accommodation if medically required;
    - nursing service;

- laboratory, radiological, and other diagnostic procedures, together with the necessary interpretations;
- drugs, biologicals, and related preparations when administered in the hospital;
- use of operating room, case room and anaesthetic facilities, including necessary equipment and supplies;
- medical and surgical equipment and supplies;
- use of radiotherapy facilities;
- use of physiotherapy facilities; and
- services provided by persons who receive remuneration from the hospital or clinic.

2. **Physician services** means any medically required services rendered by **medical practitioners**.
3. **Surgical-dental services** means any medically or dentally required surgical-dental procedures performed by a dentist in a hospital, where a hospital is required for the proper performance of the procedures.

The *Canada Health Act* (CHA) also provides the following definitions:

- **Dentist** means a person lawfully entitled to practise dentistry in the place in which the practice is carried on by that person.
- **Health care practitioner** means a person lawfully entitled under the law of a province to provide health services in the place in which the services are carried on by that person.
- **Hospital** includes any facility or portion thereof that provides hospital care, including acute, rehabilitative, or chronic care, but does not include
  - a hospital or institution primarily for the mentally disordered, or
  - a facility or portion thereof that provides nursing home intermediate care service or adult residential care service, or comparable services for children.
- **Medical practitioner** means a person lawfully entitled to practise medicine in the place in which the practice is carried on by that person.

Although not spelled out in the *Canada Health Act*, **medically required services** of general practitioners and specialists include the following:

- Diagnosis and treatment of medical conditions
- Surgical services
- Maternity services
- Anaesthesia services
- X-rays
- Lab and other diagnostic procedures in approved facilities
- Inoculations
- Vaccinations and routine physical exams
- Specialists' services upon referral

Prohibitions

The *Canada Health Act* stipulates that the following are *not* allowed:

1. **Extra-billing** is billing an amount over and above the amount paid by the Health Plan. An example is charging patients $5 or $10 for an office visit.
2. A **user charge**, also called **user fee**, is any charge for an insured health service that is covered by a Health Plan that is not payable by the Health Plan. An example is charging a **facility fee** for receiving an insured service at a hospital or clinic.
3. Any service provided by a provincial plan may be not provided by a **private clinic** for a fee.

Excluded Coverage

The *Canada Health Act* outlines two categories of **excluded insured services**:

1. A number of services provided by hospitals and physicians are considered **not medically necessary** and thus are not insured under provincial and territorial health insurance legislation.
   (a) **Uninsured hospital services** for which patients may be charged include
      i. preferred hospital accommodation unless prescribed by a physician (hospital charges for private or semi-private rooms);
      ii. private duty nursing services; and
      iii. the providing of telephones and televisions.
   (b) **Uninsured physician services** for which patients may be charged include
      i. telephone advice;
      ii. providing medical certificates for work, school, insurance purposes and fitness clubs;
      iii. medical exams for employment, life insurance, schools, camps, passports, visa or similar purposes;
      iv. testimony in court;
      v. cosmetic services, cosmetic surgery for purely aesthetic purposes; and
      vi. tattoo removal.
      However, there can be exceptions, for example, the removal of concentration camp tattoos or reconstructive cosmetic surgery following a trauma can be covered.

2. **Certain services and groups of persons** are excluded from the definitions for insured services and insured persons:
   (a) Members of the Canadian Forces
   (b) Persons appointed to a position of rank within the Royal Canadian Mounted Police
   (c) Persons serving a prison term in a federal penitentiary
   (d) Persons who have not completed a minimum period of residence in a province or territory (a period that must not exceed three months)

Optional Coverages

Some services fall outside the definition of insured health services under the *Canada Health Act*. However, these *can* be provided at provincial and territorial discretion, on terms and conditions, defined by each jurisdiction. In addition to services such as prescription drugs, ambulance services, and eye examinations, additional services might target specific population groups, such as children, seniors, or social assistance recipients and may be partially or fully covered by each health insurance plan.

All plans cover services as mandated in the *Canada Health Act* above. Additional coverages are usually available only to residents of the jurisdiction. In addition, the government plan is usually the **payor of last resort**, meaning it pays only if the cost is not covered by a private plan or another government plan, such as Workers' Compensation.

Prescription Drugs

Each province and territory has a **formulary** of **listed drugs**, a list of prescription drugs covered by its plan. Prescription drugs not on the list are not covered.

Prescription drugs are always covered if they are dispensed in a hospital, clinic, or nursing home. Over-the-counter (OTC) drugs are generally not covered even if prescribed by a physician. As shown in the following table, some jurisdictions offer better coverage than others for seniors, low-income families, palliative care (to relieve symptoms but not provide a cure), and for some chronic diseases.

Table 6.2   Prescription Drug Coverage for Health Plans

	Seniors	Other
AB	• Contracted to Alberta Blue Cross: 70% covered. The individual pays a maximum of $25 per prescription or refill over the lowest cost to a maximum of $25,000 a year for drug and certain other benefits.	
	• Entire family is covered if *anyone* is over 65.	• For those without group coverage, there is a plan with a quarterly premium. • Palliative care is 100% covered after a $1,000 deductible.
BC	• Pharmacare: The deductible is based on family income and is 0 to 2% for seniors (1.25%–3% for others) of family income. Then 75% (70%) is covered to a maximum of 1–3% (2 to 4%) of family income. Then 100% is covered.	
MB	• Pharmacare: After reaching the deductible, 100% of eligible drugs are covered. The deductible is a minimum of $100 and starts at 2.69% for income up to $15,000; goes up to 6.08% for income over $100,000.	
NB	• If receiving GIS*, seniors pay $9.05 per prescription to an annual maximum of $250. • Other low-income seniors pay $15 per prescription with no annual maximum.	• For people receiving social assistance and clients of the Department of Social Development, fees are $4 per prescription with a ceiling of $250. • For residents of nursing homes, children in the care of the Department of Social Development and children with special needs, no fees. • There are plans for people with • HIV, cystic fibrosis, growth-hormone deficiency, and solid organ transplant recipients: $50/year premium and a fee of 20% of the prescription up to $20 with annual maximum of $500 per family. • Multiple sclerosis: $50/year premium and co-pay from 0 to 100% for each prescription.
NL	• 100% of drug costs but not dispensing fees for people receiving GIS and registered for OAS.	• Pays up to 100% with co-pay based on income for low-income families and families with high drug costs. • 100% coverage for people with cystic fibrosis and growth hormone deficiency.
NS	• Pharmacare: $424 annual premium, 30% co-pay to a maximum per prescription of $30, and an annual maximum of $382.	• Low-income people are covered under Family Pharmacare, and people with diabetes are covered under the Diabetes Assistance Program. The annual deductible takes into account family income and family size. After the deductible, there is a 20% co-pay.
NT	• 100% coverage for people over 60.	• Lengthy list of diseases are covered such as asthma, lupus, and HIV. There is a plan for Métis** that covers 100%.
NU	• Seniors are 100% covered.	• First Nations, Inuit, and Innu residents of Nunavut are covered through the federal Non-Insured Health Benefits (NIHB) program. • If receiving income support, coverage is available through the Indigent Health Benefits program. • Non-Aboriginal Nunavut residents diagnosed with a disease/condition and some seniors have coverage through Extended Health Benefits (EHB).
ON	• Seniors are covered with a $100 annual deductible and a $6.11 co-pay.	• Low-income seniors and social assistance recipients are covered with a $2.00 co-pay. • Trillium Drug Program provides assistance for those with high drug costs relative to their income. There is an income-based deductible and a co-pay of $2.00. • The Special Drugs program provides coverage for people with certain diseases, such as HIV, growth hormone failure, and schizophrenia.

Table 6.2 Continued

	Seniors	Other
PEI	• Seniors pay $11 plus the dispensing fee.	• 100% coverage for people on social assistance and for people with specific diseases, such as cystic fibrosis and multiple sclerosis.
QC	• The mandatory basic government plan (RAMQ — Régie de l'assurance maladie du Québec) has premiums that are income-based and range from $0 to $585. Those in a group plan can opt out. No premiums are payable by seniors collecting GIS, low-income families, and children under 18. The monthly deductible is either $0 or $14.95, the co-pay is either 0% or 32%, and the maximum monthly contribution for a person is $0, $49.97, or $79.53.	

SK	• Seniors pay the least of:
	Under the Seniors Drug Plan, a maximum of $15 per prescription if income is less than $64,066, or
	• A $35 co-pay and
	  • for GIS recipients, a $200 semi-annual deductible
	  • for GIS recipients living in a special-care home and for Senior Income Plan (SIP) participants, a $100 semi-annual deductible.
		• The Special Support Program (SSP) is for families whose drug costs are high compared to their income. The deductible and co-pay are based on income.
		• Family Health Benefits covers low-income families. It has a $100 semi-annual deductible and 35% co-pay.
		• Palliative Care and Saskatchewan Aids to Independent Living (SAIL) covers 100% for specific diseases.

YT	• 100% coverage for seniors.	• 100% coverage for:
		  • children's Drug and Optical Program for low income families with children under 19
		  • palliative Care and Chronic Disease Program for specific chronic conditions

* GIS is the Guaranteed Income Supplement available to lower-income people over age 65 who are collecting Old Age Security (OAS). OAS is covered in Chapter 7.

** A Métis is "a person of mixed North American Indian and European ancestry, who identifies as Métis. (We also accept people who may use other words to indicate their identity, such as, 'bois brulez', 'Michif', 'half-breed', 'mixed-blood', etc.)".' Source: Métis Community of Vancouver Island, www.metis.ca

Laboratory and Diagnostic Tests

As required in the Canada Health Act, these are always covered when performed in a hospital for in-patients. B.C., Manitoba, Newfoundland and Labrador, Ontario, and Quebec also cover some listed tests when there is a prescription and they are done in an approved facility. Testing can also include screening for breast cancer and colon cancer.

Accommodation

Private and semi-private rooms are covered only if prescribed by a physician (if, for instance, the person has a contagious disease). Charges for private and semi-private rooms are legislated in Manitoba, Newfoundland and Labrador, Prince Edward Island, and Quebec and not legislated in the others. Rates range from $24 for a semi-private room in Alberta and $110–$235 in Ontario, and, for a private room, $46 in Alberta and $200–$325 in Ontario.

Ambulance

Provincial and territorial plans often cover hospital-to-hospital transfers if the patient is an in-patient. Manitoba further requires the patient be returned to the prescribing hospital within 24 hours. Nova Scotia and Yukon do not pay for ambulances at all. Ontario pays but has a $45 co-pay while the co-pay for PEI is $130 and for Alberta is $6.33. In B.C., the co-pay is $54 for the first 40 km and $0.50/km after that to a maximum of $274. Ambulance costs are covered in the Homeowners

Policy, Coverages F and H, Section II—Insurance on Your Liability to Others and may be covered in an employer's group plan.

Dental

The *Canada Health Act* requires coverage of "surgical-dental services meaning any medically or dentally required surgical-dental procedures performed by a dentist in a hospital, where a hospital is required for the prior performance of the procedures". Some jurisdictions also cover surgery to correct a cleft palate or a facial deformity. A few cover preventative dentistry for children under 12, 16, or 19.

Eye Exams

Many plans cover one eye examination for children under age 9, 17, 18, or 19 and seniors over 65—one every year in Alberta, Ontario, Quebec, and Saskatchewan, one every two years in B.C., Manitoba, Nova Scotia. Ontario also pays for one examination a year for people on social assistance or with an approved medical condition while B.C. covers all medically required exams.

Hearing Aids

Hearings aids are covered less well than eye exams, presumably because more people need glasses than need hearing aids. The following jurisdictions have some coverage:

- Manitoba covers 80% of an analog device up to $500 per ear or $1,800 for a programable device every four years with a $75 deductible for children 18 and under,
- Northwest Territories covers $500 every three years for Seniors and Métis,
- Nunavut covers one hearing aid every five years and another one if the prescription changes within the five years,
- Ontario pays up to $500 per ear every three years,
- Quebec pays for everyone who meets the hearing impairment criteria, and
- Yukon pays 100% for children under 15 and for one aid every four years for seniors.

Alternative Medical Practitioners

Canada's current health care system is based on the practice of traditional western medicine. However, some alternative health care is covered, at least partially, by some provincial and territorial health insurance plans. These services include the services of **chiropractors** (manipulation of bones and muscles), **podiatrists** (for feet), **osteopaths** (manipulation of muscles and joints), **naturopaths, licensed massage therapists** and **acupuncturists**. **Physiotherapy** is covered if it is medically required and is done in a hospital or an approved clinic. The dollar amount and number of visits are usually limited.

As health care plans face increasing cost pressures, they **delist** (take off the list of what is covered by the provincial or territorial plan) some of these coverages. For instance, in 2004, Ontario delisted chiropractic services, routine optometry exams, and physiotherapy (when not "medically required").

Table 6.3   Health Plan Coverages not Mandated by the *Canada Health Act*

	Routine Dental	Eye Exams	Hearing Aids	Alternative Practitioners
AB	No	1/year	No	Some coverage for chiropractic, podiatry, and osteopathy
BC	No	1/2 years	No	Some coverage for chiropractic, podiatry, osteopathy, naturopathy, and massage therapy
MB	No	1/2 years	Under 18	Chiropractors — 12 visits @ $10.75 ($11.30 north of 53rd parallel)

Table 6.3   Continued

	Routine Dental	Eye Exams	Hearing Aids	Alternative Practitioners
NB	No	No	No	No
NL	Yes, under 12	No	No	No
NS	No	1/2 years	No	No
NT	No	No	Seniors and Métis	No
NU	No	No	Seniors	No
ON	No	1/year	Yes	Some coverage for podiatry
PE	Yes, age 3–16	No	No	No
QC	Yes, under 10	1/year	Yes	No
SK	No	1/year	No	Some coverage for chiropractic and podiatry
YT	Yes, Grades K–8	No	Some	No

Opted-out and Non-participating Physicians

Every jurisdiction allows physicians to operate outside the provincial or territorial health insurance plans and bill their patients directly. They generally cannot operate in both the public sectors (participating in the Health Plan) and the private sector (billing patients directly) at the same time.

- **Opted-out doctors** bill the patient directly at an amount not exceeding the amount in the **Schedule of Benefits** (the maximum amount that can be charged) for the jurisdiction. The patient then submits a claim to the health care plan and is reimbursed by the plan.
- **Non-participating doctors** bill the patient directly without regard to the limits of the Schedule of Benefits and the patient *cannot* be reimbursed.

Table 6.4   Opted-out and Non-participating Doctors March 31, 2008

	Total	Opted Out			Non-Participating			Participating			
		Total	GP	Specialist	Total	GP	Specialist	Total	GP	Specialist	Other
AB	6,058	n/a			0			6,058	3,361	2,697	
BC	8,779	5	3	2	2	2		8,772	4,806	3,966	
MB	2,070	0			n/a			2,070	1,061	1,009	
NB	1,453	N/A			N/A			1,453	708	745	
NL	989	0			0			989	480	509	
NS	2,290	0			n/a			2,290	943	1,341	6
NT	300	0			0			300	57	21	**222
NU	156	0			0			156	91	65	
ON	23,900	41	10	31	0			2,3859	11,288	12,571	
PE	221	0			0			221	111	110	
QC*	17,148	148	83	65	0			17,000	8,500	8,500	
SK	1,795	0			0			1,795	1,029	766	
YT	67	0			0			67	58	9	
	65,226	194	96	98	2	2	0	65,030	32,493	32,309	228
	100.00%	0.2974%			0.0031%			99.6995%			

n/a = not applicable
N/A = not available
* All numbers for Quebec are estimates based on 2007 and 2009.
** Locum (travelling)
Source: *Canada Health Act* Annual Report, 2007–2008

Wait Times and Shortage of Doctors

In 2002, Roy J. Romanow, Q.C., was appointed Commissioner of the **Commission of the Future of Health Care in Canada**. His mandate was to talk to Canadians about the future of Canada's public health care system and to make recommendations to enure the long-term sustainability of a universal, publically funded health care system and also to find a balance between prevention and maintaining health and care and treatment. The Commission spoke with tens of thousands of people representing many interested parties and made 47 recommendations [www.cbc.ca/healthcare]. His report, *Building on Values: The Future of Health Care in Canada — Final Report*, or the *Romanow Report*, stated the following:

- Canadians support to the core values of equity, fairness and solidarity.
- Most have been well served by it.
- They want
    - it to be more comprehensive, and
    - the system to be more accountable.

There is concern about the wait times for existing services especially diagnostic services as well as access particularly in rural and remote areas.

In 2007, there were 63,682 physicians in Canada — an increase from 2003 of 7.1% when the Canadian population grew by 4.2%. Nonetheless, *Canadian Medical Association Journal* reports that in January 2009, one-sixth of Canadians were looking for a family physician. The **National Physician Survey**, 2007, indicated that 58% of family/general practitioners (FP/GPs) either were not taking new patients or were limiting the numbers of patients they would see.

Table 6.5   Percentage of Doctors Not Accepting New Patients, 2007

AB	63%
BC	64%
MB	62%
NB	71%
NL	51%
NS	65%
ON	69%
PE	76%
QC	62%
SK	51%

Source: National Physician Survey, The College of Family Physicians of Canada, *MD Pulse*, 2008 [www.nationalphysiciansurvey.ca]

The shortage of physicians, specialists, and surgeons is due to longer training requirements, fewer foreign doctors finding residency places, and cuts to medical school enrolment. In 2008/2009, there were 2,616 places in Canadian faculties of medicine. Ontario alone is short 2,500 doctors. With 23,900 doctors in Ontario, this means a shortage of over 10%. Extrapolating to the rest of the country, Canadians are short approximately 6,500 doctors. This shortage is a major factor in the wait times. Furthermore, 2,600 Ontario doctors, 11% of the doctors in Ontario, are over the age of 65 and getting ready to retire. It takes seven or eight years to train a specialist.

In addition, improvements in technology and treatment mean that people are living longer — average life expectancy in Canada has increased by seven years since the mid-1960s. This, combined with the 10% shortage of doctors, has resulted in delays of several months before seeing a specialist or getting non-emergency care and surgery.

National Wait Times Strategy

In the 1990s, governments at all levels began addressing their budget deficits. With health care accounting for about 40% of public sector spending, hospitals were closed, physicians fees were frozen or cut, nurses were laid off and spaces for medical students and medical technicians at government-funded universities and colleges were cut back. In 2004, the **First Ministers' Conference on Health Care** made a commitment to increase spending on health care over the next six years and, in the 10-year plan called a **National Wait Times Strategy**, named five **priority areas**. The provinces agreed to work toward meeting benchmarks for waiting times, as established by the federal government. The benchmarks were established in December 2005.

Table 6.6   Benchmarks Set by the National Wait Times Strategy

Priority	Wait-time Goals
Cancer Care	• Radiation therapy to treat cancer within four weeks of patients' being ready to treat.
Cardiac Treatment	• Cardiac bypass patients will receive treatment within 2 to 26 weeks, depending on the severity of the case.
Diagnostic Tests	• Breast cancer screening for women aged 50 to 69 every two years. Cervical cancer screening for women aged 18 to 69 every three years.
Joint Replacements	• Hip replacements within 26 weeks. Knee replacements within 26 weeks. Hip fracture treatment within 48 hours.
Cataract Surgeries	• Surgery to remove cataracts within 16 weeks for patients who are at high risk of losing their eyesight. (*Note: Being at risk of losing your eyesight is a very advanced stage and happens long after you simply can't drive or read unless the reading material is 6 inches from your eyes.*)

Report on Wait Times

How are the jurisdictions doing overall? The results vary by province but real progress has been made. The checkmark (✓) in the following table indicates that 75% of patients receive treatment within the benchmark.

Table 6.7   Report on Wait Times, April 2009

	Cancer — Radiation Treatment	Coronary Artery Bypass Surgery	Hip Replacements	Knee Replacements	Cataract Surgery
AB	n/a	✓	✓	No	No
BC	✓	✓	✓	No	✓
MB	✓	✓	✓	No	✓
NB	✓	✓	No	No	No
NL	✓	✓	✓	No	No
NS	n/a	n/a	No	No	✓
ON	✓	✓	✓	✓	✓
PE	✓	n/a	No	✓	No
QC	✓	n/a	✓	✓	n/a
SK	✓	✓	No	No	✓

✓ 75% of patients receive treatment within benchmark

No 75% of patients do not receive treatment within benchmark
n/a not available

Source: Canadian Institute for Health Information, Surgical Volume Trends, 2009 — Within and beyond Wait Time Priority Areas (Ottawa, Ont.: CIHI, 2009).

Final Report of the Federal Advisor on Wait Times — Dr. Brian Postl

This report, prepared by Brian D. Postl, MD, the Federal Advisor on Wait Times, was released in June, 2006 by Health Canada (www.hc-sc.gc.ca Home). His report raised urgent issues that are not being addressed at any level of government. He went beyond his mandate to address several specific issues that have implications for understanding wait times.

Wait Times for Children

Children do not fare better than adults when it comes to wait times, but clinical or surgical intervention for children is often more critical than for adults. In addition there are social, educational, and psychological effects associated with illness, hospitalization, and the inability of the child to participate in the real work of growing up. The failure to progress with his or her cohort can affect a child's life for a long time.

Surge Capacity

Surge capacity is the ability to respond to a surge in need or demand on a timely basis. It is the ability to access additional unused capacity, outside of the local region or province. Sometimes it exists and sometimes it does not and has been an issue in Canada for many years. The need for it was seen in the Severe Acute Respiratory Syndrome (SARS) event in 2001. It can also arise from a natural disaster, such as a storm or blackout; a man-made disaster, such as refinery explosion; and other unplanned events, such as multiple traumas during a prolonged period of inclement weather conditions.

Health Human Resources (HHR)

Shortages of anaesthesiologists, family doctors, psychiatrists, nurses, and other health care professionals is a concern along with delays in treatment. HHR also affects the ability to educate, train, and recruit health care professionals and to distribute them to areas where there is a shortage.

Gender-based Analysis (GBA)

Until 20 years ago, program planning, evaluation and patient care did not consider the difference between men and women, and boys and girls. GBA helps ensure that appropriate care of high quality is available to everyone. Setting wait time benchmarks has focused on the efficiency and effectiveness of the health care system to meet these benchmarks. However, idiosyncratic effects that disease and waiting for care has on men and women have not been addressed.

Cinderella Diseases

Cinderella diseases are diseases that were not recognized, or prioritized, in the five areas selected for benchmarks. They are the diseases that did not get invited to the ball. The fear anddanger is that the five benchmarked conditions will starve out all others for attention, resources and technology, leaving Cinderella diseases behind temporarily if not permanently. An Ipsos Reid poll in the fall of 2005 of both the public and by health care professionals indicated that "2 in 3 (Canadians) are concerned that meeting the wait time benchmarks in the five priority areas will come at the expense of other health care services." It is difficult to prioritize and to decide which interventions are effective. Nonetheless, the concern about "Cinderella diseases" is well taken and it is not appropriate for health care systems to be focused on limited areas to the neglect of others.

Other Provincial Priorities

In his report, Dr. Postl had the following to say about other provincial priorities:

> Canadians also need to be aware that the issue of wait times is important to different provinces and territories in different ways. Provinces, territories, regional health authorities and facilities are learning from one another about better business practices, improved use of technology and information systems. That learning will set new standards for efficiencies, appropriate wait times and satisfactory outcomes.
>
> Each province and territory has a unique set of program priorities that may not be affected by the wait time work at all .... ranging from intervention programs (crystal meth intervention might be a good example) to programs designed to address chronic conditions at various stages of their progress (diabetes would be a good example of a long term initiative).[1]

---

1   "Wait Times: Causes and Cures," Just the Facts. (www.medicare.ca)

Update from Dr. Postl

Dr. Brian Postl, in addition to being a National Wait Time advisor, is CEO of Winnipeg Regional Health Authority. In May 2009, he made a public statement about privatization — the cure that many advocate. He summarizes the reasons for longer wait times:

- Poorly organized services arising from inefficiencies, a lack of coordination, and poor planning.
- A shortage of health care workers, which causes patients to over-use emergency rooms.
- Physicians not working in teams means they do not co-ordinate appointments and procedures.
- Cuts to hospital services — between 1988 and 2002, 64,000 hospital beds were cut.
- The need for more long-term care and home care to decrease inappropriate and preventable hospitalizations and visits to emergency rooms.

> **Wait times: Why for-profit is not the answer**
>
> *People who own private for-profit clinics often make the case that by letting the wealthy pay for private services, it will take the pressure of the public system and reduce wait times for the rest of us. In fact, the evidence shows this is not true.*
>
> - **Wait times are longer where this is a parallel for-profit system** — In countries with parallel for-profit and public systems, wait times are longer, not shorter than wait times in countries where there is only a public system.
> - **For-profit clinics take doctors and nurses out of the public system** — there are limited resources in our health care system. A for-profit private clinic takes doctors and nurses out of the public system to care for those who can afford it, while the rest of us face longer public lines as a result.
> - **"Cream-skimming" in for-profit care chooses easy-to-treat patients** — this practice leaves the higher risk, higher cost patients to the public system while make money off the simple cases. This means longer wait times in the public system.
> - **For-profit care isn't as safe** — Research shows that for-profit facilities are not as good for your health. One study estimated that if all Canadian hospitals were converted to for-profit, there would 2,200 additional deaths every year. That's not the way to shorten wait times.
> - **For-profit care costs more** — Costs in a parallel system are higher than in the public system. For example, knee replacement surgery in a public hospital costs $8,000; in a private facility, between $14,000 and $18,000. That's not a cost most of us can pay.
> - **Health care should be based on need, not on ability to pay** — It's one of the strongest beliefs of most Canadians. Our public health care reflects our Canadian values of equality and fairness. We want all Canadians to get access to quality and timely care — not just those who can afford to pay out of their own pockets.[2]

Articles in both Canada and the United States support and provide documentation for these assertions by Dr. Postl. Dr. Postl's suggested solutions are as follows:

- Fund the public solutions based on successful projects.
- Put patients before profits because efficient and appropriate patient care shorten wait times.
- Have common waiting lists — all patients for a procedure go into a single list for surgery by the first available surgeon. They can still choose their own surgeon but they might have to wait longer.
- Co-ordinate better by staggering start times for surgery and standardizing surgical equipment and procedures. Where tried, wait times deceased 75% and the number of surgeries completed increased by 136%.
- Expand teamwork to eliminate duplications, improve coordination and better use scarce resources.
- Modernize electronic information systems so everyone has timely access to up-to-date and accurate patient information with no waiting for patient records.
- Improve community care by increasing long-term care, home care, and home support.
- Improve access to family health care to decrease ER visits.

An Experiment: Centralizing and Prioritizing Cataract Surgery

Until January, 1999, cataract surgeons in Manitoba performed publicly-funded cataract surgery or they performed in both the public sector and in the private sector where they charged a "tray" or

---

2   Canadian Health Coalition [www.medicare.ca], *Just the Facts, Fact Sheet #2* (Wait Times), May, 2009.)

"facility" fee of $1,000. Since January, 1999, cataract surgery in Manitoba continues to be performed in both public hospitals and privately owned clinics but Manitoba Health covers all costs, ending privately funded procedures.

In 1999, the **Manitoba Cataract Waiting List Program (MCWLP)** was implemented using a new computer program in Winnipeg, where 90% of cataract operations are performed. This program centralized and prioritized cataract surgeries using a questionnaire to determine the severity of the visual impairment. As Table 6.8 shows, the overall wait time decreased as the number of procedures increased.

Table 6.8   Results for the Manitoba Cataract Waiting List Program

System	Median Waiting Times in Weeks			
	97/98	98/99	03/04	08/09
• Private clinics	4 20.6%	5 27.4%	n/a	n/a
• Public hospitals, public-only surgeons	10 25.8%	10 23.4%	16	11
• Public hospitals, surgeons operate in both private clinics and public hospitals	21 53.6%	6 49.2%	n/a	n/a
• # of surgeries	4,389	4,929	9,287	11,303

Sources: Carolyn DeCoster, RN, MBA; Leonard MacWilliam, MSc, MNRM; Randy Walld, BSc, BCcomm, *Waiting Times for Surgery: 1997/98 and 1998/99 Update*, Manitoba Centre for Health Policy and Evaluation, Department of Community Health Sciences, Faculty of Medicine, University of Manitoba, November 2000.

Carolyn DeCoster, PhD, RN; Dan Chateau, PhD; Matt Dahl, BSc; Ruth-Ann Soodeen, MSc; Nancy McKeen, PhD; *Waiting Times for Surgery, Manitoba 1999/2000 to 2003/04*, Manitoba Centre for Health Policy and Evaluation, Department of Community Health Sciences, Faculty of Medicine, University of Manitoba, June 2007.

Manitoba Wait Time Information, *Cataract Surgery Wait Times*, Manitoba Health, June 2009.

Lorne Bellan, MD, Mathen Mathen, MD, The Manitoba Cataract Waiting List Program, *Canadian Medical Association Journal*, April 17, 2001; 164 (8), 2001.

Surgeons operating in both the public and private sectors had markedly longer wait times presumably because the higher-paying private surgeries took precedence. As shown in Table 6.4, only two doctors in Canada do not participate in the public health system.

Two-tiered System

A two-tiered system is a system where doctors perform surgery and medical check-ups in both publicly funded hospitals and private, patient-paid clinics.

The argument *for* a private system is that we should have a choice, that Canada is one of only three countries in the world where private medical care is not available. You may pay property taxes both at your cottage and at your home and yet send your children to private school. That's your choice. Some doctors argue that we should have the same choice in medical care.

The argument *against* it is this: What happens to universal health care? What happens to the people who can't afford private? Those who favour a two-tiered system argue that the waiting lists will go down when more people opt for private. This hasn't happened in other countries, such as Australia and New Zealand, that have moved to a two-tiered system because as soon as there are fewer users, the public system receives less funding.

Sweden allows doctors to work in either the public sector or the private sector, but not both. France allows both but has different funding methods for each — in the public sector, doctors are paid a salary set by the government, and in the private sector they charge fees also set by the government. Alberta, one of the first to establish a two-tiered system, has concluded that there is no market for private, pay-only practices where doctors opt out *and* people are allowed to collect from the provincial plan (see Table 6.2). Provinces and territories have, by and large, turned a blind eye to private clinics who provide medically necessary surgery for a fee (they charge a fee, which covers the "frou-frous") and also collect the fee paid by the jurisdiction). However, as efficiencies decrease the wait times, the private clinics find their supply of patients drying up.

The Manitoba Cataract Waiting List Program indicates that there is room for improved efficiencies. Health care has improved but at a cost and, unlike the manufacturing sector, hospitals are not used to operating expensive diagnostic equipment 24 hours a day in three shifts. Now that they are beginning to do so, patients and staff may have to get over their sense that it is unreasonable to have an MRI at 3:00 a.m.

Concern about the Growth in Administrative Costs

Off the record, doctors and medical consultants claim that the problem has worsened with higher administration costs as hospitals hire read MBAs in an attempt to stream-line operations. On a bad day, they claim that CEOs of hospitals, making 3/4 of a million dollars a year, have surrounded themselves with administrators to protect their position. This additional high-priced support is funded by cutting back on time for operations and reducing the number of inpatient beds available. Surgeons and general practitioners are very frustrated by these cut-backs which increases wait times for their patients. Are hospitals actually doing this? The information is difficult to get. Let's look at some financial information for two large Toronto hospitals.

University Health Network (UHN) is comprised of Toronto General Hospital, Toronto Western Hospital, and Princess Margaret Hospital (Princess Margaret does cancer research, diagnosis and treatment). For UHN, we see that revenue, including external research funding, over seven years grew by 54.5% real (adjusted for inflation) while patient activity increased by 16.2% over the same time period.

Table 6.9   University Health Network, Toronto

	2001/2002 ($000)	2008/2009 ($000)	Change nominal	real
Consumer Price Index	97.8	114.1	16.7%	
Inpatient and Outpatient Activity (000)	971	1,128		**16.2%**
Growth in Revenue ($ millions)	$822	$1,482	80.3%	**54.5%**
Growth in External Research Funding Awards ($ millions)	$130	$228	75.4%	50.3%

Source: University Health Network, Annual Reports (Corporate Reports) [www.uhn.ca]

Mount Sinai's website provides a great deal more information about its activities. It is a much smaller hospital than University Health Network and is now operating at capacity — 472 beds. In 10 years, revenue from the province increased 93.2% real and salaries increased 96.4% real while patient days increased only 52.6% and beds in service, 23.6%. Furthermore, full-time staff increased 72.6% while medical staff increased only 17.7%, meaning there was a large increase in administrative staff.

The percentage change in revenue and patient activity would seem to indicate that hospitals have indeed been re-allocating their resources to provide more for administrative salaries.
Let's put this in perspective by looking at a comparison to administration costs for the United States, where 53.4% of the population has private health care coverage. In 2008, 95.7 million Americans (31.5% of the population) were covered by

• Medicare (44.8 million for those over 65 and with disabilities), or
• Medicaid (58.7 million for low-income families), or
• both (8.8 million),

while 46 million, 15.2%, had no health insurance coverage at all.

Exhibit 6.1 illustrates the spending costs for healthcare, per capita, in both the United States and Canada. It should be noted that the total cost, per capita for the U.S. is $1,059 and $307 for Canada.

Table 6.10 Mount Sinai Hospital

	1998/1999 ($000)	2008/2009 ($000)	Change % nominal	% real
Consumer Price Index	91.3	114.1	25.0%	
Revenue				
Ministry of Health and Long-term Care	$121,542	$293,473	141.5%	93.2%
Patients	2,607	7,742	197.0%	137.6%
Preferred accommodation	6,020	8,352	38.7%	11.0%
Research funding	23,988	62,700	161.4%	109.2%
Other	10,956	56,387	414.7%	311.8%
	165,113	428,654	159.6%	107.7%
Expenditures				
Salaries	82.352	202.150	145.5%	96.4%
Employee benefits	15,276	49,602	224.7%	159.8%
General supplies and expenses	21,168	57,624	172.2%	117.8%
Medical and surgical supplies	7,170	17,867	149.2%	99.4%
Drugs	6,054	21,428	253.9%	183.2%
Amortization of equipment	7,274	16,428	125.8%	80.7%
Amortization of Building and Research Equipment, net of amortization of contributions	3,745	5,809	55.1%	24.1%
Research	23,988	62,700	161.4%	109.2%
Other	1,784	534	−70.1%	−76.0%
	168,811	434,142	157.2%	105.8%
Net income (loss)	$ −3,698	$ −5,488	48.4%	18.7%
Inpatient and Operating Room Activity				
Total admissions	17,779	25,447		43.1%
Births	3.732	6.702		79.6%
Patient days	91,803	140,068		52.6%
Average length of stays (days)	6	5		−14.3%
Beds in service	382	472		23.6%
Operations	16,494	19,431		17.8%
Ambulatory and Emergency Activity				
Emergency treatments	30,633	43,737		42.8%
Radiological exams	152,807	184,207		20.5%
Ambulatory care visits	521,200	660,100		26.7%
Ambulatory rehabilitation visits	39,437			
Hospital Staffing				
Full time	1,356	2,341		72.6%
Part time/casual	1.022	1.100		7.6%
Medical/dental staff	690	812		17.7%
Institute staff	476	675		41.8%
Medical students	280	345		23.2%
Auxiliary members	1,719	1,412		−17.9%
Volunteers	600	1,033		72.2%
Volunteer hours	103,556	115,177		11.2%

Source: Mount Sinai Hospital, Annual Reports [www.mtsinai.on.ca]

Exhibit 6.1 Costs of Health Care Administration in the United States and Canada, 1999

Source: Adapted from Steffie Woolhandler, M.D., M.P.H, Terry Campbell, M.H.A, and David U. Himmelstein, M.D., Costs of Health Care Administration in the United States and Canada, *The New England Journal of Medicine*, 2003; 349; 768–75.

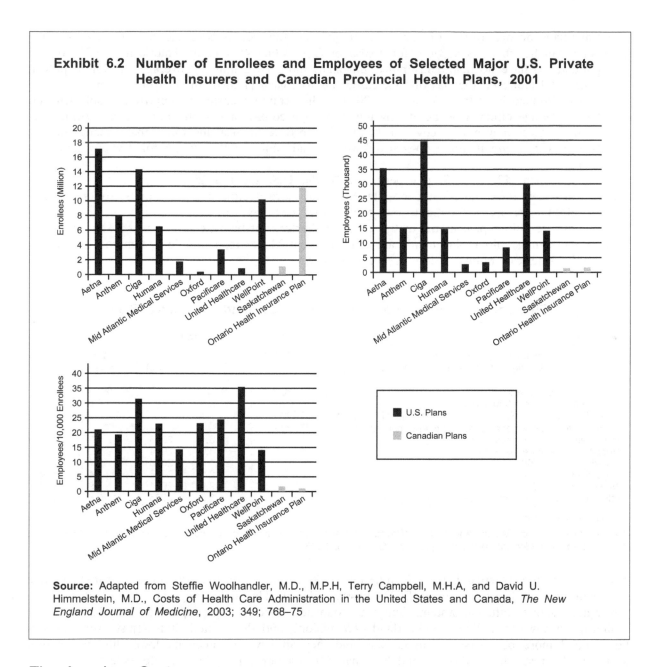

Exhibit 6.2 Number of Enrollees and Employees of Selected Major U.S. Private Health Insurers and Canadian Provincial Health Plans, 2001

Source: Adapted from Steffie Woolhandler, M.D., M.P.H, Terry Campbell, M.H.A, and David U. Himmelstein, M.D., Costs of Health Care Administration in the United States and Canada, *The New England Journal of Medicine*, 2003; 349; 768–75

The American System

The United States is the only industrialized nation that lacks some form of universal health care although it does provide universal health care for people 65 and over (**Medicare**) and for low-income people (**Medicaid**). The only other **Organisation for Economic Co-operation and Development (OECD)** countries lacking universal health care are Mexico and Turkey. By many measures, Canadians are healthier than Americans, with a longer lifespan and lower infant mortality, even though we spend much less on medical care.

- In 1970, as Canadian jurisdictions were setting up our health care system, costs in Canada and the United States were about the same, $300 per person, and American lived about one year longer than Canadians. As shown in Table 6.12, in 2007 the following was true:
  - Average life expectancy for Canadians was 81.16 while it was 78.14 for Americans in part because American who do not have health coverage don't seek medical care until their problems have become serious. Americans also have higher infant mortality rates.

- Canadians devote 10.1% of the GDP to provide full health coverage for all citizens while American health costs account for 16.0% of GDP while 46 million Americans (15.3% of the population) have no health insurance and many more have limited coverage. A Gallop poll in June 2009 indicated that lay-offs increased this to 16.6% (1 in 6) or 50.8 million in May 2009, and it dropped back to 16% in June, 2009 as the economy started to improve. People who do have coverage either at work or privately have high co-pays and high premiums and some necessary services may not be covered. In the U.S., private medical insurance that includes dental, is $300 U.S. *a month* for a 60-year-old woman and about $500 *a month* for a young family of four.
- Canada spent $3,895 U.S. per person while the U.S. spent $7,290.
- Americans have fewer nurses and hospital beds and more doctors and MRI units. American hospitals often advertise for patients but only if they can pay.
- Wait times for hip replacements in the U.S. are shorter, not because it is a market-based system but because most hip replacements are done through Medicare, a public system for the elderly and this American public system is better funded.[3]

Table 6.11 Differences in Health Care between Canada and the United States

Measure	Year	Canada		United States	
Total health care spending per capita	2007*	$3,895		$7,290	
Government spending per capita (% of total spending)	2007*	$2,727	(70.0%)	$3,310	(45.4%)
Life expectancy, years	2008*	81.16		78.14	
Infant mortality per 1,000 births	2004	5.3		6.8	
Amendable mortality (deaths before the age of 75 years from diseases amenable to treatment) per 100,000	2002–2 2003	77		110	
Physician visits per capita		6.1	2003	3.9	2002
Hospital acute care beds per 1,000		3.0	2004	2.8	2005
Bed-days per 1,000		1.0	2003	0.7	2004
Physicians per 1,000		2.2	2004	2.4	2005
Nurses per 1,000		9.9	2004	7.9	2002
MRI units per million population		5.5	2005	26.6	2004

* Numbers updated.

Source: Adapted from Marcia Angell, MD, "Privatizing Health Care is Not the Answer: Lessons from the United States", *Canadian Medical Association Journal*, October 6, 2008.

Table 6.12 compares spending on health in the 30 members of the Organisation for Economic Co-operation and Development (OECD) [www.oecd.org]. This data suggests we do not need to throw more money into the system. Only four countries, Luxembourg (population less than one-half million), Norway (4.5 million), Switzerland (7.5 million), and the United States (just over 300 million) spend more per person than Canada and they all have a somewhat lower life expectancy. Many of the rest, all of whom spend less than Canada per capita, have a life expectancy that is similar to ours and they all have public health care systems. Many also have mixed private-public systems that are regulated to some extent to prevent the public system from being undermined.

---

3   Marcia Angell, MD, "Privatizing Health Care in Not the Answer: Lessons from the United States", *Canadian Medical Association Journal*, October 6, 2008.

Table 6.12   Spending on Health and Life Expectancy

	Per Capita $US Purchasing Power Parity		Total Spending as % of GDP				Public Spending as % of Total Spending				Life Expectancy at Birth
	2007*		1970	1987	1997	2007*	1970	1987	1997	2007*	2008
Australia		85% 2006		6.6	7.6	8.7 2006		68.9	66.9	67.7 2006	81.53
Austria	3,763	97%	5.2	6.8	9.8	10.1	63.0	75.9	75.7	76.4	89.36
Belgium	3,595	92%	3.9	7.3	8.3	10.2					79.07
Canada	**3,895**	**100%**	**6.9**	**8.3**	**8.8**	**10.1**	**69.9**	**75.0**	**70.1**		**81.16**
Czech Republic	1,626	42%			6.7	6.8	96.6		90.3	85.2	76.62
Denmark	3,512	90%		8.5	8.2	9.8		84.4	82.3	84.5	78.13
Finland	2,840	73%	5.5	7.3	7.6	8.2	73.8	79.6	72.2	74.6	78.82
France	3,601	92%	5.4		10.2	11.0	75.5		79.6	79.0	80.87
Germany	3,588	92%	6.0	8.8	10.2	10.4	72.8	77.5	80.8	76.9	79.10
Greece	2,727	70%	5.4	6.6	8.4	9.6	42.6	59.9	52.8	60.3	79.52
Hungary	1,388	36%			6.8	7.4			81.3	70.6	73.18
Iceland	3,319	85%	4.7	7.8	8.1	9.3	66.2	87.3	82.1	82.5	80.55
Ireland	3,424	88%	5.1	7.1	6.4	7.6	81.7	72.9	73.9	80.7	78.07
Italy	2,686	69%			7.7	8.7			70.8	76.5	80.07
Japan		70% 2006	4.6	6.7	7.0	8.1 2006	69.8	73.7	81.5	81.3 2006	82.07
Korea	1,688	43%	3.6	4.3	6.8		28.5	41.7	54.9		78.64
Luxembourg		113% 2006	3.1	5.5	5.6	7.3 2006	88.9	93.0	92.5	90.9 2006	79.18
Mexico	823	21%			4.8	5.9			44.7	45.2	75.84
Netherlands	3,837	99%		7.6	7.9	9.8		68.4	67.8		79.25
New Zealand		66% 2006	5.2	5.7	7.3	9.2	80.3	87.2	77.3	78.0 2006	80.24
Norway	4,763	122%	4.4	7.5	8.4	8.9	91.6	86.5	81.3	84.1	79.81
Poland	1,035	27%			5.6	6.4			72.0	70.8	75.41
Portugal		58% 2006	2.5	6.2	8.0	9.9 2006	59.0	51.5	65.7	71.5 2006	78.04
Slovak Republic	1,555	40%			5.8	7.7			91.7	66.8	75.17
Spain	2,671	69%	3.5	5.4	7.3	8.5	65.4	79.7	72.5	71.8	79.92
Sweden	3,323	85%	6.8	8.3	8.1	9.1	86.0	89.9	85.8	81.7	80.74
Switzerland	4,417	113%	5.4	8.1	10.0	10.8		49.9	55.0	59.3	80.74
Turkey		18% 2005		2.1	3.1	5.7 2005		39.5	71.6	71.4 2005	73.14
United Kingdom	2,992	77%	4.5	5.9	6.6	8.4	87.0	84.3	80.4	81.7	78.85
United States	7,290	187%	7.1	10.7	13.4	16.0	36.2	40.4	44.7	45.4	78.14
Average (2007 only, not weighted)		80%	5.0	6.9	7.6	8.9	72.6	70.6	72.6	72.8	

The "percentage of Canada" calculations in the second column of numbers use Canada for 2005 and 2006 as required.

* 2007 data except as indicated.

Source: Organisation for Economic Co-operation and Development (OECD) [www.oecd.org], Directorate for Employment, Labour and Social Affairs, OECD Health Data 2009 — Frequently Requested Data.

Life Expectancy: Industry Canada, Economic and Market Research/Statistics, International Market Research.

Workers' Compensation

Provincial Workers' Compensation plans provide some health care coverage for injured employees. However, the main focus is to provide compensation for loss of income due to work-related injuries. It is covered in Chapter 7.

Supplementary Health Care Plans

Supplementary health care plans add benefits not provided by provincial or territorial plans. They are either

- group Plans through employers or associations and paid for by employers and/or employees, or
- private Plans that one pays for as an individual.

They provide for

- extended health coverage,
- dental plans, which cover dental care since most provincial plans do not cover dental care except when it is received in a hospital, and
- disability insurance, which is covered in Chapter 7.

Extended Health Care

Extended health care coverage either supplements provincial plans when the plan does not cover the entire cost or pays all or part of the cost when the cost is not covered at all by a provincial plan. Health care services commonly covered include the following the following:

- Prescription drugs
- Semi-private or private hospital accommodation
- Hospital and medical costs incurred outside of Canada
- Glasses, contact lenses and optometrists' services
- Services of a registered nurse
- Ambulance services
- Hearing aids
- Artificial limbs, prostheses and medical appliances
- Wheelchairs and other durable equipment
- Registered therapists and specialists, such as chiropractors and physiotherapists
- Orthopaedic shoes and orthotics

Coverage is either individual or family and most plans have a deductible.

Group Health Plans

Group health plans are offered by employers or associations. (A group of people cannot come together for the purpose of obtaining group insurance.) The premiums can be paid by the employer, employee, or both. Increasingly, when the employer pays, the employer covers only the amount for individual coverage, leaving the employee to pay the extra premium for family coverage. The cost of each unit of coverage in the plan is usually adjusted annually to reflect the actual cost of the plan, that is, after a year, if employees have made good use of the prescription drug coverage for instance, the cost for prescription drug coverage will increase the next year. Premiums paid by the employer are tax-deductible for the employer.

Some plans are **cafeteria plans,** whereby each employee is allocated a certain number of points and chooses the coverage he or she will spend the points on.

Deductible and Coinsurance

Group plans usually have an annual deductible of $35 or $50 which is deducted from the first claim. Plans also have a coinsurance requirement on some coverage that is different from both homeowners insurance and commercial property insurance discussed earlier. In addition, in group health plans there is no penalty for being underinsured (since rates can increase every year). For instance, a dental plan might cover 100% of the cost (based on a suggested fee guide set by provincial dental associations) for cleanings and fillings but only a dollar maximum for crowns and root canals that amounts to about 50% of the cost. Or a plan might cover 100% of all prescription and naturopath costs but set an annual ceiling of $500 for orthotics and a bi-annual maximum of $250 for glasses.

Private Plans

These plans are offered by private (non-government) companies for individuals not covered by group plans. They are allowed to offer coverage for only those expenses in excess of or not covered by provincial plans. Some plans, such as Blue Cross, are available to everyone, and some plans are offered only to members, such as CAA (Canadian Automobile Association).

A **base plan** might cover health care costs such as:

- Registered therapists and specialists, i.e., a psychologist, speech therapist, massage therapist, chiropodist, podiatrist, naturopath, physiotherapist, osteopath, and chiropractor with a schedule of coverage and annual limits

- Travel benefits to cover emergency care while outside the province of residence.

Optional coverage might include the following:

- Dental, 80%
- Hearing aids, 70%
- Hospital benefits, $200/day for semi-private or private coverage up to 90 days per/year
- Medical equipment
- Orthopedic shoes
- Prescriptions drugs, 80%,
- Private duty nursing
- Student accident benefits

Other riders are also often available such as life insurance.

The Blue Cross website [www.useblue.com] provided several quotes depending on the level of coverage desired. The quotes were for a 30-year-old female, of regular height and weight, non-smoker, enrolled in OHIP, working but without access to group benefits. The quotes ranged from a low of $20.10 to $142.56 a month. Life and health insurance companies, such as Sun Life, Manulife, and Great West Life also provide health insurance for individuals and families.

Travel Insurance

Provincial plans cover medical costs in all provinces in Canada as well as outside of Canada, but they pay only the rate for the province in which one resides (host province). This is not generally a problem in Canada, but in countries like the United States, this will not come close to covering emergency medical costs. Typically, travel insurance covers travel for less than 183 days in each 12-month period. In some jurisdictions, coverage can be extended for studies, work, missionary work, and a lifetime, two-year maximum for vacation.

Travel Health Care Insurance is provided by more than 50 insurers in Canada as well as by some gold-level credit cards. Coverage and costs vary a great deal and none cover elective surgery (like going to a Swiss spa for a facelift and tummy tuck).

Restrictions and limitations can include the following:

- Pre-existing conditions even if it is under control with medication
- High-risk sporting activities, such as sky diving
- War
- Certain destinations
- Duration of trip
- Treatment for substance abuse
- Suicide

It is important to read the fine print before you leave home. Some plans set a maximum based on total cost or will pay only a percentage of the total cost. To be adequately covered, the policy should pay for

- the entire length of your absence,
- an emergency trip home by air, and
- all members of the family.

Fiscal Agents [www.fiscalagents.com/rates] provides regular updates on the cost of travel insurance from 38 providers. For a 63-year-old person, the rates range from a low of $469 to a high of $837 for approximately 180 days. Some companies require a completed medical questionnaire. Coverage limits and medical requirements vary.

Long-term Care Insurance

This is a recent innovation in Canada and is somewhat hard to find. Generally, a person must be between the ages of 18 and 80 to apply. Once in place, coverage is for life. It applies if:

1. you have cognitive impairment, i.e., cannot think, perceive, reason, or remember, or
2. you can no longer perform two of the six **activities of daily living** unaided; i.e., bathing, eating, dressing, toileting, continence, or transferring positions of the body for more than three months.

It provides the following as part of the basic policy or as a rider:

- In-home care (home care and home health care)
- Adult daycare
- Nursing home care (long-term care facility)
- Assisted living facility
- **Respite care** (assistance given to relieve a relative or friend who is a part-time caregiver)

The benefit can range from $40 to $200 a day and the elimination period is 1 to 180 days. The maximum benefit is usually 1,000 times the daily benefit selected. Pre-existing conditions eliminate the benefit if the benefit is needed within six months of the effective date of the policy. A pre-existing condition *might* cause you to be denied coverage. In Ontario, the nursing home out-of-pocket costs are $19,000 for a ward, $22,000 for semi-private, and $26,000 for private. Non-subsidized facilities can cost $40,000 a year if personal care is required.

Policies are **reimbursement policies** that pay some or all out-of-pocket expenses, **indemnity policies** that pay the designated amount (the amount of coverage purchased), and **income policies** that pay regardless of whether or not services are received.

The Council on Aging of Ottawa [www.coaottawa.ca] has an excellent overview with warnings, such as the following:

- At the present time, all policies cover Alzheimer's and other forms of dementia but may not do so in the future.
- Initial premiums are designed to remain the same over a lifetime but usually can change for the entire class of policyholders, not just for a few people.
- Most policies have a **waiver of premiums** option that means you stop paying the premium when you start to collect the benefit.
- All current policies are guaranteed renewable although not necessarily at the same premium.
- Policies can be bought to cover 1 to 5 years or from $50,000 to $300,000 or an unlimited lifetime benefit.

Many people finance their stay in a long-term-care facility out of their retirement savings, government programs and by selling their homes and, as a result, long-term-care insurance is not selling as well in Canada as in the United States. To be useful, a person must have a spouse to provide care as people living alone would not be able to live alone with the required level of impairment.

Ellen Roseman of the *Toronto Star* suggests the following factors to consider when buying long-term care insurance:

- Is it a reimbursement policy that covers some or all out-of-pockets expenses or is it a more expensive income policy that pays benefits even if no services are received?
- What is the benefit amount for home care and for care in a long-term facility?
- How much do nursing homes, assisted living facilities, and health care agencies cost in your area before choosing a benefit amount?
- Does the policy spell out exactly what it means to be unable to feed yourself?
- What exactly is the waiting period? If you need assistance three days a week and there is a 90-day waiting period, you could wait 210 days or seven months before benefits start. A 90-calendar-day waiting period is three months?
- Does the policy have inflation protection?[4]

---

4   Ellen Roseman, "Long-term health insurance options for seniors," *The Toronto Star*, June 10, 2007.

Summary

Health care in Canada is covered in several ways. The federal government, through the *Canada Health Act*, seeks to provide universal health care for everyone living in Canada through provincial or territorial plans. The main problems in our health care plans are a critical shortage of doctors and lengthy wait times resulting from both the doctor shortage and inefficiencies. Workers' Compensation provides health coverage for people injured on the job. These plans do not cover all costs. As result, there is a strong private-insurance industry that provides additional health care benefits for both employees and people who are not employees. Travel insurance covers Canadians travelling outside of Canada — provincial and territorial plans cover them but only at the rate for the coverage of their home province or territory. Long-term-care insurance is designed to finance support for people who cannot totally look after themselves.

Sources

Building on Values: The Future of Health Care in Canada — Final Report, the Romanow Report, [www.cbc.ca/healthcare].

Canada Health Act (Health Canada, www.hc-sc.gc.ca).

Canada Health Act Annual Report, 2007–2008.

Canadian Health Coalition [www.medicare.ca], Just the Facts, Fact Sheet #2 (Wait Times), May, 2009.

Canadian Institute for Health Information, Emerging trend data show shorter waits for joint replacement and cataract surgery, Wait Times Tables — A Comparison by Province, 2009, April 23, 2009

Health Care Plans:
  • AB Alberta Health Care Insurance Plan (AHCIP) [www.health.alberta.ca].
  • BC Medical Services Plan (MSP) [www.health.gov.bc.ca].
  • MB Manitoba Health Services Insurance Plan (MHSIP) [www.gov.mb.ca/health/mhsip].
  • NB Medicare [www.gnb.ca].
  • NL Medical Care Plan (MCP) [www.health.gov.nl.ca/mcp].
  • NS Medical Services Insurance (MSI) [www.gov.ns.ca/health/msi].
  • NT Northwest Territories Health Care Plan (HCIP) [www.hlthss.gov.nt.ca].
  • NU Nunavut Health Care Plan (HCP) [www.gov.nu.ca/health].
  • ON Ontario Health Insurance Plan (OHIP) [www.health.gov.on.ca/en/public/programs/ohip].
  • PE Medicare [www.gov.pe.ca/health].
  • QC Quebec Health Insurance Plan (l'assurance maladie) [www.ramq.gouv.qc.ca].
  • SK Saskatchewan Health Services Plan [www.health.gov.sk.ca].
  • YU Yukon Health Care Insurance Plan (YHCIP) [www.hss.gov.yk.ca].

Carolyn DeCoster, RN, MBA, Leonard MacWilliam, MSc, MNRM, Randy Walld, BSc, BComm, *Waiting Times for Surgery: 1997/98 and 1998/99 Update*, Manitoba Centre for Health Policy and Evaluation, Department of Community Health Sciences, Faculty of Medicine, University of Manitoba, November 2000.

Carolyn DeCoster, PhD, RN, Dan Chateau, PhD, Matt Dahl, BSc, Ruth-Ann Soodeen, MSc, Nancy McKeen, PhD, *Waiting Times for Surgery, Manitoba 1999/2000 to 2003/04*, Manitoba Centre for Health Policy and Evaluation, Department of Community Health Sciences, Faculty of Medicine, University of Manitoba, June 2007.

Manitoba Wait Time Information, *Cataract Surgery Wait Times*, Manitoba Health, June 2009.

Lorne Bellan, MD, Mathen Mathen, MD, The Manitoba Cataract Waiting List Program, *Canadian Medical Association Journal*, April 17, 2001; 164 (8), 2001.

University Health Network, Annual Reports (Corporate Reports) [www.uhn.ca].

Mount Sinai Hospital Annual Reports [www.mtsinai.on.ca].

National Physician Survey, The College of Family Physicians of Canada, MD Pulse, 2008 [www.nationalphysiciansurvey.ca]

Steffie Woolhandler, MD, MPH, Terry Campbell, MHA, and David U. Himmelstein, MD, Costs of Health Care Administration in the United States and Canada, *The New England Journal of Medicine*, 2003; 349; 768–75

Marcia Angell, MD, Privatizing Health Care is Not the Answer: Lessons from the United States", *Canadian Medical Association Journal*, October 6, 2008.

Organisation for Economic Co-operation and Development (OECD) [www.oecd.org], Directorate for Employment, Labour and Social Affairs, OECD Health Data 2009 — Frequently Requested Data.

Life Expectancy: Industry Canada, Economic and Market Research/Statistics, International Market Research.

Ellen Roseman, Long-term health insurance options for seniors, *Toronto Star*, June 10, 2007.

Application Case

When Joanne arrives at Francesca's office, there is no espresso waiting and Francesca looks terrible. She sounds terrible too — all stuffed up. Clutching tissue and sneezing frequently, she says: "I think we will keep this really short today. And I suggest you don't get too close — I'd hate to give you this."

Francesca continues: "Let me give you the five-cent tour of this topic. Most of it will be quite familiar to you but there are some things you must know since you are going to New York in a couple of weeks to visit your friend, Anne."

A. "First of all, there are **three sources of health care benefits** and they are outlined in Table 6.1."

B. "I'll let you read through the history of the development of our current system of government health care plans. But let me point out that it has developed over many years. Saskatchewan was the first province to have universal hospital care (1946) and universal health care (1962)." And, just for fun, Kiefer Sutherland, Jack Bauer on *24*, is the grandson of Tommy Douglas, the so-called 'father of Medicare in Canada'. Tommy's daughter, Shirley Douglas, an actor, was married to the actor Donald Sutherland for a few years and Kiefer is their son" (Page 199).

C. "Do you remember how we used to have to pay part of the cost when we went to the doctor, and that your health care plan paid only 90% and we paid the rest? Many doctors didn't bother collecting the 10%, especially general practitioners, and nobody turned someone away if they couldn't pay it. In some provinces, the form was different but the effect was similar in that the provincial plan paid whatever it paid but doctors were allowed to charged extra. This is called extra billing.

   That ended in the mid-1980s when the federal government passed the *Canada Health Act,* which outlines the principles and requirements for the provinces and territories with regard to health care. The feds carry a big stick too. If provinces don't abide by the rules, the federal government gave itself the right to withhold transfer payments that cover these costs. The *Canada Health Act* outlines the **basic requirements**:
   1. **Public administration** on a non-profit basis
   2. **Comprehensiveness** with regard to coverage
   3. **Universality** meaning coverage is available to all residents of a province or territory
   4. **Portability** so that you are covered when you are not in the province where you live
   5. **Accessibility** meaning everyone has equal access to the service, doctors receive reasonable compensation and hospital costs are covered" (Pages 200–201).

D. "The *Canada Health Act* defines **two services to be included** in provincial and territorial plans:
   1. **extended health care services**, such as nursing homes and home care services, and
   2. **insured health care services**, which includes medically required services in a hospital" (Page 201–202).

E. "The *Canada Health Act* also **expressly forbids**
   1. extra-billing,
   2. user fees, and
   3. private clinics from offering a service for a fee that is covered by a provincial plan" (Pages 202).

F. "It also spells out what services are **excluded** by the *Canada Health Act* and for which patients may be charged:
   1. Services that are not medically necessary:
      (a) Uninsured hospital services such as private and semi-private rooms, telephones, televisions, and private-duty nurses.

(b) Uninsured doctors' services such as telephone advice, providing a "doctor's note", medical exams for work or school and cosmetic surgery.

2. Some groups of people are excluded, such as people in the Armed Forces and the RCMP, people doing time in a federal penitentiary, and people who do not yet meet the minimum residency requirement (which cannot be more than three months)" (Page 202–203).

G. "Some coverages can be covered by the provinces and territories if they want. This includes prescription drugs, lab tests, private and semi-private rooms. Table 6.2 outlines the coverage for prescription drugs — you can see how diverse it is — while Table 6.3 lists some other optional coverages."

H. "Every jurisdiction permits doctors to operate outside of the health care plans.
   1. **Opted-out** doctors charge the patient what they would get from the plan based on the Schedule of Benefits, but they invoice the patient directly and the patient has to submit a claim and be reimbursed by the plan.
   2. **Non-participating** doctors charge patients whatever the market will bear and patients *cannot* be reimbursed. In 2008, there were two, both in B.C.

As you can see in Table 6.4, 99.6995% of doctors participate — they are neither opted-out nor non-participating."

I. "As you know very well, there are very severe problems with our health care system. Federal funding has not kept pace with either cost-of-living adjustments and has, in fact, cut back on this funding. But also there have been many improvements to health care that increase costs because
   • things have gotten more expensive; for instance, the machines are expensive to buy and to operate; and
   • people are living longer and healthier but requiring more health care services since they are not dying off as fast from illnesses that used to be fatal."

The two fundamental problems are the long wait times and the shortage of doctors."
   1. "In 2002, Roy Romanow produced what is known as the **Romanow Report**. After consulting with thousands of Canadians, he reported that they support the core values of universal health care, most have been well served by it, and they want the system to be both more comprehensive and more accountable. The shortage of doctors can be seen in the **National Physicians Survey,** which showed the percentage of GPs that were not accepting new patients in 2007" (Table 6.5).
   2. "In 2004, the First Ministers' Conference on Health Care named **five priority areas** that would get extra funding so that **wait-time goals** could be reached" (Table 6.6).
   3. "There has been real improvement although results vary by province. Notice, however, that the checkmark (✓) in Table 6.7 indicates that 75% of patients receive treatment within the benchmark."
   4. "Dr. Brian Postl, the federal advisor on Wait Times, produced a report in 2006 outlining areas of concern with respect to the benchmarks:
      (a) The window of time to treat **children** is smaller than for most adults if the treatment is to both be effective and avoid the long-term effects of slow treatment.
      (b) There is little **surge capacity** in the system. This is the ability to draw on additional resources when something like the SARS outbreak happens.
      (c) There is a **shortage of health professionals** and the problem is more acute in some areas of the country than in others.
      (d) **Gender-based analysis (GBA)** recognizes that what might work for men might not work for women and there is concern about the lack of response to this.
      (e) **Cinderella diseases** are the ones that are not one of the priority areas — they did not get invited to the ball. There is concern that the priority areas will come at the expense of other health care services.

    (f) Different jurisdictions might have priorities that are different from other provinces and territories and that while they can and should share efficiencies, they must also be allowed to set their own benchmarks and define satisfactory outcomes for themselves" (Page 210).

5. "Dr. Postl is CEO of the Winnipeg Regional Health Authority and, in May 2009, he issued a statement *against* privatized medicine. I'll leave you to read it but note in particular that he says that between 1988 and 2002, 64,000 hospital beds were cut. He goes on to provide some recommendations that he thinks would improve wait time without resorting to private, for-profit clinics."

6. "Manitoba carried out an experiment that is worth studying because of its effectiveness. Until January 1999, Manitoba allowed cataract surgery in both public hospitals covered by Manitoba Health Services Insurance Plan (MHSIP) and private, for-profit clinics. In 1999, Manitoba started funding all cataract operations at the same rate, ending for-profit surgery. About the same time, the **Manitoba Cataract Waiting List Program (MCWLP)** was implemented. Initially it hired extra staff to deal with the backlog but the program used a new computer program to track and prioritize cataract surgeries. Priority was established by using a questionnaire to determine the level of visual impairment.

    The success of the program should be lighting the way for efficiencies in other areas and is, I think, one of the strongest arguments against a **two-tiered system** which, at the present time, has many doctors working in both the private and the public sectors in health care" (Table 6.8).

J. "There is also concern among some health professionals about the increase in administrative staff, meaning MBAs, to support increasingly well-paid heads of hospitals. It's interesting that this has generated so little press except for Dr. Postl's statement about the cuts in the number of hospital beds. It is difficult for outsiders to get a handle on this but let's look at some numbers available from the Internet for a couple of Toronto hospitals. (Tables 6.9 and 6.10)

    You'll notice in both them that the amount of patient activity has in no way kept pace with the increase in revenues. So there may be something to this criticism.

    But let's put this in perspective by looking at some data comparing Canada's health administration costs with the United States where many hospitals are for-profit and costs are generally much higher, not just in doctor's salaries but also in the cost for supplies for instance. (Exhibits 6.1 and 6.2)

K. The **United States** is the only industrialized country that lacks some form of universal health care although they do have it for people over 65 and those with disabilities (Medicare) and for low-income people (Medicaid). The American health care system is very market-driven (the latest buzz word as if the profit motive somehow automatically provides efficiencies and lower costs) with many private hospital that treat only patients who can pay — those who have either health insurance coverage or lots of money.

L "Let's end this talk about public health care plans by looking at some data from the Organization for Economic Co-operation and Development (OECD). You'll notice that only four countries spent more per capita than Canada and they all have an average life expectancy that is slightly lower than ours. I think this illustrates that we need more efficiencies, not more money. Perhaps hospitals should be hiring engineers from the manufacturing sector who, after all, are trained to look for and find efficiencies." (Table 6.12)

M. Francesca sneezes and gasps a bit. Then she continues, eyes running: "**Private insurance** is available to cover the gaps left by government plans. These **extended health care plans** provide coverage such as dental, glasses, hearings aid and many of the other things listed as optional coverage in the *Canada Health Act* section. This coverage is provided:

1. Through employers as group insurance plans. The premiums for these plans is often paid in full or in part by the employer. Some associations also provide plans for mem-

bers who pay their own premiums. However, they get a better rate than they can get in a private, individual plan, and

2. By private plans that individuals can buy. Probably the one most people have heard of is Blue Cross but other companies sell it as well." (Pages 217–219)

N. "And you need some **Travel Insurance** when you go to visit Anne. It's not likely anything will happen, but if you get sick or injured, you are covered by your provincial plan but only at that province's rate. Medical costs in the U.S. are a lot higher than here and without travel insurance, you will be personally on-the-hook to pay should anything go wrong." (Pages 219)

O. "I know you have disability insurance but you might want to think about getting some **long-term care insurance** for when you are old and frail. The most relevant feature for you is that it pays for in-home care should you unable to fully manage by yourself. A basic plan is not all that expensive and the premiums should never go up. On the other hand, many people just use their current retirement income and the equity in their home to finance this kind of help. Better hurry though, you have to sign up before you turn 80" (Page 219).

Unfortunately Francesca's attempt at a joke causes her to have a sneezing fit at which point, Joanne jumps up, grabs her coat and purse and says, "I'll call you tomorrow about another appointment." And ran out the door to get away from Francesca's germs.

Concept Questions

1. List the sources of health care benefits available to Canadians.

2. Who is called the father of medicare in Canada?

3. Which province was the first to have:
   (a) universal hospital care and in what year did this happen?
   (b) universal health care and in what year did this happen?

4. How much funding for universal health care plans did the federal government provide with the *Medical Care Act of 1966*? When did this formula change and to what?

5. What are the five mandatory requirements found in the *Canada Health Act* that regulate how the provinces provide health care?

6. Which requirement covers you when you are visiting another province or country?

7. What is:
   (a) a host province? a home province?
   (b) If you live in B.C. and need medical attention, what rate does the B.C. health care plan pay when you are visiting the following:
      i. Nunavut?
      ii. Illinois?

8. What are the three broad categories of health care services that must be included in provincial plans?

9. What three things are prohibited by the *Canada Health Act*?

10. Under what type of excluded coverage do the following fall:
    (a) Private room?
    (b) Doctors notes?
    (c) Telephones?
    (d) Medical exams to get life insurance coverage?

11. What is a formulary?

12. Which four jurisdictions cover routine dental care for all children under a certain age?

13. Which jurisdictions cover eye exams for:
    (a) everyone?
    (b) children under a certain age and seniors?

14. Which of the following statements is true about opted-out physicians?
    (a) Patients are billed directly and are reimbursed by their government health plan.
    (b) Patients are billed directly and are not reimbursed by their government health plan.

15. By what percentage did the following increase in 2007 from 2003?
    (a) Physicians
    (b) Population of Canada

16. In which province would you have had the hardest time finding a family doctor in 2007?

17. If your grandmother is waiting for a knee replacement, what is the maximum number of months she should have to wait?

18. In 2009, in which province would granny prefer to be living while she waits: Ontario, Saskatchewan, or Alberta? Why?

19. What is the name of the ability to generate extra services to meet an unexpected, high demand?

20. In countries that have a parallel for-profit system, are wait times longer or shorter than countries that have only a public system?

21. In Manitoba, what was the wait time for cataract surgery where the surgeon operated in
    (a) both the public and private sectors in 97/98?
    (b) only the public sector in 97/98?
    (c) the public sector, which was all that was available in 08/09?.

22. At University Health Network, revenue grew by 54.5% real from 01/02 to 08/09. What was the increase in patient activity?

23. At Mount Sinai Hospital, government funding increased by 93.2% real from 98/099 to 08/09. What was the increase in:
    (a) Patient days?
    (b) Emergency treatments?
    (c) The cost of drugs?

24. In 2008, what percentage of and how many Americans
    (a) are covered by Medicare and Medicaid?
    (b) are covered by private health plans or group insurance plans at work? (Answer: 53.4%, 162.3 million calculated as $[(95.7 \div .315) \times 0.534]$
    (c) have no insurance coverage?

25. In 1999, what percentage of total spending per capita was insurance overhead in
    (a) The United States, where the total cost is $1,059 per person? (Answer: 24.5%)
    (b) Canada, where the total cost is $307 per person? (Answer: 15.3%)

26. WellPoint, an American insurance, and Ontario Health Insurance Plan have about the same number of people enrolled. How many employees per enrollee does each have? (Answer: WellPoint 13.7, OHIP 1.2)

27. In 1970, whose average life expectancy was higher: Canadians or Americans? What was the average life expectancy for each in 2007?

28. In 2004, what was infant mortality in Canada and the United States?

29. Using "Total Spending as % of GDP", which countries spend

(a) more than Canada *and* have a longer life expectancy?
(b) the same or less than Canada *and* have a longer life expectancy?

30. Using "Public Spending as % of Total Spending", which countries spend
    (a) more than Canada *and* have a longer life expectancy?
    (b) less than Canada *and* have a longer life expectancy?

31. What is a supplementary health care plan?

32. Describe how a cafeteria group health insurance plan works.

33. What are some typical limitations found in travel insurance?

34. What are the six activities of daily living?

35. Regarding long-term care insurance, what is the difference between a reimbursement policy, an indemnity policy, and an income policy?

Application Questions

36. Ralph and Steven, two former politicians, decide to open up a private health care clinic. How much are they allowed to charge patients for the same type of emergency health care service found at local area hospitals?

37. After a long night partying, Mario has had too much to drink. For some reason, he decides to visit a tattoo parlour and tattoo the name of his dead goldfish, Sammy, on his arm. The next morning he is wakes up to realize what he just did. If he decides to remove his tattoo, will his provincial health care plan cover the cost of removal?

38. Which provinces and territories provide coverage for listed prescription drugs for
    (a) people with specific illnesses?
    (b) seniors?

39. If Tommy has a hearing problem, which jurisdiction provides the best support if the hearing aid he requires costs $2,000?

40. Sunny is seriously injured in a horrible car accident. His doctor recommends physiotherapy for the extensive injuries to his shoulder and neck.
    (a) Will his provincial plan cover these charges?
    (b) In which jurisdictions will his plan cover it if his doctor thinks he's all right but he wants to go anyway?

41. Nav suddenly gets a shooting pain in his lower back and he decides to see a chiropractor. Which jurisdictions will provide him with some coverage?

42. Which of the following is not covered under extended health care plans? Why or why not?
    (a) Prescription drugs
    (b) Semi-private or private hospital accommodation
    (c) Hospital and medical incurred outside of Canada
    (d) Glasses, contact lenses and optometrists' services
    (e) Services of a registered nurse
    (f) Ambulance services
    (g) Delivering a baby
    (h) Hearing aids
    (i) Artificial limbs, prostheses and medical appliances
    (j) Wheelchairs and other durable equipment
    (k) Registered therapists and specialists such as chiropractors and physiotherapists
    (l) Orthopaedic shoes and orthotics

43. Sam has decided to pursue a career in professional wrestling. While on tour through upstate New York doing some shows, he breaks his arm. For minor injuries such as a broken arm, his home health plan would have covered the injury up to the full cost, under $1,000. However, in New York the doctor charges him $3,000. Will his home health plan cover his injuries outside of Canada? For how much?

Income Protection Plans

Learning Objectives

After completing this chapter, students will understand:

A. The various ways government insurance plans provide some level of replacement for lost employment earnings.

B. How group and private individual disability coverage works.

C. The place for critical illness insurance with respect to income protection.

Introduction

Income protection is crucial for most workers during times of job loss, illness, or sickness because when someone cannot work, in addition to losing income, there are frequently additional expenses. As a result, income protection plans are, for many people, even more important than life insurance since a person has a 33% chance of being off work for at least six months due to illness or accident between the ages of 35 and 65 but only 15.6% of men and 9.4% of women die between those two ages.

All government plans are mandatory. Group and individual plans can supplement government plans in those instances where government coverage is either not available or inadequate.

Government Plans

There are three government plans that offer income protection for workers who are not able to work due to the following:

- ill health, which is covered by Workers' Compensation, Employment Insurance, and Canada Pension Plan disability benefits, and
- unemployment that is short-term and involuntary and is often covered by Employment Insurance.

Social Insurance

All of these government programs fall under the descriptor **social insurance** because their primary focus is to provide compulsory protection for personal risks. Other benefits also fall under this heading, such as Canada Pension Plan, retirement benefits, and death benefits. In this chapter we focus only on those programs that provide protection against lost income.

Social insurance exists for the following reasons:

1. To help solve social problems that result from economic changes beyond the control of both employers and employees.
2. To provide coverage for perils that are difficult to insure privately because they either
    (a) affect a very large number of people at the same time (unemployment), or

(b) are a result of workplace conditions (health and safety standards enacted by each employer).

3. To provide a base of economic security for employees.

Social insurance programs share the following **characteristics**:

1. They are compulsory — all employers and employees must participate unless the coverage is provided in another form in the organization.
2. They provide benefits that relate to income with a ceiling on both contributions and benefits.
3. The benefits are prescribed by law.
4. Benefits are not **means-tested**, that is, people receive the benefit because they qualify for it, not because they need it.
5. Contributions are made by employees, employers or both.
6. Benefits are funded, that is, contributions are made for the specific program. The benefits are paid out of the fund and are not paid out of general tax revenues as are the benefits under the Old Age Security program.

All three of the government programs — Worker's Compensation, Employment Insurance, and Canada Pension Plan — meet all of these criteria.

Workers' Compensation

Workers' Compensation was Canada's first social program. It was favoured by both workers' groups (unions) and employers hoping to avoid lawsuits. State run, compulsory compensation for injured workers was established in Britain and Germany in the late 19th century. In the early 20th century, the United States mandated systems of compensation for injured workers that were a combination of state-run, self-insurance, and combinations of these. The system in Canada arose after an inquiry by Ontario Chief Justice William Meredith, who outlined a system whose workers could be compensated for workplace injuries but they had to give up their right to sue their employers. Workers' Compensation is a provincial and territorial responsibility and, as a result, each jurisdiction has its own legislation. It was introduced at different dates in each province and territory — Ontario was first in 1915, Manitoba in 1916, British Columbia in 1917. In most provinces it is solely concerned with insurance. However, in some jurisdictions, the program also has a preventative role to ensure workplace safety.

The objectives of Workers' Compensation are as follows:

• To provide
  • substantial replacement of lost employee earnings for occupational injury and disease,
  • medical care and rehabilitation services,
  • a pension if an injury results in a permanent disability, and
  • pensions to dependants of employees who are fatally injured in the course of employment.
• To encourage safety.
• To reduce lawsuits.

There are four underlying principles to Workers' Compensation:

1. Employers bear the direct cost of compensation, that is, employers pay the premiums based on payroll, job classifications, and their history of accidents, receiving in return protection from lawsuits arising from injuries.
2. Workers give up the right to sue their employers and receive in return compensation benefits at no cost for work-related injuries.
3. Negligence and fault for the cause of injury are not considered except as premiums are increased to reflect experience.
4. The system is administered by a neutral agency having exclusive jurisdiction over all matters arising out of the enabling legislation.

The *Government Employees Compensation Act* provides for workers' compensation to all federal government employees, including employees posted outside Canada, and to employees from outside Canada who are locally engaged and are injured in the course of their duties and are not covered under any local legislation. Industrial and occupational diseases are treated in the same way as work-related injuries.

Operations of Boards

Workers' Compensation in each jurisdiction is operated by a board (WCB) that has a different names in some jurisdictions, like the Workplace Safety and Insurance Board (WSIB) in Ontario. Sometimes they are called commissions. The **Association of Workers' Compensation Boards of Canada (AWCBC)** was founded in 1919 as a non-profit organization to facilitate the exchange of information between Workers' Compensation Boards and Commissions in different jurisdictions. AWCBC refers to individual Boards and Commissions collectively as WCB/Commissions. These WCB/Commissions compensate employees for lost income, permanent disability, costs for survivors, and rehabilitation due to work-related injuries. As shown in the following table, jurisdictions having a large proportion of self-employed people, such as fishers and farmers, have lower rates of participation in Workers' Comp.

The WCB/Commissions charge employers to cover their employees and pay the injured worker or survivor directly. A few employers are **self-insured**, meaning the Board or Commission pays the cost of benefits provided to their injured workers' plan and the employer reimburses the Board. Workers' Compensation is a large industry receiving some $9 billion a year in total income and paying $9.6 billion in benefits in 2007. It also invests in Occupational Health and Safety (OHS) to reduce worker injury ($480 million in 2007).

Table 7.1   Workers' Compensation Boards and Commissions Income and Expenses, 2007 ($ millions)

	Total Premium Revenue	Benefit Costs	Administration Costs	Investment in Occupational Health & Safety	Injury Frequency* (per 100 workers)	Percentage of Workers Covered
AB	977.7	728.2	142.0	31.1	1.98	89.69%
BC	1,082.0	958.0	223.8	57.9	3.06	93.12%
MB	224.0	211.2	40.8	10.9	4.31	69.52%
NB	194.2	203.5	19.9	8.1	1.36	93.93%
NL	137.7	142.6	23.4	6.8	2.25	97.00%
NS	254.4	290.6	32.3	7.6	2.72	72.63%
NT	36.4	26.9	16.5	3.2	2.73	100.00%
ON	3,523.0	4,337.2	477.4	181.7	1.53	72.60%
PE	29.4	20.7	5.3	0.7	1.37	96.16%
QC	2,277.6	2,497.0	282.8	154.8	2.44	93.42%
SK	239.5	195.7	34.5	14.4	3.75	74.13%
YT	23.1	17.1	7.0	2.5	2.89	99.93%
Canada	8,999.0	9,628.7	1,305.7	479.7	2.26	83.63%

* Three provinces have waiting periods that may result in "Worker Injury" to be under-reported.
- NB and PE have a 3-day waiting period.
- NS has a 2-day waiting period.

Source: Key Statistical Measures for 2007, Association of Workers' Compensation Boards of Canada (AWCBC) [www.awcbc.org]

Employers' Costs

The 2007 weighted average premium rate for Canada is $1.98 for every $100 of gross insurable earnings before deductions. Premium rates for individual rate groups are recalculated annually based primarily on injury frequency and on claims costs for individual rate groups. There are 18 rate groups (Divisions).

Table 7.2 Workers' Compensation Employer Assessment Divisions (Rate Groups)

• "A" Agricultural and Related Services	• "J" Retail Trade Industries
• "B" Fishing & Trapping Industries	• "K" Finance & Insurance Industries
• "C" Logging & Forestry Industries	• "L" Real Estate & Insurance Industries
• "D" Mining, Quarrying, & Oilwell Industries	• "M" Business Service Industries
• "E" Manufacturing Industries	• "N" Government Services
• "F" Construction Industries	• "O" Educational Service Industries
• "G" Transportation Industries	• "P" Health & Social Service Industries
• "H" Communications & Other Utilities	• "Q" Accommodation, Food & Beverage
• "I" Wholesale Trade Industries	• "R" Other Service Industries

Source: General Information about the 2009 Assessment Rate Tables, AWCBC

Each Division is subdivided into a Major Group and then further subdivided. For example, Division "A", Agricultural and Related Services Industry contains two major groups:

• Major Group '01' is Agriculture, and
• Major Group '02' is Incidental Services.

Major Group '01' in Division A contains six sub-groups (011 — Livestock Farms, 012 — Other Animal Specialties, 013 — Field Crop Farms, 015 — Fruit and Vegetable Farms, 016 — Horticulture, 017 — Combination Farms). Sub-group 011 — Livestock Farms is further broken down into six categories — Dairy, Cattle, Hog, Poultry and Egg, Sheep and Goats, and Feedlots. In B.C., the rates are $1.84 for three of these categories and $6.54 for the other three. This means it matters very much which category for "Livestock Farms" a business is in since the rate is 3½ times higher for three of them in B.C. However, in Northwest Territories and Nunavut, all six categories for this sub-group, 01 — Livestock Farms, are the same, $5.84 as shown in Table 7.3.

Table 7.3 shows the following:

• **Maximum assessable earnings**, the maximum amount of earnings for each employee covered by Workers' Comp.
• The highest and lowest rates in each jurisdiction.
• The rates for each jurisdiction for Major Group '70', Deposit Accepting Intermediary in Division "K", Finance & Insurance Industries whose rates are the lowest rates in eight jurisdictions.

Table 7.3 Employer Assessment Rates for 2009

	Maximum Assessable Earnings	"K", '70' Deposit Accepting, All subgroups	2009 Estimated Assessment Rates		
			Lowest	Highest	Average
AB	$72,600	$0.24	**$0.17** "N" '82' Provincial/territorial • Provincial — Clerical/admin.	**$6.41** "F" '42' Trade Contractors 422 Structural Work • Roofing	$1.32
BC	$68,500	$0.08	**$0.08**	**$12.12** "F" '42' Trade Contractors 422 Structural Work • Structural Steel Erection • Steel Plate Erection	$1.56

Table 7.3   Continued

	Maximum Assessable Earnings	"K", '70' Deposit Accepting, All subgroups	2009 Estimated Assessment Rates		
			Lowest	Highest	Average
MB	$83,000	$.014–$0.50	**$0.14** "B" '03' Fishing & Trapping • Trapping — Wild Animals	**$35.57** "R" 995 Building Services • Window Cleaning	$1.60
NB	$55,400	$0.35	**$0.35**	**$9.69** "E" '15' Rubber Products • All subgroups	$2.03
NL	$50,379	$0.56	**$0.56**	**$27.50** "N" '83' Local Gov't Operations • Volunteer Firefighters	$2.75
NT/NU	$72,100	$0.64	**$0.48** "H" '49' Other Utilities 491 — Electric Power • Generate/distribute Power 492 — Gas Distribution • Natural Gas Distribution	**$5.84** "A" & "B" "A" '01' Agriculture '02' Incidental Services "B" '03' Fishing and Trapping • All Major Groups and all subgroups except Veterinary & Agricultural Consultant	$1.71
NS	$49,400	$0.46	**$0.46**	**$16.35** "E" '32' Transportation Equip 326 — Railroad Industry • Locomotives	$2.65
ON	$74,600	$0.18	**$0.18**	**$15.86** "F" '41' Industrial/heavy Cstr 512 Highway/Heavy Construction • Blasting	$2.26
PE	$47,500	$0.31	**$0.26** "P" '86' Health/social Svcs 863 Non Institution Health • Family Planning Services	**$17.72** "C" '04' Logging Industry '05' Forestry Industry • All subgroups	$2.16
QC	$62,000	$0.61	**$0.61**	**$21.98** "F" '41' Industrial/heavy Cstr 412 Highways/heavy Cstr. • Silos and Towers	$2.10
SK	$55,000	$0.20	**$0.20**	**$5.44** "E" '31' Machinery Industries • Install/repair Machinery & Equip	$1.66
YT	$76,842	$1.10	**$1.10**	**$11.73** "C" '04' Logging Industry 041 Logging Industry • All Subgroups	$3.00

Source: Key Assessment Rate Information for 2009, AWCBC

Why is it so much more dangerous to work in Financial Services in some jurisdictions? No idea. Rates are per $100 of assessable earnings and are based, in part, on the experience of each employer and also of the industry.

EXAMPLE 1   We-Love-Your-Money national bank has small branches in several provinces and territories. Each small branch has five employees earning an average of $40,000 each. The bank will pay Workers' Comp a total each year of:

- $160 [($200,000 ÷ 100 × $0.08] in B.C.
- $2,200 (2,000 × $1.10) in Yukon, and
- $920 ($2,000 × $0.46) in Nova Scotia for the five employees.

Some of the rates are extremely high and will add a great deal to an employer's costs. Manitoba's rate of $35.57, shown in Table 7.3, adds 35.57% of assessable wages to an employer's labour costs.

EXAMPLE 2   Juan's construction company in Manitoba has 40 hourly workers whose wages total $1,664,000 a year. His company pays Workers' Comp of $591,885 a year. [($1,664,000 ÷ 100) × 35.57] — an average of $14,797 for each hourly worker or 35.57% of their average pay of $41,600.

Benefits for Injured Workers

The maximum amount of an employee's earnings that are insurable under Workers' Comp is called the maximum earnings covered, and earnings over this amount are not covered. In all provinces and territories except Manitoba, the Maximum Assessable Earnings shown I Table 7.3 is also the maximum earnings covered. In Manitoba, there is no maximum earnings Covered even though there is a maximum assessable earnings. The *rate charged* by the Boards is based on gross earnings before deductions but *benefits* are based on 75% to 90% of net earnings (gross earnings minus income tax, CPP, and EI deductions) except in Yukon where benefits are based on 75% of gross income. Benefits also have other restrictions in some jurisdictions:

- Half of the jurisdictions require the employer to pay the worker for the day of the injury while the other half do not.
- Only Quebec requires the employer to pay for the period after the injury, 14 days, but the amount is then refunded to the employer.
- Only three provinces have an unpaid waiting period as shown in Table 7.1.
- In some jurisdictions, some benefits are offset (reduced) by any amounts received from Canada/Quebec Pension Plan.
- In most jurisdictions, the benefit may be suspended or paid to benefit a dependant when the worker is in jail, in an institution, or in a hospital.
- Maximum compensation rates of 2008 vary from a low of 79.3% of the Average Industrial Aggregate Weekly Wage in Newfoundland to a high of 124.7% in Manitoba. Ontario is 112.8%.
- Nine jurisdictions have a minimum amount of weekly payments.
- Most jurisdictions pay a lump sum to a surviving spouse as well as monthly payments. The amount and duration of the payments is affected by the number of dependent children and their ages as well as the age of the spouse.

WCB/Commissions pay benefits to injured workers or to survivors if a worker dies. There are benefits to compensate for the following:

1. **Lost Earnings,** usually referred to as an **Economic Loss**.
2. **Lost Retirement Income** because the injured worker is not earning pensionable income.
3. **Non Economic Loss**, which recognizes a physical, functional, or psychological loss. Some Boards adjust the benefit for the degree of impairment.
4. **Health Care**, which includes prescription drugs, medical devices, orthotics and transportation costs associated with a work-related injury or illness.
5. **Other benefits**, which can cover the following:
   (a) Independent Living Allowance
   (b) Burial Expenses

  (c) Transportation
  (d) Personal Care Allowance
  (e) Guide and Support Dog Allowances
  (f) Witness Fees (for hearings)
  (g) Clothing Allowance
  (h) Meal Allowance
  (i) Child Care Expenses
  (j) Escorts
  (k) Room and Board

6. **Survivor Benefits**, which provide income and retirement benefits for the survivors of workers who are killed in work-related accidents.

Many jurisdictions also have Occupational Health and Safety (OHS) programs.

Table 7.4   Schedule of Workers' Compensation Benefits for 2009

		Lost Earnings		Lost Retirement Income	Non Economic Loss
	Maximum (Gross) Earnings Covered	Percentage of Net Earnings	Maximum Annual Payments	Pension Benefits	Lump Sum Maximum
AB	$72,600		90%	$47,843	Lost earnings benefit for life	$81,606
BC	$68,500		90%	$46,971	Additional 5% set aside*	No
MB	$83,000	Adjusted for tax-free benefit	90%	$51,343	Based on pension plan contributions	$1,140 for each full % <30% and $34,200 plus $1,370 for each full % >30%.
NB	$55,400	Single	85%	$33,725	Additional 10% set aside	$55,400
		Married	85%	$35,641		
NL	$50,379	Single	80%	$29,785	CPP or RPP benefits lost	$50,379
		Equivalent to spouse	80%	$31,449		
NT/NU	$72,100		90%	$55,523	Benefits are for life	No
NS	$49,400	1st 26 wks	75%	$28,226	Additional 5% set aside	For non-physical impairment
		Then	85%	$31,989		
ON	$74,600		85%	$50,048	Additional 5% set aside	See Example 5
PE	$47,500	1st 38 wks	80%	$27,821	CPP or RPP benefits lost	For non-physical impairment
		Then	85%	$29,559		
QC	$62,000		90%	$44,796	Benefits end at age 68	$94,569 if < age 19, $46,500 at age 65
SK	$55,000		90%	$37,912	Additional 10% set aside	Impairment $45,200 Disfigurement $15,000
YT	$76,842	75% of gross		$57,474	Additional 10% set aside	$80,000 +/– 2% for each year worker is over/under age 45

*Additional set aside is invested and paid as an annuity at age 65.

Each Board or Commission has its own terminology and rules. We will use examples from a few representative jurisdictions in order get the idea of how each benefit is calculated.

Lost Earnings

In *Alberta*, maximum benefit payments are 90% of net earnings based on a maximum wage ceiling of $72,600 gross earnings for 2009. Let's assume the net earnings (gross earnings minus income tax, CPP, and EI) on $72,600 is $53,159. The maximum benefit in Alberta is $47,843 (90% of $53,159). Income received is added to taxable income and therefore affects both

- The ability of a spouse to deduct the spouse who is receiving the benefit as a dependent, and
- The amount of the child tax credit since it is added to family net income.

However, there is an **offsetting deduction**, making Workers' Comp income non-taxable. Injured workers receive the benefit until

- they are no longer impaired by the work-related injury or illness,
- they no longer have a loss of earnings, or
- age 65 in most jurisdiction but in Alberta, it is paid for life eliminating the need for a pension benefit.

EXAMPLE 3   Alice made $72,600 a year in Alberta with net earnings of $53,159 before she was permanently disabled in a work-related accident. She will receive $47,843 ($53,159 × 90%) of non-taxable income from Workers' Compensation Board of Alberta. This is the maximum she can receive even if she were making more than $72,600.

If the employee can work part-time, partial benefits are available to compensate employees for 90% of the difference between pre-accident and post-accident net earnings.

Loss of Retirement Income

Most jurisdictions set aside an additional amount as shown in Table 7.4, which is invested and used to provide a retirement annuity, usually at age 65 when Worker's Comp lost earnings benefit ends. Often employees may match this if they choose. If the employee dies before age 65, the benefit is paid to the survivors. If the death is caused by the work-related injury, the survivors receive the Survivor Benefit.

In *Saskatchewan*, an additional 10% is set aside. The maximum gross earnings covered in Saskatchewan are $55,000.

EXAMPLE 4   Dan works in uranium mining in Saskatchewan. His gross pay is $60,000 and his net earnings are $45,953. If he is injured he will receive a loss-of-earnings benefit of $37,912, the maximum (90% of the maximum net earnings of $42,124). In addition, Workers' Compensation Board of Saskatchewan will set aside $3,791 a month to be invested and used to buy an annuity at age 65.

Non Economic Loss

If the worker is permanently injured and cannot return to work, most jurisdictions provide a benefit that recognizes that there is a loss beyond the wage loss — a physical, functional, or psychological loss that causes a loss of enjoyment of life. The percentage impairment is determined — the more serious the impairment, the higher the percentage. This percentage is then multiplied by a base amount determined by law. The benefit can also be adjusted for age and inflation (which we are going to ignore).

In *Ontario*, the base amount of this benefit is $56,502.64 for 2009 and is adjusted for age at the time of the injury:

- Add $1,256.07 for each year under age 45 at the time of the injury to a maximum of $81,614.43.
- Subtract $1,256.07 for each year over age 45 to a minimum of $31,390.85. After the base non economic loss amount is adjusted for age and for inflation, it is multiplied by the percentage impairment. The result is the non economic loss benefit.

EXAMPLE 5   Marie, who is 35 years old, now has a 50% work-related impairment. She works in Ontario. She would receive a lump-sum payment of $34,531.67 [($56,502.64 base + $12,560.70 for age) × 50% for impairment] from Workplace Safety and Insurance Board (WSIB).

Occupational Health and Safety

The WCB/Commissions have programs to improve workplace safety and avoid both workplace injuries and occupational illnesses such as cancer, asthma, asbestosis and silicosis, inhalation of substances and fumes, and noise-induced hearing loss.

Survivor Benefits

When a worker dies as a result of a work-related injury or disease, the surviving spouse and other dependants receive two kinds of payments in most jurisdictions — a lump sum payment and a monthly benefit. Some jurisdictions state that the spouse must be financially dependent in order to collect the survivor benefit while other jurisdictions do not have this requirement.

A dependent child is either under age 18 or 19 or under age 25 or 30 and enrolled in an educational program. If there is no spouse, dependent children are usually entitled to the lump sum payment shared equally among them. The benefit can be paid to someone who is acting in the child or children's best interest — a surviving parent, guardian, attorney, the Public Guardian and Trustee, or another person.

Table 7.5   Workers' Compensation 2009 Survivor Benefits

	Deceased's Maximum Annual Payments	Monthly Dependency Benefit			
		Lump Sum to Surviving Spouse	Spouse Maximum Annual Benefit	Additional Benefit for Dependent Children?	Length of Dependency Benefit
AB	$47,843 90%	$1,300	• 90% ($47,843)	• No	• If gainfully employed, after youngest child is 18, benefit is 5-year reducing. If unable to work, to age 65.
BC	$46,971 90%	$2,395	• Note 1	• Yes	• For life
MB	$51,343 90%	$66,700	• $66,700	• Yes, deducted from Spouse's benefit	• 60 months or until youngest child turns 18
NB	$35,641 85%	Nil	• Year 1: 80% ($33,544) minus CPP. Then choose 85% or 60% lump sum	• Yes	• Set-aside continues to provide annuity
NL	$31,449 80%	Greater of $15,000 or ½ annual net earnings	• 80% ($31,449) less CPP Survivor Benefit	• No	• To deceased's age 65

Table 7.5   Continued

	Deceased's Maximum Annual Payments	Monthly Dependency Benefit			
		Lump Sum to Surviving Spouse	Spouse Maximum Annual Benefit	Additional Benefit for Dependent Children?	Length of Dependency Benefit
NT/NU	$55,523 90%	$21,630	• $26,648	• Yes	• For life
NS	$31,989 85% after 26 weeks	At least $15,000	• 85% ($31,989)	• Yes	• To age 65
ON	$50,048 85%	Note 2	• Note 3 40% ($23,552), or 85% ($50,048)	• Yes, deducted from Spouse's benefit	• For life
PE	$29,559 85% after 38 weeks	$10,000	• 70% ($24,343)	• Yes	
QC	$44,796 90%	$94,569 minimum	• 55% of $44,796	• Yes	• For 1 to 3 years
SK	$37,912 90%	Nil	• 90% ($37,912)	• Yes	• 5 years
YT	$57,474	Nil	• $28,816	• Yes	• For life

Note 1   BC: If the survivor is less than age 49, WorkSafeBC pays 60% of the loss-of-earnings amount (maximum $28,183) less 50% of CPP Survivor Benefits. If the survivor is less than age 50, deduct 1% from 60% for each year under the age of 50 to a minimum deduction of 30%.

Note 2   Ontario: Base lump sum of $71,697.51 plus $1,792.44 for every year under 40 years of age or minus $1,792.44 for every year over age 40 ($35,848 to $107,546).

Note 3   Ontario: Spouse only — 40% of net average earnings ($23,552) plus 1% for every year over 40 years of age or minus 1% for every year under age 40 (minimum 20%, $11,776; maximum 60%, $35,328). Spouse with 1 or more dependent children — 85% ($50,048) until youngest child is 19.

In addition, WCB/Commissions pay funeral costs, necessary costs of transporting the body, crisis intervention counseling, and labour market re-entry support. In most jurisdictions, the monthly survivor benefit continues if the survivor remarries. The surviving spouse and dependants also get monthly payments, adjusted each January 1 to reflect the change in the Consumer Price Index and often taking into account survivor benefits through the Canada or Quebec Pension Plan.

In all provinces except Newfoundland and Labrador and Quebec and in none of the three territories, the monthly survivor benefit is affected by the number and age of dependent children. Ontario is one province that also takes the survivor's age into account when calculating the amount of the benefit. Ontario, like most jurisdictions, pays a surviving spouse both a lump sum payment and a monthly benefit.

EXAMPLE 6   Alison worked in Ontario until she was killed on the job. Her spouse is age 41 and will receive a lump sum of $69,905.07 ($71,697.51 – $1,792.44).

If her spouse is age 38, her spouse will receive a lump sum of $75,282.39 [$71,697.51 + (2 × $1,792.44)].

EXAMPLE 7   If Alison and her husband have no children and he is
- 41 years of age, he will receive $24,140.80 [($50,048 ÷ 85%) × 41% – the base amount of 40% plus 1% for being one year over age 40]
- 38 years of age, he will receive $22,374.40 [($50,048 ÷ 85%) × 38% – the base amount of 40% minus 1% for being one year under age 40].

If Alison and her husband have two children, her husband will receive 85%, $50,048, until the youngest child is 19.

In Ontario, if a 19-year-old dependent child is in school or other acceptable training, the child receives a monthly benefit of 10% of the surviving spouse's monthly payment while in school and this amount is deducted from the surviving spouse's monthly payment. The 10% reverts back to the spouse when the child is no longer entitled to it. If there is no surviving spouse, dependent children receive 30% of the deceased's income plus 10% for each additional child up to a maximum of 85%. If more than one person is entitled to spousal benefits, the benefit is shared based on emotional and financial dependency on the worker.

Employment Insurance

Employment Insurance (EI), formerly Unemployment Insurance (UI), was introduced in Canada in 1940. The *Unemployment Insurance Act, 1971*, liberalized the system. In 1940, the system covered about 42% of the workforce, grew to 68% by 1970, nearly universal coverage in 1971, and is 67.4% for April 2009. The objectives of Employment Insurance are to

* provide income during short-term involuntary unemployment,
* help unemployed workers find jobs, and
* help stabilize the economy by maintaining purchasing power.

EI Premiums for Employers and Employees

Premiums for 2009 of 1.73% of insurable earnings are paid on all eligible earnings (employment income, that is not, for instance, investment income) up to the 2009 annual maximum insurable earnings of $42,300. The maximum employee contribution is $731.79 (42,300 × .0173). The employer pays an amount equal to 1.4 times the employee's premium. Employee premiums are eligible for the non-refundable tax credit while employer premiums are tax deductible for employers. Self-employed people do not pay premiums and cannot collect EI. The $42,300 is the basis for the benefit: $42,300 ÷ 52 weeks × 55% = $447 a week or $23,265 a year.

The following table shows

* the history of EI insurable earnings,
* contribution rates, as well as,
* the balance in the **Employment Insurance Account,** which holds the deficit or surplus between income received from premiums and interest and benefits and administration costs paid.

Table 7.6   EI Maximum Contributions and Balance in the EI Account

	Maximum Annual Insurable Earnings	Premium Rate: % of Insurable Earnings	Maximum Annual Contribution for Each Employee		Employment Insurance Account ($000)			GDP
			By Employee	By Employer	Change for the Year		Balance	
1993							(5,883,987)	
1994	$40,560	3.07%	$1,245.19	$1,743.27		2,282,757	(3,601,230)	4.80%
1995	$42,380	3.00%	$1,271.40	$1,779.96		4,267,269	666,039	2.81%
1996	$39,000	2.95%	$1,150.50	$1,610.70				1.62%
1997	$39,000	2.90%	$1,131.00	$1,583.40	15 months	6,634,838	7,300,877	4.23%
1998	$39,000	2.70%	$1,053.00	$1,474.20		6,344,051	13,644,928	4.10%
1999	$39,000	2.55%	$994.50	$1,392.30		7,332,188	20,977,116	5.53%
2000	$39,000	2.40%	$936.00	$1,310.40		7,225,402	28,202,518	5.23%
2001	$39,000	2.25%	$877.50	$1,228.50		7,762,101	35,964,619	1.78%
2002	$39,000	2.20%	$858.00	$1,201.20	restated	4,579,463	40,544,082	2.92%
2003	$39,000	2.10%	$819.00	$1,146.60		3,268,029	43,812,111	1.88%
2004	$39,000	1.98%	$772.20	$1,081.08		2,421,036	46,233,147	3.12%
2005	$39,000	1.95%	$760.50	$1,064.70		2,316,017	48,549,164	2.88%
2006	$39,000	1.87%	$729.30	$1,021.02		2,268,599	50,817,763	3.11%
2007	$40,000	1.80%	$720.00	$1,008.00		3,302,332	54,120,095	7.10%
2008	$41,100	1.73%	$711.03	$995.44		2,832,511	56,952,606	0.46%
2009	$42,300	1.73%	$731.79	$1,024.51				

Sources: Government of Canada, Prepared by the Receiver General for Canada, Public Accounts of Canada 2008, Volume 1, Summary Report and Financial Statements,

Department of Finance, Canada, Employment Insurance Premium Reduced to $1.95 for 2005, 2004-074.

Statistics Canada, Gross Domestic Product (GDP), expenditure-based, provincial economic accounts, annual (dollars x 1,000,000) CANSIM Table 384-0002

Employment Insurance Account

The balance in the Employment Insurance Account has been growing steadily while contributions for each employee have been decreasing for several reasons.

1. Growth as reflected by GDP was strong throughout most of the period shown.
2. The method of setting premiums has been revised in order to both
   (a) provide relatively stable premium rates over the course of a business cycle,
   (b) deal with the size of the cumulative surplus in the EI Account. The Chief Actuary estimates that a balance of between $10 and $15 billion would be sufficient. Before 1995, the EI Account was close to breakeven until 1982, in a deficit from 1983 to 1994 except for the business peak cycles of 1989 and 1990, and has had a growing surplus since 1995. The surplus is loaned to the Receiver General for Canada and the EI Account earned $1.9 billion in interest income for the year ended March 31, 2008.
3. Several revisions to the system over the years have reduced benefits. Revisions include:
   (a) Increasing the **insurable hours required** to have worked in order to be eligible for EI benefits which was eight weeks of insurable employment in 1971 and is now 12 to 20 weeks using the **Variable Entrance Requirement (VER),** which bases eligibility on the unemployment rate in the region of residence, as shown in Table 7.9.
   (b) Reducing the **maximum benefit period** (the number of weeks an **EI beneficiary** can receive benefits), which was 51 weeks in 1971 and is now 41 to 50 weeks (Table 7.10) depending on the unemployment rate in the region of residence as shown in Table 7.9.
   (c) Reducing the **replacement rate**, the percentage of earnings covered by EI benefits, which was 75% in 1971 and now stands at 55%. In addition, repeat users can have a replacement rate as low as 50% and can have to repay benefits if their earnings exceed the maximum insurable earnings.
   (d) Eliminating the **disqualification and penalty period** for claimants which was three weeks in 1971. This applies to people who quit without just cause, are fired for misconduct, and refuse to accept suitable employment. Now these people are not eligible for benefits.

Ratio of Regular Beneficiaries to Unemployed B/U Ratio

The ratio of **regular beneficiaries** (people receiving "regular" benefits as opposed to people receiving maternity or parental benefits, etc.) **to unemployed**, the **B/U ratio** is used by the Government of Canada, Human Resources and Skills Development Canada (HRSDC), and others to assess the effectiveness of EI. The B/U ratio was at its highest of 83% in 1976 and it lowest of 33% in 2006.

The B/U ratio jumped in April 2009 largely due to a new program called Work Sharing, described under EI Benefits, that allows employees to work a reduced work week and collect EI benefits for the days they are not working. This program continues until April 2010 when, hopefully, the recession will have ended.

Table 7.7 does not reflect regional disparities in EI coverage. Tightening eligibility criteria has resulted in many unemployed not qualifying for benefits and this has affected jurisdictions with low unemployment rates the most. In 2008, the B/U was over 90% in Newfoundland and Labrador but under 30% in Ontario and 22% in Alberta.

Table 7.7 Ratio of EI Regular Beneficiaries to Unemployed (B/U Ratio)

	Employed (000)			Unemployed (000)	Total Labour Force (000)	Unemployment Rate	EI "Regular" Beneficiaries	B/U
	Employees	Self-employed	Total					
1990	11,250	1,837	13,087	1,158	14,245	8.1%	854,912	74%
1991	10,962	1,896	12,858	1,479	14,337	10.3%	1,024,221	69%
1992	10,803	1,928	12,731	1,605	14,336	11.2%	1,006,009	63%
1993	10,782	2,011	12,793	1,642	14,435	11.4%	930,643	57%
1994	11,030	2,028	13,058	1,515	14,573	10.4%	772,745	51%
1995	11,212	2,083	13,295	1,394	14,689	9.5%	634,388	46%
1996	11,250	2,172	13,422	1,432	14,854	9.6%	607,186	42%
1997	11,357	2,349	13,706	1,373	15,079	9.1%	508,120	37%
1998	11,640	2,406	14,046	1,270	15,316	8.3%	484,918	38%
1999	11,974	2,433	14,407	1,182	15,589	7.6%	453,869	38%
2000	12,390	2,374	14,764	1,083	15,847	6.8%	418,771	39%
2001	12,670	2,277	14,947	1,164	16,111	7.2%	455,538	39%
2002	12,996	2,314	15,310	1,269	16,579	7.7%	488,278	38%
2003	13,270	2,402	15,672	1,286	16,958	7.6%	495,255	39%
2004	13,494	2,453	15,947	1,235	17,182	7.2%	475,041	38%
2005	13,658	2,512	16,170	1,173	17,343	6.8%	453,965	39%
2006	13,986	2,498	16,484	1,108	17,592	6.3%	431,337	39%
2007	14,251	2,615	16,866	1,079	17,945	6.0%	417,741	39%
Jul/08	14,462	2,622	17,084	1,105	18,189	6.1%	428,200	39%
Apr/09	14,187	2,687	16,874	1,465	18,339	8.0%	712,980	49%

Source: Statistics Canada [www.statcan.gc.ca]: Labour Force Catalogue No. 71-001-X, Canada, Employment Insurance Program (E.I.), beneficiaries receiving regular benefits without reported earnings by province and age group, monthly (persons), CANSIM Table 276-0002

Historical Statistical Supplement 2001/02 Catalogue No. 11-210-XIB

The Daily, Employment Insurance April 2009, Monday, June 22, 2009

As shown in Table 7.8, in 2007, 30% of unemployed people had not made EI contributions and were therefore ineligible for benefits:

- 24.8% had not worked in the previous 12 months and therefore could not contribute
- 5.2% had uninsurable employment income, which includes income such as self-employed income, scholarships, lump sum payments, research grants, payments under a wage-loss replacement plan, casual employment, and certain wages paid to non-arm's length individuals in small businesses.

Table 7.8 Coverage and Eligibility of the Unemployed for Employment Insurance Benefits for 2007

Eligible and receiving or will receive benefits *	41.0%	
Eligible based on hours worked but not receiving benefits	3.7%	44.7%
Ineligible — not enough hours	9.6%	
Ineligible — left last job for invalid reasons	15.7%	
Ineligible — no insurable employment	5.2%	
Ineligible — has not worked in previous 12 months	24.8%	55.3%
Total unemployed		100.0%

* This table is based on data for March, June, October, and December and, as a result, the B/U is slightly different from Table 7.7.

Unemployment rates vary a great deal by region. The following table is produced monthly by Human Resources and Social Development Canada (HRSDC) (www.hrsdc.gc.ca) and is used to determine eligibility for regular benefits — the required number of insurable hours based on the unemployment rate in the region of residence. The highlighted areas have had an increase in unemployment of over 50% for the month beginning June 7, 2009, over the same period in 2008 as the recession deepened.

Table 7.9 Unemployment Rates for the Employment Insurance (EI) Economic Regions

	Code	EI Economic Name	2000 Jul 9/ Aug 5	2001 Jun 10/ Jul 7	2002 Jun 9/ Jul 6	2003 Jun 8/ Jul 12	2004 Jun 6/ Jul 10	2005 Jun 12/ Jul 9	2006 Jun 11/ Jul 8	2007 Jun 10/ Jul 7	2008 Jun 8/ Jul 12	2009 Jun 7/ Jul 11
NL	1	St. John's	9.2	8.2	8.3	9.3	8.7	9.5	8.8	7.3	8.3	7.5
NL	2	Nfld — Labrador	20.1	21.9	21.2	21.6	20.6	19.2	19.5	16.9	15.6	20.7
PE	3	Prince Edward Island	11.3	12.2	11.8	12.6	12.1	10.5	10.9	10.0	10.5	12.5
NS	4	Eastern Nova Scotia	15.4	18.3	15.9	14.9	16.1	15.0	13.8	14.9	15.0	16.6
NS	5	Western Nova Scotia	8.9	10.6	10.1	9.3	10.0	8.8	9.1	8.8	8.9	10.6
NS	6	Halifax	5.5	6.7	7.6	6.9	6.2	5.8	5.2	5.2	5.0	5.9
NB	7	Fredericton — Moncton — Saint John	7.5	9.2	8.0	8.5	7.0	6.0	6.6	4.7	5.6	6.6
NB	8	Madawaska — Charlotte	10.2	15.8	12.4	11.4	11.9	11.5	10.0	9.4	10.6	11.5
NB	9	Restigouche — Albert	16.1	17.8	15.3	16.5	16.2	15.2	14.1	12.8	14.1	14.3
QC	10	Gaspésie–Iles-de-la-Madeleine	20.1	21.5	21.5	18.1	21.0	18.3	20.2	17.2	18.0	17.0
QC	11	Québec	8.3	8.1	6.5	7.4	5.8	5.7	4.3	4.9	5.1	4.5
QC	12	Trois-Rivières	10.7	8.3	11.0	9.8	11.1	10.2	8.3	7.8	8.9	8.1
QC	13	South Central Quebec	5.3	5.7	5.2	5.7	5.9	6.2	4.9	6.1	4.9	7.1
QC	14	Sherbrooke	8.7	7.9	8.1	6.1	6.3	7.7	7.7	6.4	6.0	8.8
QC	15	Montérégie	7.5	7.8	8.0	6.6	7.2	7.2	7.0	6.9	7.6	9.1
QC	16	Montréal	7.7	8.0	8.6	9.7	8.0	8.3	8.9	6.8	7.7	9.5
QC	17	Central Quebec	11.2	10.6	9.6	9.2	9.3	9.2	8.9	9.5	8.0	9.4
QC	18	North Western Quebec	17.7	17.1	15.6	15.2	18.3	10.6	10.4	12.8	10.0	12.2
QC	19	Bas-Saint-Laurent–Côte-Nord	11.2	19.3	16.0	13.1	14.1	11.8	12.0	12.2	11.1	11.8
QC	20	Hull	4.9	7.5	6.7	7.2	6.7	7.4	6.1	5.6	5.3	5.4
QC	21	Chicoutimi-Jonquière	9.7	11.0	12.7	11.5	11.0	8.3	8.9	9.7	9.5	9.4
ON	22	Ottawa	5.3	5.2	7.1	6.5	7.3	6.9	4.7	5.6	4.9	6.2
ON	23	Eastern Ontario	7.5	6.1	8.0	7.5	7.5	6.6	6.3	7.2	5.9	8.4
ON	24	Kingston	7.4	7.8	7.3	6.6	5.5	6.2	6.9	4.5	5.6	6.2
ON	25	Central Ontario	5.7	4.9	5.8	5.7	4.6	6.8	6.7	5.9	6.6	10.5
ON	26	Oshawa	5.7	5.3	7.4	5.1	5.2	6.7	6.0	5.9	8.0	7.9
ON	27	Toronto	5.3	5.9	7.1	7.6	7.8	7.5	6.4	6.9	6.5	9.1
ON	28	Hamilton	4.7	6.1	7.3	5.5	7.2	4.9	5.4	6.1	6.1	7.4
ON	29	St. Catharines	5.6	6.6	7.7	6.0	8.1	6.8	6.0	5.7	7.2	10.6
ON	30	London	6.3	6.1	7.5	6.9	5.3	6.8	5.7	6.0	7.1	10.2
ON	31	Niagara	7.6	6.5	7.5	6.5	7.0	8.5	7.9	7.9	9.4	11.2
ON	32	Windsor	5.3	6.7	8.4	7.8	7.9	8.1	9.0	9.3	7.9	13.7
ON	33	Kitchener	4.8	5.6	5.6	6.2	5.8	6.3	5.0	5.6	5.6	10.0
ON	34	Huron	6.3	9.1	7.2	7.7	7.8	7.3	6.6	8.6	8.4	10.1
ON	35	South Central Ontario	3.5	4.1	5.3	5.3	4.8	4.3	4.9	5.9	4.6	8.3
ON	36	Sudbury	7.2	8.0	10.1	7.5	9.1	7.3	7.7	5.9	6.0	8.3
ON	37	Thunder Bay	5.7	8.4	6.5	6.0	7.4	7.4	7.9	6.7	6.1	8.9
ON	38	Northern Ontario	11.1	11.7	13.0	11.3	12.1	8.8	10.2	10.4	10.4	13.6
MB	39	Winnipeg	5.4	5.1	5.6	4.9	5.3	5.2	4.8	5.0	4.3	4.9
MB	40	Southern Manitoba	4.6	5.5	5.6	5.4	6.0	6.3	4.4	5.2	5.2	5.8
MB	41	Northern Manitoba	21.9	23.0	25.2	25.5	27.5	23.5	24.9	26.2	25.6	26.5
SK	42	Regina	4.9	5.7	5.6	5.6	5.2	4.4	5.3	4.7	4.3	3.8
SK	43	Saskatoon	5.9	6.4	5.8	5.7	6.5	4.6	5.0	3.9	3.9	5.0
SK	44	Southern Saskatchewan	5.9	6.6	6.8	6.7	7.1	6.8	6.1	5.7	6.0	7.3
SK	45	Northern Saskatchewan	12.6	14.1	15.0	14.2	13.2	14.2	15.0	14.2	14.9	16.5
AB	46	Calgary	5.1	4.4	6.0	5.8	5.1	3.5	3.3	3.5	3.1	6.7
AB	47	Edmonton	5.3	5.6	5.6	5.7	4.8	4.4	3.7	3.7	4.0	6.2
AB	48	Northern Alberta	9.6	9.6	10.1	10.1	10.0	6.5	8.0	7.7	8.1	10.4
AB	49	Southern Alberta	6.3	6.0	6.4	6.7	5.8	4.6	4.2	4.7	4.4	7.2
BC	50	Southern Interior BC	10.8	9.1	10.8	11.1	8.7	6.8	6.2	5.5	6.4	10.8
BC	51	Abbotsford	7.0	6.6	6.6	8.7	6.2	6.1	5.9	4.7	4.8	7.4
BC	52	Vancouver	5.6	5.6	8.5	7.2	7.6	6.2	4.4	4.2	4.2	7.0
BC	53	Victoria	6.8	6.3	7.6	7.1	5.5	5.4	5.2	4.1	3.7	7.0
BC	54	Southern Coastal BC	8.7	10.7	11.9	10.7	12.5	8.4	5.7	6.3	5.7	8.1
BC	55	Northern BC	11.6	12.5	16.8	13.6	14.8	10.0	8.2	7.6	9.6	13.7
YT	56	Yukon	25.0	25.0	25.0	25.0	25.0	25.0	25.0	25.0	25.0	25.0
NT	57	Northwest Territories	25.0	25.0	25.0	25.0	25.0	25.0	25.0	25.0	25.0	25.0
NU	58	Nunavut	25.0	25.0	25.0	25.0	25.0	25.0	25.0	25.0	25.0	25.0

Source: Human Resources and Social Development Canada [www.hrsdc.gc.ca], Unemployment Rates for the Employment Insurance (EI) Economic Regions

These regional unemployment rates are used to determine EI eligibility as shown in Table 7.10. The highest increase in unemployment was *Calgary* where unemployment went from 3.9% to 6.7%, an 116% increase. This means that if a person became unemployed in June, 2008, he or she would have needed to have worked 700 hours or 19 35-hour weeks in the prior year to be eligible to collect EI. If this person became unemployed in June 2009, he or she would have needed 665 hours, or 20 weeks. A person in *St. John's* where the unemployment rate dropped 10%, would have needed 595 hours in 2008 but would need 630 hours in 2009.

Table 7.10   Qualifying Period: Insurable Hours Required

Regional Unemployment Rate	Required Number of Hours of Insurable Employment in the Last 52 Weeks	Number of Weeks Payable for Regular Benefits	
		Minimum	Maximum
0% to 6%	700 hours	19	41
6.1% to 7%	665 hours	20	43
7.1% to 8%	630 hours	22	45
8.1% to 9%	595 hours	23	47
9.1% to 10%	560 hours	25	49
10.1% to 11%	525 hours	26	50
11.1% to 12%	490 hours	28	50
12.1% to 13%	455 hours	29	50
13.1% and over	420 hours	37	50

Source: Human Resources and Social Development Canada, Employment Insurance (EI) Program Characteristics for the period of June 07, 2009, to July 11, 2009.

EI Benefits

Employment Insurance provides temporary financial assistance for unemployed Canadians while they look for work or upgrade their skills. There are five categories of benefits:

1. Regular benefits,
2. Maternity, parental and sickness benefits
3. Compassionate care benefits
4. Fishing benefits
5. Work sharing benefits

1. Regular Benefits

These benefits can be paid for 14 to 45 weeks if the employee loses his/her job through no fault of his/her own, for example, due to shortage of work, seasonal or mass lay-offs, and the employee is available for and able to work but can't find a job. To be eligible for regular benefits, the employee must show that

• he/she has been without work and without pay for at least 7 consecutive days, and
• in the last 52 weeks or since the last claim (this period is called the **qualifying period**), the person has worked for the required number of insurable hours, as shown in Table 7.10. The **qualifying period** is the shorter of
  • the 52 weeks immediately before the start date of a claim, or
  • the period since the start of a previous EI claim if that claim had started during the 52-week period.

Only **insurable hours** that fall within the qualifying period are used to start a **benefit period**. However, the qualifying period **may be extended** up to 104 weeks if the employee was not employed in insurable employment and not receiving EI because the employee was

• incapable of work by reason of illness, injury, quarantine, or pregnancy;

- confined in a jail, penitentiary or other similar institution;
- attending a course of instruction or other related employment activity to which he or she was referred by a Human Resources and Skills Development Canada (HRSDC)–designated authority; or
- not working because he or she was receiving a payment under a provincial law based on having stopped work because continuing to work would have entailed danger to the person, to an unborn child, or to a child being breast-fed. There is a two-week unpaid **waiting period** before EI benefits begin to be paid (the waiting period is occasionally waived). Earnings such as vacation pay or severance pay, made or allocated during the two-week waiting period, are deducted from the first 3 weeks' benefits following the waiting period.

EXAMPLE 8   For the past 15 years, Clarissa worked as a bookkeeper for a car dealership in Kitchener, where the unemployment rate was 5.6% at the time she lost her job. She was laid off on June 8, 2008, just after she returned from her annual vacation (so she was not owed any vacation pay). Since she had worked steadily for five years, she easily met the required number of hours, which was 700 hours or 20 weeks of insurable earnings. She made an immediate claim, waited the two weeks and then collected EI benefits for six weeks before finding work at another dealership where the bookkeeper was going on maternity leave. On December 14, 2008, she was laid off again when this dealership ran into financial difficulty. She had worked for just over 4 months — 18 weeks or 630 hours. Her qualifying period is the *shorter of*

- the prior 52 weeks, or
- the period since the start of the last claim, which was June 9.

Only the insurable earnings that fall within the qualifying period are used to start a benefit period. The unemployment rate in Kitchener for December 7, 2008 to January 10, 2009 had risen to 6.4%, meaning she needs 665 hours. Since she has only 630 hours, she will not be able to collect.

She *may* be able to reactivate her first claim.

Her second claim will be kept on file and when the unemployment rate increases to at least 7.1% in Kitchener, the rate that requires only the 630 hours that she has, her claim *may* be reactivated. For the period January 11 to February 7, 2009, the rate was 7.7% in Kitchener. Presumably her second claim will be reactivated on January 11 and, after waiting two weeks, she can begin collecting again for a maximum of 17 weeks, which takes her to three weeks before the first anniversary of being laid off the first time. By the time her second claim starts on January 11, she has not been paid for eight weeks since June 8,

- the first two week's waiting period in June, 2008;
- the second two week's waiting period starting January 11, 2009; and
- the four weeks between December 14 and January 11.

In addition, the 4% vacation she received when she lost her second job will be deducted from her first three EI benefit payments.

In some instances, a minimum of 910 hours or 26 weeks in the qualifying period may be needed to qualify if the person is

- in the work force for the first time, or
- re-entering the work force after an absence of two years.

For all EI benefits, the employee needs the **Record of Employment** from the employer to apply for benefits. All EI benefits are taxable income.

Amount of Benefit (for All Types of Benefits)

The amount of the weekly benefit payment depends on total earnings before deductions, including tips and commissions, in the last 26 weeks, and is calculated as follows:

1. Look at total earnings paid in the last 26 weeks ending with the last day of work.
2. Find the unemployment rate in the region where the employee lives and works and the **minimum divisor** that applies for that unemployment rate. The divisor cannot be less than 14 or greater than 26.
3. Determine the **average weekly insured earnings** by dividing total earnings in the last 26 weeks by the *greater of*
   (a) the number of weeks worked in the last 26 weeks, or
   (b) the minimum divisor number.
4. Multiply the result by 55% to obtain the weekly benefit to a **maximum benefit of $447 a week** or $23,244 a year based on annual income of $42,300 ($447 × 52 weeks = $23,244, which is roughly equal to $42,300 × 55% = $23,265).

Table 7.11   Divisor

Regional Unemployment Rate	Minimum Divisor
0% to 6%	22
6.1% to 7%	21
7.1% to 8%	20
8.1% to 9%	19
9.1% to 10%	18
10.1% to 11%	17
11.1% to 12%	16
12.1% to 13%	15
13.1% and over	14

EXAMPLE 9.1   In the last 26 weeks Sam worked for 26 weeks and earned a total of $22,880 ($877 a week). Sam lives in an area where the unemployment rate is 13.1% so the divisor is 14.
- Find the average weekly earnings: divide total earnings by the *greater of*
  - the number of weeks worked (26), and
  - the divisor (14) = $22,880 ÷ 26 = $880.
- Determine the weekly benefit rate — take 55% of $880 = **$484**.
  Since the maximum is $447, he will collect **$447**.

EXAMPLE 9.2   In the last 26 weeks, Tom worked for 12 weeks and earned a total of $8,400 ($700 a week). Tom lives in an area where the unemployment rate is 6.7% so the divisor is 21.
- Find the average weekly earnings: divide total earnings by the *greater of*
  - the number of weeks worked (12), and
  - the divisor (21) = $8,400 ÷ 21 = $400.
- Determine the weekly benefit rate: take 55% of $400 = **$220**.

EXAMPLE 9.3   In the last 26 weeks Alice worked for 17 weeks and earned a total of $12,750 ($750 a week). Alice lives in an area where the unemployment rate is 11.5% so the divisor is 16.

- Find her average weekly earnings: divide total earnings by the *greater of*
  - the number of weeks worked (17), and
  - the divisor (16) = $12,750 ÷ 17 weeks = $750.
- Determine the weekly benefit rate: take 55% of $750 = **$412.50**.

Working While on EI

A person cannot work full-time and receive EI benefits. However, a person can work part-time while receiving **regular benefits**, earning up to the greater of **$50 per week or 25%** of weekly benefits. A **pilot project**, originally for 23 regions and now extended to all the regions, shown in Table 7.9, increases this amount to the greater of **$75 or 40 % of weekly benefits**. The project has been extended to to December 4, 2010.

Any monies earned above that amount are deducted dollar for dollar from benefits. Any earnings must be reported while collecting regular benefits.

Quitting Your Job and Being Fired for Misconduct

An employee who

- voluntarily quit his or her job without just cause, or
- is fired for his or her own misconduct

is not eligible for regular benefits until he or she has worked the minimum number of insurable hours required to get regular benefits. However, a person may still be paid maternity, parental, sickness, and compassionate care benefits if he or she qualifies for these benefits.

Corporate Downsizing

When enterprises permanently reduce the size of their work force, employees are eligible for EI regular benefits. If an employer is downsizing and offers an employee the opportunity to quit his or her job in order to protect another person's job, this employee can leave the job without penalty as long as the employer shows that the layoff is permanent and that the departure protects another person's job.

Labour Disputes

If a strike, a lockout, or other form of labour dispute where the employee works

- causes him or her to lose his or her job, or
- prevents the employee from going to work,

the employee will generally not be paid EI benefits. The following conditions apply whether the employee is a union member or not and whether the job is part- or full-time. The employee may be eligible to receive benefits if he/she is *not*

- taking part in the dispute,
- giving money directly to support the dispute, and
- directly interested in the dispute — his/her wages or working conditions, etc., are not affected by the outcome of the dispute.

An employee taking part in a labour dispute is not eligible for EI until

- the strike or lockout is over, or
- the employee has found another regular job where EI premiums are paid.

If an approved absence from work was already arranged before the work stoppage started, such as sick leave, maternity leave, parental leave, or authorized training, EI benefits may still be paid.

2. Maternity, Parental and Sickness Benefits

Employment insurance is available for the following:

- **Maternity benefits** for the birth or surrogate mother to a maximum of 15 weeks,
- **Parental benefits** for either biological or adoptive parents to a maximum of 35 weeks. This benefit can be shared by both parents to a maximum total of 35 weeks, and
- **Sickness benefit** for sickness, injury or quarantine to a maximum of 15 weeks.

These benefits can be combined with each other or with regular benefits to a maximum 50 weeks which can be increased to 65 weeks if less than the maximum for either sickness or parental benefit has been received (and regular or fishing benefits have not been received). Employees are eligible for these benefits if

- regular weekly earnings have been decreased by more than 40%, and
- the employee has accumulated 600 insured hours in the last 52 weeks or since the last claim. This period is called the **qualifying period**.

The two-week unpaid waiting period applies here also.

If the employee works while on

- maternity or sickness leave, earnings are deducted dollar for dollar from the benefit, and
- parental leave, the employee can earn the higher of $75 a week or 40% of weekly income during the period of the pilot project. Any income over that amount is deducted dollar for dollar from the benefit.

3. Compassionate Care Benefits

This benefit may be paid up to a **maximum of six weeks** to a person or family who has to be absent from work to provide care or support to a gravely ill family member at risk of dying. The six weeks can be shared with other family members as long as the total benefit for each sick person does not exceed six weeks. The same eligibility requirements apply as for paternity, parental and sickness benefits. Compassionate care benefits can be received to care for one of the many relatives including one's own and a spouse or partner's grandparents, aunts, and uncles. *Partner* means a person who has been living in a conjugal relationship with that person for at least a year.

Definition of *Care* or *Support*

Care or support to a family member means

- providing psychological or emotional support,
- arranging for care by a third party, or
- directly providing or participating in the care.

4. Fishing Benefits

Fishers, self-employed people engaged in fishing, need to have earned at least $2,500 (for a regional unemployment rate of 13.1%) to $4,200 (for a regional unemployment rate of 6% and under) to qualify for fishing benefits in a maximum of the 31 weeks prior to the beginning of the claim. Those who have just started working as a self-employed fisher and those who have had an absence of one year may need $5,500 to qualify. The benefits are calculated the same way (except using 31 weeks instead of 26 weeks) using the same divisors as regular benefits.

5. Work Sharing Benefits

This program assists employees who agree to a temporary reduction in their workload when there is a temporary reduction of at least 10% in sales or orders. The employer makes the application and at least two employees must participate in the program. **Work Sharing Agreements** can last from a minimum of 6 weeks to a maximum of 52 weeks and each employee can take a minimum of one day a week to a maximum of two days a week reduction in their work activity and collect EI benefits for thee days. Seasonal and temporary employers are not eligible nor are employers who are involved in a labour dispute. Students and contract workers may not participate. Employees must meet the normal requirements for regular benefits and benefits are calculated (and pro-rated) in the same manner as regular benefits. The normal two-week waiting period is waived. Employers must continue to provide existing employee benefits. As of February 1, 2009, these benefits are available until April 3, 2010.

Canada Pension Plan (CPP)

The Canada Pension Plan provides several benefits for injured or ill CPP contributors and their dependent children as well as survivor benefits for a spouse and dependent children if a CPP contributor dies in addition to retirement benefits. Benefits are taxable and indexed annually.

CPP Disability Benefit

To qualify for disability benefits, the person must be under 65 years of age and the disability must be prolonged and severe, meaning the person cannot work regularly at any job and the condition is long term or may result in death. In addition, earnings must be at least $4,600 in 2009 and have contributed to the CPP in four of the past six years. If contributions have been made for at least 25 years, contributions must have been made in three of the past six years.

Dependent children, natural and adopted, of a disabled beneficiary also receive CPP benefits. To be dependent, the child must be either under 18 years of age or between 18 and 25 and in school full-time.

Table 7.12 Canada Pension Plan Maximum Benefits for 2009

	Per Month	Per Year	
Disability	$1,105.99	$13,271.88	122%
Retirement pension	908.75	10,905.00	100%
Survivor (under age 65)	506.38	6,076.56	56%
Survivor (age 65 and over)	545.25	6,543.00	60%
Children of disabled contributors	213.99	2,567.88	24%
Children of deceased contributors	213.99	2,567.88	24%
Survivor and retirement combined	908.75	10,905.00	100%
Survivor and disability combined	1,105.99	13,271.88	122%
Death benefit (one-time payment)	2,500.00		

The CPP disability benefit continues until age 65 at which time the retirement benefit starts — income from CPP drops by $2,367. However, at age 65 the individual can begin to collect **Old Age Security (OAS)** — $6,204 providing total maximum income of $17,109 (so income goes up by $3,837). OAS is indexed quarterly and is taxable income. In addition, OAS is subject to a special tax referred to as a **clawback**. Most other income (other than CPP retirement benefits and OAS) in excess over the threshold amount of $66,335 is subject to a special tax of 15% that reduces the OAS benefit until, at other income of $107,692, OAS is entirely clawed back.

Table 7.13 Old Age Security Maximum Benefits for July to September, 2009

	Per Month	Per year	Maximum Income
OAS pension	$ 516.96	$ 6,203.52	n/a
Allowance for the survivor	1,050.68	12,608.16	$20,664
OAS clawback threshold		66,335	
Income at which OAS is 100% clawed back		107,692	

OAS benefits are paid out of general tax revenues and, as a result, there are residency requirements both to qualify for the benefits and to continue to collect them if the beneficiary moves out of Canada.

CPP Survivor and Dependent Children's Benefit

If a CPP contributor dies, CPP survivor benefits include

- a one-time **death benefit** — a maximum of $2,500,
- a **survivor benefit** that is paid to a surviving spouse or common-law partner of either sex, and
- a **children's benefit** for dependent children (defined the same as the disability benefit).

The CPP contributor must have contributed for at least three years. If the contributory period is longer than nine years, the contributions must have been made in the *lesser of*

- one-third of the calendar years in the contributory period, or
- 10 calendar years.

A person can collect a survivor benefit and a

- disability benefit at the same time but the maximum is the same as the maximum disability benefit, or
- retirement benefit at the same time but the maximum is the same as the maximum retirement benefitas shown in Table 7.12.

The OAS Allowance for a Survivor is paid to a person 60 to 64 years old whose partner or spouse has died. Benefits end if the survivor remarries or lives in a common-law relationship for one year, moves out of Canada, or receives more income than the maximum allowed of $20,664.

Private Disability Plans

Social insurance often does not provide adequate income protection:

- Workers can lose their source of income because they are disabled for reasons not related to work.
- EI benefits do not last long, are not available to everyone, and are not all that high.
- CPP disability benefits are quite modest.

The gap is filled by private disability insurance, which covers the insured if he or she is not able to work due to illness or injury for any reason. Many companies offer this as part of group benefit plans. Individual disability insurance policies are often much more generous in their eligibility requirements than group plans and are, as a result, much more expensive.

The amount of coverage an insured can get is based on income at the time the policy is taken out although there are provisions for increasing the coverage if income increases. If the benefit is taxable, the insured might get coverage for as much as 80% of earnings. If the benefit is not taxable, the insured will be able to get coverage for only 60 to 67% of income.

The table in the following section compares the coverage between one group plan (**Group**) provided by an employer and three different individual plans (**Indiv 1, 2, and 3**) bought privately. A blank space means it is not mentioned in *that* policy. The four policies are provided to show how much policies can vary — *caveat emptor* (buyer beware)! Read your policy carefully. There isn't any point in paying monthly premiums if the policy doesn't give you the coverage you think it does.

Make sure
• you know what your coverage is before you sign up, and
• you get adequate coverage.

Policy Provisions

The following policy is divided into five parts:

Part 1   **Definitions**. This section, as outlined in Chapter 2, identifies "you" and "we" as well as providing other definitions such as own versus any occupation, full-time employment, injury and sickness, monthly earnings, and prior earnings.

Part 2   **Benefits**. This section is the insuring agreement and outlines the coverage under full, partial, proportionate, residual, recurrent, concurrent, and presumptive disability as well as any other benefits that are included in the insuring agreement.

Part 3   **Contract Provisions.** This section outlines the Conditions and Miscellaneous Provisions to the contract including the waiting period, grace period, an incontestable clause, a misstatement of age clause, and reinstatement possibilities.

Part 4   **Exclusions**. This section contains specific exclusions. Note in particular the exclusions that are included only in Individual Policy 3 (Indiv 3).

Part 5   **Riders**. Riders lists additional, optional coverages that can be bought when the policy is taken out or, perhaps, after it is in place but never while a person is collecting disability benefits (is "on disability").

Note: The following provisions have been adapted from several policies to illustrate the provisions found in policies. None represents a complete policy.

Part 1 Definitions

You and Your		Indiv 1	Indiv 2	Indiv 3
The insured named in the policy schedule.				
We, Us, and Our		Indiv 1	Indiv 2	Indiv 3
The insurance company				
Regular/Own/Your Occupation		Indiv 1	Indiv 2	Indiv 3
The occupation in which you are regularly engaged at the time you become disabled.				
Gainful/Any Occupation		Indiv 1		
An occupation for which you are fitted by reason of your education, training, or experience.				

Employed Full-Time			Indiv 2	

You are working at least 30 hours a week at the usual place of business.

Injury			Indiv 2	Indiv 3

Accidental bodily injury sustained after the Date of Issue and while your Policy is in force.

Sickness			Indiv 2	Indiv 3

Sickness or disease which first manifests itself after the Date of Issue and while your Policy is in force.

Evidence of Earned Income		Indiv 1		Indiv 3

During a period of Proportionate Disability, we may require written evidence of Earned Income as defined below. This evidence may include, but is not limited to, a true copy of one or more of the following:

* Income tax returns
* Audited income and expense statements
* Employer's salary statements

Monthly Earnings		Indiv 1	Indiv 2	Indiv 3

If you own **any portion of a business or profession**, your Monthly Earnings means

* your share of income earned by that business or profession due to your personal activities,
* less your share of business expenses which are deductible for federal income tax purposes,
* plus your salary and any contributions to a pension or profit sharing plan made on your behalf.

From any **other source of employment**, Monthly Earnings means your salary, fees, commissions, and bonuses and any other income earned for services performed.

Monthly Earnings does not include

* income from deferred compensation plans, disability policies, or retirement plans, or
* income not derived from your vocational activities.

Prior Earnings		Indiv 1	Indiv 2	Indiv 3

This means the greater of

* your average Monthly Earnings for any six consecutive calendar months during the 18 months just before your disability began, or
* your highest average Monthly Earnings for any two successive years during the five-year period just before your disability began.

Risk Class				Indiv 3

Any grouping of insureds as determined by our Risk Classification System. The variables used in determining your Risk Class are issue age, occupation, province or territory of residence, and plan type, as determined by us, for the coverage provided under this policy. This policy may be cancelled if

* you become a member of an unacceptable Risk Class due to a change in the occupation or province or territory of residence of the Insured, or
* the Risk Class of which you are a member becomes an unacceptable Risk Class, as determined by us, based on actual or anticipated adverse experience of the Plan for the occupation, province, or territory of residence of you or your plan type.

Part 2 Benefits

Total Disability	Group	Indiv 1	Indiv 2	Indiv 3

You, due directly to Injury or Sickness,

* cannot perform the important duties of the Your Regular Occupation for two years,
* thereafter, cannot work in **any Gainful Occupation**, and
* are under the regular and personal care of a physician.

Total Disability Benefit		Indiv 1	Indiv 2	Indiv 3

This benefit will begin on the Commencement Date (*also called the Start Date*). We will continue to pay it while you remain Totally Disabled. In no event will we pay beyond the Maximum Benefit Period. For periods of less than a month, we will pay $^1/_{30}$ th of the benefit for each day of disability.

We will periodically pay the Total Disability benefit during your continuous Total Disability. The monthly amount we will pay is shown on the Policy Schedule.

Partial Disability *is based on time or duties*.		Indiv 1	Indiv 2	Indiv 3

You are not Totally Disabled and are working full- or part-time in any Gainful Occupation but, due directly to Injury or Sickness

* cannot perform one or more of all the important daily duties of the Gainful Occupation, or
* suffer the necessary and continuous loss of at least ½ of the time normally spent in the daily performance of the Gainful Occupation.

Partial Disability Benefit		Indiv 1		Indiv 3

Number of months of Partial Disability	% of Total Disability Benefit Received
1 to 12	50%
13 to 24	40%
25 to 36	30%
thereafter	25%

Partial Disability Benefit			Indiv 2	

Same as Proportionate Disability for this policy.

Proportionate Disability *is based on earnings*.		Indiv 1		

You are not Totally Disabled and are working full- or part-time in any Gainful Occupation but, due directly to Injury or Sickness, are unable to earn more than 80% of the **Prior Earnings.**

Residual Disability			Indiv 2	

Because of a continuing Injury or Sickness, you are not Totally Disabled; and

* Your Loss of Earnings is equal to at least 20% of your Prior Earnings while you are engaged in your Regular Occupation or another occupation, and
* You are under the regular and personal care of a Physician.

Residual and Proportionate Disability Benefit		Indiv 1	Indiv 2	

This benefit will begin on either the Commencement Date or the day after your Total Disability ends, if later. The monthly amount we will pay equals:

(Loss of Earnings ÷ Prior Earnings) × Maximum Monthly Amount shown on the Policy Schedule Page.

Loss of Earnings for any month is the Prior Earnings minus monthly Earnings for the month which Residual Disability is claimed. This difference must be due to the Injury or Sickness causing the Residual Disability.

If the Loss of Earnings for any month is 80% or more of Prior Earnings, we will deem the loss to be 100% of Prior Earnings.

Recurrent Disability	Group	Indiv 1		Indiv 3

Successive periods of Disability, separated by 12 months or less, will be combined and deemed to continue with interruption, as long as

* the Period of Disability is not caused by a different and unrelated Injury or Sickness,
* you have worked continuously in a full-time occupation away from your home between Periods of Disability (*for Indiv 3 only*), and
* earned Income between the Periods of Disability is less than 80% of indexed Prior Earned Income.

Recurrent Disability			Indiv 2	

If after the end of a period of disability you become Disabled from the same or related causes, we will deem it a separate Disability. However, if such Disability recurs within six months of the prior period, we will deem it a continuation of the prior Disability.

Concurrent Disability		Indiv 1	Indiv 2	

If a Disability is caused by more than one Injury or Sickness or from both, we will pay benefits as if the Disability was caused by only one Injury or Sickness (*meaning you do not need to satisfy the elimination period again*).

We will not pay benefits for both Total Disability and Residual Disability for the same period, but will pay the greater of the two benefits.

Presumptive (or Assumed) Total Disability		Indiv 1	Indiv 2	Indiv 3

You will be deemed to be Totally Disabled if, due to Injury or Sickness, you suffer the total and irrevocable loss of use of the following:

* Speech
* The sight of both eyes
* The hearing of both ears
* The use of both hands or both feet
* The use of one hand and one foot

Under this provision		Indiv 1		

* the Waiting Period is waived, and
* the Premium is waived from the Date of Disability.

Contribution to Pension Plan	Group			

While benefits are payable, a portion of the benefits is paid to the employee's pension plan in accordance with the pension plan provisions.

Cosmetic Surgery Benefit			Indiv 2	

After six months from the Date of Issue, if you become Totally Disabled because you have surgery to improve your appearance or correct disfigurement, we will consider you to be Totally Disabled due to sickness.

Disability because of Normal Pregnancy			Indiv 2	

After 12 months from the Date of Issue, if you become Disabled because of normal pregnancy, we will consider you to be Disabled due to Sickness. Prior to this, no benefits for a Disability due to normal pregnancy will be payable. Complications of pregnancy will be covered during this period unless specifically excluded in your policy.

Indexation	Group			

The amount of the monthly benefit is increased by not more than 8% to reflect an increase in the Consumer Price Index for the prior year.

Integration of Benefits	Group			Indiv 3

Any income provided
* under the legislation of any government (Canada Pension Plan Disability Income, Workers' Compensation) but not Employment Insurance,
* under any other group insurance plan,
* under any retirement or pension plan as a result of a disability or medical condition, and
* as a result of the Employee's ("Your" for Individual Plan 3) membership in an association of any kind is deducted from the monthly benefit.

This **excludes** any amount provided
* under a policy which is solely an individual disability income policy, or
* any disability attachment to an individual life insurance policy.

Maximum Benefit Period	Group	Indiv 1	Indiv 2	Indiv 3
Ends at age:	65	65	65	70

Survivor Benefit		Indiv 1	Indiv 2	

If you die prior to your 65th birthday while receiving the Total Disability benefit, we will pay to your beneficiary, an amount equal to three times the Maximum Monthly Amount payable at the time you die. Your beneficiary will be your estate, or your designated beneficiary.

Transplant Surgery Benefit		Indiv 1	Indiv 2	

After six months from the Date of Issue, if you become Totally Disabled because you have surgery to transplant part of your body to someone else, we will consider you to be Totally Disabled due to Sickness.

Rehabilitation Program Benefit	Group	Indiv 1	Indiv 2	Indiv 3 Rider

This means a government sponsored or other professionally planned vocational program approved in writing by us in advance of your participation in the program. The Monthly Income Benefit for Total Disability will be paid under the Payment of Monthly Benefits provision, while you are Totally Disabled and participate in a Rehabilitation Program.

We will pay the cost of a service provided in connection with the Rehabilitation Program, as long as

- the cost of the service is not covered by any other program or plan,
- provision of the service has been approved in advance by us, and
- we have received evidence satisfactory to it of the cost of the service.

Payment will be made to the supplier of the service or to you if we receive satisfactory proof that the supplier has been paid.

Waiver of Premium Benefit	Group	Indiv 1	Indiv 2	Indiv 3

After you have been Disabled for 90 days, we will waive any premium that becomes due while you remain Disabled. Your Policy and its benefits will continue as if the premium had been paid.

We will also refund any premium that became due and was paid during those first 90 days of Disability.

When you are no longer eligible for Waiver of Premium, you can continue your Policy in force by paying the next premium that becomes due.

Group: Premiums are waived while receiving monthly benefit.

Part 3 Contract Provisions

Assignment		Indiv 1	Indiv 2	Indiv 3

We will not be bound by an assignment of your Policy or any claim unless we receive a written assignment at our Head Office before we pay the benefits claimed. We will not be responsible for the validity of any assignment.

Change in Premium				Indiv 3

We reserve the right to change the premium from time to time based on our actual or anticipated adverse experience and will not change the premium more than once in any 12--month period based on the actual or anticipated adverse experience of the Plan. **Any change in premium will be made to all policies within a particular Risk Class and will not affect only the policy of an individual insured.**

In addition, we reserve the right to change the premium, as a result of a **change in your occupation or province or territory of residence**, to the premium for the Risk Class of which you become a member.

Elimination Period or Waiting Period	Group	Indiv 1	Indiv 2	Indiv 3

The period beginning on the date of disability and ending on the Benefit Start date (*the time you wait until the benefits begin.* **The longer you can wait, the cheaper the policy.** Typically it is 60, 90, 180, or 365 days).

Group Policy: 66 working days.

Grace Period		Indiv 1	Indiv 2	Indiv 3

After the first premium has been paid, a grace period of 31 days is allowed for late payment of premium. Your Policy will remain in force during the grace period. If the premium is not paid when it is due or within the grace period, the Policy will lapse.

Elimination Period or Waiting Period	Group	Indiv 1	Indiv 2	Indiv 3

The period beginning on the date of disability and ending on the Benefit Start date (*the time you wait until the benefits begin.* **The longer you can wait, the cheaper the policy.** Typically it is 60, 90, 180, or 365 days).

Group Policy: 66 working days.

Incontestable		Indiv 1	Indiv 2	Indiv 3

After your Policy has been in force for two years, excluding any time you are disabled, we cannot contest it. This does not apply if a material fact has been fraudulently misrepresented or not disclosed to us.

No claim for loss incurred or Disability beginning after two years from the Date of Issue will be reduced or denied because a disease or physical condition existed before the Date of Issue unless it is excluded by name or specific description.

Misstatement of Age		Indiv 1	Indiv 2	Indiv 3

If your age has been misstated, the benefits under the policy will be those that the premium you paid would have purchased at your correct age.

Reinstatement		Indiv 1	Indiv 2	Indiv 3

If your Policy lapses because the premium is not paid when due or within the grace period, it will be reinstated if we or our agent accepts payment of the premium without requiring a reinstatement application.

- If we receive the premium due at our Head Office within 57 days from the date the premium was due, we will not require evidence of your insurability.
- If we receive the premium after 57 days, we will require a reinstatement application. We will issue you a conditional receipt for the premium. If we approve your application, the Policy will be reinstated as of the date of our approval.
- If we disapprove your application, we must do so in writing within 45 days of the date of the conditional receipt or the Policy will be reinstated on the 45th day.

The reinstated Policy will cover only loss due to

- injury sustained after the date of reinstatement, or
- sickness that begins more than 10 days after such date.

Except for this and any new provisions that are added to the reinstated Policy, your rights and our rights will be the same as before the Policy lapsed.

Part 4 Exclusions

Pre-Existing Condition			Indiv 2	

We will not pay benefits for a Pre-existing Condition if it was not disclosed on your application. Pre-existing Condition means a Sickness or physical condition for which prior to the Date of Issue

- symptoms existed that ordinarily would cause a person to seek diagnosis, care, or treatment, **or**
- medical advice or treatment was recommended by or received from a Physician. We will not pay benefits for any loss we have excluded by name or specific description.

Exclusions	Group	Indiv 1		Indiv 3

A benefit is not paid for a Total Disability which is due to or results from

- The hostile action of any armed forces, insurrection or participation in any riot or civil commotion,
- Intentionally self-inflicted injuries or attempted suicide (while sane or insane), and
- Commission or attempted commission of a criminal offence.

General Exceptions				Indiv 3

Benefits are not payable under this policy where Disability is contributed to or caused by

- injury sustained by the Insured while doing anything in the course of or while engaged in any occupation for remuneration or profit,
- transplant surgery of an organ or other part of the Insured's body to the body of another person,
- attempt at suicide, while the Insured is sane or insane,
- inhaling gas or fumes, whether voluntarily or otherwise,
- the use of any drug, poisonous substance, intoxicant, or narcotic, unless prescribed for the Insured by a Physician and taken by the Insured in accordance with directions given by the Physician,
- the Insured's professional participation in athletics,
- the Insured's participation in mountaineering, sky diving, parachuting, skin diving, scuba diving, motorized vehicle racing, or horse racing,
- the Insured's operating, riding in, or descending from any kind of aircraft, if the Insured is acting in any capacity other than as a fare-paying passenger on a regularly scheduled or chartered flight of a commercial airline, or other device used for the purpose of flight, or
- service in any Armed Forces at War.

Exception for Mental Disorders				Indiv 3

Benefits are not payable under this policy where Disability is contributed to or caused by any psychiatric disorder, stress, or burnout.

Exception for Chronic Fatigue Syndrome, Fibromyalgia, and Fibromyositis				Indiv 3

Benefits are not payable under this policy where Disability is contributed to or caused by any chronic fatigue syndrome, fibromyalgia, or fibromyositis.

Exception for Acquired Immune Deficiency Syndrome–Related Diseases				Indiv 3

Benefits are not payable under this policy where Disability is contributed to or caused by an opportunistic infection or other disease if the Insured either

- Had Acquired Immune Deficiency Syndrome (AIDS), or
- Tested positive for the Human Immunodeficiency Virus (HIV)

prior to the policy effective date.

Limitation for Degenerative Disk Disease				Indiv 3

Benefits will be payable for only a cumulative maximum of 15 days where Disability is contributed to or caused by degenerative disk disease. Once the cumulative maximum is reached, no further benefits will be paid.

Limitation for Strains, Sprains, and Contusions				Indiv 3

Benefits will be payable for a maximum of 15 days for each occurrence where Disability is contributed to or caused by a strain, sprain, or contusion until benefits have been paid for a cumulative maximum of 120 days for all such occurrences. Once the cumulative maximum is reached, no further benefits will be paid.

Limitation for Hernia				Indiv 3

Benefits will be payable for only a cumulative maximum of 60 days where Disability is contributed to or caused by hernia. Once the cumulative maximum is reached, no further benefits will be paid.

Cancellation				Indiv 3

We reserve the right to cancel this policy if

- the Insured becomes a member of an unacceptable Risk Class due to a change in the occupation or province or territory of residence of the Insured, or
- the Risk Class of which the Insured is a member becomes an unacceptable Risk Class, as determined by us, based on actual or anticipated adverse experience of the Plan for the occupation, province, or territory of residence of the Insured or plan type.

Part 5 Riders

Riders, optional endorsements that add benefits to the policy, are usually added at the time of the purchase of the disability policy although they can also be added afterwards but never while the insured is on disability. The first rider, Future Income Option Benefit Rider, allows the insured to buy additional coverage every two years with proof of increased income. It is usually sold to small business owners whose business is growing. It affects the amount of coverage one can collect while on disability. All of the others affect the insured when receiving disability benefits.

Future Income Option Benefit Rider *also called* Future Earnings Protector Option Rider		Indiv 1	Indiv 2	

Once every two years, on the even-numbered anniversary of the issue date of the policy, you may apply for an increase to the coverage. The amount of available increase is shown on the declarations page. If not used, a unit of available coverage can be carried forward to the next option date but not beyond that.

You do not have to provide proof of insurability but your application does have to be accompanied by proof of income.

The additional premium will be based on either

- the risk class at the time the policy was issued (note: this rate will be adjusted to reflect your present age), or
- your risk class on the option date of the increase.

Accidental Death and Dismemberment Rider		Indiv 1		Indiv 3

Basically this is a double indemnity clause whereby the insured will receive double monthly benefits if the Insured qualifies for the Presumptive Total Disability Benefit.

Cost of Living Indemnity — Total and Residual Disability Benefit Rider		Indiv 1	Indiv 2	

Beginning the day after the first anniversary of Disability, we will increase your benefits by the Consumer Price Index (only if it goes up). At the end of the period of disability, you may purchase this increased benefit without evidence of insurability if you

* are less than age 60,
* apply for the increase within 90 days of the end of the period of Disability, and
* are gainfully employed full-time.

Health Care Rider		Indiv 1		

This rider extends the definition of Sickness for Disability to include **Covered Infection**, meaning:

* Human Immunodeficiency Virus (HIV)
* Hepatitis B virus, or
* Hepatitis C virus.

Note: This rider is included even though these three were never excluded from the definition of Sickness.

Hospitalization Benefit Rider				Indiv 3

This rider provides coverage if you becomes hospitalized at any time for a period of 24 consecutive hours, due directly to Injury or Sickness except if injury is sustained while doing anything in the course of or while engaged in any occupation for remuneration or profit.

The benefit is payable for the first and each consecutive 24-hour period.

This benefit is not payable if the hospitalization is the result of a pre-existing condition, pregnancy, or child birth if it occurs within 12 consecutive months of the benefit effective date.

Own Occupation Rider		Indiv 1		

The Policy is amended by deleting the phrase " ... and is not working in any other Gainful Occupation...".

Presumptive Lifetime Benefit Rider			Indiv 2	

The benefit described above will pay for life provided the insured applies before age 65.

Reduced Elimination Period While Hospital Confined Benefit Rider			Indiv 2	

Under this rider, we will pay the Total Disability benefit for those days before the Commencement Date (the date the benefits start) that

* you are confined as a bed patient in a legally operated hospital, and
* total Disability benefits would be payable except for the Commencement Date.

Group Disability Plans

Disability insurance is often provided by employers as part of their group insurance plans. They usually offer both short- and long-term disability coverage.

Group Insurance Plans

Group insurance plans have the following characteristics in general:

* They cover many people under one contract which means they provide low cost protection because marketing and administrative expenses are reduced.
* Individual evidence of insurability is usually not required.
* Larger groups are experience-rated, meaning the rates change to reflect the number and size of claims.

Underwriting Principles

Underwriting principles for group plans of all types — disability, health, and life insurance — tend to have the same general requirements:

1. The insurance is incidental to the group, meaning the group was not formed in order to get the group insurance coverage. Some carriers will insure groups as small as two.
2. Young people enter the group as older people leave it, meaning the risk should remain about the same.
3. The insurance coverage is automatic — your disability coverage protects you for perhaps 100%, perhaps 80% of your salary.
4. A minimum percentage of employees must participate. Sometimes this is 100%.
5. A third party, the insurer, shares the cost.
6. The administration is simple and efficient with payroll deductions for any premiums paid by employees.

Eligibility Requirements

Plans tend to have the following eligibility requirements, which must be met before employees can participate in the plan:

1. Only full-time, direct employees can participate or employees working over 22 or 25 hours a week,
2. There is a probationary period or waiting period, usually three months, before a new employee can join the plan,
3. After the probationary period, the employee has to sign up during the **eligibility period**, usually 31 days, if the plan is not mandatory and the employee makes contributions. If the employee does not sign up during this time and wants to sign up later, they may be required to prove their insurability by taking a medical,
4. The employee has to be actively at work when the insurance becomes effective, and
5. Usually with small groups of 50 or so, all employees must participate. Larger companies can offer a choice and usually end up with 85–90% participation.

Short-term Group Disability Plans

Employees are far more likely to experience short-term disability than long-term disability since many injuries, like broken and sprained limbs, will not keep an employee off work for a long time. Short-term group disability plans
- pay benefits only for a short period, from 13 weeks to one or two years;
- have a short or no elimination period with provisions for 0 days if you are hospitalized (this appears in some individual policies as well) and 7 to 14 days for sickness or injury;
- may provide **non-occupational coverage,** meaning the accident or illness must happen off the job;
- provide own-occupation coverage, meaning you are not able to perform your own job;
- provide benefits that are a percentage of earnings; and
- have relatively few exclusions — most plans cover drug addiction, alcoholism, and mental and nervous disorders.

Short-term disability insurance is very expensive since most disabilities are short-term in nature. Many companies self-insure — workers receive 1.25 days per month (for example) which can accumulate up to a maximum of 85 days (again, for example). Since this is 85 working days, this gives about 4 months of short-term disability protection [(85 ÷ 5) × 7 days].

However there are benefits to employers to adding this benefit to their group insurance plans:

- The responsibility of assessing the validity of the claims is shifted away from the employer to the insurer.
- The cost of administering short-term claims is shifted to the insurer.

- The insurer may be able to reduce the number of claims and has experience helping employees return to work as soon as possible.
- Purchasing both short- and long-term disability from the same insurer can reduce the cost of the long-term disability because the insurer can help the employee treat the illness or injury before it becomes a long-term problem

Long-term Group Disability Plans

Coverage for long-term plans begins after short-term coverage ends or after a waiting period of three to six months. Long-term group plans

- offer a benefit period that may run to age 65 or longer;
- can provide coverage for both occupational and non-occupational disability;
- often use a dual definition of disability:
  - for the first two years, you are considered disabled if you cannot work at your **own** occupation,
  - after two years, you are disabled if you cannot work at **any** occupation;
- have monthly premiums and, if the employee contributes, premiums are deducted from his or her pay cheque;
- may have a provision for accrual of pension benefits, meaning pension benefits continue to accrue while the employee is on disability; and
- usually has a cost-of-living benefit, meaning it is indexed to inflation.

Some companies self-insure on their long-term disability. Eaton's of Canada, when it went bankrupt in 1999, left more than 200 employees who were on disability without coverage because they were self-insuring — there was no insurance company or trust fund to continue to pay the benefits. Some employees who had become disabled before the early 1990s continued to receive their disability through the company's pension plan. However, this was disallowed in the 1990s, leaving people who became disabled after that with no coverage. They could not receive the locked-in pension until age 55. In addition, they lost their drug plan. One 40-year-old employee with AIDS cannot get the pension and his drug bill is $14,000 a year. Another employee, a cancer patient, receives his drug therapy (chemotherapy) through a hospital and thus is covered by OHIP but has lost his disability income. Employees who are covered through an employer who self-insures may want to consider having individual coverage as well.

Cost

Group plans are as much as 75% cheaper than individual plans. The difference in cost has to do with both the quality of the coverage and with marketing costs and commissions. Policies differ widely regarding the ability to work at one's "own occupation" and "any occupation". When buying disability insurance, this can be extremely important. Little distinction is made between sickness and injury as a source of disability as compared to Workers' Compensation which covers only work-related disability. The taxation of disability benefits affects how much coverage you will need. This is covered in the next section.

Group Disability Insurance Premiums

The following rates for Table 7.14 are for the Institute of Chartered Accountants of Ontario and are taken from Kowk Ho & Chris Robinson, *Personal Financial Planning*, 4th edition, Captus Press, 2005. This group plan

- has the following cost per $100 of monthly income,
- provides maximum coverage of the lesser of
  - $8,000 per month, or
  - 50% of earned income, reduced by other disability insurance other than CPP and reduced by income continued by the employer or partnership,

- defines total disability as being unable to do the normal duties of the person's regular occupation,
- is indexed to inflation, up to 8% p.a.,
- provides no coverage for disabilities from self-inflicted injury, active participation in a criminal offense, insurrection, or war, and
- provides partial payments for partial disability.

Table 7.14 Institute of Chartered Accountants of Ontario

| | Monthly premium per Unit ($100 of monthly income) | | | |
| | Waiting Period in Days | | | |
Age	30	90	180	365
Male				
Under 40	$0.85	$0.65	$0.60	$0.50
40–49	$1.50	$1.25	$1.15	$1.00
50–64	$3.25	$2.65	$2.50	$2.00
65–69	$3.75	$3.00	$2.75	$2.50
Female				
Under 40	$1.00	$0.85	$0.75	$0.65
40–49	$1.65	$1.40	$1.25	$1.10
50–64	$2.90	$2.35	$2.25	$1.75
65–69	$3.25	$2.60	$2.50	$2.25

Individual versus Group Disability Insurance

Individual disability insurance plans tend to give better coverage to professionals than group plans do. Some high-income professionals, such doctors who work primarily in hospitals, have their own individual coverage in addition to the group coverage provided by their employer.

Taxation of Disability Income

In Canada, if a person pays for individual or group insurance him/herself or if the premiums are added to taxable income as a taxable benefit, the income is not taxable when received. As a result, the maximum gross income that can be insured is often 60 to 66% of before-tax income. If the employer pays the premiums and the premiums are not a taxable benefit, the income is taxable to the employee when the benefit is received. These plans tend to cover higher levels of income — 80 or 90% of before tax income.

Table 7.15 Taxation of Disability Benefits

	CPP/ QPP	EI	W Comp	Group Plans	Association and Individual Plans
Who pays premium — employer or employee	Both	Both	Employer	Either or both	Individual
Deductible by employer	yes	yes	yes	yes	n/a
Deductible by employee	no	no	n/a	no	no
Tax credit to individual	yes	yes	n/a	no*	no
Employer's share is taxable income (benefit) to the employee	no	no	no	depends**	n/a
Benefit is taxable	yes	yes	no	depends*	no

n/a = not applicable

* A disability tax credit can be claimed if there is no claim for expenses of a full-time attendant or care in a nursing home.

** If the **employee pays** the premium, it is not tax deductible nor is it eligible for a tax credit and the benefit is tax free. Often the employee has a choice about how the employer's contribution will be handled. If the employers' contribution is

- added to taxable income in the form of a **taxable benefit**, then the benefit is **received tax free**.
- **not** added to taxable income as a taxable benefit, then the **benefit is taxable**.

How Much Disability Coverage Should You Have?

As stated above, short-term disability premiums are very expensive. The general rule of thumb is that you should have enough savings to get you through at least three months, preferably six months. This is how much elimination period you can then take. As the elimination period increases, the premium drops considerably because your chances of being unable to work for a short time are much greater than the chances of your being unable to work for a long time.

Often, group plans will cover as much as 80% of your gross salary. In this case, the benefit is more than likely taxable. When you buy long-term disability because you are not covered through an employer, you usually cannot buy more than 60 or 66% of your gross income since the benefit will be received tax-free.

If you are not covered by a group plan, buy enough to cover all your basic expenses including saving for retirement since individual plans end at age 65 or 70. The maximum Canada Pension Plan disability benefit for 2009 is $13,272 a year, $1,106 a month. and it is taxable.

If you have investments that can cover you until you die, then you don't need any disability coverage. Most of us need enough disability insurance to pay all expenses. Buy as much as the insurance company will sell you. Insurers do not want to provide you with a disincentive to return to work so they will not allow you to cover 100% or even 80% of your income if the benefit would be tax-free.

Critical Illness Insurance

The difficulty with individual disability insurance for some people is that they have no income to insure and yet their disability would provide a real financial hardship to the family. Or a spouse may have to take time off work to care for a spouse who is sick or injured and on disability. This is the case if one parent is a stay-at-home parent. If this person became disabled, there are many functions that would still have to be performed in addition to added costs arising out of the disability.

Critical illness insurance pays a lump-sum, tax-free cash benefit if a person is diagnosed with a **covered illness** and survives for 30 days. Except for severe burns, the critical condition must result from sickness or disease such as those listed below. The purpose of the payment is to help cope with a critical illness or condition. The payment is between $10,000 to $2,000,000 and can be spent on anything — alternative or experimental medical care, pay outstanding debts, or pay for caregivers or child care.

Plans pay out only for the illnesses specified in the policy. Three conditions are generally covered in a basic policy — cancer, heart attacks, and strokes. Most policies also offer some or all of the following illnesses:

Alzheimer's disease	Heart valve replacement	Occupational HIV infection
Aortic surgery	Loss of limbs	Paralysis
Benign brain tumour	Loss of speech	Parkinson's disease
Blindness	Major organ transplant	Renal failure
Coma	Motor neuron disease	Severe burns
Deafness	Multiple sclerosis	

Some policies will:

- Return the premiums to the deceased's estate with perhaps interest compounded annually if the insured dies **claim-free,** that is, without having collected a critical illness benefit. It is payable on demand since the policy has expired with the deceased's death.
- Reimburse an additional lump sum benefit of up to $1,000 toward medical consulting services at a provider of the insured's choice within one year of receiving the benefit payment,

- People who have lots of money to spend on insurance premiums may want to have critical illness insurance in addition to disability but if the family budget is limited, critical illness insurance would be a second choice to disability insurance for people earning an income.

Cost

Like other forms of insurance, although not auto insurance, critical illness insurance is cheaper if you take it out a younger age and also for non-smokers.

Table 7.16 Cost of Critical Illness Insurance

Age	Monthly Cost for $25,000				Annual Cost for $200,000			
	Non-Smoker		Smoker		Non-Smoker		Smoker	
	Male	Female	Male	Female	Male	Female	Male	Female
18–29	8.75	9.25	9.00	9.50	840	888	864	912
30–34	9.25	10.25	10.50	11.75	888	984	1,008	1,128
35–39	10.00	12.25	14.25	15.75	960	1,176	1,368	1,512
40–44	17.25	15.75	21.00	22.00	1,656	1,512	2,016	2,112
45–49	21.00	20.75	32.50	32.25	2,016	1,992	3,120	3,096
50–54	29.75	26.25	53.25	52.00	2,856	2,520	5,112	4,992
55–59	43.00	34.00	91.25	76.25	4,128	3,264	8,760	7,320
60–64	58.75	44.75	140.25	105.00	5,640	4,296	13,464	10,080

Source: Alterna Credit Union, 2006.

Summary

There are many types of plans available to protect income during times when sickness and injury prevent people from working. Workers' Compensation provides mandatory coverage for sickness or injury that is work-related while Employment Insurance provides coverage for a maximum of 45 weeks for lay-offs in addition to some very limited non-economic leaves. Canada Pension Plan disability benefit is low while private disability insurance policies, either through group plans or individual policies, provide protection for non-work-related injuries as well as supplementing government plans for higher-income earners.

Sources

Association of Workers's Compensation Boards of Canada [www.awcbc.org]
- CPP/QPP Offset by WCBs for All Benefit Types — 2009
- Dependency Benefits — Summary — 2009
- Expense Rates Information — 2009
- Fatal Benefits Other than Pensions — 2009
- General Information about the 2009 Assessment Rate Tables
- Key Benefits Information — 2009
- Key Statistical Measures for 2007
- Survivor Benefits/Death Benefits
- Payment of Compensation Benefits Dependency Benefits
- Payment of Compensation Benefits — Types of Compensation
- Permanent Disability Awards and Escalation Benefits — Summary — 2009
- Weekly Benefits for Temporary Disability — Summary — 2009

Employment Insurance
* Canadian Labour Congress, *Falling Unemployment Insurance Protection for Canada's Unemployed, An Analysis of B/U rations (UI beneficiaries to unemployed) by age and gender from 1990 to 2001*, March 2003.
* Department of Finance, Canada, *Employment Insurance Premium Reduced to $1.95 for 2005*, 2004-074.
* Government of Canada, Prepared by the Receiver General for Canada, Public Accounts of Canada 2008, Volume 1, Summary Report and Financial Statements.
* Kerr, Kevin B., *Employment Insurance: Regular Beneficiary Trends*, Government of Canada, Depository Services Program, March 19, 1999.
* Kerr, Kevin B., *Employment Insurance Premiums: In Search of a Genuine Rate-Setting Process*, Library of Parliament, Parliamentary Information and Research Services, Social Affairs Division, February 6, 2009. [www.parl.gc.ca/information/library]
* Human Resources and Social Development Canada [www.hrsdc.gc.ca]
  * *Employment Insurance (EI) Program Characteristics for the period of June 07, 2009, to July 11, 2009.*
  * *Unemployment Rates for the Employment Insurance (EI) Economic Regions.*
* Statistics Canada [www.statcan.gc.ca]
  * *Employment Insurance Program (E.I.), beneficiaries receiving regular benefits without reported earnings by province and age group, monthly (persons)*, CANSIM Table 276-0002.
  * *Gross Domestic Product (GDP), expenditure-based, provincial economic accounts, annual (dollars x 1,000,000)* CANSIM Table 384-0002
  * Historical Statistical Supplement 2001/02 Catalogue No. 11-210-XIB
  * Labour Force Catalogue No. 71-001-X.
  * Lin, Zhengxi, *Employment Insurance in Canada: Policy Changes*, Statistics Canada, Perspectives, Summer 1998, Catalogue No. 75-001-XPE,
  * The Daily, Employment Insurance, April 2009, Monday, June 22, 2009.
* Alterna Credit Union, 2006.
* Ho & Robinson, *Personal Financial Planning*, 4th edition, Captus Press, 2005.

Application Case

Francesca is over her cold and once again has Joanne's espresso ready.

"I brought my disability insurance policy with me so we can have a look at it together when we've gone through the basics," says Joanne. "My income has increased a lot since I went out on my own five years ago. I've had offers from my insurer to increase my coverage but have never taken them up on it because money was tight. But now I am thinking their offers might not be available any more. I want to check it with you before I call them. Can we go through the basics again?"

"Sure," Francesca replies. "Let's start with an overview of all types of plans."

A. "Income protection plans provide income replacement for many people when they are not able to work and earn income due to illness or injury and unemployment. Coverage is available through three mandatory government plans as well as private plans" (Page 230).
   1. "**Government plans** fall under the heading of social insurance because they share some basic characteristics. Government plans cover you for the following:
      (a) Sickness or injury and coverage is provided by Workers' Compensation, Employment Insurance and the Canada Pension Plan
      (b) Unemployment, which is covered by Employment Insurance. Unfortunately, you are not covered by Employment Insurance since you are self-employed. There is talk of developing a plan for self-employed people since 15 to 16% of the labour force is self-employed but at this point, there is no government or private coverage available to support self-employed people when they become involuntarily unemployed."
   2. "**Private coverage** is available for ill health through both individual coverage that you buy for yourself and group plans that are available through employers or associations."

B. "Social insurance plans all share some basic characteristics:
   1. Compulsory.
   2. Contributions and benefits relate to income and have a ceiling.
   3. Benefits are determined by law.

4. Employees receive benefits because they qualify, not because they need them.

5. Contributions are made by employees, employers, or both.

6. Benefits are paid out of contributions."

C. "**Worker's Compensation** provides coverage for work-related injuries and illnesses. It usually provides between 80 and 90% of net earnings although there is a ceiling. This isn't really applicable to you — you have no regular employees on a payroll since you just hire freelancers as you need them. But for many people this is important coverage especially for small businesses since it is mandatory and many small businesses do not provide group plans for their employees."

1. "Workers' Comp has several **objectives** (Page 231):

(a) to provide substantial wage replacement when a worker is unable to work due to a work-related injury or illness, including rehabilitation to help get him or her back to work, a pension if they can never work again, and support for dependents if they are killed;

(b) to encourage safety on the job; and

(c) to reduce lawsuits."

2. "Workers Com is build around **four principles** (Page 231):

(a) Employers pay the premiums.

(b) In return, employees cannot sue.

(c) Fault is not a consideration when deciding who receives a benefit although it can affect future rates.

(d) There is a neutral government agency to administer it."

3. "Each province and territory has a Board or Commission to administer Workers Comp. As Table 7.1 shows, total premium income was almost $9 billion in 2007. As you can see from this table, 84% of the Canadian labour force is covered by Workers' Comp from a low of 70% in Manitoba to everyone in Northwest Territories."

4. "Employers are placed in rate groups called Divisions (Table 7.2), which are further sub-divided to determine the base rate for the premium."

5. "Premiums are charged on **Assessable Earnings,** which has a ceiling. As you can see in Table 7.3, rates vary a great deal with job categories that are more dangerous paying much higher rates. The rates are for each $100 of Assessable Earnings. Table 7.3 shows the highest and lowest rates for each jurisdiction and also the rate for the following:

• **Division "K"** Finance and Insurance Industries,

• **Major Group '70'** Deposit Accepting Intermediaries (there are four other major groups),

• **All sub-groups** since all the sub-groups have the same rate. The sub-groups in the Major Group 'Deposit Accepting Intermediaries' are Financial Institutions, Trust Companies, and Credit Unions.

Why does the rate for this Major Group vary so much between jurisdictions? I have no idea. The rates for each group are set by each jurisdiction and I suppose the rate reflects not only the experience of the group in each province and territory but also the overall experience for each Board."

D. "Most people know that Workers' Comp provides income for injured or sick workers but, in fact, there are several other benefits available also. Table 7.4 outlines the benefits as well as the maximum amount of earnings covered."

1. "**Lost earnings** is also called **economic loss** and is based on some percentage of net earnings. **Net earnings** is gross earnings minus income tax, CPP contributions and Employment Insurance (EI) premiums and there is a maximum gross and therefore net earnings that are covered."

2. "**Lost retirement income** in most jurisdictions means that some percentage of the lost earnings is also set aside to provide a retirement benefit if the injury or illness is permanent."

3. "**Non economic loss** to compensate for a physical, functional, or psychological impairment over and above lost earnings. The benefit is adjusted to provide a benefit based n the amount of the impairment. In Ontario, the benefit is also adjusted for age."
4. "**Health Care** cost include prescriptions and medical devices."
5. "**Miscellaneous costs** include a clothing allowance or a personal care allowance if it is appropriate."
6. "**Survivor benefits** are for dependants if a worker is killed on the job. Survivor benefits are usually adjusted for the number and ages of dependent children. There is usually a lump sum benefit as well as a monthly payment. Survivor benefits are outlined in Table 7.5."
7. "In addition, the Boards have programs to improve workplace safety."

E. "**Employment insurance** is also mandatory but not for you since you are self-employed."
1. "So-called "regular" benefits cover lay-offs during shortages of work (Page 244) but EI can also provide income for the following:
   (a) Sickness and maternity and parental leave (Page 248),
   (b) Up to sick weeks compassionate care leave to care for a dying family member (Page 248),
   (c) income for self-employed fishers, and
   (d) A new benefit — work sharing — to allow employees to temporarily reduce their workload and receive benefits for the days they don't work. This is intended to end on April 3, 2010, when it is hoped the current recession will be over.
2. Both employers and employees pay EI premiums, as shown in Table 7.6. Notice that the annual amount has been steadily decreasing but the **Employment Insurance Account** (which holds the net of the excess or deficit of premiums collected over benefits and expenses) had a surplus of $57 billion at March 31, 2008. The EI Account has been growing despite the decreasing premiums because GDP has been very strong until recently but also benefits have been dramatically reduced and it has become more difficult to collect the benefit."
3. "The **B/U ratio** compares the number of unemployed collecting 'regular' benefits to the number of unemployed people. Due to the changes already mentioned, the B/U ratio has been steadily decreasing, as shown in Table 7.7, although it jumped up in April, 2009 largely due to the work sharing program. Self-employed people never receive benefits but are included in the unemployed number. However, the percentage of people who are self-employed has remained relatively steady at 15 to 17%."
4. "In 2007, only 41% of unemployed people were collecting regular benefits (this number is different from Table 7.7 because the data for this calculation uses only four months of unemployment numbers). Notice in Table 7.8 that a quarter of the unemployed are not eligible for regular benefits because they haven't contributed, and they haven't contributed because they had not worked in the prior 12 months."
5. "One of the changes to EI over the years has been the introduction of varying levels of the number of hours one has to have worked in order to qualify for EI benefits. Now the hours of work depends on the unemployment rate in the region where the unemployed person lives. This has received much criticism recently as the recession caused high levels of unemployment in regions that normally have lower levels."
   (a) "The unemployment rates shown in Table 7.9 are issued monthly by Human Resources and Social Development Canada (HRSDC) and are the basis for determining how many hours are required to be eligible to collect and for how many weeks a beneficiary can collect. The shaded areas in Table 7.9 are areas that had an increase in the unemployment rate of over 50% from June 2008 to June 2009."
   (b) "Let's see how these rates are used. Table 7.10 shows the number of hours that a person must have worked in the **qualifying period** (the lesser of the past 52 weeks or since the beginning of the last claim) in order to qualify for EI regular benefits while Example 8 shows how the system currently works."

(c) "Now we'll look at the calculation of the benefit. It seems quite complicated but isn't really."

    i. "Start with total earnings for the past 26 weeks.

    ii. Find average earnings by dividing total earnings in the last 26 weeks by the *greater of*
- the number of weeks worked in the last 26 weeks, or
- the minimum divisor based on the unemployment rate in the region (Table 7.11).

    iii. Multiply the result by 55% to obtain the weekly benefit to a **maximum benefit of $447 a week** or $23,244 a year based on annual income of $42,300 ($447 × 52 weeks = $23,244 which is roughly equal to $42,300 × 55% = $23,265)."

(d) "EI is an important source of income for people who become unemployed. But don't kid yourself. It isn't a lot of money — the maximum is $447 a week or $23,244 a year and it is taxable. I cannot stress strongly enough the need to have three to six months of liquid savings that you can use in case your work dries up. This is especially true for you, Joanne, as a self-employed person but it is also true for employees as illustrated by Clarissa in Example 8."

F. "The **Canada Pension Plan** also provides income if someone who has paid into CPP experiences a disability that is both severe and prolonged. In addition there are benefits for dependent children and for survivors if the person dies" (Table 7.12).

    1. "CPP disability pays only until age 65. At that point, the retirement benefit begins in addition to Old Age Security" (Table 7.13).

    2. "Again, look at the amount of the benefit. Now that we are moving onto private disability plans, I cannot stress enough the need to have adequate coverage in place. Workers' Comp provides a large portion of prior earnings but EI, CPP, and OAS, while helpful, provide a really meager amount."

G. "**Private disability** is very complex because each insurer has its own definitions and rules that are different even between the various policies they offer. You have to read the policy very carefully to know exactly what coverage you have. Usually when you get the policy, you have 30 days to read it and get back to the insurer if the coverage is not what you expect. It is extremely important to check your policy to make sure it provides what you might need in the future. It is a shame to pay premiums for many years and then find out when you need it that the coverage isn't quite what you thought it would be. Let's look at a the coverage structure first although the exact layout will be different for different insurers and different policies. The example uses four disability policies — one group policy called 'Group' and three different individual policies called Indiv 1, 2, and 3. Pay close attention to the differences. Life insurance policies pay out when you die. Period. But disability policies pay out when you are disabled and that is often not so clear-cut."

    1. "**Definitions** is extremely important although some of them are pretty standard. This section explains who is meant by "we", "you", "injury", "sickness", what exactly "monthly earnings" refers to and things like that.

    (a) However, notice in particular the difference between **Regular or Own Occupation** and **Gainful or Any Occupation** (Page 251). This could matter if you are on disability for a long time. Policy Indiv 1 offers a rider (Page 258) that, for an extra premium, allows you to keep the definition of disability narrow — unable to perform the tasks of your *own* occupation, not just *any* occupation for which you might be qualified.

    (b) Notice also that Indiv 3 includes a definition of **risk class**. This was something of a surprise to me — I had not seen this before I saw this policy. The insurer includes this because this policy has a cancellation clause later (Page 257, end of Part 4) that gives them the right to cancel your policy if you change risk class."

2. "**Part 2 Benefits** outlines the various **definitions of disability** (Pages 252–255) which can matter if you are able to work part-time but not full-time.
   - (a) Note in particular that the group policy includes no definition of **partial disability**. I can conclude only that when someone covered by that policy has been on full disability and is ready to work only part-time, he or she cannot continue to receive anything from his or her group disability to cover the lost income. Scary.
   - (b) Notice too that two of the plans are **integrated** meaning disability income from other sources is deducted from the benefits. (Page 254)
   - (c) All plans have the standard **waiver of premium benefit** whereby you don't have to pay the policy premiums while you are collecting disability benefits" (Page 255).

3. "**Part 3 Contract Provisions** (Page 255) contains several standard provisions. Note in particular a few things:
   - (a) The **grace period** although it isn't really all that critical any more since the insurers usually collect the monthly premium through an automatic debit from your bank account. (Page 255).
   - (b) The **incontestability clause** which means they cannot deny a claim because of a pre-existing condition after the policy has been in effect for two years (Page 256).
   - (c) The **reinstatement clause** that allows you to start a cancelled policy again if you do so within a certain period of time" (Page 256).

4. "**Part 4** covers the **exclusions**. Notice that one of the policies, Indiv 3, has a lot of exclusions while the others have few. This is most definitely something you want to know before it is too late to look around for better coverage" (Page 256).

5. "**Part 5** covers the **Riders**. Very important. They add benefits to standard policies when you are buying the policy or possibly later but never while you are actually collecting benefits. Riders allow you to customize your policy to meet your own needs (Page 257). The part you were mentioning earlier is the Future Income Option Benefit Rider. This is the one that allows you to increase your coverage if your income goes up. Some of them seem pretty useless to me but others are extremely important. If everyone had all the money in the world to spend on premiums, you would have the maximum possible coverage in all areas of insurance. But most of us have to make choices so it is important to make a decision about additional coverage rather than just adding it on."

H. "**Group disability plans** are both cheap and easy. However, don't forget that in the policy provision section earlier, many things were not covered by that group plan. That's not to say that all group plans are the same but they generally are not as generous in their criteria for paying out benefits. That's one of the reasons they are cheaper" (Page 258):

1. "All **group plans** are based on certain **underwriting principles** (Page 259).
   - (a) The group must not have been formed in order to get the group policy.
   - (b) The average age will remain the same as younger people replace older people so the overall risk should remain about the same.
   - (c) The disability coverage is automatic and not negotiable by individuals
   - (d) A certain portion of employees must participate, often 100%.
   - (e) The insurer shares the cost.
   - (f) Administration is quite straightforward and any employee premiums are deducted from their paycheques."

2. "Group plans have **eligibility requirements**:
   - (a) Employee must work a minimum number of hours a week, perhaps 22 or 35.
   - (b) There is usually a three-month waiting period after starting work before they can join.
   - (c) If the plan is not mandatory, employees have a certain time period, perhaps 31 days, to join.
   - (d) The employee must be actively working when the insurance becomes effective.
   - (e) In smaller companies, 100% participation is usually required."

3. **"Short-term group disability plans** are very expensive and many companies self-insure by providing a certain number of sick days a year which, if not used, can accumulate until the long-term plan kicks in."

4. **"Long-term group disability plans** often define *disability* in two ways — *own* occupation for two years and then *any* occupation. In addition, if employees pay the premium or have it added to taxable income as a taxable benefit, the disability benefit is not taxable when it is received so coverage of 100% of salary is not possible or even necessary."

5. "Group disability plans can be as much as 75% cheaper than individual plans. Table 7.14 provides some sample rates for a long-term group plan. None of this affects you now but might in the future if your business continues to grow and you take on some employees."

6. "The taxation of disability benefits is important since often the benefit is not taxable. Let me summarize the taxation of all the plans we have talked about so far" (Table 7.15).

I. "Lastly, let's take a look at **critical illness insurance,** which is a good idea for people who do not have a lot of income but need to have their contribution to the family protected — namely non-working spouses. Yes, it can pay off your mortgage if you get cancer and then get better. But is this really necessary? This coverage has its uses but is generally not needed by people who have disability insurance" (Table 7.16).

Concept Questions

1. What is the purpose of income protection plans?

2. What are the characteristics of all social insurance programs?

Workers' Compensation

3. What are the objectives of Workers' Compensation?

4. What are the four underlying principles of Workers' Compensation?

5. For 2007, which jurisdiction has the
   (a) highest rate of worker injury?
   (b) lowest rate of worker injury?

6. What is the name of Assessment Division
   (a) "F"?
   (b) "B"? What is the rate for Major Group '03' in Manitoba?

7. Which jurisdiction has the
   (a) highest average assessment rate?
   (b) lowest average assessment rate?

8. Which jurisdictions cover 90% of net earnings?

9. Which jurisdiction has the:
   (a) Highest maximum annual payments?
   (b) Lowest maximum annual payments?

10. Which province does not make a provision for a life-time pension for a permanently disabled worker?

11. What is the purpose of the Non Economic Loss Benefit of Workers' Comp? Does the benefit reflect the degree of impairment?

12. What are the two types of survivor benefits that a spouse receives in most provinces and territories?

13. Which two jurisdictions do not provide an additional benefit if there are dependent children?

Employment Insurance

14. What are three objectives of employment insurance?

15. In which year did the Employment Insurance Account grow the most? What was GDP in that year?

16. For the year ended March 31, 2008, how much interest income did the EI Account earn by lending the surplus to the Receiver General?

17. What was each of the following in 1971 compared to now?
    (a) Required insurable hours
    (b) The maximum benefit period
    (c) The replacement rate
    (d) Disqualification period if you quit your job

18. The unemployment rate was 8.0% in April, 2009.
    (a) When was the last time it was higher than 8.0%?
    (b) What was the B/U ratio in that year?

19. Over 700,000 people were receiving "regular" benefits in April 2009. When was the last time more people than this were collecting regular benefits?
    (a) What was the B/U ratio in that year?
    (b) What was the B/U ratio in April 2009?
    (c) What was the B/U ratio in July 2008 before the Work Share program was implemented?

20. What percentage of unemployed people in 2007 were not eligible for benefits because they left their last job for an invalid reason, for example, they quit, were fired for misconduct, or refused to accept suitable employment?

21. In which seven economic regions did the unemployment rate go down from June 2008 to June 2009?

22. For each of the following economic regions, how many hours in June, 2009 must you have worked to collect regular EI benefits, and what is the maximum number of weeks you can collect?
    (a) Halifax
    (b) Winnipeg
    (c) Saskatoon
    (d) Ottawa
    (e) Calgary
    (f) Hamilton
    (g) Thunder Bay
    (h) PEI
    (i) Northern B.C.

23. How long does regular employment insurance last?

24. Janice quits her job because she finds that it requires too much heavy lifting. Is she eligible for regular benefits under employment insurance?

25. Peter, a famous newscaster, is forced to go on strike by his union, which is fighting for higher pay for its members. If he decides to not take part in the dispute, is he eligible for employment insurance benefits?

26. Define *care* and *support* in the context of employment insurance.

27. When is the Work Sharing program scheduled to end?

Canada Pension Plan

28. If someone who is contributing to the CPP dies, for what benefits are a surviving spouse and dependent children eligible? How much is the total annual payment if the spouse is age 42 and there is one chid age 10?

29. At what age does the CPP disability benefit end? What happens then?

Disability Insurance

30. Which definition of *occupation* will pay benefits longer: own occupation or any occupation?

31. What is included in monthly earnings in an individual disability insurance policy?

32. Jack is a welder and has Individual Policy 3.
    (a) If he moves to B.C. from New Brunswick and becomes a volunteer ski rescuer, is there any danger his policy might be cancelled? Why or why not?
    (b) Would it make a difference if he had Individual Policy 1 or 2?

33. Define *Total Disability* in a group disability insurance policy. Is it the same as the definition of total disability in an individual disability insurance policy?

34. For Individual Policy 1, what is the difference between partial disability and proportionate disability? Do all policies use the same definitions for these terms?

35. Define *residual disability* as it is found in the Individual Disability Insurance Policy 2.

36. What is a waiver of premium benefit in disability insurance? How does it work?

37. If Jack, the welder from question 32, does not find his policy cancelled when he becomes a volunteer ski rescuer, might he find that his premium has gone up? Explain.

38. What is the other name for elimination period in disability insurance? What does it mean?

39. List three exclusions often found in group disability insurance.

40. If a person attempts suicide and is left disabled as result, can he or she collect disability benefits under all three individual policies?

41. What is a future income option benefit rider? How often can you apply for an increase in coverage?

42. Explain how a cost of living benefit rider works.

43. Which of the following is not a characteristic of group disability insurance plans?
    (a) They cover many people under one contract.
    (b) They provide low-cost protection because marketing and administrative expenses are reduced.
    (c) Individual evidence of insurability is usually required.
    (d) Larger groups are experience-rated, meaning the rates change to reflect the number and size of claims.

44. What are five eligibly requirements that must be met before a group disability insurance policy can be issued?

45. What is meant by the term *non-occupational coverage* in the context of short-term group disability insurance?

46. What are the two definitions of *disability* often found in long-term disability insurance?

47. Individual disability insurance is cheaper then group disability insurance. Do you agree with this statement? Why or why not?

48. If a person pays his or her own disability insurance premiums, is he or she taxed on disability benefits when the payouts are made? How much of his or her own income can he or she generally insure if choosing to pay for it on his or her own?

49. Valerie has Multiple System Atrophy (MSA), a disease that is like have three kinds of Parkinson's Disease. She needs full-time care. If she had critical illness insurance, would it pay out if she was covered for only the illnesses listed?

Application Questions
Workers' Compensation

50. Susan's roofing company in Edmonton has 10 employees making an average of $30,000 a year each. How much will Susan pay for Workers' Comp? (Answer: $19,230)

51. James had net earnings of $70,874 ($105,000 gross pay) prior to January 23, 2009, the day he slipped down the staircase at the B.C. paint factory where he was a floor supervisor and broke his hip.
    (a) According to Workers' Compensation how much is he entitled to receive? (Answer: $46,971)
    (b) How much will be set aside and invested each year to provide him with an annuity when he reaches retirement age? (Answer: $2,348.55)

52. Mary, 37, suffers brain damage when a metal beam lands on her head while she is working on a construction site in Ontario. It is determined that the resulting percentage impairment is 60%. How much non economic loss benefit will she receive based on the 2009 rate? (Answer: $39,930.72)

53. Tim, 45, dies when his flat-bed truck swerves out of control on the Ambassador Bridge and plunges into the Detroit River while en route to deliver some automotive parts. How much will his spouse, also age 45, and children receive as their initial lump sum payment if Tim worked in Ontario? (Answer: $62,735.31)

54. If Tim from the previous question has average net earnings of $60,000 per year before he dies, how much monthly survivor benefit will Workers' Compensation pay his wife? Assume they have no children. (Answer: $2,208)

55. Caroline, a firefighter in Ontario, earns average net earnings of $65,000 per year with overtime. She has one child, Mindy, who is 14, and is married to Nick, who is a stay-at-home father. One night while out fighting a fire, Caroline loses her life. How much will Nick and Mindy receive from monthly survivor benefit? And for how long? (Anser: $3,753.60, $417.07)

Employment Insurance

56. Mark's Cook-Your-Books Limited has seven employees who make from $35,000 to $75,000 a year. How much will Mark pay in EI premiums for the employee who makes

(a) $35,000? (Answer: $847.70)

(b) $75,000? (Answer: $1,024.51)

57. Joanna lives in Economic Region 7, Fredericton-Moncton-Saint John. She recently got laid off from the warehouse where she worked.

    (a) What is the minimum insurable hours needed in the last 52 weeks or since the beginning of her last claim for her to qualify for unemployment insurance? (Answer: 665 hours)

    (b) What is the maximum number of weeks she can collect? (Answer: 43 weeks)

58. Nav earned $14,000 during the last 26 weeks of employment as a cook at a local restaurant before being laid off. Nav lives in Regina. How much is his weekly benefit? (Answer: $296.15)

59. Janet is on parental leave from work, collecting parental benefits of $125 a week. While on leave she is babysitting her neighbour's daughter for compensation of $75 a week.

    (a) Will this extra income effect her maternity leave benefit? By how much? (Answer: $25 a week reduction)

    (b) What is your answer using the amounts in the pilot project? (Answer: $0).

Private Disability Plans

60. Chris has an individual disability insurance policy that pays 60% of his earnings. He suffers a stroke and cannot work-full time for several months at his electrical engineering job for B.C. Hydro. His job paid him approximately $8,000 a month. He now only earns about $3,000 a month. How much, if any, disability insurance benefits is he eligible to collect if his policy is similar to

    (a) Individual Policy 3 and he has been on partial disability for 9 months? ($2,400)

    (b) Individual Policy 3 and he has been on partial disability for 15 months? ($1,920)

    (c) Individual Policy 2 and he has been on partial disability for 15 months? ($3,000)

61. Nathan just had laser eye surgery to correct his vision. He works as a police officer and is glad that he does not have to wear his glasses on the beat. One day, however, he wakes up and he cannot see. He gets his wife to take him to his opthamologist who confirms that he is part of the 1% of people who lose their sight due to complications from laser eye surgery. Can Nathan collect disability benefits from the individual disability insurance policy like Individual Policy 2 he purchased three months ago, even though laser eye surgery is considered an elective or cosmetic surgery?

62. Sonja, 28, is totally disabled after she suffers a stroke that leaves her with brain damage. She is a member of CAW, the powerful Canadian Automotive Workers union, which has ensured that Sonja is covered by a group disability insurance policy. She use to make approximately $80,000 a year. If her policy is the same as the group policy in the chapter, until what age can she collect disability benefits from the insurance policy?

63. Philip is 62 and has been collecting disability insurance for the past five years due to a total disability. He receives $2,500 a month, the maximum he is eligible to receive. One night while watching TV and eating nachos by himself, he chokes to death. His wife, who was out dining with her friend, comes home to find her dead husband on the floor. Can she collect any type of survival benefits under her husband's disability insurance policy if the policy is like Indiv 1? ($7,500)

64. The disability insurance agent that sold Shawn his policy incorrectly recorded Shawn's birthday and thus understated his age. Shawn's current policy premium is $250 a month for a policy that provides him with $4,000 a month of disability benefit. If his age had been recorded correctly his policy premium would have only purchased a policy of $3,700. If he becomes

disabled, how much will he collect each month because it was the agent's mistake? Why? ($3,700).

65. For each of the following independent situations, would disability insurance like Individual Policy 3 cover the resulting disability?
   (a) Jason is totally disabled after being hit by a car while working as crossing guard.
   (b) Paul suffers from skin cancer and can no longer work full-time as an interior decorator.
   (c) Mark has been left permanently disabled after an unsuccessful suicide attempt.
   (d) John is left permanently disabled after overdosing on ecstasy pills.

66. Martha has AIDS, leaving her too sick work. Can she claim disability benefits for lost wages if her policy is similar to Individual Policy 3 and she contracted AIDS after she took out the policy?

67. Much to the dismay of the owners of Try-N-Save, their employees have banded together and formed a union, which has successfully bargained for a group disability insurance policy. How much will the policy premium be for the following employees for a policy with a 30 day waiting period? *(Hint: notice that the premiums do not distinguish between smokers and non-smokers.)*
   (a) Stan, a non-smoking male aged 23. ($.85 per $100 of income)
   (b) Jas at 45 year old smoking female. ($1.65 per $ 100 of income)
   (c) Allan a non-smoking 53 year old male. ($3.25 per $100 of income)

68. Ted is covered for group insurance at work. He has a cafeteria plan, meaning he can choose between two options for his disability coverage. Ted's marginal tax rate is 40%.

   Plan A: The premium of $150 for 90% coverage, $6,000 a month, is paid by his employer.

   Plan B: The premium of $112 for 67% coverage, $4,467 a month, is paid by his employer and added to his taxable income as a taxable benefit.
   (a) If he collects the benefits, how much is his after-tax, monthly benefit for
      i. Plan A? (Answer: $ $3,600)
      ii. Plan B? (Answer: $4,467)
   (b) What is his after-tax, monthly cost for
      i. Plan A? (Answer: $0)
      ii. Plan B? (Answer: $44.80)
   (c) Which should he choose? Compare the extra coverage and the added cost of this extra coverage, bearing in mind that group coverage costs might be only 25% of the cost of individual coverage. (Answer: Plan B)

Critical Illness Insurance

69. Dianne is a stay-at-home mom with a heart condition. Her family fears that she will have a heart attack and be unable to look after the household, adding extra costs on top of having to hire people to do the tasks she now does. What insurance option would you recommend?

Life Insurance

275

Learning Objectives

After completing this chapter, students will be able to:

A. Understand various ways of evaluating the amount of insurance to buy.

B. Know the requirements and options in life insurance policies.

C. Evaluate the appropriateness of the different types of life insurance available.

Introduction

The purpose of insurance is to finance the risk of a financial loss. While there are many uses for life insurance, the primary purpose of it is to finance the risk of the premature and untimely death of a family member on whom others are financially dependent, the goal being to avoid financial deprivation for these dependants. The fundamental objective of life insurance is to provide enough money to finance future needs such as day-to-day living expenses and education costs for children, not to provide a windfall for the beneficiary or beneficiaries.

There are **three questions that need to be addressed before buying life insurance:**

1. **Do you need life insurance?** The insupportable risk is the loss of income. Thus, people need life insurance **only** if their dependants would suffer financially, that is, they would experience a material drop in their standard of living.

2. **How much life insurance is needed?** There are three ways of assessing this:
   (a) The **income approach,** which calculates the present value of the insured's future after-tax earnings. This is also called the **human life value approach**.
   (b) The **expense approach** looks at various family needs, taking into account special needs such as the future education of children, an outstanding mortgage, and retirement needs and adjusting this amount for present assets that can meet some of the financial needs. This is also called the **needs approach**.
   (c) The **capital retention approach** is much like the expense approach except that the insurance proceeds are invested and only the income is used to meet the required financial needs. The proceeds are then preserved to be distributed later to the heirs.

3. **What kind of insurance should the insured buy?** There are two basic categories of life insurance:
   (a) **Temporary life insurance** provides insurance coverage for a specific period of time. **Term insurance** is temporary insurance.
   (b) **Permanent life insurance** provides insurance for one's lifetime and the premium usually includes a savings portion. There are several types:
      i. Term-to-100 does not have a savings component. Sometimes, if the insured lives to age 100, the **face value** is paid out even if the insured is still alive.
      ii. Whole life policies have a *savings component* called a **cash surrender value**.
      iii. Universal life policies are similar to whole life policies but they have flexibility as their main feature — just about everything in the policy can be changed including the premium and the term. This is self-directed insurance where the policyholder selects the premium, the term, the investments, and several other items.

Let's look more closely at each of these questions.

Do You Need Life Insurance?

There are several reason to buy life insurance although not everyone needs it:

- Single people with no assets that will be taxed at death usually don't need any. The principle residence is exempt from capital gains tax, and financial assets such as a stock portfolio can be partially liquidated to pay final taxes.
- A spousal rollover permits registered assets such as Registered Retirement Savings Plans (RRSPs) and Registered Pension Plans (RPPs) to be rolled over to the surviving spouse with no tax consequences.

Reasons to Buy Life Insurance

However, there are many instances where life insurance can be an invaluable risk management or savings tool.

Provide for Financially Dependent Family Should You Die Prematurely

This will be illustrated with Joanne and Don, who both work and have young children. Should one of them die, the other would not be able to maintain his or her standard of living without the income of the deceased. They can manage this risk by calculating the appropriate amount of insurance coverage and buying life insurance.

Insurance to Pay the Taxes on Your Estate

In Canada, a deceased's estate can be rolled over — title changes hands without paying taxes — to the deceased's spouse. This is called a **spousal rollover** (specifically a Section 73 Rollover, referring to Section 73 of the *Income Tax Act*). However, taxes will become due on some assets when the second spouse dies. For instance, there may be a family cottage that the current owners would like to pass on to their heirs. Life insurance payable on the death of the second spouse can be used to pay the income taxes on the capital gain (which could be considerable given the recent increase in value of cottages). This topic is dealt with in more detail in the study of Estate Planning.

Finance a Buy-out by Business Partners Should One Partner Die Prematurely

Partners in a business often have a buy–sell agreement that permits the remaining partner(s) to buy the share(s) of a deceased partner(s). They may have an agreement as to the price or they might have established a formula for determining the value of the deceased's share. The survivor(s) could finance a buy-out with a sinking fund or by getting a bank loan but both of these options would tie up working capital, which most small businesses cannot readily afford. Instead, the partner(s) or the business can buy life insurance on each partner. The premiums can be paid by the following:

1. The partners in proportion to their ownership although this does not manage the varying cost of insuring each partner, which depends on his or her health and age.
2. The partnership or corporation with the beneficiaries of each policy being either
   (a) the other partner, who then has the funds for the purchase of the deceased's share.
   (b) the corporation, which can buy back the shares and distribute them or retire them.

A Tax-Advantaged Way of Saving for Retirement

A whole life policy can be set up to buy additional insurance benefits out of the dividends on participating policies, and the savings component of these policies can be accessed without terminating the policy.

The **Tax-Free Savings Account (TFSA)** allows a person 18 years of age and older to save $5,000 a year and the income is never taxed. Furthermore, one can borrow from a TFSA and repay the loan without using new contribution room. **Registered Retirement Savings Plans (RRSPs)** also grow tax-free, contributions are tax-deductible, and all withdrawals are taxed at a person's highest tax rate. Nonetheless, there could be a good reason to save using a life insurance policy, which also grows before tax. We will look at this more closely after examining the features of whole life insurance.

How Much Insurance Do You Need?

There are several ways of estimating the amount of life insurance a person should have. All of them make assumptions about the future but since there is no way to know the future, an educated guess is better than just pulling a number out of thin air. All of the following approaches base the future need in **real dollars** — dollars without inflation. As a result, we will be discounting future income at a **real interest rate** of 3%, which means inflation does not have to be added to their salaries to do this calculation. The real interest rate, which contains no inflation or adjustments for risk is between 2 and 4%.

1. Income or Human Life Value Approach

Since people's ability to earn income is their greatest asset, this is a simple, quick way to estimate the amount of insurance to buy and is a good starting point. The calculation is done by taking the present value of current after-tax income, discounted at some real interest rate. It does not take into account any special needs and is based on the assumption that present income levels will be adequate for future needs. The time the insurance is needed can be fairly short — until the children are through school; mid-term, until the surviving partner retires; or long-term, until the surviving partner dies.

EXAMPLE 1   Joanne, age 30, and Don, 31, have two children: twins, Virginia and Patrick, age 4. They want to have enough life insurance to see both their children through an undergraduate university education — about 18 years from now. Francesca, their CFP, suggests they round this up to 20 years to have a margin of safety. Joanne has life insurance at work that will pay her beneficiary two times her annual gross salary if she dies. Don's group insurance will pay three times his annual gross salary. Francesca prepares the following needs analyses for them.

Table 8.1   Income Approach

	Joanne	Don
Gross Salary	$68,000	$67,000
Take-home pay — beginning of year (BOY)	49,457	48,787
Years insurance is needed	20	20
PVA = 49,457$_{BOY}$ (PVIFA $_{3\%, 20 \text{ years}}$)	757,869	747,602
Insurance coverage at work	−136,000	−201,000
Insurance needed	**621,869**	**546,602**

If all they want to do is cover the future income of the other, should the other die, then they need to insure Joanne's life for $620,000 and Don's life for $550,000.

2. Expense or Needs Approach

This approach attempts to predict future expenses that could not be financed out of current levels of income and make an allowance for them. These needs might include the mortgage, **final expenses** such as funeral expenses, a liquidity fund to cover retirement and estate planning needs, their children's education, in addition to income replacement and support for their dependants. This approach involves looking at the following:

- Assets available to produce income minus what they owe if one spouse dies to arrive at the **available capital**.
- How much after-tax income the surviving spouse would have coming in each year and what the annual expenses would be to arrive at the **annual shortfall**.
- The present value of the annual shortfall at the real interest rate for the required number of years.
- The insurance needed by deducting the available capital from the present value of the shortfall.

EXAMPLE 2   Joanne and Don have assets as shown in the following table. Francesca does the following:

- She does not add the family home because if one dies, the other would undoubtedly prefer to remain in it. As a result, the capital invested in the family home is not available to generate income.
- She includes the mortgage on the house because they do *not* have mortgage life insurance (Chapter 4), which would pay off the mortgage in the event of either of them dying. Alternately, they could have **mortgage life insurance,** in which case the mortgage would not be included in this analysis as an additional cost.
- She includes the death benefit from the Canada Pension Plan although it is small and can easily be ignored.
- She includes Registered Retirement Savings Plans (RRSPs) but not the cash value of any Registered Pension Plan through their jobs since this money is not available to consume before retirement.

Table 8.2A Expense or Needs Approach — Available Capital

	If Joanne dies, Don has	If Don dies, Joanne has
Assets		
Bank accounts	$ 4,000	$ 4,000
Savings for emergencies	15,000	15,000
Group life insurance	136,000	201,000
Individual life insurance	0	0
CPP death benefit	2,500	2,500
RRSPs	48,000	53,000
Investments (stocks, bonds, mutual funds)	0	0
Other financial assets	0	0
	205,500	275,500
Liabilities		
Funeral expenses	15,000	15,000
Consumer debt	1,000	1,500
Mortgage, other non-life insured loans	127,000	127,000
Contingency fund	10,000	10,000
	153,000	153,500
Available Capital (= *Net Assets* = *Assets – Liabilities*)	**52,500**	**122,000**
Available Capital is available to:	**Don**	**Joanne**

Francesca now looks at their **required annual income**. Their combined after-tax income was $98,244 or about $98,000.

Income
- If one dies, the surviving spouse continues to earn his/her salary.
- Canada Pension Plan pays a survivor benefit and a Children's Benefit, and both are paid to the surviving parent. In addition, both are taxable. The amount depends on how much the deceased has contributed. We will use $5,500 for the Survivor Benefit and $4,600 for the Children's Benefit, taxable at a marginal tax rate of 40%.

Expenses
- There are cost savings if one dies because the deceased no longer needs clothes, food, a car, etc. However, there will also be more expenses because the deceased filled a role in the family and the household duties of the deceased will have to be provided by the surviving spouse and also by paying for them — child care costs, buying groceries, dropping off dry cleaning, housework, yard chores, etc. Let's add $10,000 a year to their expenses for added costs over and above the cost savings.
- Francesca has included the amount of the outstanding mortgage in the liabilities that would exist should one of them die, meaning they intend to buy enough life insurance to pay off the mortgage should one or the other die. With the mortgage paid off, the surviving spouse would have lower expenses of about $14,000 a year.

Retirement Planning
- Francesca knows that they are already using some of their take-home pay to save for retirement and their children's education so these will not be added to their future needs. If this is not the case, items like these would have to be added to their annual budget. Any education savings would not show up in the assets because this capital is not available for day-to-day spending. However, while the family would prefer to not use their RRSPs, they could if they had to.
- Both work at jobs that have pensions that are contributory plans where the employer and the employee each contribute 6% of the employee's gross salary to the company pension plan, meaning that both Joanne and Don are now saving 12% of their gross pay each year toward retirement — 6% each out of their income and 6% contributed by their respective employers. It is reasonable to assume that the insured spouse would want this saving to be replaced should one or the other die before retirement. By adding the full amount of this savings to their annual expenses, we are adding a cushion to the calculations since, at this point in their lives, they might want to assume that 10 to 20% less in the retirement fund would be enough. Each year they are saving as follows:
  - Joanne $8,160 (68,000 × 12%)
  - Don $8,040 (67,000 × 12%)

Table 8.2B Expense or Needs Approach — Annual Shortfall and Insurance Required

	If Joanne dies, Don has	If Don dies, Joanne has
Income		
Take-home pay	$ 48,787	$ 49,457
CPP Survivor Benefit	5,500	5,500
CPP Children's Benefit	4,600	4,600
Taxes on CPP @ 40% marginal rate	–4,040	–4,040
Other income	0	0
	54,847	55,517
Expenses		
Annual expenses	98,000	98,000
Additional expenses	10,000	10,000
Mortgage payments	–14,000	–14,000
Additional retirement savings	8,160	8,040
	102,160	102,040
Annual Shortfall BOY	**47,313**	**46,523**
Years insurance is needed	20	20
PVA	725,015	712,909
less Available capital (above)	–52,500	–122,000
Insurance needed	**672,515**	**590,909**
Insurance needed on:	**Joanne**	**Don**

If they want to make a provision for future expenses should either of them die, then they need to insure Joanne's life for $670,000 and Don's life for $600,000. If both of them die but the children survive and are still **minors** (under the age of 18 or 19 depending on the jurisdiction), the insurance proceeds would be put in a trust and their wills would stipulate who would be the trustee of the trust and who would be the guardians for their children.

Francesca has not made any specific provision for the children's future education costs because she has replaced the deceased spouse's income, knowing that the children's future education is being funded out of their current income.

3. Capital Retention Approach

This approach assumes that the survivor wishes to preserve the capital and live off the after-tax income generate by investing the insurance proceeds. It involves looking at the annual shortfall from the needs approach and dividing it by some expected real rate of return. (Alternatively, you could base it on the income approach and use their after-tax income instead of the annual shortfall.) Then deduct the amount of available capital to arrive at the amount of insurance needed to provide for the family without using up the capital.

EXAMPLE 3   Francesca takes their annual shortfall and divides it by the expected real rate of return of 3% to find out how much insurance they would need to have to cover the shortfall without using up the capital. They are setting up a **perpetuity** — capital that will produce income forever.

Table 8.3 Capital Retention Approach

	If Joanne dies, Don has	If Don dies, Joanne has
Shortfall BOY	$ 47,313	$ 46,523
k	3%	3%
PVA	1,577,100	1,550,767
less Available capital	–52,500	–122,000
Insurance needed	1,524,600	1,428,767

If they want have enough capital that the survivor could live off the income, preserving the capital, the **capitalized value** of the annual shortfall indicates that Joanne needs to have close to $900,000 of insurance while Don needs to be covered for about $800,000.

Summary of the Three Approaches

Francesca prepare a summary of the results of the three methods.

Insurance needed using:	on Joanne	on Don
1. Income or Human Life Value Approach	$ 621,869	$ 546,602
2. Expense or Needs Approach	672,515	590,909
3. Capital Retention Approach	1,524,600	1,428,767

The first method is quick but does not take into account any extra expenses that might be incurred. In this example, it would leave them somewhat under-insured. The third method would be favoured by people selling insurance but is it really necessary to buy insurance to provide an inheritance for one's children? It seems like overkill unless one of the children will need to be supported for his or her entire life. In this case, a perpetuity approach is appropriate. The second method is the most sound as it both replaces current income and also adjusts for assets that can produce income as well as for future possible expenses.

This analysis would be repeated every five years or so and also if there were a significant change in fortunes, such as winning the lottery or inheriting a small fortune (everyone is entitled to dream) or, more likely, a divorce or semi-permanent job loss or a permanent disability or a desire to change careers, all of which can lead to a change in insurance needs.

Settlement Options — Collecting the Insurance

If Joanne dies, Don can elect to take the face value as a lump sum or as an annuity over a few years. If Joanne bought $600,000 of insurance and died two years later, there are three ways Don can take the proceeds:

Lump-Sum Payment

Don would receive $600,000 and it is not taxable. He would invest the money to earn annual income and the annual income will be taxable.

Interest Option

This option leaves the proceeds with the insurer and interest is paid periodically to the beneficiary as taxable income. This option leaves the capital intact since only the income produced by the proceeds is consumed (the Capital Approach).

Annuity

If Don takes an annuity, only the interest portion is taxable.

EXAMPLE 4   Don takes an annuity over 15 years. He also elects to take the payments annually at the beginning of the year (BOY) (although, in reality, he would undoubtedly take the payments monthly). The insurer pays him a 7%

nominal rate of return. Francesca explains that she will use a nominal return in this illustration since taxes are applied to actual dollars, not their earning power (which is reflected in real dollars).

The following table shows the amortization of the annuity. The interest portion is taxable each year as it is earned (and, in this example, as it is received). In the first year, the payment is taken out of the $600,000 at the beginning of the year and interest is earned on the balance for the rest of the year. Don will receive $55,052.74 a year calculated as: $600,000 = PMT_{BOY} $(PVIFA_{15,\ 5\%})$.

Table 8.4 After-tax Income from an Annuity

Year	Balance BOY	Payment BOY			Balance EOY	Tax @ 40%	Payment After Tax
		Total	Interest @ 5%	Principle			
1	$600,000.00	$55,052.74	$ 0.00	$55,052.74	$544,947.26	$ 0	$55,053
2	544,947.26	55,052.74	27,247.36	27,805.37	517,141.89	10,899	44,154
3	517,141.89	55,052.74	25,857.09	29,195.64	487,946.25	10,343	44,710
4	487,946.25	55,052.74	24,397.31	30,655.42	457,290.83	9,759	45,294
5	457,290.83	55,052.74	22,864.54	32,188.19	425,102.63	9,146	45,907
6	425,102.63	55,052.74	21,255.13	33,797.60	391,305.03	8,502	46,551
7	391,305.03	55,052.74	19,565.25	35,487.48	355,817.54	7,826	47,227
8	355,817.54	55,052.74	17,790.88	37,261.86	318,555.69	7,116	47,936
9	318,555.69	55,052.74	15,927.78	39,124.95	279,430.73	6,371	48,682
10	279,430.73	55,052.74	13,971.54	41,081.20	238,349.53	5,589	49,464
11	238,349.53	55,052.74	11,917.48	43,135.26	195,214.28	4,767	50,286
12	195,214.28	55,052.74	9,760.71	45,292.02	149,922.25	3,904	51,148
13	149,922.25	55,052.74	7,496.11	47,556.62	102,365.63	2,998	52,054
14	102,365.63	55,052.74	5,118.28	49,934.45	52,431.18	2,047	53,005
15	52,431.18	55,052.74	2,621.56	52,431.18	0.00	1,049	54,004
		825,791.04	225,791.04	600,000.00			

This table shows the amortization of a **regular annuity** — the interest portion is taxable each year. This is a **non-registered annuity** since it was not bought with registered savings — a pension plan, a locked-in Registered Retirement Savings Plan (RRSP), a Registered Retirement Income Fund (RRIF), or a Locked-In Retirement Account (LIRA). As a result, Don could elect to treat the annuity as a **prescribed annuity,** meaning the total tax is amortized evenly over a maximum of 15 years — the tax is the same every year which reduces his overall tax bill. So Don would have $49,032 [$56,053 — tax of $6,021 (226,791 ÷ 15 years = 15,053 taxable interest a year × 40% tax rate)] each year.

To qualify as a prescribed annuity the following must occur:

- The payment must be the same (level, not indexed) every year but may be reduced on the first death under a **joint and last survivor annuity**.
- The joint annuitant can be only the primary annuitant's spouse, brother or sister for a Joint and Last Survivor Annuity.
- The payee (**annuitant**) must be the owner and an individual (and may be a spouse, trust or a testamentary trust) but not a corporation or a partnership.
- Cannot be **commuted** or **surrendered** (cashed-in for a lump sum).
- The annuity must be making payments since prescribed status cannot apply during a deferred period.
- The **guaranteed** or **term-certain** period cannot extend beyond the owner's 91st birthday (or joint annuitant's 91st birthday, if later).

Annuities have two fundamental determinants:

1. The time when payment begins:
   - **Immediate annuities** begin paying right away.
   - **Deferred annuity payments** do not begin until some time in the future.

2. The nature of insurer's obligation:
   - **Life annuities** provide income for life and stop when the annuitant dies.
   - **Life annuities with guaranteed number of payments** pay for a fixed period of time. They also pay for life but will continue the payouts to a beneficiary for the guaranteed number of years if the annuitant dies before the guaranteed is reached.
   - **Joint and last survivor annuities** pay until the last annuitant dies.
   - **Indexed annuity** is an annuity that increases by some predetermined percentage or by the Consumer Price Index (CPI) each year.
   - **Instalment refund annuities** pay for life to the annuitant or a beneficiary until the payments equal the purchase price.
   - **Cash refund annuities** pay the balance to the beneficiary in a lump sum when the annuitant dies.
   - **Variable annuities** pay an amount that varies each month according to the return on investment for the prior year. There are many variations on these types of annuities.

Segregated Funds

A segregated fund is an **individual variable insurance contract**. It is a pool of money held in trust by an insurance company, and the policyholder is the annuitant. As a result, while it is an annuity, it is an annuity that is payable only after the death of the policyholder or at the maturity of the segregated fund policy. The **maturity date** of a segregated fund is some predetermined number of years, such as 10 years, when the fund guarantees a certain value such as 75% and is set up at the inception of the policy. However, if all or part of the policy is terminated early, the maturity benefits are not guaranteed. Since universal life insurance policies are the only form of insurance policies that can invest in segregated funds (although segregated funds can also be purchased without using a universal life policy), they will be discussed after universal life insurance policies.

Life Insurance Policies — Common Elements

All life insurance policies share some qualities:

- The **life insured** is the person whose life is insured.
- The age of the insured is the age of the life insured at the beginning of the policy year based on the nearest or last birthday. The cost of the insurance at the inception of the policy and at any renewals depends on the insured's age.
- A **dependant of the principal life insured** is the spouse or child of the insured.
- A **joint life insurance policy** covers two or more lives. It pays out on the death of the first to die, at which point the policy terminates.
- A **last-to-die policy** covers two or more lives and pays on the death of the last to die.
- A **second-to-die policy** covers two lives and pays on the death of the second to die.
- A **premium tax** is the provincial tax on insurance policies. It is generally about 2%.
- Life insurance policies are **creditor-proof**, meaning creditors do not have access to the insurance proceeds when the insured dies and the insurer pays out the death benefit. Creditors have access to the proceeds only if
  - the proceeds are paid to the estate;
  - a beneficiary is not the spouse, child, grandchild, or parent; or
  - the policy is used as collateral on a loan, that is, the policy has been pledged as security for repayment of a loan, in which case it has been assigned to a third party.
- The **grace period** is the time after a premium is due and is unpaid but the policy and all riders remain in force, that is, the policy is not cancelled for late payment during the grace period, which is usually 31 days. If the premium is paid during the grace period, the payment is considered to have been paid on time. If the insured dies during the grace period with the premium not paid, the outstanding premium is deducted from the face value.

- **Misstatement of age** has the same effect as for disability — the face value will be adjusted to reflect the correct age.
- A **life insurance trust** is a testamentary trust set up with insurance proceeds.

Riders or Optional Coverage

Typical riders that can be bought for all types of life insurance, usually when the policy is taken out, include the following:

- An **accelerated death benefit** rider or **living benefits** rider that allows insureds who are terminally ill or who suffer from certain catastrophic diseases to collect all or part of their life insurance benefits before they die. The benefits might be to pay for the medical care they required or living expenses if there is no disability insurance or not enough to cover additional expenses such as private nursing care.
- **Child life insurance** is a rider that provides insurance on the life of a child — a child of 15 days is automatically insured. **Juvenile insurance** is insurance on children.
- **Guaranteed insurable** means the insured can increase coverage without proof of insurability. The additional insurance is available at each option date as outlined in the policy. It can be useful when major life events take place such as marriage and the birth or legal adoption of a child.
- A **waiver of premium on disability rider** waives the premium while the insured is disabled.

Beneficiaries

A **beneficiary** is the person or persons, corporation, trust, or charity who receives the **death benefit**, the proceeds of a life insurance contract. A **named beneficiary** is a person(s), company, charity, or the estate.

Beneficiary designation means the beneficiary is designated or named in the insurance contract. If there is no beneficiary named, the proceeds are paid to the insured's estate. With a designated beneficiary that is *not* the estate, there is no probate fee and no probate process — the proceeds are paid directly to the beneficiary without "going through the estate". As a result, the benefit is paid out quickly and without paying probate fees.

A beneficiary designation cannot be contested.

There are several categories of beneficiaries:

- A **primary beneficiary** is the beneficiary who is entitled to receive the proceeds first when the insured dies while a **contingent beneficiary** receives the proceeds only if the primary beneficiary dies either before the insured or before the term of a guaranteed term annuity has been paid out.
- A **revocable beneficiary** can be changed after being named without the beneficiary's consent, which means a revocable beneficiary has no enforceable rights even if he or she pays the premium. An **irrevocable beneficiary** cannot be changed once named except with the permission of the beneficiary, meaning the insured needs the consent of the beneficiary in order to make changes to the policy, including surrendering the policy for cash (cashing in the policy), changing the beneficiary, decreasing the coverage, or assigning the policy as collateral for a bank loan.
- A **specific beneficiary** is named, for example, "my children, Mildred and Hillis" while a **class of beneficiaries** is not named, for example, "my children". This can be important if the executor has to decide whether or not "my children" includes step-children, adopted children, and children born out of wedlock.

Guaranteed-Issue Policies

Guaranteed-issue policies are bought through the mail or from a television ad. They will usually advertise

- no health questions and no medical examination,

- available even if other companies declined you,
- can't be turned down, meaning all occupations and health histories are acceptable,
- fixed premium,
- guaranteed benefit never decreases with age, and
- ages 40–70 or 80.

These policies are usually very expensive since the applicant cannot get insurance anywhere else. Many plans do not actually guarantee approval since there are usually basic health questions to help the insurance company eliminate really high-risk applicants. The coverage is usually limited to between $5,000 and $50,000 of coverage perhaps with an **accidental death and dismemberment** rider or **double indemnity** rider that pays double the face value if the insured dies from an accident instead of from an illness. This rider is contrary to the analysis of the amount of life insurance required since the amount of insurance required does not double if the insured dies from an accident.

Some guaranteed-issue policies pay the full amount of the death benefit only if the insured dies in an accident. Death benefits are often **graded,** meaning if the insured person dies within a specified amount of time, usually two years, the beneficiaries receive only a portion of the death benefits.

Temporary Insurance — Term Insurance

Temporary insurance provides insurance coverage for a specified time period or term, and the only type of temporary insurance is term insurance. It is pure insurance with no savings component. The insurer promises to pay a specific amount if the insured dies within a specified period (the term of the policy). At the end of the term, if the insured is still alive, the policy terminates and protection stops. The cost of the premium for term insurance includes only the following:

- The **pure premium**, the cost to insure the person. This **pure cost of insurance** or **mortality cost** is the probability of dying times the face value of the policy.
- Expenses such as marketing, selling, and administration.
- Profit.

We will look at the pure premium for a term policy in detail in Chapter 9. There are a few differences among term policies:

- The term can be a 1, 5, 10, 15, or 20 years.
- The premium is usually level during the term. A **level premium** remains the same over the life of the policy but increases if the policy is renewed since the insured is older. However, a term policy could also have **decreasing premiums,** whereby the coverage decreases as the expiry approaches. This is useful for mortgages where the insurance covers a decreasing liability.
- The term of a term policy can vary:
  - **Level term** means the coverage is the same throughout the life of the policy.
  - **Decreasing term** is a policy in which the face value (death benefit) decreases over time but the premiums are level throughout the term.
  - **Term to age 65** has level premiums and is usually convertible to a whole life before it expires.
- **Extended term** or **paid-up term** is a term policy bought by using the cash surrender value (CSV) of a whole life policy as a lump sum premium payment on a term insurance policy.

Term policies can be tailored to the individual's needs including providing coverage to age 65 or 70 although it becomes expensive in later years. Term policies are useful if

- funds are limited, and/or
- the need for protection is temporary.

Riders on Term Policies

Riders enhance a basic term policy and, of course, increase the premium.

- Most term policies are as follows:
  - **Guaranteed convertible**, meaning it has a **conversion clause** giving the policyowner the option to convert it to a cash value policy such as whole life without evidence of insurability. At conversion, the premium is based on either the
    - **attained-age method**, the age at conversion, or
    - **original-age method**, the age when the policy is taken out.
- **Guaranteed renewable**, giving the insured the right to renew without a medical, usually at a higher premium based on the attained age — the age when the policy is renewed. Guaranteed renewable means the insurer must renew but the premium for each class may not be guaranteed. This ends at some specific age.
- **Guaranteed continuable,** meaning the insurer must renew at the same premium.
- A **cost of living rider** allows the policyowner to buy additional term insurance equal to the percentage increase in the CPI with no evidence of insurability.
- A **family coverage rider** adds a dependent to a term policy of the life insured. It is not available for group plans.
- A **disability rider** pays the premiums of a term or whole life insurance policy in the event that the insured becomes totally and permanently disabled.

Group Term Life Insurance

Group life insurance is always yearly-renewable term insurance. It provides low-cost coverage through an employer or association and is often convertible to an individual policy within 31 days after leaving the group. The major advantage is its low cost in providing coverage for everyone in the group. The premiums are usually lower due to lower marketing costs but they may not be cheaper than a private, individual term policy since the coverage pools all risks. The major disadvantage is that it is prohibitively expensive for older workers to convert to an individual plan.

Permanent Insurance

A permanent insurance policy provides lifetime coverage for the policyholder and, except for Term-to-100, is life insurance with a savings or investment component. Once in force, a permanent life insurance policy can be terminated by the insurer only if the premiums are not paid.

With all life insurance policies, in order for an insurer to offer this type of protection — to meet its contractual obligations to the insured to pay the death benefit — the insurer must set aside funds in a **policy reserve** to pay out the future **liability**, which is comprised of both the death benefit and the savings component.

The fundamental principle behind a permanent life insurance policy is that the insured receives "lifetime" protection. In term insurance, protection is in effect for only a fixed period of time — a predetermined number of years. Once the term expires the insurer is released from its contractual obligation. However, in permanent insurance, the coverage is in effect for the life of the insured and therefore the premiums collected must be set aside (and invested) by the insurer to pay out its future claims for a much longer period of time. In permanent insurance, the insurer is released from its contractual obligations only when the insured dies or cancels the policy. As a result, the premiums for a permanent insurance policy are greater than the premiums for a term policy.

In addition, the pure cost of insurance increases exponentially with age, as shown in the mortality tables in Chapter 9. In the early years of a whole life policy, excess premiums are building a pool of money called a **reserve** that will help finance the future pure cost of insurance when this cost becomes larger than the premium.

For these two reasons — the length of the contract and the increasing cost of providing insurance coverage as a person grows older — the cost of the pure insurance coverage for a permanent insurance policy for a younger person is much greater than the cost of term insurance.

The premium for permanent insurance is made even higher (other than for Term-to-100) because an excess amount or overpayment is added to the premium, which is invested to create a **cash surrender value (CSV)**, also called a **cash value**, which grows over time. A policyholder can borrow against the CSV and pay interest on the policy loan. Furthermore, if the policyholder terminates a permanent life insurance policy early — surrenders the policy before death — the insurer is then released from its contractual obligation under the insurance contract. The insurance company will then return the cash surrender value to the policyholder and will retain the balance of the reserve fund, which has been accumulating, to pay the future liability.

There are three types of permanent insurance policies:

- Term-to-100
- Whole Life
- Universal Life

Term-to-100

Term-to-100 is included in this section because it provides coverage for life but it is term insurance — it has no savings component, no CSV and, therefore, no loan value, and it does not pay dividends, that is, it is not participating. Like other insurance policies, it can be a joint-life or last-to-die policy. Sometimes the policy pays out the face value at age 100 even if insured is still alive (see "Endowment Life"). Term-to-100 insurance is usually purchased by people in mid-life who decide they need permanent insurance and for whom whole life would be very expensive.

Whole Life Insurance

Whole life insurance provides lifetime protection and generally the premiums are level — they remain the same throughout the life of the policy and the policyholder. As a result, it is *much* more expensive than term insurance in the early years but becomes cheaper than term much later in life. The savings component, the cash surrender value (CSV) or cash value, can be used to save for retirement on a tax-deferred basis since the accumulating CSV is not taxed until it is withdrawn when the policy is terminated (surrendered).

There are two basic types of whole life policies:

- **Ordinary life** or **straight life** has continuous, level premium and provides protection for life.
- **Limited payment life** is a whole life policy where the premiums are limited to a specified period of time — 10, 20, or 30 years or even one premium — but the protection continues for life.

Features of Whole Life Policies

The savings component of a whole life policy means that whole life policies have attributes that term policies cannot have. The savings component as well as the liability for future claims are invested in a **policy reserve,** which earns investment income.

Participating and Non-participating

There are two forms of permanent life insurance: participating life insurance and non-participating life insurance.

In a **non-participating life insurance policy**, the insurer assumes all the risks associated with its reserves. If the insurer underestimates its future claims, it is responsible for making up the difference in funding for those future liabilities. However, if the insurer overestimates its future claims, the insurer generates extra profits from the fund, the policy reserve, that is set aside to pay the future liabilities. Insurance companies seldom underestimate both the future liabilities and the return it can generate on the reserves although it does happen. A non-participating policy can have either

- a cash surrender value in which case the CSV is a return of premiums, or
- no CSV in which case it is just like a term-to-100 policy.

In a **participating life insurance policy**, the insurer allows the insured to "participate" in its reserve profits. By law, actuaries are required to make conservative estimates on that portion of the policy reserve that generates the guaranteed cash surrender value. Any excess income earned by the insurer is then shared with the policyholder in the form of a non-taxable **dividend**. As a result, if the reserve fund is profitable, the insurer will pay all the policyholders an annual dividend. However, the dividend is not guaranteed and if returns are less profitable, the dividend can be less than in prior years or even zero.

Most whole life policies are participating.

Paid-up Policies

A **paid-up policy** is a policy that has not matured but no further premiums are required. Once the policy is paid up, the reserve continues to earn income annually, so the cash surrender value keeps growing and the death benefit remains in place.

A **paid-up-at-age policy** is life insurance coverage that is in force during the insured's entire lifetime, but premium payments cease at a specific age, when the coverage is fully paid up. The policy is set up to be paid up at the inception of the policy.

Limited payment life insurance is a life insurance policy that covers the insured's entire life, with premium payments required only for a specified period of years. A "20 Pay" policy, for instance, is one that is set up to receive premiums for 20 years, at which time the premiums cease but the policy remains in effect.

Reduced paid-up policy is a policy where the CSV has been used to buy a paid-up policy and the amount of the paid-up insurance is less than the original death benefit.

A Note on Vanishing Premiums

Many vanishing premiums policies were set up in the early 1980s when interest rates were very high. Policy illustrations showed the premiums ending after the **premium offset date**, after perhaps 10 or 12 years when investment income and/or the dividend would be high enough that the insured no longer had to pay premiums. When interest rates fell, the reserves were not able to continue to fund the premiums and policyholders had to continue or resume paying premiums. Since the investment returns were not guaranteed, policies set up to have vanishing premiums could not produce them when interest rates declined. There were several class action law suits and the insurance companies settled. The different between a vanishing premium policy and a paid-up policy is

- in a vanishing premium policy, the end of the premiums is not guaranteed, while
- in a paid-up policy, the end of the premiums is guaranteed since the term of the premiums is in the contract — sometimes 10 years but more often 20 years.

Policy Loan

The right to a **policy loan** means the insured can borrow against the CSV. There is a maximum loan of 85 or 90% of the CSV. If the insured dies while there is a policy loan outstanding, the loan and outstanding interest, if any, are deducted from the death benefit. Since the loan reduces the value of the reserve that earns a return, a policy loan reduces dividends. The restriction of 85 or 90% provides a cushion in case the reserve's return is lower in the future. The limit ensures that the dividend will always offset the interest on the loan.. Since the interest on the policy loan is more than offset by the return on the reserve fund, the now-smaller dividend can usually continue to increase the CSV and death benefit, as shown in Example 5.

Automatic Premium Loans

Policyholders can elect to have the reserve provide automatic premium loans that pay the premiums when the premiums are in default by borrowing against the cash surrender value (CSV) as a policy loan.

Premium Vacation

A **premium vacation or holiday** means the insured can use the CSV to skip premium payments if there is enough CSV. The insured can then resume payments without penalty or cost.

A Note on Churning and Twisting

After a policyholder has built up the CSV, the agent or insurer might suggest he or she use it to buy a better policy — one that has more coverage, different features, or an improved payment schedule. Sometimes, the policyholder is *not* told that the CSV in the current policy is being used to buy the new insurance. Few policyholders know that generally

- the policy must remain in effect for a specific period of time, perhaps three years for the agent to get 70 to 80% of the commission, and
- the agent is not getting any commission trailers after seven or eight years.

So, after seven or eight years, a new policy will generate new commissions. Or the agent may have changed insurers. However, a new policy that uses the CSV to buy a new policy now has no CSV and it will have to build up again. The policyholder does not pay any premiums until the old CSV is used up and may, in fact, not have needed more insurance or a better policy. With no CSV, the policyholder cannot take out a policy loan or even surrender the policy and receive the CSV. Furthermore, since the policyholder is older, he or she will not be surprised to find that this policy costs more since the pure cost of insurance is higher.

This practice is called churning or twisting, and it is illegal.

Non-forfeiture Benefits

An insured keeps some benefits even if the policy is given up. They include the following:

- Surrendering the policy for its cash surrender value (CSV) and all other benefits cease.
- Using the CSV to buy a reduced paid-up policy.
- Using the CSV to buy paid-up term insurance equal to the original face amount for a limited period.

New Money Policies

These policies are new products that were developed to provide comparable rates of return to other kinds of savings vehicles. They were developed when tax incentives, mutual funds, and pension funds caused a decrease in the proportion of personal savings being channeled into insurance products. They include universal life, limited payment life level, or decreasing term and whole life policies where

- the insurer can change the premiums to reflect the actual cost of insurance, or
- the insured can change the face value and/or premiums to reflect the protection required.

Variable Life Insurance

These are policies where the premiums are fixed but the death benefit and the cash surrender value vary according to the investment experience of a separate account maintained by the insurer. The entire reserve in the separate account is invested in equities or other investments — the amount of the insurance coverage can be reduced but can never fall below the original face value. The CSV is not guaranteed and there is no guaranteed minimum CSV. It is suitable for insureds who are looking to improve their return on the savings portion. The risk-return trade-off applies to this type of policy — the higher the risk, the higher is the expected (but not guaranteed) return.

Endowment Life

Endowment policies are whole life policies where, at maturity — the end of a limited premium payment time — the face value is paid out even if the insured is still alive. Revisions to the *Income Tax Act* mean that the entire cash surrender value and death benefit are now taxed as income so they are no longer popular.

Maturity Date

Maturity of a life insurance policy is the point in time when the death benefit is paid usually when the insured dies. However, two types of policies pay the death benefit to the insured if the insured is still alive at the maturity date:

* endowment policies, a form of whole life policy described later, pay out at a specific date if the insured is still alive; and
* some term-to-100 policies also pay out at the insured's age 100.

Whole Life Reserves and Use of the Dividend

In Chapter 9, we look at the way an insurer calculates a level premium for a five-year term policy and the way the reserve builds up to pay the claims. A level premium means the premium remains the same over the entire five years.

In this chapter, we will now look at the way a whole life reserve builds when the dividend is reinvested. Why do we care? We care because the amount of the premium can vary a great deal on a whole life policy due to the amount of dividend that is being invested in both the cash surrender value and the death benefit.

Uses of the Dividend

Dividends are a yearly refund of a portion of the premiums to policyowners based on the company's experience and anticipated costs, that is, they are paid out of the excess of the actual return on the policy reserve over a guaranteed rate of return. They are paid out only on participating policies and are never guaranteed. Dividends arise when

* the insurer has paid out less in death benefits and operating expenses than anticipated, or
* investment returns were higher than the returns used in the guaranteed portion of the policy.

The annual dividend can be paid out or used by the policyholder in a variety of ways, and the choice can be changed after the policy is in effect, with restrictions imposed by each insurance company. There are several dividend options available to policyholders, and the dividend option does not effect the original face of the insurance policy. They are as follows:

1. The policyholder can elect to receive the dividend in cash. This annual cash dividend is a **return of premium** and a portion of the dividend is, therefore, non-taxable. With older policies the annual dividends paid out are sometimes greater than the annual premium, and create tax consequences to the policyholder.
2. Cash can be paid annually to the policyholder but *inside* the life insurance policy.
   (a) Cash can be invested in **term-like deposits,** within the life insurance policy, that earn 2–4% annually, tax-free because investment growth within a life insurance policy is not taxable. However, if the policy is **surrendered** or cancelled early, the policyholder receives the CSV and accumulated dividends within the policy, some of which is taxable.

      However, if these cash dividend are left to accumulate, they continue to accumulate tax free within the insurance policy — like an RRSP. This is an good dividend option for a conservative individual or an investor that does not have any RRSP or TFSA contribution room remaining. Permanent life insurance policies with an investment component allow people to transfer some of their wealth to their beneficiaries tax-free since the death benefit is not taxable.

(b) Be used to purchase additional insurance, as follows:

    i. Permanent insurance, which is known as **paid-up additions**, providing the insured with increasing death benefit and increasing cash value if the additional insurance is whole life. The additional insurance also earns dividends so the exponential cycle increases.

    ii. Paid-up, one-year term insurance that increases only the death benefit.

(c) The policyholder can elect to use the dividend to reduce the annual premium. This is also known as a **premium vacation** because the dividend is used to pay for the annual premium of the policy.

3. For universal life polices, but not whole life policies, the dividend can be used to purchase segregated funds.

Whole Life Reserves

Most whole life policies charge the same premium over the life of the policy. In early years, the annual premium is much higher than the cost of pure insurance. As the insured ages, the premium eventually is less than the cost of pure insurance each year. With regard to only the death benefit, the insurer has excess funds each year in the early years which accumulate and are drawn down in later years. The excess is stored in a policy reserve that accumulates to

• pay the death benefits, and
• hold the cash surrender value.

The **load** (charge for administrative, marketing, and selling costs as well as profits) is subtracted from the premium first, then the mortality charge, which is about the same as a term life premium, is subtracted. What is left is put into the reserve to earn approximately 4% a year. Because this reserve is required by law, it is also called the **legal reserve** and it continues to grow as long as the insured is alive. It is called the **accumulating reserve** in the *Income Tax Act* (ITA).

The **amount at risk** for the insurer is the difference between the face value of the whole life policy and the cash (surrender) value at any point in time. When the insured dies, the insurer pays out the death benefit (the face value) and keeps the cash value. As a result, the amount at risk decreases as the insured pays premiums and the cash value grows.

The **net amount at risk** is the face value of the policy minus the policy reserve and it also declines throughout the life of the contract. The net amount at risk is the insurer's exposure — the amount the insurer would have to draw from its own funds rather than the policy reserve were the insured to die. As the insured continues to pay premiums, the reserve grows and the net amount at risk decreases. In other words, *from the insurer's perspective*, the actual insurance coverage is decreasing, that is, the death benefit remains the same while the reserve continues to grow. For the insurer:

• the **cost of pure insurance** is the face value of the policy times the probability of dying which increases every year and can be seen in the mortality tables in Chapter 9; and
• the **net cost of pure insurance** (**NCPI**) is the probability of death times the net amount at risk.

Policy Illustration

When a person buys a whole life policy, the insurer provides a **policy illustration** that shows the following:

• The *guaranteed* cash value (cash surrender value)
• The *guaranteed* death benefit
• A **primary example** showing what *might* happen with the cash value and the death benefit, depending on
    • the options chosen for the dividend,
    • the *non-guaranteed* cash value and death benefit if the dividend it used to buy more insurance, and

• the results for the non-guaranteed portion if returns are *less* than the return used in the primary example.

Let's look at an example to understand the illustration and then compare it to a couple of other illustrations that use different dividend options.

EXAMPLE 5 Don and Joanne want to look at some policy illustrations so they can understand the options provided in whole life insurance. Francesca uses the following example for a non-smoking, 30-year-old female in a standard health class who buys $600,000 of insurance and makes annual payments. Francesca has added some column labels so she can explain the illustration.

Table 8.5A Primary Policy Illustration for $600,000 of Whole Life Insurance

End of Policy Year	Guaranteed			Current Dividend Scenario: Non-Guaranteed				
	Annual Premium Required	Cash Value	Death Benefit	Total Cash Value	Total Death Benefit	Net Cost of Pure Insurance	Adjusted Cost Base	Taxable Gain on Surrender
A	B	D	E	H	K	L	N	O
1	$10,692	$ 0	$600,000	$ 1,740	$ 617,227	$ 198	$ 10,494	$ 0
2	10,692	0	600,000	3,577	633,750	216	20,970	0
3	10,692	0	600,000	5,509	649,637	240	31,422	0
4	10,692	0	600,000	7,590	664,873	283	41,831	0
5	10,692	0	600,000	9,718	679,654	329	52,194	0
6	10,692	0	600,000	12,935	700,267	382	62,504	0
7	10,692	5,400	600,000	22,478	726,508	433	72,763	0
8	10,692	12,600	600,000	35,000	757,752	500	82,955	0
9	10,692	20,400	600,000	49,423	793,486	571	93,076	0
10	10,692	28,800	600,000	65,472	833,576	655	103,112	0
11	10,692	37,800	600,000	83,768	878,599	745	113,059	0
12	10,692	47,400	600,000	104,454	927,896	875	122,876	0
13	10,692	57,600	600,000	127,021	981,438	1,021	132,547	0
14	10,692	68,400	600,000	152,564	1,038,354	1,180	142,060	10,505
15	10,692	79,800	600,000	180,026	1,098,640	1,338	151,414	28,613
16	10,692	92,400	600,000	210,910	1,161,655	1,525	160,580	50,329
17	10,692	105,000	600,000	244,217	1,227,101	1,750	169,523	74,694
18	10,692	118,200	600,000	279,474	1,295,144	2,005	178,210	101,264
19	10,692	132,600	600,000	319,284	1,365,098	2,285	186,617	132,667
20	10,692	147,000	600,000	360,484	1,437,190	2,562	194,747	165,737
30	10,692	246,600	600,000	856,336	2,151,490	8,076	253,310	603,025
31	10,692	256,800	600,000	918,791	2,222,526	9,352	254,651	664,140
32	10,692	267,600	600,000	985,640	2,293,492	10,586	254,756	730,884
33	10,692	277,800	600,000	1,054,118	2,364,361	11,822	253,626	800,492
34	10,692	288,000	600,000	1,126,576	2,434,957	12,959	251,359	875,216
35	10,692	298,800	600,000	1,200,133	2,505,568	14,026	248,026	952,108
45	10,692	395,400	600,000	2,080,108	3,224,155	33,179	128,273	1,951,835
46	10,692	404,400	600,000	2,180,248	3,298,856	36,288	102,677	2,077,571
47	10,692	412,800	600,000	2,282,635	3,374,237	39,767	73,602	2,209,033
48	10,692	421,800	600,000	2,388,550	3,450,362	43,555	40,739	2,347,811
49	10,692	430,200	600,000	2,496,774	3,527,159	47,633	3,798	2,492,976
50	10,692	438,600	600,000	2,605,076	3,604,822	51,973	0	2,605,076
51	10,692	446,400	600,000	2,712,188	3,682,705	56,665	0	2,712,188
52	10,692	453,600	600,000	2,824,050	3,760,600	61,764	0	2,824,050
62	10,692	520,200	600,000	3,943,344	4,548,263	105,545	0	3,943,344
68	10,692	570,600	600,000	4,639,570	5,042,106	111,618	0	4,639,570
69	10,692	580,800	600,000	4,759,314	5,127,101	113,741	0	4,759,314

Needless to say, Don and Joanne would like to know what all these numbers mean so Francesca provides some details, starting with the cash value.

- **Guaranteed cash value** means this policy guarantees a certain cash (surrender) value and a guaranteed $600,000 death benefit. These are the amounts the insurer *must* pay out for the CSV if you cash in the policy or for the death benefit if the insured dies. These amounts will be the same on all versions of a policy illustration — the first one, the **primary example**, as well as the other one or two, the **reduced example(s)**, that shows the results if the **dividend scale** or actual returns are less than the "current dividend scale". The guaranteed CSV is zero for the first six years in this policy in part to pay the agent's first-year commission and **commission trailers** and also to discourage insured's from cashing the policy in (surrendering the policy).
- **Non-guaranteed cash value** reflects the amount from the dividends and depends on the rate of return earned by the investments in the reserve fund. The premium is sufficiently high generate a non-taxable dividend that could be paid to the policyholder but, more often, is allocated to the policy reserve. In this illustration, the growing policy reserve is used to buy additional paid-up insurance that generates both additional cash value and additional death benefit whose amounts are *not* guaranteed since the value of them depends on the return earned by the policy reserve.
  - **Total cash value** is the CSV from *both* the guaranteed and non-guaranteed.
  - **Total death benefit** is the total face value from *both* the guaranteed portion plus the non-guaranteed face value purchased using some of the dividends to buy paid-up insurance.

An additional illustration or two would show the amount of the cash value and death benefit if the return is lower than the illustration shown here. Francesca cannot calculated the amount of the policy reserve because she doesn't know

- the interest rate being used in the illustration, and
- the loading costs being charged to the policy.

Francesca suggests that they look at the added CSV and death benefit first (Table 8.5B). She shows the columns she has added to the illustration in a grey shade to make it easier to follow. She also points out the following:

- The added guaranteed CSV is not the same every year (column C).
- The added non-guaranteed CSV (column F) and death benefit (column I) do increase every year as the reserve grows but, of course, these amount are dependent on the return earned by the policy reserve.

Table 8.5B Analysis of Total Cash Value and Total Death Benefit

		Guaranteed			Current Dividend Scenario: Non-Guaranteed					
End of Policy Year	Annual Premiums Required	Cash Value		Death Benefit	CSV Added per Year	Total Cash Value		Additional Death Benefit		Total Death Benefit
		per year	cumulative			per year	cumulative	per year	cumulative	
A	B	C	D	E	F (G – C)	G	H	I	J (K – E)	K
1	$10,692	$ 0	$ 0	$600,000	$ 1.740	$ 1.740	$ 1,740	$17.227	$ 17.227	$ 617,227
2	10,692	0	0	600,000	1.837	1.837	3,577	16.523	33.750	633,750
3	10,692	0	0	600,000	1.932	1.932	5,509	15.887	49.637	649,637
4	10,692	0	0	600,000	2.081	2.081	7,590	15.236	64.873	664,873
5	10,692	0	0	600,000	2.128	2.128	9,718	14.780	79,654	679,654

Table 8.5B Continued

A	B										
		Guaranteed				**Current Dividend Scenario: Non-Guaranteed**					
End of Policy Year	Annual Premiums Required	Cash Value		Death Benefit	CSV Added per Year	Total Cash Value		Additional Death Benefit		Total Death Benefit	
		per year	cumulative			per year	cumulative	cumulative			
A	B	C	D	E	F	G	H	I	J (K − E)	K	
6	$10,692	$ 0	$ 0	$600,000	$ 3.217	$ 3.217	$ 12,935	$20.614	$ 100.267	$ 700,267	
7	10,692	5.400	5,400	600,000	4.144	9.544	22,478	26.240	126.508	726,508	
8	10,692	7.200	12,600	600,000	5.322	12.522	35,000	31.244	157.752	757,752	
9	10,692	7.800	20,400	600,000	6.623	14.423	49,423	35.734	193.486	793,486	
10	10,692	8,400	28,800	600,000	7,649	16,049	65,472	40,091	233,576	833,576	
11	10,692	9.000	37,800	600,000	9.296	18.296	83,768	45.023	278.599	878,599	
12	10,692	9.600	47,400	600,000	11.086	20.686	104,454	49.297	327.896	927,896	
13	10,692	10.200	57,600	600,000	12.367	22.567	127,021	53.542	381.438	981,438	
14	10,692	10.800	68,400	600,000	14.743	25.543	152,564	56.916	438.354	1,038,354	
15	10,692	11,400	79,800	600,000	16,062	27,462	180,026	60,286	498,640	1,098,640	
16	10,692	12.600	92,400	600,000	18.283	30.883	210,910	63.016	561.655	1,161,655	
17	10,692	12.600	105,000	600,000	20.707	33.307	244,217	65.446	627.101	1,227,101	
18	10,692	13.200	118,200	600,000	22.057	35.257	279,474	68.044	695.144	1,295,144	
19	10,692	14.400	132,600	600,000	25.410	39.810	319,284	69.954	765.098	1,365,098,	
20	10,692	14.400	147,000	600,000	26.800	41.200	360,484	72.091	837.190	1,437,190	
21	10,692	9,600	156,600	600,000	29,299	38,899	399,383	72,108	909,298	1,509,298	
30	10,692	10,200	246,600	600,000	51,587	61,787	856,336	70,988	1,551,490	2,151,490	
40	10,692	9,600	348,600	600,000	76,930	86,530	1,609,464	71,194	2,259,613	2,859,613	
50	10,692	8,400	438,600	600,000	99,902	108,302	2,605,076	77,663	3,004,822	3,604,822	
59	10,692	6.000	500,400	600,000	105.973	111.973	3,604,934	78.902	3.709.122	4,309,122	
60	10,692	6,600	507,000	600,000	108,004	114,604	3,719,538	79,248	3,788,370	4,388,370	
69	10,692	10,200	580,800	600,000	109,544	119,744	4,759,314	84,995	4,527,101	5,127,101	

Now Francesca explains where the taxable portion of the CSV comes from (Table 8.5C). This is taxable *only* if the policy is cashed in — surrendered — since the death benefit paid as a lump-sum is not taxable. She begins by explaining what the additional columns mean.

- Net cost of pure insurance (NCPI) for the insurers is the probability of death times net amount at risk (death benefit minus reserve). It is not calculated here but, presumably, could be using the mortality tables in Chapter 9 if she could accurately calculate the policy reserve which she can't because she doesn't know the administrative charges being deducted each year. The NCPI is increasing each year for two reasons:
  - The person is aging.
  - The total death benefit, both the guaranteed portion and the non-guaranteed portion, is increasing.
- **Adjusted Cost Base (ACB)** is
  - the annual premium required (column B)
  - the net cost of pure insurance (NCPI) (column L) for each year.
  - Since the premium is fixed for the entire 69 years,
    - the annual ACB becomes negative (−$1,130) in year 33 when the net cost of pure insurance ($11,822) becomes larger than the premium ($10,692), and
    - the cumulative ACB begins to decrease after year 33 and becomes negative in year 50 (Column N1 — the *calculated* ACB).
- **Taxable gain on surrender** is the portion of the CSV that is subject to one's marginal tax rate:
  - the total (cumulative) cash value (Column H)

– the (cumulative) adjusted cost base (ACB) (Column N1 or N2)
– cumulative dividends paid to the policyholder since they are a refund of premiums (zero in this example as all the dividends are being reinvested), and
– any non-taxable withdrawals made (again, none in this example).

Note, however, the following:
- For years 1 to 13, this taxable gain is zero until the cumulative ACB of $142,060 is greater than the CSV of $152,564 in year 14. Column O1 shows that the taxable gain is negative and, as a result, Column O2 is deemed to be zero on the illustration.
- From year 50 to year 69, the cumulative ACB becomes negative (Column N1) and again, is deemed to be zero (Column N2). At this point, the taxable gain, Column O2, is equal to the total cash value.

Table 8.5C Analysis of Taxable Gain on Surrender

	Guaranteed	Current Dividend Scenario: Non-Guaranteed						
End of Policy Year	Annual Premium Required	Total Cash Value	NCPI	Adjusted Cost Base (ACB)			Taxable Gain of Surrender	
		cumulative	per year	per year calculated	cumulative calculated	cumulative illustrated	calculated	illustrated
A	B	H	L	M	N1	N2	O1	O2
				B − L	M + prior N1		H − N1	H − N2
1	$10,692	$ 1,740	$ 198	$10,494	$ 10,494	$ 10,494	$− 8,754	$ 0
2	10,692	3,577	216	10,476	20,970	20,970	−17,393	0
3	10,692	5,509	240	10,452	31,422	31,422	−25,913	0
4	10,692	7,590	283	10,409	41,831	41,831	−34,241	0
5	10,692	9,718	329	10,363	52,194	52,194	−42,476	0
12	10,692	104,454	875	9,817	122,876	122,876	−18,422	0
13	10,692	127,021	1,021	9,671	132,547	132,547	−5,526	0
14	10,692	152,564	1,180	9,512	142,060	142,060	10,505	10,505
15	10,692	180,026	1,338	9,354	151,414	151,414	28,613	28,613
20	10,692	360,484	2,562	8,130	194,747	194,747	165,737	165,737
30	10,692	856,336	8,076	2,616	253,310	253,310	603,025	603,025
31	10,692	918,791	9,352	1,340	254,651	254,651	664,140	664,140
32	10,692	985,640	10,586	106	254,756	254,756	730,884	730,884
33	10,692	1,054,118	11,822	−1,130	253,626	253,626	800,492	800,492
34	10,692	1,126,576	12,959	−2,267	251,359	251,359	875,216	875,216
35	10,692	1,200,133	14,026	−3,334	248,026	248,026	952,108	952,108
40	10,692	1,609,464	20,627	−9,935	213,469	213,469	1,395,995	1,395,995
47	10,692	2,282,635	39,767	−29,075	73,602	73,602	2,209,033	2,209,033
48	10,692	2,388,550	43,555	−32,863	40,739	40,739	2,347,811	2,347,811
49	10,692	2,496,774	47,633	−36,941	3,798	3,798	2,492,976	2,492,976
50	10,692	2,605,076	51,973	−41,281	−37,483	0	2,642,560	2,605,076
51	10,692	2,712,188	56,665	−45,973	−83,456	0	2,795,645	2,712,188
52	10,692	2,824,050	61,764	−51,072	−134,528	0	2,958,578	2,824,050
60	10,692	3,719,538	99,966	−89,274	−722,226	0	4,441,764	3,719,538
68	10,692	4,639,570	111,618	−100,926	−1,506,091	0	6,145,661	4,639,570
69	10,692	4,759,314	113,741	−103,049	−1,609,140	0	6,368,454	4,759,314

If the insured dies, the face value or death benefit is paid out and the insurer keeps the reserve. The cash reserve (or cash surrender value, CSV) is paid to the policyholder only if
- the policy is cancelled and the policyholder receives the cash surrender value, or

- if the policyholder takes out a policy loan. If the insured dies with a policy loan outstanding, the loan is deducted from the face value.

Surrender charge is the cost to cancel a policy and it reduces the CSV.
- **Whole life**: The surrender charges are high in the early years, usually equal to 100% of the cash value. They decrease over time but generally do not disappear until year 20.
- **Universal life**: An estimate of this cost is the annual minimum charge times the number of years the policy is in force times some percentage based on the age of the contract. The surrender charges are often provided in the contract.
- **Segregated funds**: The cost is some percentage of the amount redeemed. It is similar to a deferred sales charge on a mutual fund.

Maximum Savings Component — Exempt and Non-Exempt Policies

The *Income Tax Act* does not allow the savings component to receive excessive deposits so it has rules about how large the policy reserve (accumulating fund) can be relative to the size required to pay the death benefits (mortality costs) and expenses [*Income Tax Act* Regulation 306(1)]. This applies only to policies written after December 2, 1982.

Exempt policies meet the required criteria and are exempt from a special tax. **Grandparented policies** are exempt whole life policies that were acquired before December 2, 1982.

Non-exempt policies do not meet the required criteria — insured have made deposits in excess of the amount needed to fund the death benefit and provide a reasonable level of savings. The excess gain is reportable and taxed whenever the policy is in a gain position regardless of whether or not the gain has been realized. This aspect is important when investing in universal life, which allows the contributions to vary.

Comparison of Costs of Temporary and Permanent Insurance

The following comparison is based on the following:

- A **10-year term policy** that is renewable and convertible, meaning it can be renewed without a medical up to age 80 and can be converted to a whole life policy before age 65. Most policies are renewable and convertible although the age restrictions will vary. Premiums for renewing and/or converting are set when the policy is issued and are based on the insured's attained age at renewal or conversion.
- A **Term-to-100 policy**, usually bought by someone at 50 or older who wants permanent insurance.
- A **Whole life policy** with premiums payable until age 100, at which point the coverage continues but it has become a paid-up policy. Other options include premiums payable for 10 years, 20 years, or to age 65.

This comparisons cover two 30-year-olds — a male smoker (the most expensive) and a female non-smoker (the least expensive). Table 8.6A shows the annual premium, which is the same every year for the term covered, varying from 10 years to age 100 for the three types of policies. It is obvious that if you are young and money is tight, a 10-year term policy has a great deal of appeal.

EXAMPLE 6   Joanne and Don recognize that they are underinsured and want to look at the options. While they feel they need insurance only for about 20 years, they have heard friends talk about other types of policies and want to know not only the cost of various types of insurance but the rationale behind the various costs. Francesca prepares the following examples for them. The premiums are the cost for the length of the term of the policy.

Table 8.6A Comparison of Term and Whole Life Annual Premiums for a $600,000 Life Insurance Policy Issued at Age 30

	Term Premiums			Whole Life Premiums			
	10 year	20 year	to 100	for 10 years	for 20 years	to age 65	to age 100
Female non-smoker	$240	$ 444	$1,710	$5,256	$3,024	$2,112	$2,082
Female smoker	432	768	2,268	7,386	4,212	2,976	2,856
Male non-smoker	354	600	1,980	6,120	3,504	2,448	2,436
Male smoker	678	1,104	3,054	9,312	5,376	3,696	3,396
Percentage of lowest							
Female non-smoker	100%	185%	713%	2,190%	1,260%	880%	868%
Female smoker	180%	320%	945%	3,078%	1,755%	1,240%	1,190%
Male non-smoker	148%	250%	825%	2,550%	1,460%	1,020%	1,015%
Male smoker	283%	460%	1,273%	3,880%	2,240%	1,540%	1,415%

Now Francesca compares the cost of a term policy with a term-to-100 policy and a whole life policy from age 30 to age 90. Someone for whom money is very tight might take a 10-year policy even though the children are just born because he or she might assume things will be better in 10 years when the policy has to be renewed. Francesca compares the following:

- 10-year term policy renewed several times and ending at age 90, which reflects an initial temporary need for insurance,
- Term-to-100 policy reflecting a permanent need for insurance but no need for a savings component.
- Whole life policy with premiums paid until age 100, which reflects a desire for permanent insurance. This policy pays out a death benefit (face value) on the death of the insured and the insurer keeps the cash surrender value, that is, the beneficiary does *not* collect both the death benefit and the cash surrender value on the death of the insured.

Table 8.6B Comparison of 10-Year, Term-to-100 and While Life Annual Premium of a $600,000 Life Insurance Policy Issued at Age 30

	10 year Term		Term-to-100		Whole Life, Premiums to Age 100	
	Female Non Smoker	Male Smoker	Female Non Smoker	Male Smoker	Female Non Smoker	Male Smoker
30–39	$ 240	$ 678	$1,710	$3,054	$2,082	$3,396
40–49	864	2,028	1,710	3,054	2,082	3,396
50–59	1,728	6,048	1,710	3,054	2,082	3,396
60–69	4,596	16,788	1,710	3,054	2,082	3,396
70–79	13,932	37,338	1,710	3,054	2,082	3,396
80–89	29,934	76,956	1,710	3,054	2,082	3,396
Coverage to age	90	90	100	100	Death	Death

Exhibit 8.1A shows the dramatic increase in rates for the female non-smoker. The term policy, providing only insurance coverage with no savings component, is much cheaper in earlier years but since the rate is determined by a person's age, it becomes increasingly expensive as it is renewed every 10 years. We examine how rates for term insurance are determined using mortality tables in Chapter 9, which show the probability of dying every year from age 0 to 109.

Exhibit 8.1   Annual Premiums for $600,000 of Coverage

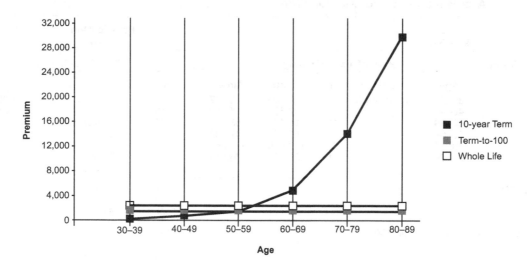

Now Francesca compares the present value of these policies at age 30. The calculation is easy enough but the rationale is not because term insurance is temporary insurance while term-to-100 and whole life are permanent insurance. Moreover, the two permanent polices have payments spread over a different number of years, which affects the amount of the premium.

Table 8.6C   Present Value at Age 30 of the Premiums if the Policies Are Held for 20 Years

k = 3%						Female Non Smoker	Male Smoker
10-year Term	**PVA of each Annuity**					**PV of each PVA**	
	Age	**PMT**	**n**	**Female**	**Male**	**n**	
	30–39	Table 8.6A	10	2,109	5,957	0	2,109	5,957
	40–49		10	7,591	17,818	10	5,649	13,258
							7,757	19,215
Term-to-100						PMT ·	1,710	3,054
						n	20	20
						PVA	26,204	46,799
Whole Life, Premiums to Age 100						PMT	2,082	3,396
						n	20	20
						PVA	31,904	52,040

Why the big difference?
* The basic rates for the insurance coverage is based on mortality rates (rates of dying). Since the premium is the same throughout the term, term-to-100 and whole life charge a lot more in the early years when mortality rates are low and relatively less in later years when people are dying at a much higher rate.
* Whole life premiums have a built-in savings component, the cash value, which adds to the cost.

Just to complete the picture, Francesca compares the present value of the premium for the same three policies but for more than 20 years:
* 10-year term policy renewed as long as possible, in this case, providing coverage for 60 years ending at age 90.
* The entire 70 years of a Term-to-100 Policy.
* The Whole Life policy where the premiums are paid to age 100.

Table 8.6D Present Value at Age 30 of the Premiums if the Policies Are Held as Long as Possible

k = 3%						Female Non Smoker	Male Smoker
10-year Term	PVA of each Annuity					PV of each PVA	
	Age	PMT	n	Female	Male	n	
	30–39	Table 8.6A	10	2,109	5,957	0	2,109	5,957
	40–49		10	7,591	17,818	10	5,649	13,258
	50–59		10	15,182	53,138	20	8,406	29,421
	60–69		10	40,381	147,501	30	16,636	60,769
	70–79		10	122,408	328,056	40	37,525	100,568
	80–89		5	263,003	676,144	50	59,993	154,233
							200,015	**488,750**
Term-to-100						PMT	1,710	3,054
						n	70	70
						PVA	**51,295**	**91,611**
Whole Life, Premiums to Age 100						PMT	2,082	3,396
						n	70	70
						PVA	**62,454**	**101,870**

So if Don and Joanne are certain they will need insurance for only 20 years or so, they should buy a term policy because it will be the cheapest by far as reflects in Table 8.6B.

Using a Policy Loan to Finance Retirement

Both Don and Joanne have a pension at work, which means they may not have very much RRSP contribution room. They also can save a total of $10,000 a year for both short- and long-term plans in a Tax-Free Savings Account (TFSA)

However, they should know the possibilities for using a whole life policy to save for retirement. This is also attractive for a small business owner who may need life insurance coverage for a longer time than Joanne and Don. This can be achieved without cashing in the policy by taking out a non-taxable policy loan — usually limited to 85 or 90% of the CSV.

EXAMPLE 7   Terry, Joanne's brother, is part of a partnership and is also married with young children. Terry chose the policy in Example 5 so that, by age 65 (at the end of Policy year 35), the policy has a death benefit of $2,505,568 and a CSV of $1,200,133.

- If he surrenders the policy, he receives $819,290 after tax (see Table 8.7) and has no insurance coverage.
- If he takes out a policy loan, he can receive $1,020,133 (85% × cash value) and still have $1,485,454 in death benefit coverage. A smaller policy loan would provide a larger death benefit.

As shown in Example 5, the policyholder has been paying a higher premium to add a lump-sum to the reserve in order to participate in the returns of the return. After the policy loan, the reserve continues to earn income each year and the resulting dividend continues to increase the death benefit. The interest charged on the $1 million policy loan will be offset by the dividend being generated by the reserve fund. The insured has **collaterally assigned** part of the death benefits to the insured, the collateral being the death benefits. When the insured dies, the insurer deducts the policy loan and interest, if any, from the death benefits and pays out the net of $1,485,454 to the beneficiary. Full and limited assignment were covered in the Sample Term Life Policy in Chapter 2.

Joanne and Don ask to see a few comparisons to other types of policies so Francesca compares the primary example as shown in Example 5 to:
• the same policy as Example 5 but the rate of return is 1% less than the primary example,
• the same policy as Example 5 but the rate of return is 2% less than the primary example,
• the same policy as Example 5 but the dividend is paid to the policyholder and not reinvested, and
• a 20 Pay policy, a whole life policy where the entire premium is paid-up after 20 years, another primary example at the optimal rate of return (k).

Table 8.7 Comparison of After-tax Cash Surrender Value with Effect of Policy Loan at Age 65

	Primary Example	k is 1% less	k is 2% less	Dividend Paid Out	20 Pay
Calculate the Adjusted Cost Base					
Total premiums paid	$ 374,220	$ 374,220	$ 374,220	$ 374,220	$ 97,200
Net cost of pure insurance	−126,194	−110,564	−103,208	−45,825	−43,978
Dividends received	0	0	0	−29,595	0
ACB	248,026	263,656	271,012	298,800	53,222
Calculate the After-Tax CSV					
CSV	1,200,133	1,005,220	926,441	298,800	410,604
ACB	−248,026	−263,656	−271,012	−298,800	−53,222
Taxable gain	952,108	741,564	655,429	0	357,382
Tax @ 40%	380,843	296,626	262,172	0	142,953
CSV after tax (CSV − tax)	819,290	708,594	664,269	298,800	267,651
Total premiums paid to end of year 35	374,220	374,220	374,220	344,625	97,200
CSV after tax ÷ total premiums paid	219%	189%	178%	87%	275%
Calculate Net Death Benefit					
Death benefit	2,05,68	2,093,486	1,926,935	600,000	664,343
Policy loan — 85% of CSV	1,020,113	854,437	787,475	253,980	349,013
Net death benefit	1,485,454	1,239,050	1,139,460	346,020	315,330
Net death benefit ÷ total premiums paid	397%	331%	304%	92%	324%

Note: First 4 policies continue to pay premiums until death.

These examples assume the entire policy is surrendered and the policyholder receives the entire CSV. For the amount of the investment, the 20 Pay policy produces the largest CSV compared to premiums paid (in this example anyway) while collecting the entire dividend produces a low return although this example does not show the result if the dividends received were invested outside the policy.

A policy loan of 85 to 90% of the CSV is not taxable when received.

Universal Life (UL)

A universal life insurance policy is a permanent life insurance policy that can be custom tailored to an individual's needs. The various components of a universal life policy are flexible and can be **unbundled** and changed at any time while the policy is in force. **Bundled** refers to the various **component parts** of a life insurance policy that are connected to each other — who is covered, investments, premiums, face value, and cash surrender value. The insured can:

• change the **initial face value** (face amount at the issue date),
• increase or decrease the death benefit,
• change a level death benefit to an increasing benefit,

- substitute one life for another,
- change the amount of the deposits (premiums),
- change the frequency of the deposits,
- change the investment strategy,
- take out a policy loan,
- sometimes withdraw cash without terminating the policy and without this withdrawal being a policy loan, and
- might be able to add other insureds.

The premiums, above and beyond the cost of the insurance, known as **contributions** or **deposits**, can be increased yearly to accumulate within the policy and are exempt from tax if left in the policy. However, if they are withdrawn, they result in taxable income. Funds in a universal life insurance policy can be invested in **segregated funds** and the income received from the segregated fund is also exempt from tax if left in the policy.

The contribution or deposits are known as the **cash value of the universal life policy**. The cash value can be withdrawn without terminating the policy (this is not a loan), and policy loans are permitted.

Other possible features are:

- The savings component can have two interest rates — one that is a guaranteed minimum, another that is the current rate.
- The expense charges can be front-end, back-end or both.
- An **investment bonus** of 1 to 1.5% p.a. might be paid to encourage insured to keeps the contract in force.
- A **side fund** might be available. It is
  - external to the policy,
  - not included in death benefit,
  - does not affect the net amount at risk, and
  - the deposits are not subject to PST.
- A **variable mortality cost option** permits the mortality cost factor to be revised each year to reflect the mortality experience of the insurer.
- **Yearly term rates** can allow premiums that are based on attained age, that is, the premiums increase each year.

In other words, almost every aspect is flexible.

Insurance agents often provide policy illustrations that illustrate what could happen. Since these policies cover a long period of time, small changes in assumptions about rates can make a large difference so a potential insured should look closely at the assumptions. However, the actual results of universal life policies, unlike whole policies, is totally transparent and the insured can see exactly what happened to the investment in the reserve.

Death Benefit Options for Universal Life

Insurers offer a variety of options for calculating the amount of the death benefit and these options are dependent on the net amount at risk (from the insurer's point of view) because it varies with the **settlement option**. The net amount at risk is

+ the amount of the death benefit payable
− the amount in the policy reserve (**account value**).

The most common are the following:

1. **Level death benefit.** The face value does not change over the life of the policy. This is the cheapest because the amount at risk decreases over the life of the policy as the account value grows. The beneficiary receives the face value and the insurer keeps the account value.

2. **Level death benefit + accumulated premium deposits**. This is one of the most expensive since the benefit is increasing to include essentially a refund of premiums after the insured dies. The amount at risk increases with every premium payment.

3. **Level death benefit + account value**. This one is also expensive since the amount at risk grows with the increase in the account value.

4. **Indexed death benefit.** The death benefit increases on a compounded basis every year. This is also expensive since the face value is continually increasing.

Comparison of Life Insurance Policies

The following tables summarize the similarities and differences among the four types of policies as well as the advantages and disadvantages of each.

Table 8.8   Comparison of Main Features

	Whole life	Universal Life	Term-to-100	Term
Period of coverage	• Life	• Flexible (usually purchased for life)	• To age 100	• 1 to 65, usually not available after age 75*
Premiums	• Guaranteed, usually level	Flexible	• Guaranteed, level	• Guaranteed for term
Cost	• Usually higher in early years but lower than term in later years of the policy	• Flexible	• More than term, but cheaper than whole life	• Cheapest form of life insurance
Death benefits	• Guaranteed and can increase depending on the dividend option selected for the policy	• Flexible	• Guaranteed	• Guaranteed
Cash surrender value (CSV)	• Guaranteed and can increase depending on the dividend return	• Flexible	• Usually none	• None
Dividends**	• Yes	• Usually no	• Usually no	• No

* This depends on the insurance company that is offering the protection. However, term policies after age 75 are rare in Canada.

** Dividends from mutual life insurance companies are a refund of premiums and are not taxable.
   Dividends from stock life insurance companies are taxed as regular dividends.

Table 8.9   Advantages and Disadvantages

ADVANTAGES			
Whole Life	**Universal Life**	**Term-to-100**	**Term**
1. Protection for life 2. Level premiums 3. Can borrow against, withdraw or use to pay premiums 4. Dividends received are non-taxable 5. Can be used to transfer wealth	Same as whole life 1. Adaptable to changing needs of insured 2. Insured controls premiums 3. Insured controls the investment 4. Can be used to transfer wealth	1. Protection for life (age 100) 2. Level premiums 3. Cheaper than participating life policies	1. Good for short-term needs (like a mortgage) 2. Cheaper than permanent 3. Often can be converted to a permanent policy without a medical

Table 8.9   Continued

DISADVANTAGES			
Whole Life	**Universal Life**	**Term-to-100**	**Term**
1. High initial cost 2. Not efficient for short-term needs 3. CSV is small in early years	1. Higher administrative expenses 2. Complexity makes it more difficult to manage 3. Insured bares sole responsible for investment returns	1. Policies are non-participating	1. Premiums increase with each renewal 2. Renewability stops at 65 or 75 3. If premiums not paid, policy cancelled in 30 days and may not be reinstated without a medical 4. Usually no CSV

Segregated Funds (SEG FUNDS)

The legal name of a Segregated Fund is **individual variable annuity contract** — it is an annuity contract between an insurance company and the policyholder in which the policyholder deposits money, known as **contributions or premiums**, in an **insurance trust,** which is used to invest in a variety of products to achieve a specific mandate. These funds in the trust are kept separate (**segregated**) from other assets of the insurance company and belong to the policyholders of the trust. For example, a fixed income segregated fund policy would invest in a fixed income fund (trust) that in turn would invest in a variety of fixed income products.

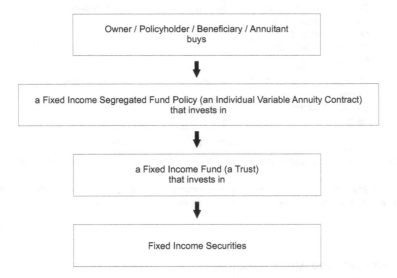

The owner of a segregated fund, unlike a mutual fund, is the *policyholder* of the individual variable insurance contract and is *also* the *beneficiary or annuitant* of the trust from the funds income. The policyholder is in a deferred annuity contract in which the policyholder promises to pay money monthly in the form of a premium to the insurance company who, in return, manages the seg fund and further guarantees at least 75% of the investment if the policyholder leaves the money in the fund until the maturity date — some specified period of time in the future, such as 10 years from the date of the contract.

The assets in a segregated fund are kept separate (are segregated) from the assets of the insurance company and are, in turn, invested in various products, such as a money market fund, a bond fund, a balanced fund, a growth fund, etc. Like mutual funds, these segregated funds have specific investment mandates and the money collected from policyholders is held in trust to carry out the investment mandate specified by the fund.

Only insurance companies can sell segregated funds which can be all or part of the investment portfolio of a UL policy and can also be purchased directly.

Only Canadian residents can purchase segregated funds but they can keep them if they subsequently become a non-resident.

Overview of Investment Funds

An investment fund pools each investors money with the money of other investors in order to buy a basket of investments. Each fund might include as many as 100 or more different individual securities or indices.

Mutual funds and segregated funds are the two most popular types of investment funds although there are also the following:

* **Labour sponsored investment funds (LSIF)** that invest in small to mid-size, unknown, junior companies. They are venture capital funds that invest in private equity and are only available to Canadian investors. LSIF provide federal and provincial tax credits to the investor who agrees to invest for a minimum number of years.
* **Income Trusts** such as
  * **royalty** and **energy income trusts** invest in oil, gas or other natural resources;
  * **real estate investment trusts (REIT)** invest in income-producing properties such as office buildings, shopping centres and apartment buildings;
  * **utility trusts** invest in pipeline, power and telecommunications companies;
  * **business investment trusts** invest in various business.
* **Income Trust Funds** or **Income Funds** are mutual funds invested in income trusts.

Mutual Funds

A **mutual fund corporation** is an open-end corporation, meaning it must provide shareholders the right of shares redemption, which a closed-end corporation and a closed-end mutual fund do not. A mutual fund corporation may elect to pay capital gains by declaring a special **capital gains dividend** which is taxed as capital gains income to the investor.

A **open-end mutual fund** issues new shares whenever an investor invests in the fund and also when it distributes mutual fund income. The fund value, the **Net Asset Value (NAV),** is the market value of the investments and units can be redeemed at any time at their **net asset value per share (NAVPS).** Most **mutual fund trusts** are open-end mutual funds.

A **closed-end mutual fund** is a fund in which the total number of units is fixed. After the initial offering, the units can be acquired only from another owner. Unit prices of closed-end funds are set by supply and demand, not net asset value, and are traded on a stock exchange.

Comparison of Segregated Funds with Mutual Funds

Segregated funds and mutual funds compete for investor dollars. They have many things in common but also some critical differences.

Unique Features of Segregated Funds

Segregated funds have two features that mutual funds do not have although they differ in the way they are taxed. Segregated funds offer

* a guarantee of some or all of the investment, and
* as an insurance policy, some of or all the death benefit and the maturity value can be creditor-protected.

1. Capital Guaranteed

Segregated funds provide policyholders a guarantee on the principal investment. The guarantee is usually based on the principal investment over a period of time and specified in the policy contract, that is, the insurer will guarantee the policyholder that it will return to them either

- at maturity of the policy, typically 10 years, 75% or more of the capital, or
- a death benefit guarantee, which can be 100% of the capital and carries a higher fee since the insurer must set aside more in the reserve for this guarantee.

2. Creditor Protection of the Insurance Proceeds

Life insurance proceeds with irrevocable named beneficiaries who are a spouse, children, grandchildren and parents do not pass through the estate and, therefore, are not available to creditors of the investor at his or her death. This is attractive to owner-managers of businesses and professional practitioners

In addition, segregated funds cannot be used as **collateral** on a loan, and policy loans are not permitted.

Similarities

- Both provide **professional money management** for the investor.
- Both are **eligible investments** for **non-registered savings**, for **registered savings** such as a Registered Retirement Savings Plan (RRSP), a Locked-in Retirement Account (LIRA) and a Locked-in RRSP (LRSP) as well as **registered retirement income plans** that are paying retirement income such as a Registered Retirement Income Fund (RRIF), a Life Income Fund (LIF), a Locked-in Retirement Income Fund (LRIF), and a Prescribed Retirement Income Fund (PRIF available in Saskatchewan and Manitoba only).
- Both provide **diversified investment options** since each fund has purchased several investments in specific categories. These funds can be as follows:
  - **Balanced funds** invested in cash-equivalent investments, bonds and stocks.
  - **Bond funds** or **(fixed) income funds** invested in government bonds, high-quality, high-yielding corporate bonds, high-yield preferred and common shares, and mortgages.
  - **Dividend funds** invested in Canadian preferred and common shares yielding high dividends.
  - **Emerging market funds** invested in small countries that are expected to grow.
  - **Equity funds** or **stock funds** invested in common stocks and, perhaps, short-term notes and other fixed-income securities.
  - **Ethical funds** guided by some moral criteria.
  - **Global funds** invested in well-diversified portfolios from every major economic region in the world.
  - **Growth funds** that are more volatile (and therefore more risky) equity funds.
  - **International funds** invested outside of Canada, such as U.S. bond funds, Japanese growth funds, Far East funds and European equity funds.
  - **Money market funds** invested in safe, short-term liquid investments.
  - **Mortgage funds** invested in high-quality (first) mortgages and maybe short-term bonds.
  - **Real estate funds** invested in income-producing real estate such as apartment buildings, office buildings, shopping malls and industrial buildings.
  - **Specialty funds** invested in
    - specific industries such as oil and gas, or
    - specific segments of the capital market such as natural resources and precious metals.
  - **Treasury-bill funds** invested only in government of Canada T-bills.
- Both charge a **management expense ratio (MER)** to cover expenses — commissions, brokerage fees, legal and audit, safekeeping charges, management fees, transfer fees, and taxes.
  - A portion of the MER in a segregated fund is used to buy insurance, which allows the insurer to offer a guarantee on the investment. The insurance guarantee increases the MER on seg funds by 0.25% to 1.5% depending on the fund's risk profile and the amount of the guarantee.

Table 8.10 Differences between Segregated Funds and Mutual Funds

	Segregated Fund	Mutual Fund
Structure	• Contracts or policies — individual variable annuity contracts. As an annuity contract, when the policy matures, the policyholder can either withdraw the accumulated value of the contract or can receive a stream of income, a single life annuity.	• Trusts usually, sometimes corporations.
	• Fund is subdivided into units.	• Fund is subdivided into trust units or corporate shares.
Regulation	• Provincial and federal insurance legislation — not securities regulation as long as it guarantees the return of at least 75% of capital.	• Provincial securities regulation.
Creditor Protection for the Fund	• The insurance company owns the assets in the fund and the policyholders are preferred creditors so the assets of the seg fund are largely creditor-proof.	• The assets of a mutual fund *trust* are owned by the financial institution, who is the trustee of the fund, and the assets are protected by trust law from claims against the trustee. The assets of a mutual fund *corporation* are owned by the fund corporation and creditors have no claim against the fund manager.
Creditor Protection for the Investor	• Yes for the death benefit and maturity value.	• No.
Value	• Value of the contract fluctuates based on the market value of the assets in the underlying fund.	• Value of the unit shares fluctuates based on the market value of the assets in the fund.
Guaranteed Value	• Value at death or maturity is guaranteed, usually between 75 and 100%.	• No.
MER	• Both charge management fees that lower the return. The fee, called a Management Expense Ratio (MER), covers management and operating expenses and is stated as a percentage. Historical returns are usually stated *before* the MER is deducted	
	• The MER also covers the cost of insurance for the seg fund.	
Redemption	• Early redemption or surrender of all or part of the policy at the net asset value (NAV) is permitted before maturity but it affects the guarantee and there may be an early redemption penalty (fee).	• Can redeem units on demand at the net asset value (NAV) of the units or shares.
	• Disposal of all or part of segregated fund and a mutual fund can lead to a capital gain or loss depending on the unit value at the time of redemption.	
Death Benefit	• Payment of the guarantee at death or maturity is taxed as a capital gain since this is a variable life annuity, not considered to be a tax-exempt life insurance death benefit.	• None.
Proceeds at Death	• Greater of guaranteed value or market value.	• Market value.
Probate	• None with a named beneficiary that is not the estate.	• Goes into the estate to be distributed after **probate fees** and capital gains taxes are paid.

Taxation

Income that **flows through** these funds mean the income "**retains its nature**".

- If the fund received **dividends from a taxable Canadian corporation**, the recipient will first gross up this income by 145% to arrive at taxable dividend income and then will use the **dividend tax credit** of 18.9655% to reduce the tax payable. This means that *both* the gross-up and dividend tax credit have flowed through:
- For **capital gains**, only 50% of
  - **net capital gains** is taxable for mutual funds;
  - **capital gains** and **capital losses** is taxable/tax-deductible for segregated funds.
- All interest income as well as dividends from foreign corporations *never* have any special tax treatment regardless of where they are invested — they are 100% taxable so while technically the income may flow through, it doesn't have any effect. However, any **foreign non-business tax credit** arising from tax withheld by foreign governments on interest and dividends earned in foreign countries also flows through.

The effect on the recipient's income taxes depends on whether or not the funds are held in a registered or a non-registered account.

- If the funds are held in a **registered account,** such as a Registered Retirement Savings Plan (RRSP), the income received by the recipient is not taxable until it is withdrawn from the registered plan, at which point it is 100% taxable. The effect is that the income does *not* flow through.
  - This is the same with *all* investment income earned by a registered plan, that is, income is not taxed until it is withdrawn, at which point it is fully taxable. While registered plans allow income to grow before tax, it *always* loses its nature and become 100% taxable when withdrawn.
- If the funds are held in a **non-registered account** (except a tax-free savings account where the income is never taxed), the income is taxed annually by the recipient as shown in Table 8.11.

Capital gains and losses are incurred in two ways:

1. The fund itself has made or lost money investing. These gains and losses can be:
   (a) **realized** — the investment was sold, or
   (b) **unrealized** — the fund is still holding the investment.
2. The investor sells units in the funds at a gain or loss.
   (a) For mutual funds, the capital gain is the proceeds from the sale *after* any fees minus the adjusted cost base. Any increase in the ACB while the units are held will decrease the amount of the capital gain (of which 50% is taxable).
   (b) For segregated funds, the capital gain is the proceeds from the sale *before* the fees minus the adjusted cost base. The fees are deducted as a capital loss.
   (c) Capital losses can be deducted only from capital gains from the prior three years or carried forward indefinitely. Dividends and interest, both domestic and foreign, are received by the fund from its investments.

Return of capital is a distribution that is over and above the annual income of the fund.

Table 8.11 Taxation and Allocation or Distribution of Income Earned by the Fund

	Segregated Fund	Mutual Fund
Type of Organization	• Deemed to be an inter vivos trust by the *Income Tax Act*.	• Is either a mutual fund *trust* or a mutual fund *corporation*.
Distribution of Income after MER and Taxation of Income Retained in the Fund	• Required by the *Income Tax* Act to *allocate all* income earned by the fund to the policyholders when it is realized. • Since it is deemed to be an inter vivos trust by the *Income Tax Act*, if income could be left in the fund, it would be taxed at the highest personal tax rates.	• Distribute income by issuing additional units or shares to investors. • All income in a mutual fund *trust* tends to be distributed at the end of the year to the unit holders on record on a specific date. Any income retained by the trust is taxed at the highest personal tax rate.
Effect of Distribution	• Increases the adjusted cost base (ACB). • Recipients do not receive a cheque from these allocations.	• **If reinvested.** Receives new units or shares, which decreases unit or share value but total value remains the same. • **If paid.** Reduces unit or share value since other investors have received additional shares but total net asset value plus cash received remains unchanged.
Flow Through for Non-Registered Plans	• All income — interest, dividends, realized capital gains and realized capital losses — retains its nature and the policyholder pays tax at his or her marginal tax rate on the allocations.	• Trusts flow through interest, dividends and *net* realized capital gains but not capital losses which have to be applied against capital gains to be used. • **Corporations** flow through dividends and capital gains dividends.
Effect for Recipient.	• Pays income tax on allocations.	• Pays income tax on distributions. Whether received as a cheque or additional shares.
Prorated Distribution	• Pays out annual income based on how long the units were owned during the year.	• Pays out annual income based on the number of units owned on the "record date".
Keeps Track of ACB	• Fund	• Investor
Sales Charges	• Are not tax deductible when acquired or redeemed and are not part of the adjusted cost base (ACB). When all or part of the fund is disposed of, the portion relating to that part of the fund that was sold is treated as a capital loss and reduces capital gains or increases capital losses.	• Are subtracted from the purchase price for front-end loads or the redemption price for deferred sales charges with the effect that they reduce the capital gain.
Taxation of Redeemed Units	• Allocated income has increased the ACB, meaning there will be less of a capital gain when units are sold.	• **Trust.** The sale of trust units can trigger a capital gain if the value of the units has increased. • **Corporation.** Since each mutual fund corporation has a different class of shares for each fund, exchanging shares within the same mutual fund does not trigger a capital gain.
Return of Capital	• Does not happen.	• Not taxable when distributed but decreases ACB, causing a larger capital gain when sold.
Unrealized Capital Gains and Losses from the Fund	• Pays out all income and capital gains created/earned by the fund throughout the year when they are realized.	• Pays out and distributes income/capital gains at the end of the year to all unit holders on record, regardless of when the gain/loss is realized.
Reset	• Allows investors to lock in market gains two to four times a year. Maturity date is extended to 10 years from the reset date. Guarantee is also reset. Is very expensive.	• Not available.

EXAMPLE 8   Don decides to buy some mutual funds and segregated funds to see what the actual difference is. He has the following transactions:

On July 1, 2008 he invests $10,000 in each when both were selling for $20 a unit and received 500 units of each.

On December 31, 2008, both funds reinvest interest income for the year:

- The segregated fund *allocates* $262.50 for the six months that he owned the seg fund.
- The mutual fund *distributes* 25.610 units at the year-end price of $20.50 per unit for a total of $525 for the entire year since he was holding 500 units on the record date of December 31, 2008.

On December 31, 2008, the segregated fund also allocated $150 of capital losses realized during the year. Mutual funds cannot flow through capital losses so this is not allocated in the mutual fund. On January 2, 2009, he invests another $7,000 and receives 333.333 units from each fund since the cost for each is the same — $20.50 per unit.

At the end of 2009, each fund reinvests income for the year:

- Both funds reinvest $944.84 of interest income for the entire year.
- Both funds reinvest $225.00 of capital gains realized during the year.
- The mutual fund is able to use the $225 of capital gains to reinvest the capital loss from the prior year since providing a *net* capital gain for the year of $75 ($225 from 2009 minus $150 from 2008).

Later in 2009, Don redeems 300 units of each fund when the price for each is $24 a unit, giving him proceeds of $7,200.

- For the mutual fund, he deducts the redemption fee of $396 from his proceeds to give him net proceeds of $6,804. He cannot deduct the seg fund surrender fee as an expense.

He calculates his capital gain on each fund (50% of the capital gain is taxable),

- The seg fund provides him the capital gain of $618.36 on this fund, from which he deducts the surrender charges of $396 as a capital loss.
- He calculates his capital gain for the mutual fund.

He also calculates the total income reinvested just to see which fund performed better.

Note: In reality, the surrender charge and the MER on the seg fund is higher than on the mutual fund to pay for the insurance built into the seg fund so he is not as well off as it appears from this example.

Table 8.12   Comparison of Segregated Fund and Mutual Fund

	Segregated Fund			Mutual Fund			Annual Allocations/ Distributions		
	Total Cost	P/unit	# units	Total Cost	P/unit	# units	Total Cost	P/unit	# units
Bought July 1, 2008	10,000.00	$20.0000	500.000	10,000.00	$20.0000	500.000			
Interest income reinvested Dec. 31, 2008	262.50			525.00	$20.5000	25.610	$525.00	$1.0500	500.000
Realized capital loss allocated	–150.00			0.00					
Adjusted cost base (ACB)	10,112.50	$20.2250	500.000	10,525.00	$20.0244	525.610			
Bought January 2, 2009	7,000.00	$21.0000	333.333	7,000.00	$21.0000	333.333			
ACB	17,112.50	$20.5350	833.333	17,525.00	$20.4030	858.943			
Interest income reinvested	944.84			944.84	$23.0000	41.080	$944.84	$1.1000	858.943
Realized capital gain reinvested	225.00			225.00	$23.0000	9.783	$225.00	$0.2619	858.943
Prior year's capital loss				–150.00	$23.0000	–6.522	–$150.00	$–0.1746	858.943
ACB before redemption	18,282.34	$21.9388	833.333	18,544.84	$20.5305	903.284			
	18,282.34	*divided by*	833.333	18,544.84	*divided by*	903.284			

Table 8.12 Continued

	Segregated Fund			Mutual Fund			Annual Allocations / Distributions		
	Total Cost	P/unit	# units	Total Cost	P/unit	# units	Total Cost	P/unit	# units
Redeemed units	7,200.00	$24.0000	300.000	7,200.00	$24.0000	300.000			
Redemption 5.5% fee	0.00			−396.00					
Proceeds	7,200.00			6,804.00					
ACB of redeemed units	6,581.64	$21.9388	300.000	6,159.14	$20.5305	300.000			
ACB of balance	11,700.70	$21.9388	533.333	12,385.70	$20.5305	603.284			
Shaded areas were input. The rest were calculated.									

Capital Gain on Redemption	Seg Fund	Difference	Mutual Fund
Proceeds	7,200.00	0.00	7,200.00
ACB	−6,581.64	422.50	−6,159.14
Expense — deferred sales charge	0.00	−396.00	−396.00
	618.36	−618.36	
Capital loss — surrender charge	−396.00	396.00	
Capital gain on redemption of units	222.36	422.50	644.86
Total income allocated / distributed	1,282.34	262.50	1,544.84

Summary

Life insurance is available to meet both short- and long-term needs. There are three ways to approach deciding how much insurance to buy. This is a decision that could change over time and needs to be reviewed when there are changes in one's life. The primary purpose of life insurance is to provide for people who are financially dependent on the insured, but life insurance can also be used to save for retirement, to buy out a business partner, and to pay taxes that become due on one's estate at death.

There are both temporary and permanent types of life insurance and the choice depends on long-term goals and also the money available to pay premiums.

Sources

Mutual Fund and Segregated Fund Flowthrough Tax Rules: Resolving the Inconsistencies, Kathleen C. Young, Toronto, 2004.
Mutual Fund Tax Guide for Your 2008 Tax Return, Mackenzie Tax and Estate Planning, Toronto, 2009.
Segregated Funds vs. Mutual Funds, Comparison, Segregated Funds Canada.
Taxation of Segregated Funds — Simplified, Standard Life, The Hughes Trustco Group Ltd, Montreal.

Application Case

Joanne arrives almost visibly quivering. Several years earlier, a friend of hers started selling life insurance and Joanne bought life insurance from her. Joanne reviewed her insurance needs with Francesca when she began seeing Francesca for financial planning advice and found out that she had a whole lot more insurance than she needed (and not enough disability insurance). Francesca helped sort that out for her but Joanne has been wary of life insurance and people who sell it ever since.

Francesca makes her a double espresso — seems like the time for something extra.

"Any particular questions?" Francesca asks.

A. "Well, since I feel I've been burned before, what questions should I be asking when I think about getting life insurance?" Joanne asks. Francesca replies:

1. "The first questions is: Do you need it all? Some people don't."
2. "Then, if you do need it, how much do you need? There are several ways of approaching this."
3. "Finally, what type of life insurance should you buy — temporary or permanent?" (Page 276)

B. "Are you saying it's possible I don't need life insurance at all?" Joanne asks and Francesca tells her: "People buy life insurance for many reasons: (Page 277)
   1. to provide for a financially dependent family should the insured die prematurely.
   2. to pay taxes on their estate.
   3. to buy out a business partner should one partner die prematurely.
   4. to save for retirement in a tax-advantaged way."

C. Now visibly relaxing, Joanne says, "I'd like to go over the ways one goes about deciding how much life insurance to buy" (Page 278).

   "There are three basic ways to make this decision. While you can just blindly follow the form, it is better if you spend a little time thinking about your own particular situation in order to make sure you are neither underinsured nor overinsured. The ways are:
   1. "The **income or human life value approach** in which you merely discount your income over the next few years or several years and then deduct any life insurance you presently have, either individually or through a group plan at work" (Page 278, Example 1 and Table 8.1).
   2. "The **expense or needs approach** endeavours to look more closely at each person's individual needs:
      (a) You first figure out what assets you have that you could use to provide investment income for living expenses.
      (b) Then subtract anything you owe and immediate expenses.
      (c) Next, you look at your spending requirements and what income you would have coming in.
      (d) Last, you repeat the income approach — take the present value for however many years in the future and deduct any insurance you already have" (Page 279 to 281, Example 2 and Tables 8.2A and 8.2B).
   3. "The **capital retention approach** figures out how much capital you need in order to produce enough income without touching the actual proceeds (or capital). Usually this is a very unrealistic approach and will lead to too much insurance *unless* you want to provide for someone, a child maybe, who will never be able to fully or even partially support him or herself. In that case, this one is ideal" (Page 281, Example 3).

D. "There are several ways you can **take the proceeds** (referred to as the **settlement options**) should you be the beneficiary of a life insurance policy. Since your son is only 16 and still a minor, you would have to name someone else, a trustee, to manage the money. In your will, you can dictate who should manage the proceeds and for how long. The trustee could take the following:"
   1. "A **non-taxable lump sum**. Of course, the trustee would invest this large amount of money after any liabilities and expenses have been paid. The income it produces would be taxable as it is earned" (Page 282).
   2. "The interest only through the **interest option**, leaving the capital with the insurance company to manage."
   3. "An **annuity**. Only the interest portion of the annuity is taxable each year. There are a great many options when it comes to annuities so the trustee would want to spend some time analysing possible future needs before deciding because most of the options cannot be changed once the annuity is set up" (Pages 282–283, Example 4 and Table 8.4).

E. "Life insurance policies have many common elements, such as the following (Page 284):
   1. The life insured
   2. The age of the insured

3. Joint-life policy
4. Last-to die policy
5. Grace period
6. Misstatement of age clause
7. **Riders** or optional coverages, such as:
   (a) an accelerated death benefit,
   (b) child life insurance,
   (c) guaranteed insurable, and
   (d) waiver of premium on disability
8. **Beneficiaries**:
   (a) named,
   (b) primary and contingent,
   (c) revokable and irrevocable, and
   (d) specific or class
9. And let me add a quick note on **guaranteed-issue policies**. You know, the ones you see on television that say no one is turned down and there isn't a medical. Let me just say that the premium is very high when compared to the coverage. It isn't likely anyone who has any assets would benefit from this kind of policy and, it seems to me, anyone who might benefit would find the premiums prohibitively expensive."

F. "**Temporary insurance** is **term insurance** — insurance for the short run, meaning 20 years or less. It is much, much cheaper than permanent insurance when you are young because you pay only for the insurance coverage, a **pure premium** based only on expected mortality which we will look at in more detail in Chapter 9, plus an **expense loading** for expenses and profit. However, all term policies are not the same" (Page 286):
   1. "The term can be 1, 5, 10, 15 or 20 years."
   2. "The premiums are usually **level** but can be decreasing."
   3. "**Extended or paid-up term policies** can be purchased using the cash value of a permanent insurance policy.
   4. "They usually have riders, such as:
      (a) **guaranteed convertible** to a whole life policy without evidence of insurability,
      (b) **guaranteed renewable** without a medical although the premium may not be guaranteed, and
      (c) **guaranteed continuable** at the same rate."
   5. "Notice that all **group life insurance** is term insurance" (Page 287).

G. "**Permanent insurance** is for people who want to build a savings component into their insurance premiums. It is in force for life and pays out when you die or, usually, when you reach age 100 (we should be so lucky). Because there is a savings component that accumulates in a **policy reserve** that is invested, the savings component is favourably taxed and some people use permanent insurance to save for retirement on a tax-deferred basis. There are several types of permanent insurance and many variations within each type so you need to understand what you might want it for."
   1. "**Term-to-100** is included only because it covers you until age 100 — there is no savings component to this one" (Page 288).
   2. "**Whole life** has a savings component called the **cash surrender value (CSV)** or just **cash value**. Some people take out whole life because they are terrible at saving money and this is a way to force themselves to save — you have a 31-day **grace period** to pay but you could lose your policy if you are later than that. So these people make paying these premiums a priority. These policies have several features not found in term insurance:
      (a) They are sometimes **non-participating**, meaning they do not pay 'dividends' out of the investment options, but most are **participating** and generate 'dividends'. I'll talk more about these dividends in a minute.
      (b) They can be **paid-up policies**, meaning, at a certain point, you no longer have to pay premiums but the coverage remains in place.

(c) You can take out a **policy loan** against the cash value. Some people use this feature in time of cash crunches but it is really most useful at retirement. We'll look at this more closely in Example 5.

(d) They can provide **automatic premium loans** that use the cash value to make premium payments if you miss a payment although this is hard to do these days since most premiums come out of your account automatically every month.

(e) They can allow you to skip payments, again using the cash value. This is called a **premium vacation or holiday**."

3. "**Variable life insurance policies** have fixed premiums but the death benefit and cash value vary according to the returns the reserve is able to earn" (Page 290).

4. "**Endowment life policies** pay out at some predetermined age even if the insured is still alive. Changes in the *Income Tax Act* mean the cash value and death benefit are fully taxable so they have fallen out of favour."

H. "Whole life policies generate a **dividend** that is not taxable. It is not the same as a dividend that shareholders receive on the shares, which is paid out of after-tax earnings. This dividend is paid when the earnings on the reserve are sufficient and the policyholder can receive them in many different ways" (Page 291).

1. "The least popular option is to receive in cash, well a cheque really. Since this is considered a **return of premium**, it is not taxable."

2. "More often, the dividend is **paid inside the policy** and can

(a) be invested to **earn interest income**,

(b) be used to **buy additional insurance** (paid-up additions), which increases both the death benefit and also the cash value if it buys more whole life insurance, or

(c) To buy paid-up term insurance that increases only the death benefit."

3. "**Universal life policies** can use the dividend to buy **segregated funds**."

4. "Before we look at a policy illustration to see how one whole life policy works, there are concepts you need to understand:

(a) The **net amount at risk** for the insurance company is the difference between the death benefit and the reserve. If you die, the insurer pays the death benefit and keeps the reserve, including the cash surrender value. So the net amount at risk is the net amount the insurer would have to pay out of its own pocket if you die. This amount is the basis for calculating the insurer's **net cost of pure insurance (NCPI)**, which we will look at shortly and is included on this illustration" (Page 293, Example 5 and Table 8.5A).

(b) **Guaranteed** means just that — the policy must provide the cash value and death benefit shown.

(c) **Non-guaranteed** depends on the rate of return earned by the reserve. There will be a **primary example** and one or two more showing the results if returns are less than the primary example.

   i. Notice that the death benefit and cash value is the *total* for both the guaranteed and non-guaranteed parts of the policy.

(d) Let's look more closely at the total cash value and total death benefit. I have added some columns shown shaded that are not on the illustration to clarify what is going on.

   i. Notice that the guaranteed cash value is zero for the first six years but the additional insurance is generating a cash value from the beginning (Page 294, Table 8.5B).

(e) The next bit is complicated but important if you want to understand why only *some* of the cash value is taxable if you cancel (**surrender**) the policy and take the cash surrender value shown in Table 8.5C (Page 296).

   i. For the insurance company, the **net cost of pure insurance (NCPI)** is
     • the probability of death × the net amount at risk, which equals
     • the death benefit — the reserve.

      ii. The **adjusted cost base (ACB)** is
- the amount you have paid over and above the cost of providing just the death benefit, which equals
- the annual premium — the NCPI.

      iii. When the **cumulative ACB** is
- greater than the cumulative or total CSV, none of the CSV is taxable (Column O2).
- positive, the taxable portion is the total CSV — the cumulative ACB.
- negative (Column N1), the **entire CSV is taxable** (Column O2) but this does not occur until Year 50 of the policy when this man is, by now, 80 years old."

    5. "One last thing. There is a rule in the *Income Tax Act* that limits the amount of the savings component since it is accumulating before tax. Policies that meet this rule are called **exempt policies** and if they don't, if they are **non-exempt policies**, the excess gain is taxable annually."

I. "Now let's compare the cost of temporary and permanent insurance because the differences explain why people buy term insurance. It is so much less money if you are young and your need is only temporary, for, say, 10 or 20 years as opposed to your whole life" (Pages 297–298, Example 6 and Tables 8.6A and 8.6B).

    1. She now shows Joanne what it would cost to buy $600,000 of insurance, basing it on the insurance needs of Joanne and Don from Examples 1, 2, and 3.

      (a) For added emphasis, she provides a graph.

      (b) To provide further insight, she calculates the present value of the premiums for each policy if the policy is held for

        i. 20 years (Table 8.6C), where term is by far the cheapest, and

        ii. as long as possible (Table 8.6D), where term becomes hideously expensive.

      (c) And yes, term-to-100 is cheaper than whole life if you keep the policy in force until age 100 but there is no CSV.

J. Now Francesca wants to show Joanne *la pièce de résistance* — using a policy loan to finance retirement (Pages 300–301, Example 7 and Table 8.7).

K. "**Universal life** is for people who want to invest time and energy in their life insurance. It is flexible — you can change the face value, the investments, the premiums, sometimes you can automatically add insureds. But it is only for people who want to think about their insurance coverage once it is in place. It also has a CSV" (Pages 301–302).

L. "Let's quickly compare the main features of each of the four type of policies we have looked at and also the advantages and disadvantages of each" (Pages 303–304, Tables 8.8 and 8.9).

M. "I know you're running out of steam but I want to provide you with information on **segregated funds** with a comparison to mutual funds because very few people who don't work with them really understand the similarities and differences." (Page 304).

    1. "First of all, a segregated fund is an **individual variable annuity contract**, an insurance policy that is invested in a trust which, in turn invests in funds similar to mutual funds. For example, a **fixed income segregated fund policy**, would invest in a **fixed income fund (trust)** that in turn would invest in a variety of **fixed income products**". (Chart on Page 304).

    2. "You may not be a fan of mutual funds because the **management expense ratio (MER)** is very high in Canada and it is even higher for seg funds because it has to finance the insurance or guaranteed portion but if you want the investment baskets and convenience that mutual funds can provide, you need to know that seg funds have two advantages over mutual funds:

      (a) Seg funds provide a **guarantee of the capital** — the amount you invest (provided you leave the money in them for the guarantee period).

(b) Seg funds are protected from creditors (**creditor proofed**) in most circumstances."
3. "Seg funds and mutual funds have several **similarities**:
    (a) Both provide professional money management.
    (b) Both are eligible investments for non-registered savings, registered savings, and registered retirement income plans.
    (c) Both provide diversified investment options.
    (d) Both charge an annual management fee, the MER, and the quoted rate of return is usually *before* the MER is deducted."
4. "But there are differences between them, also as summarized in Table 8.10."
5. "There is a slight difference in the way they are taxed. But first you need to understand that income **flows through**, that is, it **retains its nature** so that, for instance, dividend income from taxable Canadian corporations received by the fund and paid out to the owner is taxable to the owner as dividend income from a taxable Canadian corporation and is, therefore, eligible for the dividend tax credit. Likewise with capital gains.
    (a) However, capital losses flow through with seg funds while mutual funds have to be applied against capital gains to be used.
    (b) And people don't think about this but income *never flows through registered plans*. Tax advantages of dividend and capital gains are lost when they are earned in registered plans since *all income from registered plans is 100% taxable*."
6. "Now I'll illustrate the similarities and differences with an example. You have to understand that this example is quite contrived in that these funds would never cost and pay out exactly the same but I want to keep it somewhat simple so you can see how they work" (Pages –311, Example 8 and Table 8.12).

Concept Questions

1. What is the goal of life insurance?

2. What is the fundamental objective of life insurance?

3. What three questions does an individual need to ask before agreeing to purchase life insurance from a sales agent?

4. Describe briefly how the human life value approach calculates the required amount of life insurance for an individual.

5. Compare the expense approach in determining how much life insurance is required with the income approach.

6. List and describe the three types of permanent life insurance.

7. Martin, 67, and Mary, 68, are living comfortably on their company pensions and the survivor will receive 60% of the deceased's pension when the first one dies. Their only asset is their home — a principal residence that is not subject to capital gains tax.
    (a) Do they need life insurance?
    (b) Should they have bought life insurance to save for their retirement?

8. Mark's wife dies and he is named as the beneficiary in her life insurance policy. He elects to have the insurance policy pay him in a lump sum. Is the lump sum payment taxable?

9. Describe the interest option that is available to beneficiaries when the insured dies.

10. What are the two ways of amortizing annuities for tax purposes? What is the difference between them?

11. What are the two fundamental determinants of annuities?

12. List and define the seven main types of annuities.

13. What type of permanent life insurance policy can invest in a segregated fund?

14. Johann has made his estate the beneficiary on his life insurance policy. Johann has a small business that is constantly short of working capital. Is his life insurance policy creditor-proof?

15. Under what conditions would creditors have access to insurance policy proceeds?

16. What is an accelerated death benefit rider? What is its other name?

17. What is the difference between the following:
    (a) A primary and contingent beneficiary?
    (b) A revokable and an irrevokable beneficiary?
    (c) A specific beneficiary and a named beneficiary?

18. Annie lives in a rooming house on only very meager government pensions. She sees an ad on television for life insurance and thinks it would be nice to buy one of these policies so she can leave the money to the Humane Society when she dies since she is very fond of cats but cannot afford to have one. What is the name of this type of policy? Should she buy it? Why or why not?

19. Term insurance is cheaper then whole life insurance for a 23-year-old student. Is this statement true? Why or why not?

20. Define *pure premium* and *pure cost of insurance*.

21. Describe the difference between level and decreasing premiums found in term insurance.

22. Mildred wants a term policy that she can renew at the same premium she is now paying. Does she want a rider that is guaranteed convertible, guaranteed renewable, or guaranteed continuable?

23. What is the major advantage and disadvantage of group term insurance?

24. What is a policy reserve? Does it remain level throughout the length of the whole life policy?

25. What is the name of a whole life policy in which the insured pays premiums for a specified number of years and the coverage remains in place until the insured dies?

26. Describe how insurance policies can accrue and pay dividends? Are these dividends taxable?

27. Darlene, age 35, wants to buy a whole life policy. Would you expect she would pay a lower rate with a straight life policy whereby she pays premiums until she dies or a paid-up-at-age-50 policy? Why?

28. In a whole life policy, what balance dictates how much you could borrow in the form of a policy loan?

29. What is meant by a premium vacation?

30. Doug's policy has been in place for six years and he feels he has enough coverage. However, his agent is suggesting he get different coverage and can arrange for Doug to not pay premiums for at least three years without telling Doug that the current cash value will be used to pay the premiums for the three years. What is the name of this practice? Is it legal?

31. What is a new money life insurance policy?

32. Are the proceeds from an endowment life insurance policy taxable in Canada?

33. Andrea is going to use the dividends from her whole life policy to buy more permanent insurance.
    (a) Could she receive the dividends and use them to pay the premiums on another policy?

(b) If she leaves the dividends in the reserve and uses them to buy additional insurance, what is the name of the additional insurance?

34. What is the load in an insurance policy?

35. What is the name of the legal reserve in the *Income Tax Act*?

36. What are the following and do they get larger over the life of the policy?
    (a) The amount at risk for the insurer
    (b) The net amount at risk
    (c) Cost of pure insurance

37. Are the cash values and death benefits in all policy illustrations guaranteed? Why or why not?

38. Using Example 5, Table 8.5A, after 20 years
    (a) what are the total premiums paid? (Answer: $213,840)
    (b) How much is the guaranteed
        i. CSV? (Answer: $147,000)
        ii. Death benefit? (Answer: $600,000)
    (c) How much is the total
        i. CSV? (Answer: $360,484)
        ii. Death benefit? (Answer: $1,437,190)
    (d) On what does the non-guaranteed portion depend?

39. Using Example 5, Table 8.5B, in the 20th year, how much of each of the following was added:
    (a) Guaranteed CSV? (Answer: $14,400)
    (b) Non-guaranteed? (Answer: $26,800)
    (c) Guaranteed death benefits (Answer: $0)
    (d) Non-guaranteed death benefit? (Answer: $72,091)

40. Using Example 5, Table 8.5C, in the 20th year, answer the following:
    (a) What is the net cost of pure insurance? (Answer: $2,562)
    (b) What is the adjusted cost base? (Answer: $8,130)
        i. How is it calculated? (Answer: premiums for year 20 $10,692 — NCPI for year 20 $2,562)
    (c) What is the
        i. total (cumulative) cash value? (Answer: $360,484)
        ii. cumulative adjusted cost base? (Answer: $194,747)
    (d) If the policyholder gives up the policy (surrenders it) at year 20 and collects the $360,484 cash value,
        i. How much of the CSV is taxable? (Answer: $165,737)
        ii. How is this taxable amount calculated? (Answer: Total cash value $360,484 — cumulative ACB $194,747)
    (e) Does the taxable amount ever equal the total CSV? If yes, when and why? (Answer: Yes, in the 50th year of the policy when the cumulative ACB becomes negative).

41. What is an exempt policy exempt from and why is it exempt?

42. Using Example 6 and:
    (a) Table 8.6A, compared to a female non-smoker, how much does a
        i. male non-smoker pay for a 10-year policy (Answer: 180%)
        ii. male smoker pay for a 10-year term policy? (Answer: 283%)
    (b) Table 8.6B, how much does a male smoker, age 62, pay for:
        i. a 10 year term policy? (Answer: $16,788)
        ii. a term-to-100 policy? (Answer: $3,054)
        iii. a whole life policy? ($3,396)

43. What can you do with a universal life insurance policy that you cannot do with other permanent life insurance policies?

44. List and describe four ways a beneficiary can receive death benefits from universal life insurance policies.

45. What are the advantages and disadvantages of whole life insurance policies?

46. What are the advantages and disadvantages of term insurance policies?

47. What type of annuity contract is a segregated fund?

48. What are the other three names for the owner of a segregated fund?

49. How is an open-end mutual fund different from a closed-end mutual fund? What is the name of the market value of the fund?

50. What are the two main differences between a mutual fund and a segregated fund?

51. What are the four ways that segregated funds and mutual funds are similar?

52. In comparing segregated funds and mutual funds,
    (a) is there a guaranteed minimum value for both at death?
    (b) do they both provide a death benefit?
    (c) are both exempt from probate fees when the owner dies?
    (d) which has the higher MER, everything else being equal.

53. What does it mean that income "flows through"?

54. What are unrealized capital losses?

55. When the fund pays out income to the owner, what is the payout called for
    (a) segregated funds?
    (b) mutual funds?

56. When income is re-invested, what increases for a
    (a) segregated Fund?
    (b) mutual Fund?

57. What type of income can a segregated fund flow through that a mutual fund cannot flow through?

58. Are the payouts taxable to the owner if they are reinvested?

Application Questions

59. Chris and Christina have two children: Steven, 4, and Stephanie, 5. Both Chris and Christina work in construction, an occupational field which is considered quite dangerous. They wish to purchase life insurance but they don't know how much they need. Using the following information, calculate their required amount of life insurance using the income approach.
    (a) They want to have at least enough money, in case of any one of their deaths, to have their children attend university debt free.
    (b) The kids will finish university in about 15 years.
    (c) The real rate of interest in Canada is about 3%.
    (d) Chris makes $95,000 a year with take-home pay of $66,500.
    (e) Christina makes $100,000 a year with take-home pay of $70,000.
    (f) They live in Alberta so they have the same marginal tax rate of 30%.
    (g) They have insurance coverage at work that will pay them twice their gross annual salary if they die. (Answer: Chris — $627,689 or 630,000, Christine — 660,725 or 660,000).

60. Chris and Christina from the previous question have the following assets:

	If	Christina dies, Chris has	Chris dies, Christina has
Assets			
Bank accounts		$ 6,000	$ 2,000
Savings for emergencies		20,000	15,000
Group life insurance		200,000	190,000
Individual life insurance		0	0
CPP death benefits		2,500	2,500
RRSPs		30,000	53,000
Investments (stocks, bonds, mutual funds)		0	0
Other financial assets		0	0
		258,500	262,500
Liabilities			
Funeral expenses		15,000	15,000
Consumer debt		20,000	23,000
Mortgages, other non-life-insured loans		0	0
Contingency fund		10,000	10,000
		45,000	48,000
Available Capital		213,500	215,500

Assume the following:
- (a) Their present total annual expenses are $116,000.
- (b) There are cost savings if one dies because the deceased no longer needs clothes, food, a car, etc. However, there will also be higher expenses because the deceased filled a role in the family and the household duties of the deceased will have to be provided by the surviving spouse and also by paying for them — child care costs, buying groceries, dropping off dry cleaning, housework, and yard chores, etc. Let's add $20,000 a year to their expenses for added costs over and above the cost savings.
- (c) They have mortgage insurance so the mortgage is paid off, meaning the remaining spouse will have lower expenses of about $14,000 a year.
- (d) Both work at jobs that have pensions. If one dies, their required retirement income will be less but not half. We will add the annual contribution that each and their employer now makes to the required annual income of the survivor to provide a bit of a cushion (both employer and employee each contribute 6% of their gross salary to their company pension plans — add 12%).
- (e) We are assuming they are already using some of their take-home pay to, for instance, save for retirement and their children's education so these have not been added to their future needs.
- (f) CPP Survivor benefit will be $5,500 before tax for both of them.
- (g) CPP Children benefit is $4,600 before tax.
- (h) Both CPP Survivor and Children are taxable at marginal rate. Calculate the amount of insurance that each of them require using the expense approach.

  (Answer: on Chris — $478,138 or $480,000, on Christina — $529,552 or $530,000)

61. Chris and Christina believe they can earn a 5% real rate of return on their capital. How much insurance would they need to have to cover their annual shortfall without using up the capital? (Answer: Chris $995,100, Christina $912,100)

62. Ronald dies of a heart attack. His wife Rolanda decides she will choose the annuity settlement option. She selects an annuity term of 10 years on which the insurer will give a 5% rate of return. The payments will occur at the beginning of each year. The policy is for $500,000. Create an amortization schedule for this annuity.
    - (a) How much interest is paid in Year 3? (Answer: $19,929)
    - (b) If Rolanda treats the annuity as a prescribed annuity for tax purposes, how much interest will she pay tax on in Year 3? (Answer: $11,668.80)

63. Janice uses her $1,000,000 life insurance policy as collateral for a $300,000 loan from the bank. Her husband, Rico, is the named beneficiary on the policy. Janice dies before she can

pay back the loan. How much will Rico get from the insurance proceeds? (Answer: $700,000) Why?

64. Farha is 52. Her husband recently died, leaving a $25,000 life insurance policy to her. Her stepson is beginning his last year of university, and will move out and be independent within two years. Farha does not have vast amounts of money available to purchase life insurance. What type of life insurance policy would you recommend and why?

65. James purchased a whole life insurance policy 10 years ago, which now has a cash surrender value of $15,000. He is considering cashing in the policy to purchase SPINERS, which is a special type of tire rim for his Cadillac Truck. Over the policy period he has paid $4,000 in policy premiums. What will be the after-tax cash surrender value of the policy if the net cost of pure insurance is $750? His marginal tax rate is 20%. ($12,650)

66. Using Example 6, Table 8.6C, compare the cost of insurance if the policies are held for 10 years. (Answer: Female Non Smoker: $2,109, $15,024, $18,293. Male Smoker: $5,957, $26,833, $29,838)

Insurance Operations

Objectives

After completing this chapter, students will:

A. Know how insurance companies operate.

B. Understand how insurance companies calculate insurance premiums.

C. Be able to read insurance financial statements.

Introduction

Insurance operations have many facets that are unique to the insurance industry. Insurance operations encompass the following:

- Underwriting — the process of selecting and classifying applicants for insurance
- Claims settlement — the process of validating and paying claims
- Production — the sales and marketing activities of insurers
- Rate making — the process of setting insurance premiums

Insurance companies have many kinds of liabilities that are primarily large reserves for future claims. The liabilities for life and health insurers in particular are extremely long-term compared to the liabilities of other financial institutions and other industries. Property and casualty insurers also need large reserves to pay the occasional large or even huge claim when they are collecting a relatively small, annual premium. As a result, accounting practices and investment restrictions in the insurance industry reflect the special nature of their liabilities.

Underwriting

Underwriting is the process of selecting and classifying risk exposures in order to determine the appropriate rate to charge policyholders in various categories of risk. Insurance companies have underwriting principles by which they select and categorize applicants for insurance. We have looked at underwriting principles and forbidden practices in auto and home insurance.

Underwriting Principles

Underwriting principles provide guidelines so insurance companies can do the following:

1. Select insureds according to the **company's underwriting standards**. This was discussed in Chapter 3, Auto Insurance, where we saw insurance rates that made it evident that some companies prefer not to insure certain classes of drivers at all by charging very high rates.
2. Have a **proper balance within each rate classification**. While insurers try to put similar risk exposures together in the same category, some risk exposures will produce higher losses than average while others produce fewer. In both auto and home insurance, we saw that there are many criteria that insurers use to categorize policyholders. *A priori* (before the event), an insurer cannot know whether or not it has classified each policyholder correctly. However, the insurer attempts to classify insureds so that the actual loss experience will not vary greatly from the expected loss experience.

3. **Provide equity among policyholders** so that one group of policyholders does not unduly subsidize another group. If, on average, 20-year-old men have higher accident rates than 50-year-old men, the insurer will charge a 20-year-old man a higher premium even though it cannot know for certain that the final cost for the 20-year-old will be higher than for the 50-year-old. The insurer knows that the actual loss experience for an individual will be different from the expected loss experience for the group but it attempts to minimize the difference.

The principle of **adverse selection** states that those who have a greater-than-average risk of producing a loss tend to try to seek insurance more often than people who are average or less-than-average risk. This is particularly true in group insurance plans when employees have a choice about participating — those employees who are most likely to make a claim will, if given a choice, join a group insurance plan since they cannot get other insurance elsewhere or cannot get it at a better rate. Thus, while group insurance is cheaper than individual insurance, due to adverse selection it is not as cheap as one might expect since underwriters adjust group rates to reflect this adverse selection.

Rate Categories

Insurance companies have categories for policyholders and a potential policyholder may be unacceptable at one rate but acceptable at a higher rate. Generally, insurers charge the least premium they can to remain competitive and still charge each policyholder an appropriate premium.

- **Standard rates** are charged to policyholders who meet the company's average underwriting standards.
- Policyholders who are more risky will be charged a surcharge as they are **sub-standard risks**. The obvious example is charging smokers more than non-smokers for both disability and life insurance policies. These policies are called **rated policies** since the insured presents a higher than normal risk due to occupation, a hobby, or their health. The surcharge might be a flat rate — 10% or $50, for example.
- Some policyholders fall in the **preferred-risk category** — having smoke detectors and/or fire extinguishers in one's home or living close to a fire station might put a homeowner in this category since these can reduce the size of a loss if not the frequency.

Process of Underwriting

There are three steps in the underwriting process:

1. The **application** is filled in by the potential policyholder although the agent or broker may actually fill in the blanks based on information provided by the applicant. The applicant is expected to provide full, complete information — misinformation or deliberately omitted information can be the basis for voiding a policy at a later date.
2. The **agent or broker** may be able to provide additional information or validate the information on the application if the agent or broker has been involved with the applicant before. If the applicant is not known and the agent or broker has a reputation with the insurer of providing reliable applicants, the insurer may accept an applicant that would otherwise be rejected.
3. Additional information can be solicited from an external source:
   - It is the norm for insurance companies to obtain a report from a provincial motor vehicle licensing agency to check on the driving history and current status of applicants. They may or may not re-check at the time of renewal.
   - Insurers can send inspectors to check the premises or to do drive-by inspections to see if the general description is correct for a homeowner's policy.
   - They also can ask for a medical report from one's family doctor, which will include a question about how long the applicant has been a patient of the doctor.

If the policy is renewable or cancellable, the **renewal underwriting** process will re-check the assumptions under which the policy was written. At this point, the insurer may cancel the policy if possible, or may renew but at a higher rate or with a higher deductible.

Claims Settlement

Settling claims is called **loss adjustment** and involves

* verifying that a loss is covered,
* providing fair and prompt payment of claims while resisting unjust claims and overpayments, and
* assisting the insured by, for instance, helping the insured find temporary living space after a fire.

The employees in a claims department are called

* **claim representatives** or **benefit representatives** in life and health insurance companies, and
* **adjusters** in property and liability insurance where claims require more assessment and evaluation (except for disability claims, which require a great deal of monitoring and assessment).

It is the job of the adjuster to assess the facts of the claim and the extent of the coverage. There are several types of adjusters in addition to the employees of insurance companies:

* Some agents can settle small claims.
* **Independent adjusters** work for several insurance companies on a contract basis.
* **Adjustment bureaus** are adjusting organizations and are often used for catastrophic losses such as tornados where there are many losses to settle.
* **Public adjusters** represent the insureds, not the insurers. Their fee is based on the amount of the settlement.

In **health and disability insurance**, there can be coverage by more than one insurer, for instance through group plans of both spouses. In this circumstance, there are **co-insurance requirements** that decide which insurer pays how much.

* The **primary insurer** pays first and the **excess insurer** pays above the policy limits of the primary insurer.
  * There is often a **coordination-of-benefits provision** in group insurance policies to prevent double payments. If a person is covered under more than one policy, his or her own insurer is usually primary. The maximum that can be paid is 100% of the expense.
  * For children, there is often a **birthday rule** — the insurer of the parent whose birthday occurs first during the year is primary.
* **Contribution by equal shares** means that when there is more than one insurer, each insurer pays equally to the limits of the coverage.
* **Pro rata liability** clause means that when two or more policies are in place, each pays in proportion to the total amount of insurance.
* The **second payor** means the amount of the benefit is reduced by the amount of benefit under other policies covering the same risks. For example, employment insurance benefit is second payor to Canada Pension Plan disability benefit and Workers' Comp but not to individual policies. Thus, if a person is collecting EI benefits, CPP disability benefits or Workers' Comp benefits are subtracted from the EI benefit but benefits from an individual disability policy are not subtracted.

Production

Production for insurers is their sales and marketing activities. Since the sales force is often an agent or broker who is not an employee of the insurer, it is important that the limits and parameters of the agent or broker's authority and responsibilities are clearly defined.

* **Express authority** is specifically conferred, meaning the agent has the authority through the **agency agreement** to act on behalf of the insurance company. The agency agreement between agent and **principal** (the insurance company) outlines the agent's authority. For example, a life insurance agent may have the right to solicit applicants and set up medical examinations but does not have the authority to alter provisions in the contract or to extend the time for paying premiums. **Agency relationship** means the agent acts on behalf of the principal (the insurer).

- **Implied authority** means the agent has the authority to perform all incidental acts necessary to fulfill the purposes of the agency agreement. If an agent has the authority to deliver the contract, the implication is that the agent also has the authority to collect the first premium.
- **Apparent authority** means that if a third party believes an agent has certain authority, the principal is bound by the agent's actions — if the agent acts beyond his or her authority, the courts will rule that apparent authority existed if
  - the insurer did not try to stop the agent from overstepping his or her authority, and
  - the buyer had no way of knowing that the agent was overstepping his or her authority.
  For example, if an applicant for home insurance is told the coverage is in place and it turns out the insurer rejected the applicant and the applicant suffered a loss before finding out there was no insurance in place, the insurer is bound by the agent's apparent authority.

There is no presumption of an agency relationship — **presumptive agency** means there must be some evidence that an agency relationship exists, meaning an applicant cannot just take someone's word for it that an agent is an agent. The agent must provide some evidence — blank applications and the rate book of the insurer, for instance. If someone has that evidence, the principal (insurer) is responsible for the acts of agents acting within the scope of employment, and through presumptive agency, the insurance company cannot claim an agency relationship did not exist.

Agents and Brokers

An **agent** legally represents the insurer and has the authority to act on behalf of one insurance company, that is, an agent is an **exclusive agent** for one insurer or a group of related companies. Agents are also referred to as **captive insurance agents** and **career insurance agents**.

A **broker** is an independent agent who legally represents the insured and sells for more than one company. A broker does not have the authority to bind the insured — the broker can solicit the business and place it with an insurer but the insurance is not in place until the insurer accepts the business.

Property and casualty insurance is sold both by agents and brokers. Insurance companies sell:

- Life insurance only
- Life and accident & sickness (A&S)
- Personal lines and A&S
- Commercial lines and A&S

Licensing and Education

Insurance brokers, agents, and independent adjusters must be licensed by provincial regulatory bodies to conduct business. Licensing requirements vary between provinces.

A **life and health agent** (also called a representative or salesperson) is licensed in life insurance, which requires the **Full Life Licence Qualification Program (LLQP)** and includes Accident & Sickness only, which requires the **LLQP — Accident & Sickness (A&S)**. The full LLQP allows an agent to sell life, disability, A & S, critical illness insurance, and segregated funds. Life and health insurance is mostly sold through agents in Canada except for Accident & Sickness coverage which some P&C agents and brokers also sell.

A **property and casualty/general insurance salesperson** can be licensed as

- an agent, and the licence is called a **general licence** or **OTL (other than life) licence**, or
- a broker.

An insurance licensee can be an agent for one line of insurance, for example auto insurance and a broker for other personal lines of insurance, such as homeowners, tenants, and condominium insurance. However, a licensee cannot hold a licence as both a general agent and a broker in one line, that is, a person cannot be an independent representing more than one insurer and also be an agent representing only one.

The **Canadian Council of Insurance Regulators (CCIR)** [www.ccir-ccrra.org] is made up of insurance regulators from all provinces and territories to harmonize insurance policy and regulation across jurisdictions.

Table 9.1   Insurance Regulators and Licensing Bodies

	Regulators — Regular Members of CCIR	Licensing
AB	Insurance and Financial Institutions, Alberta Finance	Alberta Insurance Council
BC	Insurance Financial Institutions Commission	Insurance Council of British Columbia
MB	Financial Institutions Regulation Branch	Insurance Council of Manitoba
NB	Department of Justice	Insurance Branch
NL	Department of Government Services	Consumer and Commercial Affairs Branch, Financial Services Regulation Division
NS	Department of Environment and Labour	Financial Institutions Division
NT, NU	Department of Finance, Government of the Northwest Territories	Treasury Division
ON	Financial Services Commission of Ontario	Agents: Financial Services Commission of Ontario P&C Brokers: Registered Insurance Brokers of Ontario
PE	Office of the Attorney General	Department of Community Services
QC	*Autorité des marchés financiers*	*Chambre de l'assurance de dommages*
SK	Saskatchewan Financial Services Commission, Financial Institutions Division	Insurance Councils of Saskatchewan (there are three Councils — General, Hail, and Life)
YT	Department of Community Services	Consumer Service

Source: Associate Member: Federal Government — Office of the Superintendent of Financial Institutions Canada

CCIR developed the **education requirements** for the **LLQP**, which is the same across Canada. Several colleges and private institutions offer the LLQP in a different format from CCIR but the content is the same. The following table outlines the topics in both the full LLQP and LLQP — A&S.

Table 9.2   Education Requirements for Life and Health Licensing

Full LLQP	Accident & Sickness (A&S)
1. Insurance Industry Overview	1. Insurance Industry Overview
2. Life Insurance Products	
3. Individual Disability and Accident & Sickness Insurance Products	3. Individual Disability and Accident & Sickness Insurance Products
4. Group Insurance Products • General • Group Life Insurance • Group Disability Insurance • Group A&S Insurance • Other Types of Group Insurance	4. Group Insurance Products Only Group A&S Insurance
5. Investment Products	
6. Underwriting, Issues, and Claims	6. Underwriting, Issues, and Claims
7. Taxation	
8. Retirement Planning	
9. Needs Analysis/Risk Management	
10. Common/Contract Law Statues	10. Common/Contract Law Statues
11. Professional Standards	11. Professional Standards

Licensing requirements for P&C agents and brokers vary by jurisdiction. As a result, the education requirements are not the same in all provinces and territories and some provinces do not have education requirements — only examination requirements. All jurisdictions have more than one level of licensing for brokers and *may* have more than one level for agents. In addition, there is more than one education requirement for each level. The education requirements include courses developed by

* the **Insurance Institute of Canada (IIC)** [www.insuranceinstitute.ca] and offered by local chapters of the Insurance Institute of Canada and several community colleges,
* the **Insurance Brokers Association of Canada (IBAC)** [www.ibac.ca] and offered by provincial brokers associations and several community colleges.

In Ontario, this is further complicated by the fact that *agents* are licensed by the **Financial Services Commission of Ontario (FSCO)** [www.fsco.gov.on.ca] while *brokers* are licensed by the **Registered Insurance Brokers of Ontario (RIBO)** [www.ribo.com]. A general insurance broker in Ontario *must* pass the RIBO *exam* but can take *either*

* the Broker Preparation Courses, RIBO Levels I and II from the **Insurance Brokers Association of Ontario (IBAO)**, *or*
* RIBO Preparation Courses from the **Insurance Institute of Ontario (IIO)**.

Acceptable courses and programs for agents and brokers vary by jurisdiction but include some or all of the following for the various licensing levels:

* **General Insurance Essential (GIE)** Courses C81 and C82 developed by the Insurance Institute of Canada, and/or
* **Canadian Accredited Insurance Broker (CAIB)** program, which is a national designation designed by the Insurance Brokers Association of Canada (IBAC). It contains four courses.

General Insurance Essentials covers the following topics and is provided to give an understanding of the breadth of the program. The courses in the CAIB program cover similar topics in more detail.

Table 9.3   Topics in General Insurance Essentials (GIE)

C81 GIE Part 1	C82 GIE Part 2
• Introducing the insurance business • Insurance intermediaries • The insurance company — the insurer • Basic documents, common clauses, insurance practices • Automobile insurance — the application • The automobile policy — third-party liability, automobile accident benefits, loss of or damage to the insured automobile • Government automobile insurance plans	• The law and insurance • Insurance contracts • Government control; insurance organizations and associations • Fire insurance; the homeowner's policy • Other personal lines policies • Liability insurance • Commercial coverages — property, business interruption, crime, surety, claims, and loss adjustments • Reinsurance • Risk management • Loss prevention

The insurance industry is large and offers employment at many levels. Some licences require that a person be employed and/or sponsored by an insurance company, agency or broker before he or she can take the courses but others do not.

Table 9.4   Number Employed in the Insurance Industry

Property and Casualty 2007		Life and Health, 2007	
Insurance companies	44,253	Administration	46,200
Brokers	58,038	Agents working for 1 company	73,300
Independent adjusters and appraisers	6,344	Independent agents	6,100
	108,635		125,600
Reinsurers	1,500		
	110,135		

Sources: *IBC FACTS 2009 for Property and Casualty, CLHIA FACTS 2008 for Life and Health*

Commissions

The commission paid to an agent or broker is a percentage of the premium before provincial sales tax (PST). For agents, the commission is higher on new policies than on renewals. However, for brokers, this provides an incentive to move an insured from insurer to insurer and the commission to them reflects it — it is the same for both new policies and renewals.

Rate Making — Insurance Pricing

Insurance pricing or rate making has three objectives:

- The rates must be adequate to prevent the insurer from becoming insolvent.
- The rates should not be excessive so that insureds are paying too much for coverage.
- The rates should not unfairly discriminate — rates should be based on underwriting principles that are fair and objective and not unfair and subjective (based on race or religion, for instance).

Rates are determined by actuaries who analyse past data in order to classify insureds into predictable loss categories. There are several steps in the development of the rate the policyholder pays. Rates are applied differently for different lines of insurance:

- Life insurance is a rate for every $1,000 of coverage.
- Fire insurance and workers' compensation are for every $100 of coverage. Sample Workers' Compensation rates were shown in Chapter 7.

Rates are developed in different ways:

- In life insurance, the rate is based on mortality tables, which predict how many people will die each year at each age from age 0 to age 109. Rate making for life insurance is covered in the next section.
- Other types of insurance use specific factors as described in the chapters on auto and home insurance. These factors also apply to disability and health insurance in that there are specific factors that affect loss experiences:
  - Families with children will generally use more dental insurance benefits than families without children.
  - People who work in construction are more likely to collect disability insurance than someone who works in an insurance office.
  - Homes that are frame and joined together (row houses and townhouses) are more likely to suffer large losses than homes that are brick and detached.

Rate Making in Property and Liability Insurance

There are two basic ways of calculating insurance rates.

1. Class or manual rating which applies to a class of risk exposures. There are two methods:
   (a) Pure premium method, based on total claims and number of insureds, and
   (b) Loss ratio method, based on an adjustment to reflect actual claims.

2. Individual or merit rating, which reflects the loss experience of the individual risk. There are four methods:
   (a) Experience rating uses the loss-ratio method adjusted for the actual experience for each insured based on the past three years.
   (b) Judgment rating rates each risk exposure individually.
   (c) Schedule rating rates each risk individually using a base and adding charges based on the characteristics of the risk exposure.
   (d) Retrospective rating sets the actual premium after the period of coverage is over.

1. Class Rating

Class rating or **manual rating** places similar insureds in the same underwriting class and each insured is charged the same rate. This method is simple to apply and ideal for putting large groups of people into similar categories. For example, life insurance companies may apply the same ratings to insured individuals who are similar in age, are in good health, and are non-smokers. There are two methods of rating by class.

(a) Pure Premium Method

This method calculates a rate based on total claims and number of insureds. The **pure premium** is the portion of the premium that covers the benefits of the policy — the cost of the claims including **adjusting expenses,** which are called **adjusting losses,** but not expenses (commissions and administration) and profit. The pure premium is also referred to as the **net premium.** Let's use an example of an auto insurer who, for a certain class, has **losses (claims)** of $7,500,000 and there are 10,000 in this class of drivers.

The **pure premium** is the cost to cover all the losses that this class must pay:

Losses	÷	Exposure Units	=	Pure/net premium
$7,500,000	÷	10,000	=	$750

The **gross premium** is the price to the consumer and it covers all costs and profit. It is the net premium plus the **expense loading** to cover administrative costs, selling costs, and profits. The expense loading is generally expressed as a percentage of the **gross rate** and is called the **expense ratio.** In this example, the expense loading is 40%, comprised of 30% for expenses and 10% for profit. The gross premium is obtained by dividing the pure premium by (one minus the expense ratio):

Pure premium	÷	1 − Expense ratio	=	Gross premium
$750	÷	0.6	=	$1,250
Loss ratio	+	Expense ratio	=	Gross premium
60%	+	40%	=	100%

In Table 9.22, the financial statements for an insurance company are constructed using the same loss ratio and the expense ratio used here.

On Financial Statements	In Rate Making
Losses incurred 60% of premiums *earned*	**Loss ratio** = losses incurred ÷ premiums earned = 60%
Expenses incurred 30% of premiums *written*	Expense ratio = (expenses incurred + profit) ÷ premiums written = 40%

The **expense ratio** includes expected profit to calculate the gross rate (and the gross premium) for each policy but includes only expenses when calculated on the financial results. The terminology around the premium is also confusing because it differs depending on whether one is referring to the premium for an individual person or to the total premium income for a company. However, there is a relationship between them. Let's review the calculations we have just done and also set the stage for the financial statements in Tables 9.22 and 9.23.

Total Class		Individual	
Losses	$7,500,000		
÷ # of Exposure Units	÷ 10,000		
= **Pure premium**	= **$750**	$750 60% **+ Pure Premium** = Loses + Loss Adjusting Expenses	
÷ (1 – Expense Ratio)	÷ (1 – 40%)	500 40% **+ Expense Loading** = Sales & Administration	
		expenses + 10% before-tax Profit	
= **Gross Premium** (on 1 car)	= **$1,250**	$1,250 100% = **Gross Rate** = Pure Premium + Loading	

Financial Statements		Individual	
Loss ratio = Losses Incurred		60% **Loss Ratio** = Pure Premium ÷ Gross Premium	
÷ Premiums *Earned*	60%	40% **Expense Ratio** = Expense Loading ÷ Gross Premium	
Expense Ratio = Expense			
Incurred ÷ Premiums *Written*	30%		
Profit	10%		

The **terminology** about the rate can also be quite confusing so let's take a further look at it.

Rate is the price per
- exposure unit, or
- unit of protection, or
- unit of coverage.

Exposure unit is a unit of measure of the cost and is different for different types of coverage:

• fire insurance is per	$100 of coverage
• product liability insurance is per	$1,000 of sales
• auto collision insurance is per	1 car-year (1 car insured for a year)
• life insurance is per	$1,000 of protection
• Workers' Compensation is per	$100 of gross payroll

(b) Loss Ratio Method

The loss ratio method adjusts the rate to reflect the actual expenses as compared to the expected expenses. The **loss ratio** is the losses as a proportion of the premiums earned.

Expected losses	÷	Premiums earned	=	Expected loss ratio
$7,500,000	÷	$12,500,000	=	0.6

Without showing the calculation, let's suppose the *actual* loss ratio is 62%. Since the actual loss ratio of 62% is higher than the expected loss ratio of 60%, rates will have to increase.

(Actual loss ratio	–	Expected loss ratio)	÷	Expected loss ratio	=	Rate change
(0.62	–	0.60)	÷	0.6	=	3.33%

So the rate charged should increase by 3.33% from $1,250 to $1,292 to reflect the actual losses.

New rate =	$1,250	×	1.0333	=	$1,292

This method is also the basis for experience rating, below.

2. Individual or Merit Rating

Individual or merit rating reflects the risk of the individual insured.

(a) Experience Rating

Experience rating uses the loss ratio method, usually over a three-year period, and adjusts it by a **credibility factor,** which reflects the degree of confidence the insurer assigns to the insured's past experience to predict future losses.

For example, assume that Jamie is in the class illustrated above. In the past three years he has had no claims at all. So the insurer decides his rate should not go up by the same as everyone else in his class. He is assigned a credibility factor of 30% — the most this insurer will assign to anyone in this class. How much will his rate increase? By 2.33% instead of 3.33%. Presumably this is not enough of a modification to put him in another class but it will affect future rate changes.

Rate change	×	Credibility factor	=	Reduction in rate change	Rate change
3.33%	×	30%	=	1.00%	2.33%

(b) Judgment Rating

In this method, each exposure is individually evaluated and the rate is determined largely by the underwriter's judgment. This method is used if there is little historical data on which to base the possibility of a loss occurring or if the class is so diverse that a class rating cannot be calculated. This method is used most frequently in ocean marine insurance, which is faced with diverse ports, vessels, cargoes, and dangerous water.

(c) Schedule Rating

Schedule rating is based on the assumption that certain characteristics of the insured's operations are going to influence the insured's future loss experience. Therefore, rates are set by applying a schedule of charges and credits to some base rate to determine the appropriate rate for an individual exposure unit. It is used for commercial buildings whose loss exposure is increased or decreased depending on the construction, occupancy, protection (security and fire prevention features) and neighbourhood or location. For example, this method would apply to a hunting lodge, located on an island with no easy access by a fire department, having its own generator and fire hoses that can be run by the generator, is of wooden construction, and is 100 years old.

(d) Retrospective Rating

In retrospective rating, the actual premium is not determined until the period covered is over. In effect, the insured pays a premium that is really on a deposit against the actual premium. At the end of the insurance period, the insured receives a premium or has to pay additional premiums. The premium will be subject to a maximum and a minimum.

Rate Making in Life Insurance

Calculating life insurance premiums is very different from other types of premiums. For one thing, there is no experience rating — the insurer cannot change the rate once a policy for a given term is in place. Other types of insurance have large, periodic payouts the same way life insurance does. This is particularly true for liability insurance, where the liability can be difficult to predict and the insurer must rely on the "Law of Large Numbers" to predict losses for various categories of risk exposures. For all types of insurance, the rate is dependent on the risk exposure of the insured. In a way, life insurance is easier to understand because it pays out only in one circumstance — the insured's death.

The **pure premium** for a life insurance policy is the probability of dying (called the **rate of mortality**) times the face value of the policy. The probability of dying is found in **mortality tables,** which show the probability of living and dying for various classes of people and is calculated by looking at historical data. In this chapter, we will use only two classes — males and females.

The **gross premium** is calculated in the same way as the class premium above for the pure insurance portion of the premium. With permanent insurance such as whole life, which has a **savings component**, the savings component is also added to arrive at the gross premium.

The following mortality tables are used to illustrate how a premium for term insurance is calculated and then goes on to calculate the reserve the insurer needs in order to pay out future claims. The premium will be calculated in several steps and all calculations will use the following assumptions to make the illustrations more straightforward:

1. All premiums are collected by the insurer (and paid by the insured) at the beginning of the year (BOY).
2. All claims are for policies of $1,000 each.
3. All claims are paid at the end of the year (EOY).
4. The premiums collected earn 5% during the year between the time they are collected and the time they are paid out in claims.

Table 9.5 Standard Mortality Table — Canadian Females

Age	Alive BOY*	Deaths during the year	Probability of Surviving	Probability of Dying	Age	Alive BOY	Deaths during the year	Probability of Surviving	Probability of Dying
0	100,000	512	0.99488	0.00512	55	95,106	391	0.99590	0.00410
1	99,488	40	0.99960	0.00040	56	94,715	428	0.99547	0.00453
2	99,448	24	0.99976	0.00024	57	94,287	469	0.99502	0.00498
3	99,424	23	0.99977	0.00023	58	93,818	510	0.99457	0.00543
4	99,401	20	0.99979	0.00021	59	93,308	551	0.99410	0.00590
5	99,381	19	0.99982	0.00018	60	92,757	594	0.99359	0.00641
6	99,362	13	0.99986	0.00014	61	92,163	644	0.99301	0.00699
7	99,349	10	0.99990	0.00010	62	91,519	702	0.99233	0.00767
8	99,339	10	0.99990	0.00010	63	90,817	766	0.99157	0.00843
9	99,329	10	0.99990	0.00010	64	90,051	834	0.99074	0.00926
10	99,319	12	0.99989	0.00011	65	89,217	908	0.98982	0.01018
11	99,307	11	0.99989	0.00011	66	88,309	990	0.98879	0.01121
12	99,296	15	0.99985	0.00015	67	87,319	1,079	0.98765	0.01235
13	99,281	19	0.99981	0.00019	68	86,240	1,169	0.98644	0.01356
14	99,262	22	0.99977	0.00023	69	85,071	1,262	0.98517	0.01483
15	99,240	28	0.99973	0.00027	70	83,809	1,360	0.98377	0.01623
16	99,212	31	0.99969	0.00031	71	82,449	1,472	0.98215	0.01785
17	99,181	33	0.99966	0.00034	72	80,977	1,602	0.98021	0.01979
18	99,148	34	0.99965	0.00035	73	79,375	1,743	0.97804	0.02196
19	99,114	34	0.99966	0.00034	74	77,632	1,886	0.97571	0.02429
20	99,080	33	0.99967	0.00033	75	75,746	2,039	0.97307	0.02693
21	99,047	32	0.99968	0.00032	76	73,707	2,209	0.97003	0.02997
22	99,015	32	0.99968	0.00032	77	71,498	2,399	0.96646	0.03354
23	98,983	32	0.99967	0.00033	78	69,099	2,593	0.96246	0.03754
24	98,951	33	0.99966	0.00034	79	66,506	2,786	0.95812	0.04188
25	98,918	35	0.99965	0.00035	80	63,720	2,977	0.95328	0.04672
26	98,883	35	0.99964	0.00036	81	60,743	3,173	0.94777	0.05223
27	98,848	38	0.99962	0.00038	82	57,570	3,371	0.94143	0.05857
28	98,810	39	0.99960	0.00040	83	54,199	3,556	0.93440	0.06560
29	98,771	42	0.99958	0.00042	84	50,643	3,709	0.92676	0.07324
30	98,729	43	0.99956	0.00044	85	46,934	3,832	0.91835	0.08165
31	98,686	47	0.99953	0.00047	86	43,102	3,924	0.90898	0.09102
32	98,639	50	0.99949	0.00051	87	39,178	3,977	0.89847	0.10153
33	98,589	53	0.99946	0.00054	88	35,201	3,980	0.88694	0.11306
34	98,536	58	0.99942	0.00058	89	31,221	3,918	0.87452	0.12548
35	98,478	62	0.99937	0.00063	90	27,303	3,794	0.86102	0.13898
36	98,416	67	0.99932	0.00068	91	23,509	3,614	0.84626	0.15374
37	98,349	73	0.99925	0.00075	92	19,895	3,381	0.83007	0.16993
38	98,276	81	0.99918	0.00082	93	16,514	3,057	0.81489	0.18511
39	98,195	90	0.99909	0.00091	94	13,457	2,720	0.79786	0.20214
40	98,105	98	0.99900	0.00100	95	10,737	2,364	0.77988	0.22012
41	98,007	108	0.99890	0.00110	96	8,373	2,001	0.76096	0.23904
42	97,899	119	0.99878	0.00122	97	6,372	1,650	0.74113	0.25887
43	97,780	130	0.99867	0.00133	98	4,722	1,320	0.72043	0.27957
44	97,650	142	0.99855	0.00145	99	3,402	1,024	0.69890	0.30110
45	97,508	154	0.99842	0.00158	100	2,378	769	0.67661	0.32339
46	97,354	169	0.99827	0.00173	101	1,609	557	0.65361	0.34639
47	97,185	184	0.99810	0.00190	102	1,052	390	0.62998	0.37002
48	97,001	202	0.99792	0.00208	103	662	261	0.60580	0.39420
49	96,799	221	0.99772	0.00228	104	401	168	0.58115	0.41885
50	96,578	241	0.99750	0.00250	105	233	103	0.55612	0.44388
51	96,337	264	0.99726	0.00274	106	130	61	0.53080	0.46920
52	96,073	291	0.99697	0.00303	107	69	34	0.50529	0.49471
53	95,782	322	0.99665	0.00335	108	35	18	0.47968	0.52032
54	95,460	354	0.99629	0.00371	109	17	9	0.45408	0.54592

Statistics Canada Catalogue No. 84-537

* BOY = beginning of year

Table 9.6 Standard Mortality Table — Canadian Males

Age	Alive BOY	Deaths during the year	Probability of Surviving	Probability of Dying	Age	Alive BOY	Deaths during the year	Probability of Surviving	Probability of Dying
0	100,000	620	0.99380	0.00620	55	91,534	614	0.99330	0.00670
1	99,380	42	0.99957	0.00043	56	90,920	671	0.99261	0.00739
2	99,338	32	0.99968	0.00032	57	90,249	738	0.99182	0.00818
3	99,306	26	0.99974	0.00026	58	89,511	811	0.99094	0.00906
4	99,280	21	0.99979	0.00021	59	88,700	887	0.98999	0.01001
5	99,259	17	0.99983	0.00017	60	87,813	971	0.98895	0.01105
6	99,242	14	0.99986	0.00014	61	86,842	1,063	0.98776	0.01224
7	99,228	11	0.99988	0.00012	62	85,779	1,165	0.98641	0.01359
8	99,217	11	0.99990	0.00010	63	84,614	1,276	0.98492	0.01508
9	99,206	10	0.99990	0.00010	64	83,338	1,392	0.98329	0.01671
10	99,196	12	0.99988	0.00012	65	81,946	1,515	0.98152	0.01848
11	99,184	13	0.99987	0.00013	66	80,431	1,644	0.97956	0.02044
12	99,171	19	0.99980	0.00020	67	78,787	1,780	0.97741	0.02259
13	99,152	29	0.99971	0.00029	68	77,007	1,918	0.97510	0.02490
14	99,123	40	0.99959	0.00041	69	75,089	2,053	0.97265	0.02735
15	99,083	54	0.99946	0.00054	70	73,036	2,192	0.97000	0.03000
16	99,029	67	0.99933	0.00067	71	70,844	2,334	0.96705	0.03295
17	98,962	76	0.99923	0.00077	72	68,510	2,484	0.96374	0.03626
18	98,886	84	0.99915	0.00085	73	66,026	2,631	0.96016	0.03984
19	98,802	90	0.99909	0.00091	74	63,395	2,767	0.95636	0.04364
20	98,712	94	0.99904	0.00096	75	60,628	2,898	0.95219	0.04781
21	98,618	98	0.99901	0.00099	76	57,730	3,030	0.94752	0.05248
22	98,520	101	0.99898	0.00102	77	54,700	3,161	0.94221	0.05779
23	98,419	101	0.99897	0.00103	78	51,539	3,283	0.93630	0.06370
24	98,318	99	0.99898	0.00102	79	48,256	3,383	0.92989	0.07011
25	98,219	98	0.99900	0.00100	80	44,873	3,460	0.92290	0.07710
26	98,121	97	0.99901	0.00099	81	41,413	3,510	0.91526	0.08474
27	98,024	97	0.99901	0.00099	82	37,903	3,530	0.90687	0.09313
28	97,927	101	0.99898	0.00102	83	34,373	3,514	0.89776	0.10224
29	97,826	104	0.99893	0.00107	84	30,859	3,457	0.88797	0.11203
30	97,722	110	0.99888	0.00112	85	27,402	3,357	0.87749	0.12251
31	97,612	116	0.99882	0.00118	86	24,045	3,215	0.86630	0.13370
32	97,496	121	0.99876	0.00124	87	20,830	3,033	0.85438	0.14562
33	97,375	126	0.99870	0.00130	88	17,797	2,817	0.84173	0.15827
34	97,249	132	0.99865	0.00135	89	14,980	2,571	0.82837	0.17163
35	97,117	137	0.99859	0.00141	90	12,409	2,305	0.81428	0.18572
36	96,980	144	0.99852	0.00148	91	10,104	2,026	0.79945	0.20055
37	96,836	151	0.99844	0.00156	92	8,078	1,746	0.78384	0.21616
38	96,685	161	0.99834	0.00166	93	6,332	1,527	0.75891	0.24109
39	96,524	169	0.99824	0.00176	94	4,805	1,249	0.74006	0.25994
40	96,355	180	0.99813	0.00187	95	3,556	995	0.72027	0.27973
41	96,175	192	0.99801	0.00199	96	2,561	769	0.69956	0.30045
42	95,983	205	0.99787	0.00213	97	1,792	577	0.67793	0.32207
43	95,778	217	0.99773	0.00227	98	1,215	419	0.65541	0.34459
44	95,561	229	0.99760	0.00240	99	796	293	0.63204	0.36796
45	95,332	243	0.99745	0.00255	100	503	197	0.60785	0.39215
46	95,089	261	0.99726	0.00274	101	306	128	0.58288	0.41712
47	94,828	284	0.99700	0.00300	102	178	79	0.55719	0.44281
48	94,544	313	0.99669	0.00331	103	99	46	0.53084	0.46916
49	94,231	346	0.99633	0.00367	104	53	26	0.50388	0.49612
50	93,885	383	0.99592	0.00408	105	27	14	0.47638	0.52362
51	93,502	424	0.99547	0.00453	106	13	7	0.44841	0.55159
52	93,078	468	0.99497	0.00503	107	6	4	0.42004	0.57996
53	92,610	514	0.99445	0.00555	108	2	1	0.39135	0.60865
54	92,096	562	0.99390	0.00610	109	1	1	0.36243	0.63757

Net Premiums

The net or pure premium covers the cost of the claims and is based on **mortality rates** — the death rate or the rate at which people die during the year. In this illustration, we look at the premium for males age 25 to 29 who take out a policy with a face value (death benefit) of $1,000. Several factors play a part in this calculation.

- **Number dying during age 25.** From the mortality tables, of 100,000 males born, there are **98,219** still alive at age 25. During age 25, **98** males died during the year between the beginning of age 25 and the beginning of age 26, leaving **98,121** still alive at the beginning of age 26.
- **Value at beginning of the year of claims paid at the end of the year.** If all 98,219 25-year old males take out a life insurance policy for $1,000 for one year, the insurer will have to pay out **$98,000** (98 × $1,000 death benefit) at the end of the year because 98 died during the year. The value of this at the beginning of that year is $93,333 [Present Value (PV) = $98,000 (PVIF $_{5\%, 1 \text{ year}}$) = $93,333].
- **Premium to charge.** The insurer would have had to charge each 25-year-old **$0.95 rounded (95.025 cents)** ($93,333 ÷ 98,219 insureds) in order to be able to pay the death claims during the year: 98,219 alive $_{BOY}$ × $0.95025 each = $93,333.
- **Interest.** The premiums collected at the beginning of the year are not paid out in claims until the end of the year. Therefore, the premiums can earn interest income during the year. Using a 5% rate of interest, the $93,333 collected in premiums will grow to $98,000 [FV = $93,333 (FVIF $_{5\%, 1 \text{ year}}$)] which is the amount required to pay the claims of $1,000 each for the 98 men who died during the year.

The following tables show:

Premium Type	Table	Explanation
Net Premiums	9.7	• The annual net premium for each man for five one-year term policies. *(Note: only the men alive at the beginning of each year pay premiums — the deceased ones do not pay premiums.)*
Net Single Premiums (NSP)	9.8	• The premium for each man to cover the entire five-year period if he paid only one amount at age 25.
	9.9	• The premium for each man to cover a policy that would cover him from age 25 to age 100 (a term-to-100 policy), again paying only one amount at age 25.
Net Level Premium (NLP)	9.10	• The annual premium for a five-year term policy beginning at age 25 in which the premium *remains the same* for each year of the five years.
	9.11	• The annual premium for a term-to-100 policy beginning for a man at age 25.

In the following: "BOY" means the beginning of **each** year while "BOY 1" means the beginning of **year one**.

Net Premium for Five 1-year, $1,000 Term Policies

This table shows the calculation of the annual premium for each man for five one-year term policies. Again, only the men alive at the beginning of each year pay premiums.

Table 9.7   Net Premium for Five 1-year, $1,000 Term Policies

A	B	C	D	E	F	G
		B x $1,000				E + F
		Claims @ $1,000 each				
At Age	# of deaths (claims)	Paid $_{EOY}$	PV $_{BOY}$		# alive $_{BOY}$	Premium $_{BOY}$
			n	5.0%		
25	98	$ 98,000	1	$93,333	98,219	$0.9503
26	97	97,000	1	92,381	98,121	0.9415
27	97	97,000	1	92,381	98,024	0.9424
28	101	101,000	1	96,190	97,927	0.9823
29	104	104,000	1	99,048	97,826	1.0125

Each man alive at the beginning of the year (column F) pays enough premium (column G) to pay the $1,000 claims for those who died during the year. The claims are paid at the end of the year (column C) but the premiums are collected at the beginning of the year (column E) and earn 5% interest during the year before being paid out as claims. Table 9.12 will show the details of the rise and fall of the funds in the **reserve** (the premiums collected minus claims paid) as the premiums are collected and the claims are paid out.

Notice that the premium drops for two years as the mortality rate falls off at ages 26 and 27. However, while this doesn't show up because the premiums are rounded, the decrease is slightly offset because there are fewer men to pay premiums.

Net Single Premium (NSP)

This table shows the calculation of the premium for each man to cover the entire five-year period if he paid only one amount at age 25. This is called the **net single premium** (**NSP**).

Table 9.8   Net Single Premium (NSP) for One 5-year, $1,000 Term Policy

A	B	C $B \times \$1,000$	D	E	F	G $E \div F$
		Claims @ $1,000 each				
At Age	# of deaths (claims)	Paid EOY	PV BOY1		# alive BOY1	Premium BOY1
			n	5.0%		
25	98	$ 98,000	1	$ 93,333	98,219	
26	97	97,000	2	87,982	98,121	
27	97	97,000	3	83,792	98,024	
28	101	101,000	4	83,093	97,927	
29	104	104,000	5	81,487	97,826	
				$429,687	÷ 98,219 =	$4,3748

The rate — one premium paid at age 25 by all the men alive at age 25 that covers the entire five years — is calculated by dividing the present value at age 25 of the claims that will be paid for the men who die over the five years by the number alive at age 25. In other words, if each man alive at age 25 (column F) took out a policy and paid a premium of $4.37 to cover the entire five-year term, there would be enough to pay all the claims (column C) during the five-year period. This will be illustrated in the next section in Table 9.13 where the details of the reserve are presented.

Table 9.9 is the same calculation as Table 9.8 but for a term-to-100 policy instead of a five-year policy. The middle years are omitted for the sake of brevity.

Table 9.9   Net Single Premium (NSP) for One $1,000 Term-to-100 Policy

A	B	C $B \times \$1,000$	D	E	F	G $E \div F$
		Claims @ $1,000 each				
At Age	# of deaths (claims)	Paid EOY	PV BOY1		# alive BOY1	Premium BOY1
			n	5.0%		
25	98	$ 98,000	1	$93,333	98,219	
26	97	97,000	2	87,982		
27	97	97,000	3	83,792		
28	101	101,000	4	83,093		
29	104	104,000	5	81,487		
...	...	...	...	...		
96	769	769,000	72	22,924		
97	577	577,000	73	16,382		
98	419	419,000	74	11,329		
99	293	293,000	75	7,545		
100	197	197,000	76	4,831		
				$9,995,728	÷ 98,219 =	$101.77

Again, the present value of the death claims paid ($9,995,728) is divided by the number of men alive at age 25 (98,219) to arrive at the rate of $101.77 In other words, a 25-year-old man could pay $101.77 and have insurance coverage for the next 75 years! Sounds cheap but our example has a face value of only $1,000. For a $100,000 face value, this amount would be $10,177, and for $500,000 it would be $50,885. However, this illustrates that it is possible to figure out what the one-time pure premium would be.

Net Level Premium (NLP)

But what if the young men in the last two tables (Tables 9.8 and 9.9) want to pay the same annual premium for the entire term?

Table 9.10   Net Level Premium (NLP) for One 5-year, $1,000 Term Policy

A	B	C	D	E	F	G
	Table 9.8	Table 9.7				B ÷ F
				Premium of $1.00		
At Age	PV Claims $_{BOY1}$	# alive $_{BOY}$	Paid $_{BOY}$	PV $_{BOY1}$ n	# alive $_{BOY1}$ 5.0%	
25	$ 93,333	98,219	$98,219	0	$ 98,219	
26	87,982	98,121	98,121	1	93,449	
27	83,792	98,024	98,024	2	88,911	
28	83,093	97,927	97,927	3	84,593	
29	81,487	97,826	97,826	4	80,482	
	$429,687		÷		$445,653	= $0.9642

The annual rate of $0.9642 (96.42 cents) for $1,000 of coverage is found by dividing
- the PV (present value) of all claims paid out at the end of each year during the five years (Tables 9.8 and 9.10)

by
- the PV of all premiums paid by all men alive at the beginning of each year during the five years (Table 9.10)

$429,687

÷

445,653

By using the present value of both the premiums paid and the claims paid, the illustration takes into account the fact that the premiums collected and not yet paid out in claims are earning interest. Table 9.10 shows

- each man alive at the beginning of the year pays $0.9642 (96.42 cents) in premiums at the beginning of the year, and
- there is enough to pay all the claims during the five-year period.

Table 9.14 shows the details of the reserve that proves that this premium is the correct premium.

What is the net level premium (NLP) for a Term-to-100 or the insurance component of a whole life policy? Again, only a few years will be shown.

Table 9.11   Net Level Premium (NLP) for One $1,000 Term-to-100 Policy

A	B	C	D	E	F	G
	Table 9.9					B ÷ F
				Premium of $1.00		
At Age	PV Claims $_{BOY1}$	# alive $_{BOY}$	Paid $_{BOY}$	PV $_{BOY1}$ n	# alive $_{BOY1}$ 5.0%	
25	$93,333	98,219	$98,219	0	$98,219	
26	87,982	98,121	$98,121	1	93,449	
27	83,792	98,024	$98,024	2	88,911	
...	...	...	...	...	...	
98	11,329	1,215	$ 1,215	73	34	
99	7,545	796	796	74	22	
100	4,831	503	$503	75	13	
	$9,995,728		÷		$1,833,524	= $5.4516

PV of total claims $9,995,728
PV of premiums collected when each pays $1.00 at the beginning of each year $1,833,524
Premium that has to be charged to pay all claims $5.45

Calculating the Reserve for a Term Insurance Policy

A **policy reserve** or **legal reserve** is the funds set aside to pay future claims and is defined as the difference between

- the present value of the future benefits (claims to be made in the future), and
- the present value of the future net premiums to be collected.

This reserve is a very large portion of the liabilities for life insurance companies on the balance sheet as shown in Table 1.3 in Chapter 1. The policy reserve includes the following:

- **Terminal reserve** — the policy reserve balance at the end of the year (EOY), which is invested and monitored by insurance regulators.
- **Initial reserve** — the balance in the reserve at the beginning of the year (BOY). It is the terminal reserve from the prior year plus the current year's premiums collected.
- **Mean reserve** — the average of the terminal reserve and the initial reserve. It is used on the annual financial statement (although the simplified examples later in this chapter will not use the average to help keep the calculations clear).

We will look at three reserves:

Premium Type	Table	Based on Tables	The Reserve for:
Net Premium	9.12	9.7	• Five one-year term policies
Net Single Premium (NSP)	9.13	9.8	• One five-year term policy paid with one premium
Net Level Premium (NLP)	9.14	9.10	• One five-year term policy paid with five equal premiums

Reserve for Net Premium

If the young men buy five one-year policies, the premium collected from the young men still alive at the beginning of each year will earn enough interest so the reserve will be able to pay all the death claims for that year at the end of that year.

Table 9.12 Reserve for Net Premium for Five 1-year, $1,000 Term Policies, with Annual Premiums Paid at the Beginning of Each Year — Based on Table 9.7

A	B	C	D	E	F	G	H	I
		Table 9.7	B × C	D + I	E(1 + k)		G($1,000)	F − H
Age	# alive $_{BOY}$	Premium $_{BOY}$	Premiums Collected	Initial Reserve	Reserve + Interest $_{EOY}$ @ 5.00%	# of Deaths	Claims Paid $_{EOY}$ @ 1,000	Terminal Reserve
25	98,219	$0.9503	$93,333	$93,333	$ 98,000	98	$ 98,000	0
26	98,121	0.9415	92,381	92,381	97,000	97	97,000	0
27	98,024	0.9424	92,381	92,381	97,000	97	97,000	0
28	97,927	0.9823	96,190	96,190	101,000	101	101,000	0
29	97,826	1.0125	99,048	99,048	104,000	104	104,000	0

Table 9.12 shows that the $93,333 collected at the beginning of year 1 earns 5% interest during the year and grows to $98,000, which just enough to pay the claims for year 1, leaving a terminal reserve of zero. Since these are all one-year policies, this is repeated for each year during the five-year period — the premiums are collected, earn interest, and the entire reserve is paid out at the end of the year.

Reserve for Net Single Premium (NSP)

If the policyholders pay one premium at the beginning of year 1 to cover the entire five-year term, the reserve starts high and will decrease over the years as death claims are paid.

Table 9.13 Reserve for a Net Single Premium (NSP) for One 5-year, $1,000 Term Policy, with One Premium Paid at the Beginning of Year 1 — Based on Table 9.8

A	B	C	D	E	F	G	H	I
		Table 9.7	B × C	D + I	E(1 + k)		G($1,000)	F − H
Age	# alive BOY	Premium BOY	Premiums Collected	Initial Reserve	Reserve + Interest EOY @ 5.00%	# of Deaths	Claims Paid EOY @ 1,000	Terminal Reserve
25	98,219	$4.3748	$429,687	$429,687	$451,171	98	$ 98,000	$353,171
26				353,171	370,830	97	97,000	273,830
27				273,830	287,522	97	97,000	190,522
28				190,522	200,048	101	101,000	99,048
29				99,048	104,000	104	104,000	0

Table 9.13 shows the premium calculated in Table 9.8 being collected at the beginning of the five-year term. Each year the balance in the reserve at the beginning of the year earns interest and, at the end of the year, the claims are paid, leaving a balance in the reserve (the terminal reserve). The premium was the correct amount to pay all the claims for the entire five-year period — at the end of the five years, the reserve has a zero balance.

Reserve for Net Level Premium (NLP)

If the insureds pay the same premium for each of the five years, the reserve first builds and then falls to zero as the number available to pay premiums declines and the amount of the death claims depletes the reserve.

Table 9.14 Reserve for Net Level Premium (NLP) for One 5-year, $1,000 Term Policy, with Annual Premiums Paid at the Beginning of Each Year — Based on Table 9.10

A	B	C	D	E	F	G	H	I
		Table 9.7	B × C	D + I	E(1 + k)		G($1,000)	F − H
Age	# alive BOY	Premium BOY	Premiums Collected	Initial Reserve	Reserve + Interest EOY @ 5.00%	# of Deaths	Claims Paid EOY @ 1,000	Terminal Reserve
25	98,219	$0.9642	$94,700	$ 94,700	$ 99,435	98	$ 98,000	$1,435
26	98,121	0.9642	94,606	96,041	100,843	97	97,000	3,843
27	98,024	0.9642	94,512	98,355	103,273	97	97,000	6,273
28	97,927	0.9642	94,419	100,692	105,726	101	101,000	4,726
29	97,826	0.9642	94,321	99,048	104,000	104	104,000	0

This premium also passes the test. Even though the premium is the same every year, there is enough collected each year in premiums to earn interest and pay the death claims, leaving a reserve of zero at the end of the five years.

These examples have simplified matters a great deal — people sign up for insurance every day and die every day. But actuaries know how to take this into account — it is really just a more detailed version of the same principles. The rates shown here are pure premiums — there is nothing added on for loading. Loadings will vary by the type of policy. For example, it is more cost-efficient to write one 5-year term policy than to write five policies every year for five years and the premium will reflect this. Also not reflected in these illustrations is that one five-year policy will have a higher premium than five one-year policies because the insurance company cannot cancel the insurance if the insured gets sick whereas with five one-year policies, if the insured gets sick after year three, the insurer can refuse to renew the policy unless the insured is paying for a guaranteed renewable policy. In addition, these reserves are for a term policy, which has no accumulating cash value — it holds only the amount needed to pay out the death benefit.

We have not looked at the reserves for a term-to-100 policy but you can imagine how large it gets. We will look at the size of insurers' liabilities later in this chapter.

Office of the Superintendent of Financial Institutions (OSFI)

The Office of the Superintendent of Financial Institutions [www.osfi-bsif.gc.ca] regulates and supervises federally regulated insurance companies and has the power to intervene in insurance companies to address concerns about their financial viability. The assessments that are the result of the supervision process consider the unique circumstances of each company, including its nature, scope, complexity, and risk profile. Insurance companies face several types of risk of loss:

- **Credit risk** is the inability to meet loan payments.
- **Insurance risk** is a result of actual experience being different than expected when a product was designed or priced with the difference arising from mortality rates, morbidity rates (rates of disease and illness), and policyholder behaviour.
- **Liquidity risk** is a result of not having access to enough funds to meet cash needs.
- **Market risk** is a result of adverse investment returns arising from market volatility, interest rate changes, and detrimental changes in foreign currency rates.
- **Operational risk** arises from inadequate or unsuccessful internal processes, failures of human performance or systems, and unexpected external events.
- **Strategic risk** is a result of being unable to
  - adequately plan or implement a suitable business strategy, or
  - adapt to change in the external economic, political or regulatory environment.

The standards for all financial institutions, listed in the *Table of OSFI Guidelines*, assess the following:

- Capital adequacy requirements (solvency)
- Prudential limits and standards, for example, large exposure limits and portfolio mix
- Accounting standards, for example, non-accrual loans and derivatives disclosure
- Sound business and financial practices, for example deterring and detecting money laundering and interest rate risk management

The Table of OSFI Guidelines list the ratios required for each sector of financial services (many of the guidelines are the same for all sectors). The sectors are as follows:

- Deposit-taking institutions
  - Banks
  - Foreign bank branches
  - Trust and loan companies
  - Cooperatives
- Insurance companies:
  - Life insurance companies and fraternals (an organization operating for the benefit of their members and the communities they serve, for example ACTRA, the Alliance of Cinema, Television & Radio Artists, the Masons, the Knights of Columbus, the Independent Order of Forresters)
  - Property and casualty insurance companies.

The Guidelines involve calculating ratios to determine whether or not a financial institution is meeting the standards. The *Supervisory Guide Applicable to Federally Regulated Insurance Companies* lists the following stages/circumstances and the OSFI activities and/or interventions that can occur at each stage as the risk increases.

Table 9.15 OSFI Supervisory Guide Applicable to Federally Regulated Insurance Companies

Stage — Circumstances	OSFI Activities/interventions
No Problems/Normal Activities	
• Ongoing supervisory and regulatory activities applying to all federally regulated Canadian and foreign life and p&c insurance companies (companies), pursuant to OSFI's mandate. In addition, OSFI conducts research and analyses industry-wide issues and trends.	• reviews incorporation of new companies • reviews and monitors statutory filings and financial reports • periodic on-site examination as required by statute • informs Minister of Finance of status
Stage 1 — Early Warning	
• Deficiency in policies or procedures or the existence of other practices, conditions, and circumstances that could lead to the development of problems described at Stage 2.	• company is notified of concerns and asked to take measures to rectify the situation • monitors remedial action • may require external auditors to enlarge the scope of its examination • may require external review of actuarial methods and assumptions
Stage 2 — Risk to Financial Viability or Solvency	

• Situations or problems that, although not serious enough to present an immediate threat to financial viability or solvency, could deteriorate into serious problems if not addressed promptly, as evidenced by unsatisfactory
  • ability to meet capital and surplus requirements
  • poor earnings and operating losses
  • actuarial reserves
  • exposure to off-balance sheet risk (for example, risk associated with excessive rate of growth in premiums — **see Example 9.1**)
  • liquidity
  • deficiency in management procedures or controls
  • risks arising from, for example, rapid growth, credit rating downgrades, or qualified report from external auditors
	• senior OSFI officials meet with management and the board of directors and external auditors
	• company must present an acceptable business plan that reflects appropriate remedial measures
	• monitoring is enhanced
	• scope may be enlarged
	• Superintendent of Financial Institutions may direct the company to modify its actuarial assumptions and methods
	• business restrictions may be imposed
	• company is placed on a regulatory "watchlist" which is sent monthly to the Minister
	• status is discussed with relevant compensation funds (Assuris and PACCIC, Property and Casualty Insurance Compensation Corporation presented in Chapter 1)

Stage 3 — Future Financial Viability in Serious Doubt	
• Situations or problems described at Stage 2 are at a level where they pose a material threat to future financial viability or solvency unless effective corrective measures are applied promptly.	• Interventions are similar to Stage 2 but more so and may include posting OSFI examination staff at the company to monitor the situation on an on-going basis.
Stage 4 — Company Not Viable/Insolvency Imminent	

• Severe financial difficulties resulting in
  • failure or imminent failure to meet required capital and surplus requirements or vesting requirements in conjunction with inability to rectify the situation within a short period of time, or
  • statutory conditions for taking control being met, or
  • failure to develop and implement an acceptable business plan, thus making either of the two preceding circumstances inevitable within a short period of time.
	• increased pressure by OSFI to rectify situation
	• may impose new business restrictions
	• boards of compensation funds are notified
	• other regulatory agencies (provincial or foreign) are notified
	• *OSFI may take control of the assets* for a short period
	• *OSFI may maintain control of the assets or take control of the company* if the requirements are not met
	• the **company or OSFI may seek a winding-up order** which the Minister may overrule on the grounds of public interest only.

OSFI Guidelines provide an context for the investment mix of both life and P&C insurance companies as well as accounting policies which are, in some instances, different from the **Generally Accepted Accounting Principles (GAAP)** for most companies.

Most, but not all, insurance companies are registered both provincially and federally, meaning most companies must meet OSFI Guidelines. Insurance companies that are only provincially regulated are monitored by the regulators listed in Table 9.1.

Investments

The following table shows the investments of this industry. The heavy investment in bonds reflects the long-term nature of their reserves (see also Table 9.21). As you might expect from the previous calculations of reserves, and as reflected in premium income as a percentage of assets (shown to the right of the amount of premium income), life and health insurance companies have much larger reserves compared to the premium income for property and casualty insurers. The larger reserves for life and health insurers comes from the long-term nature of their life policies, not from the health and disability sectors. Property and casualty insurers have large reserves for liability insurance but their reserves for property insurance is on a par with the health portion of life and health insurers, which are both relatively short term.

Since insurance companies have more bonds and mortgages and less stock in their investments than many companies, there is less fluctuation in the book value of the assets.

Table 9.16   Assets — 2008 ($ millions)

	Property & Casualty		Life and Health*	
Bonds	$60,989	53.9%	$209,773	52.9%
Stocks	6,800	6.0%	22,759	5.7%
Mortgages	535	0.5%	54,639	13.8%
Real estate	76	0.1%	14,406	3.6%
Other investments	1,063	0.9%	12,766	3.2%
Term deposits	3,243	2.9%	21,625	5.5%
Policy loans			10,909	2.7%
Total investments	72,705	64.2%	346,877	87.4%
Cash	5,671	5.0%	5,560	1.4%
Receivables	26,830	23.7%	12,335	3.1%
Investment in affiliates	2,754	2.4%		
Real & fixed assets	175	0.2%		
Miscellaneous	5,054	4.5%	31,924	8.0%
	40,484	35.8%	49,819	12.6%
Total assets	113,189	100.0%	396,696	100.0%
Premium income earned	30,621	27.1%	64,718	16.3%

* without Segregated Funds

Source: *Office of the Superintendent of Financial Institutions, Regulated Entities, Insurance Companies, Financial Data*

Accounting in the Insurance Industry

By January 2011, all publicly accountable companies in Canada will be required by the **Accounting Standards Board (AcSB)** to adopt the **International Financial Reporting Standards (IFRS),** which has already been adopted by more than 100 countries including Australia, New Zealand, and the European Union but not the United States. The AcSB sets the accounting rules that are spelled out in the **CICA** (Canadian Institute of Chartered Accountants) **Handbook.**

Asset Valuation

IFRS replaces the current Canadian GAAP (Generally Accepted Accounting Principles) and has essentially been adopted by some large insurers already since they have elected to use the **fair value option**[1] Financial Instruments Implementation Guidance, Step 2 — Classification, Accounting Standards Board (AcSB) Financial Instruments Working Group, July 31, 2006, that allows financial instruments to be designated has **held for trading** ("bought and sold for the purpose of profit-taking" as described in Table 9.18) when initially classified.

The adoption of **fair value accounting** is a major change for many companies but may, in fact, have little impact on the balance sheets of insurance companies because they were already using market values under the old GAAP rules for insurance companies to value most of their investments. Table 1.3 in Chapter 1 shows the following assets for the Insurance sector at December 31, 2008.

Table 9.17 Total Assets in the Insurance Sector at December 31, 2008 ($ millions)

Investments & accounts with affiliates	$ 62,891	14.5%
Portfolio investments	235,397	54.4%
Loans	49,772	11.5%
Capital assets, net	10,094	2.4%
Other	74,415	17.2%
	432,569	

Over half of the assets are already using fair value accounting since investments are at fair value and, as shown in Table 9.16, over half of these investments are invested in bonds. High-quality bonds provide stability in an investment portfolio since, while bonds do fluctuate, they are less volatile than stocks.

Adjustments to market value are reflected as "Realized and unrealized gains (losses) on assets supporting policy liabilities and consumer notes" in Investment Income on the Income Statement. This adjustment to reflect market value has been criticized in light of the recent market downturn for requiring adjustments in the short term to asset values for assets that are intended to be held long term.

New Classification of Financial Instruments

The Accounting Standards Board (AcSB) defines[2] the IFRS categories of

- Held for trading (bought and sold for the purpose of profit-taking)
- Held-to-maturity (definitely plan to hold to maturity),
- Loans and receivables,
- Available-for-sale (any assets that is not trading or held-to-maturity), and
- Other financial liabilities.

---

1   Office of the Superintendent of Financial Institutions, Accounting for Financial Instruments Designated as Fair Value Option, February, 2007, and Financial Instruments Implementation Guidance, Step 2 — Clasification, Accounting Standards Board (AcSB), Financial Instruments Working Group, July 31, 2006.
2   Financial Instruments. Navigating new waters, Accounting Standards Board AcSB, October 1, 2006.

Table 9.18A Accounting Standards Board (AcSB) Classifications of Financial Instruments

CLASSIFY ALL FINANCIAL INSTRUMENTS

- All financial instruments must be classified into one of the categories described below. Characteristics of the instrument and your use of it determine whether you have a choice of category. Classification determines how each instrument is measured and where gains and losses are recognized.

  Reclassification is rarely possibly, so it is important to understand the implications where choice is available.

- **Financial assets and financial liabilities held for trading** — almost all derivatives are in this category, as are any instruments you buy and sell for the purpose of profit-taking. In addition, you may choose to designate any financial instrument into this category when first recognized. This may help ensure that all financial instruments managed as a portfolio are accounted for on the same basis.

- **Held-to-maturity investments** — this category is for fixed maturity financial assets with fixed or determinable payments that you have the positive intention and ability to hold to maturity — i.e., only debt instruments. This category may only be used if you are virtually certain you will hold the item to its maturity. If there are significant sales of assets within this category before maturity, you must reclassify all financial assets in the portfolio to the available-for-sale category unless the reason for the sales is outside your control. Therefore, you need to take care in allocating financial instruments to this category.

- **Loans and receivables** — this category includes all loans and receivables except debt securities. Debt securities are normally quoted in an active market and include investments in government debt, corporate bonds, convertible debt, commercial paper, securitized debt instruments such as collateralized mortgage obligations and real estate mortgage investment conduits, and interest-only and principal-only strips. Alternatively, you may designate loans and receivables as *held for trading or available for sale*.

- **Available-for-sale financial assets** — this category captures all financial assets that are not classified as *held for trading, held to maturity, or loans and receivables*. Note that investments in equity instruments may be classified only as *held for trading or available for sale*. The category might also include debt instruments that you do not wish to classify as held to maturity.

- **Other financial liabilities** — financial liabilities that are not classified as *held for trading* continue to be measured at amortized cost.

- Table 9.18B summarizes the implications of classifying financial assets and financial liabilities into the five categories.

Table 9.18B Summary of Requirements for Measurement and Recognizing Gains and Losses

	Category	Initial measurement	Subsequent measurement	Gains and losses
ASSETS	Loans and receivables	Fair value	Amortized cost** using the effective interest method	Recognized in net income when the asset is derecognized; impairment write-downs and foreign exchange. translation adjustments recognized immediately in net income
	Held-to-maturity investment			
	Available-for-sale financial assets	Fair value	Fair value*	Recognized in other comprehensive income; transferred to net income when the asset is derecognized; impairment write-downs recognized immediately in net income.
LIABILITIES	Held for trading	Fair value	Fair value	Recognized immediately in net income.
	Other	Fair value	Amortized cost using the effective interest method	Recognized in net income when the liability is derecognized; foreign exchange translation adjustments recognized immediately.

*Equity instruments that do not have a quoted market price in an active market are measured at cost.

** Amortized cost: When a bond is bought at a discount or premium and will be held to maturity, the difference between the face value and the purchase price is amortized annually with the result that the bond value equals the present value of future cash flows discounted for the number of years remaining at the yield-to-maturity discount rate.

Reserves (Liabilities) for Life Insurance Companies

Life insurance companies have several types of liabilities not generally found in most companies due to the nature of their business.

Table 9.19   Types of Reserves for Life Insurance Companies

	Liabilities	Revenue/Expenses
Policy reserves	• Cost of protection is lower in the early years so there is an accrued liability for the difference between the loss on premium income incurred and the future liability. • Cash values are accumulating.	• Earned premium income (due or receivable). Unearned premium income increases the policy reserve (liability). See Example 1.
Reserves on Supplementary Contracts like Annuities	• This occurs, for example, when someone chooses to take an annuity over 20 years rather than a lump sum death benefit.	• When someone dies, the face value is recorded as an expense whether or not it is paid out. The difference is in the Reserves on Supplementary Contracts.
Dividends Left to Accumulate	• These dividends and the income they earn are recorded as a liability.	• The dividend is recorded as an expense when it is payable.
Reserves for Unpaid Claims	• This is accrued liabilities and includes an estimate for claims not yet received.	• Losses incurred include claims received and an estimate on past experience.

Equity

The equity section of the balance sheet is somewhat different for life insurance companies because there is a section for policyholders' equity, which is the cash surrender values that belong to the policyholders should they surrender the policies.

Table 9.20   Equity: Differences for Insurance Companies

	Insurance Companies	Other Industries
	Policyholders' Equity included participating accounts for participating life insurance policies	n/a
Stock companies	Shareholders' Equity includes capital stock, contributed surplus, and retained earnings.	Same
Mutual companies	Policyholders' Surplus = retained earnings	n/a

Income Statement

Insurance companies have a couple of features unique to their incomes statements:

• All acquisition costs are recorded as incurred and not matched to earned income.

• An allowance for expected claims based on past experience is recorded as an expense annually.

Under IFRS, as shown in Table 9.18, all industries will now be recognizing unrealized gains on most investment assets. This is not new for insurance companies but is new for other industries.

Table 9.21   Income Statement: Differences for Insurance Companies

	Insurance Companies	Other Industries
Revenue		
• Premium revenue	• Revenue recorded as earned	• Same
• Investment income	• Unrealized gains and losses are recorded	• Same
• Unearned revenue	• Unearned premium reserve (liability)	• Deferred revenue (liability)
Expenses	• Acquisition costs are recorded as they are incurred, that is, there is no prepaid expense for commissions on premiums written but not yet earned. Claims expenses are recorded on an accrual basis, including an allowance for claims not yet made but expected.	• Matching principle is used — recognize revenues as they are earned and expenses on an accrual basis to match the revenues earned.

Example 1 illustrates the way new premiums written affect the liabilities when a company is growing. Notice that the company has plenty of cash but is "losing money", showing losses or little net income in the early years.

EXAMPLE 1   S. T. Ltd, a stock insurance company, is newly organized and about to go into business. Its expected costs equal actual costs:

Losses incurred   60% of premiums **earned**   **Loss ratio** = losses incurred ÷ premiums earned
Expenses incurred   30% of premiums **written** **Expense ratio** = expenses incurred ÷ premiums written
Unearned premium reserve 50% of premiums **written**

As usually happens in accounting when we learn about unearned revenue, S. T. Ltd will assume that all the premiums are received on July 1 so that, during the year, 50% of the premiums written are earned during the year while 50% are unearned at the year-end. In fact, if premiums are written evenly throughout the year, this is a fairly accurate reflection of the distribution of earned and unearned revenue.

At the beginning of year 1, S. T. Ltd issues $10 million in no-par value shares for $10 million cash. During the first year, it writes $12.5 million in premiums, and the second year, $18 million in premiums, etc. The unearned premium reserve at the end of each year equals 50% of premiums written during that year.

S. T. Ltd uses standard insurance-industry accounting policies:
• Premium revenue is recognized as earned.
• Claims (losses) are matched to revenue and are recorded as they are incurred (paid and accrued) without any deferral.
• Expenses such as underwriting costs, commissions, and administration are recognized as they are incurred, that is, on a cash basis.

Table 9.22   Financial Statements for S. T. Ltd

	BOY 1		EOY 1		EOY 2		EOY 3		EOY 4	
Cash	10,000	100%	15,000	100%	18,450	100%	22,650	100%	23,850	100%
Unearned premium reserve = 50% of premiums **written**	0	0%	6,250	42%	9,000	49%	12,000	53%	10,500	44%
Capital	10,000	100%	10,000	67%	10,000	54%	10,000	44%	10,000	42%
Surplus	0	0%	−1,250	−8%	−550	−3%	650	3%	3,350	14%
	10,000	100%	15,000	100%	18,450	100%	22,650	100%	23,850	100%
			Year 1		Year 2		Year 3		Year 4	
Premiums written			12,500		18,000		24,000		21,000	
Premiums earned:										
Written in current year			6,250		9,000		12,000		10,500	
Written in prior year			0		6,250		9,000		12,000	
			6,250		15,250		21,000		22,500	
Losses = 60% of premiums earned			3,750		9,150		12,600		13,500	
Expenses = 30% of premiums written			3,750		5,400		7,200		6,300	
Profit (Loss)			−1,250		700		1,200		2,700	
Ratio of Reserve to Premiums earned			100.0%		59.0%		57.1%		46.7%	
Cash Flow										
Cash received			12,500		18,000		24,000		21,000	
Losses paid			−3,750		−9,150		−12,600		−13,500	
Expenses paid			−3,750		−5,400		−7,200		−6,300	
Net change			5,000		3,450		4,200		1,200	
Cash − BOY			10,000		15,000		18,450		22,650	
Cash − EOY			15,000		18,450		22,650		23,850	

The percentages on the balance sheet are a *result* of the numbers, *not the cause of them*. Notice in particular that while S. T. Ltd has a positive cash flow after Year 1, it does not report positive surplus (retained earnings) until the end of Year 3.

Reinsurance

Reinsurance is risk-sharing primarily for P&C insurance companies although life insurance companies also reinsure. With reinsurance, all or part of an insurer's risk is assumed by other companies in return for part of the premium paid by the insured — the writing insurer cedes (gives up) part of the premium. In 2003, Canadian P&C insurers ceded $1.9 billion to reinsurers — about 8% of total insurance premiums written. The major reason why companies cede premiums to reinsurers is to share the risk on catastrophic losses. Several reinsurers were involved with 9/11 — the enormous cost was spread among several companies, not just one. One company would probably have become bankrupt from the cost but, because several were involved, the cost was spread around. Reinsurance also helps to stabilize earnings for the ceding insurer in addition to allowing insurers to write policies that are actually too large for them.

Insurers also reinsure because, in doing so, they reduce their unearned premium reserve. Since insurance companies must have a specified ratio of assets to unearned premium reserve, a rapidly growing insurer will find its ability to write new business restricted by this ratio as illustrated by the following example which shows the effect of reinsuring on the ratio of reserves to premiums earned when S. T. Ltd cedes 40% of the policies written in Year 3 from Table 9.22.

EXAMPLE 2 At the end of Year 2, S. T. Ltd's projected earnings are shown in Table 9.23 in "EOY 3 before reinsuring", from Example 1. S. T. Ltd wanted to rid itself of some of its risk exposure and also to bring down its ratio of:
- unearned premiums reserve to assets, projected to be 53.0%, and

- unearned premium reserve to premiums earned, projected to be 57.1%.

As a result, S. T. Ltd decided to cede 40% of premiums written in Year 3. This will reduce current year income by $4,800 and will also reduce the reserve by the same amount. The result is a reduction in
- premiums earned to $16,200 from $21,000, a $4,800 or 23% reduction,
- losses to $9,720 from $12,600, a $2,880 or 23% reduction, and
- expenses to $4,320 from $7,200, a $2,880 or 40% reduction.

As a result of reinsuring
- profit increases to $2,150 from $1,200 — a $960 or 80% increase,
- the ratio of unearned premium reserve to assets drops to 38.3% from 53.0%, an increase of 28%, and
- the ratio of unearned premium reserve to premiums earned drops to 44.4% from 57.1%, an increase of 22%.

By reinsuring, this company is free to write much more new business.

Table 9.23   Effects for S. T. Ltd of Reinsuring

	EOY 3 Before Reinsuring			Reinsuring 40%	EOY 3 After Reinsuring		
Cash		22,650	100.0%	−3,840		18,810	100.0%
Unearned premium reserve	57.1%	12,000	53.0%	−4,800	44.4%	7,200	38.3%
Capital		10,000				10,000	
Surplus		650		960		1,610	
		22,650		−3,840		18,810	
		100%		−40%		60%	
Premiums written		24,000		−9,600		14,400	
Premiums earned:							
Written in current year		12,000		−4,800		7,200	
Written in prior year		9,000				9,000	
	100.0%	21,000		−4,800	100%	16,200	
Losses = 60% of premiums earned		12,600		−2,880		9,720	
Expenses = 30% of premiums written		7,200		−2,880		4,320	
Profit (Loss)		1,200		960		2,160	
Cash Flow							
Cash received		24,000		−9,600		14,400	
Losses paid		−12,600		2,880		−9,720	
Expenses paid		−7,200		2,880		−4,320	
Net change		4,200		−3,840		360	
Cash — BOY		18,450		0		18,450	
Cash — EOY		22,650		−3,840		18,810	

Reserves are liabilities and insurance companies are restricted in the ratios of this liability to assets and to premiums earned. If this company is growing rapidly, it may prefer to write new premiums and cede some of these premiums and the liability that goes with it in order to continue to grow (as well as to reduce its risk exposure on catastrophic losses).

Summary

The insurance industry has facets that are unique to it including underwriting, claims settlement, production, and rate making. Entry level positions for those who wish to work in the insurance industry have regulated licensing requirements, which is the starting point for everything except administrative support positions. Furthermore, this industry is further unique in that insurers hold large asset balances that are invested for long periods of time since they collect premiums and hold them until they are paid out as claims. As a result, these funds being held to pay out future liabilities are a major source of investment funds for those companies who are looking to borrow funds. In this regard, while unique, it is rather like pension funds whose annual contributions are being invested long-term until they are paid out to retirees.

Sources

2008 Facts, Canadian Life and Health Insurance Association [www.clhia.ca]

2009 Facts, Insurance Bureau of Canada [www.ibc.ca]

Accounting Standards Board (AcSB)

* Financial Instruments Implementation Guidance, Step 2 — Classification, Financial Instruments Working Group, July 31, 2006
* Financial Instruments. Navigating new waters, October 1, 2006.

General Insurance Essentials, Insurance Institute of Canada (IIC) [www.insuranceinstitute.ca]

Life Licence Qualification Program, Canadian Council of Insurance Regulators (CCIR) [www.ccir-ccrra.org]

Standard Mortality Tables, Statistics Canada [www.statcan.ca] Catalogue No. 84-537

Office of the Superintendent of Financial Institutions [www.osfi-bsif.gc.ca]

* Accounting for Financial Instruments Designated as Fair Value Option, February, 2007
* Regulated Entities, Insurance Companies, Financial Data
* Table of OSFI Guidelines
* The Supervisory Guide Applicable to Federally Regulated Insurance Companies

Application Case

Joanne arrives relieved it is the last session — as interesting as all this has been, she's beginning to feel more than a little overwhelmed by it all. Francesca opens up the conversation, "We're going to cover a lot in this session but it is, in some ways, the part that will bring all the rest together. We couldn't start with this because it is important to understand the policies and what they do before you can understand why insurance companies operate the way they do. Any particular questions to start?"

"Yes," replies Joanne, "Can you tell me something about the basic operations of insurers as businesses?"

A. "There are four facets to **insurance operations** (Page 324):
1. Underwriting — selecting and classifying applicants.
2. Claims settlement — validating and paying claims.
3. Rate making — deciding on the premiums.
4. Production — sales and marketing.

In addition, we will be looking at the special accounting rules for insurance companies as well as having an idea of how these rules affect their financial statements."

B. "**Underwriting** is the process of selecting and classifying applicants so that the insurer charges each policyholder the correct rate. **Underwriting principles** include:
1. Setting standards by which each applicant is assessed.
2. Making sure each category is balanced — making sure the policyholders in each class are relatively similar as risk exposures.
3. Providing equality so that policyholders are charged fairly — that some groups are not wildly subsidizing other groups" (Pages 324–325).

C. "Insurers have underwriting categories so they can more easily figure out what to charge each applicant. There are three basic categories:
1. standard risks
2. sub-standard risks, and

3. preferred risks."

D. "The **process of underwriting** has three steps:
1. The applicant applies for coverage.
2. The agent or broker supplies additional information if he or she has any.
3. The insurer solicits information from other sources like the motor vehicle licensing bureau or a family doctor" (Page 325).

E. "**Claims settlement** involves
1. checking to make sure the claimant is covered,
2. checking the validity of a claim, and
3. assisting in some way like helping someone find alternate accommodation after a fire (Page 326).

This process is often referred to as **adjusting** even though the term adjuster applies only to P&C insurers."

F. "**Production** is the sales and marketing side of insurance operations. A couple of things are particularly important for consumers.
1. One is the various levels of authority, the ability to act on behalf of the insurance company, that the agent or broker have (Page 326).
2. Also notice the difference between agents who work for one company and brokers who sell insurance for more than one insurer." (Page 327)
3. Insurance companies are regulated and the people who sell insurance are also regulated. That means you have to be licensed to sell insurance.
   (a) **Life and health agents** have to take the Life Licence Qualification Program (LLQP) whose contents and education requirements has been established by the **Canadian Council of Insurance Regulators (CCIR)** [www.ccir-ccrra.org]. As a result, the content of LLQP is the same all across Canada. Most life insurance is sold through agents working for one company (Tables 9.1 and 9.2).
   (b) Licensing requirements for **P&C agents and brokers** varies by jurisdiction because each province and territory regulates auto insurance for its own jurisdictions.
      i. It is make further complicated by the fact that the education and licensing requirements for agents and brokers is often different within each jurisdiction. To make matters worse, in **Ontario**:
         • **brokers** are licensed by the Registered Insurance Brokers of Ontario (RIBO), while
         • **agents** are licensed by the Financial Services Commission of Ontario (FSCO).
      ii. Let's look at the contents of General Insurance Essential which is the required course in many provinces and territories for licensing to get an idea of the content (Table 9.3).
      iii. "Many agents and brokers also sell Accident and Sickness (A & S) insurance for which they need the LLQP — A & S."
4. "The insurance industry is large and offers employment at many levels. Some licences require that a person be employed and/or sponsored by an insurance company, agency, or broker before they can take the courses but other licences do not" (Table 9.4).

G. "**Rate making** is the term used to describe the process of figuring out how much to charge. These methods are used for most insurance pricing except life insurance. There are two basic ways of deciding on a premium and each way has alternatives within it (Page 330):
1. **Class rating** which puts people in classes based on certain objective criteria. We saw some of these criteria in auto and home insurance.
2. **Individual** or **merit rating,** which is done when
   (a) there is no appropriate class, or
   (b) the individual is no longer completely represented by the class.

Let's take a look at the numbers for some of these."

H. **"Rate making for life insurance** is quite different because it is based on **mortality tables** (Pages 334 and 335) which are developed to show the rate at which people die. There are many kinds of mortality tables — smokers, non-smokers for instance — but we are going to keep it simple and use only two classes — men and women. Before we start looking at how this works, we need to simplify things a little so we don't get lost in the numbers. Our example is going to look at five years of term insurance for a 25-year-old man:

    1. Number alive at the beginning of the year, number who die at age 25, etc. (Mortality Table 9.6).

    2. This example is for a $1,000 face value policy with the:

        (a) **premium** being paid at the beginning of the year (BOY) since insurance companies always collect the premium in advance, and

        (b) all **claims** being paid at the end of the year (EOY).

    3. This means the insurer has the premiums for one year before paying out the claims and can invest the funds for this year. We are going to **invest at 5%.**

We are going to look at three basic examples."

I. "Now let's check to see if these premiums are correct. We will do this by looking at the liability account (**reserve**)" (Page 339).

J. "Before we look at the ways in which accounting rules for insurance companies are different, let's get an idea of the regulatory environment in which insurance companies operate" (Page 341).

    1. "The **Office of the Superintendent of Financial Institutions (OSFI)** oversees all federally regulated insurance companies. Most, but not all, insurance companies that are provincially regulated are also registered federally. Provincial regulators oversee provincially regulated insurance companies in much the same way as OSFI. They following table outlines the activities and interventions that OSFI can take if it sees that an insurance company is getting into financial difficulty. Notice that in Stage 4, OSFI can actually take control of the company" (Table 9.15).

K. "A quick word about investments. Insurance companies have huge amounts of investments so they can pay out claims from the premiums they have received. Life insurance companies in particular have to invest funds for a very long period of time before they are paid out. And OSFI wants to make sure the funds will be there when they are needed. As the following table shows, over 50% of *total* assets are invested bonds, which are relatively low risk" (Table 9.16).

L. "Now let's looking at the **accounting rules** in the insurance industry. You can't really read financial statements for insurance companies without understanding how the rules are different from other companies, who operate using **Generally Accepted Accounting Principles (GAAP)**. And GAAP is changing because the **Accounting Standards Board (AcSB)** is requiring all publicly traded companies to adopt **International Financial Reporting Standards (IFRS)** by January 2011.

    1. We'll start with **asset valuation**. In Chapter 1, you'll remember that we looked at the insurance sector in the context of all other sectors in Canada. Let's review the total assets in this sector from Table 1.3" (Table. 9.17).

        The old accounting rules for insurance companies required them to show most investment assets at market value so the impact of IFRS may not be all that large for most of them. We are not going to study this in detail but the next time you consider investing in an insurance company, you should be aware of these rules.

    2. A large part of the **Liabilities** of insurance companies represents policyholders' money being held for future payout. We've talked about these, they are called **reserves**. Let's look at the type of reserves they have on their balance sheets. You'll be familiar with most of the categories as we've talked about them already (Table 9.19).

3. "The **Equity** section is pretty much the same except for two items:
   (a) Policyholders' equity, which holds the cash surrender values.
   (b) Policyholders' surplus for mutual insurers who, you'll recall from Chapter 1, don't have shareholders (Table 9.20).
4. The **Income Statement** also has a difference in the way acquisition costs are recognized. Everything else is pretty much the same as you learned in your accounting courses but with a different name. The recognition of unrealized losses under IFRS is not new for other industries since they were always supposed to record assets at the lower of cost or market. However, under IFRS, unrecognized gains will now be reported for many investment assets, as shown in Table 9.18" (Table 9.21).

M. "OK. Let's put this together with an example to show the interplay between the Income Statement and the unearned premium reserve and the ratio of this reserve to premiums earned (which is monitored by OSFI)." (Page 347, Example 1)

N. "This takes us to **reinsurance**, which is the process of ceding (passing off) risk and premiums to another insurer. It is done for two reasons:
   1. to reduce the possibility of a catastrophic loss for the insurer, large-risk exposures are shared with other insurers, and
   2. it reduce the reserves to premiums earned ratio allowing the insurer to write more business if it is in a strong growth position."

Let's look at S.T. Ltd as it cedes some of its premiums written and see what happens to that ratio" (Pages 348–349, Example 2).

Concept Questions

1. What are the four facets of insurance operations?

2. What are the three goals of underwriting principles?

3. Define the principle of adverse selection.

4. Describe in detail the three-step process to underwriting.

5. What are the three key elements in loss adjusting?

6. What is the main purpose of an insurance adjuster?

7. What is an adjustment bureau?

8. Discuss what is meant by primary and excess insurance, and state how the birthday rule relates to this discussion.

9. What is the difference between pro-rata liability with contribution by equal shares?

10. What is the basic difference between an insurance agent and an insurance broker?

11. What is the name of the program that all agents selling all lines of life and health insurance have to take before they can write a licensing exam?

12. Antony is a P&C broker and wants to sell travel insurance along with the auto insurance he now sells.
    (a) What is the name of the program he will have to take?
    (b) If Antony is an agent for only one P&C company, what are the two names of his licence?
    (c) If Antony sells Accident and Sickness insurance, will he study "Investment Products" in the LLQP program?

13. What two national associations offer P&C licensing programs in most jurisdictions?

14. In Ontario:
    (a) Who licences P&C:
        i. Agents?
        ii. Brokers?
    (b) What two organizations offer the education requirements to write the RIBO exam and what are the names of the programs?

15. What is the name of the national designation developed by the Insurance Brokers Association of Canada?

16. How many agents work for one company in
    (a) P&C insurance?
    (b) life insurance?

17. What are the three objectives of rate making?

18. Briefly describe the method used by life insurers to determine policy rates.

19. What are the two methods used by P&C insurers to calculate class rates.

20. List the four methods used by P&C insurance companies to set individual premiums based on merit and individual experience.

21. What is a pure premium? What is its other name?

22. What is the gross premium and what does it cover?

23. How is the expense ratio calculated for:
    (a) the total of a class of insures and financial statements?
    (b) an individual?

24. Describe how the loss ratio method figures out what new rates should be.

25. What is the credibility factor and when is it used?

26. Describe how judgement rating, schedule rating, and retrospective rating calculate individual insurance rates.

27. Why does calculating life insurance premiums provide a significant challenge when compared to calculating premiums for property insurance?

28. How is the pure premium calculated in life insurance?

29. When calculating insurance premiums, what assumption is made when each of the following occur:
    (a) Premiums are paid?
    (b) Claims are paid?

30. What is a level premium?

31. What is a policy reserve?

32. At what stage of the supervisory process can OSFI:
    (a) direct a company to modify it actuarial assumptions and methods?
    (b) decide to wind up the company?
    (c) initiate discussions with the consumer compensation agencies Assuris and PACCIC so they will know their services may be required?

33. What percentage of total investments are invested in bonds for
    (a) P&C insurers? (Answer: 83.9%)
    (b) life and Health insurers? (Answer: 60.5%)

34. What are assets:
    (a) held for trading?

(b) held-to-maturity?

(c) available-for-sale?

35. An insurance company holds Def Jam bonds that cost them $1,000,000. Def Jam records bonds that which it intends to sell. These bonds have shot up in value and sell for $2,000,000 because of massive global interest rate cuts. The company never intended to hold the bonds to maturity and may sell them now.

(a) According to IFRS, what value should these bonds be recorded at on the financial statements of the company?

(b) If it sells the bonds, is the gain recognized immediately in net income?

36. What is the name of the reserve that holds the difference between the loss on premium income incurred and the future liability?

37. What is the name of the equity account that holds a mutual insurer's retained earnings?

38. Why do property and casualty insurance companies cede their premiums to other insurance companies? What is this called?

Application Questions

39. Nav is a heavy smoker and wishes to purchase life insurance. Which rate category will he most likely fall into?

40. What is wrong with the following statement: Tim just got a job as an adjuster at a large life insurance company.

41. Carl is a shady insurance agent who works for TRY-N-SAVE auto insurance. He loves the large commission he earns on each sale. Carl's contract states that he is not allowed to tell applicants that they have insurance until the application is fully approved by the insurance company. Carl has a habit of telling customers that the insurance will be in place once the applicant signs the application. Can TRY-N-SAVE be held liable for Carl's failure to abide by his contract stipulations in a situation where a customer suffers a loss before the policy is approved by the insurer? Why or why not?

42. Luke, an insurance agent at TRY-N-SAVE auto insurance, has successfully signed up Kathy for an auto policy. The policy's net premium is $1,000, including provincial sales tax of $20. If Luke earns 5% commission on every successful sale, how much commission is he entitled to from TRY-N-SAVE? ($49)

43. TRY-N-SAVE experiences $2,000,000 of losses in a particular class of its automobile insurance business. The company has 50,000 exposure units in this class. Calculate the pure premium that must be charged to cover all losses. ($40)

44. TRY-N-SAVE from the previous question has an expense ratio of 60%. Calculate the gross premium based on the pure premium that was calculated in the previous question. ($100)

45. Assume that TRY-N-SAVE earned $5,000,000 in premiums in a particular class of auto insurance. Its losses were $2,000,000 for that class. What is the loss ratio? (40%)

46. If TRY-N-SAVE expected its loss ratio to be 44%

(a) What is the percentage difference between the expected loss ratio and the actual loss ratio? (9.09%)

(b) What will the new premium be? ($90.91)

47. Assume that a home insurance company finds that its actual loss ratio is 10% more than its expected loss ratio. Jason wants to renew his home insurance and his credibility rating is 40%. How much will his insurance premium change? Will this be an increase or decrease? (6% increase)

48. Annie is 30 years old and wants to buy a three-year term policy worth $1,000. Using an interest rate of 6%, how much is her premium if
    (a) she buys three one-year policies,
    (b) she buys one three-year policy and pays
        i. the premium at the beginning of the first year, or
        ii. an equal premium at the beginning of each of the three years?

Net Premium for Three One-year Terms

A	B	C	D E	F	G
		$B \times \$1,000$			E / F
At Age	# of deaths (claims)	$ Claims @ $1,000 each		# alive $_{BOY}$	Premium $_{BOY}$
		Paid $_{EOY}$	PV $_{BOY}$		

Net Single Premium for a 3-year Term

A	B	C	D E	F	G
		$B \times \$1,000$			E / F
At Age	# of deaths (claims)	$ Claims @ $1,000 each		# alive $_{BOY1}$	Premium $_{BOY1}$
		Paid $_{EOY}$	PV $_{BOY}1$		

Net Level Premium for a 3-year Term

A	B	C	D E F	G
	Table 2	Table 1		E / F
At Age	PV$ Claims $_{BOY1}$	# alive $_{BOY1}$	Premium of $1.00	
			Paid $_{EOY}$ / PV $_{BOY}1$	

49. Calculate the reserve for each of the above premiums

Reserve for Three 1-year Policies, Annual Premium.

A	B	C	D	E	F	G	H	I
		Table 1	$B \times C$	$D + I$	$E(1+k)$		$G(\$1,000)$	$F - H$
Age	# alive $_{BOY}$	Premium $_{BOY}$	Premiums collected	Initial Reserve	Reserve + Interest $_{EOY}$	# of deaths	Claims paid $_{EOY}$	Terminal reserve

Reserve for One 3-year Policy, One Premium

A	B	C	D	E	F	G	H	I
		Table 2	B × C	D + I	E(1+k)		G($1,000)	F − H
Age	# alive $_{BOY}$	Premium $_{BOY}$	Premiums collected	Initial Reserve	Reserve + Interest $_{EOY}$	# of deaths	Claims paid $_{EOY}$	Terminal reserve

Reserve for One 3-year Policy, Annual Premiums

A	B	C	D	E	F	G	H	I
		Table 4	B × C	D + I	E(1+k)		G($1,000)	F − H
Age	# alive $_{BOY}$	Premium $_{BOY}$	Premiums collected	Initial Reserve	Reserve + Interest $_{EOY}$	# of deaths	Claims paid $_{EOY}$	Terminal reserve

50. Insure Ltd had the following balance at the end of Year 7.

	EOY 7	
Cash	14,500	100%
Unearned premium reserve	10,000	69%
Capital	5,000	34%
Surplus	(500)	−3%
	14,500	100%

(a) If it wrote premiums of $28,000 in Year 8 and $36,000 in Year 9, what were the cash and surplus at the end of Year 9? (Answer: $25,700 and $2,700)

(b) Insure Ltd decided to cede 30% of its premiums written in Year 8.
   i. What was its Surplus before and after reinsuring? (Answer: $700, $1,540)
   ii. What was the ratio of reserves to premiums earned before and after reinsuring? (Answer: 58.3% and 49.5%)

Acronyms and Glossary

Acronyms

Chapter numbers are in brackets.

(A&S) Accident & Sickness (9)

(ACB) Adjusted cost basis (8)

(AD&D) Accidental Death and Dismemberment

(AcSB) Accounting Standards Board (9)

AcSB Accounting Standards Board (9)

AD&D Accidental Death and Dismemberment (8)

(AD) Assessment Divisions (7)

(AWCBC) Association of Workers' Compensation Boards of Canada (7)

(CAC) Consumers' Association of Canada (3)

(CAIB) Canadian Accredited Insurance Broker (9)

(CHA) Canada Health Act (6)

(CCPFSI) Canadian Consumer Protection for Financial Institution Failures (1)

(CCIR) Canadian Council of Insurance Regulators (9)

(CICA) Canadian Institute of Chartered Accountants Handbook (9)

(CLHIA) Canadian Life and Health Insurance Association (9)

(CLEAR) Canadian Loss Experience Automobile Rating System (3)

(CSV) Cash surrender value (8)

(CCIR) Canadian Council of Insurance Regulators (9)

(CCPFSI) Canadian Consumer Protection for Financial Institution Failures (1)

(CAI) Certificate of Automobile Insurance (3)

(CHA) *Canada Health Act* (6)

(CICA) Canadian Institute of Chartered Accountants Handbook (9)

(CCFC) Commission of the Future of Health Care (6)

(CAC) Consumers' Association of Canada (3)

(CSV) Cash surrender value (8)

(D&O) Directors and officers (5)

(E&O) Errors and omissions (5)

(EIA) Employment Insurance Account (7)

(FCAC) Financial Consumer Agency of Canada (1)

(FSCO) Financial Services Commission of Ontario (1) (3) (9)

(GAAP) Generally Accepted Accounting Principles (9)

(GBA) Gender-based analysis (6)

(GIE) General Insurance Essentials (9)

(HHR) Health Human Resources (6)

(HSR) Health Services Review (6)

(HIDS) *Hospital Insurance and Diagnostic Services Act* (6)

(HTA) *Highway Traffic Act* (3)

(IBAC) Insurance Brokers Association of Canada (9)

(IBAO) Insurance Brokers Association of Ontario (9)

(IBC) Insurance Bureau of Canada (3) (9)

(IFRS) International Financial Reporting Standards (9)

(IIC) Insurance Institute of Canada (9)

(IICC) Insurance Information Centre of Canada (3)

(IIO) Insurance Institute of Ontario (9)

(IFRS) International Financial Reporting Standards (9)

(LSIF) Labour Sponsored Investment Funds (8)

(LLQP) Life License Qualification Program (9)

(LSIF) Labour Sponsored Investment Funds (8)
(MER) Management expense ratio (8)
(MCWLP) Manitoba Cataract Waiting List Program (6)
(MCA) *Medical Care Act* (6)
(MRT) Minimax Regret Theory (1)
(MVAC) Motor Vehicle Accident Claim Funds (3)
(NHS) National Health Service (6)
(NPS) National Physician Survey (6)
(NWTS) National Wait Times Strategy (6)
(NAV) Net asset value (8)
(NAVPS) Net asset value per share (8)
(NCPI) Net cost of pure insurance (8)
(NLP) Net level premium (9)
(NP) Net premium (9)
(NSP) Net single premium (9)
(NHS) National Health Service (6)
(OAP) OAP Ontario Automobile Policy (3)
(OAS) Old Age Security (7)
(OHS) Occupational Health and Safety (7)
(OECD) Organization for Economic Co-operation and Development (6)
(OSFI) Office of the Superintendent of Financial Institutions (1)
(OTL) Other Than Life license (9)
(P&C) Property and Casualty Insurance (1) (5)
(PACCIC) Property and Casualty Insurance Compensation Corporation (1)
(PIPP) Personal Injury Protection Plan (Manitoba) (3)
(REIT) Real estate income trust (8)
(RAAQ) Régie de l'assurance automobile du Québec (3)
(RIBO) Registered Insurance Brokers of Ontario (9)
(RRIF) Registered Retirement Income Plans (8)
(RRSP) Registered Retirement Savings Plan (8)
(RCHF) Royal Commission on Health Services (6)
(SPF) Standard Policy Form (3)
(SAAQ) Société de l'assurance automobile du Québec (3)
(SGI) Saskatchewan Government Insurance (3)
(SHA) *Saskatchewan Hospitalization Act* (6)
(TFSA) Tax-Free Savings Account (8)
(TRIA) *Terrorism Risk Insurance Act* (5)
(UL) Universal Life Insurance (8)
(UIA) *Unemployment Insurance Act* (7)
(ULI) *Uniform Life Insurance Act* (1)
(VICC) Vehicle Information Centre of Canada (3)
(WSA) Work Sharing Agreement (7)

Glossary
Chapter numbers are in brackets.

#, A

49% rule (2) The victim must be 49% or less at fault to collect for a negligent act.

50% rule (2) The victim can collect only if the victim's negligence is not greater than the negligence of the other party.

Absolute liability (2) (3) One is liable even if there was no negligence.

Accelerated death benefit (8) A living benefits rider that allows the insured who are terminally ill or who suffer from certain catastrophic diseases to collect all or part of their life insurance benefits before they die.

Accident (5) An event that causes a loss and is sudden, unexpected and unintended.

Accident benefits (3) Benefits for insured persons if they are injured or killed in an auto accident.

Accidental death and dismemberment (8) (*also known as* double indemnity) A life insurance policy pays double if insured dies from an accident instead of from an illness.

Account value (8) The total of all investment accounts in a Universal life policy, including investment income minus deductions and expenses.

Accumulating reserve (8) The name in the *Income Tax Act* for the legal reserve or policy reserve that accumulates to hold the death benefit and cash surrender value.

Activities of daily living (6) The activities that must be impaired to collect on a long-term care policy.

Actual cash value (4) The cost less depreciation, but can have different definitions depending on the policy.

Add-on plan (3) An auto plan in which the benefits are paid on a no-fault basis and the injured person also has the right to sue. This is the case in New Brunswick.

Adhesion contract (2) A contract in which the applicant must accept the entire contract including terms and conditions and cannot bargain.

Adjusted cost basis (ACB) (8) The cumulative premiums less cumulative dividends less net cost of pure insurance (NCPI) [P(death) × net amount at risk (death benefit − accumulating fund)].

Additional living expenses (4) Expenses incurred while repairs are made to one's damaged home.

Adjuster (9) The person that assesses the facts of the claim and the extent of the coverage.

Adjusting expenses (9) The costs of settling a claim, the benefits of the policy.

Adjusting losses (9) The costs of settling a claim, the benefits of the policy.

Adjustment bureau (9) An adjusting organization and is often used for catastrophic losses, such as those from a tornado.

Adverse selection (9)   The tendency of persons with a higher-than-average chance of loss to seek insurance at standard (average) rates, which, if not controlled by underwriting, results in higher-than-expected loss levels.

Advertising injury (5) (*also known as* personal injury or personal and advertising injury)   This coverage deals with slander, libel, persecution, defamation of character, false arrest, detention or imprisonment, malicious prosecution, violation of the right of privacy, and unlawful entry or eviction.

Age of majority (2)   When a person is considered to be an adult and can legally sign a contract, usually at age 18 or 19.

Age of reason (2)   Age 7 and older.

Agency agreement (9)   An agreement between the agent and the principal (insurer) outlining the agent's authority.

Agency relationship (9)   is one in which the agent acts on behalf of the principal.

Agent (9)   The person that legally represents the insurer and has the authority to act on behalf of one insurance company.

Aggregate deductible (5)   The firm pays all the losses for the year until the deductible limit is reached.

Aleatory contract (2)   A contract where the dollar amounts exchanged may not be equal but depend on an uncertain event.

All perils (3)   A combination of collision and comprehensive having a common deductible.

All risk coverage (2) (4)   Coverage that covers everything unless it is specifically excluded.

Amount at risk (8)   For the insurer, this is the difference between the face value of a whole life policy and the cash surrender value at any point in time.

Apparent authority (9)   If a third party believes an agent has certain authority, the principal is bound by the agent's actions.

Artificial person (2)   A legal entity such as a corporation having legal rights and duties.

Assignment (7)   This transfers the benefits to another party.

Attachment bond (5)   A surety bond that guarantees that if the court rules against the plaintive who has attached the property of the defendant in a lawsuit, the defendant will be reimbursed for damages as a result of having the property attached.

Attained-age method (8)   This uses the age of the life insured at the beginning of the policy year.

Attractive nuisance (2)   A condition that can attract and injure children. Children are considered to be licensees, not trespassers because they cannot recognize danger. The occupant must keep the premises safe and take ordinary care to protect the children from harm.

Auctioneer's bond (5)   A surety bond that guarantees the accurate accounting of sales proceeds by the auctioneer.

Automatic premium loan (8)   This automatically pays premiums in default by borrowing against the CSV as a policy loan.

Average (5)   A partial loss.

B

B/U ratio (7) The ratio of regular beneficiaries (people receiving "regular" benefits as opposed to people receiving maternity or parental benefits, etc.) to unemployed.

Bail bond (5) A bond which is forfeited if a person fails to appear in court.

Bailee (5) Someone who has temporary possession of property that belongs to another for storage, repair or servicing.

Bargaining contract (2) A contract that the applicant can make counter proposals or ask for changes.

Base plan (6) A plan that outlines the health care coverage for a province or territory.

Basic policy (4) The starting point, the minimum coverage.

Beneficiary (8) The person, people, corporation, trust or charity who receives the death benefit in a life insurance contract and becomes the policyholder when the life insured dies.

Beneficiary designation (8) The beneficiary designated or named in the insurance contract.

Bid bond (5) A surety bond in which the owner (obligee) is guaranteed that the party awarded a bid on a project will sign a contract and furnish a performance bond.

Bilateral contract (2) A contract in which each party makes a legally enforceable promise.

Blanket insurance (5) Insurance that provides coverage under a single limit for two or more items or locations.

Block policy (5) A policy that cover loss to the property of a merchant, wholesaler or manufacturer including property of others in their care, custody or control, on consignment or sold but not delivered.

Boiler and machinery (5) Insurance that protects against the physical damage and financial loss that results from the sudden and accidental breakdown of boilers and other machinery and equipment.

Bonded (5) This refers to a person's status when they are covered by employee-theft insurance.

Breach of contract (2) This is wrongful non-performance, meaning one party to a contract fails to perform an obligation which is part of the contract.

Breach of warranty (5) This means the product does not do what it is intended to do.

Broad policy (4) A policy that provides "all-risks" coverage on the buildings and "named perils" coverage on the contents.

Broker (9) The person that legally represents the insured and sells for more than one company as an independent agent.

Builders risk (5) Risk that covers buildings under construction.

Bundled (8) This refers to the elements of a life insurance policy that are connected to each other.

Burglary (5) Theft using force to gain entry or exit.

Business floater (5) A policy that provides broad and comprehensive protection on property that is frequently moved from one location to another.

Business income and extra expenses (5)   Commercial insurance that covers loss of income and added expenses incurred to continue operations after a loss.

Business interruption (5) (*also known as* business income)   Insurance covers net income before taxes plus continuing expenses.

C

Cafeteria plans (6)   Group health plans where employees are allocated points and can choose the coverage on which they want to spend their points.

Capital guaranteed (8)   The amount of the capital that is guaranteed for a segregated fund.

Capital retention approach (8)   This approach preserves the capital. The steps are: determine needs, prepare a balance sheet, determine income-producing assets and determine amount of insurance required.

Capitalized value (8)   This refers to the present value of the annual shortfall when calculating the amount of life insurance needed.

Captive insurer (1) (5)   A wholly-owned subsidiary of non-insurance organizations.

Captive insurance agent (9)   An exclusive agent for one insurer or a group of related companies.

Career insurance agent (9)   A person that specializes in one insurer's products.

Cash refund annuity (8)   An annuity that pays the balance to the beneficiary in a lump sum when the annuitant dies.

Cash surrender value (CSV) (8)   A by-product of the level-premium method, not the purpose of it. It is the amount a whole life policyholder can receive if the policy is surrendered (given up).

Cash value (8)   The same as cash surrender value.

Casualty insurance (1) (5)   Insurance that covers workers compensation, liability, crime, glass and boiler coverage but   not fire and property.

Chance of loss (1)   The probability an event will occur.

Child life insurance (8)   A rider that provides insurance on the life of a child — a child as young as 15 days can be automatically insured.

Choice no-fault plan (3)   A plan that offers policyholders a choice between a cheaper no-fault insurance plan with no right to sue for personal injury, and the ability to opt out and elect the tort system, retaining the right to sue for compensation for injuries that are a result of negligence. This is the case in Saskatchewan.

Churning (8)   Using the cash surrender value on a current policy to buy a supposedly improved policy.

Cinderella diseases (6)   Diseases that were not recognized or prioritized in the five areas selected for benchmarks.

Civil law (2)   Law based on a code containing rules and principles governing private rights and remedies. It is the foundation for law in Quebec and France.

Claim representative (9)   Someone who works in the claims department of a life and health insurance company.

Claims-made policy (5)   A policy that pays for losses after a certain date (some specific time before the beginning of the policy period), but the claims are made during the policy period.

Class of beneficiaries (8)   A group of people who are beneficiaries, such as "my children".

Class rating (9) (*also known as* Manual rating)   A rating that places similar insured individuals into the same underwriting class, and each person is charged the same rate.

Clawback (7)   The 15% tax applied to Old Age Security benefits over the threshold amount.

Closed-end mutual fund (8)   A fund in which the total number of units is fixed.

Co-insurance (1) (2) (4) (5) (6) (9)   The requirement whereby the insured pay for part of the loss.

Collaterally assigned (8)   When a whole life policy has been used as collateral for a loan at a financial institution.

Collision or upset (3)   Coverage to repair a car if it is involved in a collision or tips over.

Commodity price risk (1)   Risk that arises from changes in commodity prices such as oil, gas electricity and copper.

Common law (2)   A system of laws originating in England based on precedent.

Common mistake (2)   A mistake in a contract where both parties make the same error. Each knows the intention of the other and accepts it, but each is mistaken about some underlying and fundamental fact.

Commutative contract (2)   A contract in which each party gives up goods and services of theoretically equal value.

Comparative negligence (2)   When both the injured and the injuring share the damages when both contributed to the injury.

Compassionate care benefit (7)   A type of Employment Insurance benefit.

Competent parties (2)   Individuals that are well qualified, capable, and prepared.

Completed operations (5)   Faulty work performed away from the premises after the work or operation is completed.

Compliance (1)   The legal requirement that companies, products and sales agents must comply with all applicable laws and regulations, both federal and provincial.

Component parts (8)   The aspects making up a Universal Life insurance policy.

Comprehensive (3)   Automobile insurance covers repairs to cars if they are damaged other than by collision.

Comprehensive general liability (5)   Liability coverage that insures against situations that are often excluded from general liability coverage.

Comprehensive homeowners policy (4)   A policy that covers all risks for property and contents.

Compulsory coverage (3)   Covered required as proof of insurance to register or license the car.

Concealment (2)   This occurs when an applicant fails to disclose known facts.

Concurrent disability (7)   A disability caused by more than one injury or sickness or from both.

Conditions (2) (3) (4)   Provisions that qualify or limit the insurer's promise to pay.

Condominium association (5) Insurance that covers the building, equipment and common areas.

Conduct of business operations (5) Liability due to business operations.

Consequential damage (5) A loss caused by another loss such spoiled food if a freezer breaks down.

Consequential loss (5) Added expenses that are incurred as a result of the direct loss.

Consideration (2) Something of value given in return for the performance or promise of performance to form a contract. It is usually money.

Contingent beneficiary (8) This beneficiary receives the proceeds only if the primary beneficiary dies.

Contingent business interruption (5) This covers losses arising from damage to the property of others.

Contingent liability (5) Liability that arises from work done by independent contractors.

Contract bond (5) A surety bond that guarantee that the principal will fulfill all contractual obligations.

Contract of indemnity (2) This compensates for the loss or damage while not allowing a profit. Life insurance contracts do not fall under this provision.

Contractual liability (5) Liability that arises when a business assumes the legal liability of another party in a written or oral contract — for example, a tenant assumes the legal liability when renting the entire building.

Contribution by equal shares (9) This is applied when there is more than one insurer and each insurer pays equally to the limits of the coverage.

Contributions (8) Deposits to a life insurance account.

Contributory negligence (2) When the injured person's conduct falls below the standard of care required for his or her own protection and this conduct contributed to the injury.

Conversion clause (8) This clause gives a policyowner the option to convert to permanent insurance without a medical.

Convertible (2) (8) Usually means a term policy can be converted to a cash value policy without evidence of insurability

Coordination-of-benefits provision (9) A provision within a group health policy where a benefit is covered by more than one person in the household. There is a rule which states which plan is primary.

Cost of living rider (8) The policyowner can buy 1-year term life insurance equal to the percentage change in the Consumer Price Index (CPI) with no evidence of insurability.

Court bond (5) A surety bond that protects one person (obligee) against loss in the event that the person bonded does not prove that he or she is legally entitled to the remedy sought against the obligee.

Covered property (3) This type of property includes building, business personal property of the insured, personal property of others, debris removal, preservation of property, fire department charges, pollutant clean up and removal.

Credibility factor (9) This reflects the degree of confidence the insurer assigns to the insured's past experience to predict future losses.

Credit (5)   Insurance covers customer insolvency and is for manufacturers, wholesalers and services organizations, not retailers. It covers only abnormal losses.

Credit risk (9)   The risk concerning one's inability to meet loan payments

Credit risk (1)   The risk that a receivable will become uncollectible .

Creditor-proof (8)   Creditors have access to insurance proceeds only if the proceeds are paid to the estate or the policy is collateral on a loan. Segregated funds are out of creditors' reach.

Crime (5)   A legal wrong against society punishable by fines, imprisonment or death.

Critical illness insurance (7)   Insurance that pays a tax-free lump sum if the policyholder is diagnosed with a critical illness or condition and survives for 30 days. The benefit amount is between $10,000 to $2,000,000.

Critical loss (1)   Serious financial exposure for the enterprise, possibly leading to bankruptcy.

D

Damage (3)   With respect to an automobile, this means it is not destroyed and can be repaired .

Damages (2)   Court-awarded money paid to an injured party to compensate for a legal wrong committed against the injured party.

Data (4)   The information including programs, recorded on electronic media usable in data processing operations (Homeowners Policy).

Death benefit (3) (7) (8)   This benefit is the coverage or the amount payable upon the death of the insured.

Death benefit options (8)   The options on a Universal Life policy are level death benefit, level death benefit + cumulative deposits, indexed death benefit and level death benefit + account value.

Decision Theory (1)   A theory concerned with identifying the best decision to take, assuming a fully-informed, fully-rationale decision maker who is able to predict, estimate and calculate with perfect accuracy. It arrives at a decision by calculating the expected value of the alternatives and selecting the one that incurs the lowest costs.

Declarations (2)   An insurance policy provides information about what exposures are to be covered and for how much, who is insured, the premiums and deductibles.

Decreasing premiums (8)   The coverage for a term life insurance policy decreases as the expiry approaches.

Decreasing term (8)   A policy where the death benefit declines over the term but the premiums remain the same.

Deductible (2) (3) (5) (6)   An amount subtracted from the total payment in order to reduce small claims, premiums and moral and morale hazard.

Deductive reasoning (1)   Used with probabilities where the probability is obvious from the nature of the event.

Deferred annuity payments (8)   Payments do not begin until some time in the future.

Delist (6)   To remove coverage for something from a provincial health care plan.

Demutualization (1) The process of a mutual insurer issuing stock to raise funds by acquiring shareholders.

Dependent of the principal life insured (8) The spouse or child of the policyholder.

Deposits (8) (*also known as* Contributions to a Universal Life policy) These are payments made by the insured to cover premiums or to add to the investment.

Described automobile (3) The automobile or trailer specifically shown on the Certificate of Automobile Insurance.

Direct compensation (3) Each party is paid by their own insurance company, regardless of which motorist is at fault.

Direct loss or damage (1) (3) (4) (5) Damage to or loss of property caused by a peril.

Disability rider (8) This pays the premiums of a life insurance policy in the event that the insured becomes totally and permanently disabled.

Disability waiver (2) The benefit waives the premium while the insured is disabled.

Discharged contract (2) The parties are freed from their obligation due to performance, mutual consent, frustration or breach.

Discover period (5) Often one year in duration, meaning the insured has up to one year to discover a loss after the policy ends.

Dividend scale (8) The estimated future dividends to be paid on a participating policy.

Dividends (8) These are paid out of the excess of the actual return on the policy reserve over the guaranteed rate. They occur when the operating expenses are less than anticipated or investment returns were higher than predicted. They are paid out in cash, used to reduce premiums, left to accumulate with interest or used to purchase additional paid-up insurance. They are not taxable income.

Double indemnity (8) *See* Accidental Death and Dismemberment.

Dram shop law (2) (5) A law that imputes negligence to an owner of a business that sells liquor should a customer, while intoxicated, cause injury, or damage to another person or their property.

Duress (2) Using coercion and intimidation to force another party into a contract.

Duty of care (2) A legal definition meaning "to refrain from causing harm to another person".

Dwelling (4) The building occupied by the insured as the principal residence.

Dynamic risk (1) Risk that arises from changes in the economy and is insured by governments.

E

Economic loss (7) Lost earnings for Workers' Compensation.

Eligibility period (7) The amount of time, such as three months, a new employee must wait before he or she can join an employer's group insurance plan.

Elimination period (7) (*also known as* Waiting period) The amount of time to wait before the benefits start.

Employers' liability (4)   Legal liability, as noted in a homeowners policy, for unintentional bodily injury to residence employees arising out of their employment by the insured.

Employment Insurance Account (7)   An account that holds the deficit or surplus between income received from premiums and interest and benefits and administration costs paid.

Endogenous risk (1)   Risk that is dependent on our actions.

Endorsement (2) (4)   An addition to the policy that adds, deletes or modifies provisions in the original contract. It is usually used in connection with property and casualty insurance.

Endowment life (8)   Policies in which, at the end of the limited premium payment time, the face value is paid out even if the insured is still alive. Since they are now taxed as income, they are no longer popular.

Enemy alien (2)   A person whose residence or business is located in enemy territory during war or other hostilities which are damaging to the public interest.

Entire contract clause (2)   The policy and attached application constitute the entire contract between the parties.

Errors and omissions (E&O) (5)   Covers a negligent act, error or omission.

Estoppel (2)   Prevents one party from denying a fact he has already confirmed or accepted by his own actions.

Excess coverage (3)   Adds liability, accident benefits, loss and theft coverage over the mandatory minimum to automobile insurance.

Excess insurance (5)   Insurance that provides an additional dollar amount of coverage based on the underlying policy.

Excess insurer (9)   The insurer pays above the policy limits of the primary insurer.

Exchange rate risk (1)   Risk that arises from changes in foreign exchange rates and affect businesses that import and export.

Excluded driver (3)   Someone specifically not covered by the policy when driving the described automobile. The exception is coverage for Accident Benefits required by law.

Exclusions (2) (4) (5) (6) (7)   Items or circumstances not covered by an insurance policy.

Exclusive agent (9)   An agent that sells for only one insurance company.

Exempt policy (8)   A life insurance policy which emphasizes death benefits. The accumulating fund can be greater than mortality costs and expenses but not excessively so. Term is always exempt since it has no accumulating fund.

Exogenous risk (1)   A risk which we have no control over and which is not affected by our actions.

Expense approach (8)   This approach calculates the amount of insurance required by looking at annual expenses.

Expense loading (9)   This covers administrative costs, selling costs, and profits in an insurance premium.

Expense ratio (9)   The expense loading expressed as a percentage of the gross premium.

Experience rating (9)   This rating uses the loss ratio method, usually over a three-year period, and adjusts it by a credibility factor.

Express authority (9) The agent has the authority through the agency agreement to act on behalf of the insurance company.

Extended coverage (5) Insurance that provides protection against perils not covered by the basic policy such as riots and civil commotion.

Extended health benefit plan (6) This plan covers services not covered by government insurance, such as registered therapists and specialists, travel benefits, critical care benefits, prescription drugs, dental, hospital benefits, and students accident benefits.

Extended term (8) (*also known as* paid-up term) A term policy bought by using the cash surrender value (CSV) of a whole life policy as a lump sum premium payment on a term insurance policy.

Extra billing (6) The practice of doctors charging patients extra for office visits. It is banned by the *Canada Health Act.*

F

Face value (8) The amount of death benefit.

Facilities Associations (3) The insurers of last resort. Since auto insurance is compulsory, they will provide insurance when no private insurer will.

Facility fee (6) (*also known as* a User fee) A fee for receiving an insured service at a hospital or clinic. It is banned by the *Canada Health Act.*

Fair rental value (4) The amount of rental income lost during repairs.

Fair value accounting (9) A system which records assets at their fair market value rather than using the lower of cost or market rule.

Family coverage rider (8) A rider that adds a dependent to a policy of the life insured. It is not available for group plans.

Family Purpose Doctrine (2) A doctrine which states that the owner of a car can be held responsible for the negligence of immediate family members while they are driving the car.

Fault (2) Inexcusable conduct that intentionally or carelessly causes harm.

Fault determination rules (3) Rules sometimes used to decide who is at fault in an auto accident.

Federal surety bond (5) A surety bond that guarantees that the bonded party will comply with federal standards.

Fiduciary duty (2) An obligation to perform a duty to another person in an irreproachable and trustworthy manner.

Final expenses (8) Expenses, such as funeral costs, that are incurred when a person dies.

Floater (4) A rider attached to fire and property insurance policy covering specific items.

Flow through (8) The income received and paid out "retains it nature" and is taxed the same way.

Formulary (6) Are listed drugs, a list of prescription drugs covered by a provincial or territorial health plan.

Fortuitous loss (2) Accidental, not deliberate, loss.

Franchise deductible (5) Used in ocean marine and is either a dollar amount or a percentage. The entire loss is paid once the loss is greater than the deductible.

Fraudulent misrepresentation (2) Making an incorrect statement deliberately.

Freight insurance (5) Insurance that covers the loss of earnings to ship's owners if goods are damaged or lost and are not delivered.

Frustration (2) The inability to complete a contract due to circumstances beyond the control of the contracting parties.

Fundamental risk (1) Risk that affects the entire economy or large numbers of people and is insured by governments.

Future income option (7) An option that guarantees the right to increased disability coverage, regardless of health if income has increased.

G

Gambling (1) This creates a new speculative risk.

General average (5) A loss incurred for the common good and the loss is shared by all parties. To be covered, the loss must be necessary, voluntary, successful and free from fault (it did not cause the risk).

General damages (2) Damages awarded for losses that cannot be determined and documented — for example, pain and suffering and loss of companionship of a spouse.

General insurance (5) Refers to all insurance, except life and health.

General liability (5) The legal liability arising out of day-to-day operations.

Good faith (2) The absence of intent to take advantage or defraud.

Grace period (7) (8) The period, usually 31 days, that premiums can be paid late without the policy being cancelled.

Graded death benefits (8) If the insured person dies within a specified amount of time, usually two years, the beneficiaries only receive a portion of the death benefits.

Grandparented policies (8) Exempt policies acquired before December, 1982.

Gross premium (1) (9) The pure premium plus loading costs.

Gross rate (9) The gross premium.

Group plans (8) Plans that provide life and health coverage through an employer or association.

Group term life insurance (8) Insurance that is issued as yearly renewable term. The premiums might be lower due to less marketing costs but might be higher since they are pooled for all risks.

Guaranteed annuity (8) (*also known as* term-certain annuity) An annuity that cannot extend beyond the owner's 91st birthday (or joint annuitant's 91st birthday, if later).

Guaranteed cash value (8) The amount of cash surrender value that is guaranteed in a whole life policy illustration.

Guaranteed continuable (8) Polices that the insurer must renew at same premium.

Guaranteed convertible (8)   The term policy has a conversion clause giving the policyowner the option to convert it into a cash value policy, such as whole life without evidence of insurability.

Guaranteed insurable (8)   The insured can increase coverage without proof of insurability.

Guaranteed-issue policy (8)   A policy which is bought through the mail without a medical.

Guaranteed renewable (2) (8)   The policies that the insurer must renew, but the premiums for each class may not be guaranteed. This ends at some specific age.

Guaranteed replacement cost (4)   The same as replacement cost (the cost to replace what was there without deducting depreciation) but the payment is not limited to the amount of the insurance coverage.

H

Hazard (1)   Something that creates or increases the probability of a peril. There are three types: physical, moral and morale.

Held for trading (9)   Something bought and sold for the purpose of profit-taking in fair value accounting.

Held-to-maturity (9)   The intention is to hold a debt instrument to maturity.

Hold-harmless clause (1) (5)   A clause written into a contract that releases one party from all legal liability.

Home province (6)   The province or territory where a person normally lives.

Host province (6)   The province or territory whose health services a person uses when not in the home province.

Hull insurance (5)   Insurance that covers the ship and includes a collision liability clause (a running down clause) in case the ship collides with another ship or damages the cargo of another ship. It does not cover people.

Human life value approach (8) (*also known as* income approach)   An approach that calculates the present value of the insured's future after-tax earnings.

I

Identity Fraud (4) (*also known as* Identity Theft)   Fraud that occurs when your personal information is collected and used by someone identifying him/herself as you and making transactions or requests on your account(s).

Identity Theft (4)   *See* Identity Fraud.

Immediate annuity (8)   An annuity that begins paying immediately.

Implied authority (9)   The authority whereby the public has every right to assume the agent has.

Income approach (8)   This approach calculates the face value needed to produce the current level of after-tax income for a specified number of years.

Incontestable (7)   The insurer gives up the right to dispute a claim after the policy has been in effect for a specified period of time, often two years. It can be overturned if the insured deliberately deceived the insurer.

Indemnification (2)   To restore a loss whole or in part by payment, repair or replacement.

Indemnity, contract of (2)   To compensate for the loss or damage to the insured while not allowing the insured to make a profit.

Indemnity (4)   A payment to cover all or part of a loss. The insured should not be profit from a loss.

Independent adjuster (9)   An adjuster that works for several insurance companies.

Indexed death benefit (8)   An annuity bought with the proceeds of a life insurance policy that increases annually by some pre-determined percentage or by the Consumer Price Index.

Indirect loss (1) (3) (4) (5)   A result of a direct loss.

Individual rating (9) (*also known as* merit rating)   A rating that reflects the loss experience of the individual risk.

Individual variable annuity contract (8)   A segregated fund that is an annuity contract between an insurance company and the policyholder.

Inductive reasoning (1)   Relies on the analysis of past data.

Initial face value (8)   The face amount at the issue date.

Initial reserve (9)   The reserve at the beginning of the year.

Injunction (2)   A legal order to stop one party from acting in a particular manner or that instructs that something specific is to be done.

Inland marine (5)   Insurance that covers goods being shipped on land.

Inland marine floater (5)   A policy that provides broad and comprehensive protection on property that is frequently moved from one location to another.

Innocent misrepresentation (2)   Making an incorrect statement in error.

Instalment refund annuity (8)   An annuity that pays for life to the annuitant or a beneficiary until the payments equal the purchase price.

Insurable interest (2) (4)   The insured (or a bank, etc.) will suffer a financial loss or fail to make a gain if a loss occurs. For property, the insurable interest must be present when the loss occurred. For life insurance, the insurable interest has to exist when the contract is formed. One cannot buy a life insurance policy on a person without their consent, except for spouses and parents of minor children.

Insurable risk (2)   The risk must have a large number of exposure units; losses must be accidental and unintentional; losses must be determinable and measurable; there cannot be catastrophic losses; the chance of loss must be calculable, and the premium must be economically feasible.

***Insurance Act* of Canada(3)**   An act that has given the provinces and territories legislative power to manage their automobile insurance industries.

Insurance agent bond (5)   A surety bond that indemnifies an insurer for any penalties that may result from the unlawful acts of agents.

Insurance risk (9)   A result of actual experience being different than expected when a product was designed or priced with the difference arising from mortality rates, morbidity rates (rates of disease and illness) and policyholder behaviour.

Insurance transfer (1)   A way of managing the risk of a loss by buying insurance.

Insured peril (4)   The cause of loss or damage insured.

Insured person (3)   The person or people covered by an insurance policy.

Insuring agreement (2) (4)   An agreement that summarizes the insurer's promises.

Integration of benefits (7)   The benefit is reduced if the benefits from certain other plans are available.

Interest option (8)   One of the ways the beneficiary can receive the proceeds from a life insurance policy.

Interest rate risk (1)   The risk faced by the holder of a fixed income instrument such as a bond whose price falls when interest rates increase.

Inverse liability (3)   The name used in B.C. for what is called Direct Compensation in Ontario. B.C. Autoplan covers that portion of a loss which is not the insured's fault, but for which he or she cannot sue, presumably because the state or province has no-fault where one cannot sue.

Investment bonus (8)   A bonus that is 1 to 1.5% p.a. to encourage the insured to keep the contract in force.

Invitation to treat (2)   An invitation to the general public to make an offer on a particular item.

Invitee (2)   Someone invited onto the premises for the benefit of the occupant (e.g., customers in a store, mail carriers, garbage collectors). The occupant must inspect the premises and eliminate any dangerous conditions found.

Irrevocable beneficiary (8)   A beneficiary that cannot be changed except by the beneficiary.

J

Joint-and-last-survivor annuity (8)   An annuity that pays until the death of the second spouse.

Joint life insurance (8)   Insurance that covers two or more lives. It pays on the death of the first to die, at which point the policy terminates.

Judge-made law (2) (*also known as* common law)   A system of rules based on precedents; there is no "code" or "legislation".

Judgment rating (9)   Each risk exposure is rated individually.

Judicial bond (5)   A surety bond that guarantee that the party bonded will fulfill certain obligations specified by law.

Juvenile insurance (8)   Insurance on children.

L

Last clear chance rule (2) A rule stating that the injured can recover damages if the party that caused the injury had a clear chance to avoid the accident but failed to do so.

Last-to-die policy (8) A policy that covers two or more lives and pays on the death of the last to die.

Law of large numbers (1) As the number of exposure units increases, the more closely the actual loss experience will approach the probable loss experience.

Legal duty of care (2) A legal duty to protect others from harm. In its absence, there is a legal wrong.

Legal hazard (1) A hazard that arises from characteristics of the legal system which increase the frequency and/or severity of a loss.

Legal liability (4) (5) The liability imposed by the courts.

Legal objective (2) The purpose of the contract must be legal.

Legal reserve (8) (9) (*also known as* policy reserve) The funds set aside to pay future claims.

Legal wrong (2) A violation of a person's legal rights, or a failure to perform a legal duty owed to either a certain person or to society as a whole.

Legislative compliance management (1) The legal requirement that companies, products, and sales agents must comply with all applicable laws and regulations, both federal and provincial.

Level death benefit (8) The face value of a universal life policy does not change over the life of the policy.

Level death benefit + account value (8) The amount at risk in a universal life policy grows with the increase in the account value.

Level death benefit + accumulated premium deposits (8) The benefit of a universal life policy increases to include essentially a refund of premiums after the insured dies. The amount at risk increases with every premium payment.

Level premiums (8) Premiums are the same over the life of the policy.

Level term (8) The coverage is the same throughout the life of the term insurance policy.

Liability (3) (8) Insurance covers against loss from injury to others or damage to the property of others.

Licence and permit bond (5) A surety bond that guarantees that the person bonded will comply with all laws and regulations that govern his or her activities.

Licensee (2) A person that enters or remains on the premises with the occupant's expressed or implied permission, for example, door-to-door salespersons, charity solicitors, police, fire fighters. The occupant is required to warn them of an unsafe conditions or activity but has no obligation to inspect.

Life annuity (8) An annuity that pays for the life of the annuitant.

Life insurance trust (8) A trust that is established with the proceeds of a life insurance policy.

Life insured (8) The person whose life is insured.

Limit of insurance (4) The maximum amount that will be paid for any one occurrence.

Limit of liability (4)   The maximum loss amount covered by a homeowners' policy.

Limited partnership reimbursement (5) (*also known as* or general partners liability)   Covers the management and fiduciary responsibilities of a general partner in a limited partnership.

Limited payment life (8)   A whole life policy where the premiums are limited to 10, 20 or 30 years, or even one premium.

Liquidity risk (9)   A result of not having access to enough funds to meet cash needs.

Liquor liability (5)   Liability that arises from the Dram Shop Law that imputes negligence to a owner of a business that sells liquor should a customer, while intoxicated, cause injury or damage to another person or their property.

Listed drugs (6)   The formulary, or the list of prescription drugs, covered by a health plan.

Living benefit (8)   If an insured is soon to die, the insured can receive a periodic payment.

Load (8)   The charge for administrative, marketing, and selling costs, as well as profits in a life insurance premium.

Loading costs (1)   The costs to cover operating expenses, sales commissions, profits, and contingencies.

Long-term care insurance (6)   Insurance for nursing homes and in-home care. The insured must be between 18 and 80. It is subject to an elimination period and covers for cognitive impairment (the inability to think, perceive, reason, or remember) or if one can no longer perform two of six daily living activities unaided (bathing, eating, dressing, toileting, continence or transferring positions of the body).

Loss (4) (5)   When something is entirely destroyed or missing.

Loss control (1)   This reduces the possible *severity* of a loss (loss reduction) and the *probability* of a loss (loss prevention).

Loss exposure (1)   The risk of a loss.

Loss of retirement income benefit (7)   This is a benefit of Workers' Compensation.

Loss prevention (1)   Reduces the probability of a loss.

Loss ratio (9)   The loss as a proportion of the premium earned.

Loss ratio method (9)   This method adjusts the rate to reflect the actual expenses as compared to the expected expenses.

Loss reduction (1)   This reduces the severity of a loss.

Lost-instrument bond (5)   A surety bond that guarantees the obligee against loss if the original instrument (stock certificate) turns up in the possession of another party.

M

Maintenance bond (5)   A surety bond that guarantees the workmanship will be good and that defective materials will be replaced.

Management expense ratio (MER) (8)   The annual fee charged by a segregated fund and a mutual fund to cover expenses such as commissions, brokerage fees, legal and audit, safekeeping charges, management fees, transfer fees and taxes.

Manual rating (9) (*also known as* class rating)   The rating that applies to a class of risk exposures.

Marine insurance (5)   Insurance that can cover imports and exports, domestic shipments, means of transportation, and communication, personal property floater risks and commercial property floater risks.

Market conduct regulation (1)   Regulation that focuses on protecting customers from misleading or deceptive sales practices.

Material loss (1)   Serious financial exposure leading to a reduced standard of living.

Maturity (8)   A life insurance policy occurs when the death benefit is paid, even if insured is still alive or no further premiums are required.

Maximum acceptable loss (1)   A maximum loss without unacceptable financial consequences.

Means-tested (7)   A person receives a benefit if they need it, not because the qualify for it.

Medicaid (6)   The American health care plan for low-income families.

Medicare (6)   The American health care plan for those over 65, and those with disabilities.

Mens rea (2)   The intent, knowledge, or recklessness of committing the offence.

Merit rating (9) (*also known as* individual rating)   A rating that reflects the loss experience of the individual risk.

Minimax Regret Theory (1)   A theory which states that we want to minimize our maximum loss or regret.

Minimum divisor (7)   Used to calculate employment insurance benefits.

Minor (2) (8)   Depending on the province, a person under the age of either 18 or 19. Any insurance benefits they receive must be managed by a parent or guardian.

Minor loss (1)   Financial consequences that are minor and manageable.

Misrepresentation (2)   The act of using a false statement used to persuade another to agree to a contract.

Misstatement of age (7) (8)   A clause that states the amount payable is reduced by the amount that the premiums would have been for the correct age.

Modified no-fault plan (3)   A plan that permits lawsuits if a certain threshold of damage or injury is met.

Monetary threshold (3)   If the auto claim is less than this amount, the injured person cannot sue.

Moral hazard (1)   Dishonesty or character defects that increase the frequency or severity of a loss.

Morale hazard (1)   Carelessness or indifference to a loss because of the existence of insurance.

Mortality cost (8)   The probability of death in a year multiplied by the amount at risk to the insurance company.

Mortality tables (2) (9)   Tables that show the number of expected deaths at any given age.

Mortgage default insurance (4)   Insurance that compensates the lender should someone stop making their mortgage payments.

Mortgage fraud (4)   Using a fraudulent title to a home to obtain a mortgage.

Mortgage life insurance (4) (8)   A term insurance policy payable to the financial institution that holds the mortgage. It terminates when the mortgage is terminated or transferred to another lender or if the homeowner buys another home.

Multiple-lines (5)   Insurance is property and casualty in one contract.

Mutual fund corporation (8)   An open-ended corporation, meaning it must provide shareholders the right of share redemption which a closed-ended corporation and a closed-ended mutual fund do not.

Mutual fund trust (8)   The assets are owned by the financial institution, which is the trustee of the fund, and the assets are protected by trust law from claims against the trustee.

Mutual insurers (1)   Are owned by policyholders, there is no capital stock, net income is paid out as a dividend (refund of premiums) and the board of directors is elected by the policyholders.

Mutual mistake (2)   When both parties are mistaken about the same material fact. They both make a mistake but each party's mistake is different and they are at cross purposes — that is, they cannot come to agreement.

N

Named beneficiary (8)   The person or the estate listed as the beneficiary of a life insurance policy.

Named insured (3)   The person or organization to whom the Certificate of Automobile insurance is issued.

Named perils coverage (2) (4)   Covers only what is specifically listed in the policy. If something not named, it is not covered.

Needs approach (8)   This approach adds the needs of the survivors from now until death to calculate the amount of life insurance to buy.

Negative act (2)   A failure to act.

Negligence (2) (3) (5)   The failure to exercise the standard of care required by law to protect others from an unreasonable risk of harm.

Negligent misrepresentation (2)   Carelessness in providing specialized information or advice which knowingly misleads or conceals relevant information.

Net amount at risk (8)   The risk for an insurer is the face amount of the policy minus the legal reserve.

Net asset value (NAV) (8)   The market value of the investments in a mutual fund.

Net asset value per share (NAVPS) (8)   The net asset value divided by the numbers of units outstanding.

Net cost of pure insurance (NCPI) (8)   The probability of death times the net amount at risk (the death benefit minus the accumulating fund).

Net level premium (NLP) (9)   The same annual premium for the term of the policy.

Net premium (9)   The amount of the premium before provincial and other taxes.

Net single premium (NSP) (9)   One premium paid at the beginning of the term.

New money policy (8) A permanent life policy where the insurer can change the premiums to reflect the actual cost of insurance, or the insured can change the face value and/or premiums to reflect protection required.

No-fault insurance (3) Each party collects from his or her own insurer regardless of who is at fault.

Nominal rate of return (8) A rate of return that includes inflation.

Non economic loss benefit (7) A benefit from Workers' Compensation that recognizes a physical, functional, or psychological loss.

Non-earner benefit (3) Auto insurance is paid if the injured person is not entitled to Income Replacement or Caregiver Benefits.

Non-exempt policy (8) A policy in which the insured has made deposits in excess of the amount needed to fund the death benefit and provide a reasonable level of savings. The excess gain is reportable and taxed whenever the policy is in a gain position, regardless of whether the gain has been realized.

Non-forfeiture benefits (8) The benefits an insured keeps, even if the policy is given up.

Non-insurance transfer (1) To share a risk without using insurance, such as by hedging and incorporation.

Non-occupational coverage (7) For coverage to be paid, the accident or illness must happen off the job.

Non-participating doctor (6) Doctors that bill the patient directly without regard to the limits of the Schedule of Benefits. The patient *cannot* be reimbursed by the provincial plan.

Non-participating policy (8) A whole life policy that does not pay dividends.

Non-registered annuity (8) An annuity paid out of non-registered funds.

Numismatic property (4) A collection of coins or other precious metals.

O

Objective probability (1) The probability that is determined using the long-run relative frequency of an event based on the assumptions of an infinite number of observations and no change in the underlying conditions.

Objective risk (1) The relative variation of actual loss from expected loss. As a result, the more observations, the lower the objective risk.

Obligee (5) With respect to a surety bond, this is the party who is reimbursed for damages if the principal fails to perform.

Occupant (3) Anyone, including the driver, in or on the auto, getting into, on, out or off a car.

Occurrences (5) Events that happen over a period of time resulting in continuous or repeated exposure to essentially the same harmful conditions, an accident, or a series of accidents.

Occurrence policy (5) A policy that pay for losses which occurred during the policy period, regardless of when the claim is filed.

Ocean marine (5) Covers goods being transported over water and can include legal liability.

Offer (2)   A promise by one party to undertake an obligation, subject to acceptance by the other party.

Offeree (2)   The person receiving an offer.

Offeror (2)   The person making the offer.

Offsetting deduction (7)   A deduction used for Workers' Compensation income to make it non-taxable.

Open-end mutual fund (8)   A fund that issues new shares whenever an investor invests in the fund, and also when it distributes mutual fund income.

Open perils (5)   Provides coverage for every perils except for a list of exclusions.

Operational risk (1) (9)   Risk that arises from inadequate or unsuccessful internal processes, failures of human performance, or systems and unexpected external events.

Opted-out doctor (6)   Doctors that bill the patient directly at an amount not exceeding the amount in the Schedule of Benefits (the maximum amount that can be charged) for the jurisdiction. The patient then submits a claim to the health care plan and is reimbursed by the plan.

Ordinary life insurance (8)   Whole life insurance, with continuous level premiums providing protection for life, and having a cash surrender value.

P

Paid-up addition (8)   Additional permanent life insurance coverage bought with dividends from a policy.

Paid-up-at-age policy (8)   A whole life policy that will no longer require premiums at a particular age.

Paid-up policy (8)   A life insurance policy that has not matured, but no further premiums are required.

Parental benefit (7)   Employment Insurance benefits for either biological or adoptive parents, to a maximum of 35 weeks.

Parol evidence rule (2)   The oral terms agreed to, but not included in the written contract, cannot be added later.

Partial disability (7)   When a disability allows a person to still work part-time.

Participating policy (8)   Entitles the insured to receive dividends (reduction in premiums) when the experience of mortality, interest and expenses are favourable.

Particular average (5)   A loss that falls on one party; that is, it is not covered unless the loss is caused by certain perils, such as stranding, sinking, burning, etc. It is often written as a franchise loss, such as 3%.

Particular risk (1)   A risk that affects individuals, not groups.

Pascal's Wager (1)   A wager based on the question, "God is, or he is not?"

Payment bond (5)   A surety bond that guarantees that the bills for labour and materials will be paid by the contractor when due.

Per occurrence deductible (5) (*also known as* straight deductible)   The firm pays the deductible for each separate loss.

Performance bond (5)   A surety bond that guarantees the owner that work will be completed according to contract specifications.

Peril (1) (3) (5)   This is the cause of a loss.

Permanent life insurance (8)   This includes whole life, term to 100, and universal life.

Perpetuity (8)   The policy pays forever, out of the income earned by the capital.

Personal and advertising injury (5).   *See* Advertising Injury

Personal contract (2)   The owner is insured, not the property and the contract is between the insurer and the insured. As a result, a property insurance policy cannot be assigned without the insurer's consent, although a life insurance can freely be assigned since the assignment does not change the risk.

Personal injury (5)   The false arrest, detention, imprisonment, malicious prosecution, libel, slander, defamation of character, violation of the right of privacy, unlawful entry, or eviction.

Personal liability (4)   The legal liability for unintentional bodily injury or property damage arising out of the insured's personal actions anywhere in the world including watercrafts and motorized vehicles but not cars and trailers.

Personal risk (1)   Risk that includes premature death, insufficient income during retirement, poor health, disability, and unemployment.

Philatelic property (4)   Stamps, postmarks and other items relating to postal history.

Physical hazard (1)   A physical condition that increases the chances of a loss.

Policy illustrations (8)   For permanent life insurance, these policies illustrate what could happen.

Policy loan (8)   A loan against the cash surrender value on which the insured pays interest.

Policy reserve (8) (9) (*also known as* legal reserve)   The funds set aside to pay future claims. It is called the accumulating fund in the *Income Tax Act*.

Pooling (2)   Combining one's risk exposure with others who have similar risks in order to distribute the risk among the group.

Portability (6)   The *Canada Health Act* states that health coverage must be portable from one province to another; that is, you are never not covered while in Canada. The waiting period when moving from province-to-province must not exceed three months.

Preferred-risk category (9)   For people whose mortality experience is expected to be lower than average. As a result, they can buy policies at a lower rate.

Premature death (1)   The death of a significant breadwinner with outstanding financial obligations.

Premises (4)   This includes the land and building(s) contained within the lot lines on which the dwelling is situated.

Premises and operations (5)   The exposure arising from the ownership and maintenance of a business.

Premises liability (4)   The legal liability for unintentional bodily injury or property damage arising out of the insured's ownership, use of, or occupancy of his or her premises. It does not apply to the insured's property, property in the insured's care, or the insured's property caused by non-residence employees working in the home.

Premium holiday (8) The insured can skip premium payments if there is enough cash surrender value and can resume payments without penalty or cost.

Premium offset date (8) The date on a whole life policy illustration when the accumulated dividends will be enough to pay all future premiums.

Premium tax (8) The provincial sale tax and, possibly, other taxes on an insurance policy.

Premium vacation (8) A premium holiday.

Prescribed annuity (8) An annuity whose taxable income is the same every year over a maximum of 15 years.

Presumptive agency (9) The insurance company cannot claim an agency relationship did not exist.

Presumptive total disability (7) A disability with the total and irrevocable loss of sight, hearing, speech, or two limbs (even if the insured is working).

Primary beneficiary (8) The beneficiary who is entitled to receive the proceeds first when the insured dies.

Primary example (8) The first example in a whole life policy illustration showing what *might* happen with the cash value and the death benefit.

Primary insurer (9) The entity that pays first. The excess insurer pays after the policy limits of the primary insurer.

Principal (5) (9) The insurer. In surety bonds, the principal is the party who agrees to perform certain acts or fulfil certain obligations.

Principle of Indemnity (2) The insured should not profit from the covered loss but should be restored to approximately the same financial position that existed prior to the loss.

Private law (2) Laws that govern individuals or groups of individuals. It includes contracts, property, torts, and trusts.

Private wrong (2) A tort or a violation of the rights of an individual (as opposed to the public at large).

Pro rata liability (9) When two or more policies are in place, each pays in proportion to the total amount of insurance.

Probability of a loss (1) The frequency of a loss.

Probate fees (8) The fees paid to validate a will when a person dies.

Product liability (1) (5) The legal liability of manufacturers, wholesalers, or retailers have towards persons who incur bodily injuries or property damage from a defective product.

Production (9) The sales and marketing activities of insurers.

Professional liability (2) (5) Arises from malpractices, errors, and omissions on the part of professionals.

Proportionate disability (7) Partial disability, but based on earnings.

Protection and indemnity (5) Damage to piers, docks, ship's cargo, illness or injury to passengers and crew, fines, and penalties.

Provisions (2)   The terms and conditions of an insurance policy.

Proximate cause (2)   A direct relationship exists between the act and the damages caused by the act; that is, there must be an unbroken chain of events between the negligent act and the infliction of damages.

Prudential regulation (1)   Regulation that focuses on the financial health, minimum capitalization requirements, risk management and management, and governance of insurance companies.

Public administration (6)   The administration and operation of a provincial health care plan by a public authority accountable to the provincial or territorial government on a non-profit basis.

Public adjuster (9)   The person that represents the insured, not the insurers, and is paid a fee based on the amount of the settlement.

Public law (2)   The laws that govern the relationship between individuals and the government. It includes regulatory, constitutional, and criminal law.

Public official bond (5)   A surety bond that guarantees that public officials will faithfully perform their duties for the protection of the public.

Public wrong (2)   Breaking a criminal law, which was designed to protect society at large.

Punitive damages (2)   Damages awarded to punish and to act as a deterrent.

Pure captive (1) (5)   This covers only the parent and companies the parent controls.

Pure cost of insurance (8) (*also known as* pure premium or mortality cost)   The probability of dying multiplied by the face value of the policy.

Pure no-fault system (3)   The victim cannot sue for pain and suffering.

Pure premium (1) (8) (9)   The probability of a total loss multiplied by the amount of the loss.

Pure premium method (9)   A method based on total claims and number of insured.

Pure risk (1)   Risk can have only a loss or no loss.

Pure rule (2)   Participation in a negligent act is proportional between the victim and the negligent party.

Q, R

Qualifying period (7)   The number of hours an unemployed person is required to have worked to qualify for Employment Insurance benefits.

Rate categories (9)   Categories for policyholders.

Rate making (9)   The function of establishing the risk category to set the price.

Rate of mortality (9)   The probability of death in a given year.

Rated policy (9)   A life insurance policy for someone who presents a higher than normal risk due to occupation, hobby or health.

Real interest rate (8)   An interest rate that does not includes inflation.

Real property (5)   Real estate.

Reasonable expectations (2) (4)   The insured is entitled to coverage under a policy that he or she reasonably expects it to provide and that to be effective, exclusions or qualifications must be conspicuous, plain and clear.

Rectification (2)   Rewording or rewriting a contract if it does not express what was actually agreed upon.

Recurrent disability (7)   Successive periods of disability, separated by 12 months or less, that are combined and deemed to continue with interruption.

Redlining (4)   Denying coverage in certain areas based on geographical location.

Reduced examples (8)   Examples after the primary example on a policy illustration showing the growth in the death benefit and cash surrender value if returns are lower than those on the primary example.

Reduced paid-up policy (8)   An additional policy in which the amount of the paid-up insurance is less than the original death benefit.

Regular benefits (7)   In terms of employment insurance, these are for benefits due to shortage of work or seasonal or mass lay-offs.

Regular occupation (7)   In terms of a disability benefit, this is the occupation at which a person usually works.

Reinstatement (7)   A lapsed policy can be put into effect again with certain conditions.

Reinsurance (2) (9)   Shifting of all or part of the insurance originally written by one insurer to another insurer.

Remedy of rescission (2)   Putting the plaintiff in the position he or she would have been in the contract had never been made.

Renewable (2) (8)   Term insurance gives the insured the right to renew without a medical usually at a higher premium based on attained age when renewed.

Renewal underwriting (9)   The process that re-checks the assumptions under which the policy was written.

Replacement cost (2) (4)   The cost where no depreciation has been deducted.

Replacement value (4)   The replacement cost, less depreciation.

Repudiate a contract (2)   To inform another that a contract will be disregarded.

Reputation risk (1)   The risk of a loss due to damage to one's reputation.

Reserve (8) (9)   *See* legal reserve.

Reserves (2)   Funds set aside for a special purpose.

Residence employee (4)   A person employed to perform household or domestic services to maintain or use the insured property. This does not include people working in the home in connection with a business.

Residual disability (7)   A partial disability for which a person's earnings are reduced by at least 20%.

Respite care (6)   The relieving of duty of a relative or friend who is a part-time caregiver.

Restraint of trade (2)   An action that reduces another person's ability to compete fairly in the marketplace.

Restrictions (2) Limitations on coverage that are part of the insurance policy.

Retains it nature (8) As income is received and paid out from a mutual or seg fund, the method of taxing it remains the same.

Retrospective rating (9) The rating that sets the actual premium after the period of coverage is over.

Revocable beneficiary (8) The beneficiary can be changed and has no enforceable rights, even if paying the premium.

Rider (2) (7) (8) An addition to the policy that adds, deletes, or modifies provisions in the original contract. It is usually used in connection with life and health insurance.

Right of subrogation (3) The right to collect the claim paid from the insurer of the at-fault driver.

Risk (1) The uncertainty surrounding the occurrence of a loss.

Risk management (1) The systematic process for identifying and evaluating pure loss exposures faced by an organization or individual, and for the selection and implementation of the most appropriate techniques for treating such exposures.

Risk/return tradeoff (1) The more risk one is willing to accept, the higher is the *possible* return .

Robbery (5) Theft using threats of bodily harm.

Running down clause (5) A collision liability clause in case the ship collides with another ship or damages the cargo of another ship. It does not include injury to people.

S

Salvage (5) The portion that is not damaged. It reduces the amount of the claim.

Schedule of Benefits (6) The maximum amount that can be charged for health services.

Schedule rating (9) Rates each risk individually, using a base and adding charges based on the characteristics of the risk exposure.

Scheduled coverage (5) Coverage for the named individuals or positions.

Second payor (9) The amount of benefit (from some group policy) is reduced by the amount of benefit under other policies, for example, EI benefit is second payor to CPP and Workers' Comp but not to individual policies.

Second-to-die life insurance (8) Insurance that pays on the death of the second or last insured.

Segregated funds (Seg funds) (8) Funds that are offered by an insurance company for the beneficiaries. The assets are kept separate from the assets of the insurance company. They are similar to an open-ended mutual fund but offer creditor protection.

Self-insurance (1) (5) The loss is paid out of operations, thus saving the cost of insurance premiums.

Severity of the loss (1) The amount of the loss.

Side fund (8) This is external to a Universal Life policy, and is not included in death benefit. It does not affect the net amount at risk. Deposits not subject to PST.

Single limit of insurance (4) The maximum amount the insurer will pay under one or more coverages provided under Section I in respect of one accident, or occurrence unless otherwise stated.

Social insurance (1) (7) Insurance required by governments.

Sovereign immunity (2) Governments cannot be sued because "the king can do no wrong".

Special damages (2) The damages awarded for losses that can be determined and documented.

Specific beneficiary (8) A named beneficiary, not a class beneficiary.

Specified perils (3) (4) (5) The specific perils named in the policy.

Speculative risk (1) Risk can have a loss, no change, or a gain.

Standard of care (2) The care required of a reasonably prudent person.

Standard rates (9) The rates charged to policyholders who meet the company's average underwriting standards.

Static risk (1) The risk associated with changes in the economy, and is a form of pure risk.

Statutory Conditions (3) (4) Inclusions and exclusions required by provincial legislation.

Stock insurers (1) The shareholders who elect a board of directors to manage the company.

Stop-loss provision (5) A provision that caps the amount the insured pays in total throughout the policy period.

Straight deductible (5) A deductible that is applied to each loss.

Straight life insurance (8) *See* Whole life insurance.

Strategic risk (1) (9) A risk over which the business has no control and also the failure to see that a change in direction is needed.

Strict liability (2) (5) A person is liable even if there was no negligence but can offer the defence of due diligence.

Sub-standard risks (9) Policyholders who are more risky than standard risks.

Subjective probability (1) An individual's personal estimate of a chance of loss.

Subjective risk (1) Uncertainty based on a person's mental condition or state of mind.

Subrogation (2) (3) (4) The insurer will pay the insured and is entitled to recover the loss from a negligent third party.

Supplementary health care plans (6) Plans that provide additional benefits that are not otherwise offered by provincial or territorial plans.

Supplementary payments (4) Additional expenses paid by an insurance company in defending or investigating a claim.

Surety (5) A surety bond is the party who agrees to answer for the debt, default, or obligation of another.

Surety bond (1) (5) A bond that provides monetary compensation if the bonded party fails to perform certain acts.

Surge capacity (6) The ability to respond to a surge in need or demand on a timely basis. It is the ability to access additional unused capacity, outside of the local region or province.

Surrender charge (8)   The fee paid when cancelling a life insurance policy or segregated fund prior to maturity.

Survivor benefit (7)   The benefit provided by Workers' Compensation.

T

Taxable gain on surrender (8)   The portion of the cash surrender value that is subject to tax at a person's marginal tax rate.

Temporary life insurance (8)   Life insurance coverage for a specific period of time such as 5 or 10 years.

Tenants insurance (4)   Insurance that is taken out by tenants to insure their own property and any damages they may cause to the landlord's property.

Tenants liability (4)   Liability that arises from unintentional damage to rented premises or their contents.

Term (8)   The period the policy is in effect.

Term certain annuity (8)   An annuity that pays for a defined minimum number of years.

Term insurance (8)   Insurance for a specified time period or term.

Term-like deposits (8)   Fixed-income investments similar to term deposit.

Term to age 65 (8)   Term insurance lasting to age 65.

Term-to-100 (8)   Term insurance lasting to age 100. It has no cash surrender value, no loan value, and is usually not participating. It can be a joint-life or last-to-die policy.

Terminal reserve (9)   The reserve at the end of the year.

Theft (5)   Any act of stealing.

Third party liability (3)   Claims by others (the third party) caused by insured (the first party). The insurance company is the second party.

Threshold no-fault (3)   A victim may sue for pain and suffering above a dollar or verbal threshold (Ontario). In Ontario, one cannot sue for lost income and other economic losses resulting from the injury.

Tied selling (3)   When a person selling insurance has other policies with the company.

Title insurance (4)   Insurance that protects the owner of the property or the lender of money against any unknown defects (defects to a clear title) in the title to the property under consideration.

Tort (2)   A legal wrong against a person or a group of individuals for which the law allows a remedy in the form of monetary damages.

Tort law (2)   A form of law that was established to compensate private individuals for the wrongs caused by others .

Total disability (7)   Being unable to perform each and every duty of one's occupation. *Occupation* can constitute one's own occupation, or any job for which one is qualified through training, experience, or education

Travel insurance (6) Offered by private insurers, it is for emergencies only. It never covers elective services, though it may cover emergency air ambulance, emergency return home, repatriation and the cost to return home early.

Trespasser (2) A person that enters or remains on the owner's property without the owner's consent. The owner cannot deliberately injure or a set a trap, however, since the owner has a duty of slight care.

Twisting (8) The illegal practice of using the CSV of a whole life policy to pay the premiums on a another policy.

Two-tiered system (6) A system where doctors perform surgery and medical check-ups in both publicly-funded hospitals and private, patient-paid clinics.

U

Umbrella policy (5) A policy that offers protection against a catastrophic lawsuit by providing excess insurance on all aspects of the underlying coverage.

Unbundled (8) The options (who is covered, deposits, premiums, face value, investments) are independent of each other, providing flexibility.

Underwriting (9) The process of selecting and classifying applicants for insurance.

Undue influence (2) This occurs when a person in a dominant position deprives another person of an independent decision.

Unidentified automobile (3) An automobile that leaves the scene of an accident before it can be identified (also known as hit and run).

Uniform Life Insurance Act (1) The nine common law provinces uniform (not Quebec).

Unilateral contracts (2) Contracts in which only one party makes a legally enforceable promise.

Unilateral mistake (2) A mistake where only one of the parties is in error.

Uninsured automobile insurance (3) Insurance that provides coverage if someone is hit by an uninsured driver or by a hit-and-run driver.

Universal health care (6) The same health care coverage is available to all residents of a province or territory.

Universality (6) Every provincial or territorial resident must be covered by the plan based on uniform terms and conditions.

Unjust enrichment (2) Where one party is unfairly enriched at the expense of another.

Unsatisfied judgment fund (3) A fund that compensates accident victims who have exhausted all other means of recovery; that is, the accident victim does not have to have a car and thus cannot collect from their auto policy.

User charge (6) (*also known as* User fee) Any charge for an insured health service that is covered by a Health plan but which is not payable by the health plan. It is banned by the *Canada Health Act*.

User fee (6). *See* User charge.

Utility trusts (8)   An income trust that invests in pipeline, power, and telecommunications companies.

Utmost good faith (2)   A principle that imposes a higher degree of honesty on the parties to an insurance contract than to other contracts.

V

Vacant (4)   In reference to a Homeowners' Policy, this means the occupants have moved out with no intention of returning. A newly constructed dwelling is vacant after it is completed and before the occupant moves in. The dwelling is also vacant when the occupants move out and before any new occupants move in.

Valued basis (4)   After being appraised, the insured and insurer agree on a value for something. If the item is lost, stolen or destroyed, the insured does not have to prove its value when submitting a claim.

Valued policy (2)   A policy for items whose value is difficult to determine. It pays the face value. Life insurance policies are valued policies.

Vanishing premiums (8)   Premiums that no longer have to be paid if investment income (dividends) is high enough. They are not guaranteed.

Variable annuity (8)   An annuity in which the amount of the annuity varies each month according to the return on the investment for the prior period.

Variable life insurance (8)   A permanent whole life contract with a fixed premium. The death benefit and cash surrender value vary according to the investment experience of a separate account maintained by the insurer. The amount of insurance can be reduced but can never fall below the original face value. The cash surrender value is not guaranteed and there is no guaranteed minimum cash surrender value.

Variable mortality cost option (8)   In a Universal Life policy, this is an option in which the mortality cost factor is revised each year to reflect the mortality experience of the insurer.

Verbal threshold (3)   This is for serious cases only. Plaintiffs must prove that their injuries are serious and permanent.

Vicarious liability (2) (5)   A motorist's negligence is imputed to the vehicle's owner.

Void (2)   The contract is invalid and cannot be corrected and cannot be enforced in court.

Voidable (2)   When a contract has imperfections that might be corrected.

Voluntary compensation for residence employees (4)   In a Homeowners Policy, these are payments for injury or death to residence employees while working for the insured even though the insured is not legally liable. There is a schedule of benefits for a list of injuries.

Voluntary medical payments (4)   In a Homeowners Policy, they are payments for reasonable medical expenses incurred within one year of an accident for unintentional injury to another person or unintentional injury to them while on the insured's premises even if the insured is not legally liable. Medical expenses include surgical, dental, hospital, nursing, ambulance services and funeral expenses.

Voluntary payments (4)   Payments made without being forced by a lawsuit.

Voluntary property payments (4)   In a   Homeowners Policy, they are payments for unintentional direct damage to property. For children 12 or under, this includes intentional damage.

W, Y

Waiting period (7) (*also known as* elimination period)   The amount of time to wait before the benefits start.

Waiver (2)   A voluntary relinquishment of a known legal right.

Waiver of premium benefit (6) (7) (8)   The premiums are waived if the insured becomes disabled.

Warranty (2)   A statement of fact or a promise made by the insured, which is part of the insurance contract, and which must be true if the insurer is to be held liable under the contract.

We and us (4)   Refers to the company providing the insurance.

Weekly indemnity (4)   The maximum amount an insurer will pay for injury to a residence employee in the Homeowners Policy.

Whole life insurance (8)   A cash-value policy that provides lifetime protection having fixed annual or monthly premiums.

Yearly term rates (8)   The premiums for a term life policy are based on attained age, i.e., premiums increase each year.

You and yours (4)   Refers usually to all related persons living in the same household.

Index

Index

Q, R

About the Author

Coleen Clark is an Assistant Professor of Finance at Ryerson University. She developed the Financial Planning program at Ryerson and registered the program with the Financial Planners Standards Council so that Bachelor of Commerce graduates as well as graduates in the Certificate in Financial Planning can write the national Certified Financial Planner® examination. Before coming to Ryerson, Coleen had extensive experience in the private sector in music publishing, magazine publishing, manufacturing and as a consultant to small businesses.